P9-CEN-096

WEAVING A WEBSITE

Programming In HTML, JavaScript™, Perl, and Java™

SUSAN ANDERSON-FREED

Illinois Wesleyan University

Prentice Hall
Upper Saddle River NJ 07458

Library of Congress Cataloging-in-Publication Data

Anderson-Freed, Susan.
    Weaving a Website: Programming in HTML, JavaScript, Perl, and Java/Susan Anderson-Freed.
      p. cm.
    Includes bibliographical references.
    ISBN 0-13-028220-0
    1. Website construction. 2. Programming. I. Title.

    TK5106.3.L28 2001
    005.8—dc21   2001042729
                                      CIP

Vice-president of editorial development, ECS: Marcia Horton
Acquisitions editor: Petra Recter
Editorial assistant: Karen McLean
Executive managing editor: Vince O'Brien
Managing editor: David A. George
Vice-president of production and manufacturing: David W. Riccardi
Production editor: Rose Kernan
Art director: Jayne Conte
Manufacturing buyers: Lisa McDowell and Pat Brown
Marketing manager: Holly Stark

© 2002 by Prentice-Hall, Inc.
Upper Saddle River, New Jersey 07458

The author and publisher of this book have used their best efforts in preparing this book. These efforts include the
development, research, and testing of the theories and programs to determine their effectiveness. The author and
publisher make no warranty of any kind, expressed or implied, with regard to these programs or the documentation
contained in this book. The author and publisher shall not be liable in any event for incidental or consequential
damages in connection with, or arising out of, the furnishing, performance, or use of these programs.

Printed in the United States of America

10 9 8 7 6 5 4 3 2 1

ISBN 0-13-028220-0

10-28-02

Pearson Education LDT., *London*
Pearson Education Australia PTY, Limited, *Sidney*
Pearson Education Singapore, Pte. Ldt
Pearson Education North Asia Ldt., *Hong Kong*
Pearson Education Canada, Ldt., *Toronto*
Pearson Educación de Mexico, S.A. de C.V.
Pearson Education -- Japan, *Tokyo*
Pearson Education Malaysia, Pte. Ldt.

To my parents,
Donald Anderson and Jeanette DeCremer Anderson

Contents

CHAPTER 6   FRAMES AND IMAGES   **120**

CHAPTER 7   CASCADING STYLE SHEETS   **150**

CHAPTER 15   THE STRING, REGEXP, AND DATE OBJECTS

PART III PERL   364

CHAPTER 16   INTRODUCTION TO PERL: WEB BASICS AND SCALARS   364

Preface

A decade ago, the World Wide Web was nonexistent. Today, it is a pervasive part of our everyday lives. Web sites exist for every imaginable topic. The best sites are well-designed, easy to use, interactive, and error free. Since these sites typically include JavaScript™ scripts, Java™ applets, or Perl® scripts, creation of such sites requires programming.

Programming is not an obscure art form accessible only to computer science majors or hackers; it is a craft that shares many similarities with other crafts, such as woodworking, quilting, or model building. Mastery of any craft requires plenty of practice, the right tools, and knowledge of the vocabulary associated with the craft.

Practice is crucial because mastery of any craft depends upon experience. Throughout this book, readers are asked to think about the problem and a solution before they examine the code. Additionally, each chapter contains several practice exercises.

A programmer's key tool is the programming language used. Just as apprentices use simpler tools and techniques than do experienced craftpersons, a newcomer to programming will experience less frustration working in a simpler language. The book begins with the simplest of the web languages, HTML. This is only a mark-up language; the beginner learns to create simple, but static pages. The introduction of frames and images to HTML in chapters 5 and 6 produces visually appealing pages. These images were created with PhotoShop® (a commercial product available from Adobe Systems and not included with this text.) The book also covers three programming languages: JavaScript, Perl, and Java. Of the three programming languages discussed in this book, JavaScript is by far the easiest. The book also covers this language first, so that we can concentrate on learning programming fundamentals. Many of the concepts, vocabulary, and conventions that are introduced in the discussion of JavaScript apply to Perl and Java. Thus, learning the later languages will be easier.

An experienced programmer always wields an arsenal of testing techniques to ensure that pages are error free. These techniques are stressed throughout the book. Most web programming books do not discuss these techniques. Either they don't care, or they assume that the reader's code will work correctly.

As a teacher with more than twenty years experience, I know that programming can be a frustrating experience for beginners. It requires a level of accuracy and attention to detail that many of us initially lack. I believe in a progressive, hands-on approach. Any individual, if given clear instructions and visual examples, can learn to program. The examples chosen for the text cover a wide variety of topics. The book includes pages containing recipes, football terms, crossword puzzles, multilanguage dictionaries, suggestion boxes, opinion polls, Shakespearean quizzes, and bird identification pages. The examples are designed to rouse your interest and to encourage you to develop creative and imaginative web pages. I hope that you enjoy reading the book as much as I enyoyed writing it.

ACKNOWLEDGMENTS

First, I would like to thank the many students who helped class-test this book. Students in the *Introduction to the Web* class used drafts of Parts I and II. Computer Science students used drafts of Parts III and IV in upper-level courses. Special thanks to the *Introduction to the Web* instructors, Moreena Tiede, Paul Kapitza, and Roussanka Loukanova, for their many helpful suggestions.

I am also indebted to my office suite mates, Jörg Tiede, Lon Shapiro, and Chris Boucher. Jörg patiently corrected my German in the several German-English pages. All my suite mates provided ongoing support for this project. Thanks also to Harold Grossman, Clemson University; Bert Lundy, Naval Postgraduate School; Scott Henninger, University of Nebraska; Rayford Vaughn, Mississippi State University; Marc Loy, Galileo Systems; and Jesse Heines, University of Massachusetts, Lowell, who reviewed early drafts of this manuscript.

I would also like to thank our technical reviewers who took the time to review the manuscript: Harold C. Grossman, Computer Science Department, Clemson University; Berty Lundy, Computer Science Department, Naval Postgraduate School; Scott Henninger, University of Nebraska; Rayford B. Vaughn, Missisipi State University; Marc Loy, Galileo Systems, LLC; and Jesse Heines, University of Massachussetts—Lowel.

I would also like to thank Petra Recter, Senior Acquisitions Editor, Prentice-Hall, for her ongoing support and encouragement. I thank Amy Waller, Publisher's Representative, Prentice-Hall, for bringing the manuscript to Prentice-Hall's attention. Thanks also to all of the other individuals at Prentice Hall who helped bring this book to fruition, with special thanks to Sarah Burrows and Rose Kernan.

I especially thank my husband, John, and my daughter, Jenny, for their ongoing support and patience. I appreciate their willingness to assume family chores so that I had additional time to write. And I owe a special debt of gratitude to my parents, Don and Jeanette Anderson, for all their assistance and encouragement over the years.

Susan Anderson-Freed
Bloomington, Illinois

PART I HTML

Introduction to HTML

GETTING STARTED

We begin our excursion into Web programming with the simplest of Web languages: HTML. HTML stands for HyperText Markup Language. A *HyperText* language is one that lets the user move easily between different documents or parts of the same document. This makes HTML a superb navigational tool for moving around the World Wide Web, which derives its name from the intricate complexity of its links. A *Markup* language uses symbols to specify the appearance of a document. HTML calls these mark-up symbols *tags*. You can insert HTML tags into a page manually, or you can use an HTML editor to create them. The way that editors generate the tags automatically, gives you less control over a page's appearance. This book focuses on the more laborious task of generating the tags by hand. Creating tags by hand furnishes an understanding of the relation between the tags and a page's appearance. This knowledge lets us fine-tune the tags produced by an HTML editor.

System Requirements

Creating HTML pages requires the following software:

Text Editor. HTML pages are created as *plain text*, also called ASCII, files. Plain-text editors are available on all platforms: Macintosh systems provide the *Simple Text* editor; an IBM PC provides the *Notepad* editor; Unix and Linux systems provide several editors, including *vi* and *emacs*.

Browser. Displaying an HTML page requires a browser. The two browsers most frequently used are Netscape and Internet Explorer. Most systems come equipped with one, if not both, of these browsers.

Internet Service Provider (ISP). Connecting to the World Wide Web requires an Internet Service Provider. Creating Perl scripts (Part III) requires `cgi-bin` privileges.

THE STRUCTURE OF AN HTML PAGE

An HTML page is divided into a *head* and a *body*. The *head* of the page contains tags that provide a title for the page, that load scripts, or that provide information for search engines. The *body* of a page contains the page's information. Figure 1.1 contains an annotated version of our first web page as it appears in a Netscape browser. (Internet Explorer displays the page in a similar fashion, but with a white background.) The title appears at the top of the page. The *body* of the page appears below the **Netsite:** window. The **NetSite** window contains the URL (or link) to the page. The URL is divided into the following pieces:

Protocol. The URL begins with a protocol. In this example, the protocol is **http://**, which stands for *HyperText Transfer Protocol*. Other protocols exist including **ftp://**, **gopher://**, and **mailto://**. (Protocols are discussed in Chapter 5.)

Server Name: The server name follows the protocol. This name is provided by the Internet Service Provider. In Figure 1.1, the server is **www.iwu.edu**.

The last portion of the server name identifies the type of server (if it is in the United States) or the country of the server (if it is outside). Server types include **.edu** for educational institutions, **.com** for commercial, **.gov** for government, **.org** for organization, and **.net** for networks. Country names include **.jp** for Japan, **.ca** for Canada, and **.de** for Germany.

Page Location. The last portion of the URL specifies the page's location. A tilde (~) indicates that the URL is located in the home directory of the page's creator. In this example, the file is in the home directory, **~sander/**. The name of the page is **first.html**. HTML pages always have the extension **.html** (or **.htm** on systems that permit only three-letter extensions).

Figure 1.2 contains the HTML that produced the page displayed in Figure 1.1.

This simple program contains several HTML tags that control the appearance of the text. Comparing Figure 1.1 with Figure 1.2 shows the difference between text and tags: the text appears on the page, the tag does not. Notice that anything appearing inside angular brackets, <>, is not written on the Web page. In fact, all HTML tags are encased in angular brackets.

The first tag is a comment tag. Comment tags begin with <!-- and end with -->. Comments are a page's long-term memory. The details of a page's construction often are forgotten with time, so programmers use comments to help them remember these details. Inclusion of comments makes it easier to revise a page later. Browsers ignore comments, so comments don't appear on a displayed page; a user can select the *View Source* option in the *Edit* menu to see what comments the programmer included.

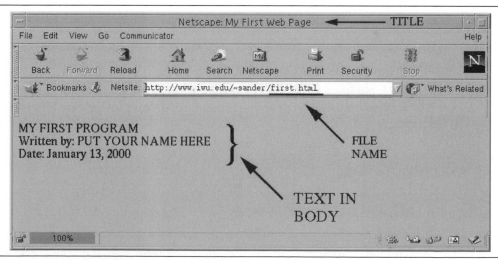

Figure 1.1 The *First Web* Page

```
<!-- File Name: first.html -->
<!DOCTYPE HTML PUBLIC "-//W3C//DTD HTML 4.0 Transitional//EN">
<HTML>
<HEAD><TITLE>My First Web Page</TITLE></HEAD>
<BODY>
MY FIRST PROGRAM<BR>
Written by: PUT YOUR NAME HERE<BR>
Date: January 13, 2000
</BODY></HTML>
```

Figure 1.2 HTML for the *First Web* Page

The **<DOCTYPE>** tag follows the comment tag. Only comment tags should appear before this tag, because the **<DOCTYPE>** tag tells a browser which HTML version and which language were used to write the page. The **<DOCTYPE>** tag in Figure 1.2 indicates that the *First Web* page was written in *HTML 4.0 transitional* with *English* as the language.

The **<HTML>** tag always follows the **<DOCTYPE>** tag. This tag indicates that the page is written in HTML. Notice the last line of the page: **</HTML>**. The **<HTML>** tag has this corresponding end tag to indicate the end of the HTML. These two tags form a container into which we place all of our HTML statements.

The **<HEAD>** follows the **<HTML>** tag. This tag and its corresponding end tag, **</HEAD>**, form a container for the head of the page. The head should contain a title, which is placed between the **<TITLE>** and **</TITLE>** tags. The *body* of the page is placed after the head. The page's content is placed inside the body of the page. You might try modifying the text in the body of the *First Web* page so that it contains your name and the current date. Save the page and load it into your browser. The page's overall appearance remains unchanged, but your text replaces the text in the original page.

HTML BASICS

HTML is a "forgiving" language. It has a few simple rules and a great deal of flexibility. Anything that HTML cannot understand it ignores. The rules governing tags are also simple; they can be summarized as follows:

Rule 1. Tag Names.   Each tag has a name that identifies it. Because HTML is not case sensitive, the tag names can be written by using any combination of upper- and lower-case letters. For example, the **<HEAD>** tag can also be written as **<head>** or **<Head>**. Most programmers use only upper-case letters for HTML tags to make the tags stand out.

Rule 2. Tags as Containers.   Many HTML tags come in pairs; the two tags bound a container, into which the programmer places text or other tags or both. Figure 1.2 contains several examples of tags as containers, including **<HTML>...</HTML>**, **<HEAD>...</HEAD>**, **<TITLE>...</TITLE>**, and **<BODY>...</BODY>**.

Figure 1.2 also contains a tag that does not have a corresponding end tag: **
**. This tag breaks the line on a page.

Rule 3. Tag Attribute Names.   Almost all HTML tags have at least these five attributes: **ID**, **CLASS**, **STYLE**, **DIR**, and **LANG**. These attributes are used with cascading style sheets. (See Chapter 7.) In addition, many tags have attributes that control alignment, color, size, or other features of the text associated with the tag. These attribute names are also case insensitive. The end of each HTML chapter contains a summary of the HTML tags discussed in that chapter. The summary lists the attributes and details the values associated with each attribute. In most cases, the attributes are optional. The attributes are listed in alphabetical order, but we can use them in any order.

Rule 4. Tag Attribute Values.   Tag attributes frequently require an associated value. For example, the paragraph tag, **<P>**, tag has an alignment attribute that lets the programmer center, left-justify, or right-justify paragraphs. Thus, the tag that creates a centered paragraph is:

    <P ALIGN = "CENTER">

In this statement, the tag name is **P**, the attribute name is **ALIGN**, and the attribute's value is **"CENTER"**. HTML determines the choice of values for this attribute. When HTML provides the values, they are case insensitive. Some attributes, particularly those associated with forms, do not have a preset value. The page's author chooses appropriate values. These values *are* case sensitive.

Rule 5. Spacing.   HTML does not like spaces immediately after the opening angular bracket or before the closing bracket. For example, **< HEAD>** or **<HEAD >** can produce subtle errors.

Rule 6. Nested Tags.   Figure 1.2 contained nested tags. For example, the **<TITLE>...</TITLE>** tags must be placed inside the **<HEAD>...</HEAD>** tags. When a tag is a container for another tag, the programmer must ensure that the inner tag is truly contained. This means that the end tag of the enclosed tag should appear before the end tag of the outer tag. Figure 1.3 shows nested and crossed tags. Crossed tags often produce pages that don't "look right."

The <BR> and <P> Tags

Two tags that are frequently used in the body of web pages are the **
** (*BReak*) and **<P>** (*Paragraph*) tags. The **
** tag is HTML's equivalent of pressing the *Enter* or *Return* key in a word processor. This tag has no ending tag. It can be repeated consecutively to create several blank lines. For example, **

** creates two blank lines. The **
** tag has a single attribute, **CLEAR**; it is often used in conjunction with tables.

The **<P>** tag creates a new HTML paragraph. HTML does not indent the first line of a paragraph, as a word processor typically would. Instead, HTML uses a blank line to indicate the start of a new paragraph. The **<P>** tag has a corresponding end tag, **</P>**; however, this tag is optional, and most people leave it out. The **<P>** tag has one attribute, **ALIGN**; it sets the alignment of the paragraph. Alignment values are **"LEFT"** (default), **"CENTER"**, **"RIGHT"**, and **"JUSTIFY"**. The **"JUSTIFY"** value does not always work.

(a) Nested Tags	**(b) Crossed Tags**
`<HEAD>`	`<HEAD>`
`<TITLE>My First Web Page</TITLE>`	`<TITLE>My First Web Page</HEAD>`
`</HEAD>`	`</TITLE>`

Figure 1.3 Nested and Crossed Tags

THE *WEATHER FORECAST* PAGE

Figure 1.4 Contains an HTML page with a local weather forecast. The page uses both **
** and **<P>** tags. You are encouraged to write the HTML for this page before examining the code in Figure 1.5.

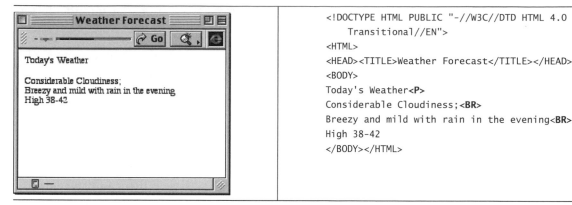

Figure 1.4 The *Weather Forecast* Page

Figure 1.5 HTML for the *Weather Forecast* Page

Figure 1.5 contains the HTML for the *Weather Forecast* page. Notice the first line in the body of the HTML page. It ends with a **<P>** tag, so a blank line appears between *Today's Weather* and *Considerable Cloudiness*. The remaining lines use the **
** tag.

HEADING TAGS

The *Weather Forecast* page used a **<P>** tag to create a heading. HTML has a separate *heading* tag that creates six different levels of headings. Because this heading tag is a container, it has beginning and ending tags. The beginning tag is **<Hn>**, where *n* is a number between 1 and 6. The ending tag is **</Hn>**, where *n* is the same number used in the beginning tag. The **<Hn>** tag contains an **ALIGN** attribute that uses the same values as the paragraph's **ALIGN** attribute. Most browsers display a heading in **bold** font. All browsers insert a paragraph tag when the heading ends. Figure 1.6 shows the six headings. The larger the heading number, the smaller the size of the heading.

Figure 1.7 contains the HTML that produced the *Heading* page. The heading tags are highlighted.

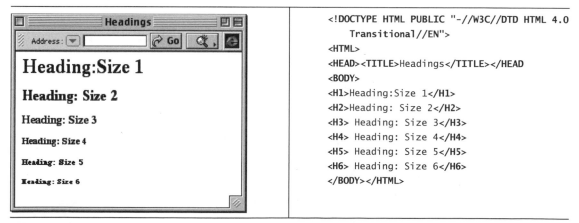

Figure 1.6 The *Heading* Page

Figure 1.7 HTML for the *Heading* Page

Figure 1.8 contains a page listing *The Grand Sauces in French Cooking*. Each of the lines is centered. The first line uses an **<H1>** heading. The remaining lines use an **<H2>** heading. Try writing the HTML for the page before examining Figure 1.9

```
<!DOCTYPE HTML PUBLIC "-//W3C//DTD HTML 4.0
      Transitional//EN">
<HTML>
<HEAD><TITLE>Grand Sauces</TITLE></HEAD>
<BODY>
<H1 ALIGN = "CENTER">The Grand Sauces in French
      Cooking</H1>
<H2 ALIGN = "CENTER"> Sauce Espagnole</H2>
<H2 ALIGN = "CENTER"> Demi-Glace</H2>
<H2 ALIGN = "CENTER"> Sauce Bechamel</H2>
<H2 ALIGN = "CENTER"> Tomato Sauce</H2>
<H2 ALIGN = "CENTER"> Hollandaise Sauce</H2>
</BODY></HTML>
```

Figure 1.8 The *Grand Sauces* Page

Figure 1.9 HTML for the *Grand Sauces Page*

Figure 1.9 contains the HTML for the *Grand Sauces* page. Notice the repeated use of the **<H2>** tag.

Because the *Grand* Sauces pages uses a separate heading for each sauce, a blank line is inserted between each of the sauces. Using a single **<H2 ALIGN = "CENTER">** tag before the first heading reduces the number of tags. Placing a **<P>** tag at the end of the sauce's name creates a blank line between the sauces. Using a **
** tag creates single-spaced text. Figure 1.10 contains the *Grand Sauces* page that results from using a single **<H2 ALIGN = "CENTER">** tag and **
** tags.

Figure 1.11 contains the HTML for the new version of the *Grand Sauces* page. This version illustrates nested HTML tags.

```
<!DOCTYPE HTML PUBLIC "-//W3C//DTD HTML 4.0
      Transitional//EN">
<HTML>
<HEAD><TITLE>Grand Sauces 2</TITLE></HEAD>
<BODY>
<H1 ALIGN = "CENTER">The Grand Sauces in French
      Cooking</H1>
<H2 ALIGN = "CENTER"> Sauce Espagnole<BR>
Demi-Glace<BR>
Sauce Bechamel<BR>
Tomato Sauce<BR>
Hollandaise Sauce</H2>
</BODY></HTML>
```

Figure 1.10 The *Grand Sauces* Page, version 2

Figure 1.11 HTML for the *Grand Sauces* Page, version 2

A Note of Caution: Computer screens and printers do not use the same font size for headings. Typically, a printer will display a heading in a much larger font than the computer screen. In many cases, the font size is obnoxiously large.

HORIZONTAL RULES

The Horizontal Rule tag, **<HR>**, places a beveled line on the page. There is no corresponding end tag. Figure 1.12 contains a *Newspaper Sections* page. Horizontal rules separate each section.

The HTML for the *Newspaper Sections* page appears in Figure 1.13. The **<HR>** tag automatically breaks at the end of the line, so **
** tags are not needed to terminate the lines.

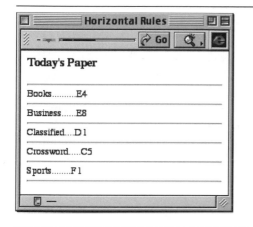

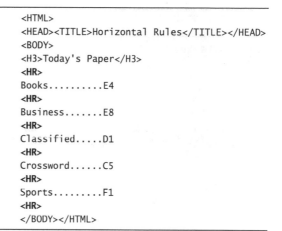

```
<HTML>
<HEAD><TITLE>Horizontal Rules</TITLE></HEAD>
<BODY>
<H3>Today's Paper</H3>
<HR>
Books..........E4
<HR>
Business.......E8
<HR>
Classified.....D1
<HR>
Crossword......C5
<HR>
Sports.........F1
<HR>
</BODY></HTML>
```

Figure 1.12 The *Newspaper Sections* Page   **Figure 1.13** HTML for the *Newspaper Sections* Page

The NOSHADE Attribute

The **<HR>** tag contains several attributes that let us vary the appearance of the line. The easiest of these attributes is **NOSHADE**. This attribute produces a solid line rather than the airy, default line. Figure 1.14 contains a revision of the *Newspaper Sections* page. In the new version, the **NOSHADE** attribute is used for all of the odd-numbered lines.

Figure 1.15 contains the HTML for the new version of the *Newspaper Sections* page.

The WIDTH and ALIGN Attributes

The **<HR>** tag contains an **ALIGN** attribute identical to the **ALIGN** attribute for the **<P>** and **<Hn>** tags. A horizontal rule extends, by default, across the entire width of the browser, but the **ALIGN** attribute can be used in conjunction with the **WIDTH** attribute to produce interesting effects. The **WIDTH** attribute requires a value specifying the desired width. The value can be a percentage of the browser's width or the number of pixels. For example, the statement

```
<HR WIDTH = "50%">
```

draws a line that covers 1/2 of the browser's width. By contrast, the statement

```
<HR WIDTH = "144">
```

draws a line that is 144 pixels long. In each case, the default alignment is **LEFT**.

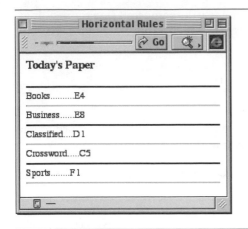

Figure 1.14 The *Newspaper Sections* Page, version 2

```
<HTML>
<HEAD><TITLE>Horizontal Rules</TITLE></HEAD>
<BODY>
<H3>Today's Paper</H3>
<HR NOSHADE>
Books..........E4
<HR>
Business.......E8
<HR NOSHADE>
Classified.....D1
<HR>
Crossword......C5
<HR NOSHADE>
Sports.........F1
<HR>
</BODY></HTML>
```

Figure 1.15 HTML for the *Newspaper Sections* Page, version 2

Figure 1.16 contains an advertisement for the fictitious *Muskrat Mounds Tree Farm*. The page uses horizontal rules to create a simple logo for this company.

The HTML for the *Tree Farm* page appears in Figure 1.17. The tree logo uses center alignment and a percentage increase in the width of each line. Since the tree's size is based on a percentage of the browser's width, the tree grows and contracts as we increase or decrease the browser's width.

Figure 1.16 The *Muskrat Mounds Tree Farm* Page

```
<!DOCTYPE HTML PUBLIC "-//W3C//DTD HTML 4.0
         Transitional//EN">
<HTML>
<HEAD><TITLE>Tree Farm 1</TITLE></HEAD>
<BODY>
<HR ALIGN ="CENTER" WIDTH= "5%" NOSHADE>
<HR ALIGN ="CENTER" WIDTH= "10%" NOSHADE>
<HR ALIGN ="CENTER" WIDTH= "20%" NOSHADE>
<HR ALIGN ="CENTER" WIDTH= "30%" NOSHADE>
<HR ALIGN ="CENTER" WIDTH= "40%" NOSHADE>
<HR ALIGN ="CENTER" WIDTH= "50%" NOSHADE>
<HR ALIGN ="CENTER" WIDTH= "60%" NOSHADE>
<HR ALIGN ="CENTER" WIDTH= "10%" NOSHADE>
<HR ALIGN ="CENTER" WIDTH= "10%" NOSHADE>
<HR ALIGN ="CENTER" WIDTH= "10%" NOSHADE>
<P ALIGN ="CENTER">
The Muskrat Mounds Tree Farm
</BODY></HTML>
```

Figure 1.17 HTML for the *Tree Farm* Page

Figure 1.18 contains a second logo created via the use of horizontal rules. In this example, the lines use a right alignment and give the illusion of a road disappearing in the horizon.

Figure 1.19 contains the HTML for the *Chamber of Commerce* page. The width is based on the percentage of the browser's width. The alignment is right.

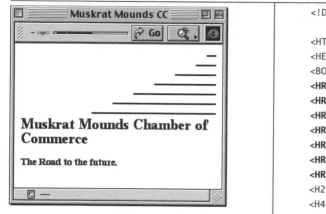

```
<!DOCTYPE HTML PUBLIC "-//W3C//DTD HTML 4.0
    Transitional//EN">
<HTML>
<HEAD><TITLE>Muskrat Mounds CC</TITLE></HEAD>
<BODY>
<HR ALIGN = "RIGHT" WIDTH = "5%" NOSHADE>
<HR ALIGN = "RIGHT" WIDTH = "10%" NOSHADE>
<HR ALIGN = "RIGHT" WIDTH = "20%" NOSHADE>
<HR ALIGN = "RIGHT" WIDTH = "30%" NOSHADE>
<HR ALIGN = "RIGHT" WIDTH = "40%" NOSHADE>
<HR ALIGN = "RIGHT" WIDTH = "50%" NOSHADE>
<HR ALIGN = "RIGHT" WIDTH = "60%" NOSHADE>
<H2>Muskrat Mounds Chamber of Commerce</H2>
<H4>The Road to the future.</H4>
</BODY></HTML>
```

Figure 1.18 The *MM Chamber of Commerce* Page

Figure 1.19 HTML for *MM Chamber of Commerce* Page

The SIZE Attribute

HTML uses a default height of two pixels for horizontal rules. The **SIZE** attribute changes the height of a horizontal rule. The value must be specified in pixels. Figure 1.20 contains a new version of the *Tree Farm* page. The tree is more substantial, because the **SIZE** attribute changes the height of the lines to twelve pixels.

The HTML for the second version of the *Tree Farm* page appears in Figure 1.21.

```
<!DOCTYPE HTML PUBLIC "-//W3C//DTD HTML 4.0
    Transitional//EN">
<HTML>
<HEAD><TITLE>Tree Farm 2</TITLE></HEAD>
<BODY>
<HR ALIGN = "CENTER" WIDTH = "5%" NOSHADE SIZE ="12">
<HR ALIGN = "CENTER" WIDTH = "10%" NOSHADE SIZE = "12">
<HR ALIGN = "CENTER" WIDTH = "20%" NOSHADE SIZE = "12">
<HR ALIGN = "CENTER" WIDTH = "30%" NOSHADE SIZE = "12">
<HR ALIGN = "CENTER" WIDTH = "40%" NOSHADE SIZE = "12">
<HR ALIGN = "CENTER" WIDTH = "50%" NOSHADE SIZE = "12">
<HR ALIGN = "CENTER" WIDTH = "60%" NOSHADE SIZE = "12">
<HR ALIGN = "CENTER" WIDTH = "10%" NOSHADE SIZE = "12">
<HR ALIGN = "CENTER" WIDTH = "10%" NOSHADE SIZE = "12">
<HR ALIGN = "CENTER" WIDTH = "10%" NOSHADE SIZE = "12">
<P ALIGN = "CENTER">
The Muskrat Mounds Tree Farm
</BODY></HTML>
```

Figure 1.20 The *Tree Farm* Page, version 2

Figure 1.21 HTML for the *Tree Farm* Page, version 2

THE <CENTER> AND <DIV> TAGS

The **<CENTER>** tag and its corresponding end tag, **</CENTER>**, center things on a web page. This tag is simply a shorthand way of writing **<DIV ALIGN = "CENTER">**. Figure 1.22 contains a classified ad for a newspaper. The entire ad is centered on the page. Notice the use of the different heading tags.

Figure 1.23 contains the HTML for the *Classified Ad* page. Notice how the **<CENTER>...</CEN-TER>** tags form a container for the advertisement.

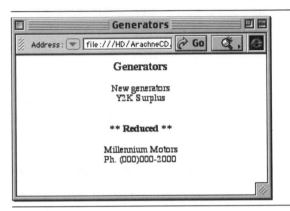

Figure 1.22 The *Classified Ad* Page

```
<!DOCTYPE HTML PUBLIC "-//W3C//DTD HTML 4.0
    Transitional//EN">
<HTML>
<HEAD><TITLE>Generators</TITLE></HEAD>
<BODY>
<CENTER><H3>Generators</H3>
New generators<BR>
Y2K Surplus<BR>
<H4>** Reduced **</H4>
Millennium Motors<BR>
Ph. (000)000-2000</CENTER>
</BODY></HTML>
```

Figure 1.23 HTML for the *Classified Ad* Page

The <DIV> Tag Attributes

The division tags,**<DIV>...</DIV>**, contain an **ALIGN** attribute that uses the same values as the paragraph **ALIGN** attribute. The division tag differs from the paragraph tag in two respects:

1. The division end tag, **</DIV>**, is required; the paragraph end tag, **</P>**, is optional.
2. The division tag does not separate page divisions with a blank line; the paragraph tag does.

Figure 1.24 contains a *Tree Conservation* page created with a **<DIV>** tag. The center alignment and **
** tags form the text into a tree shape.

The HTML for the *Tree Conservation* page appears in Figure 1.25. Notice how the **<DIV>...</DIV>** tags form a container for the text.

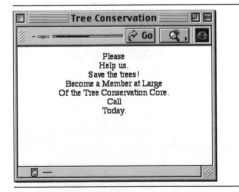

Figure 1.24 The *Tree Conservation* Page

```
<!DOCTYPE HTML PUBLIC "-//W3C//DTD HTML 4.0
    Transitional//EN">
<HTML>
<HEAD><TITLE>Tree Conservation</TITLE></HEAD>
<BODY>
<DIV ALIGN = "CENTER">Please<BR>
Help us.<BR>
Save the trees!<BR>
Become a Member at Large<BR>
Of the Tree Conservation Core.<BR>
Call<BR>
Today.</DIV>
</BODY></HTML>
```

Figure 1.25 HTML for the *Tree Conservation* Page

➤ EXERCISES

Directions: *Create a separate web page for each exercise. Include an appropriate title for the page. The exercises use various combinations of the*
, <P>, <DIV>, <Hn>, *and* <HR> *tags.*

1. **An *Online Business* Page.** Figure 1.26 contains an information sheet for a fictitious store. Recreate this page.

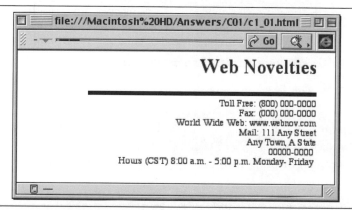

Figure 1.26 An *Online Business* Page

2. **A *Business Card* Page.** Figure 1.27 contains a fictitious business card. Recreate this card.

Figure 1.27 A *Business Card* Page

3. **A *Spring Schedule* Page.** Figure 1.28 contains a portion of a spring schedule for a school. Recreate this schedule.

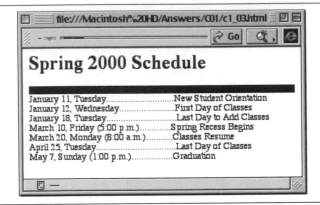

Figure 1.28 A *Spring Schedule* Page

4. **An *Event Calendar* Page.** Find an event calendar for a local or national organization. Recreate this calendar as a web page.

5. **The *Dinette* Page.** Figure 1.29 contains a "specials" menu for a restaurant. Recreate this menu.

Figure 1.29 The *Dinette Menu* Page

6. **The *Grocery Specials* Page.** Figure 1.30 contains a list of weekly specials for the Muskrat Mounds Grocery Store. Recreate this advertisement. Add your own specials.

Figure 1.30 The *Grocery Specials* Page

7. **The *Kite Company* Page.** Figure 1.31 contains the logo for a fictitious kite company. Recreate this logo.

Figure 1.31 The *Kite Company* Page

8. **The *Softball League* Page.** Figure 1.32 contains an announcement for a fictitious softball league. Recreate this announcement. Feel free to improve upon its roughly diamond shape.

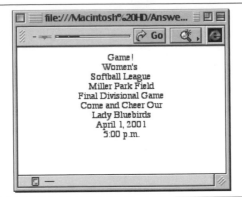

Figure 1.32 The *Softball League* Page

9. **The *Omelette* Page.** Figure 1.33 contains the ingredients for two of Escoffier's omelettes. Recreate these recipes (at least in HTML Form).

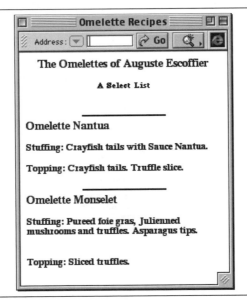

Figure 1.33 The *Omelette* Page

10. **The *Roasting Garlic* Page.** Figure 1.34 contains the technique for roasting garlic. Reproduce this page.
11. **The *Technique* Page.** Pick an area of interest to you. Create a step chart similar to the one found in the previous example.
12. **The *Open House* Page.** Figure 1.35 contains the announcement for a fictitious open house. Recreate this announcement.

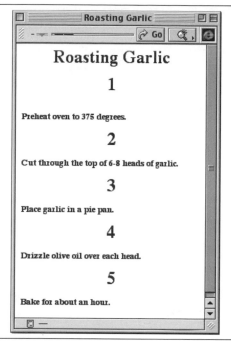

Figure 1.34 The *Roasting Garlic* Page

Figure 1.35 The *Open House* Page

13. **The *Hollandaise Sauce* Page.** Figure 1.36 contains the definition of Hollandaise sauce and its derivatives. Recreate this definition list.

Figure 1.36 The *Hollandaise Sauce* Page

14. **The *Used Book Ad* Page.** Figure 1.37 contains a fictitious advertisement for a used bookstore. Recreate this ad.

Figure 1.37 The *Used Book Ad* Page

15. **The *Color Symbolism* Page.** Figure 1.38 displays a page listing the symbolism associated with the color red. Recreate this list.

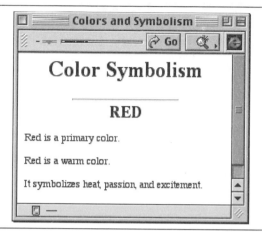

Figure 1.38 The *Color Symbolism* Page

16. **The *Color Classification* Page.** Figure 1.39 contains a list of the primary and secondary colors. Recreate this list.

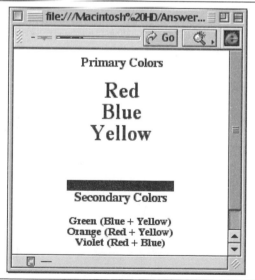

Figure 1.39 The *Color Classification* Page

17. **The *Sports Announcement* Page.** Figure 1.40 contains a news announcement for a fictitious organization. Recreate this announcement.

Figure 1.40 The *Sports Announcement* Page

18. **A *Child's Poem* Page.** Figure 1.41 contains a short poem. Reproduce this poem.

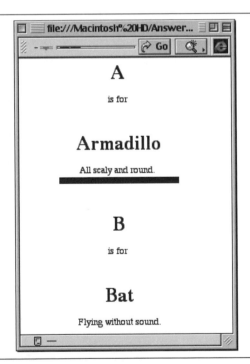

Figure 1.41 A *Child's Poem* Page

19. **A *Knitting Pattern* Page.** Figure 1.42 contains a simple knitting pattern. Recreate this pattern.

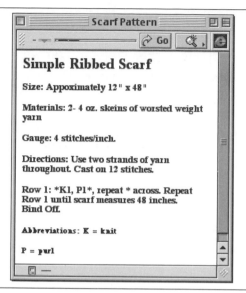

Figure 1.42 A *Knitting Pattern* Page

➤ ## HTML TAGS FOR CHAPTER 1 (in alphabetical order)

**
.**   The line **BR**eak breaks the line.

Syntax:
```
<BR CLEAR = "ALL" | "LEFT" | "RIGHT" | "NONE">
```

<BODY>....</BODY>.   These tags encase the body of an HTML program.

Syntax:
```
<BODY ALINK = "ColorName" | "#RRGGBB"
     BACKGROUND = "ImageFile"
     BGCOLOR = "ColorName" | "#RRGGBB"
     LINK = "ColorName" | "#RRGGBB"
     TEXT = "ColorName" | "#RRGGBB"
     VLINK = "ColorName" | "#RRGGBB">
```

The **<BODY>** tag must appear after the **<HEAD>** tag. The attributes appearing in the **<BODY>** tag let programmers customize a page's colors.

<CENTER>....</CENTER>.   These tags center text. The **<CENTER>** tag is a shorthand form of **<DIV ALIGN = "CENTER">**.

<DOCTYPE>.   The **<DOCTYPE>** tag is the first line of an HTML program. It specifies the HTML version and the language.

Syntax:
```
<!DOCTYPE HTML PUBLIC "-//W3C//DTD HTML 4.0 Transitional//EN">
```

<DIV>...</DIV>. The **DIV**ision Block tags encase a block of text.

Syntax:
```
<DIV ALIGN = "CENTER" | "LEFT" | "RIGHT" | "JUSTIFY"> .... </DIV>
```

<HEAD>...</HEAD>. These tags encase the head of a page. They should appear after the **<HTML>** tag. Only **<TITLE>, <BASE>, <META>,** and **<SCRIPT>** tags (and the corresponding closers) may be put in the head.

<HTML>...</HTML>. These tags encase an HTML page. The **<HTML>** tag should appear after the **<DOCTYPE>** tag. The **</HTML>** tag should be the last statement in an HTML program.

<Hn>...<Hn>. The **H**eading tag uses values from 1 through 6 for *n*. "1" is the largest heading, while "6" is the smallest.

Syntax:
```
<Hn ALIGN = "CENTER" | "LEFT" | "RIGHT" | "JUSTIFY"> ... </Hn>
```

<HR>. The **H**orizontal **R**ule tag (HR) creates a line.

Syntax:
```
<HR ALIGN = "CENTER" | "LEFT" | "RIGHT" | "JUSTIFY"
    NOSHADE
    WIDTH = "pixels | percentage%"
    SIZE = "pixels>
```

<P>...</P>. The **P**aragraph tag is used to denote the start of a new paragraph. The end tag, **</P>**, is optional.

Syntax:
```
<P ALIGN = "CENTER" | "LEFT" | "RIGHT" |"JUSTIFY"> ... </P>
```

<TITLE>*Title of Page***</TITLE>.** These tags encase a page's title as it appears in a browser's title line.

HTML TIPS

1. **Tag and Attribute Names.** HTML tag and attribute names are *not* case sensitive. The tag and attribute names can be written in upper-case letters, lower-case letters, or a combination. Many programmers use only UPPERCASE letters because it's easier to see the tags.

2. **Attribute Values.** Attribute values might be case sensitive. This is especially true for form-related attributes.

3. **Nested Tags.** Tags must be nested rather than crossed.

4. **Tag Spacing.** Do not leave any spaces between < and the tag name. Do not leave any spaces before the > symbol. Spaces can cause unpredictable errors.

5. **Incorrect Tag Names and/or Attributes.** Browsers ignore tag names or attributes that are written incorrectly. If a page looks incorrect, check the spelling of the attribute and tag names.

6. **Comments.** Use comments to document a page.

2 Fonts, Colors, and Character Entities

The HTML tags discussed in Chapter 1 offer little control over the appearance of a page's text. HTML provides several tags that change the style of text. All of the style tags form containers into which we place text or other style tags. The style tags are divided into two groups: *physical style tags* and *logical style tags*.

PHYSICAL STYLE TAGS

These tags dictate the physical appearance of the text they enclose. For example, **bold** or *italics* represent physical styles. Since the physical style tags form containers for text, they have beginning and ending tags. We can nest the tags to produce a combined style, for example, ***bold italics***. The physical style tags available in HTML are as follows:

Bold.   The `<B>` ... `</B>` tags display the enclosed text in **bold**.

Big.   The `<BIG>` ... `</BIG>` tags display the enclosed text in a font that is larger than the standard HTML font size.

Blink.   The `<BLINK>` ... `</BLINK>` tags make the enclosed text blink on and off. This tag is available in Netscape Navigator, but not in Internet Explorer. This tag should be used cautiously, because a page full of blinking text can cause seizures in individuals viewing the page.

Italics.   The `<I>` ... `</I>` tags display the enclosed text in *italics*.

Small.   The `<SMALL>` ... `</SMALL>` tags display the enclosed text in a font that is smaller than the standard HTML font size.

Strike.   The `<STRIKE>` ... `</STRIKE>` tags cross out the enclosed text.

Subscripts.   The `<SUB>` ... `</SUB>` tags write the enclosed text as a subscript.

Superscripts.   The `<SUP>` ... `</SUP>` tags write the enclosed text as a superscript.

Monospaced. The <TT> ... </TT> tags display the enclosed text in a style reminiscent of old teletype machines or typewriters.

Underline. <U> ... </U> tags underline the enclosed text.

The Web page displayed in Figure 2.1 contains an example of each of the physical font tags. Try to write the page before examining the HTML in Figure 2.2.

Figure 2.1 The *Physical Style Tags* Page   **Figure 2.2** HTML for *Physical Style Tags* Page

Figure 2.2 contains the HTML for the physical font page. Notice the **<BODY BGCOLOR = "white">** tag. The **BGCOLOR** attribute of the body tag changes the background color of the page. Netscape uses a gray background color that produces an unsightly page. Later in the chapter, we look at other background color possibilities.

LOGICAL STYLE TAGS

HTML logical style tags affect the content of the enclosed text rather than its physical appearance. These tags let the browser determine the physical appearance. The logical style tags are as follows:

Citation. The **<CITE>** and **</CITE>** tags indicate that the enclosed text is a citation. Many browsers display citations in italics.

Code. The **<CODE>** and **</CODE>** tags indicate that the enclosed text is a computer program. By convention, computer programs are displayed in a monospaced font.

Emphasis. The `<EM>` and `</EM>` tags indicate that the enclosed text is to be emphasized. In most browsers, emphasized text is displayed in italics.

Keyboard Input. The `<KBD>` and `</KBD>` tags indicate that the enclosed text is keyboard input. For example, the text might be a user's response to a prompt given by a computer program. Keyboard input is usually displayed in a monospaced font.

Character Sequence. The `<SAMP>` and `</SAMP>` tags indicate that the enclosed text is a literal sequence of characters, or *wysiwyg* ("what you see is what you get"). Literal character sequences are usually displayed in a monospaced font.

Strong. Use the `<STRONG>` and `</STRONG>` tags when you really want to make a statement that no one will miss. Most browsers display strong text in bold.

Variable. The `<VAR>` and `</VAR>` tags indicate that the enclosed text is a variable in a mathematical expression or a computer program. By mathematical and computer science conventions, variables are displayed in italics.

Figure 2.3 contains a web page that provides an example of each of the logical font style tags. Try to write the HTML for this page before examining Figure 2.4.

Figure 2.4 contains the HTML for the *Logical Style Tags* page.

Which of the style tags is preferable? The answer depends upon a page's audience. To reach the largest possible audience, web page developers use logical style tags. Physical style tags represent an older visual specification of text. In contrast, the logical style tags reflect a spoken style. A physical style tag conveys little information to a Braille browser, but a logical style tag does. A logical style tag offers clues to intonation if the browser is capable of speech. If the browser is only textual, it can translate the logical tags into a physical appearance that still conveys the tag's content.

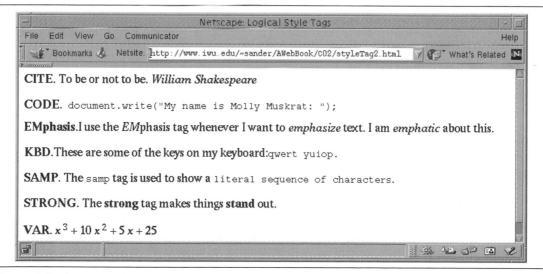

Figure 2.3 The *Logical Style Tags* Page

```
<!DOCTYPE HTML PUBLIC "-//W3C//DTD HTML 4.0 Transitional//EN">
<HTML>
<HEAD><TITLE>Logical Style Tags</TITLE></HEAD>
<BODY BGCOLOR = "white">
<B>CITE</B>. To be or not to be. <CITE>William Shakespeare</CITE><P>
<B>CODE</B>.<CODE>document.write("My name is Molly Muskrat: ");</CODE><P>
<B>EMphasis</B>. I use the <EM>EM</EM>phasis tag whenever I want to <EM>emphasize</EM> text. I am
<EM>emphatic</EM> about this.<P>
<B>KBD</B>.These are some of the keys on my keyboard:<KBD>qwert yuiop.</KBD> <P><B>SAMP</B>. The
<SAMP>samp</SAMP> tag is used to show a <SAMP>literal sequence of characters</SAMP>.<P>
<B>STRONG</B>. The <STRONG>strong</STRONG> tag makes things <STRONG>stand</STRONG> out.<P>
<B>VAR</B>. <VAR>x</VAR><sup>3</Sup> + 10 <VAR>x</VAR><SUP>2</SUP> + 5 <VAR>x</VAR> + 25 <P>
</BODY></HTML>
```

Figure 2.4 HTML for the *Logical Style Tags* Page

THE <PRE> TAG

HTML has the annoying habit of removing extra spaces from any text that we write. What do we do if we want to preserve the text's formatting? We use the **<PRE>** tag. The tag's name stands for *preformatted text*, which means that the browser displays the text exactly as we entered it on the page. Spaces and blank lines are preserved.

The **<PRE>** and its corresponding end tag, **</PRE>**, form a container for the preformatted text and any style tags that are used with the text. HTML prints the encased text in a monospaced font, and leaves a blank line before and after the text contained within **<PRE>...</PRE>** tags.

Figure 2.5 contains a simple dessert menu that was constructed with a **<PRE>** tag. Periods are used to align the weekdays and the desserts. Spaces could have been used to create the same effect. Notice the monospaced font.

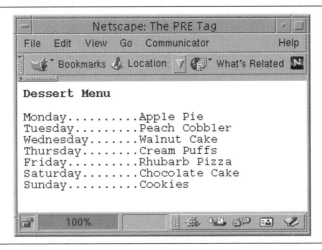

Figure 2.5 A *Dessert Menu* Page

Figure 2.6 contains the HTML for the *Dessert Menu* page. The menu heading was written in bold to highlight it. The remainder of the menu is in a plain font. The blank line between *Dessert Menu* and Monday's offering is preserved when the page is displayed.

```
<!DOCTYPE HTML PUBLIC "-//W3C//DTD HTML 4.0 Transitional//EN">
<HTML><HEAD><TITLE>The PRE Tag</TITLE></HEAD>
<BODY BGCOLOR = "white">
<PRE><B>Dessert Menu</B>

Monday..........Apple Pie
Tuesday.........Peach Cobbler
Wednesday.......Walnut Cake
Thursday........Cream Puffs
Friday..........Rhubarb Pizza
Saturday........Chocolate Cake
Sunday..........Cookies</PRE>
</BODY></HTML>
```

Figure 2.6 HTML for the *Dessert Menu* Page

Although the monospaced format used by the **<PRE>** tag works well when displaying computer programs, it produces a less pleasing appearance in most other applications. The **<PRE>** tag usually produces the same monospaced font as the **<TT>** tag, but placing a **</TT>** tag *within* a **<PRE>** *tag turns off the monospace font.* Figure 2.7 contains a *Dinner Menu* page. The menu is preformatted; however, the first line uses the browser's default font rather than the monospaced font.

Figure 2.8 contains the HTML for the *Dinner Menu* page. The **</TT>** tag immediately inside the **<PRE>** tag turns off the monospaced font. Thus, *Dinner Menu* is printed in the browser's default font. The **<TT>** tag after *Dinner Menu* switches the font back to monospaced for the remainder of the page.

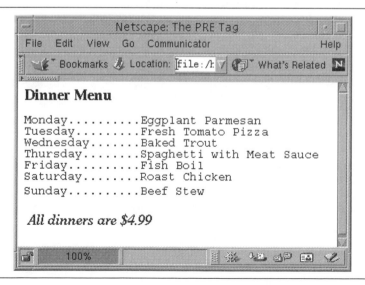

Figure 2.7 A *Dinner Menu* Page

```
<!DOCTYPE HTML PUBLIC "-//W3C//DTD HTML 4.0 Transitional//EN">
<HTML><HEAD><TITLE>The PRE Tag</TITLE></HEAD>
<BODY BGCOLOR = "white">
<PRE></TT><B>Dinner Menu</B><TT>

Monday..........Eggplant Parmesan
Tuesday.........Fresh Tomato Pizza
Wednesday.......Baked Trout
Thursday........Spaghetti with Meat Sauce
Friday..........Fish Boil
Saturday........Roast Chicken
Sunday..........Beef Stew</TT>
<I> All dinners are $4.99</I></PRE>
</BODY></HTML>
```

Figure 2.8 HTML for the *Dinner Menu* Page

THE <BLOCKQUOTE> TAG

Block quotations refer to quotations that extend beyond two or three lines of text. By convention, these quotations are indented from both the left and right margins. The **<BLOCKQUOTE>** tag and its corresponding end tag, **</BLOCKQUOTE>**, create a block quotation in HTML. Figure 2.9 contains a *Custom Colors* page that uses the **<BLOCKQUOTE>** tag to indent the definition of an *HTML Custom Color* doubly.

The HTML for the *Custom Colors* page appears in Figure 2.10. The heading, *HTML Custom Colors*, is placed inside the **<BLOCKQUOTE>** tag; as a result, the heading and definition use the same indentation. The **<BLOCKQUOTE>** tag leaves a blank line before and after the block quotation. Physical and logical style tags can be used to change the appearance of the text contained within the **<BLOCKQUOTE>** ... **</BLOCKQUOTE>** tags.

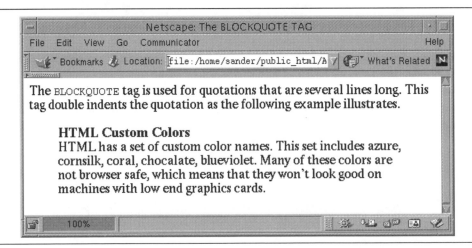

Figure 2.9 The *Custom Colors* Page

```
<!DOCTYPE HTML PUBLIC "-//W3C//DTD HTML 4.0 Transitional//EN">
<HTML><HEAD><TITLE>The BLOCKQUOTE TAG</TITLE></HEAD>
<BODY BGCOLOR = "white">
The <TT>BLOCKQUOTE</TT> tag is used for quotations that are several lines long.
This tag double indents the quotation as the following example illustrates.
<BLOCKQUOTE><B>HTML Custom Colors</B><BR>
HTML has a set of custom color names. This set includes azure, cornsilk,coral, chocolate,
blueviolet. Many of these colors are not browser safe, which means that they won't look good on
machines with low end graphics cards.
</BLOCKQUOTE>
</BODY></HTML>
```

Figure 2.10 HTML for the *Custom Colors* Page

THE <FONT> TAG

The **<FONT>** tag contains attributes that can change the font size, color, and face of the text that follows this tag. The values associated with the attributes remain in effect until the **</FONT>** tag is encountered. The **</FONT>** tag resets the font to the browser's default settings.

Colors

HTML provides tags that change the background color of a page or a table (per Chapter 4) and the font color for displaying text or links (per Chapter 5). We change the background and text colors for a page in the **<BODY>** tag. We change the font color in the **<FONT>** tag. Figure 2.11 contains the syntax for both tags.

(a) The BODY Tag	(b) The FONT Tag

`<BODY BGCOLOR = "ColorName" |`
`"#RRGGBB"`
`TEXT = "ColorName" | "#RRGGBB">`
	`<FONT COLOR = "ColorName" |`
	`"#RRGGBB">`

Figure 2.11 Body and Font Tags

The **<BODY>** tag contains attributes that change the background and foreground (or font) color of an entire page.

Background Color.   The **BGCOLOR** attribute changes the background color of the page. The standard background color in Netscape Navigator is gray. The standard background color in Internet Explorer is white.

Text Color.   The **TEXT** attribute changes the text color (or font color) for the *entire* page. The **COLOR** attribute of the **<FONT>** tag changes only the text contained between the **<FONT>** and **</FONT>** tags.

As Figure 2.11 indicates, we can use an HTML color name or an RGB value for the color.

Color Names

HTML contains two sets of color names: standard and custom. Figure 2.12 contains a page displaying the standard color names. Each line of text is written in the color. These colors look the same on all monitors, operating systems, and browsers. Colors that appear identical on all systems are called *browser-safe* colors.

Figure 2.13 contains the HTML for the *Standard Colors* page. Each **<FONT>** tag changes the font color to a different standard color.

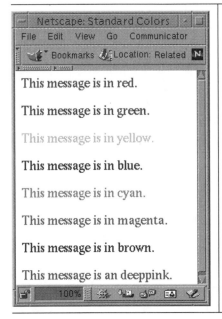

```
<!DOCTYPE HTML PUBLIC "-//W3C//DTD HTML 4.0 Transitional//EN">
<HTML>
<HEAD><TITLE>Standard Colors</TITLE></HEAD>
<BODY BGCOLOR = "white">
<FONT COLOR = "red"> This message is in red.</FONT><P>
<FONT COLOR = "green"> This message is in green.</FONT><P>
<FONT COLOR = "yellow"> This message is in yellow.</FONT><P>
<FONT COLOR = "blue"> This message is in blue.</FONT><P>
<FONT COLOR = "cyan"> This message is in cyan.</FONT><P>
<FONT COLOR = "magenta"> This message is in magenta.</FONT><P>
<FONT COLOR = "brown"> This message is in brown.</FONT><P>
<FONT COLOR = "deeppink"> This message is in deeppink.</FONT>
</BODY></HTML>
```

Figure 2.12 The *Standard Colors* Page

Figure 2.13 HTML for the *Standard Colors* Page

HTML also contains a set of approximately 100 additional color names. The set includes names such as *papayawhip, peachpuff,* and *thistle*. Unfortunately, most of these colors are not browser-safe: Some browsers will not display some of these colors correctly.

RGB Values

We can create custom colors by using RGB ("*Red, Green, Blue*") values. The format for these custom colors is **#RRGGBB**, where RR represents a two-digit hexadecimal red value, GG a two-digit hexadecimal green value, and BB a two-digit hexadecimal blue value. Theoretically, this means that we could create $256 \times 256 \times 256 = 16,777,216$ distinct colors; however, only 216 of these RGB combinations are browser-safe. Figure 2.14 contains a table listing the browser-safe RGB values. Figure 2.14(a) lists the hexadecimal values required by HTML. Figure 2.14(b) contains the decimal equivalents.

(a) Hexadecimal	(b) Decimal Equivalent
00	0
33	51
66	102
99	153
CC	204
FF	255

Figure 2.14 RGB Values for Browser-Safe Colors

The RGB values for black and white are **#000000** and **#FFFFFF**, respectively. Figure 2.15 contains a *Vegetable Colors* page that illustrates browser-safe RGB values.

Figure 2.16 contains the HTML for the *Vegetable Colors* page. Try experimenting with various values to create other browser-safe colors.

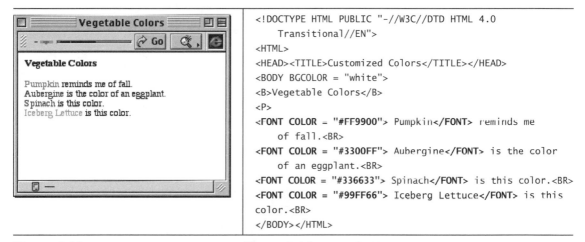

```
<!DOCTYPE HTML PUBLIC "-//W3C//DTD HTML 4.0
    Transitional//EN">
<HTML>
<HEAD><TITLE>Customized Colors</TITLE></HEAD>
<BODY BGCOLOR = "white">
<B>Vegetable Colors</B>
<P>
<FONT COLOR = "#FF9900"> Pumpkin</FONT> reminds me
    of fall.<BR>
<FONT COLOR = "#3300FF"> Aubergine</FONT> is the color
    of an eggplant.<BR>
<FONT COLOR = "#336633"> Spinach</FONT> is this color.<BR>
<FONT COLOR = "#99FF66"> Iceberg Lettuce</FONT> is this
color.<BR>
</BODY></HTML>
```

Figure 2.15 The *Vegetable Colors* Page   **Figure 2.16** HTML for the *Vegetable Colors* Page

Font Size

As its name implies, the **SIZE** attribute changes the font size. This attribute requires a value between 1 and 7, where 1 is the smallest font size, 3 is the default size, and 7 is the largest font size. For example, the statement

```
<FONT SIZE = "5"> This is a bigger font.</FONT>
```

prints the enclosed message in font size 5. We can also use + and − to change the font. Thus, the following statement changes the font size to 5 if the *current* font size is 3:

```
<FONT SIZE = "+2"> This is a bigger font.</FONT>
```

Figure 2.17 contains a sample page illustrating the font size attribute.
Figure 2.18 contains the HTML for the *Font Size* page.

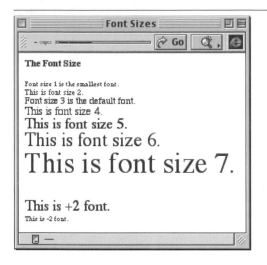

Figure 2.17 The *Font Size* Page

```
<!DOCTYPE HTML PUBLIC "-//W3C//DTD HTML 4.0
    Transitional//EN">
<HTML>
<HEAD><TITLE>Font Sizes</TITLE></HEAD>
<BODY BGCOLOR = "white">
<B>The Font Size</B>
<P>
<FONT SIZE = "1">Font size 1 is the smallest
    font.</FONT><BR>
<FONT SIZE = "2">This is font size 2.</FONT><BR>
<FONT SIZE = "3">Font size 3 is the default
    font.</FONT><BR>
<FONT SIZE = "4">This is font size 4.</FONT><BR>
<FONT SIZE = "5">This is font size 5.</FONT><BR>
<FONT SIZE = "6">This is font size 6.</FONT><BR>
<FONT SIZE = "7">This is font size 7.</FONT><BR>
<BR><BR>
<FONT SIZE = "+2">This is +2 font.</FONT><BR>
<FONT SIZE = "-2">This is -2 font.</FONT>
</BODY></HTML>
```

Figure 2.18 HTML for the *Font Size* Page

Font Faces

The **FACE** attribute changes the face of the font. Most Web programmers do not use this attribute because IBM, MAC, and UNIX systems have different default font faces. This means that the face might not be available on the user's browser. Figure 2.19 lists several face names. Notice what happens when the font is not built into the system.

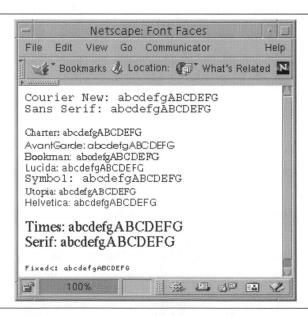

Figure 2.19 The *Font Face* Page

As Figure 2.19 indicates, the browser chooses a font face if the user's system doesn't have the requested font face. Thus, the face names from Charter through Helvetica use the same font.

Figure 2.20 contains the HTML for the *Font Face* page.

```
<!DOCTYPE HTML PUBLIC "-//W3C//DTD HTML 4.0 Transitional//EN">
<HTML>
<HEAD><TITLE> Font Faces</TITLE></HEAD>
<BODY BGCOLOR = "white">
<FONT FACE = "Courier New"> Courier New: abcdefgABCDEFG</FONT><BR>
<FONT FACE = "Sans Serif"> Sans Serif: abcdefgABCDEFG</FONT><BR><BR>
<FONT FACE = "Charter"> Charter: abcdefgABCDEFG </FONT><BR>
<FONT FACE = "Avantgarde"> AvantGarde: abcdefgABCDEFG</FONT><BR>
<FONT FACE = "Bookman"> Bookman: abcdefgABCDEFG</FONT><BR>
<FONT FACE = "Lucida"> Lucida: abcdefgABCDEFG</FONT><BR>
<FONT FACE = "Symbol"> Symbol: abcdefgABCDEFG</FONT><BR>
<FONT FACE = "Utopia"> Utopia: abcdefgABCDEFG</FONT><BR>
<FONT FACE = "Helvetica"> Helvetica: abcdefgABCDEFG</FONT><BR><BR>
<FONT FACE = "Times"> Times: abcdefgABCDEFG</FONT><BR>
<FONT FACE = "Serif"> Serif: abcdefgABCDEFG</FONT><BR><BR>
<FONT FACE = "Fixed"> Fixed<: abcdefgABCDEFG</FONT><BR><BR>
</BODY></HTML>
```

Figure 2.20 HTML for the *Font Face* Page

To compensate for differences in systems, Web programmers choose several compatible font faces when using the **FACE** attribute. For example, a font statement that works on most, if not all, browsers is

```
<FONT FACE = "Times, Serif, Times New Roman">
```

COMBINING THE FONT, PHYSICAL STYLE, AND LOGICAL STYLE TAGS

Thus, far we've used the font style tags in isolation. The font style tags can be combined to produce interesting effects. Figure 2.21 contains a short story that illustrates the versatility of HTML. The page integrates many of the tags that we've discussed. For example, the *Magic Mango* in the story is always in a mango color. When Freddie Ferret talks about blinking, the text blinks. Look at the page and try to write the HTML that produced it.

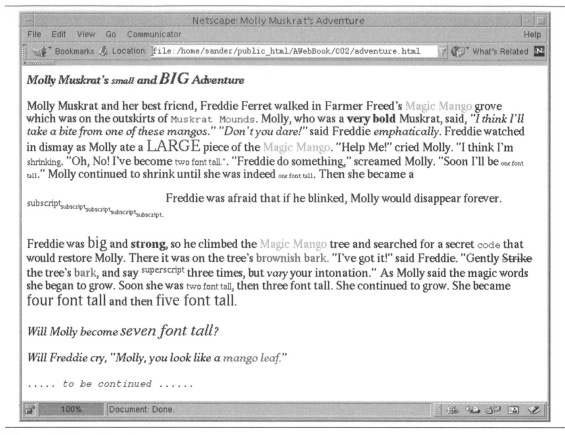

Figure 2.21 *Molly's Adventure* Page

Figure 2.22 contains the HTML for *Molly's Adventure* page. The tags are highlighted. Notice how easy it is to create interesting effects.

THE `<BASEFONT>` TAG

The `<BASEFONT>` tag changes the default font size for an entire page. It has a single attribute, **SIZE**, on Netscape Navigator. On Internet Explorer, this tag also has **FACE** and **COLOR** attributes. We can still change the text size from the new default by using `<FONT>` tags. When the browser encounters the `</FONT>` tag, it reverts to the base font. Figure 2.23 contains a *Base Font* page. The default font size is set to 2.

Figure 2.24 contains the HTML for the *Base Font* page.

CHARACTER AND NUMERIC ENTITIES

There are times that we'd like to write such statements as **a + b < c**. Unfortunately, the *less than* symbol, <, also indicates the start of an HTML tag, so a browser would interpret the *less than* symbol as the start of a tag named *c*. To handle this situation, we use HTML character entities. Character enti-

```
<!DOCTYPE HTML PUBLIC "-//W3C//DTD HTML 4.0 Transitional//EN">
<HTML>
<HEAD><TITLE>Molly Muskrat's Adventure</TITLE></HEAD>
<BODY BGCOLOR = "white">
<B><I>Molly Muskrat's <SMALL>small</SMALL> and <BIG>BIG</BIG> Adventure</I></B>
<P> Molly Muskrat and her best friend, Freddie Ferret walked in Farmer Freed's <FONT COLOR =
"#FF9999">Magic Mango</FONT> grove which was on the outskirts of <SAMP>Muskrat Mounds</SAMP>.
Molly, who was a <B>very bold</B> Muskrat, said, <CITE>"I think I'll take a bite from one of these
mangos."</CITE> <EM>"Don't you dare!"</EM> said Freddie <EM>emphatically</EM>. Freddie watched in
dismay as Molly ate a <BIG>LARGE</BIG> piece of the <FONT COLOR = "#FF9999">Magic Mango</FONT>.
"Help Me!" cried Molly. "I think I'm <SMALL>shrinking</SMALL>. "Oh, No! I've become <FONT SIZE =
"2">two font tall."</FONT>. "Freddie do something," screamed Molly. "Soon I'll be <FONT SIZE = "1">
one font tall</FONT>." Molly continued to shrink until she was indeed <FONT SIZE = "1"> one font
tall</FONT>. Then she became a <SUB>subscript<SUB>subscript
<SUB>subscript<SUB>subscript<SUB>subscript.<SUB> </SUB></SUB></SUB></SUB></SUB> Freddie was
afraid that if he <BLINK>blinked</BLINK>, Molly would disappear forever.
<P>Freddie was <BIG>big</BIG> and <STRONG>strong</STRONG>, so he climbed the <FONT COLOR =
"#FF9999">Magic Mango</FONT> tree and searched for a secret <CODE>code</CODE> that would restore
Molly. There it was on the tree's <FONT COLOR = "brown"> brownish bark.</FONT> "I've got it!" said
Freddie. "Gently <STRIKE>Strike</STRIKE> the tree's <FONT COLOR = "brown"> bark</FONT>, and say
<SUP>superscript</SUP> three times, but <VAR>vary</VAR> your intonation." As Molly said the magic
words she began to grow. Soon she was <FONT SIZE = "2">two font tall</FONT>, then <FONT SIZE =
"3">three font tall</FONT>. She continued to grow. She became <FONT SIZE = "4"> four font
tall</FONT> and then <FONT SIZE = "5">five font tall</FONT>.
<P> <EM>Will Molly become <FONT SIZE = "7">seven font tall</FONT>?</EM><P>
<EM> Will Freddie cry, "<T>Molly, you look like a <FONT COLOR = "green">mango leaf.</FONT>"</EM>
<P>
<TT>..... to be continued ......</TT>
</BODY></HTML>
```

Figure 2.22 HTML for *Molly's Adventure* Page

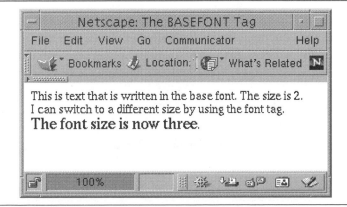

Figure 2.23 The *Base Font* Page

```
<!DOCTYPE HTML PUBLIC "-//W3C//DTD HTML 4.0 Transitional//EN">
<HTML><HEAD><TITLE>The BASEFONT Tag</TITLE></HEAD>
<BODY BGCOLOR = "white">
<BASEFONT SIZE = "2">
<!-- IE also has COlor and FACE attributes -->
This is text that is written in the base font. The size is 2.
I can switch to a different size by using the font tag. <FONT SIZE = "3">
The font size is now three</FONT>.
</BODY></HTML>
```

Figure 2.24 HTML for the *Base Font* Page

ties begin with an ampersand, **&**, and end with a semicolon. Each character entity contains an abbreviation for the desired character. For example, the character entity for *less than* is **<**.

Character entities exist for mathematical symbols, such as ×, and for letters not in the English alphabet, such as Ö. Appendix A contains a list of the HTML character entities. Each entity also has a corresponding numeric entity.

Figure 2.25 lists the character entities used in Germanic words. We'll use several of these characters to create a short list of German sentences.

Figure 2.26 contains a *German Sentences* page. Notice the umlauts and the sz ligature.

Symbol	HTML	Meaning	Symbol	HTML	Meaning
Ä	Ä	*A* Umlaut	ä	ä	*a* Umlaut
Ë	Ë	*E* Umlaut	ë	ë	*e* Umlaut
Ï	Ï	*A* Umlaut	ï	ï	*i* Umlaut
Ö	Ö	*O* Umlaut	ö	ö	*o* Umlaut
Ü	Ü	*U* Umlaut	ü	ü	*u* Umlaut
β	ß	*SZ* Ligature			

Figure 2.25 German Character Entities

Figure 2.26 The *German Sentences* Page

Figure 2.27 contains the HTML for the *German Sentences* page. The HTML character entities are highlighted.

```
<!DOCTYPE HTML PUBLIC "-//W3C//DTD HTML 4.0 Transitional//EN">
<HTML>
<HEAD><TITLE>German Sentences</TITLE></HEAD>
<BODY BGCOLOR = "white">
Das M&auml;dchen i&szlig;t die Kartoffel!<BR>
<I> The girl eats the potato.</I><P>
&Ouml;ffnet die T&uuml;r!<BR>
<I>Open the door</I><P>
Gr&uuml;&szlig; Gott!</BR>
<I>Hello. (Austria and Southern Bavaria)</I>
</BODY> <HTML>
```

Figure 2.27 HTML for the *German Sentences* Page

A NOTE ON FRACTIONS

HTML provides character entities for only three fractions: 1/4, 1/2, and 3/4. We can mimic this form for other fractions with the following HTML:

```
<FONT SIZE = "2"><SUP> x </SUP>/<SUB>y</SUB></FONT>
```

For example, the fraction **1/3** is written as

```
<FONT SIZE = "2"><SUP>1</SUP>/<SUB>3</SUB></FONT>
```

This font looks better than **1/3**.

➤ **EXERCISES**

*Directions: Many of these exercises ask you to recreate a portion of a newspaper. Use the font and color tags introduced in this chapter. Do not use header tags (**<Hn>**) unless explicitly asked to do so. Try writing two versions of the pages. Use **<PRE>** tags in the first version, **<P>** and **
** tags in the second version. Many of the exercises use colors. The directions give color suggestions. Feel free to experiment with other colors.*

1. **The *Classifieds Ads* Page.** Figure 2.28 contains classified ads for miscellaneous merchandise. Recreate these ads. Consult your local newspaper, and then add two additional ads of your choice.

2. **The *Weekly Specials* Page.** Figure 2.29 contains a list of weekly specials for an on-line grocery store. Recreate the specials, and add two of your own. The first line should be in blue.

3. **The *Advertisement* Page.** The *Less than a Buck* on-line store is running its weekly special. Figure 2.30 contains the specials. Recreate the advertisement. Add two more specials of your choice. (*Note: The first heading should be in green, the second in red.*)

Figure 2.28 The *Classified Ads* Page

Figure 2.29 The *Weekly Specials* Page

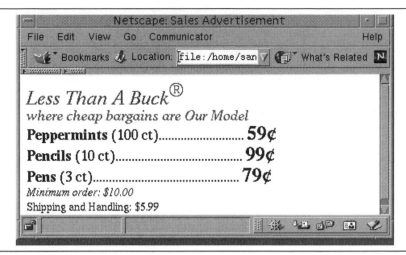

Figure 2.30 The *Advertisement* Page

4. **The *Sports Schedule* Page.** Figure 2.31 contains a fictitious radio/TV sports schedule. Recreate this table, or find a similar table in your local newspaper. The heading is in blue, and the sports are in green.

Figure 2.31 The *Sports Schedule* Page

5. **The *Sports Standings* Page.** Figure 2.32 contains the standings for a fictitious basketball conference. Recreate this display. Make the heading red and the local team's record blue.

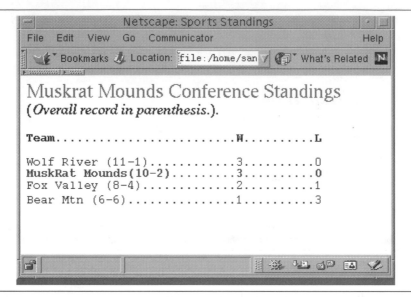

Figure 2.32 The *Sports Standings* Page

6. **The *Employment Listings* Page.** Figure 2.33 contains a fictitious set of help-wanted ads. Recreate the ads in this figure. Consult your local newspaper, and add two additional listings.

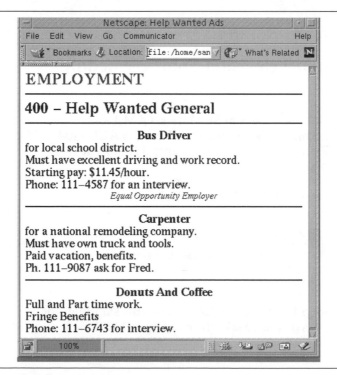

Figure 2.33 The *Employment Listings* Page

7. **The *Newspaper* Page.** Figure 2.34 contains the publication information for a fictitious newspaper. Recreate this information sheet.

Figure 2.34 The *Newspaper* Page

8. **The *Debate* Page.** Figure 2.35 contains the information sheet for a fictitious debate. Recreate this information sheet. The first line should be in blue; the *who, when, where* (and so on) titles should be in red.

Figure 2.35 The *Debate* Page

9. **The *Color and Font Coded HTML* Page.** Figure 2.36 contains an HTML page that uses color and font style to illustrate the tags, attributes, and comments. Recreate this page.

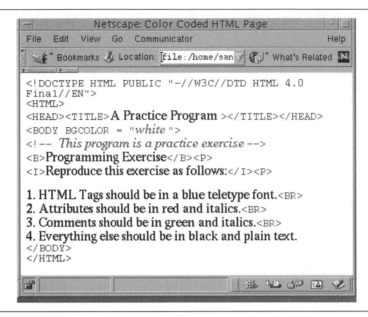

Figure 2.36 The *Color and Font Coded HTML* Page

10. **The *Catalog* Page.** Figure 2.37 contains a fictitious catalog page. The items listed with "A." and "B." are in blue. The *Sale* line is in red. Recreate this sales listing.

Figure 2.37 The *Catalog* Page

11. **The** *Character Entities* **Page.** Figure 2.38 contains five examples that use character entities. Write the HTML that produces these examples.

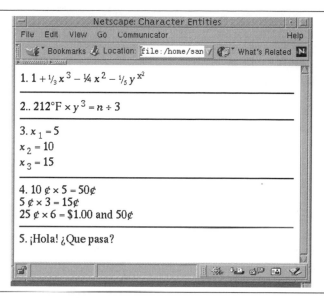

Figure 2.38 The *Character Entities* Page

12. **The** *German Conversation* **Page.** Figure 2.39 contains a simple German conversation page. Jörg's name is in blue, Maria's in red. Recreate this conversation.

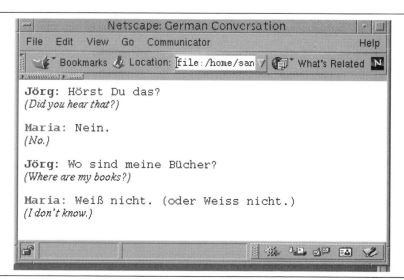

Figure 2.39 The *German Conversation* Page

13. **The** *Local Forecast* **Page.** Figure 2.40 contains information on the local forecast. Recreate this table, or find a similar table, in your local newspaper. You may use **<PRE>** tags for this table. Use different colors for the headings.

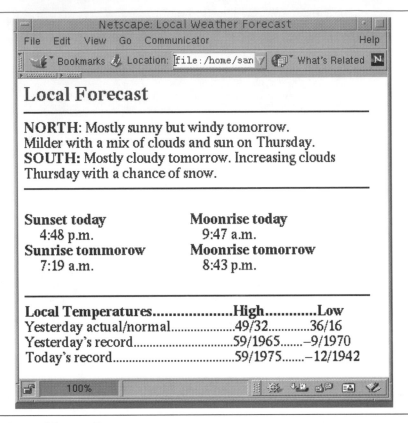

Figure 2.40 The *Local Forecast* Page

14. **The *Browser-Safe Colors* Page.** Create eight browser-safe colors. Write eight different messages in these colors. The message should contain the color code and a color name. Figure 2.41 shows several examples.

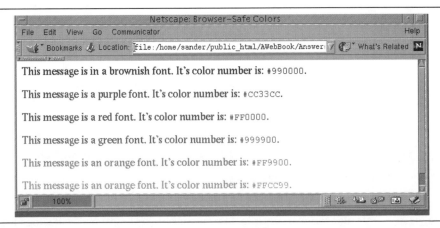

Figure 2.41 The *Browser-Safe Colors* Page

15. **The *Color-Coded Story* Page.** Figure 2.42 contains a simple story. The words are color-coded with the standard colors—for example, blue things are printed in blue.

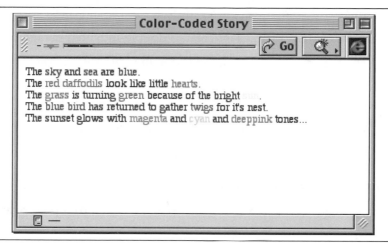

Figure 2.42 The *Color-Coded Story* Page

16. **The *Short Story* Page, version 2.** Create your own short story with color-coded words. Use browser-safe colors to create your story.

17. **The *German Grammar* Page.** Figure 2.43 contains a simple grammar sheet for the German verb *grüßen*. Recreate this grammar page.

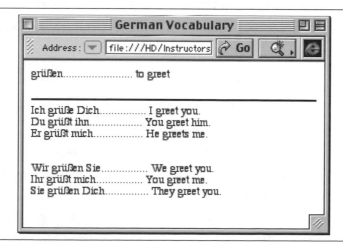

Figure 2.43 The *German Grammar* Page

➤ HTML TAGS (IN ALPHABETICAL ORDER)

<B>...</B>. These tags display the enclosed text in *bold.* (*Physical Style Tag*)

<BASEFONT>...</BASEFONT>. These tags set the base font for the page. Netscape recognizes only the **SIZE** attribute. Internet Explorer recognizes the **SIZE, FACE**, and **COLOR** attributes.

<BLOCKQUOTE>...</BLOCKQUOTE>. These tags create a double-indented paragraph.

<BIG>...</BIG>. The tags display the enclosed text in big letters. (*Physical Style Tag*)

<BLINK>...</BLINK>. The tags make the enclosed text blink. This tag is available only in Netscape Navigator. Use this tag cautiously, because it can cause seizures. (*Physical Style Tag*)

<CITE>...</CITE>. These tags are used to display citations. Most browsers use italics for citations. (*Logical Style Tag*)

<CODE>...</CODE>. These tags are used to display code, that is, computer programs. Most browsers use a monospaced font for code. (*Logical Style Tag*)

<EM>...</EM>. These tags *emphasize* text. Most browsers use italics to emphasize text. (*Logical Style Tag*)

<FONT>...</FONT>. These tags let the programmer determine the color, face, and size of the text that they enclose. (*Note:* the vertical bar used with the color attribute indicates that we can specify a color name or an RGB value.)

Syntax:
```
<FONT COLOR = "Name | #RRGGBB"
    FACE = "FaceName"
    SIZE = 1...6>
... Place text here ....
</FONT>
```

<KBD>...</KBD>. These tags display the enclosed text as plain text as if from a keyboard. Most browsers use a monospaced font for the keyboard style. (*Logical Style Tag*)

<I>...</I>. These tags display the enclosed text in italics. (*Physical Style Tag*)

<PRE>...</PRE>. These tags create **PRE**formatted text.

<SMALL>...</SMALL>. These tags display the enclosed text in small letters. (*Physical Style Tag*)

<STRIKE>...</STRIKE>. These tags cross out the enclosed text. (*Physical Style Tag*)

_{...}. These tags create a subscript. (*Physical Style Tag*)

^{...}. These tags create a superscript. (*Physical Style Tag*)

<TT>...</TT>. These tags display the enclosed text as plain text as if from a teletype. Most browsers use a monospaced font for teletype text. (*Physical Style Tag*)

<U>...</U>. These tags underline the enclosed text. (*Physical Style Tag*)

<VAR>...</VAR>. These tags indicate that enclosed text is a variable. Most browsers use italics for variables. (*Logical Style Tag*)

➤ HTML TIPS

1. **Background and Text Color.** Use `BGCOLOR` and `TEXT` attributes in the `<BODY>` tag to change the background and text color. You may use a standard color, an HTML color (not recommended), or an RGB value (written as `#RRGGBB`).

2. **Browser-Safe Colors.** Use only browser-safe colors. Browser-safe colors use the following RGB values: 00, 33, 66, 99, CC, FF.

3. **Spacing.** Use `<PRE>...</PRE>` tags to place extra spaces in your text. To change the default monospaced font used by the `<PRE>` tag, use a `<TT>` tag immediately after the `<PRE>` tag. Use the `</TT>` tag to change back to the monospaced font within PRE.

4. Use the `<FONT FACE = "Times, Serif, Times New Roman">` tag immediately after the `<PRE>` tag. Use the `</FONT>` tag to change back to monospaced font.

5. **Character and Numeric Entities.** Use character or numeric entities for mathematical symbols and foreign words. The complete list appears in Appendix A.

6. **Simulating Fractions.** Use `<SUP>`x`</SUP>`/`<SUB>`y`</SUB>` to create "better looking" fractions.

3 Lists

Pick up a local newspaper and glance through the pages. Unless it's an unusual day, you should see several examples of lists. Some lists use bullets to distinguish between the list items. Other lists use numbers. Lists are popular because they present information in a format that is easy to understand. In this chapter, we examine HTML tags that create lists.

HTML offers three list alternatives: unordered lists, ordered lists, and definition lists. Earlier versions of HTML provided menu lists and directory lists; however, these lists offered no advantages, because the same effects can be achieved with one of the other list types.

UNORDERED LISTS

Unordered lists resemble the bullet lists often found in newspapers or magazines. These lists are created with the **<UL>...</UL>** tags. The tags form a container for the list items that are created with **<LI>** tags. Each list item has a separate **<LI>** tag. Figure 3.1 contains a *Special Teams* page. The page uses an unordered list. Notice the small bullet that appears before each special team. HTML calls this type of bullet a **DISC**.

The HTML for the *Special Teams* page appears in Figure 3.2.

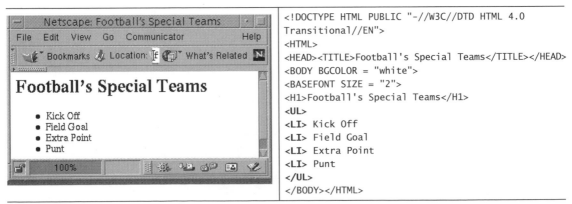

```
<!DOCTYPE HTML PUBLIC "-//W3C//DTD HTML 4.0
Transitional//EN">
<HTML>
<HEAD><TITLE>Football's Special Teams</TITLE></HEAD>
<BODY BGCOLOR = "white">
<BASEFONT SIZE = "2">
<H1>Football's Special Teams</H1>
<UL>
<LI> Kick Off
<LI> Field Goal
<LI> Extra Point
<LI> Punt
</UL>
</BODY></HTML>
```

Figure 3.1 The *Special Teams* Page

Figure 3.2 HTML for the *Special Teams* Page

The browser indents all items contained within a list. Each list item automatically appears on a separate line; we do not need to use **
** tags to separate the items.

THE *PICKLE RECIPE* PAGE

Figure 3.3 contains a *Pickle Recipe* page that was created with two unordered lists. The first list contains the starting ingredients. The second list contains additional ingredients. The lists are printed in italics. Notice the changes in indentation as the lists open and close.

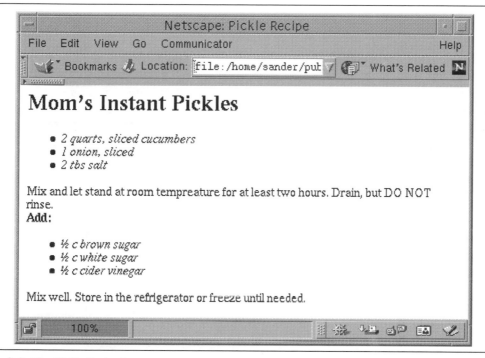

Figure 3.3 The *Pickle Recipe* Page

Figure 3.4 contains the HTML for the *Pickle Recipe* page. The *italic* tags are completely contained in the **<UL>...>/UL>** tags. This prevents subtle errors from creeping into the page.

THE TYPE ATTRIBUTE FOR UNORDERED LISTS

The **<UL>** tag has a single attribute, **TYPE**. It changes the type of bullet used for the list items. The **TYPE** values recognized by HTML are **DISC** (the default), **CIRCLE**, and **SQUARE**. Figure 3.5 contains a *Healthy Shopping* page that uses squares to denote the list items.

Figure 3.6 contains the HTML for the *Healthy Shopping* page. The **TYPE** attribute in the **<UL>** tag changes the bullet type to a square.

```
<!DOCTYPE HTML PUBLIC "-//W3C//DTD HTML 4.0 Transitional//EN">
<HTML>
<HEAD><TITLE>Pickle Recipe</TITLE></HEAD>
<BODY BGCOLOR = "white">
<BASEFONT SIZE = "2">
<H1>Mom's Instant Pickles</H1>
<UL><I>
<LI> 2 quarts, sliced cucumbers
<LI> 1 onion, sliced
<LI> 2 tbs salt</I>
</UL>
<P>
Mix and let stand at room tempreature for at least two hours. Drain, but DO NOT rinse.<BR>
<B>Add:</B><P>
<UL><I>
<LI> &frac12; c brown sugar
<LI> &frac12; c white sugar
<LI> &frac12; c cider vinegar</I>
</UL>
<P>
Mix well. Store in the refrigerator or freeze until needed.
</BODY></HTML>
```

Figure 3.4 HTML for the *Pickle Recipe* Page

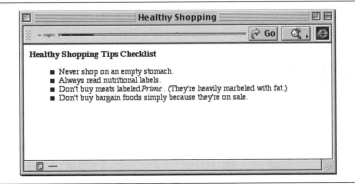

Figure 3.5 The *Healthy Shopping* Page

```
<!DOCTYPE HTML PUBLIC "-//W3C//DTD HTML 4.0 Transitional//EN">
<HTML>
<HEAD><TITLE>Healthy Shopping</TITLE></HEAD>
<BODY BGCOLOR = "white">
<B>Healthy Shopping Tips Checklist</H1>
<UL TYPE = "SQUARE">
<LI>Never shop on an empty stomach.
<LI>Always read nutritional labels.
<LI>Don't buy meats labeled <EM>Prime</EM>. (They're heavily marbeled with fat.)
<LI>Don't buy bargain foods simply because they're on sale.
</UL>
</BODY></HTML>
```

Figure 3.6 HTML for the *Healthy Shopping* Page

THE *UNORDERED LISTS TYPES* PAGE

The **<LI>** tag also contains a **TYPE** attribute that changes the bullet type of a list item. This is the only attribute allowed for items in an unordered list. Figure 3.7 shows an unordered list using each of the **TYPE** values.

Figure 3.8 contains the HTML for the *Unordered List Types* page. Each **<LI>** tag uses a different type.

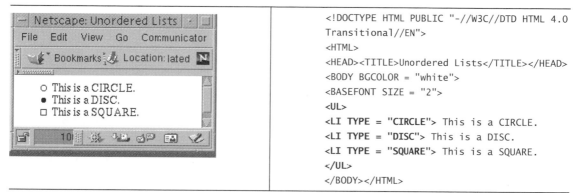

```
<!DOCTYPE HTML PUBLIC "-//W3C//DTD HTML 4.0
Transitional//EN">
<HTML>
<HEAD><TITLE>Unordered Lists</TITLE></HEAD>
<BODY BGCOLOR = "white">
<BASEFONT SIZE = "2">
<UL>
<LI TYPE = "CIRCLE"> This is a CIRCLE.
<LI TYPE = "DISC"> This is a DISC.
<LI TYPE = "SQUARE"> This is a SQUARE.
</UL>
</BODY></HTML>
```

Figure 3.7 The *Unordered List Types* Page

Figure 3.8 HTML for the *Unordered List Types* Page

NESTED UNORDERED LISTS

Figure 3.9 contains a set of unordered lists that show the scoring system used in football. Each level of indentation indicates the start of a new list. So does the change in the type of bullet; the browser uses a different type of bullet for each level of indentation.

Figure 3.9 uses the indentation provided by unordered lists to illustrate football scores: the higher the level of indentation, the lower the score. Items at the same level of indentation have

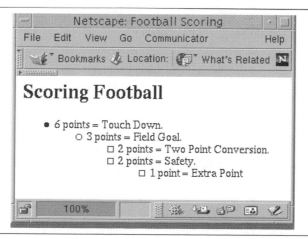

Figure 3.9 The *Football Scoring* Page

the same score. HTML automatically changes the indentation and the default type with each list. Figure 3.10 contains the HTML for the *Football Scoring* page.

```
<!DOCTYPE HTML PUBLIC "-//W3C//DTD HTML 4.0 Transitional//EN">
<HTML>
<HEAD><TITLE>Football Scoring</TITLE></HEAD>
<BODY BGCOLOR = "white">
<BASEFONT SIZE = "2">
<H1>Scoring Football</H1>
<UL>
<LI> 6 points = Touch Down.
<UL>
<LI> 3 points = Field Goal.
<UL>
<LI> 2 points = Two Point Conversion.
<LI> 2 points = Safety.
<UL>
<LI> 1 point = Extra Point
</UL></Ul></UL></UL>
</Body></HTML>
```

Figure 3.10 HTML for the *Football Scoring* Page

Suppose we wish to maintain the indentation levels for the *Football Scoring* page while using the same bullet type for all of the lists. Figure 3.11 contains a new version of the *Football Scoring* page. In this version, a **SQUARE** is used consistently through all of the lists.

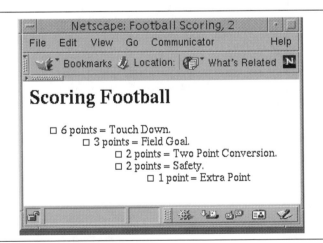

Figure 3.11 The *Football Scoring* Page, version 2

Figure 3.12 contains the HTML for the second version of the *Football Scoring* page. In this version, the type is explicitly set to **SQUARE** in each of the **<UL>** tags. As usual, the key features are typed in bold for teaching emphasis; naturally, you would not need to use bold in the HTML code in everyday applications.

```
<!DOCTYPE HTML PUBLIC "-//W3C//DTD HTML 4.0 Transitional//EN">
<HTML>
<HEAD><TITLE>Football Scoring, 2</TITLE></HEAD>
<BODY BGCOLOR = "white">
<BASEFONT SIZE = "2">
<H1>Scoring Football</H1>
<UL TYPE = "SQUARE">
<LI> 6 points = Touch Down.
<UL TYPE = "SQUARE">
<LI> 3 points = Field Goal.
<UL TYPE = "SQUARE">
<LI> 2 points = Two Point Conversion.
<LI> 2 points = Safety.
<UL TYPE = "SQUARE">
<LI> 1 point = Extra Point
</UL></Ul></UL></UL>
</BODY></HTML>
```

Figure 3.12 HTML for the *Football Scoring* Page, version 2

ORDERED LISTS

As the name implies, an ordered list contains items that are arranged according to some ordering principle. Ordered lists appear frequently in our everyday lives. For example, newspapers print lists of the top 10 best-selling works of fiction and nonfiction; they print lists of the top 10 movies or videos. These lists use a numeric ordering that implies that the first element in the list is more popular than the last element. Dictionaries or phone books use a different ordering principle, one based on the alphabet. Term papers or scholarly works often use a third ordering system that is based on Roman numerals. We can create each of these ordering systems with the HTML ordered list tags, `<OL>...</OL>`.

The `<OL>... </OL>` tags form a container for ordered list elements. Ordered lists use the same list item tag, `<LI>`, as unordered lists; however, the `<LI>` tag has additional attributes when used with ordered lists. The `<OL>` tag contains attributes that set a list's **TYPE** and **START**ing value. The `<LI>` tag for ordered lists also contains attributes for the list item's **TYPE** and **VALUE**.

THE *FAVORITE MOVIES* PAGE

The simplest ordered list uses the defaults provided by HTML. These defaults create a numerically ordered list that begins with 1. Figure 3.13 contains a list of favorite movies, presented in ascending numeric order.

Figure 3.14 contains the HTML for the *Favorite Movies* page. Because the page uses the default settings, this list involves little programming effort.

```
<!DOCTYPE HTML PUBLIC "-//W3C//DTD HTML 4.0
     Transitional//EN">
<HTML>
<HEAD><TITLE>Favorite Movies</TITLE></HEAD>
<BODY BGCOLOR = "white">
<B>Favorite Movies</B>
<OL>
<LI> Arsenic and Old Lace
<LI> Mulan
<LI> It Happened One Night
<LI> Miracle on 34<sup>th</SUP> Street
<LI> Bringing Up Baby
</OL>
</BODY></HTML>
```

Figure 3.13 The *Favorite Movies* Page   **Figure 3.14** HTML for the *Favorite Movies* Page

THE TYPE ATTRIBUTE FOR ORDERED LISTS

The **TYPE** attribute of the **<OL>** tag changes a list's ordering principle. The allowed types are **"1"** (default), **"A"**, **"a"**, **"I"**, and **"i"**. The **"A"** and **"a"** types produce upper-case and lower-case alphabetical lists, respectively. The **"I"** and **"i"** types produce upper- and lower-case Roman numerals, respectively.

    Figure 3.15 contains a web page that uses the **TYPE** attribute with a value of **"A"**. The result is a small initial portion of a child's alphabet. Notice the periods after the letters.

    Figure 3.16 contains the HTML for the *Alphabet* page. Notice the **TYPE** attribute in the **<OL>** tag.

```
<!DOCTYPE HTML PUBLIC "-//W3C//DTD HTML 4.0 Transitional//EN">
<HTML>
<HEAD><TITLE>Alphabet</TITLE></HEAD>
<BODY BGCOLOR = "white">
<BASEFONT SIZE = "2">
<OL TYPE = "A">
<LI> is for <B>Airplane</B>.
<LI> is for <B>Bed</B>.
<LI> is for <B>Coin</B>.
<LI> is for <B>Day</B>.
</OL>
</BODY></HTML>
```

Figure 3.15 The *Alphabet* Page   **Figure 3.16** HTML for the *Alphabet* Page

THE START ATTRIBUTE FOR ORDERED LISTS

Ordered lists don't have to start with "1", "A", "a", "I", or "i", because the **START** attribute of an ordered list can change the beginning value. Unfortunately, the **START** attribute requires a numeric value, even if the list **TYPE** is not numeric. For example, suppose we want to construct an animal alphabet starting with the letter "**d**". The **<OL>** tag that creates this list is

      `<OL TYPE = "a" START = "4">`

Because "**d**" is the fourth letter of the alphabet, we set the starting value to "4". Figure 3.17 contains an *Animal Alphabet* page.

Figure 3.18 contains the HTML for the *Animal Alphabet* page. The HTML would be easier to write if the value used in the **START** attribute matched the list **TYPE**, but the use of a numerical starting value is only slightly annoying.

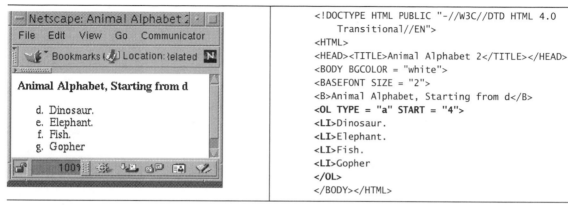

Figure 3.17 The *Animal Alphabet* Page   **Figure 3.18** HTML for the *Animal Alphabet* Page

THE VALUE ATTRIBUTE OF THE <LI> TAG

The **<LI>** tag contains **TYPE and VALUE** attributes when used with ordered lists. The **TYPE** attribute changes the list element's type. The recognized **TYPE** values are "**1**", "**A**", "**a**", "**I**", and "**i**". The **VALUE** attribute changes the ordering of list elements. For example, we could use this attribute to create a list of odd- or even-numbered elements.

Figure 3.19 contains a Web page containing a popular nursery rhyme. Notice the numbering used for the list's items.

Figure 3.20 contains the HTML for the *Nursery Rhyme* page. The **<LI>** tags use the **VALUE** attribute to count the odd numbers.

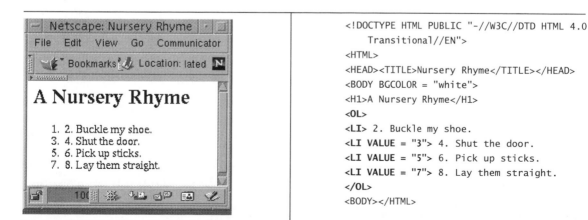

Figure 3.19 A *Nursery Rhyme* Page   **Figure 3.20** HTML for the *Nursery Rhyme* Page

The **VALUE** attribute works with nonnumeric lists; however, we must furnish a numeric value. Figure 3.21 contains a second version of the *Animal Alphabet* page. This version contains a list that displays every other alphabetical character.

Figure 3.22 contains the HTML for the second version of the *Animal Alphabet* page. Notice the numeric values in the **<LI>** tags.

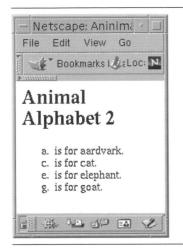

```
<!DOCTYPE HTML PUBLIC "-//W3C//DTD HTML 4.0 Transitional//EN">
<HTML>
<HEAD><TITLE>Aninimal Alphabet 2</TITLE></HEAD>
<BODY BGCOLOR = "white">
<H1>Animal Alphabet 2</H1>
<OL TYPE = "a">
<LI>is for aardvark.
<LI VALUE = "3"> is for cat.
<LI VALUE = "5"> is for elephant.
<LI VALUE = "7"> is for goat.
</OL>
<BODY></HTML>
```

Figure 3.21 The *Animal Alphabet* Page, version 2

Figure 3.22 HTML for the *Animal Alphabet* Page, version 2

NESTED ORDERED LISTS

Ordered lists can be nested in much the same way that unordered lists are nested. Unlike nested unordered lists, which use a different bullet type for each enclosed list, nested ordered lists always begin with a default value of "1". This means that we must specify the **TYPE** if we want to change the ordering.

Figure 3.23 shows a simple list of chores. The two chores, *Shoe Tying* and *Bed Making*, form the outermost list. Each of these chores is subdivided into a list of tasks necessary to complete the chore.

Figure 3.24 contains the HTML for the *Simple Chores* page. The sublists require no **TYPE** value; they use the default value, of "1".

COMBINING ORDERED AND UNORDERED LISTS

Ordered lists can be nested inside unordered lists, and *vice versa*. In fact, HTML's flexibility lets programmers create interesting effects. For example, Figure 3.25 contains a fictitious spring sweater collection. An alphabetical list identifies the sweaters. Each letter in the alphabetical lists contains a bullet list of the available colors and sizes.

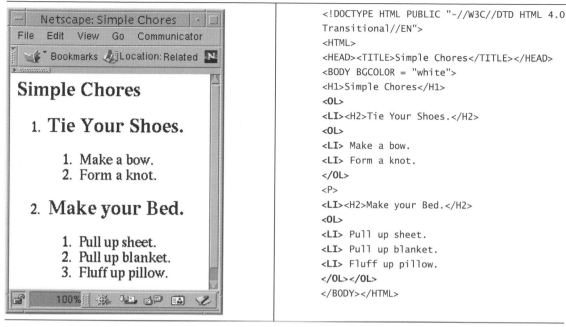

Figure 3.23 The *Simple Chores* Page

Figure 3.24 HTML for the *Simple Chores* Page

```
<!DOCTYPE HTML PUBLIC "-//W3C//DTD HTML 4.0
Transitional//EN">
<HTML>
<HEAD><TITLE>Simple Chores</TITLE></HEAD>
<BODY BGCOLOR = "white">
<H1>Simple Chores</H1>
<OL>
<LI><H2>Tie Your Shoes.</H2>
<OL>
<LI> Make a bow.
<LI> Form a knot.
</OL>
<P>
<LI><H2>Make your Bed.</H2>
<OL>
<LI> Pull up sheet.
<LI> Pull up blanket.
<LI> Fluff up pillow.
</OL></OL>
</BODY></HTML>
```

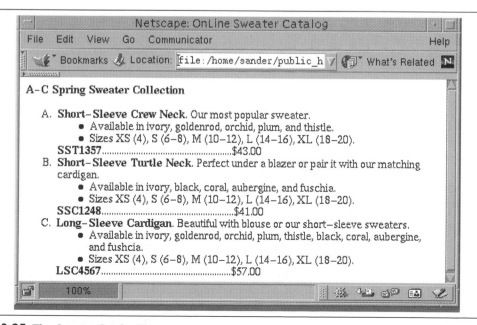

Figure 3.25 The *Sweater Catalog* Page

Figure 3.26 contains the HTML for the *Sweater Catalog* page. Notice how each list item in the alphabetical list is followed by an unordered list showing the available colors and sizes. Since the same format is used for each sweater, it's easy to copy the HTML for the unordered lists and modify it to match each alphabetical list item.

```
<HTML>
<HEAD><TITLE>OnLine Sweater Catalog</TITLE></HEAD>
<BODY BGCOLOR = "white">
<B>A-C Spring Sweater Collection</B>
<OL TYPE = "A">
<LI> <B>Short-Sleeve Crew Neck</B>. Our most popular sweater.
<UL TYPE = "DISC">
<LI> Available in ivory, goldenrod, orchid, plum, and thistle.
<LI> Sizes XS (4), S (6-8), M (10-12), L (14-16), XL (18-20).
</UL>
<B>SST1357</B>...............................................$43.00
<LI> <B>Short-Sleeve Turtle Neck</B>. Perfect under a blazer or pair it with our matching cardigan.
<UL TYPE = "DISC">
<LI> Available in ivory, black, coral, aubergine, and fuchsia.
<LI> Sizes XS (4), S (6-8), M (10-12), L (14-16), XL (18-20).
</UL>
<B>SSC1248</B>...............................................$41.00
<LI> <B>Long-Sleeve Cardigan</B>. Beautiful with blouse or our short-sleeve sweaters.
<UL TYPE = "DISC">
<LI> Available in ivory, goldenrod, orchid, plum, thistle, black, coral, aubergine, and fuchsia.
<LI> Sizes XS (4), S (6-8), M (10-12), L (14-16), XL (18-20).
</UL>
<B>LSC4567</B>...............................................$57.00
</BODY></HTML>
```

Figure 3.26 HTML for the *Sweater Catalog* Page

DEFINITION LISTS

Definition lists construct a list of terms and definitions. These lists use three different tags:

Definition List Tags. The <DL> ... </DL> tags form a container for a definition list. The definition terms and the definitions are placed in this list.

Definition Term Tags. The <DT> ... </DT> tags form a container for a definition term. The term may be a single word or a phrase. Each term should be followed by at least one definition tag.

Definition Tags. The <DD> ... </DD> tags form a container for a definition. HTML uses left indentation for the definition. Thus, the definitions "hang" beneath their associated terms.

Figure 3.27 contains a definition list of *Green Bay Football Terms*. Notice the appearance of the terms and definitions. The terms are displayed in a bold font to highlight them.

Figure 2.38 contains the HTML for the *GB Football Terms* page. Notice how few HTML tags are needed to create this definition list.

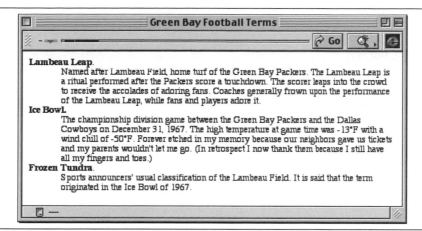

Figure 3.27 The *GB Football Terms* Page

```
<!DOCTYPE HTML PUBLIC "-//W3C//DTD HTML 4.0 Transitional//EN">
<HTML>
<HEAD><TITLE>Green Bay Football Terms</TITLE></HEAD>
<BODY BGCOLOR = "white">
<DL>
<DT><B>Lambeau Leap</B>.</DT>
<DD> Named after Lambeau Field, home turf of the Green Bay Packers. The Lambeau Leap is a ritual
performed after the Packers score a touchdown. The scorer leaps into the crowd to receive the
accolades of adoring fans. Coaches generally frown upon the performance of the Lambeau Leap, while
fans and players adore it.</DD>
<DT><B>Ice Bowl.</B></DT>
<DD> The championship division game between the Green Bay Packers and the Dallas Cowboys on
December 31, 1967. The high temperature at game time was -13&deg;F with a wind chill of -50&deg;F.
Forever etched in my memory because our neighbors gave us tickets and my parents wouldn't let me
go. (In retrospect I now thank them because I still have all my fingers and toes.)
</DD>
<DT><B>Frozen Tundra</B></DT>.
<DD> Sports announcers' usual classification of the Lambeau Field. It is said that the term
originated in the Ice Bowl of 1967.
</DD></DL>
</BODY></HTML>
```

Figure 3.28 HTML for the *GB Football Terms* Page

A NESTED DEFINITION LIST

Ordered and unordered lists can be placed inside a definition list, and *vice versa.* Figure 3.29 contains a *Cholesterol* page. The definition of **Cholesterol** contains an unordered list with the cholesterol-level classification. Unordered lists containing a single bullet are used to indicate the acceptable HDL and LDL levels. Examine this page and try to construct the HTML for it.

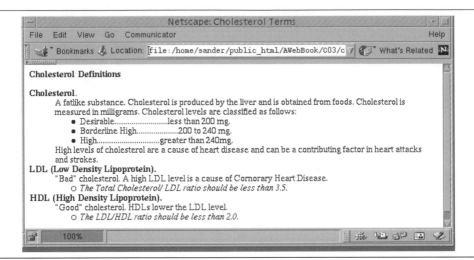

Figure 3.29 The *Cholesterol* Page

Figure 3.30 contains the HTML for the *Cholesterol* page. Notice the unordered lists contained inside each definition tag.

```
<HTML>
<HEAD><TITLE>Cholesterol Terms</TITLE></HEAD>
<BODY BGCOLOR = "white">
<BASEFONT SIZE = "2">
<B>Cholesterol Definitions</B>
<DL>
<DT><B>Cholesterol</B>.</DT>
<DD>A fatlike substance. Cholesterol is produced by the liver and is obtained from foods.
Cholesterol is measured in milligrams. Cholesterol levels are classified as follows:
<UL TYPE = "DISC">
<LI> Desirable..........................less than 200 mg.
<LI> Borderline High.....................200 to 240 mg.
<LI> High...............................greater than 240mg.
</UL>
High levels of cholesterol are a cause of heart disease and can be a contributing factor in heart
attacks and strokes.</DD>
<DT><B>LDL (Low Density Lipoprotein).</B></DT>
<DD> "Bad" cholesterol. A high LDL level is a cause of Coronary Heart Disease.
<UL>
<LI><I>The Total Cholesterol/ LDL ratio should be less than 3.5.</I>
</UL>
<DT><B>HDL (High Density Lipoprotein).</B>
<DD> "Good" cholesterol. HDLs lower the LDL level.
<UL>
<LI><I>The LDL/HDL ratio should be less than 2.0.</I>
</UL></DT></DL>
</BODY></HTML>
```

Figure 3.30 HTML for the Cholesterol Page

We've examined three different types of lists in this chapter, and we've combined them in several ways. By experimentation, you should be able to develop interesting lists that convey information in an easy-to-read format.

> ## EXERCISES

Directions: *Each of the following exercises asks you to create a list. Several of the exercises use nested lists. Try to produce the lists as they appear in the figure.*

1. **The *Low-Fat Fish* Page.** Figure 3.31 contains a list of low-fat fishes. Recreate this list. The list is ordered by grams of fat. Find an additional low-fat fish and add it to the list.

Figure 3.31 The *Low-Fat Fish* Page

2. **A *Recipe* Page.** Create a list that reproduces the simple recipe appearing in Figure 3.32.

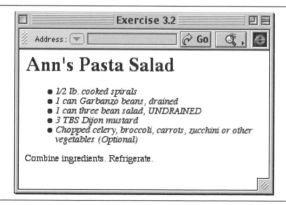

Figure 3.32 A *Recipe* Page

3. **A *Weaving Patterns* Page.** Figure 3.33 contains a list of weaving patterns. Recreate this list.

Figure 3.33 A *Weaving Patterns* Page

4. **A *Patchwork Quilt* Page.** Figure 3.34 contains a small list of patchwork quilt blocks. Recreate this list.

Figure 3.34 A *Patchwork Quilt* Page

5. **A *Leaf Classification* Page.** Figure 3.35 contains a simplified list for leaf classification. Recreate this list.

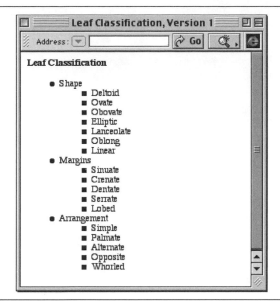

Figure 3.35 A *Leaf Classification* Page

6. **A *Favorite Books* Page.** Figure 3.36 contains a list of favorite books. The book and its author are listed. Reproduce this list, or create your own list of favorite books and authors.

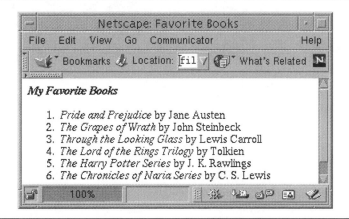

Figure 3.36 A *Favorite Books* Page

7. **An *Animal Alphabet* Page, version 3.** Figure 3.37 contains another animal alphabet page. Add your own animals and insects to complete this list.

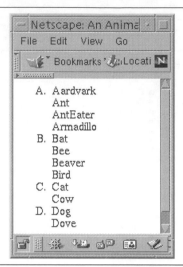

Figure 3.37 The *Animal Alphabet* Page, version 3

8. **The *American Presidents* Page.**   Figure 3.38 contains a partial list of American presidents and their years in office. Recreate this list. Add the next two presidents (or more, if you're so inclined) to this list.

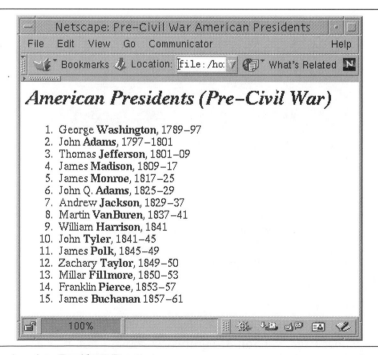

Figure 3.38 The *American Presidents* Page

9. **The *Ice Creams, Toppings, and Sauces* Page.** Figure 3.39 contains a list of favorite ice creams, sauces, and toppings. Recreate this list. Add your own favorites to it.

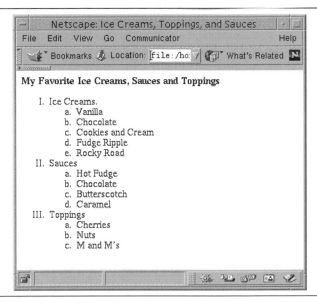

Figure 3.39 The *Ice Creams, Toppings, and Sauces* Page

10. **A *Leaf Classification* Page.** Figure 3.40 contains the table of contents for a paper on leaf classification. Recreate this list.

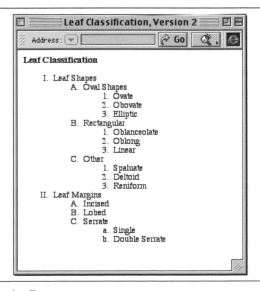

Figure 3.40 A *Leaf Classification* Page

11. **The *Term Paper* Page.** Create a list for a term paper of your choice. Use the *Leaf Classification* page in Figure 3.40 as your model.

12. **The *Yarn Terms* Page.** Figure 3.41 contains a simple set of yarn definitions. Recreate this list.

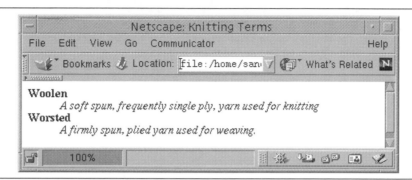

Figure 3.41 The *Yarn Terms* Page

13. **A Dictionary of White Sauces.** Figure 3.42 contains a *Dictionary of White Sauces*. Recreate this list.

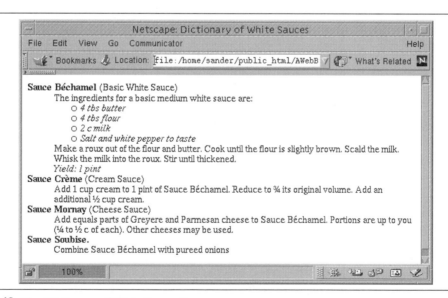

Figure 3.42 The *Dictionary of White Sauces* Page

14. **The *Count Down* Page.** Figure 3.43 contains a list that counts down until the weekend.

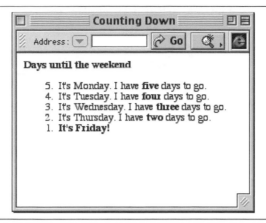

Figure 3.43 The *Count Down* Page

15. **The *Repetition Definitions* Page.** Figure 3.44 contains definitions of computer repetition statements. Recreate this list.

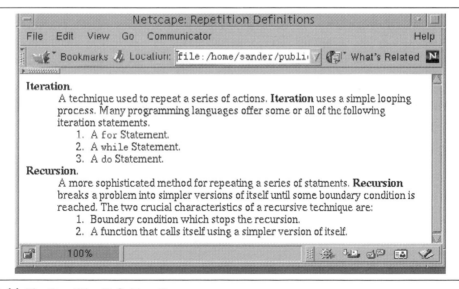

Figure 3.44 The *Repetition Definitions* Page

16. **Another *Catalog* Page.** Find a mail-order catalog. Pick a section that contains a group of labeled products. Recreate the section as a Web page. (See Figure 3.25 for an example.)

17. **Another *Football Scoring* Page.** Figure 3.45 contains a list for scoring football. Recreate this list.

17. **The *Sports Scoring* Page.** Pick a sport of your choice. Create a list similar to the one appearing in Figure 3.45.

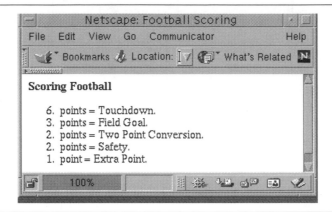

Figure 3.45 A *Football Scoring* Page

> ### HTML TAGS

<DD>...</DD>. The **<DD>...</DD>** tags form a container for *Definition Data*. These tags are used with *Definition Lists*. They contain the definition of a term.

<DL>...</DL>. The **<DL>...</DL>** tags form a container for a *Definition List* composed of definition terms (**<DT>...</DT>**) and data (**<DD>...</DD>**).

<DT>...</DT>. The **<DT>...</DT>** tags form a container for a *Definition Term*. Each **<DT>** tag should have at least one corresponding **<DD>** tag.

<LI>. The **<LI>** tag adds a *List Item* to ordered or unordered lists. Ordered and unordered lists can contain a **TYPE** attribute. The attribute's value depends on the type of list. For unordered lists, the value must be chosen from **"CIRCLE"**, **"SQUARE"**, and **"DISC"**. For ordered lists, the value must be chosen from **"1"**, **"I"**, **"i"**, **"a"**, and **"A"**.

The **VALUE** attribute can be used with *ordered* list items to change the numbering of a list item.

<OL>...</OL>. The **<OL>... </OL>** tags create an *Ordered List*.

Syntax:
```
<OL START = "number"
    TYPE = "1" | "a" | "A" | "i" | "I">
```

The default type is **"1"**, as is the default starting value.

<UL>...</UL>. The **<UL> ... </UL>** tags create an *Unordered List*.

Syntax:
```
<UL TYPE = "CIRCLE" | "SQUARE" | "DISC">
```
The default value is **"DISC"**.

➤ **HTML TIPS**

1. **Isolated Bullets.** The `<LI>` tag can be used to create isolated bullets within a web page. HTML assumes that these tags are part of an implicit unordered list.

2. **VALUE.** Use the **VALUE** attribute with the `<LI>` tag to change an item's value in an ordered list.

3. **TYPE.** Use the **TYPE** attribute to change the default list type.

4. **START.** Use the **START** attribute to change the starting value in an ordered list. The value must be numeric, even if the list type is not.

5. **Nested Lists.** Nested unordered lists change the default type with each new list. Nested ordered lists always have a default type of **"1"**.

6. **Indented Text.** If your text is indented and you don't want it to be, check the list end tags. Chances are, you forgot to add one.

4 Tables

In previous chapters, we used the **<PRE>...</PRE>** tags to create simple tables of information. Although **<PRE>...</PRE>** tags work well with text written in a monospaced font, alignment is difficult when other fonts are used. The HTML table tags contain a rich set of attributes that let us create sophisticated tables. We explore tables and table attributes in this chapter.

TABLE BASICS

HTML contains five distinct table tags, each with its own set of attributes:

- *The Table Tags.* The **<TABLE>...</TABLE>** tags form a container for an HTML table. The **<TABLE>** tag contains several optional attributes that change the table's background color, alignment, border, cell padding and spacing, and width.
- *The Caption Tags.* The **<CAPTION>...</CAPTION>** tags form a container for the table's caption. The caption is optional. If one is present, HTML by default centers it and places it at the top of the table. The **ALIGN** attribute changes the caption's alignment. The alignment values are **"TOP"** (default), **"BOTTOM"**, **"LEFT"**, and **"RIGHT"**. Using **"LEFT"** or **"RIGHT"** has *no effect* on the caption's alignment: it is still centered at the top of the page. The **"BOTTOM"** alignment centers the caption at the bottom of the table.
- *The Row Tags.* The **<TR>...</TR>** tags create the rows of the table. The rows contain either headings or data.
- *The Table Heading Tags.* The **<TH>...</TH>** tags create heading cells. Headings are centered and written in a bold font.
- *The Table Data Tags.* The **<TD>...</TD>** tags create data cells. Table data are left-aligned and are written in a plain font.

THE *COLOR TABLE* PAGE

Figure 4.1 contains a *Color Table* page that lists the primary and secondary colors. A caption appears above the table. The table heading cells identify the columns as *Primary* or *Secondary*.

Figure 4.2 contains the HTML for the *Color Table* page. The **<TABLE>** tag contains a **BORDER** attribute with a value of one. This creates a one-pixel border between the table cells. A default padding of one pixel separates the border from the cell's contents. Notice the table heading (**<TH>...</TH>**) and data (**<TD>...</TD>**) tags. These tags must be contained within the row tags.

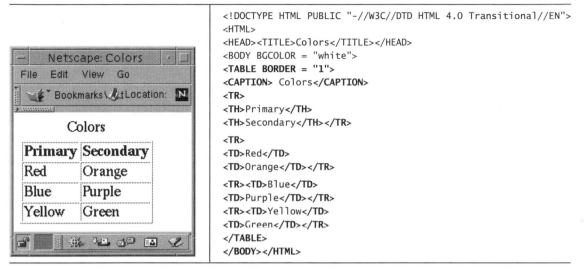

```
<!DOCTYPE HTML PUBLIC "-//W3C//DTD HTML 4.0 Transitional//EN">
<HTML>
<HEAD><TITLE>Colors</TITLE></HEAD>
<BODY BGCOLOR = "white">
<TABLE BORDER = "1">
<CAPTION> Colors</CAPTION>
<TR>
<TH>Primary</TH>
<TH>Secondary</TH></TR>

<TR>
<TD>Red</TD>
<TD>Orange</TD></TR>

<TR><TD>Blue</TD>
<TD>Purple</TD></TR>
<TR><TD>Yellow</TD>
<TD>Green</TD></TR>
</TABLE>
</BODY></HTML>
```

Figure 4.1 A *Color Table* Page   **Figure 4.2** HTML for the *Color Table* Page

THE *LITERARY CHARACTERS* PAGE

Figure 4.3 contains a table of character entities that a copy editor might use. The caption is placed below the table. The **Literary Symbol** heading in the first row does not contain a **
** tag; nonetheless, the heading is displayed on two lines, because the browser's width was not large enough to accommodate this heading. The browser automatically breaks lines if they won't fit. We can exert partial control over where breaks occur by inserting **
** tags or by setting the width of the cells or table.

Figure 4.4 contains the HTML for the *Literary Characters* page. Notice the

```
ALIGN = "BOTTOM"
```

attribute in the **<CAPTION>** tag.

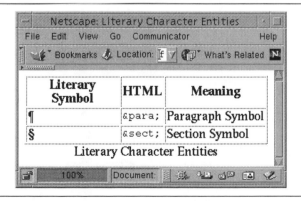

Figure 4.3 The *Literary Characters* Page

```
<!DOCTYPE HTML PUBLIC "-//W3C//DTD HTML 4.0 Transitional//EN">
<HTML>
<HEAD><TITLE>Literary Character Entities</TITLE></HEAD>
<BODY BGCOLOR = "white">
<TABLE BORDER = "1" CELLPADDING = "5">
<CAPTION ALIGN = "BOTTOM"> Literary Character Entities</CAPTION>
<TR><TH>Literary Symbol</TH>
<TH>HTML</TH>
<TH>Meaning</TH></TR>

<TR><TD>&para;</TD>
<TD><TT>&para;</TT></TD>
<TD>Paragraph Symbol</TD></TR>

<TR><TD>&sect;</TD>
<TD><TT>&sect;</TT></TD>
<TD>Section Symbol</TD></TR>
</TABLE>
</BODY></HTML>
```

Figure 4.4 HTML for the *Literary Characters* Page

PADDING, SPACING, AND BORDERS

The **<TABLE>** tag contains three attributes that control the overall appearance of a table: **BORDER**, **CELLSPACING**, and **CELLPADDING**. Each of these attributes uses a pixel value. That is, we specify the number of pixels we want for the border, cell spacing, or cell padding. The difference between spacing and padding is best illustrated with an example. Figure 4.5 contains the HTML for a table that has a border of 60 pixels, a cell spacing of 80 pixels, and a cell padding of 45 pixels. The table uses the **BGCOLOR** attribute to change the background color of the table to **#CC9999**.

Figure 4.6 shows an annotated version of the table created by the HTML appearing in Figure 4.5. When used together, the border, padding, and spacing attributes create a table that resembles a button. Each attribute has a specific function.

```
<!DOCTYPE HTML PUBLIC "-//W3C//DTD HTML 4.0 Transitional//EN">
<HTML>
<HEAD><TITLE>Button Tables</TITLE></HEAD>
<BODY BGCOLOR = "white">
<TABLE  BORDER = "60"  CELLSPACING = "80" CELLPADDING = "45" BGCOLOR = "#CC9999">
<TR><TD>Click me!</TD></TR>
</TABLE>
</BODY></HTML>
```

Figure 4.5 HTML for the *Table* Page

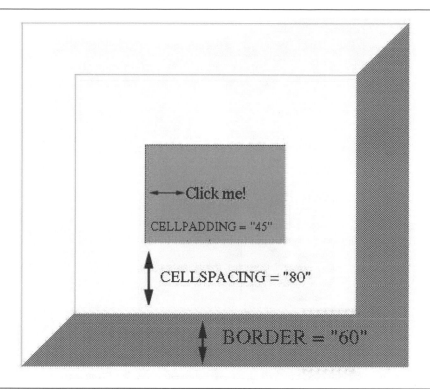

Figure 4.6 The *Table* Page

The **BORDER** *Attribute.*   When used in isolation the border attribute creates an outside border of the desired size and sets the cell padding and spacing to one. HTML bevels the border. As the size of the border increases, the three-dimensional effect of the beveling becomes more dramatic.

The **CELLPADDING** *Attribute.*   The **CELLPADDING** attribute establishes the minimum number of pixels to appear on the inside of a cell. A cell padding of "45" indicates that 45 pixels separate the cell's contents from the top, bottom, left, and right borders of the cell.

The **CELLSPACING** *Attribute.*   The **CELLSPACING** attribute establishes the size of the inner borders. When the table contains a single cell, the cell spacing creates the space between the inside of the cell and the border.

Figure 4.7 shows the relation between the border, the cell spacing, and the cell padding when the table contains more than one cell. This table uses a border of 15 pixels, a cell padding of 25 pixels, and a cell spacing of 10 pixels. The **CELLPADDING** attribute indicates that a minimum of 25 pixels separates the cell's contents from the top, left, right, and bottom borders of the cell. The **CELLSPACING** attribute indicates that 10 pixels separate the cells from each other and from the outer border.

Figure 4.8 contains the HTML for the *Multiple Cell* page.

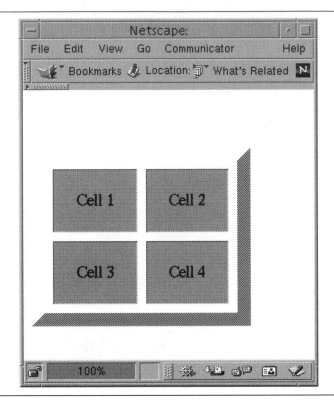

Figure 4.7 The *Multiple Cell* Page

```
<!DOCTYPE HTML PUBLIC "-//W3C//DTD HTML 4.0 Transitional//EN">
<HTML>
<HEAD><TITLE></TITLE></HEAD>
<BODY BGCOLOR = "white">
<BR><BR><BR>
<TABLE BORDER = "15" CELLPADDING = "25" CELLSPACING = "10"  BGCOLOR = "#CC9999">
<TR><TD>Cell 1</TD>
<TD>Cell 2</TD></TR>
<TR><TD>Cell 3</TD>
<TD>Cell 4</TD></TR>
</Table>
</BODY></HTML>
```

Figure 4.8 HTML for the *Multiple Cell* Page

A *MINIATURE BUTTON* PAGE

Figure 4.9 contains a miniature version of the table appearing in Figure 4.6. The table looks like a clickable button that links to another web page.

Figure 4.10 contains the HTML for the *Miniature Button* page. Because the button does not contain any link tags, nothing happens when it is clicked. In Chapter 5, we will transform this table into a functioning button.

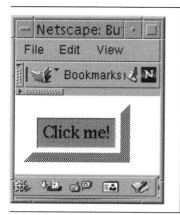

```
<!DOCTYPE HTML PUBLIC "-//W3C//DTD HTML 4.0 Transitional//EN">
<HTML>
<HEAD><TITLE>Button Tables</TITLE></HEAD>
<BODY BGCOLOR = "white">
<TABLE Border = "10" CELLSPACING = "5" CELLPADDING = "5" BGCOLOR =
"#CC9999">
<TR><TD>Click me!</TD></TR>
</TABLE>
</BODY></HTML>
```

Figure 4.9 A *Miniature Button* Page

Figure 4.10 HTML for the *Miniature Button* Page

THE *MUSKRAT MOUNDS RECYCLING* PAGE

We can change the horizontal alignment of an entire row or individual heading or data cells by using the **ALIGN** attribute in the **<TR>**, **<TH>**, or **<TD>** tags, respectively. The alignment values are **"CENTER"**, **"LEFT"**, **"RIGHT"**, and **"JUSTIFY"**. As mentioned previously, the default alignment is **"CENTER"** for heading cells and **"LEFT"** for data cells. Figure 4.11 displays the fictitious *Muskrat Mounds Recycling* page. The table headings, specifying the items suitable and unsuitable for recycling, are aligned with the left edge of the cell. Notice how the browser centers the contents of the second, shorter column vertically.

Figure 4.12 contains the HTML for the *Muskrat Mounds Recycling* page. The absence of a border gives the table a two-column appearance. Each heading tag sets its alignment to the left with the statement

    <TH ALIGN = "LEFT">

We can also set the alignment in the row tag as follows:

    <TR ALIGN = "LEFT">

This eliminates the need to set the alignment in each of the heading tags.

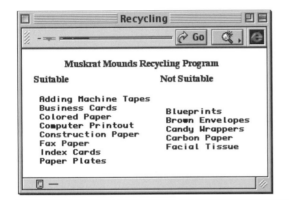

```
<HTML>
<HEAD><TITLE>Recycling</TITLE></HEAD>
<BODY BGCOLOR = "white">
<TABLE CELLPADDING = "5">
<CAPTION><B>Muskrat Mounds Recycling
Program</B></CAPTION>

<TR><TH ALIGN = "LEFT">Suitable</TH>
<TH ALIGN = "LEFT">Not Suitable</TH></TR>
<TR><TD><FONT SIZE = "2"><PRE></TT><B> Adding
     Machine Tapes

Business Cards
Colored Paper
Computer Printout
Construction Paper
Fax Paper
Index Cards
Paper Plates</B></PRE></FONT></TD>

<TD><FONT SIZE = "2"><PRE></TT><B> Blueprints
Brown Envelopes
Candy Wrappers
Carbon Paper
Facial Tissue</B></PRE></FONT></TD></TR>
</TABLE>
</BODY></HTML>
```

Figure 4.11 The *Muskrat Mounds Recycling* Page

Figure 4.12 HTML for the *Recycling* Page

The table contains only two columns of data. Each column uses a font size of 2 with pre-formatted text. The **<FONT>** tag must be placed before the **<PRE>** tag, because the **<PRE>** tag ignores font size changes contained within it. A **</TT>** tag is placed immediately inside the **<PRE>** tag so that the columns are not printed in a monospaced font.

THE *MUSKRAT MOUNDS RECYCLING* **PAGE (VERTICALLY ALIGNED VERSION)**

The *Muskrat Mounds Recycling* page centers the list of items that are not suitable for recycling vertically, because this list is shorter than the items that can be recycled. HTML provides a **VALIGN** attribute for the **<TR>**, **<TH>**, and **<TD>** tags that changes the default vertical alignment. The allowed values are **"MIDDLE"** (default), **"TOP"**, **"BOTTOM"**, and **"BASELINE"**. Figure 4.13 contains a new version of the *Muskrat Mounds Recycling* page. Notice the list of unsuitable items: it is now aligned with the top of the column.

Figure 4.14 contains the HTML for the new table. Notice the **<TD VALIGN = "TOP">** tag in the second row of the table. This tag aligns the unsuitable items with the top of the column. The remainder of the HTML is identical to the HTML appearing in Figure 4.12.

```
<TABLE CELLPADDING = "5">
<CAPTION><B>Muskrat Mounds Recycling
Program</B></CAPTION>

<TR ALIGN = "LEFT"><TH>Suitable</TH>
<TH>Not Suitable</TH></TR>
<TR><TD><FONT SIZE = "2"><PRE></TT><B> Adding
    Machine Tapes

Business Cards
Colored Paper
Computer Printout
Construction Paper
Fax Paper
Index Cards
Paper Plates</B></PRE></FONT></TD>
<TD VALIGN = "TOP"><FONT SIZE = "2"><PRE></TT><B>
Blueprints
Brown Envelopes
Candy Wrappers
Carbon Paper
Facial Tissue</B></PRE></FONT></TD></TR>
</TABLE>
```

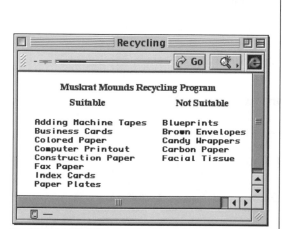

Figure 4.13 The *Recycling* Page (vertically aligned)

Figure 4.14 HTML for *Recycling* Page (vertically aligned)

BASELINE ALIGNMENT

In Figure 4.14, we used the statement

        <TD VALIGN = "TOP">

to align the second column vertically with the top of the cell. We also could have used a *baseline* alignment to produce the same effect. Thus, the statement

        <TD VALIGN = "BASELINE">

produces a page that is identical to the one appearing in Figure 4.13.

The vertical alignments produce different effects when the table cells contain text written in different font sizes. For example, consider the table appearing in Figure 4.15. The headings, which were written with **<H1>...</H1>** tags, occupy the first column of the table. The remaining columns of each row contain color names written in the default font face and size. The first row uses a baseline alignment that creates an invisible baseline for the text in every cell of this row. The browser uses the largest font to establish the baseline. The second row uses the default, middle alignment. Notice how the smaller fonts sink below the heading. The third row uses a top alignment, which causes the smaller text to rise above the heading. The final row uses a bottom alignment, which places the smaller text next to the bottom inner border. The heading does not sink, because the browser inserts a blank line after every **<H1>** heading.

Figure 4.16 contains the HTML for the *Vertical Alignments* page. The **VALIGN** attribute was set for the table rows, but this attribute can also be used to change the alignment for specific heading or data cells.

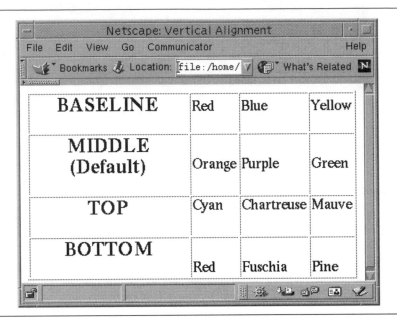

Figure 4.15 The *Vertical Alignments* Page

```
<HTML>
<HEAD><TITLE>Vertical Alignment</TITLE></HEAD>
<BODY BGCOLOR = "white" CELLPADDING = "5">
<TABLE BORDER = "1">
<TR VALIGN = "BASELINE">
<TH><H1>BASELINE</H1></TH>
<TD>Red</TD><TD>Blue</TD>
<TD>Yellow</TD></TR>

<TR><TH><H1>MIDDLE (Default)</H1></TH>
<TD>Orange</TD><TD>Purple</TD>
<TD>Green</TD></TR>

<TR VALIGN = "TOP">
<TH><H1>TOP</H1></TH>
<TD>Cyan</TD><TD>Chartreuse</TD>
<TD>Mauve</TD></TR>

<TR VALIGN = "BOTTOM">
<TH><H1>BOTTOM</H1></TH>
<TD>Red</TD><TD>Fuschia</TD>
<TD>Pine</TD></TR>
</TABLE>
</BODY></HTML>
```

Figure 4.16 HTML for the *Vertical Alignments* Page

THE *SPECIAL TEAMS* **PAGE**

We can create cells that span several rows or columns by using the **ROWSPAN** and **COLSPAN** attributes of the **<TH>** and **<TD>** tags. For example, suppose we want to create a *Special Teams* page like the one appearing in Figure 4.17. The **Special Teams** label occupies the entire first column of the table. The second column contains the names of the special teams.

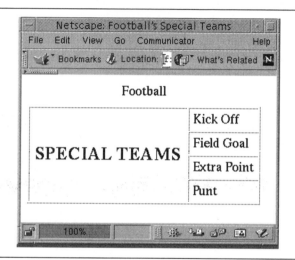

Figure 4.17 The *Special Teams* Page

To create the *Special Teams* label, we use the following statement:

```
<TR><TH ROWSPAN = "4"><H1>SPECIAL TEAMS</H1></TH>
```

The **<TH>** tag indicates that *Special Teams* cell extends through the first four table rows. The data cell for the first special team is placed after the table heading. The remaining special teams are listed in separate rows. Figure 4.18 contains the HTML for the *Special Teams* page.

```
<!DOCTYPE HTML PUBLIC "-//W3C//DTD HTML 4.0 Transitional//EN">
<HTML>
<HEAD><TITLE>Football's Special Teams</TITLE></HEAD>
<BODY BGCOLOR = "white">
<TABLE BORDER = "1" CELLPADDING = "5">
<CAPTION>Football</CAPTION>
<TR><TH ROWSPAN = "4"><H1>SPECIAL TEAMS</H1></TH>
<TD>Kick Off</TD></TR>
<TR><TD>Field Goal</TD></TR>
<TR><TD>Extra Point</TD></TR>
<TR><TD>Punt</TD></TR>
</TABLE>
</BODY></HTML>
```

Figure 4.18 HTML for *Special Teams* Page

Rows two through four of the *Special Teams* page contain a single data cell that holds the name of a special team. The browser puts these data cells in the table's second column because the header cell created in the first row occupies four rows.

THE *FOOTBALL NUMBERS* PAGE

The **COLSPAN** attribute creates table cells that extend through several columns. This attribute can be used with either the **<TH>** or **<TD>** tags. Figure 4.19 contains a *Football Numbers* page that illustrates the **COLSPAN** attribute. The football jersey numbers in the heading cells span three columns. The heading cells have a background color of **#CC9999**. The football positions associated with the jersey numbers appear below the heading row.

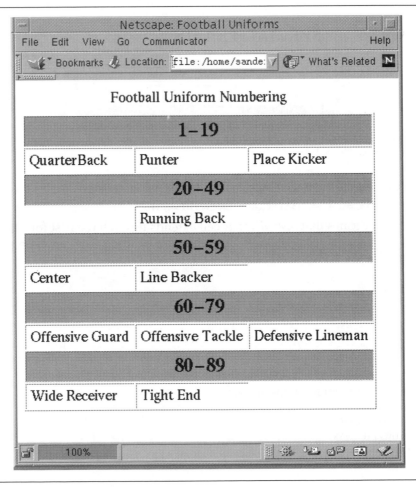

Figure 4.19 The *Football Numbers* Page

Figure 4.20 contains the HTML for the *Football Numbers* page. The heading cells span an entire row, so the HTML is easy to follow.

```
<!DOCTYPE HTML PUBLIC "-//W3C//DTD HTML 4.0 Transitional//EN">
<HTML>
<HEAD><TITLE>Football Uniforms</TITLE></HEAD>
<BODY BGCOLOR = "white">
<TABLE BORDER = "1" CELLPADDING = "5">
<CAPTION>Football Uniform Numbering</CAPTION>
<TR><TH COLSPAN = "3" BGCOLOR = "CC9999"><H1>1-19</H1></TH></TR>
<TR><TD>QuarterBack</TD>
<TD>Punter</TD>
<TD>Place Kicker</TD></TR>

<TR><TH COLSPAN = "3" BGCOLOR = "CC9999"><H1>20-49</H1></TH></TR>
<TR><TD></TD>
<TD>Running Back</TD></TR>
<TR><TH COLSPAN = "3" BGCOLOR = "CC9999"><H1>50-59</H1></TH></TR>
<TR><TD>Center</TD>
<TD>Line Backer</TD></TR>

<TR><TH COLSPAN = "3" BGCOLOR = "CC9999"><H1>60-79</H1></TH></TR>
<TR><TD>Offensive Guard</TD>
<TD>Offensive Tackle</TD>
<TD>Defensive Lineman</TD></TR>
<TR><TH COLSPAN = "3" BGCOLOR = "CC9999"><H1>80-89</H1></TH></TR>
<TR><TD>Wide Receiver</TD>
<TD>Tight End</TD></TR>
</TABLE>
</BODY></HTML>
```

Figure 4.20 HTML for *Football Uniforms* Page

THE *CHEESE HEAD SURVEY* PAGE

We can combine the **ROWSPAN** and **COLSPAN** attributes to create larger areas for headings. Figure 4.21 contains a fictitious cheese survey. The survey's bias is clearly displayed in the large *Go CheeseHeads!* message that appears in the upper left corner of the table. Both **ROWSPAN** and **COLSPAN** attributes are used to change the heading's dimensions. The *Likes Cheese* and *Gender* headings use the **COLSPAN** and **ROWSPAN** attributes, respectively, to extend these labels past their normal boundaries.

Creating complex tables requires prior planning. The design process is simplified by using graph paper to delineate the table's layout. Figure 4.22 contains an outline of the *Cheese Head Survey* page. The outline shows the **ROWSPAN** and **COLSPAN** attributes and the row placement for the various cells. Comments identify the rows to make it easy to translate this sketch into HTML tags.

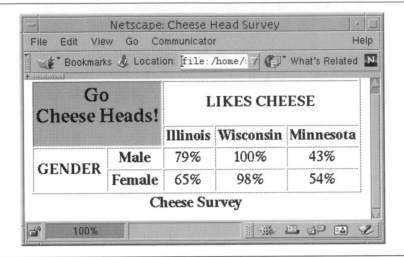

Figure 4.21 The *Cheese Head Survey* Page

— Row 1 — ROWSPAN = "2" COLSPAN = "2"		— Row 1 — COLSPAN = "3"		
		— Row 2 —	— Row 2 —	— Row 2 —
— Row 3 — ROWSPAN = "2"	— Row 3 —	— Row 3 —	— Row 3 —	— Row 3 —
	— Row 4 —	— Row 4 —	— Row 4 —	— Row 4 —

Figure 4.22 Layout for the *Cheese Head Survey* Page

Figure 4.23 contains the HTML for the *Cheese Head Survey* page. Compare the item placement in the HTML with the sketch appearing in Figure 4.22.

THE *MUSKRAT MOUNDS HOCKEY LEAGUE* **PAGE**

Newspaper often uses tables similar to the one appearing in Figure 4.24. The alternation of light and dark background colors in the table rows adds interest and keeps the attention of readers. Although Figure 4.24 resembles the *Football Numbers* page (Figure 4.19), the *Hockey League* page is substantially more complex. Try recreating this table, using a background color of #CC9999 for every other row. Compare your results with the results displayed in Figure 4.24. If you use a border of 1 pixel, your table will contain a one-pixel vertical border separating the team name and the attendance. Figure 4.24 contains no vertical line!

```
<!DOCTYPE HTML PUBLIC "-//W3C//DTD HTML 4.0 Transitional//EN">
<HTML>
<HEAD><TITLE>Cheese Head Survey</TITLE></HEAD>
<BODY BGCOLOR = white>
<TABLE BORDER = "1" CELLPADDING = "2">
<CAPTION ALIGN = "BOTTOM"><B>Muskrat Mounds Cheese Survey</B></CAPTION>
<TR><!-- Row 1 -->
<TD COLSPAN = "2" ROWSPAN = "2" BGCOLOR = "#FF9900" ALIGN = "CENTER">
<H1>Go<BR>Cheese Heads!</H1></TD>
<TH COLSPAN = "3" HEIGHT = "50">LIKES CHEESE</TH></TR>

<TR><!-- Row 2 -->
<TH>Illinois</TH>
<TH>Wisconsin</TH>
<TH>Minnesota</TH>
</TR>

<TR ALIGN = "CENTER"><!-- Row 3 -->
<TH ROWSPAN = "2" HEIGHT = "50">GENDER</TH>
<TH>Male</TH>
<TD>79%</TD>
<TD>100%</TD>
<TD>43%</TD>
</TR>

<TR ALIGN = "CENTER"><!-- Row 4 -->
<TH>Female</TH>
<TD>65%</TD>
<TD>98%</TD>
<TD>54%</TD></TR>
</TABLE>
</BODY></HTML>
```

Figure 4.23 HTML for the *Cheese Head Survey* Page

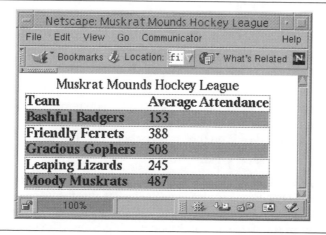

Figure 4.24 The *Muskrat Mounds Hockey League* Page

To create the illusion of solid rows, we use a separate table for each row, even the row with the heading cells. The odd-numbered rows have a white background; the even-numbered rows have a background color of **#CC9999**. The outer table, which contains the nested tables, has a border of 1. The tag that creates the outer table is

```
<TABLE BORDER = "1" CELLPADDING = "0" CELLSPACING = "0">
```

The tag that creates the odd-numbered inner tables is

```
<TABLE BORDER = "0" CELLPADDING = "0" CELLSPACING = "0">
```

The tag that creates the even-numbered inner tables is

```
<TABLE BORDER = "0" BGCOLOR = "#CC9999" CELLPADDING = "0" CELLSPACING = "0">
```

The cell padding and spacing of all tables is set to zero. This not only eliminates the one-pixel vertical border separating the two columns, it also ensures that the background color in the even rows completely fills the table's boundaries.

Placing each inner table in a separate data cell on a separate row leads to a new problem: The number of characters in each data cell varies, so the inner tables do not align correctly to produce even columns of information. Setting the **WIDTH** attribute of each data cell in the inner tables easily solves this problem. The same width, 160 pixels, works well for both columns of information.

The HTML for the *Hockey League* page appears in Figure 4.25. A blank line separates the table rows. This makes it easy to check the table. Because the complete table is composed of several smaller tables, it's easy to forget a table tag. The usual result is either a disappearing table or a table with information "floating" above the table. Adding the inner tables one at a time helps show error locations.

THE *CROSSWORD PUZZLE* PAGE

Our last table example is a *Crossword Puzzle* page. The puzzle, which appears in Figure 4.26, contains HTML tags. Some of the tags appear in later chapters.

Creating the crossword puzzle is tedious, but not difficult. The design process begins with a sketch of the puzzle's layout on graph paper. The puzzle depicted in Figure 4.26 contains 12 rows and 13 columns. The cells that are not to contain letters are darkened in the layout. The cells that contain word starts are numbered numerically.

After sketching the puzzle's layout, we create a template for the table rows. The template is

```
<TR><TD></TD> <TD></TD> <TD></TD> <TD></TD> <TD></TD> <TD></TD>
<TD></TD> <TD></TD> <TD></TD> <TD> </TD> <TD></TD> <TD></TD>
<TD></TD></TR>
```

This template creates a table row with 13 data cells. The template is duplicated 11 times to produce the structure for the entire crossword puzzle.

We transform the darkened cells on the graph paper into HTML columns with the statement

```
<TD BGCOLOR = "black"><PRE> </PRE></TD>
```

Using `<PRE>...</PRE>` tags forces the browser to place borders between adjacent empty cells. The `<PRE>...</PRE>` tags create columns with similar widths. Once the column widths are established in the early rows of the table, we can use the "nonbreaking space" character entity, ** **, to force a border in the data cells of the remaining rows. The light data cells are created in a similar fashion, with superscripts used to indicate the word starts.

```
<!DOCTYPE HTML PUBLIC "-//W3C//DTD HTML 4.0 Transitional//EN">
<HTML>
<HEAD><TITLE>Muskrat Mounds Hockey League</TITLE></HEAD>
<BODY BGCOLOR = "white">
<TABLE BORDER = "1" CELLPADDING = "0" CELLSPACING = "0">
<CAPTION>Muskrat Mounds Hockey League</CAPTION>
<TR><TD>
<TABLE BORDER = "0" CELLPADDING = "0" CELLSPACING = "0">
<TR>
<TH ALIGN = "LEFT" WIDTH = "160">Team</TH>
<TH ALIGN = "LEFT" WIDTH = "160">Average Attendance</TH></TR>
</TABLE></TD></TR>

<TR><TD>
<TABLE  BORDER = "0" BGCOLOR = "#CC9999" CELLPADDING = "0" CELLSPACING = "0">
<TR>
<TD WIDTH = "160"><B>Bashful Badgers</B></TD>
<TD  WIDTH = "160">153</TD></TR></TABLE></TD></TR>

<TR><TD>
<TABLE BORDER = "0"  CELLPADDING = "0" CELLSPACING = "0"><TR>
<TD WIDTH = "160"><B>Friendly Ferrets</B></TD>
<TD WIDTH = "160">388</TD></TR></TABLE>

<TR><TD>
<TABLE BORDER = "0"  BGCOLOR = "#CC9999" CELLPADDTNG = "0" CELLSPACING = "0">
<TR>
<TD WIDTH = "160"><B>Gracious Gophers</B></TD>
<TD WIDTH = "160">508</TD></TR></TABLE>

<TR><TD>
<TABLE BORDER = "0" CELLPADDING = "0" CELLSPACING = "0" CELLSPACING = "0">
<TR>
<TD WIDTH = "160"><B>Leaping Lizards</B></TD>
<TD WIDTH = "160">245</TD></TR></TABLE>

<TR><TD>
<TABLE BORDER = "0"  BGCOLOR = "#CC9999" CELLPADDING = "0" CELLSPACING = "0">
<TR>
<TD WIDTH = "160"><B>Moody Muskrats</B></TD>
<TD WIDTH = "160">487</TD></TR></TABLE></TD>
</TR>
</TABLE>
</BODY></HTML>
```

Figure 4.25 HTML for the *Hockey League* Page

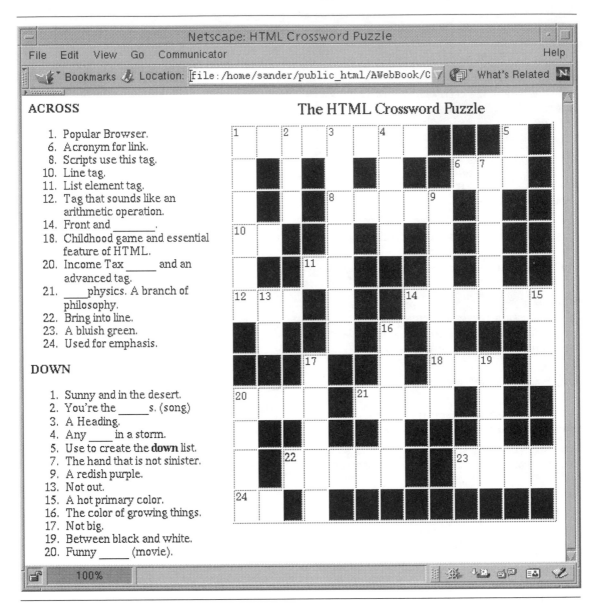

Figure 4.26 A *Crossword Puzzle* Page

The <TABLE> tag for the crossword puzzle sets the table alignment to RIGHT. The crossword puzzle clues were placed below the table, so a RIGHT alignment indicates that the clues will appear to the left of the table when the page is loaded. Figure 4.27 contains the first two rows of the crossword puzzle. The remaining rows were created by using the technique discussed previously. We use ordered lists for the ACROSS and DOWN clues. The HTML for the ACROSS list appears in Figure 4.27. We create the DOWN list in a similar fashion.

```
<!DOCTYPE HTML PUBLIC "-//W3C//DTD HTML 4.0 Transitional//EN">
<HTML>
<HEAD><TITLE>HTML Crossword Puzzle</TITLE></HEAD>
<BODY BGCOLOR = white>
<BASEFONT SIZE = "2">

<TABLE BORDER = 1 ALIGN = RIGHT>
<CAPTION>The HTML Crossword Puzzle</CAPTION>
<!-- Row 1-->
<TR><TD><PRE><Sup>1</SUP> </PRE></TD><TD><PRE>
</PRE></TD><TD><PRE><SUP>2</SUP> </PRE></TD>
<TD><PRE> </PRE></TD><TD><PRE><SUP>3</SUP> </PRE></TD><TD><PRE> </PRE></TD>
<TD><PRE><Sup>4</SUP> </PRE></TD><TD><PRE> </PRE></TD>
<TD BGCOLOR = "black"><PRE> </PRE></TD>
<TD BGCOLOR = "black"><PRE> </PRE></TD><TD BGCOLOR = "black"><PRE> </PRE></TD>
<TD><PRE><SUP>5</SUP> </PRE></TD><TD BGCOLOR = "black"><PRE> </PRE></TD></TR>

<!-- Row 2-->
<TR><TD> </TD><TD BGCOLOR = "black"> </TD><TD> </TD>
<TD BGCOLOR = "black"> </TD><TD></TD><TD BGCOLOR = "black"> </TD>
<TD> </TD><TD BGCOLOR = "black"> </TD><TD BGCOLOR = "black"> </TD>
<TD><PRE><SUP>6</SUP> </PRE></TD><TD><PRE><SUP>7</SUP> </PRE></TD>
<TD> </TD><TD BGCOLOR = "black"> </TD></TR>

<!-- Row 3-->
<!-- Row 4-->
<!-- Row 5-->
<!-- Row 6-->
<!-- Row 7-->
<!-- Row 8-->
<!-- Row 9-->
<!-- Row 10->
<!-- Row 11-->
<!-- Row 12-->
<!-- Row 13-->
</TABLE>

<B>ACROSS</B>
<OL>
<LI>Popular Browser.
<LI VALUE = "6">Acronym for link.
<LI VALUE = "8">Scripts use this tag.
<LI VALUE = "10"> Line tag.
<LI VALUE = "11">List element tag.
<LI VALUE = "12">Tag that sounds like an arithmetic operation.
<LI VALUE = "14">Front and _____.
<LI VALUE = "18">Childhood game and essential feature of HTML.
<LI VALUE = "20">Income Tax _____ and an advanced tag.
<LI VALUE = "21">____physics. A branch of philosophy.
<LI VALUE = "22">Bring into line.
<LI VALUE = "23">A bluish green.
<LI VALUE = "24">Used for emphasis.</OL>
<B>DOWN</B>
```

Figure 4.27 HTML for the *Crossword Puzzle* Page

> ## EXERCISES

Directions: *Each of the following exercises asks you to create a table. You should reproduce the table exactly as it appears in the exercise.*

1. **The *European and American Shoe* Page.** Figure 4.28 contains a table of European shoe sizes for women's shoes and their American equivalents. Recreate this table.

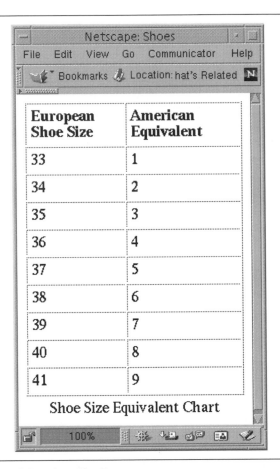

Figure 4.28 The *European and American Shoe* Page

2. **The *Knitting Needles* Page.** Figure 4.29 contains a table of U.S. knitting needle sizes and their metric equivalents. Recreate this table.
3. **The *Favorite Books* Page.** Figure 4.30 contains a list of favorite books, their years of publication, and their authors. Recreate this table, or create a table of your own favorite books.

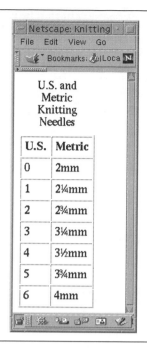

Figure 4.29 The *Knitting Needles* Page

Netscape: Favorite books

My Favorite Books

Title	Publication Date	Author
Pride and Prejudice	1813	Jane Austen
East of Eden	1952	John Steinbeck
Howard's End	1910	E.M. Forrester
Out of the Silent Planet	1965	C. S. Lewis
The Sound and the Fury	1929	William Faulkner

Figure 4.30 The *Favorite Books* Page

4. **The *Household Equivalents* Page.** Create a chart of household equivalents similar to the one appearing in Figure 4.31.

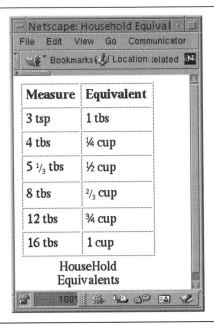

Figure 4.31 The *Household Equivalents* Page

5. **The *Mathematical Symbols* Page.** Figure 4.32 contains a chart of mathematical symbols. Reproduce this chart.

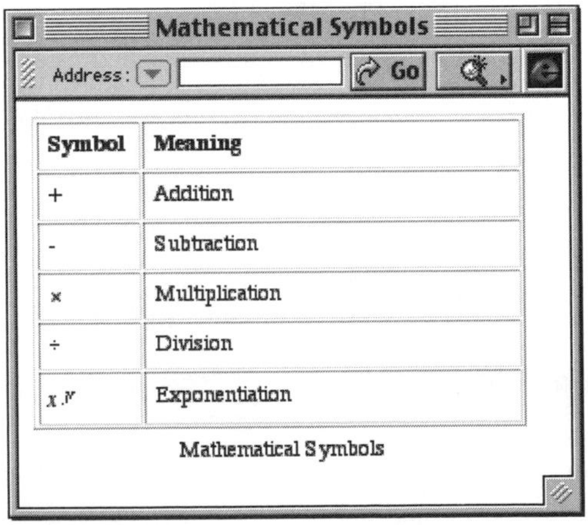

Figure 4.32 The *Mathematical Symbols* Page

6. **The *Household Chores* Page.** Figure 4.33 contains a child's checklist of daily chores. Reproduce the table. Feel free to change the list of chores.

Figure 4.33 The *Household Chores* Page

7. **The *Rainfall* Page.** Look up the rain amounts for your area, and create a table similar to the one appearing in Figure 4.34.

1999 Rainfall
The Holiday Gazette, January 15, 2000
Measurement recorded at Muskrat Mounds

Month	Avg. Rainfall (in inches)	1999 Rainfall (in inches)
January	1.06	1.77
February	0.68	0.39
March	4.742	3.69
April	5.28	7.36
May	4.87	5.00
June	5.25	7.67
July	1.67	3.37
August	2.22	4.12
September	5.46	3.26
October	4.78	6.87
November	2.15	1.40
December	0.20	3.19

Figure 4.34 The *Rainfall* Page

8. **The *State Flora and Fauna* Page.** Create a table of state flora and fauna similar to the one appearing in Figure 4.35.

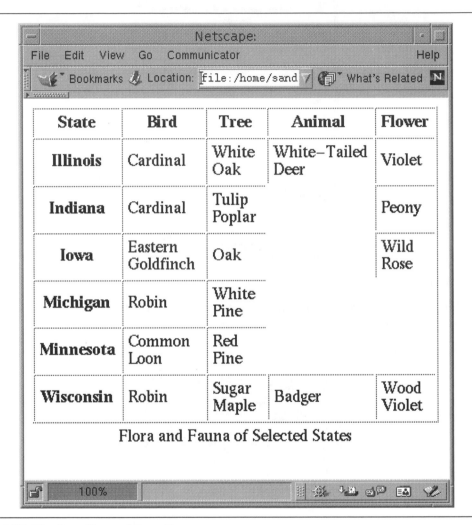

Figure 4.35 The *State Flora and Fauna* Page

9. **The *Recipe* Page.** Figure 4.36 contains a recipe. Recreate this recipe as a table.

10. **The *Generic Food Label* Page.** Figure 4.37 contains a generic food label. Recreate the label; then, find two labels, and create on-line labels for these foods.

11. **The *Food Pyramid* Page.** Figure 4.38 contains a checklist for the food pyramid.

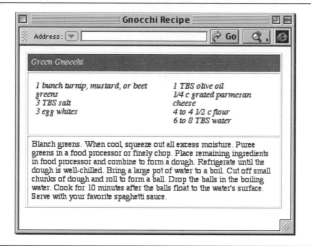

Figure 4.36 A *Recipe* Page

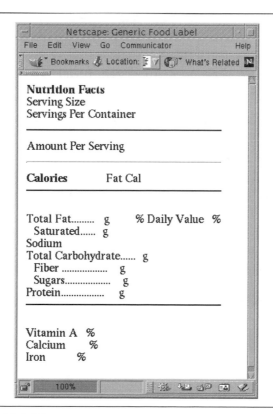

Figure 4.37 A *Generic Food Label* Page

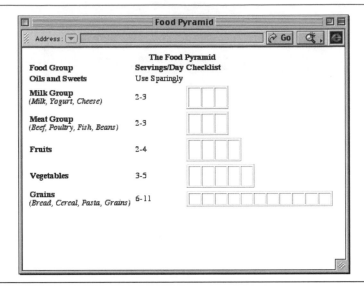

Figure 4.38 The *Food Pyramid* Page

12. **The *Your Recipes* Page.** Find two favorite recipes. Create tables for the recipes. Color-code the recipe name so that it matches the type of recipe—that is, pick a different color for each of the following categories: Vegetables, Appetizers, Breads, Desserts, Entrees.

13. **The *Invoice* Page.** Create a customer order form similar to the one appearing in Figure 4.39.

14. **The *Tudor Genealogy* Page.** Figure 4.40 contains a truncated genealogy of the Tudor line. Reproduce this genealogy.

15. **The *Color-Coded Genealogy* Page.** Repeat Figure 4.40, but add a *color codes* legend, as displayed in Figure 4.41.

16. **Your Genealogy Page.** Create a three-generation genealogy for your family tree. Include your grandparents, your parents, yourself, and your siblings.

17. **The *Football* Page.** Use the official NFL page to complete the table appearing in Figure 4.42. You may pair divisions to produce equal alignments. Use a different color for each division. (*Hint: The team names are available at the NFL Web page: http://www.nfl.com/, or you can use your local newspaper, if it's football season.*)

18. **The *Monetary Symbols* Page.** Figure 4.43 contains a table of monetary symbols. Recreate this table. (Use Appendix A to obtain the appropriate HTML character entities.)

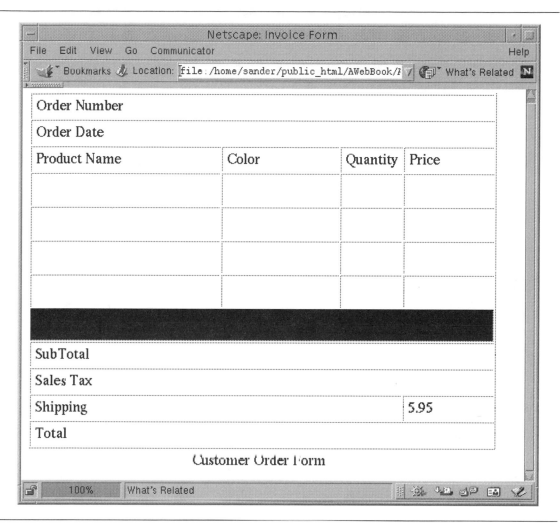

Figure 4.39 The *Invoice* Page

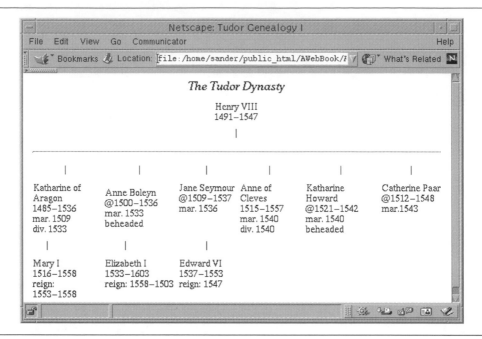

Figure 4.40 The *Tudor Genealogy* Page

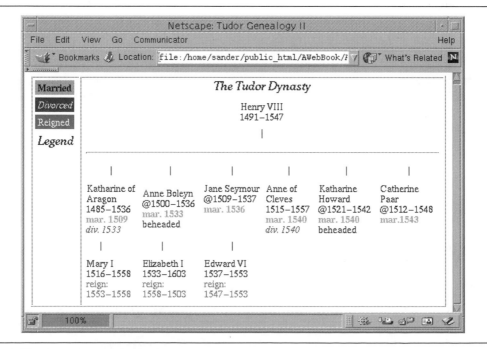

Figure 4.41 The *Color-Coded Genealogy* Page

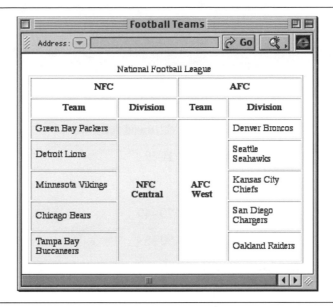

Figure 4.42 The *Football* Page

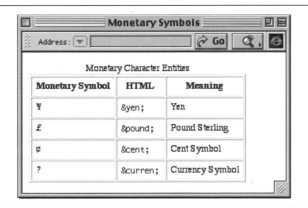

Figure 4.43 A *Monetary Symbols* Page

19. **The *Snowfall* Page.** Create a *Snowfall* page similar to the *Rainfall* page. Create the chart with the even rows in one color and the odd rows in a different color.

20. **The *Football Numbers* Page (table version).** Figure 4.44 contains a table listing football positions and valid uniform numbers. Recreate this page.

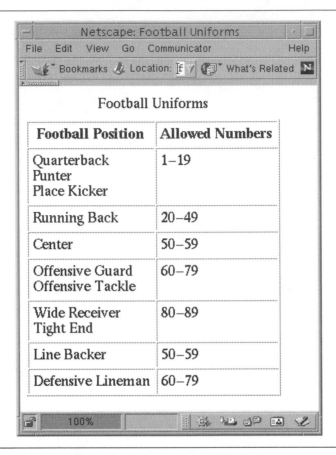

Figure 4.44 The *Football Uniform* Page (table version)

➤ HTML TAGS

<CAPTION>...</CAPTION>. The **<CAPTION>...</CAPTION>** tags create a caption for a table.

Syntax:
```
<CAPTION ALIGN = "TOP" | "BOTTOM" | "LEFT" | "RIGHT">
```

<TABLE>...</TABLE>. The **<TABLE>...</TABLE>** tags create a table.

Syntax:
```
<TABLE ALIGN = "CENTER" | "LEFT" | "RIGHT"
       BGCOLOR = "name" | "#RRGGBB"
       BORDER = "pixels"
       CELLPADDING = "pixels"
       CELLSPACING = "pixels"
       WIDTH = "pixels" | "percent%">
```

<TD>...</TD>. The **<TD>...</TD>** tags create a data cell in a table.

Syntax:
```
<TD ALIGN = "CENTER" | "LEFT" | "RIGHT"| "JUSTIFY"
    BGCOLOR = "name" | "#RRGGBB"
    COLSPAN = "number"
    HEIGHT = "pixels"
    NOWRAP
    ROWSPAN = "number"
    VALIGN = "BASELINE"| "BOTTOM"|"MIDDLE"| "TOP"
    WIDTH = "pixels" | "percent%">
```

<TH>...</TH>. The **<TH>...</TH>** tags create a table heading. Table headings are (by default) centered and in a bold font.

Syntax:
```
<TH ALIGN = "CENTER" | "LEFT" | "RIGHT"| "JUSTIFY"
    BGCOLOR = "name" | "#RRGGBB"
    COLSPAN = "number"
    HEIGHT = "pixels"
    NOWRAP
    ROWSPAN = "number"
    VALIGN = "BASELINE"|"BOTTOM"| "MIDDLE" | "TOP"
    WIDTH = "pixels" | "percent%">
```

<TR>...</TR>. The **<TR>...</TR>** tags create a table row.

Syntax:
```
<TR ALIGN = "CENTER" | "LEFT" | "RIGHT"| "JUSTIFY"
    BGCOLOR = "name" | "#RRGGBB"
    VALIGN = "BASELINE"| "BOTTOM"|"MIDDLE"|"TOP">
```

➤ HTML TIPS

1. **Internet Explorer versus Netscape Navigator.** Internet Explorer is much more forgiving than Netscape Navigator when it comes to table creation errors. Internet Explorer displays tables with missing table tags; Netscape Navigator will not. Make sure that you check your tables on *both* browsers to ensure that they will work correctly no matter who views them.

2. **End Tags.** Always use the appropriate end tag for table headings, data, and rows. Internet Explorer is forgiving, but Netscape Navigator is not. Failure to use the proper end tags can lead to obscure errors. Additionally, the programming languages discussed in later chapters are less forgiving. Failure to use the end tags when using these languages usually produces improperly formatted tables.

3. **Disappearing Tables.** If a table does not appear on the page, check to make sure that you included the end table tag, **</TABLE>**. If this tag is present, check the other tags. Make sure that the > symbol appears at the end of each tag.

4. **Forcing Borders Between Rows and Columns.** Browsers do not display borders between empty cells. To force the border lines, use either `<PRE>`...`</PRE>` tags with embedded spaces or the "nonbreaking space" character entity, ` `.

5. **No Borders.** Use tables without borders to create simple line drawings. See, for example, the genealogies.

6. **Cell Padding.** Use a cell padding of 2–5 for all tables with borders.

7. **Borders and Spacing.** Use border and cell spacing values greater than 10 to simulate buttons.

8. **Text Displayed Above A Table.** Figure 4.45 contains a frequently occurring error. Part of the table's content appears above the table. The usual source of this error is text placed between `</TD>` and `<TD>` tags.

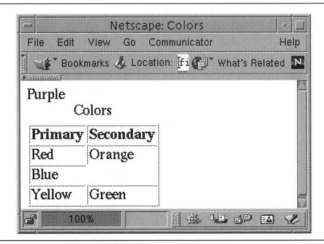

Figure 4.45 A Table Error

9. **BaseFont and Tables.** The `<BASEFONT>` tag does not apply to a table's contents. For example, if we use the tag `<BASEFONT SIZE = "2">`, the table's caption or heading and data cells will be written with a font size of 3. The only way to change the font size of a caption or table heading or data cell is to place a `<FONT>` tag *within* the caption heading or data cell, by creating a cascading sheet style for the heading and data cells.

5 Links and Images

PROTOCOLS

In our previous pages, we used the **http://** (Hyper Text Transfer Protocol) protocol. The Internet recognizes several other protocols:

ftp (File Transfer Protocol)—Many web sites contain archival information. This information can represent collections of programs, graphics, movie, or sound files. Because the file sizes are large, archivists frequently place such files in tape archives (**.tar** files). The tape archives can be compressed further by "zipping" them (**.zip** or **.gz** files). To transfer archival information from a host machine to our machine, that is, to *download* information, we use the **ftp** protocol. The syntax of this protocol is

```
ftp://serverName/DirectoryName/FileName.tar
```

Notice the **.tar** extension that appears with the file name. If the file is also zipped, it will have the extension *FileName*.**tar.gz** (for gnu zip) or *FileName*.**tar.zip**; once you've transferred the archive to your machine, you must unzip the file (if it has been zipped) and untar it. You'll need to consult your machine's reference manual to find the appropriate utilities to accomplish these tasks.

The **ftp** protocol is an *authenticated* protocol; a user can be forced to provide a user name and password before being allowed to access the archives. Many sites do, however, offer *anonymous ftp*, so that anyone can use the archives.

File The **file** protocol indicates that the browser should load the page *without connecting to the Internet*. This protocol works with any page that does not link to files outside local directories. You can use the **file** protocol to develop pages and check their appearance without paying connect charges. This protocol works with both HTML and image files. To load a file in Netscape Navigator, use the **File>Open>Page in Navigator** option. To load a file in Internet Explorer, use the **File>Open File** option.

mailto Web pages often contain a link that lets users email comments or questions to the page's developer or to the site's webmaster. To provide an email access link, add a link of the form:

```
mailto://UserName@ServerName
```

where *UserName* represents your email name and *ServerName* is the name of your email provider.

In addition to the **http**, **ftp**, **file**, and **mailto** protocols, the internet recognizes several less frequently used protocols. Among them are the following:

telnet This protocol establishes a **telnet** session. Because **telnet** is an authenticated protocol, a user must furnish a valid user name and password before being allowed to gain access to the system.

news Use this protocol to connect to any newsgroups to which you belong. The format of this link is

```
news://NewsGroup
```

where *NewsGroup* is the name of a newsgroup.

nntp The **nntp** protocol provides access to specific articles in the Usenet news system. The format of this link is

```
nntp://ServerName/NewsGroup/ArticleNumber
```

Note that the articles are identified by a numeric code, so accessing them does not use a *user-friendly*.

gopher The **gopher** protocol is an old protocol, dating from before the creation of the World Wide Web; it is rarely used today.

DEFAULT LINK COLORS

Many web pages contain links to other web pages. Figure 5.1 shows a page of links as displayed by Internet Explorer. By default, both Internet Explorer and Netscape underline all links. Internet Explorer displays visited links in green and unvisited links in blue. Netscape uses blue for unvisited links and purple for visited links. If you find the underlining of links a distraction, you can turn off this feature by selecting **Edit>Preferences** from the pull-down menu. Click the **Underline Links** check box to uncheck the option.

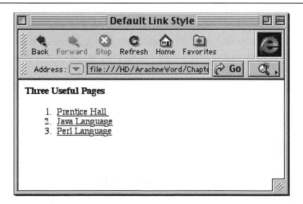

Figure 5.1 The *Link* Page

We can also change the default link colors. For example, Figure 5.2 contains a new version of the *Link* page displayed in Figure 5.1. The links are no longer underlined. In addition, the visited links are tan and the unvisited links are red.

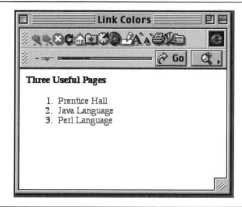

Figure 5.2 The *Link Colors* Page

The default link colors can be changed by adding **VLINK**, **ALINK**, and **LINK** attributes to the **<BODY>** tag. The **LINK** attribute changes the default color for unvisited links; the **VLINK** attribute does the same thing for visited links. The **ALINK** attribute changes the default color for the active link. Unless your system is terribly slow, you will not see the active link color; it represents the color of a clicked link only while the browser is loading the selected page.

The **LINK**, **VLINK**, and **ALINK** attributes require a value that is either an acceptable color name or an RGB value of the form **#RRGGBB**. The **<BODY>** tag of the *Link Colors* page uses browser-safe RGB values to change the unvisited, visited, and active link colors. The HTML for the **<BODY>** tag is

```
<BODY BGCOLOR = "white" LINK = "#FF0000" VLINK = #996666" ALINK = "#FF9966">
```

where the **ALINK** color is a deep orange.

ABSOLUTE LINKS

The *Link Colors* page contains a list of links. Thus, clicking on a page's name not only changes the link color, it loads the selected page into the browser. Adding links to pages requires anchor tags, **<A>...</A>**. The **<A>** tag contains three attributes: **HREF**, **NAME**, and **TARGET**. The **HREF** attribute creates a link to another page. The **NAME** attribute creates a target for a link within a Web page. (This type of target is called a *fragment*). The **TARGET** attribute indicates that the file associated with an **HREF** attribute should be loaded into the frame associated with the **TARGET** attribute. We examine frames in Chapter 6.

The general syntax for creating a link is

```
<A HREF = "URL">Label</A>
```

where *"URL"* represents the URL of the page and *Label* represents an identifying label of our choice.

Let's consider the Prentice Hall link. The URL for Prentice Hall is

```
http://www.prenhall.com/
```

the HTML that creates the Prentice Hall link is

`<A HREF = http://www.prenhall.com/>`Prentice Hall`</A>`.

Figure 5.3 contains the HTML for the *Link Colors* page. Notice the **LINK**, **ALINK**, and **VLINK** attributes in the **<BODY>** tag and the **<A HREF>** tags that create the links to the Prentice Hall, Java, and Perl home pages.

```
<HTML><HEAD><TITLE>Link Colors</TITLE></HEAD>
<BODY BGCOLOR = "white" LINK = "#FF0000" VLINK = #996666" ALINK = "#FF9966">
<B>Three Useful Pages</B>
<P>
<OL>
<LI><A HREF = "http://www.prenhall.com/">Prentice Hall</A>
<LI><A HREF = "http://java.sun.com/">Java Language</A>
<LI><A HREF = "http://www.perl.com/perl">Perl Language</A>
</OL>
</BODY>
</HTML>
```

Figure 5.3 HTML for the *Link Colors* Page

THE *BUTTON TABLE* PAGE

The *Link Colors* page uses *absolute links*. An *absolute link* contains a full specification of the URL for a page. When linking to files in the current directory, we can use the shortened type of URL referred to as a *relative link*. Figure 5.4 contains a *Button Table* page. Clicking a button loads the desired page into the browser.

Figure 5.4 The *Button Table* Page

The *Button Table* page requires four HTML files. The files reside in the *firstLink* directory. Figure 5.5 contains a picture of this directory. The *buttonTable* file contains the HTML for the *Button Table* page. The three remaining files each contain the HTML for one of the linked pages.

The HTML for the *buttonTable* file appears in Figure 5.6. This page creates a borderless table for the three button tables. Each button table uses the same width to ensure that the buttons will be the same size. The **<A HREF>** tags contain only the HTML file name. The full URL is not necessary, because the linked pages reside in the same directory as the page that contains the links.

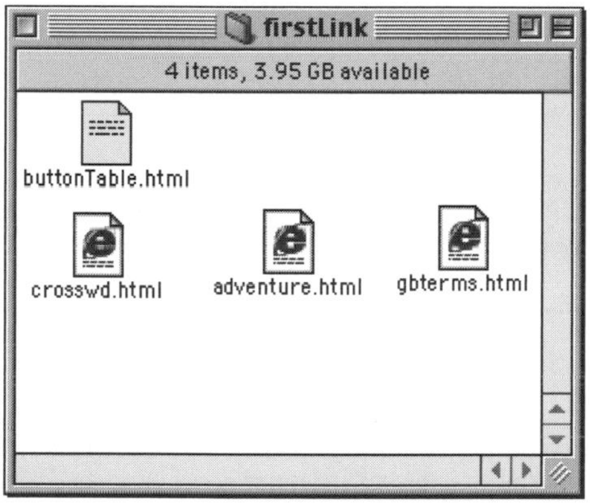

```
<!DOCTYPE HTML PUBLIC "-//W3C//DTD HTML 4.0
    Transitional//EN">
<HTML>
<HEAD><TITLE>Button Tables</TITLE></HEAD>
<BODY BGCOLOR = "white" LINK = "black">
<TABLE>
<CAPTION><H1>My Favorite Pages</H1></CAPTION>
<TR>
<TD>
<TABLE BORDER = "5" CELLSPACING = "5"
    CELLPADDING = "5" BGCOLOR = "#CC9999">
<TR><TD WIDTH = "90">
<A HREF = "adventure.html">Molly's Adventure</A>
</TD></TR></TABLE></TD>
<TD>
<TABLE BORDER = "5" CELLSPACING = "5"
    CELLPADDING = "5" BGCOLOR = "#FFFFCC">
<TR><TD WIDTH = "90">
<A HREF = "crosswd.html">CrossWord Puzzle</A>
</TD></TR></TABLE></TD>
<TD>
<TABLE BORDER = "5" CELLSPACING = "5"
    CELLPADDING = "5" BGCOLOR = "#33FFFF">
<TR><TD WIDTH = "90">
<A HREF = "gbterms.html">GB Football</A>
</TD></TR></TABLE></TD>
</TABLE>
</BODY></HTML>
```

Figure 5.5 The *firstLink* Folder

Figure 5.6 HTML for the *ButtonTable* File

We can use relative links to access any file within any of our directories by using the following formats.

Format 1. File in Same Directory. The format is

```
<A HREF = "fileName">
```

Format 2. File in a Subdirectory. The format is

```
<A HREF = "Directory/fileName">
```

We can use the same format to access files in sub-subdirectories. For example, the statement

```
<A HREF = "wool/cheviot/color.html">
```

creates a link to the file named *color.html* that is located in the **cheviot/** directory. This directory is a subdirectory of the **wool/** directory. The **wool/** directory is a subdirectory located in the current directory.

Format 3. File in the Parent Directory. The format is

```
<A HREF = "../fileName">
```

For example, suppose we have a page named **Chapter2.html**, located in the **Chp2** directory. An index page in the parent directory lists all of the chapters. The **<A HREF>** tag that creates a link to the index page in the parent directory is

```
<A HREF = "../index.html">
```

(See Figure 5.20.)

We can create a link to a file in a grandparent directory (two levels up) by using a similar strategy. For example, the tag

```
<A HREF = "../../topLevel.html">
```

creates a link to the **topLevel.html** file that is located in a directory that is the grandparent of the current directory.

Format 4. File in a Subdirectory of a Parent Directory. The format is

```
<A HREF = "../Directory/fileName>
```

For example, suppose Chapter 2's page contains a link to Chapter 1's index page. The latter page is located in the **Chp1** directory, which is located in the parent directory. The **<A HREF>** tag that creates this link is

```
<A HREF = "../Chp1/index.html">
```

We combine Formats 2 and 4 to create a link to a sub-subdirectory of a parent directory. We combine Formats 3 and 4 to create a link to a subdirectory of a grandparent directory.

THE *GLOSSARY* PAGE

We can use the **<A HREF>** tag to link to a place within a page if we mark the desired location with an **<A NAME>** tag. These internal links are called *fragments*. For example, Figure 5.7 contains a small glossary of HTML tags that begin with B, C, or D. The page uses a line with letter labels before the start of each letter. This line lets us jump to the start of a letter: clicking on *B* moves us to the start of the B tags, clicking on *C* moves us to the start of the C tags, and clicking on *D* moves us to the start of the D tags.

The syntax for creating a fragment is

```
<A NAME = "fragmentName">Label</A>
```

where *fragmentName* is a unique identifier for the fragment. *Label* is optional text. The fragments in the *Glossary* page are anchored to the first tag for each letter. For example, the fragment for *B* is anchored to the **<BODY>** tag. The following statement creates the fragment:

```
<A NAME = "B"> &lt;BODY&gt;....&lt;/BODY&gt;.</A>
```

The fragments for C and D are created in a similar manner.

Once the fragments exist, we can use **<A HREF>** tags to link to them. The syntax for linking to a fragment contained in the same page as the **<A HREF>** tag is

```
<A HREF "#fragmentName">Label</A>
```

Figure 5.7 The *Glossary* Page

The link line that appears before the start of each letter is created with the following HTML statements:

```
<A HREF = "#B">[B]</A>
<A HREF = "#C">[C]</A>
<A HREF = "#D">[D]</A>
```

Figure 5.8 contains the HTML for the *Glossary* page. The **<A NAME>** and **<A HREF>** tags are highlighted.

We can create **<A HREF>** tags that access fragments in any page or directory by using the following formats.

Format 1. **<A HREF> tag is in the same page as the fragment.**   The format is

```
<A HREF = "#fragmentName">
```

Format 2. Absolute Link.   The format is

```
<A HREF = "URL#fragmentName">
```

For example, suppose we have the absolute link

```
http://www.xyz.com/myPage.html
```

which contains a fragment named *hobbies*. The **<A HREF>** tag that links to the *hobbies* fragment is

```
<A HREF = http://www.xyz.com/myPage.html#hobbies>
```

Format 3. Fragment is in a different page in the same directory.   The format is

```
<A HREF = "fileName.html#fragmentName">
```

```
<HTML>
<HEAD><TITLE>HTML TAGS: B-D</TITLE></HEAD>
<BODY BGCOLOR = "white">
<A HREF = "#B">[B]</A> <A HREF = "#C">[C]</A> <A HREF = "#D">[D]</A>
<PRE></TT>
<A NAME = "B">&lt;BODY&gt;....&lt;/BODY&gt;.</A>
These tags encase the body of your HTML program.

Syntax: &lt;BODY ALINK = "ColorName" | "RRGGBB"
           BACKGROUND = "ImageFile"
           BGCOLOR = "ColorName" | "RRGGBB"
           LINK = "ColorName" | "RRGGBB"
           TEXT = "ColorName" | "RRGGBB"
           VLINK = "ColorName" | "RRGGBB"&gt;

&lt;BR&gt;. The line BReak breaks the line.

Syntax: &lt;BR CLEAR = "ALL" | "LEFT" | "RIGHT" | "NONE" &gt;

<A HREF  = "#B">[B]</A><A HREF = "#C">[C]</A><A HREF  = "#D">[D]</A>

<A NAME = "C">&lt;CENTER&gt;...&lt;/CENTER&gt;.</A>This tag centers text.

The tag is a short-hand form of  &lt;DIV ALIGN = "CENTER"&gt;.

<A HREF  = "#B">[B]</A><A HREF  = "#C">[C]</A><A HREF = "#D">[D]</A>

<A NAME = "D">&lt;DIV&gt;....&lt;/DIV&gt;.</A>The DIVision Block tags encase a block of text.

Syntax: &lt;DIV ALIGN = "CENTER" | "LEFT" | "RIGHT" | "JUSTIFY"&gt; .... &lt;/DIV&gt;

&lt;DOCTYPE&gt;. The &lt;DOCTYPE&gt; tag is the first line of an HTML program. It specifies the
HTML version and the language.

Syntax: &lt;!DOCTYPE HTML PUBLIC "-//W3C//DTD HTML 4.0 Transitional//EN"&gt;
</PRE>
</BODY></HTML>
```

Figure 5.8 HTML for the *Glossary* Page

For example, to create a link to a fragment *cooking* in the file *worldCuisine.html*, we write

```
<A HREF = "worldCuisine.html#cooking">
```

We can create links to fragments in parent directories, subdirectories, and so on by combining the fragment formats and the relative link formats.

IMAGES

Web pages often contain images, ranging from simple line drawings to photographs. Not all browsers can process images. The two most popular browsers, Netscape and Internet Explorer, recognize GIF and JPEG image files. A third image format, PNG, is not yet widely available, but it should be in the near future. All graphics formats use compression to reduce the size of an image file. Generally, the larger the size of the file, the more slowly it loads into a browser. Most users won't wait for a slow page, so a good Web-page developer chooses image files that are of high quality yet of the smallest possible size, to increase the chances that site visitors will wait until the page loads. Generally, GIF files are smaller than JPEG files; however, GIF files are not suitable for all images.

GIF Format

"GIF" stands for Graphics Interchange Format and is pronounced with a soft "g" like a brand of peanut butter. GIF files have an extension of `.gif`. GIF uses a lossless, proprietary compression method. Because *lossless* comprehension preserves *all* information in the original image, the decompressed image has the same quality as the original. GIF files are created by using the LZW (Lempel-Ziv-Welch) compression method. Currently, pages containing GIF files do not pay a fee to use the proprietary LZW compression method, but that could change in the future.

The GIF format uses a single byte to store a color, so it can represent only 2^8, or 256, distinct colors. GIF images use the standard RGB palette and one *transparent* color. An image with a transparent background blends into any background color. Because GIF files have a limited color palette, a color in the original image could fail to exist within the GIF palette. The GIF format approximates the original color by blending pixels from different colors within the GIF palette. This blending process is called *dithering*. The quality of a dithered image varies. Generally, the GIF format works well with images that have large areas of a solid color, for example, line drawings. These images require little dithering, so the overall quality is good. The GIF format does not work well with a highly detailed image that contains many different colors—for example, photographs.

Figure 5.9 displays a Wood Duck carving stored as a GIF file. The carving contains several large areas of solid color. Slight dithering occurs in the chest area. The GIF file requires only 8K bytes of storage (8,000 bytes)! An image of this size loads very quickly.

Figure 5.9 A Wood Duck Carving (GIF format)

The GIF89a format supports *interlacing*. Interlacing is useful for large images because an interlaced GIF file is displayed in pieces. The first piece appears after 1/8 of the file has been read. The other pieces are added as the browser loads the pieces. This lets users know that the browser is working and increases the probability that users will wait while a large file loads. The GIF 89a format also supports animation.

JPEG FORMAT

"JPEG" stands for Joint Photographic Experts Group and is pronounced like two nicknames, "Jay-Peg." The JPEG format uses 24 bits to store each color, so this format recognizes 2^{24} (or 16,777,216) colors. This format is called "Millions Of Colors." JPEG files have an extension of `.jpeg` or `.jpg`.

The JPEG format uses a *lossy compression* method. This means that it does not preserve all of the details in the original image. Most graphics programs let users choose between low, medium, and high levels of compression. Generally, the higher the level of compression, the greater the loss of details, but highly compressed files are significantly smaller than less-compressed files. Most graphics programs use "medium compression" as the default. Figure 5.10 contains a photograph taken at Glacier National Park. The photograph is stored as a JPEG file with medium compression. The details were preserved, but the file size was 92K (or approximately 92,000 bytes).

Figure 5.10 Glacier National Park (JPEG format)

The JPEG format does not support transparency or animation. The Progressive JPEG format supports interlacing.

PNG

PNG is a new image format. "PNG" stands for Portable Network Graphics. PNG supports two image techniques: PNG-8 and PNG-24. PNG-8 uses 8 bits to store a color, PNG-24 uses 24 bits. The PNG format supports animation, transparency, and interlacing. It uses a nonproprietary compression method. This format can preserve the sharpness of the original image.

At present, displaying PNG files requires QuickTime Pro. Figure 5.11 contains a PNG file of the Canadian Rockies as displayed in Netscape Navigator.

PNG files are memory hogs. The PNG file displayed in Figure 5.11 required 1.6M of storage. On the positive side, PNG files have a clarity not seen in the other formats.

OBTAINING IMAGES

There are several ways to obtain images for a Web page. You can use a search engine, such as Yahoo, Lycos, or Magellan, to locate sites that offer free images. The relevant search topics are Clip Art, Borders, or Bullets. You can also purchase CDs containing clip-art images. Finally, you can create your own images. This approach requires a graphics package, such as PhotoShop, and a digital camera or a scanner. The images appearing in this book were created by using the last approach.

Figure 5.11 Canadian Rockies (PNG format)

THE *DUCK CARVER'S* PAGE, VERSION 1

We've used the attributes of the **<BODY>** tag to change the background, text, and link colors. The **BACKGROUND** attribute of the **<BODY>** tag uses an image file as the background for a page. The syntax to add a background image is

```
<BODY BACKGROUND = "imageFile">
```

where *imageFile* is an image stored in the GIF or JPEG format. Background images should be selected carefully, because some images detract from a page's appearance or readability.

Figure 5.12 contains an example of a "bad" background image. This page uses the Wood Duck image found in Figure 5.9 as the background for the *Duck Carver's* page. The text is difficult to read, and the multicolored wood ducks are a distraction.

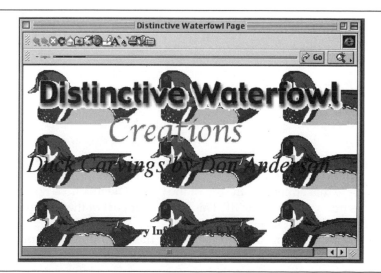

Figure 5.12 The *Duck Carver's* Page, version 1

Figure 5.13 contains a gray-scale version of the wood duck decoy. The image is stored as a GIF. The file size is only 4K.

Figure 5.13 Gray-Scale Wood Duck

Figure 5.14 contains a new version of the *Duck Carver's* page that uses the gray-scale duck. The `<BODY>` tag is

```
<BODY BACKGROUND = "woody2Back.gif">
```

The text is easy to read, and the gray-scale ducks are not a distraction. The page contains links to a picture gallery, to information about the carver, and to the carver's email address.

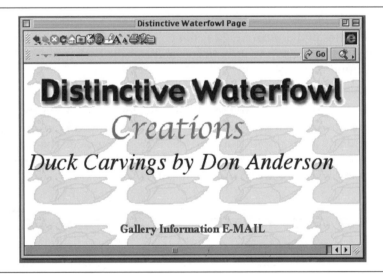

Figure 5.14 The *Duck Carver's* Page, version 2

THE IMG TAG

The *Duck Carver's* page displayed in Figure 5.14 contains two GIF files. The first file, *woody2Back.gif*, provides the background image for the page. The second file, *name2.gif*, displays the *Distinctive Waterfowl Creations* title that appears at the top of the page. The title does not blend into the background, because it is not a transparent GIF. This title is not part of the background, so we use an `<IMG>` tag to add it to the page.

The `<IMG>` tag contains several attributes. Most of these attributes are optional. The required attribute is

```
SRC = "imageFile"
```

where *imageFile* is a file in GIF or JPEG format.

The other attributes associated with the `<IMG>` tag are as follows:

ALT = `"alternate text"`. Some browsers do not have graphic capabilities; the **ALT** attribute specifies text that should be displayed on such browsers. Using the **ALT** attribute makes a page accessible to everyone, regardless of the browser in use.

BORDER = `"Number"`. The **BORDER** attribute specifies the image's border. Images that do not serve as *hot links* have by default a border of zero pixels. An image that serves as a hot link (by virtue of the fact that the image is contained within `<A HREF>` ... `</A>` tags) has by default a border of one pixel. Most web-page developers remove the borders on clickable images. Simply include **BORDER** = `"0"` in the `<IMG>` tag to remove the border.

HEIGHT = `"pixels"` *and* `WIDTH` = `"pixels"`. The **HEIGHT** and **WIDTH** attributes change the scale of the image. Many graphics programs include proportional scaling. This means that a change in an image's height produces a corresponding change in the image's width, or vice versa. Images that do not use proportional scaling often look distorted. Therefore, be careful when using the **HEIGHT** and **WIDTH** attributes; the browser does not check an image's proportions, so it's easy to create distorted images with these attributes.

ISMAP and *USEMAP*. The **ISMAP** and **USEMAP** attributes are used with image maps. We will examine this topic in Chapter 6.

ALIGN = "LEFT" | "RIGHT". The **ALIGN** attribute wraps text around an image. Left alignment places the image on the left side of the page. Text written after the `<IMG>` tag is placed to the right of the image. Right alignment places the image on the right side of the page, with the text appearing to the left of the image.

The HTML for the *Duck Carver's* page (version 2) appears in Figure 5.15. Notice the `<IMG>` tag used to add the page's title. This tag contains a **HEIGHT** attribute that increases the height of the original image. An **ALT** tag is not necessary because the message that appears below the title, *Duck Carvings by Don Anderson*, conveys the same information as the title GIF.

```
<HTML>
<HEAD><TITLE>Distinctive Waterfowl Page</TITLE></HEAD>
<BODY BACKGROUND = "woody2Back.gif">
<IMG SRC = "name2.gif" HEIGHT = "130"><BR>
<FONT SIZE = "7"><I>Duck Carvings by Don Anderson</I></FONT>
<BR><BR><BR><BR><BR><BR>
<CENTER><TABLE>
<TR><TD><A HREF = "gallery.html">
<H2>Gallery</H2></A></TD>

<TD><A HREF = "info.html">
<H2>Information</H2></A></TD>
<TD><A HREF = "mailto:djander@gbw.duc.org">
<H2>E-MAIL</H2></A></TD></TR>
</TABLE>
</BODY></HTML>
```

Figure 5.15 HTML for Duck Carving Page, version 2

TILES WITH SEAMS

The gray-scale duck decoy produces a nicely tiled background image. Since there is white space surrounding the decoy, the duck images appear to form a seamless background. Figure 5.16 contains a second background image, one composed of small spider webs. The web lines don't connect, so, this background image contains *seams* that detract from the page's appearance.

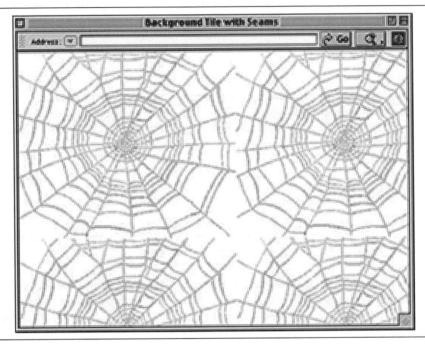

Figure 5.16 A Background Image with Seams

If you have access to a graphics program, you can easily transform an image that creates seams into a seamless one. Figure 5.17 uses our transformed spider-web image as the background. To create a seamless image in PhotoShop 5.5®, use the following steps.

Step 1. Determine Width and Height.   Select `Image>ImageSize` from the PhotoShop menu, and read the width and height in pixels. The original spider web was 288 × 245 pixels.

Step 2. Split Width and Height.   Divide the width and height by two. For the spider-web image, half of the width is 144 pixels, and half of the height is 123 pixels.

Step 3. Shift Image.   Select `Filter>Other>Offset` from the pull-down menu. Enter 144 and 123 for the offsets. This shifts the image so that the seams are prominently displayed in the middle of the image.

Step 4. Remove Seams.   Remove the seams by drawing connecting lines.

This technique works with any image. Remember to keep the background image simple.

THE *WEB EXERCISES* PAGE

Figure 5.17 contains a *Web Exercises* page that applies our knowledge of links and images. The page contains a sampling of the exercises for the first three chapters.

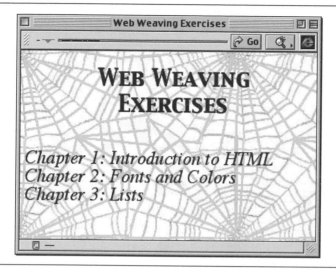

Figure 5.17 The *Web Exercises* Page

The *Web Exercises* page contains a title image stored as a transparent GIF. Links to the first three chapters follow the title. Unvisited links are displayed in purple, visited ones in black. Figure 5.18 contains the HTML for the *Web Exercises* index page.

```
<HTML>
<HEAD><TITLE>Web Weaving Exercises</TITLE></HEAD>
<BODY BACKGROUND =  "web.gif"  VLINK = "black" LINK = "#330033">
<CENTER><IMG SRC = "title.gif"></CENTER>
<BR>
<FONT SIZE = "6" ><I>
<A HREF = "Chp1/index.html">Chapter 1:  Introduction to HTML</A><BR>
<A HREF = "Chp2/index.html">Chapter 2:  Fonts and Colors</A><BR>
<A HREF = "Chp3/index.html">Chapter 3:  Lists</A><BR>
</I></FONT>
</BODY>
</HTML>
```

Figure 5.18 HTML for the *Web Exercises* Page

The *Web Exercises* page contains links to the index pages for the first three chapters of the book. Notice the relative links used for each chapter. The links indicate that a separate directory exists for each chapter. Each chapter directory also contains an *index.html* file that holds the link table for the chapter. Figure 5.19 shows an annotated directory structure for the *Web Exercises* page.

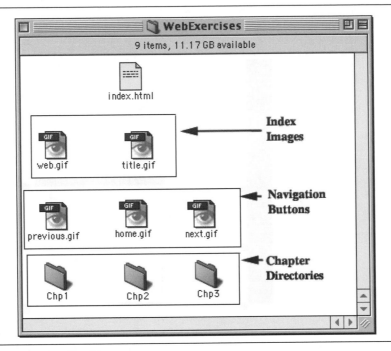

Figure 5.19 The *Web Exercises* Directory

The *Web Exercises* directory contains a subdirectory for each chapter. The `index.html` file is the starting point for the *Web Exercises* page. The `web.gif` file contains the background image for the page, and the `title.gif` file contains the transparent GIF for the title. The three remaining files, `home.gif`, `next.gif`, and `previous.gif`, contain button images used by the index pages in the chapter directories.

Figure 5.20 shows the index page for Chapter 2. This page contains a table of links to the three completed exercises. The completed exercises are represented as GIF files. A second table contains the navigation buttons represented as GIF files. Since the `<IMG>` tags are placed inside the `<A HREF>...</A>` tags, these images serve as clickable buttons. For example, clicking the *Previous* button sends the user to the Chapter 1 index page. Clicking the *Next* button sends the user to the Chapter 3 index page. Clicking the *Home* button sends the user to the home page.

Figure 5.21 contains the HTML for the Chapter 2 index page. Relative links are used for the GIF exercise files, because these files are contained within the directory. By contrast, the *Previous*, *Home*, and *Next* images reside in the parent directory. This means that the `<A HREF>` tags must use `"../"` to obtain access to these image files.

The `<IMG>` tags for the *Previous*, *Next*, and *Home* images contain **ALT** and **BORDER** attributes. The **ALT** tag furnishes alternative text for nongraphic browsers. The border is set to 0 to remove the blue box that is drawn around link images.

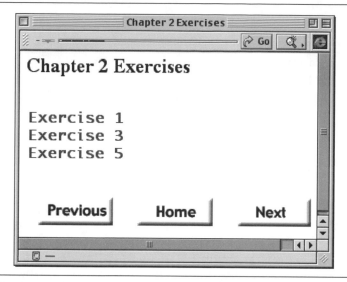

Figure 5.20 The Chapter 2 Index Page

```
<HTML>
<HEAD><TITLE>Chapter 2 Exercises</TITLE></HEAD>
<BODY BGCOLOR = "white">
<H1>Chapter 2 Exercises</H1>
<P>
<TABLE><TR><TD><PRE></TT><H1>
<A HREF = "ex2_01.gif">Exercise 1</A>
<A HREF = "ex2_03.gif">Exercise 3</A>
<A HREF = "ex2_05.gif">Exercise 5</A></H1>
</TD></TD></TABLE>
<TABLE><TR><TD >
<A HREF = "../Chp1/index.html">
<IMG SRC = "../previous.gif" BORDER = "0" ALT = "Previous Page">
</A></TD>>
<TD><A HREF = "../index.html">
<IMG SRC = "../home.gif" BORDER = "0"  ALT = "Home Page"></A></TD>>
<TD><A HREF = "../Chp3/index.html">
<IMG SRC = "../next.gif" BORDER = "0" ALT = "Next Page"></A>
</TD></TR></TABLE>
</BODY></HTML>
```

Figure 5.21 HTML for the Chapter 2 Index Page

THE *DUCK CARVER'S* PAGE (FINAL VERSION)

Figure 5.22 contains the final version of the *Duck Carver's* page. This version contains text and button links to the gallery and information pages and the carver's (fictitious) email address. The user can click on the text or on the small *Green Teal* buttons.

Figure 5.22 The *Duck Carver's* Page (final version)

The *Green Teal* buttons were scaled down in the *Duck Carver's* page by using the **WIDTH** and **HEIGHT** attributes. Each button is about one inch high by $1\frac{1}{2}$ inches wide. Originally, I tried to scale the images in my graphics program; however, the image is highly dithered, so it began to "break apart" when I reduced it beyond a certain threshold. The **HEIGHT** and **WIDTH** attributes reduced the image with no additional deterioration in quality. Figure 5.23 contains the HTML for the final version of the *Duck Carver's* Page.

```
<HTML>
<HEAD><TITLE>Distinctive Waterfowl Page</TITLE></HEAD>
<BODY BACKGROUND = "woody2Back.gif">
<IMG SRC = "name2.gif" HEIGHT = "130" ><BR>
<FONT SIZE = "7"><I>Duck Carvings by Don Anderson</I></FONT>

<BR><BR><BR><BR><BR><BR>
<CENTER>
<TABLE>
<TR>
<TD><A HREF = "gallery.html">
<IMG SRC = "but2.gif"  HEIGHT = "72" WIDTH = "125" BORDER = "0">
<H2>Gallery</H2></A></TD>

<TD><A HREF = "info.html">
<IMG SRC = "but2.gif" HEIGHT = "72" WIDTH = "125" BORDER = "0">
<H2>Information</H2></A></TD>
<TD><A HREF = "mailto:djander@gbw.duc.org">
<IMG SRC = "but2.gif" HEIGHT = "72" WIDTH = "125"  BORDER = "0">
<H2>E-MAIL</H2></A></TD>
</TR>
</TABLE>
</BODY>
</HTML>
```

Figure 2.23 The *Duck Carver's* Page (final version)

➤ EXERCISES

The exercises in this chapter include links and images. The CD that accompanies this book contains image files that you can use for several of the exercises. If you have a graphics program, feel free to substitute your own images.

1. **The *Button Tables* Page.** Using Figure 5.4 as your guide, create a five-button table that contains links to your five favorite pages.

2. **The *Birding Links* Page.** Find 5–10 birding pages on the Web. Create an ordered list that contains the name of the birding page. Each name should serve as a link to the page that it describes.

3. **The *Sports Teams* Page.** Find Web pages for your favorite sports teams. Create an unordered list that contains the names of the sports teams. Each name should serve as a link to the page that it describes.

4. **The *Address Book* Page.** Create an online address book. The book should contain the name, address, phone number, and birthday of several friends or relatives. Create fragments for the names. You can create alphabetical fragments of the form `[A][B]...[Z]`, or last name fragments of the form `[Apple][Baker]...[Hill]`. Create as many fragments as you need. Model your page after Figure 5.7.

5. **The *Definition List* Page.** Select a definition list from Chapter 3. Transform each definition term into a fragment. Use a line of links to move between the definitions. Model your page after Figure 5.7.

6. **The *Football Facts* Page.** Chapters 3 and 4 contained several football pages. These pages covered special teams, scoring, football uniforms, and definitions. Create a page that links to each of these pages.

7. **The *Local News, Weather, and Sports* Page.** The CD that accompanies this book contains GIF files with buttons for News, Weather, and Sports. Find Web pages for the local or regional newspaper(s), radio and TV stations, weather forecasts, and sports teams. In a separate page, create a fragment for each category. Each fragment should be followed by a list of links to the appropriate pages. The buttons should link to the appropriate fragment in the new page.

8. **Your *Home* Page.** Find or create appropriate images that will serve as buttons for your home page. Find buttons to represent a hobby, local news/weather, and your email address. Link the first two buttons to appropriate pages and the last button to your email.

9. **The *Web Exercises* Page.** Modify the *Web Exercises* page appearing in Figure 5.17. Create separate directories for the first five chapters. Create links to the HTML files for the exercises that you've completed. Add the navigational buttons to each chapter.

10. **The *Favorite Places* Page.** Find JPEG files of your favorite places. If the images are under copyright, be sure to request permission to use these files from the page's author. Create a page that has an ordered list of links to your ten favorite places. Label the image files appropriately, and be sure to include ALT tags for nongraphic browsers.

11. **The *Web Definitions* Page.** Create a definition list of terms used in this chapter. Your definition list should include GIF, JPEG, PNG, dithering, interlacing, transparency, and animation. Pick at least three image files (you may use the examples in this book) to illustrate your definitions. Each definition should serve as a fragment. Create references that move back and forth between the definitions. Use Figure 5.7 as your model.

12. **The *Web Resources* Page.** Search the Web for pages related to HTML, JavaScript, Java, Perl, and Clip Art. Create fragments for each topic, followed by a list of links to your resources. Create reference tags that let you move back and forth between the Web-resource categories.

13. **The *Gardening* Page.** Develop a gardening page for your region. The page should indicate your climate zone and the plants, flowers, and trees that grow within your region. Find image files for at least two plants, flowers, or trees. Place the information and images on the page.

14. **The *Child's Animal Alphabet* Page.** Find or create images of animals. Create a page that lists the letters of the alphabet. Each letter should link to a page that contains a picture of the animal, with an appropriate message (for example, A is for Anteater).

15. **The *Child's Shape* Page.** Create a page with the names of several simple shapes—for example, triangle, square, circle, star, heart. Each name should link to a page that contains a picture of the shape. Display an appropriate message with the shape.

16. **The *Science* Page.** Pick a scientific topic of your choice. Search the Web for relevant links. Create a page that contains information on your topic and has appropriate images and links.

➤ **HTML TAGS**

<A>...</A>. The `<A>...</A>` tags form a container for an anchor.

Syntax:

```
<A HREF = "URL"
    NAME = "target"
    TARGET = "name">
```

<IMG>. The **<IMG>** tag embeds an image into a Web page.

Syntax:

```
<IMG ALIGN = "LEFT" | "RIGHT" | "WIDTH"
     ALT = "alternate text"
     BORDER = "pixels"
     HEIGHT = "pixels"
     ISMAP
     SRC = "name"
     USEMAP
     WIDTH = "pixels">
```

The **ISMAP** and **USEMAP** attributes are used to create image maps. (Chapter 6.)

➤ HTML TIPS

1. **Links.** Check all links before making a page public. Periodically recheck the links to ensure that they are still correct.

2. **Invisible Links.** If a link does not appear on your page, check for the corresponding `</A>` tag. If this tag is present, check for closing quotation marks.

3. **Underlined Links.** Netscape and Internet Explorer let you turn off the underlining for links. To remove underlining, go to the `Edit>Preferences` option, and click on the *underline links* checkbox.

4. **Link Color.** Use the `LINK` attribute of the `<BODY>` tag to change the default color of visited links. Use the `VLINK` attribute of the `<BODY>` tag to change the default color of visited links.

5. **Images as Buttons.** Use `BORDER` = "0" in the `<IMG>` tag to remove the border that is automatically placed around clickable images.

6. **ALT Attribute.** Use the `ALT` attribute of the `<IMG>` tag to provide information to nongraphic browsers.

7. **Image Size.** Reduce your images to the smallest byte size. This will make your pages load more quickly.

8. **Transparent GIF Files.** Use transparent GIF files when you want your image to blend into the background.

9. **Seamless Tiles.** Use only seamless tiles for background images.

6 Frames and Images

FRAMES

Chapter 5 contained an HTML glossary that used a row of letters to link to fragments within the page. (See Figure 5.7.) We repeated this row of letters at the start of each set of tags beginning with a new letter. Although the links work correctly, the *Glossary* page is neither "user friendly" nor pleasing in appearance. HTML provides a better alternative. Rather than repeating rows of links in a single page, we divide our page into *frames*. Figure 6.1 contains an example of a frame-based page displayed with the default layout. This default layout uses a narrow border to separate frames. Internet Explorer uses a light gray line to depict this border; Netscape uses a solid gray border. Both browsers add scrollbars if the contents of the frame do not fit in the specified dimensions. In the *Basic Frame* page illustrated in Figure 6.1, the left frame does not quite fit, so the browser automatically adds horizontal and vertical scrollbars.

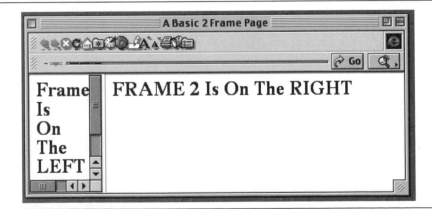

Figure 6.1 The *Basic Frame* Page

A frame-based page requires at least one HTML file for each frame in the page. The page also requires a separate file that creates the layout for the entire page. Figure 6.2 contains the directory for the *Basic Frame* page. The *basic.html* file contains the page's layout, while *frame1.html* and *frame2.html* contain the contents of the left and right frames, respectively.

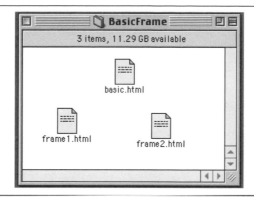

Figure 6.2 The *Basic Frame* Directory

Frame Tags

HTML provides three sets of tags for the creation of frame-based pages.

The <FRAMESET>...</FRAMESET> *tags.* The <FRAMESET>...</FRAMESET> tags form a container into which we place <FRAMESET>...</FRAMESET>, <FRAME>, or <NOFRAMES>...</NOFRAMES> tags.

The <FRAMESET> tag contains three attributes that determine a page's layout. The **COLS** attribute divides a page into vertical frames, either by percentage of the browser's width or by absolute pixels. The **ROWS** attribute divides a page into horizontal frames, either by percentage of the browser's length or by absolute pixels. We can use the **ROWS** and **COLS** attributes independently or we can combine them. For example, the *Basic Frame* page divides the page into left and right vertical frames. The final **FRAMESET** attribute, **BORDER**, specifies the width of the border appearing between frameset components. Setting the border to zero **(BORDER = "0")**, produces a seamless appearance.

The <NOFRAMES>...</NOFRAMES> *tags.* These tags form a container into which we place text for browsers that do not support frames. All major browsers support frames, so these tags are now obsolete. In fact, most developers use the <NOFRAMES>...</NOFRAMES> tags merely to display a simple message that indicates that the page requires frames.

The <FRAME> *Tag.* The <FRAME> tag contains attributes that specify a frame's appearance or identify it. The four appearance attributes are **MARGINHEIGHT**, **MARGINWIDTH**, **NORESIZE**, and **SCROLLING**. The **MARGINHEIGHT** and **MARGINWIDTH** attributes specify the size of these margins in pixels. The **NORESIZE** attribute tells the browser that it should not resize (or scale) the frame if it does not fit in the indicated dimensions. The **SCROLLING** attribute controls the frame's scrollbars. To permanently disable the scrollbars in a frame, use **SCROLLING = "no"**. To permanently enable the scrollbars—that is to make them appear even when not needed—use **SCROLLING = "yes"**. To let the browser automatically add scrollbars only when necessary, use **SCROLLING = "auto"**.

The **NAME** attribute identifies the frame so that we can use it as a target for URLs. Many of the examples that follow name one frame as the target for all references.

The previous attributes are all optional; the only required **FRAME** attribute is **SRC**. This attribute contains the URL of the page that will be loaded into the frame.

THE FRAMESET FOR THE *BASIC FRAME* PAGE

The *basic.html* file contains the **FRAMESET** for the *Basic Frame* Page. The HTML for this file appears in Figure 6.3. A frameset file contains **<HEAD>** and **<TITLE>** tags, but not **<BODY>...</BODY>** tags.

```
<HTML>
<HEAD><TITLE>A Basic 2 Frame Page</TITLE></HEAD>
<FRAMESET COLS = "20%, *">
<FRAME SRC = "frame1.html" NAME = "leftFrame">
<FRAME SRC = "frame2.html" NAME = "rightFrame">
<NOFRAMES>
   This page requires frames.
</NOFRAMES>
</FRAMESET>
</HTML>
```

Figure 6.3 HTML for the *Basic Frame* Page, Frameset **(Basic.html)**

The **<FRAMESET>** tag creates two vertical frames. The first frame occupies 20% of the browser's width. The second frame uses the remaining space. Since the remaining space is 80% of the width, we could have written the **<FRAMESET>** tag as

<FRAMESET COLS = "20%, 80%">

The asterisk (*) accomplishes the same effect: it indicates that the browser should use any remaining space for the last frame.

The two **<FRAME>** tags follow the **<FRAMESET>** tags. The browser loads the frames from left to right. This means that *frame1.html* is loaded into the left frame, and *frame2.html* is loaded into the right frame. The **SRC** attribute places the page into its frame. The **NAME** attribute serves no purpose in this example, because we will not use these frames as targets. Figure 6.4 contains the HTML for the left frame; Figure 6.5 contains the HTML for the right frame.

```
<HTML>
<HEAD><TITLE>The Left Frame</TITLE></HEAD>
<BODY BGCOLOR =  "white">
<H1>Frame1 Is On The LEFT</H1>
</BODY></HTML>
```

```
<HTML><HEAD><TITLE>The Right Frame</TITLE></HEAD>
<BODY BGCOLOR = "white">
<H1>FRAME 2 Is On The RIGHT</H1>
</BODY></HTML>
```

Figure 6.4 HTML for the *Basic Frame* Page, Left Frame (*Frame1.html*)

Figure 6.5 HTML for the *Basic Frame* Page, Right Frame (*Frame2.html*)

The pages displayed by Figures 6.4 and 6.5 use the same structure as the pages created in previous chapters. The files contain **<HEAD>**, **<TITLE>**, and **<BODY>** tags. These pages are fully functional; they can be used independently. When one is loaded as a "stand-alone" page, its title is displayed in the browser. When it is instead placed in a frameset, the frameset's title takes precedence, and the frame's title is not displayed.

The *Midwestern States Info* Page

Figure 6.6 contains a snapshot of the *Midwestern States Info* page. The page is divided into left and right frames. The left frame contains the names of five Midwestern states. Clicking on a state name displays a fact sheet for the state in the right frame. Initially, the page contains the state names in the left frame and a set of directions in the right frame. Figure 6.6 shows the page after the *Illinois* button was clicked. The page has a nice, clean appearance because both frames use a white background, and the scrollbars and borders have been removed.

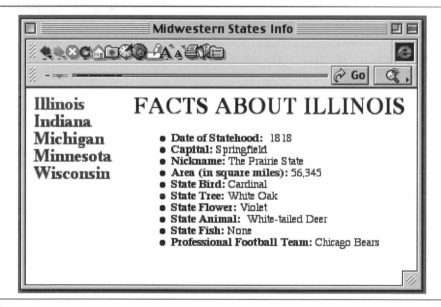

Figure 6.6 The *Midwestern States Info* Page

Figure 6.7 shows the *midWestFrame* directory. The topmost file, *midStateFrame.html*, contains the frameset for the page. The source file for the left frame is *stateNames.html*. The remaining files serve as source files for the right frame. *Directions.html* is the initial source file for the right frame. A state file becomes a source file for the right frame when a state name is clicked.

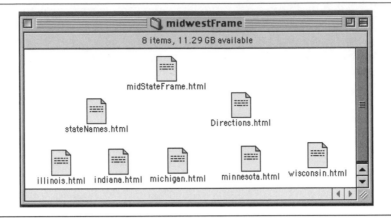

Figure 6.7 The *midWestFrame* Directory

Figure 6.8 contains the HTML for the *midStateFrame.html* file. The **<FRAMESET>** tag creates two frames: a left frame occupying 25% of the browser's width, and a right frame occupying the remaining space. The **<FRAMESET>** tag also removes the border between the left and right frames (**BORDER = "0"**). The first **<FRAME>** tag loads the *stateNames.html* file into the left frame. The tag indicates that the page is not scrollable. The second **<FRAME>** tag loads the *Directions.html* file into the right frame. Scrolling is not permitted. This frame tag contains a **NAME** attribute that identifies this frame as the *rightFrame*.

```
<HTML><HEAD><TITLE>Midwestern States Info</TITLE></HEAD>
<FRAMESET COLS = "25%, *" BORDER = "0">
<FRAME SRC = "stateNames.html" SCROLLING = "NO">
<FRAME SRC = "Directions.html" SCROLLING = "NO" NAME = "rightFrame">
</FRAMESET></HTML>
```

Figure 6.8 HTML for the *Midwestern State Info* Page, Frameset (*midStateFrame.html*)

Once a frame has a name, we can use it as a target for a reference. To do this, we create an **<A>** tag, using the form

    <A HREF = "*URL*" TARGET = "*frameName*">

When the user clicks on the link field, the URL is loaded into the targeted frame. The *stateNames* page used in the left frame contains the **<A>** tags that establish the relation between the state information files and the right frame. Figure 6.9 contains the HTML for the *stateNames* page. Each **<A>** tag uses *rightFrame* as its target.

Figure 6.10 contains the HTML for the Illinois fact sheet. This page uses an unordered list to present the state information.

The information pages for the remaining states follow the model displayed in Figure 6.10. The CD that accompanies this text contains the complete set of files for the *Midwestern States Info* page. Try loading the page into your browser. Click on the names and watch the right frame after each mouse click.

```
<HTML><HEAD><TITLE></TITLE></HEAD>
<BODY BGCOLOR = "white">
<H2><A HREF = "illinois.html" TARGET = "rightFrame">Illinois</A><BR>
<A HREF = "indiana.html" TARGET = "rightFrame">Indiana</A><BR>
<A HREF = "michigan.html" TARGET = "rightFrame">Michigan</A><BR>
<A HREF = "minnesota.html" TARGET = "rightFrame">Minnesota</A><BR>
<A HREF = "wisconsin.html" TARGET = "rightFrame">Wisconsin</A><BR></H2>
</BODY></HTML>
```

Figure 6.9 HTML for the *Midwestern States Info* Page, Left Frame (`stateNames.html`)

```
<HTML><HEAD><TITLE>Illinois Facts</TITLE></HEAD>
<BODY BGCOLOR = "White">
<H1>FACTS ABOUT  ILLINOIS</H1>
<UL>
<LI><B>Date of Statehood:</B> 1818
<LI><B>Capital:</B> Springfield
<LI><B>Nickname:</B> The Prairie State
<LI><B>Area (in square miles):</B> 56,345
<LI><B>State Bird:</B> Cardinal
<LI><B>State Tree:</B> White Oak
<LI><B>State Flower:</B> Violet
<LI><B>State Animal:</B> White-tailed Deer
<LI><B>State Fish:</B> None
<LI> <B>Professional Football Team:</B> Chicago Bears
</UL>
</BODY></HTML>
```

Figure 6.10 HTML for the *Midwestern States Info* Page, Right Frame (`illinois.html`)

Areas of Common Shapes

Figure 6.11 contains an example of horizontal frames. The upper frame contains images of three shapes. When the user clicks on either a shape's image or its name, simple statistics with an accompanying diagram appear in the lower frame. For example, when the user clicks on the rectangle, the lower frame displays the formulas for the area and perimeter of a rectangle.

Figure 6.12 shows the *Areas* directory. Although this directory contains twelve files, each file contains only a few HTML statements.

The Frameset Page

The `areaFrame.html` file contains the frameset for the *Area* page. The frameset divides the page into two equal, horizontal frames. The first (or upper) frame displays the shapes with corresponding labels. Initially the lower frame holds a blank page. When the user clicks on either a name or shape, the appropriate statistics page is loaded into the lower frame. Figure 6.13 contains the HTML for the frameset page.

The **<FRAMESET>** tag uses the **ROWS** attribute to divide the page into two horizontal frames, each occupying 50% of the page length. The **BORDER = "0"** attribute removes the border separating the two

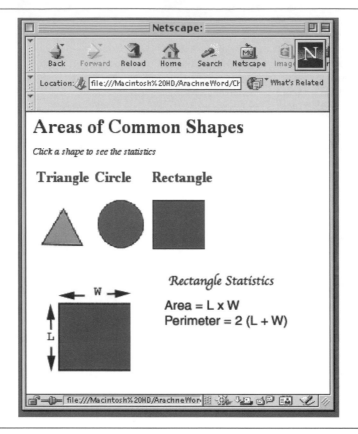

Figure 6.11 The *Areas* Page

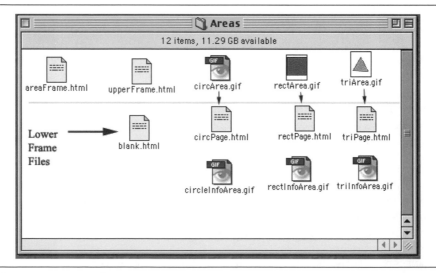

Figure 6.12 The *Areas* Directory

```
<HTML><HEAD><TITLE>Shapes Statistics</TITLE></HEAD>
<FRAMESET ROWS = "50%,*" BORDER = "0">
<FRAME SRC = "upperFrame.html"   SCROLLING = "no"  NAME = "topFrame">
<FRAME SRC = "blank.html"  SCROLLING = "no" NAME = "lowerFrame" >
</FRAMESET></HTML>
```

Figure 6.13 HTML for *Areas* Page, Frameset (`areaFrame.html`)

frames. The first **<FRAME>** tag places the *upperFrame.html* file in the first (or upper) frame. This frame does not permit scrolling. The second **<FRAME>** tag places the *blank.html* file in the lower frame.

The Upper Frame Page

The source page for the upper frame is the *upperFrame.html* file. This page uses three GIF files, *circArea.gif*, *rectArea.gif*, and *triArea.gif*, to display the circle, rectangle, and triangle shapes. Figure 6.14 contains the HTML for the upper frame.

```
<HTML><HEAD><TITLE></TITLE></HEAD>
<BODY BGCOLOR = "white">
<H1>Areas of Common Shapes</H1>
<I>Click a shape to see the statistics</I><P>
<TABLE>
<TR><TD><A HREF = "triPage.html" TARGET = "lowerFrame"><H2>Triangle</H2>
<IMG SRC = "triArea.gif" BORDER = "0"></A></TD>

<TD><A HREF = "circPage.html" TARGET = "lowerFrame"><H2>Circle</H2>
<IMG SRC = "circArea.gif" BORDER = "0"></A></TD>
<TD> <A HREF = "rectPage.html" TARGET = "lowerFrame"><H2> Rectangle</H2>
<IMG SRC = "rectArea.gif" BORDER - "0"></A></TD>
</TR></TABLE>
</BODY><HTML>
```

Figure 6.14 HTML for the *Areas Page,* Upper Frame (*upperFrame.html*)

The upper-frame file contains the HTML for a borderless table that creates a set of coordinated name and image links. For example, consider the following statement:

```
<A HREF = "triPage.html" TARGET = "lowerFrame"><H2>Triangle</H2>
<IMG SRC = "triArea.gif" BORDER = "0"></A>
```

This anchor tag creates a link to *triPage.html*, the statistics file for the triangle. The **<A> ...</A>** tags form a container that holds a label, **<H2>Triangle</H2>**, and an image, **<IMG SRC = "triArea.gif">**. The lower frame is the anchor's target; clicking on either the label or the image loads the *triPage.html* page into the lower frame. The anchor tags for the rectangle and circle were created in a similar manner.

The Lower Frame

Initially, the lower frame displays the product of the HTML code in the *blank.html* file. The HTML appears in Figure 6.15. This file creates a white background for the lower frame. Because Netscape uses a gray background for frames, the blank page produces a seamless appearance between the upper and lower frames.

The browser displays the blank page in the lower frame only when the *Areas* page is initially loaded. Once the user clicks on a label or image, the lower frame displays the appropriate statistics page. Figure 6.16 contains the HTML for the triangle's statistics page. The page displays the GIF file containing the statistics for the shape. Although a browser can display a GIF file directly, Netscape displays the image against a gray background. If your intended audience only uses Internet Explorer you can link directly to the GIF file, and thus eliminate half of the files used to construct the lower frame. For example, you would rewrite the anchor tag for the triangle link in *upperFrame.html* as

```
<A HREF = "triInfoArea.gif TARGET = "lowerFrame">
```

```
<HTML>
<HEAD><TITLE></TITLE></HEAD>
<BODY BGCOLOR = "white"></BODY>
</HTML>
```

```
<HTML><HEAD><TITLE></TITLE></HEAD>
<BODY BGCOLOR = "white">
<IMG SRC = "triInfoArea.gif">
</BODY></HTML>
```

Figure 6.15 HTML for the *Areas* Page, Initial Lower Frame (*blank.html*)

Figure 6.16 HTML for the *Areas* Page, Triangle Lower Frame

The *Color* Page (version 1)

Figure 6.17 displays a page containing four frames. The frames are arranged in a 2 × 2 grid, with each frame using a different background color.

Figure 6.18 shows the directory structure for the *Color* page. The directory contains five files: one for each color, and one for the frameset. The directory's structure shows the page's structure. The frameset file, *colorFrame.html*, is the top file in the directory. The frame files are arranged by rows and columns.

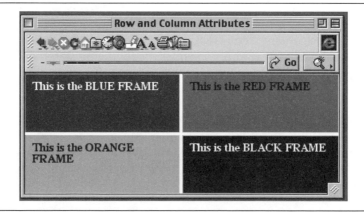

Figure 6.17 The *Color* Page (version 1)

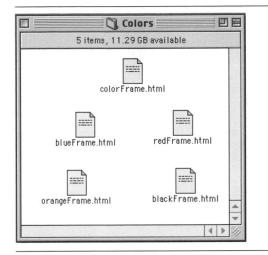

Figure 6.18 Directory for the *Color* Page

```
<HTML><HEAD><TITLE>Row and Column
Attributes</TITLE></HEAD>
<FRAMESET ROWS = "50%,*" COLS = "50%,*">
<FRAME SRC = "blueFrame.html" SCROLLING = "NO">
<FRAME SRC = "redFrame.html" SCROLLING = "NO">
<FRAME SRC = "orangeFrame.html" SCROLLING = "NO">
<FRAME SRC = "blackFrame.html" SCROLLING = "NO">
</FRAMESET></HTML>
```

Figure 6.19 HTML for the *Color* Page, Frameset (`colorFrame.html`)

The **<FRAMESET>** tag that creates the layout for the *Color* page uses the **ROWS** and **COLS** attributes to divide the page symmetrically into two rows, each using 50% of the browser's length, and two columns, each using 50% of the browser's width. The **<FRAMESET>...</FRAMESET>** tags contain the four frames, which are entered by rows. Using the color names to indicate placement, we enter frames in the following order: blue, red, orange, and black. Figure 6.19 contains the HTML for the frameset. Compare the **<FRAME>** tags with the placement of the frames in Figure 6.17.

Figure 6.20 contains the HTML for the blue frame. The remaining frame pages follow the same model.

```
<HTML><HEAD><TITLE></TITLE></HEAD>
<BODY BGCOLOR = "blue" TEXT = "white">
<H3>This is the BLUE FRAME</H3>
</BODY></HTML>
```

Figure 6.20 HTML for the *Color* Page, Blue Frame (`blueFrame.html`)

The *Color* Page (version 2)

Figure 6.21 contains a second version of the *Color* page. This page uses six frames arranged in a 2 × 3 grid.

The new *Color* page also uses a symmetrical arrangement. The two rows each occupy 50% of the browser's length. Within each row, the first and last columns each occupy 33% of the

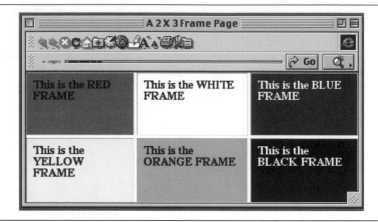

Figure 6.21 The *Color* Page (version 2)

browser's width. The middle column occupies the middle 34% of the width. The **<FRAMESET>** tag that creates this layout is

    <FRAMESET ROWS = "50%,*" COLS = "33%,*,33%">

The frame tags are placed into the frameset by rows, with the first row's frames entered before the second row's frames. The frames representing the columns are entered from the leftmost column to the rightmost column. Using the color names to indicate placement, we enter frames in the following order: red, white, blue, yellow, orange, black. Figure 6.22 contains the HTML for the frameset page.

```
<HTML><HEAD><TITLE>A 2 X 3 Frame Page</TITLE></HEAD>
<FRAMESET ROWS = "50%,*" COLS = "33%,*,33%">
<FRAME SRC = "redFrame.html" SCROLLING = "NO">
<FRAME SRC = "whiteFrame.html" SCROLLING = "NO">
<FRAME SRC = "blueFrame.html" SCROLLING = "NO">
<FRAME SRC = "yellowFrame.html" SCROLLING = "NO">
<FRAME SRC = "orangeFrame.html" SCROLLING = "NO">
<FRAME SRC = "blackFrame.html" SCROLLING = "NO">
</FRAMESET></HTML>
```

Figure 6.22 HTML for the *Color* Page (version 2), Frameset

The Birder's Checklist Page

Figure 6.23 contains a *Birder's Checklist* page. This frame-based page contains two rows. The first row contains frames that link to a set of directions and checklists for Falcons, Eagles, and Hawks. When the user clicks on a frame in the top row, the appropriate page is loaded into the lower frame. In Figure 6.23, the Falcons frame was clicked to obtain a checklist for Falcons. The checklist includes the bird's name, a checkbox to indicate a bird sighting, and a place to indicate the date of the sighting. To print a copy of the checklist, click a mouse button anywhere in the lower frame and select **Print Frame** from the browser's file menu.

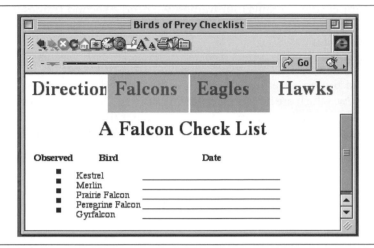

Figure 6.23 The *Birder's Checklist* Page

Figure 6.24 shows the directory for the *Birder's Checklist* page. The directory structure appears complicated, but the files in the upper frame use a similar format, as do the files in the lower frames. The *birdFrame.html* file contains the frameset for the page. The *start*, *falcons*, *eagles*, and *hawks* files contain the HTML for the pages loaded into the first frame row. The lower frame row initially contains a blank page (*blank.html*). When the user clicks on a frame in the upper row, the browser loads the corresponding directions or checklist page into the lower frame. The arrows show the connections between the files in the upper and lower frames.

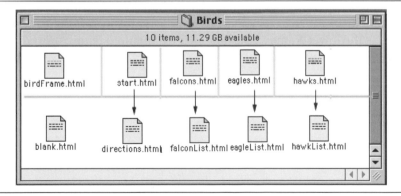

Figure 6.24 Directory for the *Birder's Checklist* Page

Unlike the previous frame examples, the *Birder's Checklist* page does not use a symmetrical frame layout. The first row contains four frames, while the second row contains a single frame. Nonsymmetrical layouts require nested **<FRAMESET>** tags. The outer frameset tag determines the size of the two rows. The *Birder's Checklist* page uses a 25%–75% division. That is, the *Directions* row occupies 25% of the browser's length, while the checklists displayed in the lower frame use the remaining 75% of the length. The **<FRAMESET>** tag that creates this layout is

```
<FRAMESET ROWS = "25",*" BORDER = "0">
```

Because the upper row contains four frames, we need a second frameset to specify its layout. Because the column space is divided equally between the four frames, the **<FRAMESET>** tag that creates the upper row's layout is

<FRAMESET COLS = "25%,25%,25%,*">

Having created the frameset tags, we're now ready to add the frames. We begin with the frames for the first row, which are added in left-to-right order. Once we've added all of the frames, we add the ending tag for the inner frameset. Next, we enter the single frame for the lower frame followed by the ending tag for the outer frameset. Figure 6.25 contains the frameset file for the *Birder's Checklist* page.

```
<HTML><HEAD><TITLE>Birds of Prey Checklist</TITLE></HEAD>
<FRAMESET ROWS = "25%, *" BORDER = "0">
<FRAMESET COLS = "25%,25%,25%, *">
<FRAME SRC = "start.html" NORESIZE SCROLLING = "no">
<FRAME SRC = "falcons.html" NORESIZE SCROLLING = "no">
<FRAME SRC = "eagles.html" NORESIZE SCROLLING = "no">
<FRAME SRC = "hawks.html" NORESIZE SCROLLING = "no">
</FRAMESET>
<FRAME SRC = "blank.html" NORESIZE NAME = "lowerFrame">
</FRAMESET></HTML>
```

Figure 6.25 HTML for the *Birder's Checklist* Page, Frameset (*birdFrame.html*)

The Frame Pages for the *Birder's Checklist* Page

The frame files for the upper row of the *Birder's Checklist* page use a similar format. Each file sets the background to a different color. An anchor tag links to the appropriate directions or checklist page and targets the lower frame as the link file's destination. Figure 6.26 contains the HTML for the *Falcons* frame in the upper row.

```
<HTML>
<HEAD><TITLE></TITLE></HEAD>
<BODY BGCOLOR = "#66CCCC">
<A HREF = "falconList.html" TARGET = "lowerFrame"> <H1>Falcons</H1></A>
</BODY></HTML>
```

Figure 6.26 HTML for the *Birder's Checklist* Page, Upper Row (*Falcons.html*)

The lower frame uses three different types of files. The lower frame contains a blank page (*blank.html*) when the page is first loaded. If the user clicks on the *Directions* frame in the upper row, an ordered list of instructions appears in the lower frame. Figure 6.27 shows the HTML for the *Directions* file.

If the user clicks on any of the bird species in the upper row, a checklist page is loaded into the lower frame. The checklist pages use a similar format, illustrated in Figure 6.28. This figure contains the HTML for the Falcon checklist.

```
HTML>
<HEAD><TITLE></TITLE></HEAD>
<BODY BGCOLOR = "white">
<H1><I>DIRECTIONS</I></H1>
<H2><OL>
<LI>Click the desired bird species.
<LI>The checklist appears in the lower frame.
<LI>Click in the lower frame.
<LI>Select File>Print Frame  to print the bird identification list.</OL></H2>
</BODY></HTML>
```

Figure 6.27 HTML for the *Birder's Checklist* Page, Lower Row (*directions.html*)

```
<HTML>
<HEAD><TITLE></TITLE></HEAD>
<BODY BGCOLOR = "white">
<H1 ALIGN = "CENTER">A Falcon Check List</H1>
<TABLE>
<TR><TH>Observed</TH><TH>Bird</TH><TH>Date</TH></TR>
<TR><TD><UL TYPE = "SQUARE"><LI><LI><LI><LI><LI></UL>
</TD>
<TD>Kestrel<BR>
Merlin<BR>
Prairie Falcon<BR>
Peregrine Falcon<BR>
Gyrfalcon</TD>
<TD>_____<BR>
_____<BR>
_____<BR>
_____<BR>
_____</TD></TR></TABLE>
</BODY></HTML>
```

Figure 6.28 HTML for the *Birder's Checklist* Page, Lower Row Frame (*falconList.html*)

The CD that accompanies this text contains all of the files used in the *Birder's Checklist* page. Load the page into your browser and click on the links. Try printing a checklist.

IMAGE MAPS

Most Web-page developers use frames to separate a page into two or more sections, in which one frame serves as the target for URLs created in the other frames. An image map performs a similar function for images. An image map divides an image into clickable regions, each region being associated with a URL. Typically, the image map resides in one frame. The URL associated with a region is loaded into another frame when the user clicks in the region.

HTML provides two types of image maps: server-side maps and client-side maps. A server-side map processes the image map from the creator's server. This means that the creator must have `cgi-bin` privileges. A client-side map processes the image map on the client's (user's) machine, so `cgi-bin` privileges are not necessary. In this text, we cover client-side image maps, because they are accessible to anyone with a graphics package.

Figure 6.29 contains our first image map. The page resembles the *Areas* page appearing in Figure 6.11. The *shapes* image map divides the page into two frames. The first frame contains the image map. One GIF file contains the entire image. The map divides the image into regions. When the user clicks inside a shape region, the browser loads the HTML statement that created this region. Thus, the *Shapes* page uses an image map to present a tutorial on image maps.

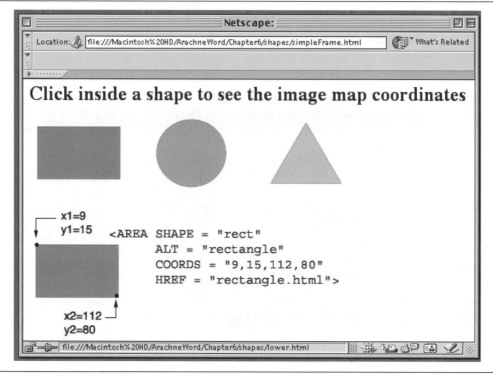

Figure 6.29 The *Shapes* Image Map

Figure 6.30 contains the directory for the *shapes* image map. The *shapeFrame* file contains the frame set for the *shapes*. The upper (or top) frame contains the image map. The lower frame initially contains a blank page. When the user clicks on an image map region, the corresponding tutorial for that region is loaded into the lower frame.

Figure 6.31 contains the HTML for the frameset page. The frame set divides the page into two equal horizontal frames. Neither frame is scrollable. The second frame serves as the target for the image map.

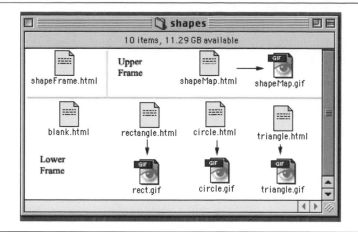

Figure 6.30 Directory for the *Shapes* Page

```
<HTML><FRAMESET ROWS = "50%,*"  BORDER = "0">
<FRAME SRC = "shapeMap.html"    SCROLLING = "no">
<FRAME SRC = "blank.html" NORESIZE SCROLLING = "no"
      NAME = "lowerFrame">
</FRAMESET></BODY></HTML>
```

Figure 6.31 HTML for the *Shapes* Page, Frameset (`shapeFrame.html`)

Figure 6.32 contains the *shapeMap* GIF used to construct the image map.

Figure 6.32 The *shapeMap* GIF File

The `<MAP>...</MAP>` and `<IMG>` Tags

Constructing a client-side image map requires three distinct HTML tags. We begin with the `<MAP>...</MAP>` tags, which form a container for the `<AREA>` tags that define the clickable regions. Because a page could contain more than one image map, the `<MAP>` tag requires a `NAME` attribute that identifies the image map. The `<IMG>` tag that appears after the `</MAP>` tag includes a `USEMAP` attribute that identifies the map that should be used with this image. Figure 6.33 shows the relation between the `<MAP>`, `<AREA>`, and `<IMG>` tags for the *shapes* image map. Notice the relation between the `NAME` attribute in the `<MAP>` tag and the `USEMAP` attribute in the `<IMG>` tag.

```
<MAP NAME = "shapes" ><!-- Start of image map -->
            <AREA ...><!-- Define the first region -->
              ... .
            <AREA...><!-- Define the last region -->
</MAP>
<IMG SRC = "shapeMap.gif" BORDER = "0" USEMAP = "#shapes">
```

Figure 6.33 HTML Tags Used to Create an Image Map

The <AREA> Tag

The **<AREA>** tag defines a clickable region within the image file. An **<AREA>** tag can contain the following attributes:

SHAPE = "*value*". The **SHAPE** attribute defines the shape of the area. Allowed values are **"circle"**, **"rect"**, **"polygon"**, and **"default"**. The **"rect"** value defines a rectangular area; the **"default"** value catches any previously undefined areas.

COORDS = "*shape coordinates*". The **COORDS** attribute contains a list of the coordinates (in pixels) required to create the shape. The coordinate list varies according to the shape.

ALT = "*alternate text*". The **ALT** attribute provides alternate text for browsers that do not recognize image maps. All the major browsers recognize image maps; however, including an **ALT** attribute is a simple safeguard that lets everyone use a page.

HREF = "*URL*". The **HREF** attribute contains the name of the file that will be loaded when the area is clicked.

TARGET = "*frameName*". If present, this attribute specifies the frame that is the target for the URL specified by the **HREF** attribute.

The *shapes* image map uses each of the allowed shapes to create the complete image map. This lets us examine the coordinate lists for each shape. HTML uses the standard coordinate system found in all digital graphics systems. This system divides the image into pixels. A particular point on the image is described by its column (x) and row (y) positions. The coordinates of the upper left corner of the image are (0,0). The column values increase as we move to the right, and the row values increase as we move down.

Rectangular Areas

To create a rectangular region, we must know the (x, y) coordinates for the rectangle's upper left corner and its lower right corner. Many graphics programs display the (x, y) coordinates of the current location when the mouse is placed over a location. Figure 6.34 contains the tutorial for rectangular areas. The coordinates, $(x1, y1)$ define the upper left corner; the coordinates, $(x2, y2)$ define the lower right corner. The **COORDS** attribute contains the list of these coordinates. The upper left corner coordinates are always listed first, then the lower right coordinates.

Circular Areas

A circular area requires the (x, y) coordinates for the circle's origin (or center) and the length of the circle's radius. To construct the circular area, we read the pixel coordinates for the circle's top and bottom. Because the x coordinate's value does not change when we move from the circle's highest to its lowest point, this value represents the x coordinate of the origin. The circle's diam-

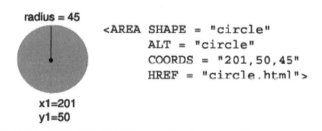

```
           x1=9
            y1=15    <AREA SHAPE = "rect"
                            ALT = "rectangle"
                            COORDS = "9,15,112,80"
                            HREF = "rectangle.html">

           x2=112
           y2=80
```

Figure 6.34 The Rectangular Area

eter is the difference between the bottom and top values for *y*. The *y* coordinate for the origin is the average of the bottom and top values; the length of the radius is half of the difference. Increasing the radius by ten pixels ensures that it covers the entire circle. Figure 6.35 contains the GIF file for the circular area.

```
     radius = 45
                     <AREA SHAPE = "circle"
                            ALT = "circle"
                            COORDS = "201,50,45"
                            HREF = "circle.html">

        x1=201
        y1=50
```

Figure 6.35 The Circular Area

Polygonal Areas

The coordinates for a polygonal area require a set of (x, y) coordinates for each point on the polygon. Usually, a last set of coordinates closes the polygon. Figure 6.36 shows the points used for the triangular area. The **COORDS** list begins and ends with the same (x, y) coordinates (345,8).

```
     x1=x4=345
     y1=y4=8
                    <AREA SHAPE = "polygon"
                           ALT = "triangle"
                           COORDS = "345,8,389,85,
                                     301,85,345,8"
     x3=301    x2=389   HREF = "triangle.html">
     y3=85     y2=85
```

Figure 6.36 The Polygonal Area

The Default Area

The default area is the easiest to create. This area has no **COORDS** attribute, because the browser automatically groups any undefined areas. An image map does not need a default area. Default areas are used to handle mouse clicks that occur outside the areas. The *shape* image map contains a default area that reloads the blank page when the user clicks on an area that is not associated with the other three shapes. The tag that creates this default area is

```
<AREA SHAPE = "default" HREF = "blank.html"
      TARGET = "lowerFrame">
```

Figure 6.37 contains the HTML for the upper frame (*shapeMap.html*) page. Each **<AREA>** tag contains a **TARGET** attribute that specifies the lower frame as the target.

```
<HTML><HEAD><TITLE>A Shape Image Map</TITLE></HEAD>
<BODY BGCOLOR = "white">
<H1>Click inside a shape to see the image map coordinates</H1>
<MAP NAME="shapes">
<AREA SHAPE="rect" ALT="rectangle" COORDS="9,15,112,80"HREF="rectangle.html" TARGET = "lowerFrame">
<AREA SHAPE="circle" ALT="circle" COORDS="201,50,45" HREF="circle.html" TARGET = "lowerFrame">
<AREA SHAPE="polygon" ALT="triangle" COORDS="345,8,389,85,301,85,345,8" HREF="triangle.html" TARGET
= "lowerFrame">
<AREA SHAPE = "default" HREF = "blank.html" TARGET = "lowerFrame">
</MAP>
<IMG SRC="shapeMap.gif" BORDER=0 USEMAP="#shapes">
<P><HR NOSHADE SIZE = "4">
</BODY></HTML>
```

Figure 6.37 HTML for the *Shapes* Image Map, Upper Frame (*shapeMap.html*)

Image Maps Using PhotoShop 5.5 and ImageReady 2.0 (OPTIONAL)

Creating image maps manually is tedious, boring, and error-prone. The *shape* image map was created twice. The first time, I created this map manually. The second time, I used PhotoShop 5.5® and ImageReady 2.0®. These software packages automate image map creation. The *shape* image map created with PhotoShop 5.5 and ImageReady 2.0 took substantially less time, yet was as accurate as the original image map.

Our final example of image maps uses PhotoShop 5.5 and ImageReady 2.0. Once you've used these packages, you'll never again create an image map manually. As our example, we revisit the *Midwestern States Info* Page. Figure 6.38 contains a new version of the page. This page uses an image map of the Midwestern states. Each state is a separate area of the image map. Clicking on a state loads the state's fact page into the right frame. The CD accompanying this text contains the complete program. Try loading the page into a browser. Click on a state or in the water or land, and watch the changes in the right frame.

Creating the *Midwestern States* image map begins with a GIF containing a simple line drawing of the states. Figure 6.39 contains this image. The image is available on the CD. If you have

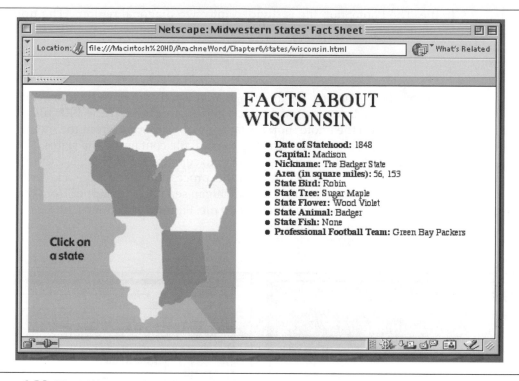

Figure 6.38 The *Midwestern States Image Map* Page

Figure 6.39 The Midwestern States GIF

PhotoShop 5.5, you can recreate the image map appearing in Figure 6.38. The first step involves coloring each of the states.

Creating the Background

The GIF file serves as the basis for the image map, but this file will not contain the image map itself. The image map resides in a new PhotoShop file. This file should be slightly larger than the original GIF file. The PhotoShop file is divided into two diagonal regions. The upper diagonal is painted blue to represent the Great Lakes. The lower diagonal is painted tan to represent the land.

Creating the Layers

ImageReady 2.0 creates the `<AREA>` tags for the image map. Each area must be represented as a PhotoShop layer. To create a layer, we move back and forth between the GIF file and the PhotoShop file. To begin, select the PhotoShop file, and choose **Layer>New** from the menu. Name the new layer after one of the states, then switch to the GIF file containing the states. Using the "magic wand" tool, click inside a state. Select **Edit>Copy** to copy the state. Next, use the Marquee tool to drag the copy to the image-map file. Repeat this process until you have a layer for each state. Michigan requires two layers, because Lake Michigan separates the upper from the lower peninsula. Figure 6.40 shows the completed PhotoShop file. Figure 6.41 contains the *Layers Menu*, showing the layers used in the image map file.

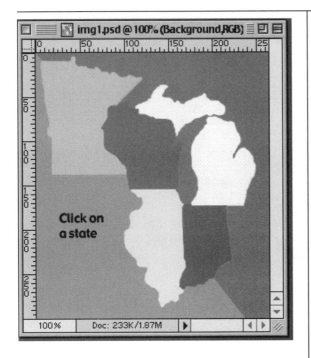

Figure 6.40 The *Midwestern States* Image Map, PhotoShop File

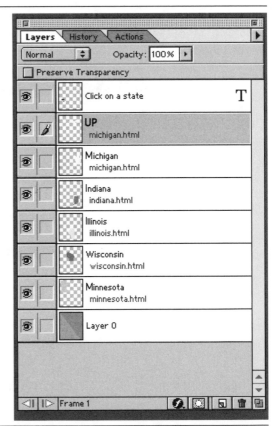

Figure 6.41 The Layers Menu with the State Layers

Image Ready

After completing the layers, create a copy of the image file, close the original file, and jump to ImageReady 2.0. Select the *Optimize* menu, and switch the settings to those found in Figure 6.42.

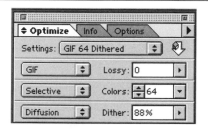

Figure 6.42 The ImageReady Optimize Menu

Creating the Areas

To create an image-map area, double-click on a layer. This opens the *Layer Options* menu. Check the *Use Layer as Image Map box*. Use a polygon for each area, and accept the default tolerance (2.0). Add the URL of the appropriate state facts file.

Figure 6.43 shows the completed *Layer Options* menu for the Minnesota layer.

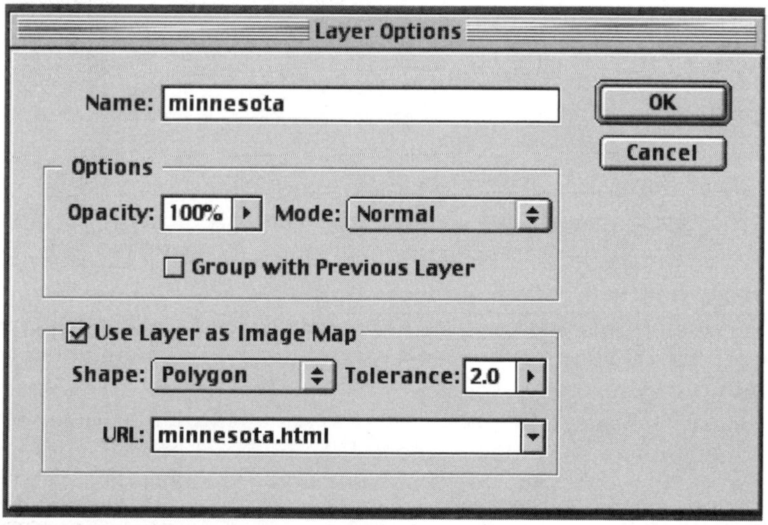

Figure 6.43 The ImageReady *Layer Options* Menu

When you've finished creating the areas, select the

`File>Save Optimized As`

option. This opens a menu similar to the one appearing in Figure 6.44.

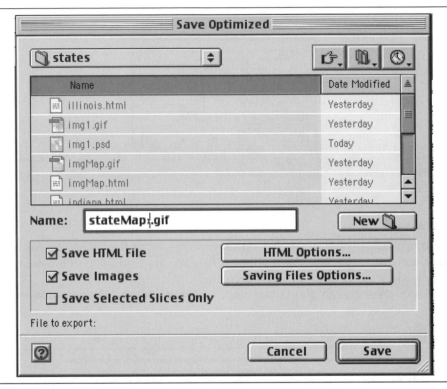

Figure 6.44 The ImageReady *Save Optimized* as Menu

Enter the GIF name, and make sure the *Save HTML File* and *Save Images* options are checked. Click the *Save* button. ImageReady 2.0 creates the GIF image and a corresponding HTML file containing the image-map tags.

Figure 6.45 contains the *stateMap.html* file. Only the **TARGET** attributes and a default area need to be added to the HTML file produced by ImageReady. The highlighted code was added to the HTML produced by ImageReady 2.0.

The *Midwestern States Image Map* page uses the same HTML files as the frame-based version, so the only remaining task is the creation of the frameset page. Figure 6.46 contains the code for this page.

```
<HTML><HEAD><TITLE></TITLE>
<META HTTP-EQUIV="Content-Type" CONTENT="text/html; charset=iso-8859-1">
</HEAD>
<BODY BGCOLOR="white">
<!-- ImageReady Slices (img1.psd) -->
<MAP NAME="ImageMap31358">

<AREA SHAPE="polygon" ALT="up" COORDS="150,39, 145,49, 154,52, 173,53, 194,47, 201,53, 210,56,
215,63, 212,71, 177,78, 164,88, 157,94, 152,77, 115,67, 114,63, 115,57, 128,50, 141,36"
HREF="michigan.html" TARGET = "rightFrame">

<AREA SHAPE="polygon" ALT="michigan" COORDS="215,76, 226,81, 233,101, 232,108, 241,110, 247,121,
247,142, 238,165, 234,173, 175,169, 182,152, 178,134, 176,102, 202,72" HREF="michigan.html" TARGET
= "rightFrame">

<AREA SHAPE="polygon" ALT="indiana" COORDS="216,175, 217,237, 203,250, 197,256, 185,263, 182,263,
161,262, 164,249, 168,238, 167,171" HREF="indiana.html"
TARGET = "rightFrame">

<AREA SHAPE="polygon" ALT="illinois" COORDS="161,158, 167,170, 164,256, 166,267, 165,272, 161,278,
155,282, 145,285, 138,285, 132,266, 121,257, 119,242, 112,239, 109,232, 98,215, 101,199, 104,187,
107,179, 119,170, 116,164, 107,154" HREF="illinois.html"
 TARGET = "rightFrame">

<AREA SHAPE="polygon" ALT="Wisconsin" COORDS="107,55, 108,61, 117,65, 121,68, 157,80, 162,98,
165,100, 154,158, 104,154, 97,126, 75,101, 79,74, 83,60" HREF="wisconsin.html" TARGET =
"rightFrame">

<AREA SHAPE="polygon" ALT="minnesota" COORDS="45,6, 48,14, 80,21, 93,25, 103,24, 120,31, 83,72,
78,91, 83,111, 98,124, 105,135, 102,139, 17,135, 13,96, 13,84, 10,8, 39,4" HREF="minnesota.html"
TARGET = "rightFrame">

<AREA SHAPE = "default"  HREF = "blank.html" TARGET - "rightFrame">
</MAP>
<IMG SRC="stateMap.gif" WIDTH=264 HEIGHT=300 BORDER=0 USEMAP="#ImageMap31358">
<!-- End ImageReady Slices -->
</BODY></HTML>
```

Figure 6.45 The ImageReady Image Map (`stateMap.html`)

```
<HTML><HEAD><TITLE>Midwestern  States' Fact Sheet</TITLE></HEAD>
<FRAMESET COLS = "45%,*" BORDER = "0">
<FRAME SRC = "stateMap.html"  SCROLLING = "no">
<FRAME   SRC = "blank.html" SCROLLING = "no" NAME = "rightFrame">
</FRAMESET></HTML>
```

Figure 6.46 HTML For the *Midwestern States Image Map* Frameset

➤ **EXERCISES**

The exercises in this chapter include simple modifications of the frame-based pages. They also ask you to create new frame-based pages or image maps. Two problems that contain images with labeled coordinates are included for readers who do not have a graphics program. The accompanying CD contains the original images with no markings. This lets you create an image map without a graphics program.

1. **The *Glossary* Page, Revisited.** Revise the *Glossary* page (Figure 5.7) so that it uses frames. Place the letter links in the left frame and the glossary in the right frame.

2. **A *Row-Based Glossary* Page.** Revise the *Glossary* page (Figure 5.7) so that the letter links appear in the top frame and the glossary appears in the bottom frame.

3. **The *Color* Page (version 3).** Revise the *Color* Page (version 2) so that the frames are arranged in a 3 × 2 grid. (See Figure 6.21.)

4. **The *Color* Page (version 4).** Create three additional color pages of your choice. Revise the *Color* page (version 2) so that the frames are arranged in a 3 × 3 grid. (See Figure 6.21.)

5. **The *Resume* Page.** Create an online resume in which the resume categories appear in the left frame and the resume appears in the right frame. Use a 1% border to separate the two frames. The resume categories should reference fragments in the right frame. Figure 6.47 contains a sample layout.

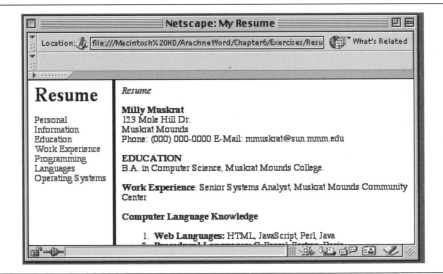

Figure 6.47 A *Resume* Page

6. **The *Cooking Links* Page.** Create a page that contains cooking categories in the left frame and links to cooking pages on the right frame. The categories in the left frame link to fragments in the page on the right frame. Figure 6.48 contains a small sample page.

7. **The *Local News, Weather, and Sports* Page.** Create a page that contains links to Web pages about your local news, weather, and sports. Figure 6.49 contains a sample page.

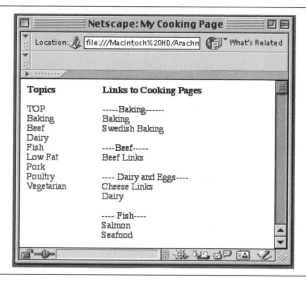

Figure 6.48 A *Cooking Links* Page

Figure 6.49 A *Local News Links* Page

8. **The *Special Interests* Page.** Create a frame-based page that contains a list of special-interest categories in the left frame. Find Web links to the special interests. Create a page that contains all of these links. Use fragments in the left frame page to link to the lists in the right frame.

9. **The *Football* Page.** Chapters 1 through 5 contain several examples of pages related to football. Create a frame-based page that links these pages together. Place the topics in the left frame. Link to the pages in the right frame. Topics should include uniform numbering, scoring, special teams, and definitions. Include a category that contains the name of your favorite football team. Find the address of this team, and link to it.

10. **The *Sports* Page.** Pick your favorite sport. Find links to this sport. Put the link categories in the left frame. Load the pages in the right frame. Add a 1% border between the frames.

11. **The *Book Exercises* Page.** Create a page that contains your answers to the exercises in this and the previous chapters. Place the chapter numbers in the TOP frame. Put a list of exercises that you've completed in the MIDDLE frame. This list should change as the user selects a category in the TOP frame. The BOTTOM frame should load the page the user selects by picking a link in the MIDDLE frame.

12. **The *Web Resources* Page.** Create a page of Web resource links. The left frame should contain the following categories: HTML, JavaScript, Perl, Java, Clip Art. Use a search engine to find links related to each topic. Place the URLs for these links in a page that is loaded into the right frame. Use an approach similar to the one found in Exercise 2.

13. **The *Bird Links* Page.** Make a list of birder's pages. Create a frame-based page that contains the birds in the left frame. Clicking the name in the left frame links to the official page for the corresponding organization or birding group, which appears in the right frame. (*Hint: There are official pages for raptors and bluebirds.*)

14. **The *Travel Links* Page.** Pick your favorite country. Search the Web for links related to this country. Develop link categories that you'll place in a TOP frame. Use the BOTTOM frame to display the linked page.

15. **The *Sports Team* Page.** Pick a professional sports organization of your choice. Find the home pages for at least five teams. Create a frame-based page in which the team names appear in the left frame. When the user clicks on a team name, load the official page for the team in the right frame.

16. **The *Cooking Shows on the Web* Page.** Many cooking shows have Web pages that list weekly recipes and/or offer cooking tips. Create a page that lists the names of five cooking shows in the top frame. When the user clicks on a name, load the show's page in the bottom frame.

17. **Your *Home* Page.** Personalize your home page. Develop link categories for your interests, your resume, etc. Place these categories in a frame. Use a second frame to display the linked information.

18. **A *House* Image Map Page.** Figure 6.50 contains a picture of a house with the (x, y) coordinates specified. The CD contains a GIF file, `house1.gif`, without the coordinates. Create an

Figure 6.50 The *House* Image Map

image map for the specified regions. Place this image map in a frame. Create a second frame that prints out an appropriate message for a small child clicking on a house section. For example, you might print "The house is green" or "The roof is red".

19. **A *New Shapes* Image Map Page.** Figure 6.51 contains a figure with a parallelogram and a trapezoid. The (x, y) coordinates are given for each point. The accompanying CD contains a GIF labeled *newShape.gif* that contains the same figure without the coordinates. Create an image map for the GIF. When the user clicks in one of the shapes, you should display the appropriate formula for the area in a second frame.

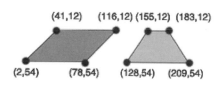

Figure 6.51 The *New Shapes* Image Map

20. **The *Colonial States* Page.** Create an image map for the Colonial United States. Place this image map in a frame that resides on the left side of the page. Find appropriate facts for each of the states and display these facts when the user clicks inside one of the states.

21. **The *European Travel* Page.** Find a regional map for a country in Europe. Develop a travel brochure page that contains an image map depicting the regions. Each region should have a separate page that displays tourist information for the region. Place the image map in the top frame and the tourist information in the bottom frame.

➤ **HTML TAGS**

<AREA>. The **<AREA>** tag defines a region of an image map. The syntax varies with the area's **SHAPE** attribute. The options are as follows:

```
<AREA SHAPE = "CIRCLE"
              COORDS = "centerX, centerY, radius"
              HREF = "URL"
              ALT = "alternative text"
              TARGET = "frame name">
<AREA SHAPE = "SQUARE"
        COORDS = "x1,y1,x2,y2"
        HREF = "URL"
        ALT = "alternative text"
        TARGET = "frame name">
<AREA SHAPE = "POLYGON"
        COORDS = "x1,y1,x2,y2,...,x1,y1"
        HREF = "URL"
        ALT = "alternative text"
        TARGET = "frame name">
```

<FRAME>. The **<FRAME>** tag specifies the parameters of a frame within a frameset.

Syntax:
```
<FRAME FRAMEBORDER = "0" | "1"
        MARGINHEIGHT = "pixels"
        MARGINWIDTH = "pixels"
        NAME = "frameName"
        NORESIZE
        SCROLLING = "yes" | "no" | "auto"
        SRC = "URL">
```

<FRAMESET>...</FRAMESET>. The **<FRAMESET>...</FRAMESET>** tags form a container for the frames of a page or a frameset.

Syntax:
```
<FRAMESET BORDER = "0" | "1"
          COLS = "pixels" |  "xx%"
          ROWS = "pixels" | "xx%">
```

The **COLS** and **ROWS** attributes contain a comma-separated list of the frameset's layout. The sizes may be in terms of pixels or of percentage. Use an asterisk (*****) to specify a leftover portion of a dimension.

<MAP>...</MAP>. The **<MAP>...</MAP>** tags form a container for the **<AREA>** tags used to define an image map.

Syntax:
```
<MAP NAME = "name">
      <AREA ... .>
      </MAP>
```

<NOFRAMES>...</NOFRAMES>. These tags furnish alternate text for browsers that do not recognize frames. If you use these tags, be sure to include a link to a non-frame-based page or a statement that the page needs to be viewed by means of a frame-capable browser.

➤ **HTML TIPS**

1. **Frameset.** In a frameset page, the **<FRAMESET>...</FRAMESET>** tags replace the **<BODY>...</BODY>** tags. If your frames do not load, make sure that you did not include the **<BODY>** tag.

2. **Image Maps.** If you have access to Photoshop 5.5 and ImageReady 2.0, use the guidelines in the optional section to create your image maps. Although the first image map will take time, once you understand the process you'll be able to create image maps much more quickly than you can by hand.

3. **Image Maps versus Tables.** A page with an image map typically loads more slowly than a page without one. Before creating an image map, consider whether you can achieve the same effect without the map. For example, the *shapes* image map could be replaced by a simple table, as in Figure 6.11. By contrast, the *Midwestern States* image map creates a visually appealing page. Compare this page with the original frame-based page found in Figure 6.6.

4. **Default.** Use the **SHAPE = "default"** attribute to trap any leftover areas in an image map. Link these areas to a blank page in the desired background color.

7 Cascading Style Sheets

The final HTML chapter explores Cascading Style Sheets (CSS). *Cascading Style Sheets* are used to create a reusable set of styles. Not only does this give pages a consistent appearance; it cuts the time needed to develop them. For example, suppose we want to create a table in which the font size of every data cell (**<TD>...</TD>**) is two. We cannot use the **<BASEFONT>** tag, because it ignores table cells. Without style sheets, we must place a **<FONT SIZE = "2">** tag in every data cell. With style sheets, we create a style for the **<TD>** tag that sets the font size. The style is set once and the browser automatically applies the style to every **<TD>** tag.

The *W3* organization maintains a web site that contains both the HTML 4.0 specification and the CSS1 and CSS2 specifications. The URL for the HTML specification is

```
http://www.w3.org/TR/
```

The URL for the CSS1 specification is

```
http://www.w3.org/TR/CSS1
```

The URL for the CSS2 specification is

```
http://www.w3.org/TR/CSS2
```

Internet Explorer and Netscape both provide limited support for the CCS1 specification. Neither browser supports the CSS2 specification. Of the two browsers, Internet Explorer currently provides a fuller implementation of the CSS1 specification. Because neither browser fully implements this specification, pages using style sheets should be carefully examined in both browsers before releasing them to the public.

The CSS1 specification includes font, border, background, margin, link, and list styles. We can embed the styles in a page or we can create an external style sheet that is loaded into a page. We can apply a style to a single tag or to a set of tags. We can create different styles for the same tag. We will explore all of these possibilities in this chapter.

EMBEDDED STYLE SHEET BASICS

Creating an embedded style sheet requires **<STYLE>...</STYLE>** tags. These tags are placed within the **<HEAD>...</HEAD>** container to ensure that the browser loads the style sheet before the page's body. The **<STYLE>** tag requires a **TYPE** attribute with a value of **"text/css"** (for cascading style sheet). Typically, the styles are placed inside HTML comment tags. This ensures that browsers that do not support style sheets will ignore the styles. The simplest styles attach the style to a specific tag.

THE *FIRST STYLE* PAGE

Figure 7.1 contains the *First Style* page. This page uses a body style to create the yellow background and green text.

The CSS1 specification includes **background** and **color** properties that set the style for a tag's background color and text color, respectively. These properties can be used with any tag that contains color attributes. Examples of such tags include **<BODY>**, **<TABLE>**, **<TR>**, **<TD>**, **<TH>**, **<H1>**, **<P>**, and **<PRE>**. The properties require a color value that is a recognized color name or a number written as **#RRGGBB** or **rgb (0...255, 0...255, 0...255)**. For example, to create a yellow background, we use

```
background:yellow
```

or

```
background: "#FFCC00"
```

Similarly, to create a green text color, we use

```
color: green
```

or

```
color: rgb(66,99,66)
```

Figure 7.2 shows how to associate properties with a specific tag.

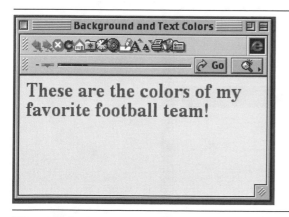

```
TAG {property₁ : value₁;
        ...
     propertyₙ:valueₙ}
```

Figure 7.1 The *First Style* Page

Figure 7.2 Creating a Tag-Specific Style

As this figure indicates, the property–value pairs are enclosed in braces. Semicolons separate the pairs. The tag name appears to the left of the style list. Figure 7.3 contains the HTML for the *First Style* page. The **<STYLE>** ... **</STYLE>** tags are placed after the page's **<TITLE>**...**</TITLE>** tags.

```
<HTML><HEAD><TITLE>Background and Text Colors</TITLE>
<STYLE TYPE = "text/css">
<!--
  BODY { background: yellow;
         color: green}
-->
</STYLE></HEAD>
<BODY>
<H1>These are the colors of my favorite football team!</H1>
</BODY></HTML>
```

Figure 7.3 HTML for the *First Style* Page

THE *POEM* PAGE (VERSION 1)

The CSS1 specification contains several font and text properties. A summary of these properties appears at the end of the chapter. The text properties include horizontal alignment (**text-align**), indentation (**text-indent**), style (**text-style**), and decoration (**text-decoration**). A transformation property (**text-transform**) converts text to uppercase or lowercase letters. The font properties include size (**font-size**), weight (**font-weight**), and family (**font-family**).

Figure 7.4 contains a simple poem that illustrates several of the font and text properties. The page defines styles for the **<H1>** and **<PRE>** tags. The **<H1>** style uses a black background and white text written in a bold font. The **<PRE>** style uses a 14-point italic Times Roman font.

Figure 7.4 The *Poem* Page (version 1)

THE <H1> STYLE

Creating the <H1> style requires the **background** and **color** properties. These properties have values of *black* and *white*, respectively. The bold style uses the **font-weight** property. The acceptable values are **bold, bolder, lighter, normal,** and numbers between 100 and 900. (The higher the number, the bolder the font.) The complete style for the <H1> tag is

```
H1 {background:black;
    color:white;
    font-weight:bold}
```

The order of the property–value pairs is irrelevant.

THE STYLE FOR THE <PRE> TAG

The <PRE> style uses the **font-family** property to set the font. Acceptable values include logical font families, such as *Serif, Sans Serif,* and *Monospaced,* and specific font names, such as Helvetica, Courier, and Times New Roman. Generally, logical families are preferable. A font face should not be used in isolation, because the user's browser may not support the font. Always include several font faces (or a logical family name) when using the **font-family** property. This gives the browser a choice if a specific font is not available. The style used for the <PRE> tags contains Times New Roman and Serif as the **font-family** values.

The **font-size** property sets the font size. The size can be measured in pixels (**px**), points (**pt**), inches (**in**), or centimeters (**cm**). For example, the statement

```
font-size:14pt
```

creates a 14-point font. Available font sizes vary, so be sure to test the page.

The **text-style** property creates an italic font. Acceptable values for this property are **italic**, **oblique**, and **normal**.

Figure 7.5 contains the HTML for the *Poem* page. The <H1> and <PRE> styles are found in the head of the page.

```
<HTML>
<HEAD><TITLE>Font And Text Tags</TITLE>
<STYLE TYPE = "text/css">
<!--
BODY {background: white}
PRE {font-family: "Times New Roman, serif";
     font-size: 14pt;
     font-style: italic}
H1 { background: black;
    color: white;
    font-weight: bold}

-->
</STYLE></HEAD>
<BODY>
<H1> My Poem </H1>
<PRE> Roses are red.
   Violets are blue.
HTML's cool,
    And Java is too.</PRE></BODY></HTML>
```

Figure 7.5 HTML for the *Poem* Page (version 1)

THE *POEM* PAGE (VERSION 2)

Virtually all HTML tags contain an optional **ID** attribute. This attribute associates a tag with a "generic" style. Figure 7.6 contains a new version of the *Poem* page. This version contains bold and italic styles that can be used with any HTML tag. The page contains **<H1>**, **<H3>**, and **<P>** tags written with the default HTML style and the newly defined bold or italic styles. The bold style uses bold red text; the italic style uses italic blue text.

Figure 7.7 shows the syntax for creating a style associated with an **ID** attribute. The style uses the pound symbol (#) as a prefix.

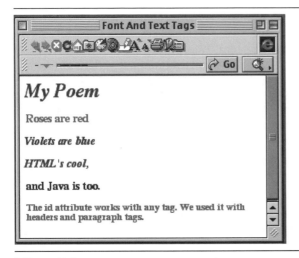

```
#Style {property₁ : value₁;
        ...
        propertyₙ:valueₙ}
```

Figure 7.6 The *Poem* Page (version 2)　　　　**Figure 7.7** **ID** style specification

The *Bold* style used in the second version of the *Poem* page is defined as

```
#Bold{ font-weight: bold; color: red}
```

The *Ital* style is defined as

```
#Ital {font-style:italic; color: blue}
```

The styles are accessed by placing an **ID** attribute with the style name inside the desired tag. Tags without an **ID** attribute use the default HTML style.

For example, the statement

```
<H3> How are you ?</H3>
```

displays *How are you?* in HTML's default style. By contrast, the statement

```
<H3 ID = "Ital">I am fine.</H3>
```

displays *I am fine.* in a red italic font.

Figure 7.8 contains the HTML for the *Poem* page, version 2. Notice the **ID** attributes in the tags.

```
<HTML><HEAD><TITLE>Font And Text Tags</TITLE>
<STYLE TYPE = "text/css">
<!--
BODY { background: white}

#Bold{ font-weight: bold;
       color: red}
#Ital {font-style:italic;
       color: blue}
-->
</STYLE></HEAD>
<BODY>
<H1 ID = "Ital"> My Poem </H1>

<H3 ID = "Bold"> Roses are red</H3>
<H3 ID = "Ital"> Violets are blue</H3>
<H3 ID = "Ital"> HTML's cool,</H3>
<H3> and Java is too.</H3>
<P ID = "Bold"> The id attribute works with any tag. We used it with headers and paragraph
tags.</P> </BODY>
</BODY></HTML>
```

Figure 7.8 The *Poem* Page (version 2)

THE CLASS ATTRIBUTE

Style classes offer a second method for creating generic styles. Figure 7.9 illustrates the syntax for creating a style class. The syntax is almost identical to the identification style. In fact, the only difference is the prefix: Identification styles use a pound symbol (#); style classes use a period (.).

```
.Style {property₁ : value₁;
           ...
        propertyₙ:valueₙ}
```

Figure 7.9 The Style Class Specification

THE FONT CLASS PAGE

Figure 7.10 contains a *Font Class* page that displays the message *Hello World!* in several different styles. The first line of this page uses the default font style. Each of the remaining lines uses a style class to display the text.

Creating the upper-case font displayed on the second line of the *Font Class* page requires the **text-transform** property. The allowed values are **uppercase**, **lowercase**, and **capitalize**. The class style is defined as

```
.upper {text-transform:uppercase}
```

To use the new style, we add a **CLASS** attribute to the desired tags. For example,

```
<P CLASS = "upper"> Hello, world!</P>
```

displays HELLO, WORLD! in uppercase letters. By contrast,

```
<P>Hello, world!</P>
```

displays the message in the default style.

The **.lower** class is also created with the **text-transform** property.

Creating the **.underline** class requires the **text-decoration** property. The valid values for this property are **underline**, **overline**, **line-through**, and **blink**. (Internet Explorer does not recognize the **blink** property.) The statement

```
.underline {text-decoration:underline}
```

creates the **underline** class.

The **.italic** class uses the **font-style** property discussed earlier.

Figure 7.11 contains the HTML for the *Font Class* page.

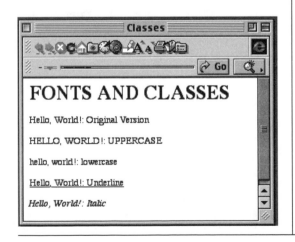

```
<HTML><HEAD><TITLE>Classes</TITLE>
<STYLE TYPE = "text/css">
<!--
 BODY { background: white}
.upper { text-transform: uppercase}
.lower {text-transform: lowercase}
.strike {text-decoration: linethrough}
.underline {text-decoration: underline}
.italic {font-style: italic}
-->
</STYLE></HEAD>
<BODY>
<H1 CLASS = "upper">Fonts and Classes</H1>
<P> Hello, World!: Original Version</P>
<P CLASS = "upper"> Hello, World!: Uppercase</P>
<P CLASS = "lower"> Hello, World!: Lowercase</P>
<P CLASS = "underline">Hello, World!:
    Underline</P>
<P CLASS = "italic"> Hello, World!: Italic </P>
</BODY></HTML>
```

Figure 7.10 The *Font Class* Page   **Figure 7.11** HTML for the *Font Class* Page

SPANNING CLASSES

A *spanning* class combines styles from two different classes. Figure 7.12 contains the syntax for a spanning class.

```
<TagName CLASS = "ClassName"> This message was created with ClassName.
<SPAN CLASS = "SecondClass"> This message uses both classes</SPAN>.
This message uses only ClassName</TAG>
```

Figure 7.12 *Spanning Class* Syntax.

For example, assume that the page contains a **.upper** class. We can use a spanning class to underline and capitalize text within a paragraph. The statement is

```
<P CLASS = "upper">
<SPAN CLASS = "underline"> This is uppercase, underlined text</SPAN></P>
```

Figure 7.13 contains several examples of spanning classes. Try to write the statements that produced this page before examining the HTML appearing in Figure 7.14.

Figure 7.14 contains the HTML for the *Spanning Class* page. The *strike* class, which is new to this page, was created with the **text-decoration** property.

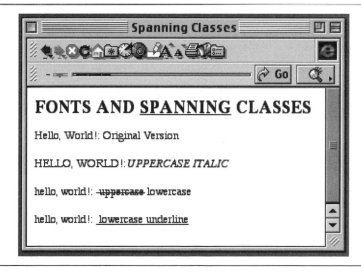

Figure 7.13 The *Spanning Class* Page

```
<HTML><HEAD><TITLE>Spanning Classes</TITLE>
<STYLE TYPE = "text/css">
<!--
BODY { background: white}
.upper { text-transform: uppercase}
.lower {text-transform: lowercase}
.strike {text-decoration: line-through}
.underline {text-decoration: underline}
.italic {font-style: italic}
-->
</STYLE>
<BODY>
<H2 CLASS = "upper">Fonts and <SPAN CLASS = "underline">Spanning</SPAN> Classes</H2>
<P> Hello, World!: Original Version</P>
<P CLASS = "upper"> Hello, World!: <SPAN CLASS = "italic">uppercase italic</SPAN> </P>
<P CLASS = "lower"> Hello, World!: <SPAN CLASS = "strike"> uppercase</SPAN> lowercase</P>
<P CLASS = "lower">Hello, world!: <SPAN CLASS = "underline"> lowercase underline</SPAN></P>
</BODY></HTML>
```

Figure 7.14 HTML for the *Spanning Class* Page

TAG-SPECIFIC IDENTIFICATION STYLES AND CLASSES

The identification styles and classes created thus far are generic. This means that they can be used with any appropriate tag. We can also create tag-specific identification styles or classes. Figure 7.15 contains the syntax for creating each style.

Tag-Specific Identification Style	*Tag-Specific Class*
Tag#Style {property$_1$: value$_1$; ... property$_n$:value$_n$}	Tag.Style {property$_1$: value$_1$; ... property$_n$:value$_n$}

Figure 7.15 Syntax for Tag-Specific Identification Styles and Classes

For example, the following statement creates an uppercase class for the **<H1>** tag:

H1.Upper{text-transform:uppercase}

Because the class name *Upper* is attached to the **<H1>** tag, this class applies only to the **<H1>** tag. Similarly, the following statement creates an identification style that is unique to the **<H3>** tag:

H3#Bold{font-weight: bold;
        color: red}

When defined in this manner, the *Bold* style works only with the **<H3>** tag. The browser ignores any **ID = "Bold"** attribute that appears in any other tag.

Figure 7.16 contains a *Tag-Specific Style* page. Try creating the styles and the HTML tags before examining the HTML contained in Figure 7.17.

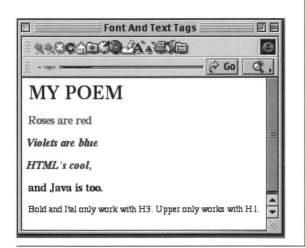

```
<HTML><HEAD><TITLE>Font And Text Tags</TITLE>
<STYLE TYPE = "text/css">
<!--
BODY { background: white}
H1.Upper{text-transform:uppercase}
H3#Bold{ font-weight: bold;
         color: red}
H3#Ital {font-style:italic;
         color: blue}
-->
</STYLE>
<BODY>
<!-- Bold and italic ONLY work with H3 -->
<!-- Upper only works with H1 -->
<H1 CLASS = "Upper"> My Poem </H1>
<H3  ID = "Bold"> Roses are red</H3>
<H3 ID = "Ital">   Violets are blue</H3>
<H3 ID = "Ital"> HTML's cool,</H3>
<H3> and Java is too.</H3>
<P CLASS = "Upper">Bold and Ital only
    work with H3.
Upper only works with H1.</P> </BODY>
</HTML>
```

Figure 7.16 The *Tag-Specific Style* Page   **Figure 7.17** HTML for the *Tag-Specific Style* Page

Figure 7.17 contains the HTML for the *Tag-Specific Style* page. The HTML is straightforward. However, be sure to compare the last statement in Figure 7.16 with the statement used to create it:

```
<P CLASS = "Upper">Bold and Ital only work with H3.
Upper only works with H1.</P>
```

The **<P>** tag includes a **CLASS = "Upper"** attribute, which the browser ignores because the *Upper* class is not defined for the **<P>** tag.

THE *FOURTH OF JULY* PAGE (VERSION 1)

The CSS1 specification contains two *list style* properties: **list-style-type** and **list-style-image**. The **list-style-type** property changes the default type for an ordered or unordered list. The acceptable values for an unordered list are **disc**, **circle**, and **square**. The acceptable values for an ordered list are **decimal**, **upper-roman**, **lower-roman**, **upper-alpha**, and **lower-alpha**. The **list-style-image** property creates an image-based bullet for an unordered list.

Figure 7.18 contains a *Fourth of July* page. This page uses alternating red and blue bullets to list the events.

Two GIF files, *redBullet.gif* and *blueBullet.gif*, create the two bullets. Alternating the red and blue bullets requires two identification styles for the **<LI>** tag. The definition of the *redBullet* style is

```
LI#redBullet {list-style-image: url(redBullet.gif)}
```

The definition of the *blueBullet* style is

```
LI#blueBullet {list-style-image: url(blueBullet.gif)}
```

These styles use the **list-style-image** property, which always takes a **url(***imageFile***)** as its value. The image file must be stored as a GIF or JPEG. Figure 7.19 contains the HTML for the fourth of July page (version 1).

```
<HTML><HEAD><TITLE> List with Buttons</TITLE>
<STYLE TYPE = "text/css">
<!--
LI#redBullet {list-style-image:
    url(redBullet.gif )}
LI#blueBullet {list-style-image:
    url(blueBullet.gif)}
 -->
</STYLE></HEAD>
<BODY BGCOLOR = "white">
<H1> The Muskrat Mounds Independence
    Day Celebration
<UL >
<LI ID = "redBullet"> Games
<LI ID = "blueBullet">Pony Rides
<LI ID = "redBullet" > Cook Out
<LI ID = "blueBullet"> Sing Along
</UL></H1>
</BODY></HTML
```

Figure 7.18 The *Fourth of July* Page (version 1)

Figure 7.19 HTML for the *Fourth of July* Page (version 1)

THE *FOURTH OF JULY* PAGE (VERSION 2)

Figure 7.20 contains a second version of the *Fourth of July* Page. The list elements use alternating red discs, white circles, and blue squares. The text color of the list item matches the bullet color. (The white circle is actually a black circle with a white interior.)

The second version of the *Fourth of July* page creates red, white, and blue identification styles for the **<LI>** tag. Each style contains a **color** property set to the appropriate text color and a **list-style-type** property set to the appropriate bullet type. For example, the definition of the *red* style is

```
LI#red {color:red; list-style-type: disc}
```

Figure 7.20 The *Fourth of July* Page
(version 2)

```
HTML><HEAD><TITLE> Unordered List Types</TITLE>
<STYLE TYPE = "text/css">
<!--
LI#red {color:red;
        list-style-type: disc}
LI#blue {color:blue;
         list-style-type:square}
LI#white {color:black;
          list-style-type:circle}
-->
</STYLE>
</HEAD>
<BODY BGCOLOR = "white">
<H2> The Muskrat Mounds Independence Day Celebration
<UL >
<LI ID = "red"> Games
<LI ID = "white">Fun
<LI ID = "blue">Pony Rides
<LI ID = "red" > Cook Out
<LI ID = "white"> CampFire
<LI ID = "blue"> Sing Along
</UL>
</H2>
</BODY></HTML>
```

Figure 7.21 HTML for the *Fourth of July* Page
(Version 2)

The *blue* and *white* **<LI>** identification styles were created in a similar manner. Figure 7.21 contains the HTML for the second version of the *Fourth of July* page.

THE *FOURTH OF JULY* PAGE (VERSION 3)

The color styles used in the second version of the *Fourth of July* page apply the **color** property both to the bullet and to the text that follows the bullet. For example, the items with red discs display the text in red, and the items with blue squares display the text in blue. Suppose we want to alternate the colors of the bullets, while displaying all of the text in black, as illustrated in Figure 7.22.

This last version of the *Fourth of July* page uses the **<LI>** identification styles created for the second version. However, this version encases the item's text in **<FONT COLOR = "black"> </FONT>** tags. The final version also includes an identification style for the **<H2>** tag that centers the text. Figure 7.23 contains the HTML for the final version of the *Fourth of July* page. Notice the use of the **<FONT>** tags with the *red* and *blue* identification styles. The *white* identification style does not require **<FONT>** tags, because it already uses black.

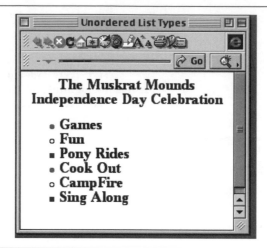

Figure 7.22 The *Fourth of July* Page (final version)

```
<HTML><HEAD><TITLE> Unordered List Types</TITLE>
<STYLE TYPE = "text/css">
<!--
H2#Center {text-align:center}
LI#red {color:red;
        list-style-type: disc}
LI#blue {color:blue;
         list-style-type:square}
LI#white {color:black;
          list-style-type:circle}
-->
</STYLE>
</HEAD>
<BODY BGCOLOR = "white">
<H2 ID = "Center"> The Muskrat Mounds<BR> Independence Day Celebration</H2>
<H2><UL>
<LI ID = "red"> <FONT COLOR = "black">Games </FONT>
<LI ID = "white">Fun
<LI ID = "blue"><FONT COLOR = "black">Pony Rides</FONT>
<LI ID = "red" > <FONT COLOR = "black">Cook Out</FONT>
<LI ID = "white"> CampFire
<LI ID = "blue"> <FONT COLOR = "black">Sing Along </FONT></UL></H2>
</BODY></HTML>
```

Figure 7.23 HTML for the *Fourth of July* Page (final version)

Combining styles with HTML tags does not always work, because the style sheets do *cascade*. (This term means that the styles form a hierarchy in which lower styles automatically inherit features of higher styles.) In the third version of the *Fourth of July* page, the styles and the **<FONT>...</FONT>** tags work together. If they do not, the styles have precedence over the HTML tags.

THE *TERM PAPER* PAGE

We can use the **list-style-type** property to change the default bullets used for nested, unordered lists or the default numbers used for nested, ordered lists. Figure 7.24 contains a *Term Paper* page that uses uppercase Roman numerals for the outermost list items, uppercase letters for the middle list items, and numbers for the innermost list items.

To create this nested list style, we begin with the outermost list. We define an **<OL>** style that uses the **list-style-type** property with an **upper-roman** value. The style tag is:

```
OL {list-style-type: upper-roman}
```

Next, we create the middle list style. The middle list is only an ordered list contained within another ordered list, so the style tag is

```
OL OL {list-style-type: upper-alpha}
```

The style for the innermost list is

```
OL OL OL {list-style-type: decimal}
```

We can repeat this process to specify the ordering for a fourth level. For example, suppose we decided to use lowercase letters for this level; then the style would be:

```
OL OL OL OL {list-style-type: lower-alpha}
```

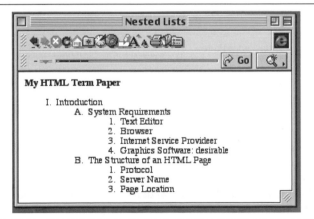

Figure 7.24 The *Term Paper* Page

Figure 7.25 contains the HTML for the *Term Paper* page. Notice the simplicity of the `<LI>` tags used for each level.

```
<HTML><HEAD><TITLE>Nested Lists</TITLE>
<STYLE TYPE = "text/css">
<!--
    OL {list-style-type: upper-roman}
    OL OL {list-style-type: upper-alpha}
    OL OL  OL {list-style-type: decimal}
-->
</STYLE>
</HEAD>
<BODY BGCOLOR = "white">
<B>My HTML Term Paper</B>
<OL>
<LI> Introduction
<OL>
<LI> System Requirements
<OL>
<LI> Text Editor
<LI> Browser
<LI> Internet Service Provideer
<LI> Graphics Software: desirable
</OL>
<LI> The Structure of an HTML Page
<OL>
<LI> Protocol
<LI> Server Name
<LI> Page Location
</OL>
</BODY></HTML>
```

Figure 7.25 HTML for the *Term Paper* Page

Although the *Term Paper* page uses ordered lists, we can create nested list styles for unordered lists by using the same procedure.

THE *HALLOWEEN* PAGE

We can create styles for table captions and for data or header cells by using previously discussed styles. In addition, we can also use **border** and **padding** properties to create a border style for a table or to define the padding between various cell components. Figure 7.26 contains a table of Halloween colors and things. The page contains styles for the `<TABLE>`, `<CAPTION>`, `<TH>`, and `<TD>` tags.

The data cells in the *Halloween* table use an orange background. A 12-point Serif font is used for the left-aligned text. A padding of five pixels separates the text from the inner border. The only new property required for this style is **padding**. This property requires a numeric value represented as pixels (**px**), points (**pt**), inches (**in**), or centimeters (**cm**). The ordering of the properties within the style is irrelevant. Figure 7.27 contains the specification of the **TD** style:

Figure 7.26 The *Halloween* Page

```
TD {background:orange;
    font-size:12 pt;
    font-family:serif;
    text-align:left;
    padding:5px}
```

Figure 7.27 The **TD** Style

The table header cells use a black background with a white 14-point Serif font. The text is left aligned. A padding of five pixels separates the text from the inner border. Try writing the style specification before examining the specification contained in Figure 7.28.

The caption uses an 18-point bold Serif font. A padding of seven pixels separates the caption from the table's outer border. Try writing the specification for the caption style before examining Figure 7.29.

```
TH {background:  black;
    color: white;
    font-size: 14 pt;
    font-family: serif;
    text-align: left;
    padding: 5px}
```

Figure 7.28 The **TH** Style

The table uses the **border** property to create a thin solid black border. The **border** property is not fully implemented on either Internet Explorer or Netscape. The Style Sheet Summary at the end of the chapter shows the different border styles. Carefully check them on your browser.

Figure 7.29 contains the HTML for the *Halloween* page. Notice the simplicity of the **<TD>** and **<TH>** tags. The styles created in the head of the page do all of the work.

```
<HTML><HEAD><TITLE> CSS and Tables</TITLE>
<STYLE TYPE = "text/css">
<!--
BODY {background: white}
TABLE { border : thin solid black}

TD {background:  orange;
    font-size: 12 pt;
    font-family: serif;
    text-align: left;
    padding: 5px}

TH {background:  black;
    color: white;
    font-size: 14 pt;
    font-family: serif;
    text-align: left;
    padding: 5px}

CAPTION {font-size: 18pt;
        font-family: serif;
        font-weight: bold;
        padding: 7px}
-->
</STYLE></HEAD>
<BODY BGCOLOR = "white">
<TABLE>
<CAPTION> Halloween</Caption>
<TR><TH>Colors</TH><TH>Things</TH></TR>
<TR><TD>Orange</TD><TD>Ghosts</TD></TR>
<TR><TD>Black</TD><TD>Witches</TD></TR>
<TR><TD>White</TD><TD> Goblins</TD></TR>
<TR><TD> </TD><TD>Bats</TD></TR>
</TABLE>
</BODY></HTML>
```

Figure 7.29 HTML for the *Halloween* Page

THE *LINK STYLES* **PAGE**

The CSS1 specification contains properties to change the default link styles. Recall that Netscape uses blue for unvisited links and purple for visited links, while Internet Explorer uses blue for unvisited links and green for visited links. Active links usually display too quickly to note the color change. The **A:active**, **A:link**, and **A:visited** properties create styles for the active, unvisited, and visited links, respectively. Figure 7.30 contains a page with three absolute links. The page displays unvisited links in a bold red font and visited links in a bold tan font.

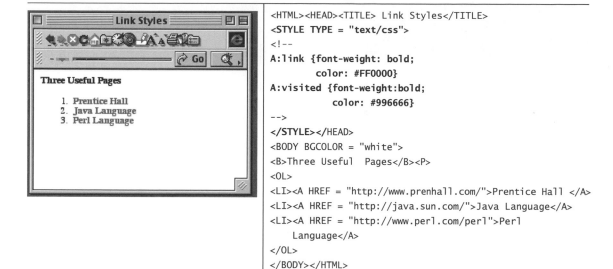

Figure 7.30 The *Link Styles* Page

Figure 7.31 HTML for the *Link Styles* Page

The *Link Styles* page uses the **color** and **font-weight** properties discussed previously. Figure 7.31 contains the HTML for the *Link Styles* page.

We can create the link styles illustrated in Figure 7.30 without using an embedded style sheet; however, the technique requires more effort and is error prone. Without style sheets, we would use the **LINK** and **VLINK** attributes to change the link colors in the **<BODY>** tag. To produce the bold font, we would need to encase the link text in **<B>...</B>** tags. The link styles automatically change both the color and the font weight.

THE *HOLIDAY COLORS* PAGE

An external style sheet is a set of styles stored in a separate file. The styles exist independently, and so we can use them in many different pages. Figure 7.32 contains a page that uses an external style sheet. This sheet contains a paragraph style and styles for the table components.

An external style sheet file must have an extension of **.css** . The *Holiday Colors* page uses a style sheet file named *myStyles.css*. The text of this file is simply a listing of the various paragraph and table styles. As an example, consider the paragraph displayed in Figure 7.32. The paragraph style uses left and right margins of 20 pixels and top and bottom margins of 5 pixels. The CSS1 specification includes a **margin** property that sets the top, bottom, left, and right margins to the same size. This specification also includes **margin-left**, **margin-right**, **margin-top**, and **margin-bottom** properties that individually set the four margins. Figure 7.33 contains the paragraph style used in Figure 7.32.

We can also specify a margin value in inches (**in**), points (**pt**), or centimeters (**cm**).

The **TABLE** style uses a thin solid black border. The **CAPTION** style uses a 14-point bold Serif font. The bottom of the caption uses a 10-pixel margin to prevent the caption from sliding into the table's border. The **TD** and **TH** styles use a 12-point left-aligned Serif font. A padding of five

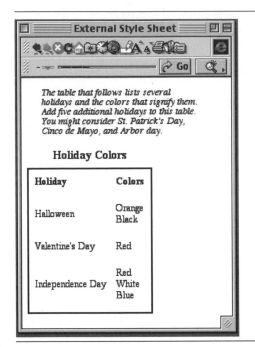

The table that follows lists several holidays and the colors that signify them. Add five additional holidays to this table. You might consider St. Patrick's Day, Cinco de Mayo, and Arbor day.

Holiday Colors

Holiday	Colors
Halloween	Orange Black
Valentine's Day	Red
Independence Day	Red White Blue

Figure 7.32 The *Holiday Colors* Page

```
P {margin-left:20px;
   margin-right:20px;
   margin-top:5px;
   margin-bottom:5px}
```

Figure 7.33 The Paragraph Style

pixels surrounds the cell contents. The CSS1 specification makes possible a comma-separated list of tags using the same style. Figure 7.34 contains the external style sheet.

To use an external style sheet, we place a **<LINK>** tag in the head of the page. This tag requires three attributes: a **REL** attribute with a value of *StyleSheet*, a **TYPE** attribute with a value of *text/css*, and an **HREF** attribute specifying the file name of the external style sheet. Figure 7.35 contains the HTML for the *Holiday Colors* page. The **<LINK>** tag that loads the external style sheet is highlighted.

```
BODY {background: white}

TABLE {border: thin solid black}

CAPTION {font-family: serif;
         font-weight: bold;
         font-size: 14pt;
         margin-bottom: 10px}
TD, TH {padding: 5px;
         font-family: serif;
         text-align:  left;
         font-size: 12pt}
P {margin-left: 20px;
   margin-right: 20px;
   margin-top: 5px;
   margin-bottom: 5px}
```

Figure 7.34 The *myStyles.css* File

```
<HTML><HEAD><TITLE>External Style Sheet</TITLE>
<LINK REL = "StyleSheet"  TYPE = "text/css" HREF = "myStyles.css">
</HEAD>
<BODY>
<P><I>The table that follows lists several holidays and the colors that signify them.
Add five additional holidays to this table. You might consider St. Patrick's Day,  Cinco de Mayo,
and Arbor day.</P>
<TABLE BORDER = "1"><!-- The internal border -->
<CAPTION>Holiday Colors</CAPTION>
<TR><TH>Holiday</TH><TH>Colors</TH></TR>
<TR><TD>Halloween</TD>  <TD>Orange<BR>Black</TD></TR>
<TR><TD>Valentine's Day</TD><TD>Red</TD></TR>
<TR><TD>Independence Day</TD><TD>Red<BR>White<BR>Blue</TD></TR>
</TABLE>
</BODY></HTML>
```

Figure 7.35 HTML for the *Holiday Colors* Page

➤ EXERCISES

The exercises cover both internal and external style sheet. Although the exercises focus on the styles, you must create a page that tests each of the styles created in an exercise.

1. **The *Halloween List* Page.** Find or create appropriate Halloween images. Create a list of Halloween things using your images as the bullets for an unordered list. Figure 7.36 contains an example.

Figure 7.36 The *Halloween List* Page

2. **The *Fall Colors* Page.** Create a table of fall things that contains columns of orange and yellow things. Create a separate style for each column. List the things that you associate with these colors. Figure 7.37 contains an example.

Figure 7.37 The *Fall Colors* Page

3. **The *Headings* Page.** Create three different **H1** heading styles. Make the first style bold, the second italic, and the third bold italic. Use the default font-size. Create a page that tests your different headings.

4. **The *Paragraph* Page.** Create three different paragraph styles. Each style should have a different alignment. The first style should be centered, the second should be right aligned, and the third style should resemble the double-indent style found on many word processors.

5. **The *Ordered List* Page.** Create a set of ordered list style tags. The outermost (or first) list uses decimal numbering, the second list uses upper-case letters, the third list uses lower-case roman numerals, and the last (or innermost) list uses lower-case letters.

6. **The *Division Blocks* Page.** Create a set of styles for the **DIV** tag. Your styles should alter the text and background colors and the font size.

7. **The *Sports Links* Page.** Pick your favorite sports team. Create a page that uses the team's colors for the visited and unvisited links. Include links to the official team page and any unofficial pages.

8. **A *Tables* Page.** Pick an exercise from Chapter 4. Recreate the table with a style sheet. You should modify the **TABLE**, **CAPTION**, **TH**, and **TR** attributes. Use a different padding property for each tag, and observe how it affects the table's appearance.

9. **The *Font* Page.** Create a set of classes that represent different font styles. Include bold italic, upper-case, lower-case, small, and large font styles.

10. **The *Color-Coded Division Blocks* Page.** Create at least three different styles for division tags. The styles should vary the foreground and text color of the text enclosed in the **<DIV>...</DIV>** tags. Use **CLASS** styles attached to the **DIV** tag to create the styles.

11. **The *Unordered Lists* Page.** Find or create two bullet images that appeal to you. Create a style for unordered lists that uses one image for an outer list and the other image for an inner (second-level) list.

12. **The *Valentine's Day Essay* Page.** Create a page that discusses Valentine's Day and all of the things associated with it. Use the **<SPAN>** tag to print words related to Valentine's Day in red.

13. **Another *Headings* Page.** Create **H1**, **H2**, and **H3** styles with the following characteristics: all **H1** headings are in white bold italics with a blue background; all **H2** headings are in white italics with a green background; all **H3** headings are in red with a white background.

14. **The *Paragraph ID* Page.** Create three different paragraph styles, **P1**, **P2**, and **P3**. **P1** should contain left and right margins of 30 pixels; text contained within it should be written in italics. **P2** should contain right and left margins of ten pixels and top and bottom margins of two pixels. Use different top, bottom, left, and right margins for **P3**.

15. **The *External Style Sheet* Page.** Create a style sheet for your home page and any pages linked to it. Develop a set of styles that you wish to use consistently throughout your pages. Make sure that each page uses the external style sheet.

16. *Underlined Links* **Page.** Create new link styles for unvisited and unvisited links, ones that always underline the link. Pick text colors and font sizes that appeal to you.

➤ STYLE SHEET PROPERTIES

Border and Related Properties

padding.   The **padding** property changes the inside space of an object. The padding can be measured in pixels (**px**), points (**pt**), inches (**in**), or centimeters (**cm**). The padding can be set separately by using **padding-top**, **padding-bottom**, **padding-right**, and **padding-left**.

margin.   The **margin** property sets the top, bottom, left, and right margins to the same size. The margin can be measured in pixels, points, inches, or centimeters. The margins can be set individually by using **margin-top**, **margin-bottom**, **margin-left**, and **margin-right**.

border.   The **border** property specifies the width, style, and color of an object's border. Values for the width are **normal**, **thick**, and **thin**. Style values are **solid**, **outset**, **ridge**, **inset**, and **double**. Color values may be either a color name or number written as **#RRGGBB** or **rgb(0...255, 0...255, 0.255)**. The borders can be set separately by using **border-top**, **border-right**, **border-left**, and **border-bottom**. The width can be set separately by using **border-width** (or any of the variants, such as **border-top-width**).

The **border-color** property sets the color of the border. The **border-style** property sets the style of the border.

Color Properties

background.   The **background** property changes the background color or adds a background image. The general form is

```
{background transparent |  colorName | #RRGGBB | rgb(0..255, 0..255, 0..255) |
url(imageName)}
```

background-color. The **background-color** property changes only the background color of an object. The color value can be a valid color name, a hexadecimal RGB value (#RRGGBB), or a decimal RGB value written as **rgb(0...255, 0...255, 0...255)**.

color. The **color** property changes the foreground (text) color. The acceptable values are identical to the **background-color** values.

Font and Text Properties

font-family. The **font-family** property sets the font options. The options may be a logical family name, such as **serif**, **sans-serif**, **cursive**, **fantasy**, or **monospaced**, or a face name, such as Times or Courier.

text-align. The **text-align** property sets the horizontal alignment. The syntax is

```
text-align: right | left | center | justify
```

text-vertical-align. The **text-vertical-align** property sets the vertical alignment. The syntax is

```
text-vertical-align: baseline | sub | super | top | text-top | middle | bottom |
text-bottom
```

Unfortunately, no browser currently supports this property.

text-indent. The **text-indent** property sets the indentation for the left and right margins.

font-weight. The **font-weight** property sets the "boldness" of a font. Named values are **bold**, **bolder**, **normal**, and **lighter**. Numeric value range from 100 to 900; the higher the number, the bolder the font.

font-size. The **font-size** property sets the font size. Named values are **xx-small**, **x-small**, **small**, **medium**, **large**, **x-large**, and **xx-large**. Numeric value can be written in points (**pt**) or pixels (**px**).

text-decoration. The **text-decoration** property sets the "embellishments." Values are **underline**, **blink**, **line-through**, and **overline**.
Note: Internet Explorer does not recognize the **blink** value.

text-style. The **text-style** property sets the font's style. Values are **normal**, **oblique**, and **italic**.

text-transform. The **text-transform** property changes the font's overall appearance. Values are **capitalize**, **uppercase**, and **lowercase**.

Link Properties

A:active. The **A:active** property changes the appearance of active links.

A:link. The **A:link** property changes the appearance of unvisited links.

A:visited. The **A:visited** property changes the appearance of visited links.

List Properties

`list-style-image.`   The `list-style-image` property creates bullets from images. The syntax is

`{list-style-image: url(imageFile)}`

`list-style-type.`   The `list-style-type` property changes the default bullets or numbering for unordered and ordered lists, respectively. The values for unordered lists are `disc`, `circle`, and `square`. The values for ordered lists are `decimal`, `upper-roman`, `lower-roman`, `upper-alpha`, and `lower-alpha`.

➤ HTML TIPS

1. **Style Sheet Specification.** The official style sheet specification is available at

   `http://www.w3.org/TR/REC-CSS1.`

2. **Browser Limitations.** Remember that the styles in the CSS1 specification might not be fully implemented on your browser. Be sure to check pages under both the Internet Explorer and the Netscape browser and under the browser used by your targeted audience.

3. **External Style Sheets.** Use external style sheets to create a uniform appearance for all of your pages.

PART II   JavaScript

8   Introduction to JavaScript

In Part I, we learned how to use HTML, a Web-based mark-up language. As a mark-up language, HTML resembles many of the early versions of word processing programs and some contemporary systems such as troff, a UNIX-based typesetter, and Latex, a mathematically specialized word processor. All of these systems use tags to specify page layouts: There are tags to turn on and off bold or italics, tags to create lists or tables, and tags to embed images.

Learning any markup language is relatively easy: we simply memorize the relevant tag for the desired task. When we use HTML to produce Web pages, we are doing little more than word processing. In essence, we are creating a manuscript that the whole world can view. Although the pages might be informative and well designed, they are static. Users read these pages as they would read a book; they cannot interact with them. We're about to change that scenario. By learning a Web-based programming language, we can turn our static "Web books" into interactive sites that engage our viewers.

Parts II through IV of this text successively cover three Web-based programming languages: JavaScript, Perl, and Java. These languages are arranged from the simplest, and thus easiest to learn, to the hardest. If you have never programmed before (and I'm going to assume that this is the case), you'll soon discover that programming is a craft that shares many similarities with crafts like woodworking, model building, and quilting. Mastery of any craft requires plenty of practice, the right tools, and knowledge of the vocabulary associated with the craft.

Practice is crucial because mastery of any craft depends upon experience. The more experience you have, the more your skills improve. If all you do is read the chapters in this book, you will not become a programmer. You should run and modify the examples in the book and try out each of the practice exercises until you feel comfortable with the material.

A programmer's key tool is the programming language used. Just as apprentices use simpler tools and techniques than experienced craftpersons, a newcomer to programming will experience less frustration by beginning with a simpler language. Of the three languages discussed in this book, JavaScript is by far the easiest. We begin with this language so that we can concentrate on learning programming fundamentals. Many of the concepts, vocabulary, and conventions that we discuss in our excursion through JavaScript apply to Perl and Java. Thus, learning the latter languages will be easier.

Before we begin, a word of caution: Programming can, and often is, a very frustrating pursuit, particularly in the beginning stages. It requires a level of accuracy and attention to detail that many

174

of us initially lack. A failure to follow the rules of a programming language results in a very obvious (but not necessarily very informative) error message that must be eliminated before the program will work. To facilitate learning a new programming language, I tell my students to keep small spiral-bound-notebooks at their computers. The notebook should contain coded examples that work correctly and the output produced by the example. It should also contain common mistakes. When an error message appears, compare the erroneous code with the correctly coded example.

JAVASCRIPT HISTORY

As indicated previously, JavaScript is the easiest of the web programming languages. (Originally, it was called LiveScript.) The language's development began in 1995 at Netscape. LiveScript was intended to be a client-based language able to interact with applets written in Java. In late 1995, Netscape and Sun Microsystems joined creative forces and LiveScript became JavaScript. The language is embedded in all Netscape browsers greater than Netscape 2.0 and Internet Explorer browsers greater than IE3.0. JavaScript is used to provide simple interactions with users, navigate through pages, and validate form information. The language is "client-based"—that is, it works through the user's computer rather than your system server. As a result, there are many things that JavaScript cannot do. For example, JavaScript cannot write files to the system server or the client's machine and it cannot read files from the client's machine. You need to learn Perl or Java if your applications require file facilities. JavaScript also does not have graphics capabilities. For these tasks, you might want to learn Java, which has extensive graphics facilities.

A FIRST JAVASCRIPT PROGRAM

As our first JavaScript programming exercise, we reproduce the Web page appearing in Figure 8.1.

The first line of this page is written in HTML. A JavaScript (JS) script generates the remaining two lines. The code for the page appears in Figure 8.2. Boxes separate the HTML portion of the page from the JS portion.

Figure 8.1 The First JavaScript Page

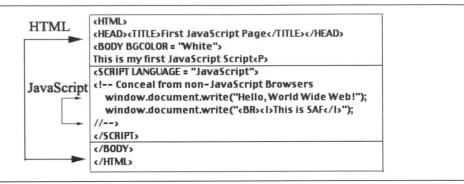

Figure 8.2 Code for the *First JavaScript* Page

Figure 8.2 contains a new set of HTML tags: **<SCRIPT>**...**</SCRIPT>**. These tags form a container for a script. The **<SCRIPT>** tag contains several optional attributes, as is illustrated in Figure 8.3.

```
<SCRIPT DEFER
        LANGUAGE = "Scripting Language"
        SRC = "External File"
        TYPE = "mime type">
```

Figure 8.3 The **<SCRIPT>** tag

The first JavaScript script uses the **LANGUAGE** attribute to indicate that the script is written in JavaScript. A **TYPE** attribute would indicate the mime type of the script. The mime type for JavaScript is *text/javascript*. A **SRC** attribute would indicate the source of a script, when the script is external to the program. External scripts conceal the script code from users. External JavaScript files should have an extension of **.js**. The **DEFER** attribute tells the browser that it may defer execution of a script.

Although all the popular browsers recognize JavaScript, our pages might attract users with browsers that cannot process JavaScript scripts. Such browsers display the JavaScript code in the browser window. Since this is unsightly, programmers embed scripts inside HTML comment tags. Browsers that recognize JavaScript scripts ignore the comments and execute the script; browsers that cannot process JavaScript ignore the script. The statement

```
<!-- Conceal from non-JavaScript Browsers
```

begins the HTML comment. The JavaScript script appears immediately after the comment. From this point on, The browser is processing the script, so we cannot end the HTML comment directly. The HTML comment must be embedded inside a JavaScript comment. The statement immediately before the **</SCRIPT>** statement ends the HTML comment. The statement is **//-->**.

The JavaScript script contains only two statements:

```
window.document.write("Hello, World Wide Web!");
```

and

```
window.document.write("<BR> <I>This is SAF</I>");
```

The first statement prints the message *Hello, World Wide Web!* on the page. The second statement inserts a **
** tag and then writes *This is SAF* in italics. Notice the use of HTML tags in this statement.

Creating, Running, and Correcting the Sample JS page

I would like you to try your hand at creating and running this program. Although you could copy the program from the accompanying CD, you will learn more if you type in the example yourself. With any luck, you will make several mistakes. Here are the steps to follow:

1. Create the page.   Using your favorite text editor, enter the code shown in Figure 8.2. Make sure that the file is written in plain text or ASCII. Save the file under the name `firstJS.html` or `firstJS.htm`.

2. Load the page into a browser.   Open up a browser and enter the page's name into the `Net-Site:` or `Location:` space. The browser must be capable of handling JavaScript (JS) scripts. Both Netscape 2.0 (or higher) and Internet Explorer 3.0 (or higher) recognize JavaScript scripts.

3. Correct errors.   If you entered the script correctly, you should see a page that resembles the one displayed in Figure 8.1. Now remove the ending quotation mark from the statement

```
window.document.write("<BR><I>This is SAF</I>);
```

JavaScript expects matched quotation marks, so this triggers an error when the page is re-loaded. How the error is handled depends on the browser and the computer system. Generally, browsers won't execute a script with errors, and they won't print an error message. This means that you must carefully search through your script to find the erroneous code. Both Internet Explorer and Netscape Navigator let the user turn on *error debugging*. For example, to activate debugging on IE 4.0, select **Edit>Preferences>WebBrowser>WebContent**. Under **"ActiveContent, Active scripting error alerts"** select **"Expert(Debugging)"**. Click on the **"Show unsupported scripting language errors"** box. Once you activate debugging, Internet Explorer displays an error box like the one shown in Figure 8.4. This box clearly indicates that we have an unterminated string constant on line 6. Unfortunately, Internet Explorer counts only JavaScript lines. This means that *Line 6* is the 6th JavaScript line, not the 6th line in the file. This makes error correction a challenge.

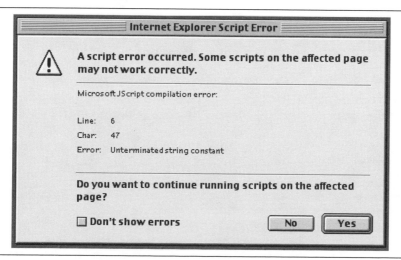

Figure 8.4 An Internet Explorer Error Box

Netscape Navigator uses a different approach to error handling. An error condition is signaled by a message in the status line at the bottom of the browser window. If you're not paying attention, it's easy to miss the message. To display the error messages, activate the error window by typing **javascript:** into the *Netsite:* window as illustrated in Figure 8.5.

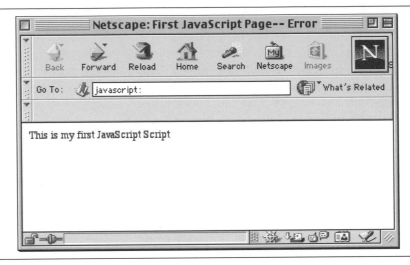

Figure 8.5 Handling Errors in Netscape, Part I

Netscape Navigator opens a *Communicator Console* window that lists the JavaScript errors. Not only does Netscape display the offending lines, it uses a caret to indicate the probable loca-

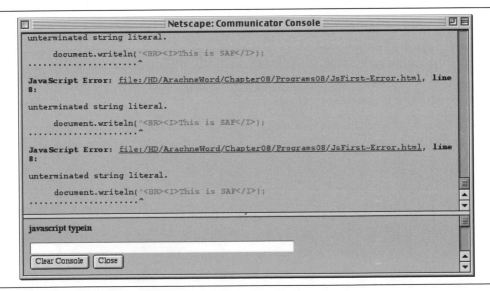

Figure 8.6 Handling Errors in Netscape, part 2

tion of the error. Figure 8.6 shows the *Communicator Console* for the *JavaScript Error* page.

The Communicator Console keeps a running list of errors. Figure 8.6 indicates that the last error occurred on line 8. A small caret appears underneath the start of the error. The error portion of the line is written in red.

Common JavaScript Errors

Common sources of JavaScript errors involve the following aspects of the code:

Case.　Unlike HTML, JavaScript is case sensitive. This means that JavaScript distinguishes between upper-case and lower-case letters. Most built-in features of JavaScript must be written in lower case.

Matching Quotation Marks.　JavaScript expects beginning and ending quotation marks. In Figure 8.6, the error message indicates that we have an `unterminated string literal`. The human translation of this error message is, "You forgot one of your quotation marks."

Errors in the HTML Tags.　Errors can also occur in the `<SCRIPT>...</SCRIPT>` tags. For example, the following tag has a missing quotation mark:

```
<SCRIPT LANGUAGE = "JavaScript>
```

Because this is an HTML error and not a JavaScript error, the JavaScript interpreter will not issue an error message. The browser will also not load the script.

AN INTRODUCTION TO OBJECTS

JavaScript belongs to a family of programming languages referred to as "object-oriented" (OO). An object-oriented approach models entities (objects). The model not only captures an object's crucial characteristics, but also controls a user's access to these characteristics. In the real world, an object could be a person, place, or thing. This characterization also applies to the cyberworld, but here objects are much more likely to be things.

JavaScript uses a specialized vocabulary to describe objects. Objects contain *properties*, *methods*, and *event handlers*. Objects are also related to each other hierarchically. In the remainder of this chapter, we examine several simple properties and methods of the `window` object.

Properties

A **property** is an attribute of an object. As an example, think about a circle that is drawn on a Web page. This circle has a center point, denoted by x (row) and y (column) coordinates, and it has a radius. The *radius* and the (x, y) coordinates are properties of the circle object. Similarly, JavaScript contains a **string** object that is defined as a sequence of characters. All JavaScript strings have a **length** property, which stores the number of characters in the string.

Accessing a property requires both the object name and the property name. Figure 8.7 illustrates this accessing technique with the **defaultStatus** property of the **window** object. The object's name appears to the left of the dot (.) separator; the property appears to the right of the separator.

Before we proceed, some explanation is in order, because I'm sure you're wondering about **window** objects and **defaultStatus** properties. First, let's consider the **window** object. Open your favorite browser, and look at the information that appears on the page. If you are in Netscape, you should see a menu bar containing **File**, **Edit**, **View**, and related options. You also should see a

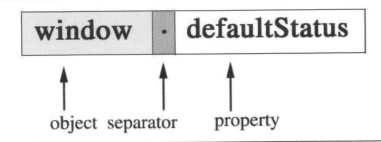

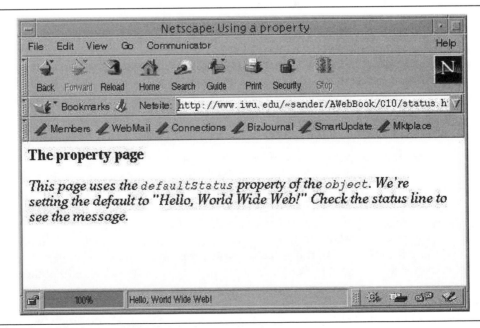

Figure 8.7 The `window.defaultStatus` property

tool bar containing a series of buttons labeled **Back**, **Forward**, **Home**, and so on. Your page should have scrollbars on the right side and bottom of the page and a status line on the bottom. Your page also contains the page's contents, which appears to the left of and above the scrollbars. This page, with everything that it contains (menu bars, tool bars, scroll bars, status line, and so on), is a **window** object to JavaScript.

The **defaultStatus** property refers to the message that appears in the status line of a page. Web page developers frequently use the status line to provide additional information on page links. A developer can place a default message in the status line, as illustrated in Figure 8.8. In this example, the message *Hello, World Wide Web!* appears in the status line at the bottom of the page.

To reproduce this page, place the desired message inside quotation marks. (The message is now a JavaScript string.) Next, assign the string to the **window.defaultStatus** property by using

Figure 8.8 The `window.defaultStatus` Property Page

the JavaScript assignment operator, =. The message appears to the right of the assignment operator, and the property appears to the left. Figure 8.9 shows the complete code for this page.

```
<HTML>
<HEAD><TITLE>Using a property</TITLE></HEAD>
<BODY BGCOLOR = 'white'>
<B>The property page</B>
<P>
<I> This page uses the <TT>defaultStatus</TT> property of the <TT>object</TT>. We're setting the
default to "Hello, World Wide Web!"  Check the status line to see the message.</I>
<P>
<SCRIPT LANGUAGE = "JavaScript">
<!-- Conceal from non-JS browsers
    window.defaultStatus = "Hello, World Wide Web!";
/-->
</SCRIPT>
</BODY></HTML>
```

Figure 8.9 HTML Code for the *Property* Page

Methods

Methods are pieces of code that extract information about an object or change an object's properties. Verbs are frequently used to name a method. For example, **write()**, **open()**, and **close()** are names of JavaScript methods. Notice the parentheses that appear after the method names. JavaScript properties are easily distinguished from methods because methods always use parentheses, but properties never use them. The parentheses hold the information required by the method. Each piece of information is called a **parameter**. Some methods require no parameters, some require a single parameter, and some require several parameters.

Figure 8.10 contains an illustration of the **write()** method of the **document** object. The method always contains a single parameter, which is a JavaScript string. The string appearing in Figure 8.10 is referred to as a *literal*, because the page displays exactly what appears between the quotation marks.

The code in Figure 8.10 indicates that **document** contains a method called **write()**. This method writes whatever appears between the quotation marks onto the browser page. Figure 8.10

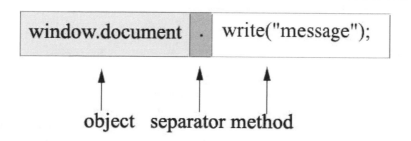

Figure 8.10 The **window.document.write()** method, unraveled

also indicates that the **document** object is a property of the **window** object. Thus, this single statement includes both a method and a property. In addition, notice the semicolon (;) appearing at the end of the **window.document.write()** method. The semicolon turns this method into a JavaScript statement. JavaScript prefers a terminating semicolon at the end of each statement.

Object Hierarchies

JavaScript objects do not exist independently of each other. Instead, they are related in a hierarchical fashion that resembles an organizational chart. Within this hierarchy, the **window** object is the one of highest order. The **document** object is one property of the **window** object. This relation is illustrated in Figure 8.11.

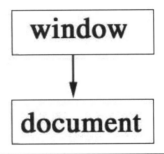

Figure 8.11 The **window** and **document** Objects

JavaScript programmers frequently omit the **window** object as a prefix when using **window** methods or properties. For example, the statement

```
window.document.write("Hello, World Wide Web!");
```

can be written as

```
document.write("Hello, World Wide Web!");
```

Similarly, the statement

```
window.defaultStatus = "Hello, World Wide Web!";
```

can be written as

```
defaultStatus = "Hello, World Wide Web!";
```

THREE LITTLE BOXES:
THE *ALERT, CONFIRM,* **AND** *PROMPT* **WINDOWS**

Browsers often use three small windows to send information to or request information from the user. The boxes are known as the *alert, confirm,* and *prompt* windows. The JavaScript **window** object contains three methods that create these miniature pop-up windows. These methods are easy to use and to understand, so we will use them throughout the next several chapters to obtain input from users and send them information.

The *Alert Window* Page

As its name implies, the **alert()** method creates a pop-up window that alerts the user to some special condition. Netscape displays this alert window as an *error* box; Internet Explorer identifies it only as an *alert*. Figure 8.12 shows an Internet Explorer alert window. The window remains on the page until the user clicks the *OK* button.

The alert window contains a single statement that identifies the window as an alert window. The **alert()** method lets us place any message in this popup window. Figure 8.13 contains the HTML and JavaScript for the *Alert Window* page. The relevant JavaScript statements are highlighted.

```
<HTML><HEAD><TITLE>The alert box</TITLE></HEAD>
<BODY BGCOLOR = 'white'>
<B>The <TT>window.alert()</TT> method</B>
<P>
<I> This page displays an alert box.
    Click the OK button to close the box</I>
<P>
<SCRIPT LANGUAGE = "JavaScript">
<!--
    window.alert("This is an alert box");
//-->
</SCRIPT>
</BODY></HTML>
```

Figure 8.12 The *Alert Window* Page

Figure 8.13 Code for the *Alert Window* Page

A few cautionary notes apply to the **alert()** method. These notes are also relevant to the **confirm()** and **prompt()** methods, which we will we examine shortly.

1. As a precautionary measure, a **<P>** tag should be placed before a JS script. Otherwise, the browser might not display text that appears before the script until after the user responds to the window.

2. The string passed as a parameter to an **alert(), prompt(),** or **confirm()** method should not contain HTML tags, such **<B>** or **
**. The tags would be displayed literally in the pop-up windows.

3. The *new line* character, **\n**, can be used to insert lines in the string parameter. For example, the following statement displays two lines of text in the alert window:

```
alert("This is an alert box.\n Look at the two lines.");.
```

The *Confirm Window* Page

The confirm window presents a question and two buttons, *OK* and *Cancel*, to the user. If the user clicks the *OK* button, the browser sends (returns) a *true* to the script. If the user clicks the *Cancel* button, the browser sends (returns) a *false* to the script. Figure 8.14(a) shows a typical confirm window. The window asks users whether they want to learn about confirm boxes. Figure 8.14(b)

(a) The Confirm Window

(b) After Clicking OK

Figure 8.14 The *Confirm Window* Page

shows the page after a user has clicked the *OK* button. Notice the new line added to the page. The line indicates that the user clicked the *OK* button (*true*). If the user had clicked the *Cancel* button, the page would have printed *You picked false*.

Unlike an alert window, a confirm window saves the user's choice as a *true/false* value. To access this value, we must create a variable. In JavaScript, or any other programming language, a variable is just an identifier associated with a memory location. It lets us store or change information without knowing the physical (binary) address of the information within the computer. Creating a variable is easy in JavaScript: We simply put the variable name of our choice to the left of the assignment operator (=) and the value we wish to place in the variable to the right of the assignment operator. For example, to create a variable named *animal* that holds the name of a pet, we write

```
animal = "Pandora";
```

We can explicitly indicate that we are creating a new variable by placing a **var** in front of the variable name. The JavaScript statement is

```
var animal = "Pandora";
```

Processing a Confirm Window

Creating and responding to a confirm window is a three-step process.

Step 1. Call the `window.confirm()` *Method.*   Call the `window.confirm()` method with an appropriate question passed as a parameter. The call used in Figure 8.14 is

```
confirm("Would you like to learn how to create confirm boxes?");
```

Step 2. Store the User's Response in a Variable.   Create a variable to hold the user's answer. Place this variable on the left-hand side of an assignment operator. Place the `confirm()` method on the right-hand side. The *Confirm Window* page uses *reply* as the variable. The code that invokes the `confirm()` method and places the returned value in *reply* is

```
var reply =confirm("Would you like to learn how to create confirm boxes?");
```

Notice that JS is not picky about spaces (blanks) before or after the assignment operator.

Step 3. Process the User's Information.   The *Confirm Window* page appends the user's response to the string literal *You picked*. Although the `document.write()` method requires a single string parameter, we can use the concatenation operator (+) to create one string from several. The `document.write()` call used in the *Confirm* Window page is

```
document.write("<P>You picked " + reply + ".");
```

The parameter creates a new string by concatenating three distinct strings.
Figure 8.15 shows the complete code for the *Confirm Window* page displayed in Figure 8.14.

```
<HTML>
<HEAD><TITLE> The Confirm Box</TITLE></HEAD>
<BODY BGCOLOR = "white">
<B>The <TT>window.confirm()</TT> method</B>
<P>
<I>Click a button to close the box.</I>
<P>
<SCRIPT LANGUAGE = "JavaScript">
<!--
 var reply = confirm("Would you like to learn how to create confirm boxes?");
  document.write("<P>You picked " + reply + ".");
//-->
</SCRIPT> </BODY></HTML>
```

Figure 8.15 Code for the *Confirm Window* Page

The *Prompt Window* Page

A *prompt* window contains a question, a small message space called a *text field*, and three clickable buttons (*OK, Clear,* and *Cancel*). The text field displays a default message, **"undefined"**, which must be cleared before the user can enter information. The buttons determine how the browser handles the information that currently resides in the text field.

Clear.   Pressing this button erases everything that appears in the text field. The value in the text field is set to **null**. Clicking the *Clear* button does not close the window. The user must press either the *OK* or the *Cancel* button to accomplish this task.

OK. Pressing this button closes the prompt window and sends the information appearing in the text field to the JS script. Closing the window with an empty text field returns a **null** value to the JS script. As its name implies, **null** indicates that "nothing" was sent to the script.

Cancel. Pressing this button cancels the current operation. The window is closed and a **null** value is returned to the JS script, no matter what was in the text field at the time.

Figure 8.16(a) shows the *Prompt Window* page after a user has entered her name, but before she has selected a button. Figure 8.16(b) shows the page after the *OK* button was clicked.

(a) The Prompt Window

(b) After clicking OK

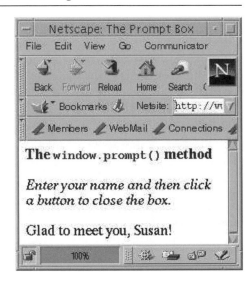

Figure 8.16 The *Prompt Window* Page

Creating a prompt window requires the same three-step process used to create a confirm window.

Step 1. Use the **window.prompt()** method to present a question to the user. This method has two parameters, the second of which is optional. The first parameter holds the question, usually written as a string literal. The second parameter specifies the initial value for the text field. If the second parameter is omitted, the value **"undefined"** is written in the text field. Most programmers prefer to use a null string as the initial value. Two consecutive occurrences of a double quotation mark create this string. The code is

```
prompt("What's your first name?", "")
```

Step 2. Create a variable to hold the user's answer. The variable name appears on the left-hand side of the assignment operator. The **prompt()** method appears on the right-hand side.

Step 3. Print a message with the user's reply.

Figure 8.17 contains the JS Script for the *Prompt Window* page.

```
<HTML><HEAD><TITLE> The Prompt Box</TITLE></HEAD>
<BODY BGCOLOR = "white">
<B>The <TT>window.prompt()</TT> method</B>
<P>
<I>Enter your name and then click a button to close the box.</I>
<P>
<SCRIPT LANGUAGE = "JavaScript">
<!--
  var name = prompt("What's your first name?", "");
  document.write("<P>Glad to meet you, " + name + "!");
//-->
</SCRIPT> </BODY></HTML>
```

Figure 8.17 Code for the *Prompt Window* Page

EVENT HANDLERS

Event handlers are code segments that execute when a user performs some action (known as an event). Typical events include clicking a mouse button, moving the mouse over a link, and opening or closing a window. Event handlers always begin with the word **on**. Examples of event handlers include **onMouseOver**, **onMouseOut**, **onClick**, **onLoad**, and **onUnLoad**. Figure 8.18 contains an example of a JavaScript event handler.

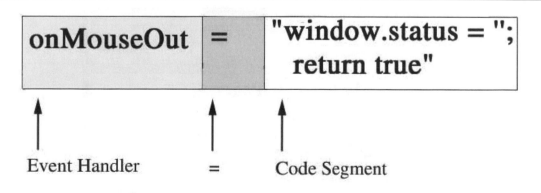

Figure 8.18 The **onMouseOut** Event Handler

As Figure 8.18 indicates, the name of the event handler appears on left-hand side of the assignment operator. The code that implements the event handler appears on the right-hand side of the assignment operator and is enclosed by double quotation marks.

The **onMouseOut** event handler is usually coupled with the **onMouseOver** event handler. The **onMouseOver** event handler executes code when the mouse passes over an area of the page; the **onMouseOut** handler executes code when the mouse passes out of an area. The code segment appearing in Figure 8.18 executes two JavaScript statements when the mouse passes out of the indicated area.

1. The first statement, **window.status = '';**, sets the **status** property of the **window** object to the empty string. The empty string, also called a null string, is usually denoted by a set of adjoining double quotation marks (**""**); here however, they would trigger an error, because JavaScript would view the first double quotation mark as the end of the event handler code. Therefore, we replace the double quotation marks with **two single quotation marks**. (It might look like a double quotation mark, but it's really two single ones.) The **status** and **defaultStatus** properties both change the message in the status line. They differ in one way: The **status** property must be associated with an event handler, such as **onMouseOut** or **onMouseOver**; the **defaultStatus** property is not associated with an event handler.

2. The second statement, **return true**, signals the successful completion of the event handler. An event handler that executes without error should always returns the value *true*. Returning the value *false* denotes an error condition.

A SIMPLE *MOUSE HANDLER* PAGE

As indicated previously, web page developers frequently write descriptive messages that are displayed in the status line whenever the mouse passes over a link. Figure 8.19 contains the *Favorite Links* page discussed in Chapter 5. When the snapshot of the page was taken, the mouse was passing over the *Molly's Adventure* link. Notice the message that appears in the status line of the browser. A different message appears as the mouse passes over each link. As the mouse moves out of a link area, the message is set to the null string.

Figure 8.19 A *Simple Mouse Handler* Page

Event handlers use embedded JavaScript. An embedded script does not require **<SCRIPT>** and **</SCRIPT>** tags. The script is placed inside an HTML tag. To create the status line messages in the *Simple Mouse Handler* page, we place the JavaScript event handlers inside the **<A HREF>** tags.

Let's think about the *Molly's Adventure* link in Figure 8.17. In Chapter 5, we created the link with the following **<A HREF>** tag:

```
<A HREF = "adventure.html"> Molly's Adventure</A>
```

When the mouse moves over this link, the status line should display the string. The modified page appearing in Figure 8.19 uses the **onMouseOver** event handler to display the message *Molly Muskrat visits a magic Mango Grove* in the status line. Figure 8.20 contains the code for this event handler.

```
onMouseOver = "window.status='Molly Muskrat visits a magic Mango Grove';
                              return true"
```

Figure 8.20 The **onMouseOver** Event Handler for the *Molly's Adventure* Link

Let's examine this code in more detail.

1. Notice that the event handler appears on the left-hand side of the assignment operator and the code that it executes appears on the right-hand side. A pair of double quotation marks always surrounds the code for the event handler.

2. The event handler returns a *true* value to indicate that it successfully completed its task.

The **onMouseOut** event handler for our *Molly's Adventure* link changes the window's status property to a null string. Figure 8.21 contains the complete set of event handlers for *Molly's Adventure* link.

```
<A HREF = "adventure.html"
 onMouseOver = "window.status='Molly Muskrat visits a magic Mango Grove';
                               return true"
   onMouseOut = "window.status = ''; return true">Molly's Adventure</A>
```

Figure 8.21 Molly's Adventure Link with Event Handlers

The event handlers for the remaining links are created in a similar manner. Figure 8.22 contains the URLs and messages for the remaining link fields. Try to write the event handlers for these links before looking at the code appearing in Figure 8.23.

URL	Message
crosswd.html	*A HTML and JavaScript Crossword puzzle*
gbterms.html	*Green Bay Packer Football Definitions*

Figure 8.22 URLs and Messages for Link Fields

Figure 8.23 contains the complete code to produce the new version of the *Favorite Links* page.

```
<!DOCTYPE HTML PUBLIC "-//W3C//DTD HTML 4.0 Transitional//EN">
<HTML>
<HEAD><TITLE>Button Tables</TITLE></HEAD>
<BODY BGCOLOR = "white" LINK = "black">
<TABLE>
<CAPTION><H1>My Favorite Pages</H1></CAPTION>
<TR>
<TD>
<TABLE BORDER = "5" CELLSPACING = "5" CEllPADDING = "5" BGCOLOR = "#CC9999">
<TR><TD WIDTH = "90">
<A HREF = "adventure.html"
 onMouseOver = "window.status='Molly Muskrat visits a magic Mango Grove';
                                    return true"
   onMouseOut = "window.status = ''; return true">Molly's Adventure</A>
</TD></TR></TABLE></TD>
<TD>
<TABLE BORDER = "5" CELLSPACING = "5" CEllPADDING = "5" BGCOLOR = "#FFFFCC">
<TR><TD WIDTH = "90">
<A HREF = "crosswd.html"
 onMouseOver = "window.status='An HTML and JavaScript Crossword puzzle';
 return true"
   onMouseOut = "window.status = ''; return true"> CrossWord Puzzle</A>
</TD></TR></TABLE></TD>
<TD>
<TABLE BORDER = "5" CELLSPACING = "5" CEllPADDING = "5" BGCOLOR = "#33FFFF">
<TR><TD WIDTH = "90">
<A HREF = "gbterms.html"
 onMouseOver = "window.status='Green Bay Packer Football Definitions';
  return true"
   onMouseOut = "window.status = ''; return true">GB Football</A>
</TD></TR></TABLE></TD>
</TABLE></BODY></HTML
```

Figure 8.23 The Revised *Favorite Links Page*

➤ EXERCISES

1. **Check out the source code for the cnn.com page**. Use the *View > Page Source* option of your browser to examine the code for the page. Notice the multiple uses of JavaScript.

2. Find several Web pages that you like. Use the *View > Page Source* or *View > Frame Source* options on your browser to determine whether the page uses JavaScript.

3. Start your JavaScript notebook by copying your corrected program to it. If you made a mistake, add the mistake, the error message, and the correction.

4. Redo the sample program, but purposely add mistakes. Trying leaving out quotation marks or capitalizing part of the **document.write()** method. Forget a parenthesis. Examine the error messages. Keep a list of them and the solutions.

5. Modify the first program so that it prints out your name. Add your street address and city on separate lines.

6. **The title property.** The JS **document** object contains a **title** property that holds the title of the web page as contained between the HTML **<TITLE>** and **</TITLE>** tags. Although you cannot change the title, you can print it out. Write a page that prints out the page's title.

7. **An alert() Page.** Create a page with an **alert()** window that displays the following message:

   ```
   JavaScript requires:
   Practice
   Vocabulary
   Tools
   ```

8. **An alert() Page.** Create a page with an **alert()** window that contains a line of JavaScript code with an error.

9. **An alert() Page.** Create a page with an **alert()** window that reminds the user to keep a notebook of JavaScript code.

10. **A confirm() Page.** Create a page with a **confirm()** window that displays the following message: *Have you practiced your JavaScript today?* Print a message similar to the one displayed in Figure 8.12(b). Look at the results when you click the *OK* button. Compare them to the results you obtain when you click the *Cancel* button.

11. **A confirm() Page.** Create a page with two **confirm()** windows. The first window asks the user whether JavaScript requires practice. The second asks the user whether JavaScript is harder than HTML.

12. **A prompt() Page.** Create a page that asks the user to enter a favorite Web language. Print the user's choice on the screen.

13. **A prompt() Page.** Create a page that contains a **prompt()** window that asks the user to enter a first name. Next, create a **prompt()** window that asks the user to enter a last name. (Don't worry! JavaScript only displays a single prompt at a time.) Print out the results in the following manner:

    ```
    First Name: Jane
    Last Name Smith
    ```

14. **A prompt() Page.** Modify the last exercise by adding a **prompt()** window for the middle initial. Print out a message similar to the following:

    ```
    Name: Jane A. Smith
    ```

15. **An onMouseOver, onMouseOut Page.** Pick six of your favorite HTML pages from Part I. Write the links with descriptive messages as an ordered list. Write **onMouseOver** and **onMouseOut** event handlers for each link. You should display a description of the page for the **onMouseOver** event and a null string for the **onMouseOut** event.

16. **An onMouseOver, onMouseOut Page.** Repeat the previous exercise, but place your links in a table. In addition, each link should have an image associated with it; include an **<IMG>** tag with your link.

➤ ▌ **JAVASCRIPT VOCABULARY** ▐

This chapter introduces several concepts related to object-oriented programming. The crucial concepts are the following:

Concatenation.   Concatenation is *string addition*. We use concatenation to "glue" strings together to create a larger string. For example, the statement

```
document.write("Hello " + yourName + "!");
```

creates a string composed of the literals *Hello* and *!* and the contents (value) of the variable *yourName*.

Event Handler.   An event handler responds to actions such as a mouse click, the opening or closing of a page, and the passing of the mouse over a link. We examined the **onMouseOver** and **onMouseOut** event handlers in this chapter.

Literal.   A literal is something that means exactly what the user sees and requires no further explanation. We used several string literals in this chapter. We create a string literal by placing text inside single or double quotation marks. For example, *"This is a string literal."* is an example of a string literal.

Method.   A method is an operation associated with an object. Methods can change an object's properties or report on the status of a property. We examined the **alert()**, **confirm()**, and **prompt()** methods of the **window** object. We also used the **write()** method of the **document** object. A method in an object-oriented programming language corresponds to a verb in a natural language.

Object.   An object corresponds to a noun; it describes a person, a place, or a thing. In JavaScript, an object contains methods, properties, and event handlers. We briefly examined two objects in this chapter: **window** and **document**.

Parameter.   A method can contain one or more parameters. The parameters are placed in a parenthesized list when we use the method. For example, the **alert()** method uses a single parameter. This parameter contains the message that we wish to display in the alert window. By contrast, the **prompt()** method contains two parameters, the second of which is optional. The first parameter contains the message that we wish to display in the prompt window. The second parameter can contain a default value for the prompt window's text field.

Property.   A property is a noun that describes an attribute of an object. The **document** object is a property of the **window** object.

String.   A string is a sequence of characters. We use strings to display messages in JavaScript. JavaScript uses **null** to indicate that a string is empty—that is, that it contains no value.

Variable.   A variable is a name that we give to a memory location. We use variables to store information used by, or obtained from, a script. We use the assignment operator to place a value in a variable. For example, the statement

```
var day = "April 16, 2000";
```

creates a variable, *day*, that contains the string *"April 16, 2000"*.

9 Arithmetic Statements

MATHEMATICAL FOUNDATIONS

Web pages frequently require mathematical calculations. For example, international weather pages offer to calculate the Fahrenheit temperature for "Celsius-challenged" Americans. A food page might offer to calculate the percentage of calories from fat. A geometry page might let students check their calculations for the areas of standard shapes.

The JavaScript Arithmetic Operators

Programming-language designers use the *"Law of Least Surprises"* when implementing a language. This law states that the designer should confuse the least number of programmers for the smallest amount of time. When it comes to mathematical formulas, we all know that mathematics has a set of rules for evaluating equations. The principles of precedence and associativity determine the evaluation sequence. Although no programming language defies the laws of mathematics, a designer is free to add new operators if they "make sense." Figure 9.1 contains the arithmetic operators for JavaScript. The operators are arranged in order of precedence. Operators within the same box have the same precedence.

Mathematical	JavaScript	Description
	++	Increment
	--	Decrement
-	-	Unary Minus
× •	*	Multiplication
÷	/	Division
	%	Modulus
+	+	Addition
-	-	Subtraction
=	=	Assignment
	*= /= %= += -=	Combined Assignment

Figure 9.1 Mathematical Operators and Their JavaScript Equivalents

As Figure 9.1 indicates, JavaScript provides operators for the standard mathematical operations of addition, subtraction, multiplication, and division. There is no operator for exponentiation because JavaScript uses a method in the **Math** object to handle this operation. JavaScript also provides several "new" operators, which are shaded in Figure 9.1. For instance, there are increment and decrement operators, which we use whenever we wish to add or subtract by one. They enable us to abbreviate statements like x = x + 1 or y = y - 1 to x++ and y--, respectively. Similarly, there are several combined assignment operators, they let us abbreviate, for example x = x + 2 or n = n / 2 to x += 2 and n /= 2, respectively. Finally, JavaScript provides a modulus operator that produces the remainder after an integer division.

A Brief Review of Precedence

Before we create our sample arithmetic pages, let's quickly review the mathematical rules of precedence. These rules state the following:

Rule 1.　Operators are evaluated in the order of their precedence; higher-order operators are evaluated before lower order operators.

Rule 2.　Operators of the same precedence are evaluated according to their associativity. Left-associative operators (addition, subtraction, multiplication, division, and modulus) evaluate same-precedence operators from left to right. Right-associative operators (assignment) evaluate operators from right to left.

Rule 3.　Parentheses are used to override precedence.

Rule 4.　Parenthesized expressions are evaluated from the innermost to the outermost set of parentheses.

A *Simple Precedence* Page

To illustrate the mathematical operators, we create a small JavaScript script that evaluates two mathematical expressions. Figure 9.2 contains a sample page.

Figure 9.3 lists the arithmetic expressions and the anticipated results. The results are evaluated in a series of substeps that illustrate the order of precedence of the operators.

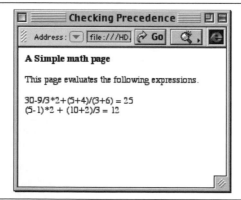

Figure 9.2 A *Simple Precedence* Page

Arithmetic Expression	Anticipated Result
`30-9/3*2+(5+4)/(3+6);`	=30-3*2+(9)/(9) =30-6+1 =25
`(5-1)*2 + (10+2)/3`	=(4)*2+(12)/3 =8+4 =12

Figure 9.3 Arithmetic Expressions and Anticipated Results

Figure 9.4 contains the HTML and JavaScript code that produces the *Simple Precedence* page. The JS script contains two string variables that represent the left-hand side of the expressions appearing in Figure 9.2. The first string, *string1*, was assigned a value of **"30-9/3*2+(5+4)/(3+6)"**. The second string, *string2*, was assigned a value of **"(5-1)*2 + (10+2)/3"**. The JS script also contains two arithmetic variables, *expression1* and *expression2*. These variables hold the results of the arithmetic expressions depicted in the *Simple Precedence* page. The assignment statements that create these variables are the following:

```
var expression1 = 30-9/3*2+(5+4)/(3+6);
var expression2 = (5-1)*2 + (10+2)/3;
```

The string variables display the expressions assigned to the arithmetic variables. Notice the use of quotation marks to encase the string literals assigned to *string1* and *string2*. This contrasts sharply with the arithmetic variables, *expression1* and *expression2*, which do not use quotation marks.

```
<HTML>
<HEAD><TITLE>Checking Precedence</TITLE></HTML>
<BODY BGCOLOR = "white">
<B>A Simple math page</B>
<P>
This page evaluates the following expressions.
<P>
<SCRIPT LANGUAGE = "JavaScript">
<!--
  var string1 = "30-9/3*2+(5+4)/(3+6)";
  var string2 = "(5-1)*2 + (10+2)/3";
  var expression1 =30-9/3*2+(5+4)/(3+6);
  var expression2 = (5-1)*2 + (10+2)/3;
  document.write(string1 + " = " + expression1);
  document.write("<BR>" + string2 + " = " + expression2);
//-->
</SCRIPT>
</BODY>
</HTML>
```

Figure 9.4 Code for the *Simple Precedence* Page

The *Test Score* Page

Percentages pop up in the strangest places. Football fanatics see them in a quarterback's percentage of completed passes, which is defined as

$$\frac{\text{Completed passes}}{\text{Total Passes}} \cdot 100$$

Dieters confront them when calculating the percentage of calories from fat. This is defined as

$$\frac{\text{Fat grams} \cdot 9}{\text{Total Calories}} \cdot 100$$

Students see them whenever they obtain a test grade. Grades are usually defined as the percentage of correct answers to total questions. Mathematically, this is defined as

$$\frac{\text{Correct Answers}}{\text{Total Questions}} \cdot 100$$

We use the last example to illustrate our first interactive arithmetic Web page. All of these formulas involve simple percentages, so we can easily modify this example to produce pages that calculate completed passes or percentages of calories from fat.

The *Test Score* page uses prompt windows to obtain the correct answers and total questions. Figure 9.5 contains a sample page.

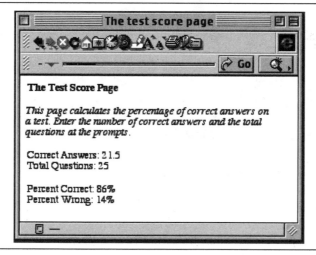

Figure 9.5 The *Test Score* Page

Test Plans

Developing the *Test Score* page requires more planning than our previous pages, because mathematical formulas introduce a new source of errors. In our previous pages, only one type of error plagued us: *syntax errors*. These errors occur whenever a programmer violates a JavaScript grammar rule.

The translation of mathematical formulas to JavaScript arithmetic statements can lead to *logic errors*. As its name implies, a logic error stems from a flaw in the program's design. In other words, the program runs but it produces the wrong results. JavaScript cannot detect these errors: we must develop a test plan to prevent them. A test plan must take into account two distinct types of errors.

Erroneous Data. A mathematical formula could fail to apply to the entire spectrum of numbers. For example, a formula involving division cannot have a denominator of zero. Similarly, a formula for a square root cannot have a negative number under the radical. A well-designed program eliminates the possibility of erroneous data by checking all user input. Erroneous data is trapped in an *error loop*, a topic that we will discuss in Chapter 11.

Erroneous Results. An erroneous result occurs when a programmer translates a mathematical formula incorrectly. We detect these errors by developing test data, that is, a set of input values that we use to determine the correctness of our calculations. Simple formulas, like the test score equation, typically require a single set of test values. More complicated formulas, like the quadratic equation, might require several data sets. We "plug" our test data into the equation by hand or by calculator, so that we know what the answer should be. If the program produces a different answer, we recheck both our hand calculations and the computer's output. When the answers agree, we can be confident that our program works correctly.

Figure 9.6 contains a test plan for the *Test Score* page. Compare the test data results with the results displayed in Figure 9.5.

Erroneous Data	Test Data		
1. Total Questions is 0	Correct Answer	$= 21.5$	
2. Correct Answers $>$ Total Questions	Total Questions	$- 25$	
	%Correct	$- \dfrac{21.5 \cdot 100}{25}$	
		$= .86 \cdot 100$	
		$= 86\%$	
	%Wrong	$= 100 - 86$	
		$= 14\%$	

Figure 9.6 Test plan for the *Test Score* Page

PARSING NUMBERS

When we use a prompt window to obtain user input, JavaScript stores this information as a string. A string is only a sequence of characters; we cannot apply mathematical operators to it. We must convert the string to its numeric equivalent. *Parsing* is the official name for this conversion process, and JavaScript provides two functions that handle it for us. (A *function* is a method that is not attached to any object.)

Integers. For integers, that is, numbers that do not take a decimal point, we use the `parseInt()` function. This function requires a string parameter; it returns the integer equivalent. To use this function, we place a variable on the left of the assignment operator and the `parseInt()` function on the right. For example, the following statement asks the user to enter the total questions, parses this to an integer, and places the result in the variable *total*.

```
var total = parseInt(prompt("Total questions: ", ""));
```

Notice how the **prompt()** method is placed inside the **parseInt()** function. If this appears too complicated, try the following instead:

```
var totalString = prompt("Total questions: ", "");
var total = parseInt(totalString);
```

Floating-Point Numbers. A floating-point number can have a decimal portion. The **parseFloat()** function handles these conversions. For example, if a teacher assigns partial credit for answers, we should use the **parseFloat()** function to obtain the answer. The following statement accomplishes this task:

```
var correct = parseFloat(prompt("Correct answers: ", ""));
```

Again, we can divide this statement into two statements. The first statement would create a variable that holds the string returned by the **prompt()** method. The second statement would convert the string variable created in the first statement to a floating-point variable. The statements are as follows:

```
var correctString = prompt("Correct answers: ", "");
var correct = parseFloat(correctString);
```

Code for the *Test Score* Page

Figure 9.7 contains the code for the *Test Score* page. The code for the JavaScript script is highlighted.

```
<HTML>
<HEAD><TITLE>The test score page </TITLE></HEAD>
<BODY BGCOLOR = "white">
<B>The Test Score Page</B>
<P>
<I> This page calculates the percentage of correct answers on a test. Enter the number of correct
answers and the total questions at the prompts.</I>
<P>
<SCRIPT LANGUAGE =  "JavaScript">
<!--
    var correct = parseFloat(prompt("Correct answers: ", ""));
    var total = parseInt(prompt("Total questions: ", ""));
    var percentCorrect = correct/total*100;
    var percentWrong = 100 - percentCorrect;

    document.write("Correct Answers: " + correct);
    document.write("<BR>Total Questions: " + total);
    document.write("<P>Percent Correct: " + percentCorrect + "%");
    document.write("<BR>Percent Wrong: " + percentWrong + "%");
//-->
</SCRIPT>
</BODY></HTML>
```

Figure 9.7 Code for the *Test Score* page

THE Number OBJECT

At some point in your programming career, you will see a page that resembles the one depicted in Figure 9.8. In this example, the user forgot to enter the number of correct answers at the prompt. Recall that JavaScript returns the **null** string whenever this happens. A null string is clearly *not a number* (**NaN**), and this is what JavaScript tells us in abbreviated form.

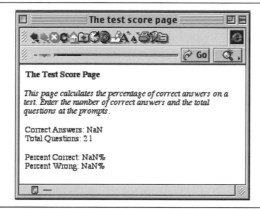

Figure 9.8 The *NaN* (Not a Number) Page

NaN is a property of the **Number** object. This object contains five properties. Two properties, **MAX_VALUE** and **MIN_VALUE**, contain the maximum and minimum values for a browser, respectively. Figure 9.9(a) contains a page that prints the numeric limits of a browser. Figure 9.9(b) shows the results for a Netscape browser running under a Unix operating system.

(a) Code

(b) Sample Page

```
<HTML>
<HEAD> <TITLE>Maxmimum and Minimum Values</TITLE></HEAD>
<BODY BGCOLOR = "white">
<B>The Boundary Page</B>
<P>
<I> Your browser has the following numeric limits.</I>
<P>
<SCRIPT LANGUAGE = "JavaScript">
<!--
   document.write("Largest Number: ");
   document.write(Number.MAX_VALUE);
   document.write("<BR>Smallest Number: ");
   document.write(Number.MIN_VALUE);
//-->
</SCRIPT>
</BODY></HTML>
```

Figure 9.9 The *Boundaries* Page

JavaScript uses the remaining three properties to signal error conditions:

NaN. We already know that JavaScript uses this property to indicate that nonnumeric data was used in a mathematical equation.

POSITIVE_INFINITY indicates the number is greater than **MAX_VALUE**.

NEGATIVE_INFINITY indicates that the number is smaller than **-MAX_VALUE**.

THE Math OBJECT

Previously, we saw that JavaScript does not have an exponentiation operator. We can still carry out exponentiation, because JavaScript has a **Math** object that contains methods that perform a variety of common mathematical tasks. This method also contains several constants. The complete list of **Math** methods and constants is found in Figure 9.10. The constants are written in upper-case letters in deference to Java conventions.

Constants		Math Methods		Trig Methods	
Name	**Meaning**	**Method**	**Meaning**	**Method**	**Meaning**
E	2.718281828459045	`ceil(x)`	Integer above	`cos(x)`	Cosine
PI	3.141592653589793	`floor(x)`	Integer below	`sin(x)`	Sine
LOG10E	.4342944819032518	`round(x)`	Round	`tan(x)`	Tangent
LOG2E	1.4426950408889634	`abs(x)`	Absolute value	`acos(x)`	Arc cosine
SQRT1_2	.7071067811865476	`sqrt(x)`	Square root	`asin(x)`	Arc sine
SQRT2	1.4142135623730951	`min(x,y)`	Minimum	`atan(x)`	Arc tangent
LN2	.6931471805599453	`max(x,y)`	Maximum		
LN10	2.302585092994046	`pow(x,y)`	x^y		

Figure 9.10 The **Math** Object

We end this chapter by developing two programs that use a variety of mathematical operators and **Math** methods.

THE *LET'S MAKE CHANGE* PAGE

Have you ever encountered a store clerk who has trouble returning the correct coinage from a purchase? We're going to solve this problem by creating a page that returns the correct number of quarters, dimes, nickels, and pennies. We assume that the maximum purchase is $1.00; however, we can easily extend the example to include any purchase. Figure 9.11 contains a sample page. In this example, the purchases totaled 56 cents. The output indicates that we are due 44 cents: 1 Quarter, 1 Dime, 1 Nickel, and 4 Pennies. Prove to yourself that this is correct.

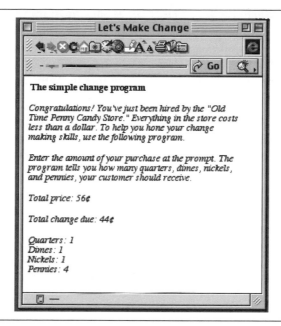

Figure 9.11 The *Let's Make Change* Page

The process of verifying the correctness of Figure 9.11 makes us think about the programming strategy necessary to solve this problem. The most efficient solution involves long division and the remainder (modulus) from division. Figure 9.12 indicates the correct approach.

As Figure 9.12 indicates, we begin by dividing the total change due (44 cents) by the value of a quarter (25 cents). The quotient (1) is the number of quarters the customer receives. The remainder (19) is plugged into the dime equation. The second equation divides the value of a dime (10 cents) by the remaining change. This gives us 1 dime and a remainder of 9 cents. We divide the 9 cents by the value of a nickel (5 cents). This gives us 1 nickel and a remainder of 4 cents. The remainder is the number of pennies. Try using this approach with a total purchase of 23 cents. What answer did you receive? (You should get 3 quarters and 2 pennies.)

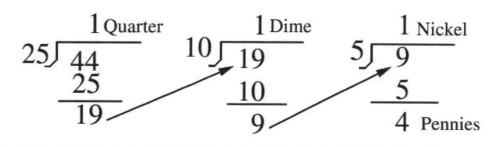

Figure 9.12 Change-Making Logic

The JavaScript solution to the *Let's Make Change* page must mimic our pencil and paper approach. We must perform the following steps:

Perform an integer division. An integer division discards the fractional portion of the result. By design, JavaScript retains the fractional portion, so we use the **Math.floor()** method to reduce the result to the lowest integer. For example, the statement that finds the correct number of quarters is

```
var quarters = Math.floor(pennies / 25);
```

In this statement, *pennies* refer to the current number of pennies.

Find the remaining pennies. We use a modulus operation to find the remaining number of pennies. For example, the statement that finds the remaining pennies after the quarters have been extracted is

```
pennies = pennies % 25;
```

These two statements are repeated for dimes and nickels, with appropriate changes in the variable names. The pennies are whatever remains after the quarters, dimes, and nickels have been extracted. The complete code for the *Let's Make Change* page appears in Figure 9.13.

```
<HTML>
<HEAD><TITLE>Let's Make Change</TITLE></HEAD>
<BODY BGCOLOR = "white">
<B>The simple change program</B>
<P>
<I>Congratulations! You've just been hired by the "Old Time Penny Candy Store." Everything in the
store costs less than a dollar. To help you hone your change making skills, use the following program.
<P>
Enter the amount of your purchase at the prompt. The program tells you how many quarters, dimes,
nickels, and pennies, your customer should receive.
<P>
<SCRIPT LANGUAGE = "JavaScript">
<!--
    var price = parseFloat(prompt("Enter the purchase price: ", ""));
    var pennies = 100 - price;  // save the price
    var amountChange = pennies;

    var quarters = Math.floor(pennies / 25);
    pennies = pennies % 25;
    var dimes = Math.floor(pennies / 10);
    pennies %= 10;

    var nickels = Math.floor(pennies / 5);
    pennies %= 5;

    document.write("Total price: " + price + "&cent;");
    document.write("<P>Total change due: " + amountChange + "&cent;<P>");
    document.write("Quarters: " + quarters);
    document.write("<BR>Dimes: " + dimes);
    document.write("<BR>Nickels: " + nickels);
    document.write("<BR>Pennies: " + pennies);
//-->
</SCRIPT></BODY></HTML>
```

Figure 9.13 Code for the *Let's Make Change* Page

THE *SALES TAX* PAGE

Our final mathematical example calculates the sales tax and the total price on a single item purchase. The user enters the purchase price and the tax rate (as a percentage). The page prints the purchase price, tax rate, sales tax, and total price. Figure 9.14 contains a sample page. Try to work out the example by hand to verify that the results are correct. Think about the process that you used to check the results.

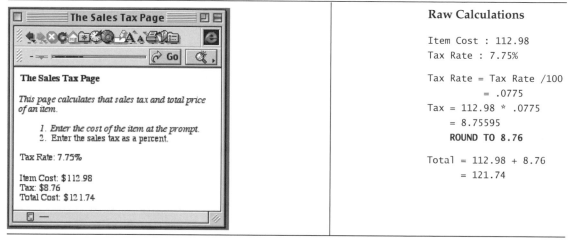

Figure 9.14 The *Sales Tax* Page

Figure 9.15 Test Data for the *Sales Tax* Page

Figure 9.14 shows the results obtained for test data that were developed prior to creating the JS script. The item cost was $112.98, and the tax rate was 7.75% percent. Figure 9.15 the test data and the expected results. Although a total tax of 8.75595 is correct, customers expect a sales tax and total cost in *dollar and cents* format. The test plan indicates that we must round the total tax to two decimal places.

Unfortunately, JavaScript does not round numbers for us. If we want numbers in *dollars and cents* format, we must do it ourselves, via the following steps:

Step1: Multiply by the correct power of 10.   For two decimal places, we multiply the number by `Math.pow(10,2)`; for three decimal places, we multiply by `Math.pow(10,3)`; and so on. In our example, multiplying the tax (8.755595) by 100 yields 875.5595.

Step2: Round the result by using the `Math.round()` method.   Applying this method to the previous step yields 876.

Step3: Divide by the correct power of 10.   For two decimal places, we divide by `Math.pow(10,2)`, and so on. For example, because we multiplied our tax by `Math.pow(10,2)` to start this process, we now divide by `Math.pow(10,2)` to obtain our final answer. Thus, our tax becomes 8.76.

We can combine our three steps into the following line of code:

```
amountTax = Math.round(amountTax * Math.pow(10,2))/Math.pow(10,2);
```

Figure 9.16 contains the complete code for the *Sales Tax* page. As the code indicates, we calculate the tax, *amountTax,* and then round the results. We use the same process to calculate the total cost.

```
<HTML><HEAD><TITLE>The Sales Tax Page</TITLE></HEAD>
<BODY BGCOLOR = "white">
<B>The Sales Tax Page</B>
<P>
<I> This page calculates that sales tax and total price of an item.
<OL>
<LI> Enter the cost of the item at the prompt.
<LI> Enter the sales tax as a percent.
</OL>
<P>
<SCRIPT LANGUAGE = "JavaScript">
<!--
    var itemCost = parseFloat(prompt("Enter the item's cost: ", ""));
    var salesTax = parseFloat(prompt("Enter the sale's tax as a percent: ", ""))/100;
    var amountTax = (itemCost * salesTax);
    var totalCost = itemCost + amountTax;
//convert the numbers to dollars and cents format: $XXXX.XX
    amountTax = Math.round(amountTax * Math.pow(10,2))/Math.pow(10,2);
    totalCost = Math.round(totalCost * Math.pow(10,2))/Math.pow(10,2);
    document.write("Tax Rate: " + salesTax*100 + "%<P>");
    document.write("Item Cost: $" + itemCost);
    document.write("<BR>Tax: $" + amountTax);
    document.write("<BR>Total Cost: $" + totalCost);
//-->
</SCRIPT>
</BODY></HTML>
```

Figure 9.16 Code for the *Sales Tax* Page

➤ **PRACTICE EXERCISES**

The practice exercises range from simple translations of arithmetic formulas to pages that assist foreign travelers. For each exercise, create a "friendly" interface for the user. Make sure that you have test data so that you can verify the correctness of your formula translations.

1. **The *Fat Grams* Page.** Create a page that calculates the percentage of calories from fat. Modify the *Test Score* page (Figure 9.5).

2. **A *Football* Page.** It's NFL time, so grab your sports section and find all the uses of percentages. Typical examples include percentages of completed passes, percentage of wins, and percentage of losses. Create a page that reports the NFL statistics of your favorite team.

3. **The *Circle* Page.** Create a page that calculates the area and circumference of a circle (Figure 9.17). Ask the user to enter the radius. Print the radius, the area, and the circumference.

$$\text{Area} = \text{PI} \cdot R^2$$

$$\text{Circumference} = 2 \cdot \text{PI} \cdot R$$

Figure 9.17 Circle Formulas

4. **The *Roots of the Quadratic Function* Page.** Create a page that calculates the positive and negative roots of the quadratic equation (Figure 9.18). The user should enter the values for a, b, and c. Print these values and the two roots. Use only a test data set that produces two roots.

$$\frac{-b \pm \sqrt{b^2 - 4ac}}{2a}$$

Figure 9.18 Roots of the Quadratic Equation

5. **The *Parallelogram* Page.** Create a page that calculates and displays the area of a parallelogram. (Figure 9.19). Use prompt boxes to obtain the width and height of the parallelogram. Your page should display the width, height, and area with appropriate messages.

$$\textbf{Area = Base} \cdot \textbf{Height}$$

Figure 9.19 Area of a Parallelogram

Display the base, height, and area on the page with appropriate messages.

6. **The *Triangle* Page.** Create a page that calculates and displays the area of a triangle (Figure 9.20). Use prompt windows to obtain the base and height of the triangle.

$$\text{Area} = 1/2 \cdot \text{Base} \cdot \text{Height}$$

Figure 9.20 Area of a Triangle

Your page should display the formula as it appears in Figure 9.20. (Use the HTML character entities.) Display the formula with the user's information. Figure 9.21 shows the desired output.

Triangle Formula: Area = $1/2 \cdot$ Base $\cdot$ Height

Base: 2

Height: 3

Result: $3 = 1/2 \cdot 2 \cdot 3$

Figure 9.21 Sample Output for the *Triangle* Page

7. **The *Trapezoid* Page.** Create a page that calculates and displays the area of a trapezoid (Figure 9.22). Use prompt windows to obtain the two bases and the height. Print the user's responses and the area.

Area $= 1/2 \cdot$ Height $\cdot$ (Base$_1$ + Base$_2$)

where Base$_1$ = width of top

and Base$_2$ = width of bottom

Figure 9.22 Area of a Trapezoid

8. **The *Box* Page.** Create a page that calculates the area and perimeter of a box (Figure 9.23). Use prompt windows to obtain the length and width. Display the length, width, area, and perimeter.

Perimeter $= 2$ (length + width)

Area = length $\cdot$ width

Figure 9.23 Box Formulas

9. **The *Let's Travel to Germany* Page.** Create a page that helps North Americans plan a trip to Germany. Your page should let the user do the following:
   - convert Fahrenheit temperatures to Celsius. (Figure 9.24.)
   - convert Dollars to Marks. (Check the financial page of your newspaper.)

Celsius $= 5/9$(Fahrenheit $- 32$)

Figure 9.24 The Celsius Formula

10. **The *Let's Travel to the USA* Page.** Create a page that reverses the German page. This time, assume that a German visitor wishes to travel to the United States. The Fahrenheit formula is found in Figure 9.25.

Fahrenheit $= 9/5$ Celsius $+ 32$

Figure 9.25 The Fahrenheit Formula

11. **The *Monetary Conversion* Page.** Find the monetary conversion rates in your local paper (or try the New York Times). Ask the user to enter an amount in US dollars. Convert this amount to the foreign currencies listed in the NY Times or in your local paper.

12. Create a page that calculates the formula depicted in Figure 9.26.

$$\sqrt{\frac{n}{2}} + \sqrt{\frac{n}{3}}$$

Figure 9.26 A Square Root Formula

13. Create a page that calculates the formula depicted in Figure 9.27.

$$\sqrt[3]{\frac{PI \cdot n}{2} + \frac{n}{3}}$$

Figure 9.27 A Cube Root Formula

14. Create a page that calculates the formula depicted in Figure 9.28.

$$\left| \frac{(-k) * (i + n)}{2} \right|$$

Figure 9.28 An Absolute Value Formula

15. Create a page that calculates the formulas depicted in Figure 9.29.

A floor Function   **A Ceiling Function**

$$\left\lfloor \frac{1}{4} n^2 - \frac{1}{2} n + c \right\rfloor \qquad \left\lceil \frac{1}{4} n^2 - \frac{1}{2} n + c \right\rceil$$

Figure 9.29 Floor and Ceiling Functions

16. Create a page that calculates the formula depicted in Figure 9.30.

$$z = 3x^3 + 8y^3 + 5x^210y^2 + xy - 5$$

Figure 9.30 An Exponentiation Formula

➤ JAVASCRIPT VOCABULARY

Associativity. Associativity is the order of evaluation of mathematical operators of the same precedence. Addition, subtraction, multiplication, division, and modulus are left-associative operators. The assignment operator is right associative.

Constant. A constant is a name that holds an unchanging value. The **Math** object contains several constants including, **PI** and **E**.

Decrement. The decrement operator subtracts one from a number. The decrement operator in JavaScript is --.

Floating Point. A floating-point number is stored in scientific notation (mantissa and exponent). Floating-point numbers typically have six digits of precision to the right of the decimal point. The **parseFloat()** function converts a string to a floating-point number.

Function. A function executes a set of code. It is similar to a method, except that methods are attached to objects, but functions exist independently of any object.

Increment. The increment operator adds one to a number. The increment operator in JavaScript is ++.

Integer. An integer is a number that does not take a decimal point. Frequently, integers are called *whole numbers* or *counting numbers*. The **parseInt()** function converts a string into an integer.

Law of Least Surprises. The *Law of Least Surprises* states that a language developer should confuse the smallest number of programmers for the least amount of time. In other words, the language constructs reflect common usage.

Logic Error. A logic error is a flaw in the design of a program. A program with logic errors runs, but produces erroneous results.

Modulus. Modulus is the remainder after integer division. The modulus operator in JavaScript is **%**.

Precedence. Precedence indicates the order of evaluation for mathematical operators. The mathematical order indicates that multiplication and division have a higher precedence than addition and subtraction.

Syntax Error. A syntax error is a violation of a grammar rule in a programming language. Browsers will not execute a script if it contains syntax errors.

Test Plan and Data. A test plan specifies the types of errors that the programmer can expect the program to encounter. It also contains a set of test data that the programmer uses to verify the correctness of the program.

10 Selection Statements

The previous JavaScript chapters concentrated on statements that obtained input from the user (**prompt()**), printed results on a web page (**document.write()**), or calculated mathematical equations. These pages were necessarily simple and straightforward; they could not control whether a **prompt()** window appeared, nor repeat a segment of code. Creating interesting and complex web pages requires programming statements that select between alternate segments of code or repeat a series of statements. Selection statements are the focus of this chapter; repetition statements are the topic of the next chapter.

JavaScript provides two distinct types of selection statement:

The **if** *statement.* The **if** statement and its variations (**if ... else, if ... else if...else**) use an expression to select between alternative code segments.

The **switch** *statement.* The **switch** statement executes code segments based on specific values in a selector variable.

Since the **if** statements is the more general of the statements, we begin with it.

THE if STATEMENT

Consider a simple example from every day life. We would like to plant azaleas in our backyard. We live in a climate that is hospitable to azaleas. However, the landscaper told us that we must check the *pH* level of our soil. As he stated:

If the pH level is 5.5 or lower, you can plant azaleas.

The landscaper could have phrased this statement in several other ways, including:

You can grow azaleas only if the pH level of your soil is less than 5.6.

Azaleas require a soil pH level of 5.5. or lower, if they are to survive.

In each case the landscaper's response suggests that we must:

Step 1. Find the *pH* level of our soil.

Step 2. Determine if the *pH* level is less than or equal to 5.5.

Step 3. Plant azaleas only if the answer to Step 2 is *true*.

We can easily transform our landscaping problem into JavaScript code. The implementation introduces the JavaScript **if** statement. Figure 10.1 contains the syntax of this statement.

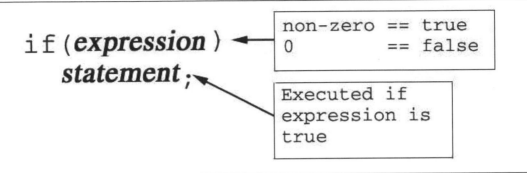

Figure 10.1 Syntax for the **if** statement

As Figure 10.1 indicates, the JavaScript **if** statement contains a parenthesized expression. Although we can view this expression in *true/false* terms, JavaScript does not. In JavaScript, an expression is *false* if it produces a value of zero. An expression is *true* if it produces a value that is not zero. This definition of *true* and *false* is both confusing and a cause of logic errors for beginning programmers.

Relational Operators

In the *Azalea* problem, the landscaper phrased the requirements using mathematical relational operators. These relational operators are found in virtually every programming language. Figure 10.2 contains the JavaScript relational operators. (Notice the lower precedence of the equality and inequality operators.)

Operator	Meaning	
<	Less than	*Highest Precedence*
<=	Less than or equal	
>	Greater than	
>=	Greater than or equal	
==	Equal	*Lowest Precedence*
!=	Not Equal	

Figure 10.2 JavaScript Relational Operators

As Figure 10.2 indicates, the JavaScript relational operators differ slightly from their mathematical counterparts. For example, mathematicians use < and > for the *less than or equal* and *greater than or equal* operators, while JavaScript substitutes <= and >=. Similarly, mathematicians use = for both assignment and equality; while JavaScript uses = for assignment and == for equality.

THE AZALEA PAGE: VERSION 1

We're now ready to translate our *Azalea* problem into a simple Web page. This page asks the user to enter the *pH* level of the soil. We print a message if the soil is suitable for growing azaleas. Figure 10.3 contains two samples of our *Azalea* page. Figure 10.3(a) shows a *pH* level in the correct range for azalea growing. Figure 10.3(b) shows a *pH* level that is above the range.

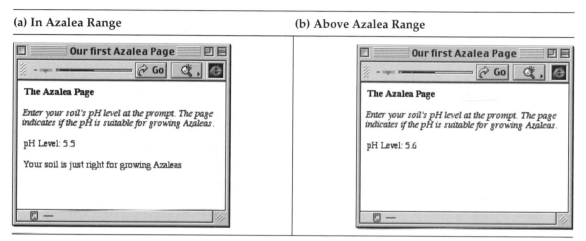

(a) In Azalea Range

(b) Above Azalea Range

Figure 10.3 The *Azalea* Page, version 1

TEST DATA FOR AN if STATEMENT

Figure 10.3 contains sample pages produced by a *true* and a *false* expression. The *pH* levels were not selected randomly. Prior to writing the code, we develop test data for the page. Whenever we selectively execute segments of code, we must check each of the alternatives. Never assume that code works correctly. Inevitably, it is the one piece of code that is not checked that is erroneous. Errors typically occur at the boundaries, so test data should be chosen so that the boundaries are checked. Figure 10.4 shows the test data for the *Azalea* page, version 1. The first test occurs at the upper boundary for azalea growing (5.5). The second test occurs just above this boundary.

Test Case	Anticipated Result
pH = 5.5	Your soil is just right for growing Azaleas
pH = 5.6	*Nothing is printed on the page*

Figure 10.4 Test data for the *Azalea* Page, version 1

Figure 10.5 contains the JS script for the *Azalea* page. The **if** statement is highlighted. The HTML code for the page's title and user's instructions has been omitted to conserve space. The HTML is easily generated by examining Figure 10.3.

```
<SCRIPT LANGUAGE = "JavaScript">
<!--
   var pH = parseFloat(prompt("Enter the pH level of your soil: ", ""));
   document.write("pH Level: " + pH + "<P>");
   if (pH <= 5.5)
   document.write("Your soil is just right for growing Azaleas");
//-->
</SCRIPT>
```

Figure 10.5 JS Script for the *Azalea* Page, version 1

THE AZALEA PAGE: VERSION 2 (THE if...else STATEMENT)

The first version of the *Azalea* page responds only if the *pH* level is in the correct range. Many users will find it disconcerting that an "out-of-range" level is ignored. We solve this problem by printing two different messages. One message indicates that the *pH* level is in the correct range for azaleas. The second message indicates that the *pH* level is too high for azaleas. To implement this code, we use a variation of the **if** statement: the **if...else** statement. Figure 10.6 shows the structure of this statement.

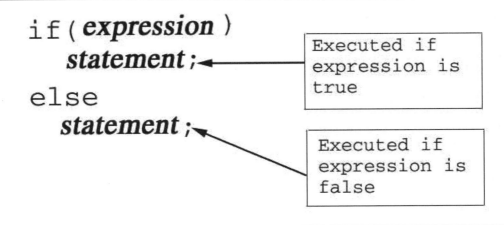

Figure 10.6 The **if...else** Statement

As Figure 10.6 indicates, JavaScript executes the statement after the expression if the expression is *true*. If the expression is *false*, it executes the statement after the **else**. The statements associated with the **if** and **else** blocks are indented to show the structure of the code.

Figure 10.7 illustrates the second version of the *Azalea* page. Figure 10.7(a) shows the page when the user enters a *pH* level in the correct range for growing azaleas. Figure 10.7(b) shows the page when the *pH* level is too high for growing azaleas.

The two versions of the *Azalea* page produce the same results when the expression is *true*. They differ in their approach to a *false* expression. Thus, Version 1 prints nothing when the expression is *false* (Figure 10.3(a)), but Version 2 indicates that the user cannot grow azaleas

(a) In Azalea Range   **(b) Above Azalea Range**

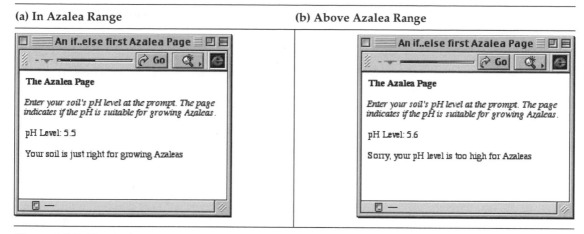

Figure 10.7 The *Azalea* Page, version 2

(Figure 10.7(b)). The two versions of the *Azalea* page use the same set of test data. They differ in their expected results for the **else** clause.

Figure 10.8 contains the JS script for the second version of the *Azalea* page. The **if...else** statement is highlighted.

```
<SCRIPT LANGUAGE = "JavaScript">
<!--
    var pH = parseFloat(prompt("Enter the pH level of your soil: ", ""));
    document.write("pH Level: " + pH + "<P>");
    if (pH <= 5.5)
        document.write("Your soil is just right for growing Azaleas");
    else
        document.write("Sorry, your pH level is too high for Azaleas");
//-->
</SCRIPT>
```

Figure 10.8 JS Script for the *Azalea* Page, version 2

THE AZALEA PAGE: VERSION 3 (COMPOUND STATEMENTS)

JavaScript syntax rules state that only one statement can appear after the expression in an **if** statement. Similarly, only one statement can appear after the **else** in an **if...else** statement. If we need to execute several statements for either the **if** or the **else** alternative, we must use a *compound statement* (also known as a *block*). A block is simply a set of statements enclosed in braces: **{ }**. Figure 10.9 shows a new version of our *Azalea* page. This version prints several messages when the *pH* level is in the proper range.

Figure 10.10 contains the JS script. Notice the use of braces to group the *true* statements together. The statements are indented under their respective **if** or **else** clauses so that structure of the code is obvious. The indentation aids in error detection. Although the **else** clause still contains a single statement, we could have created a block to print several messages if the *pH* level was too high.

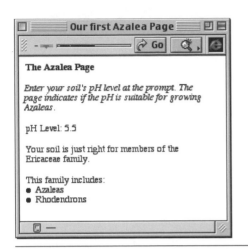

Figure 10.9 The *Azalea* Page, version 3

```
<SCRIPT LANGUAGE = "JavaScript">
<!--
var pH = parseFloat(prompt("Enter the pH level
of your soil: ", ""));
document.write("pH Level: " + pH + "<P>");
if (pH <= 5.5) {
document.write("Your soil is just right for
members ");
document.write("of the Ericaceae family.");
document.write("<P>This family includes: </BR>");
document.write("<LI>Azaleas<BR>");
document.write("<LI>Rhodendrons");
}
else
document.write("Sorry, your pH level is too
high for Azaleas");
//-->
</SCRIPT>
```

Figure 10.10 The Azalea Page, version 3

A NOTE ON LEXICOGRAPHIC ORDER

The *Azalea* pages use relational operators to compare numeric information. Most programming languages extend the meaning of these operators so that they can be used to compare strings. Programming languages use lexicographic (or dictionary) order to compare strings. Suppose that we have two strings, *word1* and *word2*. If *word1* appears before *word2* in the dictionary, *word1* will be treated by Java Script as less than *word2*. Similarly, if *word1* appears after *word2* in the dictionary, *word1* is greater than *word2*. Figure 10.11 contains a sample page that illustrates lexicographic order.

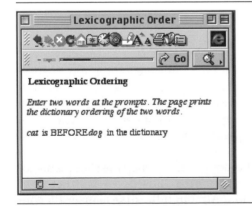
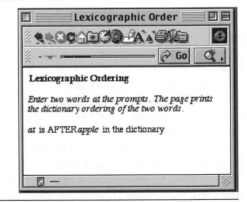

Figure 10.11a, b The *Lexicographic Order* Page

The JS Script for this page appears in Figure 10.12. Try testing this code with a variety of words.

```
<SCRIPT LANGUAGE = "JavaScript">
<!--
  var word1 = prompt("First Word: ", "");
  var word2 = prompt("Second Word: ", "");
  document.write("<I>" + word1 + "</I>");

  if (word1 < word2)
    document.write(" is BEFORE ");
  else if (word1 == word2)
    document.write(" is the SAME as ");
  else
    document.write(" is AFTER ");

  document.write("<I>" + word2 + "</I> in the dictionary");
//-->
</SCRIPT>
```

Figure 10.12 JS Script for the *Lexicographic Order* Page

Figure 10.12 shows an interesting variation of the **if...else** statement: an **else if** clause. An **else if** clause simply indicates that another **if** statement is executed when the original expression is *false*. By using **else if** clauses we can create multiway branches, not just *true/false* alternatives. Figure 10.13 uses pseudocode to show the logic behind the *Lexicographic Order* page. Pseudocode combines English and a programming language. Programmers use pseudocode only to design programs and to explain solutions to other programmers, so there are no strict rules for creating pseudocode.

```
if (word 1 < word 2)
     write "Less than"
else if (word 1==word 2)
     write "Equal"
else
     write "Greater than"
```

Figure 10.13 Pseudocode Version of the **if...else if ...else** Statement

Notice how the pseudocode in Figure 10.13 illustrates the flow of the code without actually resorting to strict JavaScript. Pseudocode lets us think about programming solutions without becoming bogged down in the syntax of a specific programming language.

We'll see several additional examples of **else if** statement before we finish this chapter. These statements require more sophisticated test data than does a simple **if...else** statement. Because the lexicographic page has three possible courses of action, the test data set must address all three possibilities. Figure 10.12 illustrated two of the possibilities: *less than* and *greater than*. The third possibility occurs when the two words are identical.

LOGICAL OPERATORS

Sometimes relational operators are not sufficient. Consider the following English sentences:

1. *If I'm lying, I'm **not** telling the truth.*
2. *If your test score is between 90 **and** 100, then you'll receive an A.*
3. *If your favorite color is red, blue, **or** yellow, then you like primary colors.*

Each of these statements uses a *logical operator*. JavaScript contains symbols that represent each of these operators. The *not* operator, !, has the highest precedence. The *and* operator, &&, is second in precedence. The *or* operator, ||, has the lowest precedence. Additionally, the &&, *and*, and || operators have a lower precedence than the relational operators. (See Appendix B for the complete JavaScript precedence hierarchy.)

Computer scientists and logicians use *truth tables* to describe the results of applying a logical operator. We will examine each of the truth tables separately.

The not Truth Table.   Figure 10.14 contains the truth table for the *not* operator. The *not* operator, !, is a unary, prefix operator. A unary operand requires a single operand. A prefix operator is placed before its operand. The first column in Figure 10.14 uses *A* to represent any valid expression. The second column show the results when the *not* operator is applied to the operand.

A	! A
false	*true*
true	*false*

Figure 10.14 The *not* Truth Table

As Figure 10.14 indicates, the operand, *A*, can have only two possible values: *false* and *true*. Applying the *not* operator to *A* changes the expression to its opposite. Thus, if is *A* is initially *false*, the expression !A is *true*. Similarly, if *A* is initially *true*, the expression !A is *false*.

The and Truth Table.   Figure 10.15 contains the truth table for the *and* operator. The *and* operator, &&, is a binary, infix operator. A binary operator requires two expressions. An infix operator is placed between these expressions. Because binary operators require two operands, there will be four distinct sets of *true*/*false* combinations. In Figure 10.15, *A* and *B* denote any two valid expressions. As this figure indicates, an expression created with an *and* operator is *true* only if *both* of the constituent expressions are *true*.

A	B	A && B
false	*false*	*false*
false	*true*	*false*
true	*false*	*false*
true	*true*	*true*

Figure 10.15 The *and* Truth Table

The or Truth Table.   Figure 10.16 contains the truth table for the *or* operator. The *or* operator, ||, is also a binary, infix operator. Although logicians use two types of *or* operators, *inclusive* and *exclusive*, programming languages generally implement only the former. An *inclusive or* is so named because it includes the *and* operator. Thus, an expression of the form **A || B** is *true* if either A is *true* or B is *true*. It is also *true* if both A and B are *true*.

A	B	A || B
false	false	false
false	true	false
true	false	true
true	true	true

Figure 10.16 The *or* Truth Table

We're now ready to examine three simple pages that illustrate these logical operators.

A "NOT" PAGE

As an example of negation, we create a simple page that reproduces the *not* truth table. The page uses a confirm window to ask users whether they understand negation. If the user presses the OK button, a value of *true* is returned. If the user presses the *Cancel* button, a value of *false* is returned. The page prints the opposite value. Figure 10.17 shows the sample pages.

(a) Not True   **(b) Not False**

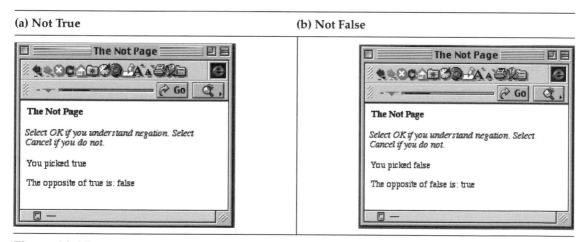

Figure 10.17 The *not* Page

Figure 10.18 contains the script for the *not* page. The line containing the *not* operator is highlighted.

```
<SCRIPT LANGUAGE = "JavaScript">
<!--
    var reply = confirm("Do you understand negation?");
    document.write("You picked " + reply + "<BR><BR>");
    document.write("The opposite of " + reply + " is: ");
    document.write(!reply);
//-->
</SCRIPT>
```

Figure 10.18 JS script for the *not* Page

THE TEST GRADE PAGE

In Chapter 9, we created a *Test Score* page. This page asked the user to enter the number of correct answers and the number of total questions on a test. The page calculated the percentage of correct and incorrect answers. As an example of the *and* operator, we will extend that page. After the percentages are calculated, we will print a letter grade for the test. Figure 10.19 contains a sample page.

We assume that the teacher uses a straight scale when determining the grade. With this assumption, we can use pseudocode to write a solution to the problem. Figure 10.20 contains one pseudocode solution. Several other solutions are possible. You might want to sketch out other possible solutions.

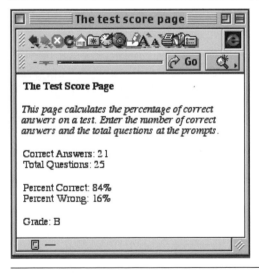

Figure 10.19 The *Test Grade* Page

```
if (Score ≥ 90 && Score ≤ 100)
    Letter Grade = A
if (Score ≥ 80 && Score < 90)
    Letter Grade = B
if (Score ≥ 70 && Score < 80)
    Letter Grade = C
if (Score ≥ 60 && Score < 70)
    Letter Grade = D
if (Score ≥ 0 && Score < 60)
    Letter Grade = F
```

Figure 10.20 Pseudocode for *Test Grade* Page

Solution 1: A set of independent **if** *statements.*   The pseudocode appearing in Figure 10.20 uses five separate **if** statements to determine the user's letter grade. Figure 10.21 contains the JavaScript implementation of the pseudocode.

```
<SCRIPT LANGUAGE = "JavaScript">
<!--
   var correct = parseInt(prompt("Correct answers: ", ""));
   var total = parseInt(prompt("Total questions: ", ""));
   var percentCorrect - correct/total*100;
   var percentWrong = 100 - percentCorrect;

   document.write("Correct Answers: " + correct);
   document.write("<BR>Total Questions: " + total);
   document.write("<P>Percent Correct: " + percentCorrect + "%");
   document.write("<BR>Percent Wrong: " + percentWrong + "%<P>");

   if (percentCorrect >= 90 && percentCorrect <= 100)
      document.write("Grade: A");
   if (percentCorrect >= 80 && percentCorrect < 90)
      document.write("Grade: B");
   if (percentCorrect >= 70 && percentCorrect < 80)
      document.write("Grade: C");
   if (percentCorrect >= 60 && percentCorrect < 70)
       document.write("Grade: D");
   if (percentCorrect >= 0 && percentCorrect < 60)
       document.write("Grade: F");
//-->
</SCRIPT>
```

Figure 10.21 The *Test Grade* Page, solution 1

The solution appearing in Figure 10.21 is inefficient, because the JavaScript interpreter must always check each of the **if** statements even though only one **if** statement will be selected.

Solution 2: Interconnected **if...else if...else** *statements.*   We can also code the *Test Grade* problem by using a single **if...else** statement. This solution is more efficient than the first solution, because JavaScript stops evaluating the expressions when it finds the expression that is *true*. Figure 10.22 contains the JS script for this solution. (Only the **if** statements are included.)

```
if (percentCorrect >= 90 && percentCorrect <= 100)
   document.write("Grade: A");
else if (percentCorrect >= 80 && percentCorrect < 90)
   document.write("Grade: B");
else if (percentCorrect >= 70 && percentCorrect < 80)
   document.write("Grade: C");
else if (percentCorrect >= 60 && percentCorrect < 70)
    document.write("Grade: D");
else
    document.write("Grade: F");
```

Figure 10.22 The *Test Grade* Page, solution 2

Solution 3: Interconnected **if...else if ..else** *statements with only the lower bounds.*   Whenever we have a series of **if** statements that include the full spectrum of values, we can simplify the expressions: the **else** clauses in the problem always signify a failure, so we can omit the upper bound for each of the expressions in the **else if** clauses. For example, consider the first two clauses:

```
if (percentCorrect >= 90 && percentCorrect <= 100)
    document.write("Grade: A");

else if (percentCorrect >= 80 && percentCorrect < 90)
    document.write("Grade: B");
```

If the JavaScript interpreter evaluates the **else if** clause, we know that the *percentCorrect* must be less than 90—otherwise, the JavaScript interpreter could not evaluate this clause. The same argument applies to the remaining **else if** clauses. The simplified **if...else if...else** statement appears in Figure 10.23.

The three solutions to the *Test Grade* page produce similar results. The last solution is the simplest and most efficient.

```
if (percentCorrect <0 || percentCorrect >100)
    document.write("Error! Invalid Data.");
else if (percentCorrect >= 90)
    document.write("Grade: A");
else if (percentCorrect >= 80)
    document.write("Grade: B");
else if (percentCorrect >= 70)
    document.write("Grade: C");
else if (percentCorrect >= 60)
    document.write("Grade: D");
else
    document.write("Grade: F");
```

Figure 10.23 The *Test Grade* Page, solution 3

THE *PRIMARY COLORS* PAGE

As our last example of the **if** statement and its variants, we create a *Primary Colors* page. The user is asked to enter a color. If the color is red, yellow, or blue, the page displays the message *Primary Color*. If the color is orange, purple, or green, the page displays message *Secondary Color*. For any other colors, the message *Not a primary or secondary color* is displayed. Figure 10.24 contains two sample pages.

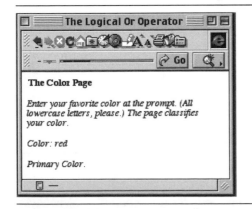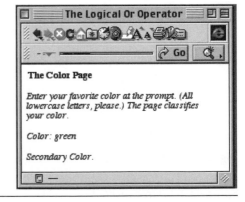

Figure 10.24 The *Primary Colors* Page

Figure 10.25 contains the JS script for the *Primary Colors* page. A nested **if ...else if...else** statement is used for the classification. The code is simple, but you must remember to repeat the variable name *color* for each equality check.

```
<SCRIPT LANGUAGE = "JavaScript">
<!--
   var color = prompt("Enter a color: ", "");
   document.write("Color: " + color);
   if (color == "red" || color == "blue" || color == "yellow")
      document.write("<P> Primary Color.");
   else if (color == "green" || color == "purple" || color == "orange")
      document.write("<P>Secondary Color.");
   else
      document.write("<P>Not a primary or secondary color.");
//-->
</SCRIPT>
```

Figure 10.25 JS script for the *Primary Colors* Page

THE switch STATEMENT

The expressions evaluated in JavaScript **if** and **if...else** statements can easily become complex and confusing. For example, consider the arithmetic page displayed in Figure 10.26. As Figure 10.26(a) indicates, the user can select the desired arithmetic operation by typing its number, its symbol, or its name. Figure 10.26(b) shows the results when the user selects the modulus operator.

(a) Prompt   **(b) Result**

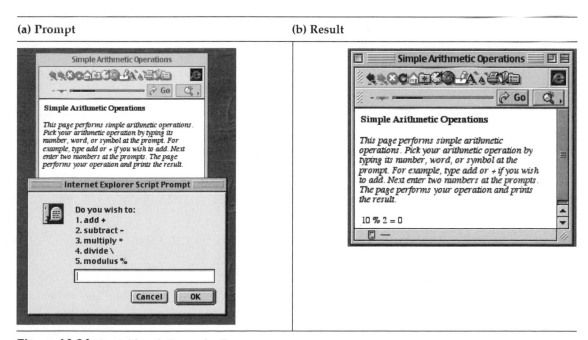

Figure 10.26 An *Arithmetic Expression* Page

Think about the expressions required to implement this page by using **if...else** statements. Try to write the code before examining the code in Figure 10.27.

```
<SCRIPT LANGUAGE = "JavaScript">
<!--
    var choice = prompt("Do you wish to:\n1. add +\n2. subtract -\n" +
    "3. multiply *\n4. Divide \\ \n5. modulus %", "");
    var x = parseFloat(prompt("First number: ", ""));
    var y = parseFloat(prompt("Second number: ", ""));
    if (choice == "add" || choice == "+" || choice == "1")
        document.write(x + " + " + y + " = " + (x+y));
    else if (choice == "subtract" || choice == "-" || choice == "2")
        document.write(x + " - " + y + " = " + (x-y));
    else if (choice == "multiply" || choice == "*" || choice == "3")
        document.write(x + " * " + y + " = " + (x*y));
    else if (choice == "divide" || choice == "/" || choice == "4")
        document.write(x + " / " + y + " = " + (x/y));
    else if (choice == "modulus" || choice == "%" || choice == "5")
        document.write(x + " % " + y + " = " + (x%y));
    else
        document.write("Sorry! I don't recognize your choice.");
//-->
</SCRIPT>
```

Figure 10.27 The *Arithmetic Expressions* Page: **if..else** version

The expressions in Figure 10.27 are cumbersome and offer plenty of opportunities for the commission of logical errors. Often, the JavaScript **switch** statement provides a cleaner, less cumbersome solution to a programming problem. The basic form of this statement appears in Figure 10.28.

```
switch (variable) {
  case value: statement₁;
            ...
            statementₙ;
            break;
  case value: case value: statement₁;
                        ...
                        statementₙ;
                        break;
  defaultₒₚₜᵢₒₙₐₗ: statement₁;
              ...
              statementₙ;
}
```

Figure 10.28 The JavaScript **switch** Statement

The **switch** statement is divided into the following parts:

switch *(variable)* **{ ... }.**   JavaScript uses the word **switch** to denote the start of a **switch** statement. The entire statement is always enclosed in braces **{ }**. A parenthesized variable is placed immediately after the word, **switch**. Any type of variable except **null** and **undefined** can be used in a **switch** statement.

case *value.*   The **case** statement is a value selector. We use it to associate values with code segments. Each value must have its own **case** statement. A value cannot be used more than once in a **switch** statement. A list of statements to be executed follows the **case** list. Braces are not necessary because the **switch** statement executes all statements after a matched value. The statements are executed until the JavaScript interpreter either reaches the end of the **switch** statement or encounters a **break** statement.

break.   As its name suggests, the **break** statement terminates execution of a **switch** statement.

default.   The optional **default:** statement is used when JavaScript cannot match the variable's current value with any of the values appearing in the **case** statements.

The JavaScript **switch** statement frequently produces cleaner code than the equivalent **if...else** statements. This is particularly true when the **if** statements use logical *or*s to select among only a few alternatives. Reexamine the **if...else** statements in Figure 10.27, then look at the equivalent **switch** statement appearing in Figure 10.29. I think you'll find that the version using the **switch** statement is easier to read and to code.

```
<SCRIPT LANGUAGE = "JavaScript">
<!--
   var choice = prompt("Do you wish to:\n1. Add +\n2. subtract -\n" +"3. multiply *\n4. divide \\
\n5. modulus %", "");
   var x = parseFloat(prompt("First number: ", ""));
   var y = parseFloat(prompt("Second number: ", ""));
   switch (choice) {
      case "add": case "1":  case "+":
          document.write(x + " + " + y + " = " + (x+y));
          break;
      case "subtract": case "2": case "-":
          document.write(x + " - " + y + " = " + (x-y));
          break;
      case "multiply": case "3": case "*":
          document.write(x + " * " + y + " = " + (x*y));
          break;
      case "divide": case "4": case "/":
          document.write(x + " / " + y + " = " + (x/y));
          break;
      case "modulus": case "5": case "%":
         document.write(x + " % " + y + " = " + (x%y));
         break;
      default:  document.write("Sorry! I don't recognize your choice.");
   }
//-->
</SCRIPT>
```

Figure 10.29 The *Arithmetic Expressions* Page: **switch** version

➤ **PRACTICE EXERCISES**

Write web pages for each of the following exercises. Prior to writing the web page, you should

1. *create a pseudo-code outline of your solution;*
2. *develop test data appropriate to the problem.*
   Make sure that your user interface is friendly. Thoroughly test your solution.

1. **The *Freshwater Aquarium* Page.** Freshwater fish require *pH*, nitrate, and temperature levels within the ranges indicated in Figure 10.30. Create a web page that asks the user to enter the *pH*, nitrate, and temperature. Use an alert window to signal any level that is out of the proper range.

pH Level	6.5 to 7.5
Nitrate Level	Less than 100mg/liter
Temperature	68 to 83 degrees Fahrenheit

Figure 10.30 The *Freshwater Aquarium* Chart

2. **The *Garden* Page.** Create a page that indicates what type of garden a user should plant. Gardens vary in the amount of sunlight they receive. Figure 10.31 contains the appropriate information. Ask the user to enter the hours of shade, then print the appropriate type of garden.

More than 11 hours of shade	Shade garden
One to 11 hours of shade	In-between garden
Less than one hour of shade	Sunny garden

Figure 10.31 The *Garden* Chart

3. **The *Wind Chill* Page.** Scientists use the *wind chill* index to determine the level of danger in severe winter conditions. Figure 10.32 contains temperature ranges and frostbite risk. Develop a page that asks the user to enter the wind chill. Display the wind chill and the frostbite risk.

Temperature Range	Effect
9 above zero to 10 below zero	Unpleasant
11 below to 25 below zero	Frostbite is possible
26 below to 65 below zero	Frostbite Danger. Flesh freezes in a minute
66 below or lower	Frostbite Warning. Flesh freezes in 30 seconds

Figure 10.32 The *Wind Chill* Chart

4. **The *Breeze Classification* Page.** Scientists use the *Beaufort Scale* (Figure 10.33) to classify breezes. The user should enter the wind speed. Display the speed and the breeze classification.

5. **The *Hurricane* Page.** Scientists use the *Saffir–Simpson Scale* (Figure 10.34) to classify hurricanes. Create a page that asks the user to enter the wind speed in miles per hour (mph). Print out the wind speed, pressure, hurricane description, storm surge, and damage.

Wind Speed (Kilometers/hour)	Description
Below 6	Calm
6-11	Light Breeze
12-19	Gentle Breeze
20-29	Moderate Breeze
30-38	Fresh Breeze
39-50	Strong Breeze

Figure 10.33 The Beaufort Scale

Wind Speed	Pressure (mb)	Description	Storm Surge	Damage
22-39		Tropical Depression		
40-73		Tropical Storm	1-3 ft	
74-95	>980	Category One Hurricane	4-5 ft	Minimal
96-110	979-965	Category Two Hurricane	6-8 ft.	Moderate
111-130	964-945	Category Three Hurricane	9-12 ft	Extensive
131-155	944-920	Category Four Hurricane	13-18 ft	Extreme
>155	<920	Category Five Hurricane	>18 ft	Catastrophic

Figure 10.34 The Saffir–Simpson Scale

6. **The *Tornado* Page.** Scientists use the *Fujita Scale* (Figure 10.35) to classify tornadoes. Create a page that first lets the user enter a wind speed, then prints the wind speed description and the F-scale number.

Wind Speed	Description	F-Scale
42-72 mph	Gale Tornado	F0
73-112	Moderate Tornado	F1
113-157	Significant Tornado	F2
158-206	Severe Tornado	F3
207-260	Devastating Tornado	F4
261-318	Incredible Tornado	F5
319-379	Inconceivable Tornado	F6

Figure 10.35 The Fujita Scale

7. **The *Richter Scale* Page.** Scientists use the *Richter Scale* (Figure 10.36) to classify the severity of an earthquake. Ask the user to enter the Richter scale value, then print this value and the TNT equivalent and damage level.

8. **The *Heat Index* Page.** Create a page that lets the user enter the current heat index. The page should print the heat index and the risk from heat exhaustion or heat stroke. Figure 10.37 contains the relevant information.

Richter Magnitude	TNT Equivalent (Tons)	Damage
Less than 3.5	<1000 pounds	Not felt
3.5 to 5.4	1000 pounds to 499 tons	Minor Damage
5.5 to 6.0	500-6370 tons	Slight Damage
6.1 to 6.9	6371-198,999 tons	Moderate Damage
7.0 to 7.9	199,000 to 6.26 million tons	Major Earthquake: serious damage
8 or greater	>= 6.27 million tons	Great Earthquake: Total destruction

Figure 10.36 The Richter Scale

Heat Index	Danger Zone
Below 84° F	No Risk
84° to 94° F	Caution
95° to 105° F	Extreme Caution
Above 105° F	Danger

Figure 10.37 The *Heat Index* Page

9. **A *Character Classification* Page.** Figure 10.38 contains a set of characters and their classification. Create a page that asks a user to enter a letter. Display the letter and its classification.

Character	Classification
A to Z	Upper-case letter
a to z	Lower-case letter
0 to 9	Digit
+ − * /	Arithmetic Operator
$	Monetary
#	Pound
@	At
%	Percent
Anything else	Other

Figure 10.38 Character Classification Scale

10. **The *Light Classification* Page.** Scientists classify light based on the wavelength as measured in microns (μ) (Figure 10.39). Create a page that asks a user to enter the light type. Display the light type and the micron range for the type.

Light Type	Microns
Red light	0.710μ to 0.647μ
Orange light	0.646μ to 0.585μ
Yellow light	0.584μ to 0.575μ
Green light	0.574μ to 0.491μ
Blue light	0.490μ to 0.424μ
Violet light	0.423μ to 0.400μ
Error	Anything else

Figure 10.39 Light Classification Scale

11. **The *Quadratic Roots* Page.** Finding the roots of the quadratic equation depends on the values of *a*, *b*, and *c*. Figure 10.40 shows the rules. Create a page that asks the user to enter the values of *a*, *b*, and *c*. Print the values and the appropriate rule and message. You do not have to calculate the roots.

Rule	Message
Rule 1: a, b, c are zero	Infinite real roots
Rule 2: a and b are zero but c is not	No real roots
Rule 3: Only a is zero	No real roots
Rule 4: $b^2 < 4*a*c$	No real roots
Rule 5: $b^2 == 4*a*c$	1 real root
Rule 6: $b > 4*a*c$	2 real roots

Figure 10.40 Rules for the Quadratic Equation

12. **The *Humiture* Page.** The *humiture*, short for humidity and temperature, is a hot-weather equivalent of the heat index. Figure 10.41 contains the humiture formula. Figure 10.42 contains a table of *humit* values.

$$Humiture = Temperature + Humits$$

Figure 10.41 The Humiture Formula

Dew Point	<55	55-59	60-64	65-69	70-74	75-79	80-84	≥85
Humits	2	5	8	11	15	19	25	31

Figure 10.42 The Humit Scale

Create a page that asks the user to enter the temperature and dew point. Print the temperature, dew point, humits, and humiture.

13. **The *Grams of Fat* Page.** Create a page that asks the user to enter the name of a food and the grams of fat for the food. Calculate the percentage of fat for the food. If the percentage is greater than 30, indicate that this is a high fat food. Otherwise, indicate that it is an acceptable food.

14. **The *Pets* Page.** Ask the user to enter the type of pet he or she has. Print an appropriate message for the type pet. For example, if the user enters "dog," you might indicate that you also like dogs.

15. **The *Multiple Choice Test* Page.** Create a multiple-choice question. Ask the user to enter the correct answer. If the user answers correctly, print a message indicating that the user was correct; otherwise, tell the user that he or she was wrong.

16. **The *Exclusive Or* Page.** Create a page that asks the user two *true/false* questions. Print out a message that indicates whether an expression formed from the two statements is *true* or *false*. Use the definition of the *exclusive or* that appears in the **JavaScript Vocabulary** section.

> ## JAVASCRIPT VOCABULARY

Block. A block is a piece of connected code. For example, the **switch** statement and its included **case**, **break**, and **default** statements is a JavaScript block. Braces **{}** are used to bound a block of code.

Compound Statement. A compound statement is a set of JavaScript statements encased in braces. Since the **if...else** statements allows only a single statement after the **if** or **else** clauses, we create a compound statement to execute multiple statements.

Exclusive or. An *exclusive or* is an *or* statement that is *true* only if exactly one of the expressions is *true*. It is *false* if both of the expressions are *false* or if both of the expressions are *true*. The *exclusive or* is so named because it excludes the *and* operator.

Inclusive or. An *inclusive or* is so named because it include the *and* operation. Hence, an expression is *false* only if both of the expressions linked by the *or* operator are *false*. Most programming languages implement an *inclusive or* operator.

Lexicographic Order. We use lexicographic, or dictionary, order when comparing strings. One string is less than a second string if it appears before the second string in the dictionary. Similarly, a string is greater than a second string if it appears after the second string in the dictionary.

Logical Operator. The three logical operators, in order of precedence, are *not* (**!**), *and* (**&&**), and *or* (**||**).

Ordinal Variable. Ordinal refers to any type that has obvious predecessor and successor values. For example, everyone knows that the predecessor of 10 is 9 and the successor of 10 is 11; integers are ordinal values.

   Similarly, we know that the letter that comes before *c* is *b* and the letter that comes after *c* is *d.* Integers and characters are ordinal; floating-point numbers and strings are not.

Pseudocode. Pseudocode combines English and programming-language constructors. Programmers use pseudocode to develop solutions to programming problems and to summarize solutions for other programmers. Because pseudocode is language independent, a pseudocode solution can be translated into many programming languages.

Relational Operator. JavaScript contains six relational operators: **<, >, <=, >=, ==**, and **!=**. The equality and inequality operators have a lower precedence than the other relational operators.

Selection Statement. We use selection statements to indicate which pieces of code we wish to execute. The **if** statement bases its selection on an expression. The **switch** statement uses specific variable values to determine which segment of code to execute.

Truth Table. A *truth table* is a table that indicates the truth value of an expression composed of logical operators.

> ## TRAPS AND PITFALLS

We conclude this chapter by discussing typical traps and pitfalls that ensnare beginning programmers.

JavaScript Expressions. As indicated previously, JavaScript expressions use a peculiar concept of *true* and *false*. This concept can lead to subtle logic errors, as is illustrated by the JavaScript appearing in Figure 10.43.

```
<SCRIPT LANGUAGE = "JavaScript">
<!--
   var x = parseInt(prompt("Pick a number: ", ""));
   if (x)
      document.write(x + " is the same as <TT>true</TT>");
   else
      document.write(x + " is the same as <TT>false</TT>");
//-->
</SCRIPT>
```

Figure 10.43 JavaScript Expressions

The JS script in Figure 10.43 asks the user to pick a number. This number, and this number alone, becomes the expression used in the **if** statement. Based on the value in the number, the script prints a *true* or *false* message. Figure 10.44 shows both possibilities.

(a)False   **(b) True**

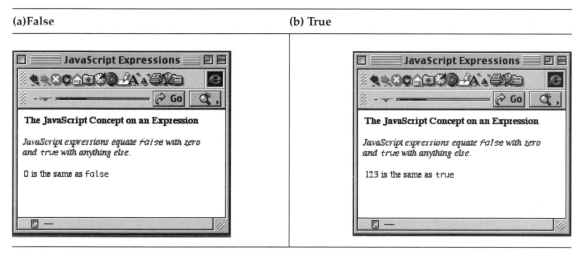

Figure 10.44 Examples of JavaScript Expressions

In Figure 10.44(a), "0" was entered at the prompt. The page indicates that this number is equivalent to *false*. In Figure 10.44(b), "123" was entered at the prompt. JavaScript indicates that this is equivalent to *true*. In fact, any number other than zero is equivalent to *true*.

Now consider the JavaScript statements appearing in Figure 10.45.

```
var x = parseInt(prompt("Pick a number: ", ""));
if (x = 3)
   document.write(x + " is the same as 3");
else
   document.write(x + " is different from 3");
```

Figure 10.45 An Incorrect **if** Statement

In this example, an assignment operator, =, was erroneously used instead of an equality operator, ==. JavaScript prints a warning message, which ALL users will see each time they access this page. The message indicates that the programmer used the wrong operator. JavaScript graciously changes the operator, but the page still looks erroneous to users.

Incomplete Complex Expression.   Beginning programmers frequently write shorthand expressions. For example, consider the JavaScript statement appearing in Figure 10.46.

```
if (x == 3 || 4 || 5)
      document.write("<BR>3, 4 or 5");
else
      document.write("<BR>Not 3,4, or 5");
```

Figure 10.46 Incorrect use of a logical Or

JavaScript will NOT issue a warning or error message if you write code like this. It also won't correctly evaluate the expressions. In sample runs, JavaScript always evaluated the expression as *true*. The correct version of this statement appears in Figure 10.47.

```
if (x == 3 || x == 4 || x== 5)
      document.write("<BR>3, 4 or 5");
else
      document.write("<BR>Not 3,4, or 5");
```

Figure 10.47 The Correct Use of a Logical Or

11 Iteration Statements

Suppose you're planning a trip to Alberta, Canada. It's late spring and you'd like to know what type of clothes to pack. You check the international weather pages and quickly discover that the forecast is measured in Celsius. You'd like a chart that contains the Fahrenheit equivalents for a range of Celsius temperatures. Writing a JavaScript script to accomplish this task is easy once you understand iteration. Iteration is a commonly used technique for repeating segments of code. JavaScript provides three iteration statements. The three iteration statements, listed by order of popularity among programmers, are:

*The **for** statement.* The **for** statement is the most general and flexible of the iteration statements. Any problem requiring iteration can be implemented using a **for** statement.

*The **while** statement.* Generally, the **while** statement is used to write error loops. With a little more effort, we can create a **while** statement that does exactly the same thing as a **for** statement.

*The **do...while** Statement.* The **do...while** statement is the least popular of the iteration statements because it always executes a code segment **at least once**. It is most frequently used to create repeatable menus in which the user can continue to select a menu option until selecting the *quit* option.

THE for STATEMENT

Because the **for** statement is the most popular of the iteration statements, we will discuss it first. The syntax of this statement appears in Figure 11.1.

---

for (*Initial Expression ; Test Expression ; Change Expression*)
    Statement;

Figure 11.1 Syntax of the **for** statement

     The **for** statement is divided into two parts: a *header* and a *body*. The header, which always begins with the word **for**, contains a set of parenthesized expressions. The body contains a single JavaScript statement. The body can contain several statements if they are enclosed in braces: **{ }** . This creates a *compound statement*, as discussed in Chapter 10.

The **for** statement uses a variable, called an *index*, to link the three expressions appearing in the header. Each expression has a distinct task:

Initial Expression.   The initial expression assigns a starting value to the *index* variable.

Test Expression   The test expression controls repetition. The statement in the body is executed as long as the expression is *true*. The loop terminates when the test expression becomes *false*. If the test expression is *false* initially, the body of the **for** statement is ignored. The test expression must use the *index* variable to ensure proper termination.

Change Expression.   The change expression changes the value in the *index* variable so that it moves closer to loop termination.

These expressions are all optional. Although we can omit any of the expressions, we must retain the semicolons; JavaScript uses the semicolons to determine which expressions are included in the header. Thus, the *initial expression* always appears before the first semicolon, the *test expression* always appears between the first and second semicolons, and the *change expression* always appears after the second semicolon.

The *Celsius To Fahrenheit Table*

As our first illustration of the **for** statement, we create a page that prints the Celsius-to-Fahrenheit table discussed at the beginning of the chapter. Figure 11.2 shows a sample page. In this example, the high

(a) Data Entry

(b) C to F table

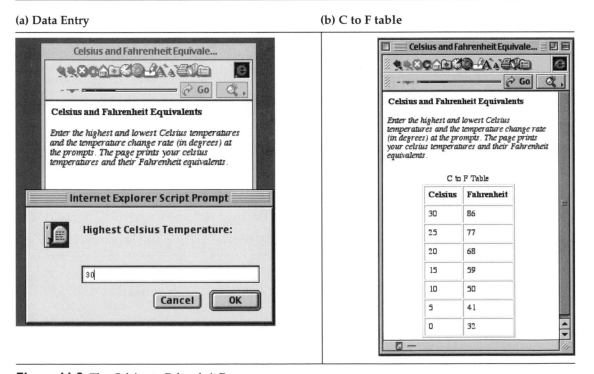

Figure 11.2 The *Celsius to Fahrenheit* Page

and low temperatures were 30°C and 0°C, respectively. The temperature change was five degrees. Figure 11.2(a) shows a portion of the data entry process. Figure 11.2(b) shows the completed table.

Stepwise Program Development

Because this page is our most complicated to date, we use a stepwise approach to programming. A stepwise approach, also called *stepwise refinement*, creates a large program from smaller pieces. This means that we write a few lines of JavaScript script and run them. When we're sure that these lines work correctly, we add the next set of lines. We continue this process until the page is complete. To begin the process, we list the steps necessary to complete the page. Frequently, this list expands and contracts as we write code segments. What's important is putting ideas on paper. Look at Figure 11.2 and try to develop a set of tasks or steps, then look at the list contained in figure 11.3. This figure contains the pseudo-code for the *Celsius to Fahrenheit* page.

Step 1.   Use prompts to obtain the highest and lowest Celsius temperatures and the temperature change.

Step 2.   (a) Use `document.write()` to create the table border, caption, and headings.

Step 3.   Use a **for** statement to:

    * Convert a Celsius temperature to Fahrenheit.

    * Put the Celsius and Fahrenheit temperatures in the table.

Step 4.   (b) Close the table.

Figure 11.3 Pseudo-code for the Celsius to Fahrenheit Page

Since the first two steps in Figure 11.3 are also the easiest to code, we implement them in the order listed. Generally, when we write a program we always start with the easiest tasks and move progressively to the more complicated ones. We don't necessarily begin with the first task on the list.

Step 1: Obtaining the Celsius Temperatures.   By now you should be able to write prompt windows in your sleep. In our current project, we need three prompt windows. When using stepwise refinement, we obtain **and print** the user's input. This means that the intermediate pages contain temporary `document.write()` statements: one for each variable. These statements are left in the program until the last step is completed. They are removed when we have verified that the program works correctly. Often logical errors occur because a programmer uses the wrong variable in a calculation. Printing the variables provides a useful starting point for removing errors. Figure 11.4 contains a sample page and the JS script that implements the first step. The temporary `document.write()` statements are highlighted.

(a) Sample Page	**(b) JS Script**
| 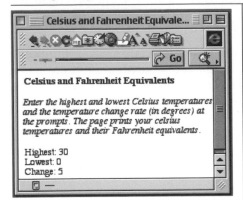 | ```javascript
<SCRIPT LANGUAGE = "JavaScript">
<!--
   var high = parseInt
     (prompt("Highest Celsius Temperature: ", ""));
  var low = parseInt
     (prompt("Lowest Celsius Temperature: ", ""));
   var change = parseInt
     (prompt("Temperature Change: ", ""));
   document.write("Highest: " + high);
   document.write("<BR>Lowest: " + low);
   document.write("<BR>Change: " + change + "<BR>");
//-->
</SCRIPT>
``` |

Figure 11.4 Step 1: Obtain and Check Temperatures

Step 2: Create the table. Browsers are usually quite forgiving in their interpretation of HTML table tags. A programmer can leave out **</TD>**, **</TH>** and **</TR>** tags with abandon. In Internet Explorer, the programmer can also leave out **</TABLE>** tags. The browser infers the correct termination of a statement without the ending tag. Unfortunately, Web programming languages, including JavaScript, Java, and Perl, require strict compliance with the HTML rules. Beginning tags must have their corresponding ending tags. Forgetting the ending tags often leads to strange results: tables don't appear, or their row and column structure is wrong. Thus, the second step in the development of the *Celsius to Fahrenheit* page is the creation of the table's caption and headers. Figure 11.5 contains a sample page and the JS script that implements this step. The new code is highlighted.

(a) Sample Page	**(b) JS Script**
| 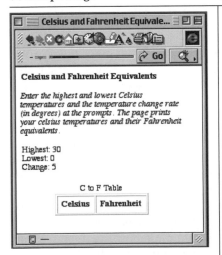 | ```javascript
<SCRIPT LANGUAGE = "JavaScript">
<!--
   var high = parseInt
     (prompt("Highest Celsius Temperature: ", ""));
   var low = parseInt
     (prompt("Lowest Celsius Temperature: ", ""));
   var change = parseInt(prompt("Temperature Change: ", ""));
   document.write("Highest: " + high);
   document.write("<BR>Lowest: " + low);
   document.write("<BR>Change: " + change + "<BR>");
   var celsius;
   document.write("<CENTER><TABLE BORDER = '1'
     CELLPADDING = '5'>");
   document.write("<CAPTION>C to F Table</CAPTION>");
   document.write("<TR><TH>Celsius</TH><TH>Fahrenheit
     </TH></TR>");
   //Put the for statement here
   document.write("</TABLE></CENTER>");
//-->
</SCRIPT>
``` |

Figure 11.5 Step 2: Create Table Captions and Titles

Step 3: The **for** *statement.*   The final step in the *Celsius to Fahrenheit* page is the creation of the **for** statement that fills the table with *Celsius* values and their *Fahrenheit* equivalent. The **for** statement must write the temperatures from the highest to the lowest while using the *change* variable to control the temperature interval. The loop focuses on Celsius temperatures, so the loop index variable is called *celsius*. Creating the **for** statement header requires establishing initial, test, and change expressions that use the index variable.

Initial Expression.   Because the temperature table begins with the highest Celsius temperature, the initial expression should assign the value in *high* to the loop index, `celsius`. Thus, the initial expression is `celsius = high`.

Test Expression.   The page prints the temperatures from the highest to the lowest. This means that table rows are printed as long as `celsius >= low`.

Change Expression.   The *change* variable determines the correct decrement. In this example, *change* holds the decrement entered by the user. The change expression is `celsius -= change`.

Putting these three expressions together gives us the **for** statement header:

```
for (celsius = high; celsius >= low; celsius -= change)
```

The body of the **for** statement converts the current Celsius temperature into Fahrenheit and prints a table row with the Celsius and Fahrenheit temperatures. We break these tasks into three statements. The first statement creates a new table row and a new column that holds the current Celsius value. The statement is

```
document.write("<TR><TD>" + celsius + "</TD><TD>");
```

Notice that we also start the column that will contain the Fahrenheit value.

Next, we calculate the Fahrenheit value. The statement that does this is

```
fahrenheit = 9/5*celsius + 32;
```

Finally, we write the Fahrenheit value, and we close the column and row. The statement that accomplishes this task is

```
document.write(fahrenheit + "</TD></TR>");
```

Figure 11.6 contains the complete JS script for the *Celsius to Fahrenheit Table* page. The **for** statement is highlighted. The temporary `document.write()` statements have been removed from the final version of the page.

```
<SCRIPT LANGUAGE = "JavaScript">
<!--
   var high = parseInt(prompt("Highest Celsius Temperature: ", ""));
   var low = parseInt(prompt("Lowest Celsius Temperature: ", ""));
   var change = parseInt(prompt("Temperature Change: ", ""));
   var celsius;
   document.write("<CENTER><TABLE BORDER = '1' CELLPADDING = '5'>");
   document.write("<CAPTION>C to F Table</CAPTION>");
   document.write("<TR><TH>Celsius</TH><TH>Fahrenheit</TH></TR>");
   for (celsius = high; celsius >= low; celsius -= change){
   document.write("<TR><TD>" + celsius + "</TD><TD>");
   fahrenheit = 9/5*celsius + 32;
   document.write(fahrenheit + "</TD></TR>");
   }
   document.write("</TABLE></CENTER>");
//-->
</SCRIPT>
```

Figure 11.6 JS Script for the *Celsius to Fahrenheit Table* Page

Sums and Products

Many statistical and monetary formulas require the calculation of sums or products. Examples of such programs include tax depreciation schedules, earned interest tables, and arithmetic means and medians. Calculating a sum or product with a computer program differs from hand calculation or calculations using a calculator. An extra step is needed to ensure the accuracy of the results. In this section, we create simple pages that illustrate the techniques used to find the sums and products.

The *Total Calories* Page

Figure 11.7 contains a table that determines the total calories consumed in a day. The page asks the user to enter the calories consumed for breakfast, lunch, dinner, and two snacks. Figure 11.7(a) illustrates the data entry process for the second snack. Figure 11.7(b) shows the completed page. The page prints the calories consumed at each meal as well as the total calories consumed.

Any program that adds a series of numbers must initialize a summing variable to zero prior to the start of the summing loop. The statement that accomplishes this here is

```
var sum = 0;
```

(a) Data Entry

(b) Final Result

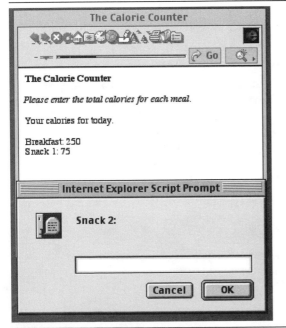
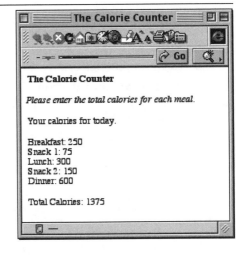

Figure 11.7 The *Total Calories* Page

A **for** statement is typically used to add the numbers. The header of the statement establishes the initial, test, and change expressions. The *Total Calories* page uses *i* as the loop index. This index has an initial value of 0. Since the user enters five meals, the test expression is i < 5. The change expression is i++. The complete header for the **for** statement is

```
for (i=0; i < 5; i++)
```

The body of the **for** statement contains a **switch** statement that uses the index variable *i*, to construct the selector values for the **case** statements. Each **case** statement contains a prompt for the current meal and a **document.write()** statement that prints the meal and the calories consumed at that meal.

After the user provides the calories for the meal, an arithmetic statement adds the calories to the current sum. The statement is

```
sum += calories;
```

Figure 11.8 contains the code for the *Total Calories* page.

```
<SCRIPT LANGUAGE = "JavaScript">
<!--
      var sum = 0; //initialize sum to 0
      var calories;
      var i;
      document.write("Your calories for today.<P>");
      for (i=0; i < 5; i++) {
        switch (i) {
        case 0:  calories = parseInt(prompt("Breakfast: ", ""));
                 document.write("Breakfast: " + calories);
                 break;
        case 1:  calories = parseInt(prompt("Snack 1: ", ""));
                 document.write("<BR>Snack 1: " + calories);
                 break;
        case 2:  calories = parseInt(prompt("Lunch: ", ""));
                 document.write("<BR>Lunch: " + calories);
                 break;
        case 3: calories = parseInt(prompt("Snack 2: ", ""));
                 document.write("<BR>Snack 2: " + calories);
                 break;
        case 4:  calories = parseInt(prompt("Dinner: ", ""));
                 document.write("<BR>Dinner: " + calories);
        }
         sum += calories;
      }
      document.write("<P>Total Calories: " + sum);
//-->
</SCRIPT>
```

Figure 11.8 JS Script for the *Total Calories* Page

WALK-THROUGHS

Although the script in Figure 11.8 correctly adds the total calories consumed in a day, the code used is often puzzling to beginning programmers. Experienced programmers use walk-throughs to understand loop processing and to verify that a looping statement works correctly. When walk-throughs are used to verify the correctness of a looping structure, they double as test data.

A *walk-through* is simply a table that contains all of the relevant variables and the test expression. Rows of the table contain entries for each iteration of the **for** statement. The table also contains rows that show the "pre-loop" and "post-loop" status of variables. Figure 11.9 shows the walk-through for the *Total Calories* page.

i	i < 5	switch(i)	sum
	Pre-Loop		0
0	0 < 5	Breakfast: 250	250 ← 0 + 250
1	1 < 5	Snack 1: 75	325 ← 250 + 75
2	2 < 5	Lunch: 300	625 ← 325 + 300
3	3 < 5	Snack 2: 150	775 ← 625 + 150
4	4 < 5	Dinner: 600	1375 ← 775 + 600
5	5 == 5 *Loop stops*		
	Post-loop	Total Calories	1375

Figure 11.9 A Walk-through for the *Summing* Page

As Figure 11.9 indicates, *sum* contains the initial value "0" prior to the start of the **for** statement. This is the first statement in any program that adds numbers. All programming languages prohibit undefined variables in arithmetic expressions; we cannot write statements such as **sum = sum + i;** without providing an initial value for *sum*. This statement indicates that we wish to add *i* to *sum* and place the result back in *sum*. If *sum* does not have an initial value, JavaScript cannot perform the first (or subsequent) additions.

Figure 11.9 also shows the loop iterations. JavaScript begins each iteration by evaluating the test expression, **i < 5**. If the test expression is *true*, the body of the loop is executed, and then the value in *i* is incremented. The iterations terminate when the test expression becomes *false*. At this point, *sum* contains the final result.

THE *FACTORIAL* PAGE

The technique for calculating products is similar to the one used for summing. To illustrate this technique, we create a page that calculates factorials. Figure 11.10 shows a sample page that contains the definition of a factorial and the calculation of the factorial for *n = 6*.

Figure 11.10 contains the rules for calculating factorials. The rules lend themselves to pseudocode. You might want to create pseudocode for the *Factorial* page before examining the pseudocode appearing in Figure 11.11.

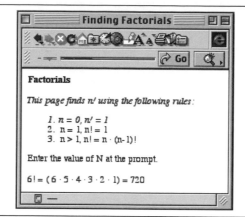

Figure 11.10 The *Factorial* Page

Step 1.   Use a prompt to obtain *n*,   **`n = parseInt(prompt(....));`**

Step 2.   **(a)** if *n* == 0,   **`document.write("0! == 1");`**
   (b) **else** *Use a for statement to calculate the factorial,*

Example n = 6, 6! = 6 × 5 × 4 × 3 × 2 × 1

Figure 11.11 Pseudocode for the *Factorial* Page

The pseudocode contained in Figure 11.11 translates the mathematical rules for factorials into two steps. Steps 1 through 2(a) are simple programming tasks. A preliminary version of this page should implement and test these steps. Once that has been accomplished, we concentrate on Step 2(b): calculating factorials when *n* is *greater than or equal to 1*.

Calculating Factorials When n is Not Zero

When $n \geq 1$, we use a **for** statement to calculate the factorial. Prior to the start of the **for** statement, we initialize a variable to hold the product. The appropriate initial value for a product is one since $1 \times i = i$, where *i* is any numeric value. The statement that initializes the product for the *Factorial* page is

```
var product = 1;
```

The **for** statement header uses the index variable *i*. The initial expression is i = n, the test expression is i >= 1, and the change expression is i--. The complete **for** statement header is

```
for(i=n; i >= 1; i--)
```

The body of the **for** statement multiples *factorial* by *i* and places the result into *factorial*. The body also prints the current value of *i* and a middot character (·) if *i* is greater than one.

Figure 11.12 contains the JS script for the *Factorial* page. The code for Step 2(b) is highlighted.

```
<SCRIPT LANGUAGE = "JavaScript">
<!--
    var n = parseInt(prompt("Enter N: ", ""))
    if (n == 0)
      document.write("0! == 1");
    else {
      var factorial = 1;
      var i;
      document.write(n + "! = ( ");
      for (i=n; i >= 1; i--) {
         factorial = factorial * i;
         document.write(i);
         if (i > 1)
            document.write(" &middot; ");
      }
      document.write(") = " + factorial);
    }
//-->
</SCRIPT>
```

Figure 11.12 JS Script for the *Factorial* Page

NESTED for LOOPS

Having successfully written a program requiring multiplication, we're ready to tackle a more sophisticated problem: multiplication tables. Figure 11.13 contains a sample page. The user enters the first and last values; we generate a multiplication table using these values. Elementary teachers could easily modify the table to quiz students; we consider that variation in the practice exercises.

Examine the multiplication table in Figure 11.13. You might want to jot down a list of program steps using both English and JavaScript statements before examining the pseudocode for the *Multiplication Table* page contained in Figure 11.14.

The first two steps and the last step in Figure 11.14 involve previously discussed techniques. The initial versions of the *Multiplication Table* page should incorporate only these steps. The third step contains a simple **for** statement that prints the white column headings against a black background. Before continuing, try to write and test the JavaScript code to implement these steps. Make sure that you close the table as your last step. Don't worry about the fourth step at this stage.

Nesting for Statements

Unlike the *Factorial* page, which produced a single row of information, the *Multiplication Table* page must generate several rows of information. Processing or printing tables requires a set of nested **for** statements. One **for** statement processes the rows, while the second **for** statement processes the columns within a row. Figure 11.15 shows a simple set of nested **for** statements. These **for** statements print the values of *i* and *j* on the page. This simple example illustrates the inner (and outer) workings of nested loops.

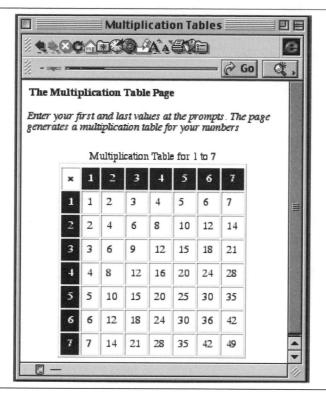

Figure 11.13 The *Multiplication Table* Page

Step 1. Use prompts to obtain the highest and lowest numbers:
```
var start = parseInt(prompt("Starting value", ""));
var stop = parseInt(prompt("Ending value" , ""));
```

Step 2. Create a table shell that contains the caption.
```
document.write("<CENTER><TABLE BORDER = '1' CELLPADDING = '5'>");
document.write("<CAPTION> Multiplication Table for " + start);
document.write(" to " + stop + "<CAPTION>");
```

Step 3. Use a **for** statement to create the first row of the table:
```
for (i = start; i <= stop; i++)
   document.write("<TH bgcolor = black> <FONT COLOR = white>" + i + "</FONT></TH>");
document.write("</TR>");
```

Step 4. Create a loop that generates the rest of the table.

Step 5. Close the table.
```
      document.write("</TABLE></CENTER>");
```

Figure 11.14 Pseudocode for the *Multiplication Table* Page

```
for (i = 1; i <= 2; i++)
    for (j = 1; j <= 3; j++)
        document.write(i + " " + j + "<BR>");
```

Figure 11.15 Nested **for** statements

The **for** statement that uses the index *i* is referred to as the *outer loop*. This loop is also the *slow loop*, so named because the values of *i* change more slowly than the values of *j*. The **for** statement that uses the index *j* is referred to as the *inner loop*. This loop is the *fast loop*, because each index change in the outer loop causes the inner loop to execute completely. For example, while *i* is one, *j* changes from 1 to 4. Figure 11.16 contains a walk-through for the loops shown in Figure 11.15. Notice the *i* and *j* values for each iteration of the inner and outer loops.

i	j	i <= 2	j <= 3	Output
1	1	1 <= 2	1 <= 3	1 1
1	2	1 <= 2	2 <= 3	1 2
1	3	1 <= 2	3 <= 3	1 3
1	4		*j loop stops*	
2	1	2 <= 2	1 <= 3	2 1
2	2	2 <= 2	2 <= 3	2 2
2	2	2 <= 2	3 <= 3	2 3
2	4		*j loop stops*	
3		*i loop stops*		

Figure 11.16 Walk-through for Figure 11.15

The *Multiplication Table* Nested **for** Loop

Creation of the multiplication table begins with a simple modification of the **for** statement headers used in Figure 11.15. These modifications reflect user input, that is, the multiplication table is based on the starting and stopping values provided by the user. Figure 11.17 contains the pseudocode for the *Multiplication Table's* loop structure. The **for** statement headers represent actual JavaScript code. The loop bodies contain comments that indicate the loop's task lists.

```
for (i = start; i <= stop; i++) {
    //print the row number in white with a black background
    for (j = start; j <= stop; j++)
    //print the "answer" for this row and column
    //end the current table row
}
```

Figure 11.17 Pseudocode for the *Multiplication Table's* Loop Structure

Compare the loop structures in Figure 11.15 and Figure 11.17. Notice their structural similarity. This structure is the starting point for any page that requires tabular data. Figure 11.17 is also a *pseudocode* version of the last program step, so you might want to write the JavaScript statements from the pseudocode before examining Figure 11.18. This figure contains the complete script for the *Multiplication Table* page. The nested for loops are highlighted.

```
<SCRIPT LANGUAGE= "JavaScript">
<!--
   var start = parseInt(prompt("Starting value", ""));
   var stop = parseInt(prompt("Ending value" , ""));
   var i,j;
   document.write("<CENTER><TABLE BORDER = '1' CELLPADDING = '5'>");
   document.write("<CAPTION> Multiplication Table for " + start);
   document.write(" to " + stop + "<CAPTION>");
   document.write("<TR><TH>&times;</TH>");

   //**print column numbers**
   for (i = start; i <= stop; i++)
      document.write("<TH BGCOLOR = 'black39><FONT COLOR = 'white'>" + i + "</FONT></TH>");
   document.write("</TR>");

   //**print the body of the multiplication table**
   for (i = start; i <= stop; i++) {
     document.write("<TR><TH BGCOLOR = 'black'> <FONT COLOR = 'white'>" + i + "</FONT></TH>");
     for (j = start; j <= stop; j++)
        document.write("<TD>" + (i*j) + "</TD>");
     document.write("</TR>");
   }
   document.write("</TABLE></CENTER>");
//-->
</SCRIPT>
```

Figure 11.18 JS Script for the *Multiplication Table* Page

THE while STATEMENT

The **while** statement has a simpler syntax than the **for** statement. As Figure 11.19 indicates, the **while** statement header contains the word **while** followed by a test expression. The statement in the body of the loop is executed as long as the expression is *true*. If the test expression is initially *false*, the body of the **while** statement is ignored. The body can contain either a single JavaScript statement or several statements encased in braces **{ }**.

```
while(Test Expression)
     Statement;
```

Figure 11.19 The while Statement

The Sales Tax Page, Revisited

Programmers use `while` statements to create error loops. An *error loop* is a code segment that checks for erroneous data and traps the user in a loop until they submit acceptable data. The user is always informed of the error and asked to resubmit data. For example, let's reconsider the *Sales Tax* page developed in Chapter 9. Recall that this page asks the user to enter an item's cost and the tax rate. The page calculates the sales tax and the total cost. Assume that the user isn't paying attention and presses the *Enter or Return* key before entering the item's cost. Figure 11.20 shows the resulting page.

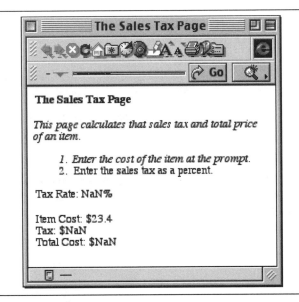

Figure 11.20 The Original *Sales Tax* Page

The *NaN*s appearing through out Figure 11.20 are confusing. Most users will not realize that *NaN* stands for *Not a Number* and that this error stems from erroneous user data. Instead, users will attribute the lack of a correct result to poor programming—and they will be justified!

Now consider the *Sales Tax* page appearing in Figure 11.21. In Figure 11.21(a), the user once again hits the *Enter* key before entering the item's cost. In this case, however, an error message appears, and the user is asked to re-enter the cost. Figure 11.21(b) shows the results. All errors are trapped; the user must enter appropriate data before the JS script calculates and prints any results.

Creating loops that trap nonnumeric data is a relatively easy task, because JavaScript provides an `isNan()` function that checks for nonnumeric data. Figure 11.22 describes the `isNaN()` function.

(a) Error Trapping

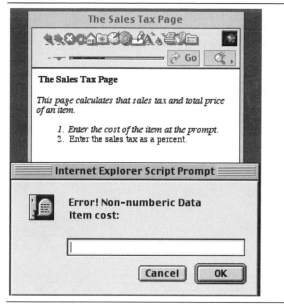

(b) Page Results

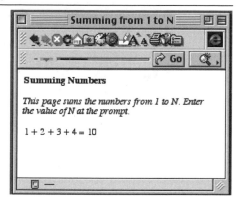

Figure 11.21 The *Sales Tax* Page with Error Trapping

---

isNaN(*value*)
returns *true* if *value* is Not a Number
returns *false* if *value* is a number

Figure 11.22 The `isNaN()` Function

Creating an error loop for nonnumeric data involves the following steps:

Step 1. Obtain the user's input in the normal fashion. For example, we obtain the item cost via the statement

```
var itemCost = parseFloat(prompt("Item cost: ", ""));
```

Step 2. Create an error loop that uses the `isNaN()` function as the test expression. For example, the error loop for the item cost is

```
while (isNaN(itemCost))
    itemCost = parseFloat(prompt("Item cost: ", ""));
```

This statement indicates that, as long as *itemCost* is not a number, the script asks the user to reenter the cost. This two-step approach is repeated for each numeric variable. The *Sales Tax* page asks the user to enter the item cost and the sales tax, so the script must include an error loop for each variable. Figure 11.23 contains the revised *Sales Tax* page. The code for the error loops is highlighted.

```
<SCRIPT LANGUAGE = "JavaScript">
<!--
    var itemCost = parseFloat(prompt("Item cost: ", ""));
    while (isNaN(itemCost))
        itemCost = parseFloat(prompt("Error! Non-numberic Data\nItem cost: ", ""));
    var salesTax = parseFloat(prompt("Sale's tax:", ""));
    while (isNaN(salesTax))
        salesTax = parseFloat(prompt("Error! Non-numeric Data\n Sales tax: ", ""));
    salesTax /= 100; //convert to a proportion
    var amountTax = (itemCost * salesTax);
    var totalCost = itemCost + amountTax;
    //convert the numbers to dollars and cents format: $XXXX.XX
    amountTax = Math.round(amountTax * Math.pow(10,2))/Math.pow(10,2);
    totalCost = Math.round(totalCost * Math.pow(10,2))/Math.pow(10,2);
    document.write("Tax Rate: " + salesTax*100 + "%<P>");
    document.write("Item Cost: $" + itemCost);
    document.write("<BR>Tax: $" + amountTax);
    document.write("<BR>Total Cost: $" + totalCost);
//-->
</SCRIPT>
```

Figure 11.23 JS Script for the Revised *Sales Tax* Page

Changing for Statements into while Statements

The JavaScript **for** and **while** statements do exactly the same things but in different ways. This redundancy gives programmers flexibility and coding alternatives. Alternatives are always desirable, because sometimes we get stuck trying to correct logical errors. Switching to a different coding strategy often reveals errors in our thinking. Converting a **for** statement into an equivalent **while** statement is a relatively easy task. To illustrate this conversion process, we use a simple page that sums the numbers from 1 to *n*. Figure 11.24(a) contains a sample page, and Figure 11.24(b) contains the JS script for the page.

(a) The *Summing* **Page**

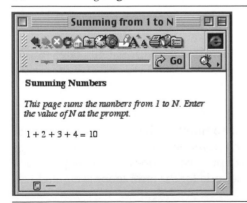

(b) JS Script for the *Summing* **Page**

```
<SCRIPT LANGUAGE = "JavaScript">
<!--
    var n = parseInt(prompt("Enter N: ", ""));
    var sum = 0;
    var i;
    for (i=1; i<=n; i++) {
        sum += i;
        document.write(i);
        if (i < n)
            document.write(" + ");
    }
    document.write(" = " + sum);
//-->
</SCRIPT>
```

Figure 11.24 The *Summing* Page

The *Summing* page contained in Figure 11.24 uses the same structure as the *Factorial* page. The summing variable is initialized to zero prior to the start of the **for** statement. The **for** statement header contains the initial expression i = 1, the test expression i <= n, and the change expression i++.

Figure 11.25 converts the **for** statement used in the *Summing* page into the equivalent **while** statement.

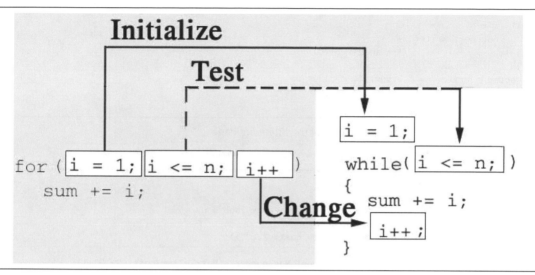

Figure 11.25 Converting a **for** Statement into a **while** Statement

The four steps in this conversion process are as follows:

Step 1. Initialization. The initial expression in the **for** statement is placed **before** the **while** statement header.

Step 2. Test Expression. The test expression in the **for** statement becomes the expression in the **while** statement header.

Step 3. Body. The body of the **for** statement becomes the body of the **while** statement.

Step 4. Change Expression. The change expression in the **for** statement header becomes the last statement in the body of the **while** statement.

Figure 11.26 contains the code to implement the summing page by using a **while** statement. The page's appearance in a browser is identical to the **for** statement version.

We also can use Figure 11.25 to convert a **while** statement into the equivalent **for** statement. Typically, the transformation produces code that is harder to read, but it can be done. For example, Figure 11.27 shows the error loops in the *Sales Tax* page written as **for** statements.

Let's examine the code for each of these loops. The error loop for the item cost places all of the code in the **for** statement header. The code for this loop is as follows:

```
for (itemCost = parseFloat(prompt("Item cost: ", "")); 
    isNaN(itemCost); 
    itemCost = parseFloat(prompt("Error! Non-numberic Data\nItem cost: ", ""))) 
    ; //Empty body
```

```
<SCRIPT LANGUAGE = "JavaScript">
<!--
    var n = parseInt(prompt("Enter N: ", ""));
    var sum = 0;          //**initialize sum to 0**
    var i = 1;            //**initialize i**
    while (i <= n) {      //**test condition**
    sum += i;
    document.write(i);
    if (i < n)
        document.write(" + ");
    i++;                  //**change i **
    }
    document.write(" = " + sum);
//-->
!/SCRIPT>
```

Figure 11.26 A **while** Statement Version of the *Summing* Page

```
<SCRIPT LANGUAGE = "JavaScript">
<!--
    //Everything coded in for statement header, empty loop body
    var itemCost;
    for (itemCost = parseFloat(prompt("Item cost: ", ""));
        isNaN(itemCost);
        itemCost = parseFloat(prompt("Error! Non-numberic Data\nItem cost: ", "")))
            ; //Empty body

    //only test expression in for statement
    var salesTax = parseFloat(prompt("Sale's tax:", "")); //initialize
    for(;isNaN(salesTax);)
        salesTax = parseFloat(prompt("Error! Non-numeric Data\n Sales tax: ", "")); //change

    //Rest of page is unchanged
//-->
!/SCRIPT>
```

Figure 11.27 Error Loops Written as **for** Statements

The initial expression obtains an item cost from the user. The abbreviated test expression indicates that the body of the loop is executed as long as *itemCost* is not a number. The change expression prompts the user for another number. Now, notice the body of this **for** statement. It contains only a semicolon. The **for** statement header does all of the work, so the body is empty.

Now, let's consider the second **for** statement. The code is as follows:

```
var salesTax = parseFloat(prompt("Sale's tax:", "")); //initialize
for(;isNaN(salesTax);)
    salesTax =
    parseFloat(prompt("Error! Non-numeric Data\n Sales tax: ", ""));
```

The **for** statement includes only a test expression and a change expression. An initial expression is unnecessary, because the statement that immediately precedes the **for** statement asks the user to enter the sales tax. The first semicolon in the header indicates that the initial expression is absent.

This **for** statement also has an empty body, as denoted by the semicolon that appears after the header. This code is more obscure, because the semicolon is buried. The initial **for** statement placed the semicolon on a separate line and included a comment indicating that the body of the loop was empty.

THE do...while **STATEMENT**

The **for** and **while** statements always check the test expression *before* executing the statement in the body. In contrast, the **do...while** statement checks the test expression **after** it executes the statement in the body. This means that the body of the **do...while** statement always executes **at least once**. The body can contain a single statement or multiple statements encased in braces, **{}**. Figure 11.28 shows the syntax of this statement.

```
do
    statement;
while(Test Expression);
```

Figure 11.28 The **do...while** Statement

Most programming problems need a constraint of **zero or more iterations**, so the **do...while** statement is used less frequently than the other two iteration statements. The calculation of factorials when *n* is greater than 1 constitutes a perfect application of the **do...while** statement. Figure 11.29 shows the *Factorial* page written with a **do...while** statement. The page produced by this code is identical in appearance to the page produced by the **for** statement version (Figure 11.10).

```
<SCRIPT Language = "JavaScript">
<!--
    var n = parseInt(prompt("Enter N: ", ""))
    if (n == 0)
      document.write("0! == 1");
    else {
       document.write(n + "! = ( ");
       var factorial = 1;
       var i = n;//initialize
       do {
          factorial *= i;
          document.write(i);
          if (i > 1)
             document.write(" &middot; ");
          i--;
       }while(i >= 1);
       document.write(") = " + factorial);
    }
//-->
</SCRIPT>
```

Figure 11.29 A **do...while** Version of the *Factorial* Page

LOOPING PITFALLS

Looping statements introduce a new set of errors to the programming process. The two most common errors are the following:

Infinite Loops.   As its name suggests, an *infinite* loop is a loop that never terminates. The usual cause of such errors is an erroneous or absent change expression or an erroneous test expression. For example, let's think about the factorial page. Suppose we write the **for** statement header as

```
for (i=n; i >= 1; i++)
```

Because the change expression, i++, increments *i*, the test expression, i >= 1, will **always** remain *true*. The result is a page of ever-changing numbers that never halts. You can try pressing the *stop* button on your browser: it won't do any good. You can try to exit your browser. This works if the browser's program space hasn't been corrupted. (You'll know if it's corrupted: The browser will start to fade.) If everything else fails, you can turn off the machine and hope for the best.

Creating a walk-through for a loop will detect nonterminating loops. A few iterations are usually sufficient to determine whether the change and test expressions work correctly.

Off-by-one Errors.   An *off-by-one error* means that the loop performs one too many or one too few iterations. The usual cause of these errors is an erroneous test expression. Always check the relational operators used in an expression; they are the usual culprits. For example, <= is often written when we really need <, and *vice versa*. Similarly, >= is often erroneously written instead of >, and *vice versa*. A walk-through table and test data are the best strategies for finding and correcting *off-by-one errors*.

In addition the equality, ==, and inequality, !=, operators should not be used with floating-point numbers. Because conversion errors occur when floating-point numbers are converted to binary, the binary number can differ from its decimal counterpart. Always rephrase equality and inequality operators as <= or >=. For example, the **for** statement header

```
for (a = 2.5; a!=10.2; a += 5)
```

should be rewritten as

```
for (a = 2.5; a < 10.2; a+=5)
```

➤ PRACTICE EXERCISES

The practice exercises that follow include translations of mathematical functions, tables of English-to-metric conversions, and error loops. Try creating different versions of the pages by using the loops discussed in this chapter. Make sure that you have appropriate test data. Use walk-throughs to verify that your loops work correctly.

1. **Counting the numbers in an interval.** Create a page that asks the user to enter beginning and ending values and an increment. Print the numbers in the interval and print a count. *Hint: Counting is similar to summing, except that you always add one.*

2. **The *Fibonacci* Page.** Create a page that asks the user to enter a value for *n*. Write an error loop to make sure that *n* is numeric. Generate the Fibonacci number for *n*. Figure 11.30 contains the Fibonacci formula.

n = 0, fib(n) = 1
n = 1, fib(n) = 1
n > 1, fib(n) = fib(n − 1) + fib(n − 2);

Figure 11.30 The Fibonacci Formula

Figure 11.31 shows the Fibonacci numbers for values of *n* from 0 to 8.

n	0	1	2	3	4	5	6	7	8
fib(n)	1	1	2	3	5	8	13	21	34

Figure 11.31 The Fibonacci Numbers from 0 to 8

3. **The Harmonic Function.** Figure 11.32 contains the mathematical formula for the harmonic function. Create a web page that asks the user to enter the value of *n*. Print out the function as it appears in Figure 11.33, and print out the sum.

$H(n) = 1 + 1/2 + 1/3 + 1/4 + ... + 1/n$

Figure 11.32 The Harmonic Function

Hint: 1 is the same as 1/1.

4. **An Alternating Series Function.** Figure 11.33 contains the formula for an alternating series. Create a web page that asks the user to enter the value of *n*. Print the function as it appears in Figure 11.33. Print the sum.

$F(n) = 1 + 1/2 − 1/3 + 1/4 − 1/5 + ... + 1/n$

Figure 11.33 An Alternating Series Function

Hint: To change the signs, use **pow(-1, i)**. When *i* is even, this expression will be positive; when *i* is odd, it will be negative.

5. **The *Measuring Mountains* Page.** Europeans and Canadians measure their mountains in meters; citizens of the United States prefer feet (or sometimes yards). Create a page that asks the user to enter the highest and lowest meters. Print the meters from highest to lowest at 200-meter decrements and the foot and yard equivalents. Figure 11.34 contains the relevant formulas.

Metric to U.S.	U.S. to Metric
feet = meters / 0.3048	Meters = feet / 3.28
yards = meters / 0.9144	meters = yards / 1.09

Figure 11.34 English and Metric Conversions (Meters)

6. **Teaspoons and Tablespoons to Cubic Centimeters.** Cookbooks in the United States use teaspoons and tablespoons; Europeans prefer cubic centimeters (cm^3). Create a page that asks the user to enter the lowest and highest teaspoon values. Assume a change of 1 teaspoon. Print out the cubic centimeters. Also, print out tablespoons where appropriate. Remember that 3 teaspoons = 1 tablespoon. So, for every three teaspoons, you should print the tablespoon measure. Figure 11.35(b) contains the appropriate formulas.

(a) Metric to U.S.	(b) U.S. to Metric
TSP $=$ cm^3 / 4.929	cm^3 $=$ teaspoons / 0.20
TBS $=$ cm^3 / 14.788	cm^3 $=$ tablespoons / 0.06.76

Figure 11.35 English and Metric Conversions (Cubic Centimeters)

7. **Cubic Centimeters to Teaspoons and Tablespoons.** Reverse the previous exercise. Ask the user to enter the lowest and highest cubic centimeters. Print the teaspoon equivalent in a separate column. Figure 11.35(a) contains the appropriate formulas.

8. **The *Kitchen Conversion* Page for Liquid Measures.** Europeans and Canadians use liters to measure liquids; citizens of the United States prefer cups, pints, quarts, and gallons. Ask the user to enter the lowest and highest liters. Assume a one-liter change. Print a table that contains the liters and their equivalents in cups. Figure 11.36(a) contains the appropriate formula.

(a) Metric to U.S.	(b) U.S. to Metric
cups $=$ liters / 0.2366	liters $=$ cups / 4.23
pints $=$ liters / 0.4732	liters $=$ pints / 2.11
quarts $=$ liters / 0.9463	liters $=$ quarts / 1.06
gallons $=$ liters / 3.785	liters $=$ gallons / 0.26

Figure 11.36 Liquid Conversions

9. **The *Liquid Measures* Page, Revisited.** Ask the user to enter the lowest and highest number of cups. Convert the cups to pints, quarts, gallons, and liters. Create columns for cups, pints, quarts, gallons, and liters. Use Figure 11.35(b) and Figure 11.37.

2 cups $=$ 1 pint
2 pints $=$ 1 quart
4 quarts $=$ 1 gallon

Figure 11.37 Cups, Pints, Quarts, and Gallons

10. **The *Dry Measures Conversion* Page.** Europeans and Canadians also use liters to measure dry goods; citizens of the United States prefer pecks and bushels. Create a page that lets the user

enter the lowest and highest liters. Convert the liters into pecks and bushels. Present the results in a table. Figure 11.38(a) contains the appropriate formulas.

(a) Metric to U.S.	(b) U.S. to Metric
pecks = liters / 8.809	liters = pecks / 0.1135
bushels = liters / 35.24	liters = bushels / 0.26

Figure 11.38 Dry Measures

11. **The *Weight Conversion* Page.** Many doctor's offices measure weight in kilograms, while the rest of us still use pounds. Create a page that lets the user enter the lowest and highest weight in Kilos. Also let the user enter a weight increment. Create a table that prints the weights in Kilos and their pound equivalents. Figure 11.39(a) contains the appropriate formula.

(a) Metric to U.S.	(b) U.S. to Metric
Ounces = grams / 28.3495	grams = ounces / 0.035
pounds = kilos / 0.4536	kilos = pounds / 2.2

Figure 11.39 Weight Formulas

12. **Modifying the *Multiplication* Page, version 1.** Modify the multiplication page so that it prints only the answers on the diagonal (i.e., 1 · 1, 2 · 2, and so on).

13. **Modifying the *Multiplication* Page, version 2.** Use a prompt to ask the user whether to generate a multiplication or an addition table. Create the appropriate table for the user.

14. **Letter Boxes and Rectangles.** Create a page that asks the user to enter a *width*, *length*, and *letter*. Create a box of *width* × *length* letters. For example, if *width* = 5, *length* = 3, and *letter* = S, the box should be:

```
SSSSS
SSSSS
SSSSS
```

15. **The *Celsius Table* Page, Revisited.** Modify the *Celsius to Fahrenheit* page (Figure 11.6) so that it contains a error loop.

16. **The *Multiplication* Page, Revisited.** Modify the *Multiplication Table* page (Figure 11.19) so that it contains error loops.

17. **The *Test Score* Page, Revisited.** Modify the *Test Score* page (Figure 10.17) so that it contains error loops.

18. **The *Azalea* Page, Revisited.** Modify the *Azalea* page (Figure 10.9) so that it contains an error loop if the user enters a negative pH level.

19. **Arithmetic Exercises.** Modify one of the pages in the arithmetic exercises in Chapter 9 so that your script contains an error loop.

➤ **JAVASCRIPT VOCABULARY**

Error Loop.   Programmers use error loops to trap erroneous data. The error loop, which is typically coded by using a `while` statement, prints an error message and asks the user to reenter data. The user is trapped in the loop until having correctly entered the information.

Index (or Index Variable).   An index variable is used in a `for` statement. The index is given an appropriate initial value. The increment expression changes the index, and the test expression compares the index with some final value.

Infinite Loop.   As its name implies, an infinite loop never terminates. Incorrect test expressions are the usual cause of infinite loops. Sometimes they are caused by *conversion errors*. Conversions errors usually occur when the computer cannot correctly translate a floating-point number into exactly equivalent binary, so you should never use strict equality (`==`) or inequality (`!=`) when testing floating-point expressions.

Iteration.   Iteration is one way of repeating a set of JavaScript statements.

Nested Loop.   A nested loop is a `for` statement that contains a second `for` statement.

Off-by-one Errors.   Off-by-one errors occur when a loop executes one too few or one too many times. An appropriate set of test data will detect off-by-one errors.

Pseudocode.   Pseudocode is a combination of English and programming code. We use pseudocode to help us think about a programming problem.

Stepwise Refinement.   Stepwise refinement is a program development technique. It emphasizes coding small segments and building these segments into a larger program.

Walk-through.   A walk-through is a table that is used to hand-test a looping statement. It contains the index variable and the expression. Walk-throughs can detect off-by-one errors and infinite loops.

12 Functions and Objects

The *stepwise refinement* method, introduced in Chapter 11, involves more than writing and testing small code segments. This method also emphasizes "tweaking" code until an elegant, efficient, and reliable programming solution is obtained. As an example, consider the *Sales Tax* page. We've now written two versions of this page. The first version, introduced in Chapter 9, did not include error traps. The second version, introduced in Chapter 11, added traps for nonnumeric data. A portion of the JS script appears in Figure 12.1. As the comments indicate, the *Sales Tax* script is full of redundant code, that is, repeated instances of identical or nearly identical code. The code to obtain and check a numeric variable is always the same; so is the code to round a number.

```
<SCRIPT LANGUAGE = "JavaScript">
<!--
  //Code for itemCost and salesTax is redundant
var itemCost = parseFloat(prompt("Item cost: ", ""));
while (isNaN(itemCost))
    itemCost = parseFloat(prompt("Error! Non-numberic Data\nItem cost: ", ""));
var salesTax = parseFloat(prompt("Sale's tax:", ""));
while (isNaN(salesTax))
    salesTax = parseFloat(prompt("Error! Non-numeric Data\n Sales tax: ", ""));
salesTax /= 100; //convert to a proportion

//Code for rounding is redundant
var amountTax = (itemCost * salesTax);
var totalCost = itemCost + amountTax;
//convert the numbers to dollars and cents format: $XXXX.XX
amountTax = Math.round(amountTax * Math.pow(10,2))/Math.pow(10,2);
totalCost = Math.round(totalCost * Math.pow(10,2))/Math.pow(10,2);

//Rest of script goes here
//-->
</SCRIPT>
```

Figure 12.1 JS Script for the *Sales Tax* Page

Redundant code is neither efficient nor reliable. In this chapter, we learn to create reusable code. The two vehicles that let us accomplish this feat are programmer-defined functions and objects. We have used JavaScript objects (`window, document`) and functions (`parseFloat()`, `parseInt(), isNaN()`). Now, we are going to create our own objects and functions. Before we begin, let's review object and function terminology.

A JavaScript object contains properties and methods. The *properties* represent an object's attributes. For example, the JavaScript `window` object contains a `document` property. *Methods* are functions that are associated with an object. For example, the `document` object has a `write()` method. A function is a reusable piece of code that is not attached to an object. JavaScript provides several built-in functions, including `parseFloat()`.

Now, let's consider some additional terminology for programmer-defined functions.

JAVASCRIPT PROGRAMMER-DEFINED FUNCTIONS

Before we can create functions, we must acquire a new vocabulary. Here's an initial vocabulary list:

Function Call: When we use a function, we *call* it.

Function Caller.   The caller is the statement that invoked or called the function. If a function returns a value, the value goes to the caller.

Parameters.   Most functions require user-supplied information to complete their task. Each piece of information is a parameter. The function definition determines the number of parameters.

Return Value.   Many functions return information to the user. For example, `parseFloat()` returns a floating point number. When used in the context of a function, *return* means "send back to the caller." Many beginning programmers assume that *return* means print on the page. It doesn't.

To illustrate this vocabulary, consider this statement from Figure 12.1.

```
var itemCost = parseFloat(prompt("Item cost: ", ""));
```

The statement combines calls to a function (`parseFloat()`) and a method (`window.prompt()`) in a single line. It is easier to see the relation between the caller, the parameter(s), and the return value if we break this statement into two parts, as illustrated in Figure 12.2. This figure creates a variable, *stringCost*, that holds the value returned by the `prompt()` method. We pass *stringCost* as a parameter to the `parseFloat()` function, which returns the floating-point counterpart of *stringCost*.

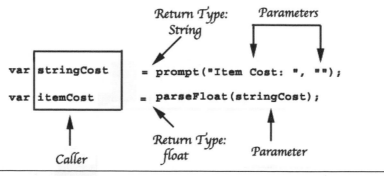

Figure 12.2 Illustrating Function Terminology

As Figure 12.2 indicates, the `prompt()` method uses two parameters. The first parameter is a prompt string (`"Item Cost: "`). The second, optional parameter, is a default value (`""`). The implicit return type is a string that the `prompt()` method returns to its caller, `stringCost =`. The `parseFloat()` function requires a single string parameter. We pass the string variable *stringCost*. The `parseFloat()` function returns a floating-point number (or `NaN`) to its caller, `itemCost =`.

Function Definitions

Creating a new function begins with a function definition. Figure 12.3 shows the JavaScript syntax for a function definition.

---

function *Name* (*ParameterList*)
{
  statement₁;
    ....
  statementₙ;
}

Figure 12.3 Function Definition Syntax

The *function definition* contains the code that implements the function. This definition contains a header and a body. The header is the first line of the function definition. The body is the list of statements that appears inside the braces. As Figure 12.3 indicates, the header contains the function's name and a parameter list. The latter is simply a comma-separated list of names. The function designer determines the number of parameters, their names, and their order in the parameter list.

Function Design Rules

We're now ready to begin the function creation process. If you ask any experienced programmer how she or he creates functions, you'll probably get a list of *Do's and Don'ts*. This is my list:

Rule 1. A function should perform one and only one task. The name of the function should accurately reflect this task.   For example, a function that obtains a floating-point number from the user should have a name like `getFloat()`. If the function has a name like `findAreaAndCircumference()` you've missed the mark. This function has limited usefulness because users may not want to find both the area and circumference. Functions that do more than one thing have limited usability.

Rule 2. Keep function users on a need to know basis.   This means that function details should be concealed from users. The parameters should be kept to the minimum necessary to complete the task. For example, consider a function that calculates the area of a circle $(PI \bullet R^2)$. Circles have different radii, so the function requires a single parameter: the radius. Pi should not be passed as a parameter, because we can use the built-in `Math` constant.

Rule 3. Return results to the function caller.   Let's consider the `area()` function again. A function that calculates the area of a circle should return the area to the user. The function should NOT print the area on the page. The only functions that print information should be ones that have `print` in their names. Returning information to the function caller increases the usefulness of a function.

The `roundPlaces()` Function

As our first excursion into function design, we create a **roundPlaces()** function. Reexamine the rounding code that appears in Figure 12.1. Determine the information that the user must provide to the function. Determine what the function should return to the user. After you have finished, look at Figure 12.4. It contains a description of the **roundPlaces()** function.

roundPlaces()	
PURPOSE	Round a floating-point number.
SYNTAX	**roundPlaces** (*number, places*)
PARAMETERS	
number	The floating-point number to be rounded.
places	The number of decimal places.

Figure 12.4 Description of the **roundPlaces()** Function

A *function description* provides information on a function's purpose, syntax, and parameters. Programming reference manuals provide descriptions of all built-in functions and methods. Function designers should create similar descriptions. A notebook of these descriptions is worthwhile even if you're the only function user. The meanings of parameters and the exact purposes of functions are quickly forgotten.

The description of the **roundPlaces()** function indicates that the user supplies a number and the desired decimal places. The function returns the rounded number. Because the function returns (sends back) a number, we can use the function *anywhere* that we would use a number. Figure 12.5 shows the function description and two function calls. Although we have not written the function definition, the function description should provide enough information to create function calls.

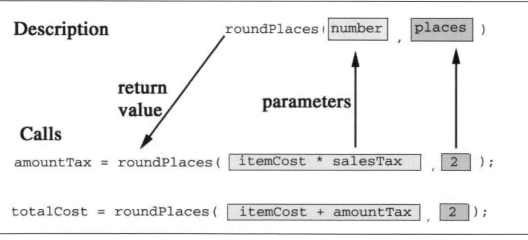

Figure 12.5 Using Function Descriptions to Create Calls

The first call in Figure 12.5 calculates the amount of sales tax and rounds this tax to two decimal points. The call uses the expression, `itemCost*salesTax` as the *number* parameter. This is perfectly legal. In fact, we can use any numeric literal, expression, variable, or function returning a number as a parameter. The function returns the rounded result, which is assigned to the variable *amountTax*. The second call uses `itemCost + amountTax` as the *number* parameter and 2 as the *places* parameter. The rounded result is placed in the variable *totalCost*.

In addition to supplying information to users, a function description is our guide to creating the function definition. We form the function header by placing the word **function** in front of the syntax description. Thus, the function header for the **roundPlaces()** function is

```
function roundPlaces(number,places)
```

To create the function body, we rewrite the rounding statement so that it uses the parameters in the function header. We're using *number* and *places* as parameters, so the new rounding code is:

```
Math.round(number * Math.pow(10,places))/Math.pow(10,places)
```

To return the results to a user, we create a *return statement* by placing the word **return** in front of our rounding code. A semicolon ends the statement.

A return statement does two things:

It stops execution of the function. Any JavaScript statements below a return statement are ignored. To stop execution of a function, we need only write **return** ;.

It returns a value to the caller. This value is placed to the right of **return**. The value can be a literal, a variable, an expression, or a function call. Returning a value also stops execution of the function.

Because the **roundPlaces()** function must return the rounded results, the **return** statement is

```
return Math.round(number * Math.pow(10,places))/Math.pow(10,places);
```

Figure 12.6 contains the complete definition of the **roundPlaces()** function.

```
function roundPlaces(number, places)
{//round number to desired decimal places
    return Math.round(number * Math.pow(10,places))/Math.pow(10,places);
}
```

Figure 12.6 The **roundPlaces()** Function

Because the **roundPlaces()** function is not built into the JavaScript language, we must place the function definition inside a script before we can issue function calls. Web programmers typically place function definitions in a script located in the head of the page. We'll look at the complete revision of the *Sales Tax* script shortly. This script illustrates the correct placement of the function definitions and calls.

LOCAL VARIABLES

A second function, **getFloat()**, removes the redundant code associated with getting a floating point number from the user. Figure 12.7 contains a function description.

---

getFloat()

PURPOSE	Return a valid floating point number.
SYNTAX	**getFloat** (*message*)
PARAMETERS	
message	The prompt displayed to the user.

Figure 12.7 Description of the **getFloat()** function

The description of the **getFloat()** function clearly indicates that this function returns only a valid floating-point number. Thus, the function encapsulates the error handling code. The programmer supplies the desired prompt. We use this function to obtain the *itemCost* and *salesTax* information from the user. Reexamine the redundant code in Figure 12.1. The **getFloat()** function reduces this redundant code to the following two lines:

```
var itemCost = getFloat("Item Cost: ");
var salesTax = getFloat("Sales Tax: ")/100;
```

The definition of the **getFloat()** function appears in Figure 12.8. This function uses a parameter, *message*, and a local variable, *x*. A *local variable* is one that has meaning only within its defining function. Because *x* is defined in **getFloat()**, we cannot use it outside **getFloat()**.

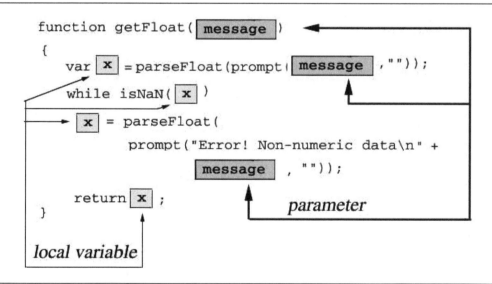

Figure 12.8 The **getFloat()** Function

The **getFloat()** function definition uses the local variable *x* to hold the parsed floating-point number obtained from the user. Function designers can create as many local variables as they need, and they can reuse the same variable name in different functions. Local variables are one way of concealing unnecessary details from function users.

We're now ready to examine our new version of the *Sales Tax* script. This version appears in Figure 12.9. Compare the new code with the version appearing in Figure 12.1. The new version is both reliable and elegant.

```
<SCRIPT LANGUAGE = "JavaScript">
<!- -
  function getFloat(message)
  {/* print the message for the prompt
     Use an error loop to check for non-numeric data */
    var x = parseFloat(prompt(message, ""));
    while (isNaN(x))
      x = parseFloat(prompt("Error! Non-numeric data\n" + message, ""));
    return x;
  }
  function roundPlaces(number, places)
  {//round number to desired decimal places
     return Math.round(number * Math.pow(10,places))/Math.pow(10,places);
   }
  var itemCost = getFloat("Item Cost: ");
  var salesTax = getFloat("Sale's tax:")/100;
  var amountTax = roundPlaces(itemCost * salesTax, 2);
  var totalCost = roundPlaces(itemCost + amountTax,2);
  document.write("Tax Rate: " + salesTax*100 + "%<P>");
  document.write("Item Cost: $" + itemCost);
  document.write("<BR>Tax: $" + amountTax);
  document.write("<BR>Total Cost: $" + totalCost);
//-->
</SCRIPT>
```

Figure 12.9 Revised JS Script for *Sales Tax* Page

CALLING FUNCTIONS WITHIN A FUNCTION

The concept of reusability also emphasizes building new functions from old ones. For example, suppose a script requires integer values. We can create a **getInt()** function with almost no effort if we use the **getFloat()** function. After all, an integer is only a floating-point number that's been rounded. Thus, to create the **getInt()** function, we call the **getFloat()** function and round the result. The function definition appears in Figure 12.10.

```
function getInt(message)
{//get an integer
   return Math.round(getFloat(message));
}
```

Figure 12.10 The **getInt()** Function

The new functions reduce the time taken to write new scripts. Whenever we need one of these functions, we simply copy the code to the script. Functions can also be stored in a separate file with an extension of **.js**. This would let us load the functions into any script. Because we tested the functions when we created them, we know that they will work reliably.

PROGRAMMER-DEFINED OBJECTS

We now turn our attention to programmer-defined objects, also referred to as *custom objects*. Although JavaScript provides several built-in objects, it cannot provide objects for every conceivable area. Instead it provides facilities that let programmers define new objects of their choice. Once they are defined, a programmer can use these objects as though they were built-in. Of course, the programmer must include the object definition in every script that requires this object.

To illustrate object creation, think about a circle. As an object, a circle must have both properties and methods. Try to list a circle's properties and methods. Figure 12.11 contains a model for a *Circle* object. This object contains a single property, *radius*. Other properties, such as the *x* and *y* coordinates of the circle's center, could have be included. The *Circle* object contains methods that return the area, circumference, and radius of a *Circle* object. Additional methods change the radius and print the information about a *Circle* object.

Circle		
Properties	radius	
Methods	Circle()	//Constructor
	setRadius()	//Change a Circle object's radius
	getRadius()	//Return a Circle object's radius
	area()	//Return the area
	circumference()	//Return the circumference
	print()	//Print the circle's radius, area and circumference

Figure 12.11 Model for the *Circle* Object

Figure 12.12 contains a sample page that uses *Circle* objects. The page creates two *Circle* objects: a default circle with a radius of 5, and a circle with a radius of the user's choice. Figure 12.12(a) shows the page as the user enters the radius. Figure 12.12(b) shows the completed page. The final page uses all of the *Circle* methods contained in Figure 12.11.

Creating the Circle Object

Creating a new object is a two-step process:

Step 1. Create Function Definitions.   Every method specified in the object model must have a corresponding function definition. The function names do not need to match the method names; a constructor links the methods with the functions. This lack of correspondence lets us create similar methods for different objects. For example, suppose we want to create a *Circle* and a *Rectangle* object. Both objects will have an **area()** method, and so both objects will need an **area()** function definition. We cannot name both functions **area()**, because JavaScript would view this practice as a duplicate function definition. Duplicate function definitions are illegal, and the JavaScript interpreter would trigger an error message. We get around this problem by choosing different names for the functions—for example, **cArea()** and **rectArea()**. In contrast, duplicate

(a) Data Entry

(b) Completed Page

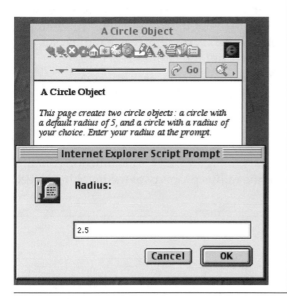
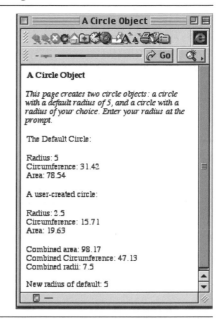

Figure 12.12 The *Circle Object* Page

method names are perfectly legal. Thus, *Circle* and *Rectangle* objects may both have an **area()** method. Methods do not exist independently of their defining objects, so JavaScript can easily determine a method's owner.

Step 2. Create an Object Constructor. A *constructor* is a specialized function that contains an object's properties and links the object's methods to the function definitions created in Step 1. The first letter of each word in the constructor's name is always capitalized, in deference to JavaScript and Java conventions. The constructor is used to create instances of an object.

We're now ready to apply this process to our *Circle* object.

Step 1: Create the Function Definitions for the *Circle* Object

The object model contains **getRadius()** and **setRadius()** methods. By convention, a **set** method lets the user change a property's value; a **get** method returns the property's value to the caller. The Java programming language provides **get** and **set** methods for virtually all of its built-in classes. We'll follow Java's example when we create objects.

The definition of the **getRadius()** function appears in Figure 12.13.

```
function getRadius()
{//retrieve the radius
   return this.radius;
}
```

Figure 12.13 The **getRadius()** Function

The body of the **getRadius()** function contains a single line of code:

return this.radius;

The code uses standard object notation: a dot separates the property, *radius*, from the object, **this**. The object's name, **this**, is a *self-reference*. A programmer can create several instances of an object, each with its own radius, so JavaScript must be able to return the correct radius. For example, the *Circle Object* page (Figure 12.12) uses two circle objects: *defaultCircle*, with a radius of 5, and *yourCircle*, with a radius of 2.5. The following statements print the radius of each object:

document.write("Radius of Default Circle: " + defaultCircle.getRadius());
**document.write("
 Radius of Your circle: " + yourCircle.getRadius());**

When **defaultCircle.getRadius()** is called, **this** refers to the *defaultCircle* object. When **yourCircle.getRadius()** is called, **this** refers to the *yourCircle* object. In each example, **getRadius()** refers back to the invoking object or, in other words, *this object*.

The definition of the **setRadius()** function appears in Figure 12.14. This function contains a *radius* parameter. It places the parameter's value in the radius property of the invoking object.

```
function setRadius(radius)
{//change the radius
    this.radius = radius;
}
```

Figure 12.14 The **setRadius()** Function

Suppose we want to change the radius of the *defaultCircle* object to 12.5. The following statement accomplishes this task:

defaultCircle.setRadius(12.5);

The remaining *Circle* functions are easy to write; however, most of these functions require the **roundPlaces()** method developed earlier in the chapter. The complete script also uses the **getFloat()** function. These function definitions must be copied into the *Circle Object* script. Figure 12.15 contains the definitions of the remaining functions.

```
function cArea()
{ //return the area of a Circle object
    return roundPlaces(Math.PI * Math.pow(this.radius, 2),2);
}
function cCircumference()
{//return the circumference of a Circle object
    return roundPlaces(2 * Math.PI * this.radius, 2);
}
function cPrint()
{//print a Circle's radius, area and circumference
    document.write("<P>Radius: " + this.radius);
    document.write("<BR>Circumference: " + this.circumference());
    document.write("<BR>Area: " + this.area() + "<P>");
}
```

Figure 12.15 Additional Function Definitions for the *Circle* Object

Notice the function names appearing in Figure 12.15. Each function contains the prefix c (for circle), to identify it as a *circle* function. For example, the function that determines the area of a circle is called **cArea()**. The actual area method for the *Circle* object will be called **area()**. Using an object prefix associates functions with objects. For example, we could create an **rArea()** method for rectangular objects and a **tArea()** function for triangular objects.

Step 2: The *Circle* Constructor

An object constructor establishes initial values for the object's properties, and it links the function definitions to the object's methods. Initial values for properties are handled through parameters. The linking of functions with methods is handled through assignment statements. The general form of these assignment statements is

```
this.MethodName = FunctionName;
```

The parameter lists, if any, are not included in these assignment statements—only the function and method names.

Figure 12.16 contains the constructor for the *Circle* object.

```
function Circle(radius)
{ //constructor for the circle object
   this.radius = radius;

   this.area = cArea;
   this.circumference = cCircumference;
   this.getRadius = getRadius;
   this.setRadius = setRadius;
   this.print = cPrint;
}
```

Figure 12.16 The *Circle* Constructor

Using Custom Objects

Using custom objects begins with creating a new instance for each object. Instance creation takes the following form:

VariableName = **new** *objectConstructor* (Parameter List);

For example, the statement that creates the *defaultCircle* object is

```
defaultCircle = new Circle(5);
```

The statements that create the *yourCircle* object are as follows:

```
radius = getFloat("Radius: ");
yourCircle = new Circle(radius);
```

Figure 12.17 contains the script for the *Circle Object* page. The functions that implement the *Circle* methods appear at the beginning of the script. The **roundPlaces()** and **getFloat()** functions must appear first, because the *Circle* functions contain calls to these functions. The order of the *Circle* functions is irrelevant.

```
<SCRIPT LANGUAGE = "JavaScript">
<!--
    function getFloat(message)
    {/* print the message for the prompt
        Use an error loop to check for non-numeric data */
      var x = parseFloat(prompt(message, ""));
      while (isNaN(x))
        x = parseFloat(prompt("Error! Non-numeric data\n" + message, ""));
      return x;
    }

    function roundPlaces(number, places)
    {//round number to desired decimal places
        return Math.round(number * Math.pow(10,places))/Math.pow(10,places);
    }

    function cArea()
    { //return the area of a Circle object
        return roundPlaces(Math.PI * Math.pow(this.radius, 2),2);
    }

    function cCircumference()
    {//return the circumference of a Circle object
        return roundPlaces(2 * Math.PI * this.radius, 2);
    }

    function cPrint()
    {//print a Circle's radius, area and circumference
        document.write("<P>Radius: " + this.radius);
        document.write("<BR>Circumference: " + this.circumference());
        document.write("<BR>Area: " + this.area() + "<P>");
    }

    function getRadius()
    {//retrieve the radius
        return this.radius;
    }

    function setRadius(radius)
    {//change the radius
        this.radius = radius;
    }

    function Circle(radius)
    { //constructor for the circle object
        this.radius = radius;

        //circle methods
        this.area = cArea;
        this.circumference = cCircumference;
        this.getRadius = getRadius;
        this.setRadius = setRadius;
        this.print = cPrint;
    }
```

Figure 12.17 JS Script for the *Circle Object* Page

```
  var defaultCircle = new Circle(5); //declare a circle object
  document.write("The Default Circle: ");
  defaultCircle.print();

  var radius = getFloat("Radius:");
  var yourCircle = new Circle(radius);
  document.write("A user-created circle: ");
  yourCircle.print();

  //Find the combined radii, areas and circumferences
  var combinedArea = defaultCircle.area() + yourCircle.area();
  document.write("<P>Combined area: " + combinedArea);
  document.write("<BR>Combined Circumference: ");
  document.write(defaultCircle.circumference() + yourCircle.circumference());
  document.write("<BR>Combined radii: ");
  document.write(defaultCircle.getRadius() + yourCircle.getRadius() + "<BR>");
  defaultCircle.setRadius(getFloat("New radius for default: "));
  document.write("<BR>New radius of default: " + defaultCircle.getRadius());
//-->
</SCRIPT>
```

Figure 12.17 *(continued)*

A NOTE ON PARAMETER PASSING

Programming languages have different techniques for passing the parameters used in a call (referred to as *arguments* or *actual parameters*) to the parameters appearing in a function header (referred to as *formal parameters*). Many languages let the programmer select the passing method that best fits the programming problem. JavaScript does not. In JavaScript, the passing method is determined by the type of information that is passed, not by the programmer. This can lead to problems for programmers who don't understand JavaScript's parameter-passing defaults.

Before we discuss these defaults, let's look at the three parameter-passing techniques that JavaScript uses.

Pass by value. The pass-by-value technique evaluates the parameter used in the call. For example, if the parameter is *x+y*, the JavaScript interpreter adds *x* and *y*. The result is copied and used as the formal parameter. The function works with a copy, and so changes made in the formal parameter do not affect the actual parameter. The technique is equivalent to xeroxing. You can change a xerox as much as you like, but it has no effect on the original.

Pass by reference. A reference is computer lingo for a memory location. Literals, such as "3" or "Hi", and expressions, such as *x+y*, do not have memory locations; therefore you cannot pass them by reference. This technique requires *variables* as the actual parameters. The pass-by-reference technique sends the actual parameter's memory location to the function. As a result, changing the value in a formal parameter produces the same change in the corresponding actual parameter.

Pass by constant reference. Because copying values can waste time, programming languages use a intermediate technique for efficiency. The pass-by-constant-reference technique passes the actual parameter's memory location (reference), but it prevents the programmer from permanently changing the contents of the actual parameter (constant).

Figure 12.18 shows the parameter-passing technique that JavaScript uses for each built-in type.

Pass by value	Numbers	Booleans (*true* and *false*)
Pass by value	Numbers	Booleans (*true* and *false*)
Pass by reference	Objects	Arrays
Pass by constant reference	Strings	Functions

Figure 12.18 Parameter Passing in JavaScript

> **EXERCISES**

Many of the practice exercises that follow ask you to rewrite exercises that appeared in previous chapters. Compare your early versions with the newer versions.

1. **The *Fibonacci* Page.** Revise the *Fibonacci* page (Figures 11.30 and 11.31). Use a function to calculate the nth Fibonacci number. Return this number.

2. **The *Harmonic Function* Page.** Revise the *Harmonic Function* page (Figure 11.32). Use a function to calculate H(n), where the user supplies the value of *n*. Return this number.

3. **The *Alternating Series* Page.** Revise the *Alternating Series* page (Figure 11.33). Use a function to calculate F(n), where the user supplies the value of *n*. Return this number.

4. **The *Percentage* Page.** Create a percentage page that lets the user enter the numerator and denominator. Use a function to return the percentage rounded to 5 decimal places.

5. **The *Humiture* Page.** Revise the *Humiture* page (Figures 10.41 and 10.42). Use a function to calculate and return the humiture.

6. **The *Radians* Page.** Laypersons measure an angle in degrees; scientists and computer functions measure it in *radians*. Create a page that lets the user enter the size of the angle in degrees. Return the size of the angle in radians. The formula is found in Figure 12.19.

---
radians = PI/180 × degrees

Figure 12.19 The Radian Formula

7. **The Quadratic Object.** Create a `Quadratic` object based on the model in Figure 12.20. (*Hint:* Figure 9.18 contains the quadratic formula.)

Quadratic		
Properties	*a*	
	b	
	c	
Methods	Quadratic()	//Constructor
	setA()	//Change a
	setB()	//Change b
	setC()	/Change c
	checkRoots()	//Return the positive root
	posRoot()	//Return the number of roots
	negRoot()	//Return the negative root
	print()	//Print the values in a, b, c

Figure 12.20 Model for the *Quadratic* Object

8. **The Rectangle Object.** Create a *Rectangle* object based on the model in Figure 12.21. (*Hint*: Figure 9.23 contains the rectangle formulas.)

Rectangle		
Properties	*length*	
	width	
Methods	Rectangle()	//Constructor
	getLength()	//Return the length
	setLength()	//Change the length
	getWidth()	//Return the width
	setWidth()	//Change the width
	perimeter()	//Return the perimeter
	area()	//Return the area
	print()	//Print the length and width

Figure 12.21 Model for the *Rectangle* Object

9. **The Trapezoid Object.** Create a *Trapezoid* object based on the model in Figure 12.22. (*Hint*: Figure 9.22 contains the trapezoid formulas.)

Trapezoid		
Properties	*height*	
	base1	
	base2	
Methods	Trapezoid()	//Constructor
	getBase1()	//Return $base_1$
	setBase1()	//Change $base_1$
	getBase2()	//Return $base_2$
	setBase2()	//Change $base_2$
	getHeight()	//Return height
	setHeight()	//Change height
	area()	//Return area
	print()	//Print the two bases and the height

Figure 12.22 Model for the *Trapezoid* Object

10. **The *Triangle* Object.** Create an object based on the model in Figure 12.23. (*Hint*: Figure 9.20 contains the triangle formulas.)

Triangle		
Properties	*base*	
	height	
Methods	Triangle()	//Constructor
	getHeight()	//Return height
	setHeight()	//Change height
	getBase()	//Return base
	setBase()	//Change base
	area()	//Return area
	print()	//Print the width and height

Figure 12.23 Model for the *Triangle* Object

11. **The *Point* Object.** Create an object based on the model in Figure 12.24.

Point		
Properties	*x*	//column position
	y	//row position
Methods	Point()	//Constructor
	getx()	//return the column position
	gety()	//return the row position
	setx()	//change the column position
	sety()	//change the row position
	print()	//print the column and row values

Figure 12.24 Model for the *Point* Object

12. **The *Bird* Object.** Create a *Bird* object based on the model in Figure 12.25.

Bird		
Properties		**Example**
	commmonName	*American Goldfinch*
	latinName	*Carduelis Tristis*
	sightingYear	*1995*
	numberOfSightings	*32*
Methods	Bird()	*//Constructor*
	changeSightings()	*// Change number of sightings*
	changeYear()	*// Change sighting year*
	print()	*// Print information on a bird*

Figure 12.25 Model for the *Bird* object

13. **The Person Object.** Create an object that describes a person. Obvious properties include name and address. Add other properties and methods of your choice.

14. **The *Pet* Object.** Create an object that describes household pets. Pick appropriate properties and methods of your choice.

15. **The *Ice Cream Float* Object.** Create an *IceCreamFloat* object. Develop properties and methods of your choice.

16. Create an object of your choice. Develop the object model. Use this model to create the function definitions and constructor. Write application code that uses your new object.

➤ **JAVASCRIPT VOCABULARY**

Constructor. A constructor is a function associated with an object. The constructor creates new instances of an object.

Global variable. A global variable is a variable that is declared outside of any function or method. As its name implies, we can use a global variable in any function or method without passing it as a parameter. This is usually considered a dangerous programming practice.

Local variable. A local variable is a variable that is declared inside a function or a method. A local variable has meaning only within its enclosing function or method.

Function. A function is a block of self-contained code that is not part of an object.

Function definition. The function definition contains a function header and a body. The function header contains the function's name and its parameter list. The function body contains the executable code.

Function call.   A function call is the use of a function. The caller must supply appropriate parameters.

Parameter.   A parameter holds input for the function or output from the function.

Pass by value.   *Pass by value* occurs when the JavaScript interpreter copies the values used in the call. JavaScript automatically passes numbers and booleans by value. The JavaScript interpreter is using only a copy of the original values; any changes made to the parameter in the function body will not affect the parameter in the calling body.

Pass by reference.   *Pass by reference* occurs when the JavaScript interpreter uses the memory address of the variable used in the call. JavaScript automatically passes objects and arrays by reference. Here the JavaScript interpreter is working with a memory location, so any changes made to an object or array in the function's body will affect the original value in the calling body.

Pass by constant reference.   *Pass by constant reference* indicates that the parameter passed in the call is immutable. JavaScript passes strings and functions by constant reference because it is more efficient to pass the address than to copy a string or function. Although the address (reference) is passed, the string or function passed in the call will not be altered (constant).

Return value.   A function or method can contain one or more **return** statements. These statements terminate the execution of a function or method. A **return** statement sends the expression (if any) that appears after **return** to the caller.

13 Arrays

We used variables many times in previous chapters. We also, created simple assignment statements, such as these two:

```
var x = 1;
var myPet = "cat";
```

Each of these assignment statements places a single *value* into a variable. Now, look at the information in Figure 13.1. Figure 13.1(a) contains a list of numbers that might be used by a mathematician. Figure 13.1(b) contains a list of barnyard animals.

(a)	x	50 45 35 8 9 13
(b)	**BarnYard Animals**	*pig ox horse chicken*

Figure 13.1 List

Suppose we want to place these *lists* into variables named *x* and *barnyardAnimals*, respectively. How could we do this? We might consider creating an object for each list. This solution poses problems, however, because objects are not designed to encapsulate lists. An object's properties represent different attributes. For example, a rectangle object has width and length properties; it does not have a list of width properties. When we want to represent lists of similar things, we use an *array*.

ARRAY CONCEPTS

An array is a concept borrowed from mathematics. Mathematicians frequently use lists of numbers that are almost invariably named *x*. Each individual number has a *subscript* that identifies its position in the array. Let's consider the list of numbers appearing in Figure 13.1(a). Figure 13.2 shows this list with its associated subscripts. As Figure 13.2(b) indicates, mathematicians use subscripts from 1 to n, where n represents both the size and the last number in the list. The first number in the list is referred to as x_1 (pronounced "x sub 1"). Similarly, the last number in the list is referred as x_n (pronounced "x sub n"). Computer keyboards do not have subscripts, so most programming languages use square brackets, [], to represent array subscripts. Figure 13.2(c) shows the subscript notation used by JavaScript, Perl, and Java. These programming languages label subscripts from zero through n-1. Thus, in JavaScript, 50 is now in the position **x[0]** (pronounced "x sub 0"), and 13 is now in the position **x[5]**.

(a) x	(b) Mathematical Notation	(c) JavaScript Notation
50	x_1	x[0]
45	x_2	x[1]
35	x_3	x[2]
8	x_4	x[3]
9	x_5	x[4]
13	x_6 or x_n	x[5]

Figure 13.2 Array Notation

JavaScript implements arrays through an *Array* object. Figure 13.3 contains the *Array* object model. As this figure indicates, an array has a property, *length*, that contains the number of elements in the array. JavaScript also provides a facility for creating additional properties or methods. This facility, known as a *prototype*, applies to all arrays created within a program. Figure 13.4 also lists the *Array* object methods. The *Old Methods* work with all JavaScript versions. The *New Methods* require JavaScript 1.2 or higher.

Array

Properties	*length*	// Number of elements in the array
	Array.prototype.*name*	// Name of prototype, if any
Old Methods	Array()	// Constructor
	join (*separatorString*)	// Create a string from the array elements
	reverse ()	// Reverse the array elements.
	sort (*compareFunction*_{*optional*})	// Sort using lexicographic order or compare function
New Methods (JS 1.2)	push(*element*)	//Add to the end of the array, e.g. x[n]
	unshift(*element*)	// Add to the end of the array, e.g. x[0]
	pop()	// Remove from end of the array, e.g. x[n]
	shift()	// Remove from beginning of the array, e.g. x[0]
	slice(*lower, upper*)	// Extract the elements from **lower** to **upper**-1
	concat(*arrayObject*)	// Append arrayObject to the array

Figure 13.3 The *Array* Object Model

PRELOADED ARRAYS, SIMPLE METHODS, AND A PROTOTYPE

As our first foray in programming with arrays, we recreate the page appearing in Figure 13.4. This page contains an array of barnyard animals. The animals are displayed in their original order, and then in reversed and in sorted order. The built-in **sort()** and **reverse()** methods are used to sort and reverse the *barnyardAnimals* array. We create a prototype method, **print()**, to print the arrays.

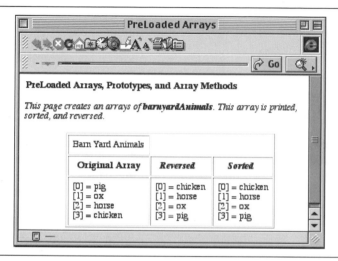

Figure 13.4 A *First Array* Page

Pre-Filling an Array

This first array example uses the simplest technique for filling an array: the values are placed into the array as it is created. (We'll call this technique *preloading* or *prefilling*.) The general form for preloading an array is

```
ArrayName = new Array(Comma separated list of values);
```

Notice that we use **new** to create a new *Array* object. We place the list of array values inside parentheses. We use an assignment statement to place this new object in a JavaScript variable. Applying this form to the barnyard animals list appearing in Figure 13.1 yields the following array declaration:

```
var barnyardAnimals = new Array("pig", "ox", "horse", "chicken");
```

Notice the use of double quotation marks to indicate that the animal names are string literals.

Printing an Array

Having created an array, we'd like to print it. In a typical application, we would print only the elements in an array. In this example, we print both the subscript and the value for each array element. Beginning programmers frequently confuse the subscript with the contents contained at the subscripted position. Therefore, printing both subscripts and contents illustrates the differences. We implement the **print()** method as a prototype so that we can reuse it.

ADDING *ARRAY* METHODS

Creating a new *Array* method requires a two-step technique similar to the one used to create methods for custom objects.

1. Create a JavaScript Function. We create a JavaScript function that implements the desired task. This function uses self-reference to refer to the current array object. Typically, a **for** statement is used to process the array elements.

2. Create an array prototype. The prototype links the function to the *Array* object. The general form of the prototype statement is

```
Array.prototype.Name = functionName;
```

A print() Method

Creating a **print()** *method* for *Array* objects begins with a *function* definition. Here, the function is named **printWithSubscript()** to reflect the current task. In the course of this chapter, we develop other functions that we can use as prototypes for printing arrays. This gives us flexibility in picking an appropriate **print()** method for our current needs. Figure 13.5 contains the definition of the **printWithSubscript()** function.

```
function printWithSubscript()
{//print the contents of the array
   var i;
   for (i = 0; i < this.length; i++)
     document.write("[" + i + "] = " + this[i] + "<BR>");
}
```

Figure 13.5 The **printWithSubscript()** Function

The **printWithSubscript()** function contains a single **for** statement that loops through all the elements in an array. The initial expression sets *i* to zero, because zero is the starting subscript for all arrays. Because the last subscript in any array is *length-1*, the test expression is always **i < this.length**. The change expression increments *i*. The body of the **for** statement prints the current array subscript, **i**, in brackets. The content of the current position, **this[i]**, is also printed.

The statement that makes the **printWithSubscript()** *function* a new *Array method* for the current JavaScript program is

```
Array.prototype.print = printWithSubscript;
```

After creating the prototype, we can use the **print()** method as though it were a built-in JavaScript *Array* method. Figure 13.6 contains the JavaScript code that produces the page in Figure 13.4. The calls to the **print()** method are highlighted; so are the calls to the **reverse()** and **sort()** methods.

```
<SCRIPT LANGUAGE = "JavaScript">
   function printWithSubscript()
   {//print the contents of the array
      var i;
      for (i = 0; i < this.length; i++)
         document.write("[" + i + "] = " + this[i] + "<BR>");
   }
   Array.prototype.print = printWithSubscript;
   var barnyardAnimals = new Array("pig", "ox", "horse",  "chicken");
  //put the results in a table
   document.write("<CENTER><TABLE BORDER = '1' CELLPADDING = '5'>");
   document.write("<CAPTON>Barn Yard Animals</CAPTION>");
   document.write("<TR><TH>Original Array</TH>");
   document.write("<TH><I>Reversed </TH>");
   document.write("<TH><I>Sorted </TH></TR>");
   document.write("<TR><TD>");
   barnyardAnimals.print();
   document.write("</TD><TD>");

   //reverse the array
   barnyardAnimals.reverse();
   barnyardAnimals.print();

   document.write("</TD><TD>");
   //sort the array
   barnyardAnimals.sort();
   barnyardAnimals.print();

   document.write("</TD></TR></TABLE></CENTER>");
//-->
</SCRIPT>
```

Figure 13.6 JS Script for the *First Array* page

NEW JAVASCRIPT (1.2) METHODS

As a second array example, we create a web page that lets the user add elements to either end of an array of household pets. The page uses several of the new *Array* methods. These new methods incorporate Perl's array-handling facilities. Although the method names might sound peculiar to laypersons, they are part of the everyday vocabulary of a computer scientist.

1. push().   Pushing an element appends it to the right-hand end of the array. The right-hand end contains the higher subscripts. A push increases an array's length by one.

2. pop().   Popping removes the *last* element in the array. The last element is the one with the highest subscript. A pop reduces the array's length by one.

3. unshift().   Unshifting an element appends it before the *front* (left-hand end) of the array. The new element now resides in the [0] position, and all the remaining elements are shifted to the right by one position. An unshift increases the length of the array by one.

4. shift(). Shifting removes the *first* element in an array. The remaining array elements are shifted to the left by one—that is, the element in position **[1]** is moved to position **[0]**, and so on. A shift reduces the length of the list by one.

The *New Methods* page contains an array with *cat* and *dog* as household pets. The page presents a menu to the user. A loop lets the user select a menu option until choosing the *Quit* option. Figure 13.7(a) contains the initial page with the user prompt. Figures 13.7(b) through Figure 13.7(e) show the array after various menu selections.

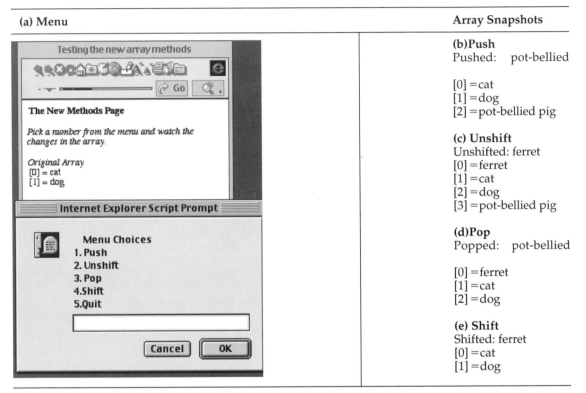

(a) Menu	Array Snapshots

(b) Push
Pushed: pot-bellied

[0] =cat
[1] =dog
[2] =pot-bellied pig

(c) Unshift
Unshifted: ferret
[0] =ferret
[1] =cat
[2] =dog
[3] =pot-bellied pig

(d) Pop
Popped: pot-bellied

[0] =ferret
[1] =cat
[2] =dog

(e) Shift
Shifted: ferret
[0] =cat
[1] =dog

Figure 13.7 The *New Methods* Page

The *New Methods* page uses the **printWithIndex()** function developed in the last example. The page contains an additional function that creates a menu loop. Figure 13.8 contains the definition of the **menuLoop()** function.

The **menuLoop()** function requires three local variables:

1. promptString. The *promptString* variable holds the message displayed in the prompt window. Because the JavaScript interpreter invokes the **prompt()** method before and during the **do...while** loop, it's easier to store the message in a variable.

2. choice. The *choice* variable holds the user's menu selection. The **do...while** statement contains a **switch** statement with **case** options for each selection except *Quit*.

```
function menuLoop()
{//create a loop to process choices until the user selects quit
   var promptString = "Menu Choices\n1. Push\n2. Unshift\n3. Pop\n4.Shift\n5.Quit"

   var name;
   do {
       var choice = prompt(promptString, "");
       switch(choice) {
       case "1" : name = prompt("Animal name: " , "");
                  housePets.push(name);
                  document.write("<BR><I>Pushed: " + name + "</I><BR>");
                  break;
       case "2" : name = prompt("Animal name: ", "");
                  housePets.unshift(name);
                  document.write("<BR><I>Unshifted: " + name+ "</I><BR>");
                  break;
       case "3" : name = housePets.pop();
                  document.write("<BR><I>Popped: " + name + "</I><BR>");
                  break;
       case "4" : name = housePets.shift();
                  document.write("<BR><I>Shifted: " + name + "</I><BR>");
   }
   housePets.print();
   } while (choice != "5");
}
```

Figure 13.8 The **menuLoop()** Function

3. name.   The use of this variable depends on the user's choice. If the user selects *Push* or *Unshift, name* holds the animal to be added to the array. We pass *name* as a parameter to the **push()** or **unshift()** methods. If the user selects *Pop* or *Shift, name* contains the animal removed from the array.

The **menuLoop()** function carries out the user's selection, prints the array so that the user can see the result, and asks the user to make another selection. The remainder of the script for the *New Methods* page contains three simple statements. Figure 13.9 contains the JS script.

```
<SCRIPT LANGUAGE = "JavaScript">
<!--
The printWithIndex() method goes here
Array.prototype.print = printWithIndex;
//The menuLoop() method goes here
var housePets = new Array("cat", "dog");
document.write("<I>Original Array</I><BR>");
housePets.print();
menuLoop();
//-->
</SCRIPT>
```

Figure 13.9 JS Script for the *New Methods* Page

SORTING NUMERIC ARRAYS

The *Array* **sort()** method sorts array elements based on lexicographic (dictionary) order. This ordering principle does not work for numeric arrays, as Figure 13.10(b) clearly indicates. By design, the **sort()** method has an optional parameter that lets us specify a different ordering principle. Creating new ordering principles for numeric arrays is an easy task and is the subject of the next web page. Figure 13.10(a) shows the test array, *y*, and the user prompt. Figures 13.10(b) through 13.10(d) contain snapshots of the three sort orders.

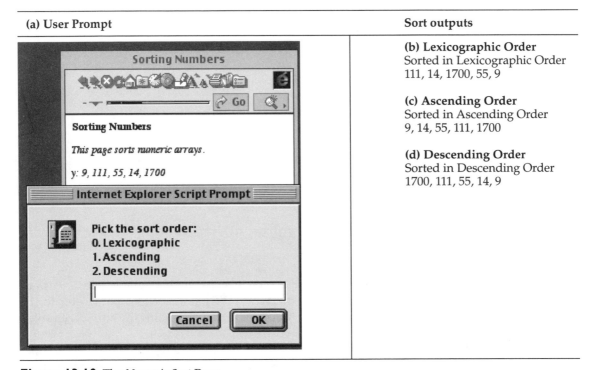

(a) User Prompt	Sort outputs
	(b) Lexicographic Order Sorted in Lexicographic Order 111, 14, 1700, 55, 9 **(c) Ascending Order** Sorted in Ascending Order 9, 14, 55, 111, 1700 **(d) Descending Order** Sorted in Descending Order 1700, 111, 55, 14, 9

Figure 13.10 The *Numeric Sort* Page

Sorting a numeric array begins with the creation of a comparison function. The function contains two parameters, named *x* and *y*. The function's body compares the two parameters and returns a result. An ascending sort uses the following comparisons:

1. If x < y, return a negative number.
2. If x == y, return zero.
3. If x > y, return a positive number.

A descending sort reverses *x* and *y* in the comparisons. Although we can easily translate this pseudo-code into JavaScript **if** statements, we can achieve the same effect with a simple subtraction. Figure 13.11 uses the subtraction technique to create ascending and descending functions. Hand check these functions with different combinations of *x* and *y* to verify that they produce that same results as a set of **if** statements.

(a) Ascending	(b) Descending

```
function ascending(x, y)      function descending(x, y)
{                             {
   return (x-y);                 return (y-x);
}                             }
```

Figure 13.11 Ascending and Descending Functions

The *Numeric Sort* page uses a second function, **getSortOrder()**, that obtains the user's choice and sorts the array according to this choice. The function definition is found in Figure 13.12. The calls to the **sort()** method are highlighted.

The *Numeric Sort* page prints a comma-separated list of array elements. The new **print()** function and the remainder of the code for this page is found in Figure 13.13.

```
function getSortOrder()
{
  var promptString = "Pick the sort order: \n0. Lexicographic\n1. Ascending\n2. Descending";
  var choice = prompt(promptString, "");
  switch (choice) {
  case "0": document.write("<P>Lexicographic Order</P>");
            y.sort();
            y.print();
            break;
  case "1": document.write("<P>Sorted in Ascending Order<P>");
            y.sort(ascending);
            y.print();
            break;
  case "2": document.write("<P>Sorted in Descending Order<P>");
            y.sort(descending)
            y.print();
  }
}
```

Figure 13.12 The **getSortOrder()** Function

THE SEQUENTIAL SEARCH

Sorting and searching are the two array tasks most frequently performed. We have sorted numeric and string arrays. Now we turn our attention to searching. We use a numeric array in our example, but the search method, **seqSearch()**, also works for string arrays. This method uses the simplest searching technique: a sequential search. Figure 13.14 shows the *Sequential Search* page. Figure 13.14(a) shows the sample array and the user prompt. As the figure indicates, the page uses a loop that lets the user search for several numbers. The loop ends when the user enters a zero.

```
<SCRIPT LANGUAGE = "JavaScript">
<!--
// Put the ascending() function here
// Put the descending() function here
// Put the getSortOrder() function here
  function print()
  {//print the contents of the array
     var i;
     for (i = 0; i < this.length; i++)
        if (i < this.length -1)
          document.write(this[i] + ", ");
        else
          document.write(this[i] + "<P>");
  }
  Array.prototype.print = print;
  y = new Array (9, 111, 55, 14, 1700);
  document.write("<P>y: ");
  y.print();
  getSortOrder();
//-->
</SCRIPT>
```

Figure 13.13 JS Script for the *Numeric Sort* Page

Figure 13.14(b) shows the page after several searches. Notice how the subscript is printed if the number is in the array. If the number is not in the array, a message is printed to that effect.

The sequential search is a brute-force technique that works well on small arrays. This search begins with the first array position and examines each element in the array until it finds

(a) User Prompt

(b) Search Examples

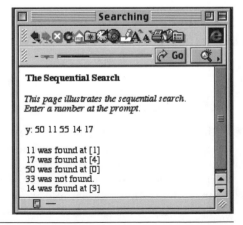

Figure 13.14 The *Sequential Search* Page

the element or it reaches the end of the array. The number's subscript is returned if the search finds the number. If the number is not found, the function returns an invalid subscript: negative numbers are never valid subscripts, so the function returns a minus-one when the number is not in the array. Figure 13.15(a) contains the function definition and Figure 13.15(b) contains the array prototype.

(a)Function

```
function seqSearch(number)
{//return position if number is found; return -1 otherwise
  var i;
  for (i = 0; i < this.length; i++)
    if (this[i] == number)
      return i;
  return -1;
}
```

(b) Prototype

```
Array.prototype.seqSearch = seqSearch;
```

Figure 13.15 The **seqSearch()** Function

The *Array Search* page also uses a **searchLoop()** function that lets a user try several searches. Although this function uses the array, it is not an array method. The function obtains a number from the user, calls the **seqsearch()** method, and reports the result. Its primary tasks are not related to arrays, so we do not make it an *Array* method. The function definition appears in Figure 13.16.

```
function searchLoop(anArray)
{//Obtain number, search for it, report result
  var index;
  var number = getFloat("x: (0 to quit): ");
  while (number > 0) {
    index = anArray.seqSearch(number);
    if (index >= 0 )
      document.write(number + " was found at ["  + index + "]<BR>");
    else
      document.write(number + " was not found. <BR>");
    number = getFloat("x: (0 to quit): ");
  }
}
```

Figure 13.16 The **searchLoop()** Function

The **searchLoop()** function has a single array parameter. The function uses two local variables: *index* and *number*. The first variable, *index,* holds a valid subscript (or minus-one). The second variable, *number,* holds the user's number. The **getFloat()** function developed previously is used to obtain this number. The body of the function contains a **while** statement that reports the results and obtains the next number. We could easily have used a **do...while** statement to code the loop, and the exercises ask you to explore this possibility. The **searchLoop()** function can be

```
<SCRIPT LANGUAGE = "JavaScript">
<!--
  // Put the print() function  here
   // Put the getFloat() function  here
   // Put the seqSearch() function here
   // Put the searchLoop() function here

  Array.prototype.print = print;
  Array.prototype.seqSearch = seqSearch;
  var y = new Array (50, 11, 55, 14, 17);
  document.write("<P>y: ");
  y.print();
  searchLoop(y);
//-->
</SCRIPT>
```

Figure 13.17 JS Script for the *Numeric Search* Page

modified to work with string searches. You must change the test expression used in the **while** statement, and you must obtain string data. The modification appears in the exercises.

The remainder of the code for the *Numeric Search* page is found in Figure 13.17.

SUMS AND AVERAGES

Laypersons often find mathematical formulas obtuse and confusing. After all, they use a lot of Greek symbols. However, many mathematical formulas are easily translated into JavaScript (or any other programming language). Statistical formulas, in particular, are good candidates for programming solutions, because the formulas use arrays and the notation can be translated into a **for** statement. As an example, we calculate rushing, passing, and total-yard averages for a football team. Figure 13.18(a) shows a sample page after four games. Figure 13.18(b) shows the averages after five games.

(a) After Game 4

Football Statistics

It's football time. The statistics for my team are produced below.

Statistics through Game: 4
Passing Yards: 110 150 90 55
Rushing Yards: 78 110 60 100
Total Yards: 188 260 150 155

Averages:
Passing: 101.25
Rushing: 87
Total: 188.25

(b) After Game 5

Football Statistics

It's football time. The statistics for my team are produced below.

Statistics through Game: 5
Passing Yards: 110 150 90 55 134
Rushing Yards: 78 110 60 100 85
Total Yards: 188 260 150 155 219

Averages:
Passing: 107.8
Rushing: 86.6
Total: 194.4

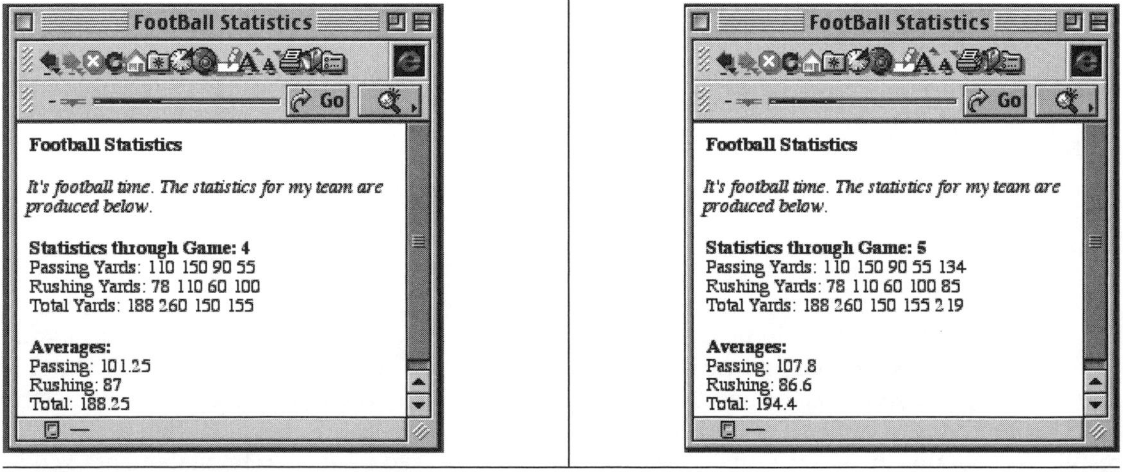

Figure 13.18 The *Football Statistics* Page

The *Football Statistics* page uses two pre-filled arrays, *rushingYards* and *passingYards*. The array declarations looked like this after the first four games:

```
passingYards = new Array(110, 150, 90, 55);
rushingYards = new Array(78, 110, 60, 100);
```

As the season progresses, we simply add the passing and rushing yards for the last game to the end of each array. The page automatically calculates the new statistics.

The *Football Statistics* page uses a third array, *totalYards*, which contains the combined passing and rushing yards for a particular game. The declaration that creates this array is

```
totalYards = new Array();
```

Notice that this array does not pre-load the values. After all, we'd have to add the passing and rushing yards for each game to prefill the *passingYards* array. Because JavaScript adds so much more reliably than we do, we instead create a function, **setTotalYards()**, to fill this array. The function definition appears in Figure 13.19.

```
function setTotalYards()
{//set values for the totalYards array
  var i;
  for (i=0; i< passingYards.length; i++)
    totalYards[i] = passingYards[i] + rushingYards[i];
}
```

Figure 13.19 The **setTotalYards()** Function

The **setTotalYards()** function is not an *Array* method: its purpose is too limited to declare it as a method. In addition, the function does not use parameters. Instead, we use the array names directly in the body of the function. When used in this way, the three arrays are *global* variables. Heavy use of global variables, rather than of the passing of variables as parameters, is a dangerous practice, because we could inadvertently change a variable's contents. However, JavaScript passes arrays by reference, so even a parameter doesn't prevent accidental changes to an array's contents.

FINDING THE ARITHMETIC MEAN

Having taken care of all the preliminary work, we're ready to tackle the arithmetic mean. Figure 13.20 contains the arithmetic formulas in all their gory details.

(a) Sum   **(b) Mean**

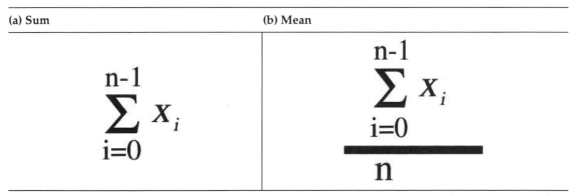

$$\sum_{i=0}^{n-1} x_i \qquad\qquad \frac{\sum_{i=0}^{n-1} x_i}{n}$$

Figure 13.20 Formulas for the Sum

Figure 13.20(a) contains the mathematical formula for summing a list of numbers. The Greek symbol *sigma* (Σ) always signifies summation. The starting subscript for the summation appears below the *sigma*, while the last subscript appears above the *sigma*. The variable to the right of the *sigma* is the name of the array to be summed. Thus, Figure 13.20(a) tell us to add the values in *x*, beginning with x_0 and continuing until we reach x_{n-1}. Figure 13.20(b) defines the arithmetic mean as the sum divided by the number of elements in the array.

An arithmetic formula like the one appearing in Figure 13.20(a) is easily translated into a **for** statement. Figure 13.21 shows this translation process.

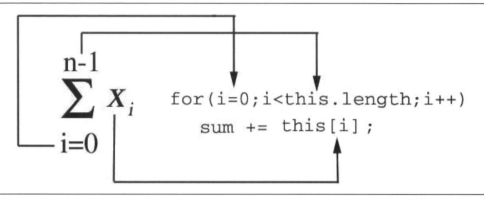

Figure 13.21 Translating Mathematical Notation

Notice the correspondence between the boundaries in the mathematical formulas and the expressions in the **for** statement header. This correspondence suggests a set of translation rules that we can apply to any statistical formula.

1. *Initial Expression.* The initial subscript (*lower bound*) in the mathematical formula is used to create the initial expression in the **for** statement header. If no initial subscript is given, assume **i=0**.

2. *Test Expression.* The last subscript (*upper bound*) in the mathematical formula is used to create the test expression. If the entire array is processed or if no upper bound is given, the test expression is: **i < this.length**.

3. *Change Expression.* The change expression is always **i++**.

4. *Loop Body.* x_i is translated into **this[i]**. The summing variable must be initialized to zero prior to the start of the **for** statement.

Figure 13.22 contains the definition of the **sum()** function.

```
function sum()
{//sum the elements in an array
  var sum = 0;
  for(i = 0; i < this.length; i++)
    sum += this[i];
  return sum;
}
```

Figure 13.22 The **sum()** Function

   The **sum()** function uses the same technique as the summing loops developed in Chapter 11, but the switch to arrays increases the usefulness of the technique. We can now permanently store and reuse a list of values whenever we choose.

   Once we create the summing function, we use it to find the arithmetic mean. The function definition appears in Figure 13.23. The function body contains a single line of code.

```
function mean()
{//return the arithmetic average (mean)
    return (this.sum()/this.length);
}
```

Figure 13.23 The **mean()** Function

   The script for the *Football Statistics* page appears in Figure 13.24. Included in the code are prototypes that create the **print()**, **sum()**, and **mean()** methods. The remainder of the code consists largely of **document.write()** statements.

```
<SCRIPT Language = "JavaScript">
<!--
  // The print() function goes here
  // The getTotalYards() function goes here
  // The sum() function goes here
  // The mean() function goes here

  Array.prototype.print = print;
  Array.prototype.sum = sum;
  Array.prototype.mean = mean;

  passingYards = new Array(110, 150, 90, 55);
  rushingYards = new Array(78, 110, 60, 100);
  totalYards = new Array();
  setTotalYards();

  //Print the arrays
  document.write("<P><B>Statistics through Game: " + passingYards.length + "</B>");
  document.write("<BR>Passing Yards: ");
  passingYards.print();
  document.write("<BR> Rushing Yards: ");
  rushingYards.print();
  document.write("<BR> Total Yards: ");
  totalYards.print();

  //Find and print the averages
  document.write("<P><B> Averages: </B>");
  document.write("<BR> Passing: " + passingYards.mean());
  document.write("<BR> Rushing: " + rushingYards.mean());
  document.write("<BR> Total: " + totalYards.mean());
 //-->
</SCRIPT>
```

Figure 13.24 JS Script for the *Football Statistics* Page

A Note on Test Data. Developing test data for statistical pages is crucial. To develop test data for the *Football Statistics* page, we must calculate the average passing yards for the sample data. The sample data could consist of the first four weeks. The hand calculation is used to check the page results. Once we've verified that the averages are correct for the first four weeks, we can add additional information into the football arrays.

AN ARRAY OF OBJECTS

Having created several string and numeric arrays, we end the chapter with an array of *objects*. Figure 13.25 contains a sample web page. The page contains the names of several Rocky Mountains passes. The height of each pass is recorded in meters (for the Europeans and Canadians) and feet (for the U.S. citizens). The original array is printed in a table. A second table containing the sorted array follows the original table.

Creation of this page begins with a constructor, **Pass()**. The constructor has properties for the the name, the meters, and the feet. Methods are not necessary in this example; this page requires only array methods. The constructor appears in Figure 13.26.

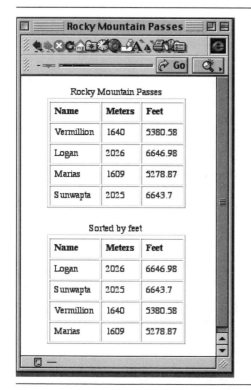

```
function Pass(name, meters)
{ // constructor for the pass object
    this.name = name;
    this. meters = meters;
    this.feet = roundPlaces(meters/0.3048, 2);
.}
```

Figure 13.25 The *Passes* Page

Figure 13.26 The **Pass()** Constructor

The **Pass()** constructor contains two parameters: *name* and *meters*. (Most of these passes are in the Canadian Rockies, so the height was listed in meters.) The meters are used to find the height in feet. You can easily reverse the process if you prefer the U.S. Rockies.

Creating an array of passes requires the creation of a new *Array* object and of a new *Pass* object for each pass in the array. The statements that create the *Array* object and its *Pass* elements are listed in Figure 13.27.

```
var RockyMountainPasses = new Array();
RockyMountainPasses[0]  = new Pass("Vermillion", 1640);
RockyMountainPasses[1]  = new Pass("Logan", 2026);
RockyMountainPasses[2]  = new Pass("Marias", 1609);
RockyMountainPasses[3]  = new Pass("Sunwapta", 2025);
```

Figure 13.27 Creating the *RockyMoutainPasses* Array

Sorting the passes by feet requires a descending function. This function varies slightly from the **descending()** function appearing in Figure 13.11(b). The new version must indicate the comparison property. We want to arrange the passes from the highest pass as measured in feet to the lowest pass, so the comparison property will be

pass2.feet - pass1.feet

Figure 13.28 contains the code for the **descending()** function.

```
function descending(pass1, pass2)
{ //compare for descending sort
   return (pass2.feet - pass1.feet);
}
```

Figure 13.28 The **descending()** Function: *Rocky Mountain Passes*

The last step is the creation of a method that prints the object's properties in columns. Accessing a property or method of an object that is part of an array requires a new notation that combines array and object notation. The general form is

ArrayName[Subscript].PropertyOrMethod

As the notation indicates, the array subscript appears before the dot operator used to extract the property or method.

The **tablePrint()** function and the remaining code for the *Passes* page are found in Figure 13.29.

The **tablePrint()** function appearing in Figure 13.29 contains a parameter for the table caption. The function prints a table header for each property. A **for** statement is used to print the properties of the current object in the columns.

```
<SCRIPT LANGUAGE = "JavaScript">
<!--
   function roundPlaces(number, places)
   {//round number to desired decimal places
       return Math.round(number * Math.pow(10,places))/Math.pow(10,places);

    }
   function Pass(name, meters)
   { // constructor for the pass object
      this.name = name;
      this. meters = meters;
      this.feet = roundPlaces(meters/0.3048, 2);
    }
    function tablePrint(caption)
    {//print a table of the rocky mountain passes
        document.write("<P><CENTER><TABLE BORDER = '1' CELLPADDING = '5'>");
        document.write("<CAPTION>" + caption + "<CAPTION>");
        document.write("<TR><TH ALIGN = 'left'>Name</TH>");
        document.write("<TH ALIGN = 'left'>Meters</TH>");
        document.write("<TH ALIGN = 'left'>Feet</TH></TR>");

        for (i = 0; i < this.length; i++) {
            document.write("<TR><TD>" + this[i].name + "</TD><TD>");
            document.write(this[i].meters + "</TD><TD>");
            document.write(this[i].feet + "</TD></TR>");
        }
        document.write("</TABLE></CENTER><P>");
    }
    function descending(pass1, pass2)
    { //compare for descending sort
        return (pass2.feet - pass1.feet);
    }

    Array.prototype.print = tablePrint;

    //Create the arrays
    var RockyMountainPasses = new Array();
    RockyMountainPasses[0]  = new Pass("Vermillion", 1640);
    RockyMountainPasses[1]  = new Pass("Logan", 2026);
    RockyMountainPasses[2]  = new Pass("Marias", 1609);
    RockyMountainPasses[3]  = new Pass("Sunwapta", 2025);

    RockyMountainPasses.print("Rocky Mountain Passes");
    RockyMountainPasses.sort(descending);
    RockyMountainPasses.print("Sorted by feet");

//-->
</SCRIPT>
```

Figure 13.29 JS Script for the *Passes* Page

EXERCISES

1. **A *Stack* Page.** Stacks are frequently used in computer-science applications. A *stack* is defined as a last in, first out (LIFO) structure. This means that stack elements are always added to and removed from the right-hand end of the stack. Create a menu-driven page that lets the user add and remove elements for a stack.

2. **A *Queue* Page.** Queues are also frequently used in computer-science applications. A queue is defined as a first in, first out (FIFO) structure. This means that stack elements are always added at the right-hand end and removed from the front (left-hand end, or beginning, of the array). Create a menu-driven page that lets the user add and remove elements for a queue.

3. **A *User-Inputted Arrays* Page.** Create a page that asks the user to enter the number of elements in an array. Next, create a function that lets the user enter the array elements. Print the original array, then print the array in sorted and reversed orders.

4. **A *Search and Replace* Page.** Fill an array with values of your choice. Ask the user to enter a search value and a replacement value. Search for the value. If it's in the array, replace it with the new value.

5. **A *String Search* Page.** Modify the *Numeric Search* page (Figures 13.14 through 13.17) so that it works for an array of strings. Replace the `while` statement with a `do...while`. (*Hint:* Use the null string to terminate the loop.)

6. **The *Defensive Football Player Searc* Page.** Create a defensive player, using the object model in Figure 13.30. Create a loop that asks the user to enter the football player's last name. If the player is found, print his defensive statistics. If the player is not found, indicate this.

7. **The *Football Statistics* Page.** You'd like to keep your own statistics for your favorite football team. Modify the *Football Statistics* page so that it offers a more complete set of statistics for a football season. Figure 13.31 contains a list of typical statistics. These statistics involve averages, summations, and percentages. Create a table of statistics. The statistics should occupy the row positions. The games should occupy the columns.

8. **An Array of *Circle* Objects.** Create an array of *Circle* objects, using the object model developed in Figure 12.11. Develop sort and print methods for your array. Let the user select an object by its subscript. Find and print the area and radius for this object.

9. **The *Pick A Sport* Page.** Pick a sport of your choice. Create a page that reports that statistics for a team of your choice. Create arrays that can be updated on a weekly basis. Make sure that you report averages in the relevant categories.

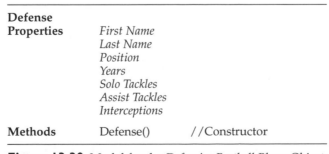

Defense	
Properties	*First Name*
	Last Name
	Position
	Years
	Solo Tackles
	Assist Tackles
	Interceptions
Methods	Defense() //Constructor

Figure 13.30 Model for the *Defensive Football Player* Object

---

Statistics

First Downs	Total
	Rushing
	Passing
	Penalty
Rushing	Total
	Average/Game
	Average/Play
Passing	Total
	Average/Game
	Average/Play
Punts	Total
	Average Yards
Possession	Average Time
Passes	Percent Completed
	Attempted
Fourth Down	Made
	Percent

Figure 13.31 Football Statistics

10. **The *Slicing Arrays* Page.** The `slice()` method (Figure 13.3) lets us copy part or all of an array into a new array. The method copies array elements from the *lower bound* to the *upper bound minus one*. The upper bound is optional. If absent, `slice()` copies array elements from the lower bound to the end of the array. You must create a new array object prior to placing a slice from another array into it. Create a page that lets the user select the lower and upper bounds for the slice. Slice an array of your choice. Print the sliced array.

➤ STATISTICAL EXERCISES

The following exercises use mathematical notation. Most of the formulas include test data and an explanation. The formulas are easily translated into JavaScript code.

11. **The *Products* Page.** Figure 13.32 contains the formula for finding the product of an array. (The Greek symbol, π, signifies multiplication. The starting subscript for the multiplication appears below the π, while the last subscript appears above π. The variable to the right of π is the name of the array to be multiplied.) Add a product function to the *Array* object. Remember that the variable holding the product should be given an initial value of 1.

12. **The *Medians* Page.** A median is an "average" obtained by finding the value associated with the middle position in a sorted array. Figure 5.33 contains the median passing yards (per Figure 13.18) for Week 4 and Week 5 of the *Football Statistics* page. As this figure shows, calculation of the median depends on whether the array contains an odd or even number of elements. If the array contains an odd number of elements, we return the value in the middle position. If the array contains an even number of elements, there are two middle positions. We find and return the arithmetic mean of these two positions. Modify the *Football Statistics* page so that the median statistics are reported.

$$\prod_{i=0}^{n-1} x_i$$

Figure 13.32 The Product Formula

(a) Even	(b) odd

(a) Even

[0]   55
[1]   90
[2]   110   → $\dfrac{90+110}{2}$ =100
[3]   150

(b) odd

[0]   55
[1]   90
[2]   110
[3]   134
[4]   150

Figure 13.33 Median Examples

Hint 1: Use the modulus operator to determine whether a number is odd or even.

Hint 2: Use `Math.floor()` method to find the middle position.

13. **The *Lows and Highs* Page.** Create *Array* prototypes that return the highest and lowest value in an array. You cannot sort the original array (although you can sort a copy of it.)
    Hint: Slice the array and sort the slice.

14. **The *Range* Page.** Create an *Array* prototype that returns the range. The range is defined as *highest value* − *lowest value* + 1.

15. **The *Variance* Page.** The variance is a statistical measure of *dispersion* (as is the range). Figure 13.34 contains the mathematical formula for the variance.

$$\frac{\sum_{i=1}^{n} (X_i - \bar{X})^2}{n}$$

Figure 13.34 The Variance

Translation	Example		
Find the mean (X-bar in the formula).	**X**	**X_i-Mean**	**$(X_i$-Mean$)^2$**
Subtract a score (X_i) from the mean.	50	20	400
Square each difference	40	10	100
Sum the squared differences	30	0	0
Divide the summed squared differences by n	20	−10	100
	10	−20	400
	SUM		1000
	s^2		200

Figure 13.35 Variance Example

Figure 13.35 contains an "English" translation of this formula, along with an example that you can use as test data.

16. **The *Standard Deviation* Page.** Most statisticians use the standard deviation as their measure of dispersion. The standard deviation is defined as the square root of the variance. For example, if the variance is 200 (as it was in the previous example), the standard deviation is 14.14. Create a standard deviation prototype for arrays. Use the variance function in your calculations.

17. **Z-score.** Standardized tests use z-scores (also called standardized scores) to determine an individual's variation from the mean. The z-score formula is given in Figure 13.36.

$$Z_i = \frac{X_i - \bar{X}}{S}$$

Figure 13.36 The Z-Score Formula

Unlike the previous formulas, which returned a single value, we usually return a new array that contains a z-score for every value in the original array. Remember that JavaScript passes arrays by reference, so this is easy. The z-score distribution for the example array is found in Figure 13.37. This Figure also contains an "English" translation of the z-score formula.

	Translation	Example	
Subtract X_i from the mean.	**X**	**X_i-Mean**	**z_i**
Divide result by the standard deviation.	50	20	1.41
	40	10	0.71
	30	0	0
	20	−10	−0.71
	10	−20	−1.41

Figure 13.37 A Z-Score Example

# 14 Forms and Form Elements

INTRODUCTION

In previous chapters, we used prompt windows to obtain information from the users. These windows are convenient and easy to use; however, they are not designed to obtain massive amounts of data. A form is our best bet when we need several pieces of information. This chapter covers the HTML tags that create forms and the JavaScript objects that process them. Because JavaScript is client-based, its form-processing capabilities are limited. Full form processing requires a server-based language such as Perl. Nevertheless, we can create and process many interesting forms, even when using only JavaScript.

THE FORM TAG AND OBJECT

HTML provides a set of tags to create a form and the elements that go into it. The HTML **<FORM>** tag and its corresponding JavaScript object appear in Figure 14.1.

(a) HTML Form Tag	(b) JavaScript **form** Object	

```<FORM NAME = "form.name"opt```
     `ACTION = "URL"opt`
     `METHOD = "POST | GET"opt`
     `ENCTYPE = "mimeType"opt`
     `TARGET = "Target Page or Frame"opt`
     `onSubmit = "eventHandler"opt`
     `onReset = "eventHandler"opt>`
     `formElement1`
        `....`
     `formElementn`
 `</FORM>`
	`name`
	 `action`
	 `method`
	 `encoding`
	 `target`
	 `elements[]`
	 `length`
	
	 `onSubmit =`
	 `onReset=`
		Properties
		
		 Event Handlers

Figure 14.1 The HTML **<FORM>** Tag and Corresponding JS Object

295

As Figure 14.1(a) indicates, HTML forms are constructed with a pair of tags: `<FORM>`...`</FORM>`. The form's elements are placed between these opening and closing tags. All of the attributes of the `<FORM>` tag are optional, as denoted by the subscript $_{opt}$. As Figure 14.1(b) indicates, each HTML attribute has an associated JavaScript *form* object property. The same applies to the two optional event handlers. The purpose of these attributes and event handlers is as follows:

The `NAME` *Attribute.* Because a Web page can contain several forms, the `NAME` attribute can be used to identify each particular form.

The `ACTION` *Attribute.* The `ACTION` attribute specifies the URL of the script that processes the form. This attribute is used in server-side script processing (e.g., Perl script processing). The `ACTION` attribute is also used to email form results in JavaScript.

The `METHOD` *Attribute.* The `METHOD` attribute specifies how form information is passed to a server-side script. Server-side script handling can use either the `GET` or the `POST` method. In JavaScript, the only relevant method is `POST`, and it is used only to email form results.

The `ENCTYPE` *Attribute.* Form data is URL encoded. We examine this encoding technique when we switch to Perl. In JavaScript, encryption is relevant only when emailing form results. When we create an email quiz later in the chapter, we will set the `ENCTYPE` attribute to `"plain/text"`.

The `TARGET` *Attribute.* The `TARGET` attribute is used to place form results into a frame. Typically, it's easier let the JavaScript script choose the frame.

The `onSubmit` *Event Handler.* The `onSubmit` event handler is relevant only when one is using server-side form processing or is emailing form results. This event handler is associated with a *submit* button. When the user clicks this specialized button, the event handler is activated.

The `onReset` *Event Handler.* The `onReset` event handler also has a corresponding *reset* button. When the user clicks this button, the form is reset to its original state. Resetting does NOT change JavaScript properties; it affects only the outer appearance of the form. The `onReset` event handler in JavaScript does not work well, so it is safer to leave it out of a form. This event handler is better suited to server-side script handling.

The HTML `<FORM>`...`</FORM>` *Tags.* These create a container into which we put form elements. JavaScript uses an array, `elements[]`, to store the form's elements. The `length` attribute holds the number of elements in a form. We can extract form information by using the `elements[]` array or by using the form element's name. We use both techniques in this chapter.

Most form elements are created with an HTML `<INPUT>` tag. This tag is used to create text fields, buttons, radio buttons, and check boxes. The syntax of the `<INPUT>` tag is

```
<INPUT TYPE = "type" NAME = "name" OtherAttributes>
```

All elements created with an `<INPUT>` tag have `TYPE` and `NAME` attributes. The remaining attributes are determined by the element's type.

Text Fields

A text field provides a single line of text into which the user places the desired information. We can use a text field to obtain string data—for example, a person's name, street address, city, state, zip code, or email address. We can also use a text field to obtain numeric information, such as the

(a) HTML for a text field	(b) The JavaScript text Object	
```<INPUT TYPE = "text" NAME = "Field Name" VALUE = "Field Contents"opt SIZE = "Columns in Use"opt MAXLENGTH = "Maximum Columns"opt onBlur = "Event Handler"opt onFocus = "Event Handler"opt onSelect = "Event Handler"opt onChange = "Event Handler"opt>```	type	**Properties**
	name	
	defaultValue	
	value	
	blur()	**Methods**
	focus ()	
	select ()	
	onBlur =	**Event Handlers**
	onFocus =	
	onSelect =	
	onChange =	

Figure 14.2 The <INPUT> Tag and its Corresponding JavaScript **text** Object

income of or the number of computers in a household. Figure 14.2 contains the HTML tag and its corresponding JavaScript **text** object.

The HTML attributes have the following interpretations.

The NAME *Attribute.*   The NAME attribute identifies the text field. JavaScript uses this name to obtain the information that the user enters in a text field.

The TYPE *Attribute.*   The TYPE attribute identifies the form element as **text**, HTML's abbreviation for a text field.

The VALUE *Attribute.*   The VALUE attribute contains default text for a text field. For example, suppose we have a phone text field; we could use the VALUE attribute to show our users the desired format: VALUE = "(123) 456-7890". The VALUE attribute becomes the **defaultValue** property in the JavaScript **form** object, while the **value** property holds the user's entry.

The SIZE *and* MAXLENGTH *Attributes.*   The SIZE and MAXLENGTH attributes both specify the number of columns that appear in the text field. The SIZE attribute contains the desired number of columns. HTML uses a default size if this attribute is omitted. These attributes have no corresponding JavaScript properties.

The remaining HTML attributes specify handlers for text field events. The event handlers should be used cautiously, because a single event can trigger more than one event handler. Typically, the JavaScript text-field methods are used to simulate an event. Programmers do not use the event handlers to respond to text-field events.

The onFocus *Event Handler.*   Pressing a mouse button or typing text in a text field brings a text field into focus. A user cannot type or press a mouse button in several text fields simultaneously, so only one text field is in focus at any give time. The text field currently in focus has a bold, blinking cursor. The JavaScript **focus()** method changes the focus to a text field of our choice.

The onBlur *Event Handler.*   A text field is *blurred* when it goes out of focus. This happens when the user types text in another text field or moves the mouse somewhere else. Bringing one text field in focus causes a second text field to blur, so using *both* the **onBlur** and the **onFocus** event handlers for text fields simultaneously usually causes unpredictable results. The JavaScript **blur()** method blurs a text field.

The **onSelect** *Event Handler.* Selecting text occurs when the user drags the mouse button over an area of text. Because JavaScript does not have a property that holds the selected text, the **onSelect** event handler is relatively useless. However, we can use the JavaScript **select()** method to select a text field. This highlights the box that surrounds the text field.

The **onChange** *Event Hander.* The **onChange** event handler is invoked when text is added to or deleted from a text field.

The Button Object

Take a look at Web pages containing forms. These pages almost inevitably have a *Submit* button that's used to invoke a script that processes the form. As indicated previously, the *Submit* button has limited usefulness in JavaScript. Fortunately, JavaScript provides a *button* object that we can use to signal the completion of a form. Upon completing the form, the user clicks a JavaScript button. An event handler associated with the button processes the form. The HTML tag and corresponding JavaScript *button* object appear in Figure 14.3.

(a) HTML	(b) The JavaScript *button* Object	

`<INPUT TYPE = "button"`
`      NAME = "Button Name"`
`      VALUE = "Label Name"`$_{opt}$
`      onClick = "Event Handler"`$_{opt}$`>`
	type
	name
	value
	onClick =
		Properties
		
		Event Handler

Figure 14.3 The **<INPUT>** Tag with a *Button* Object

The purpose of these attributes and the event handler is as follows:

The **NAME** *Attribute.* The **NAME** attribute identifies the button. We use the corresponding **name** property to determine which button a user clicked.

The **TYPE** *Attribute.* The **TYPE** attribute indicates that the form element is a **button**.

The **VALUE** *Attribute.* The **VALUE** attribute holds the label that appears on the button's "face."

The **onClick** *Event Handler.* The **onClick** event handler specifies the action to be taken when a button is pressed. JavaScript also provides a **click()** method that is intended to simulate a button click, but this method does not work.

THE *FIRST FORM* PAGE

The *First Form* page appears in Figure 14.4. The page contains a text field and a button. Figure 14.4(a) shows what happens when the user clicks the *Done* button without entering a name. Notice that an alert window appears with an error message. The text field is also brought

(a) The *First Form* Page

(b) The Output Page

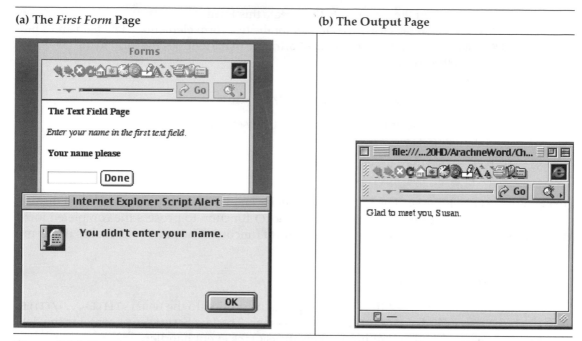

Figure 14.4 The *First Form* Page

into focus. Figure 14.4(b) shows the processed form. It consists of a simple message containing the user's name. This message is displayed on a new web page.

Creating a form typically is easier than processing it. Most HTML books discuss form creation, but few discuss form processing. Form creation requires only knowledge of the relevant HTML tags. Processing requires programming in a language such as JavaScript or Perl. In this example, we begin with the creation of the form in HTML. Form creation always occurs in the body of the page. Once we've created the form, we write the script that processes it. We can place the script in either the head or the body of the page. Most Web programmers place event-handling scripts in the head of a page. This ensures that the event handler is fully loaded before the user enters information into the form. Figure 14.5 contains the body of the *First Form* page. The form is highlighted.

```
<BODY BGCOLOR = 'white'>
<B>The Text Field Page</B>
<P>
<I> Enter your name in the first text field.</I>
<P><B>Your name please</B><P>
<FORM NAME = "firstForm">
<INPUT TYPE = "text" NAME = "yourName" SIZE = "10">
<INPUT TYPE = "button" VALUE = "Done" onClick = "check(this.form)">
</FORM>
</BODY>
```

Figure 14.5 Body of the *First Form* Page

Let's examine each of the statements that create this form.

The `<FORM>...</FORM>` tags form a container for the two form elements: a text field and a button. The `<FORM>` tag requires no more than a `NAME` attribute that identifies the form to the JavaScript script that processes this form.

The first `<INPUT>` tag,

```
<INPUT TYPE = "text" NAME = "yourName" SIZE = "10">
```

creates a text field, *yourName*, with ten columns for the user's input.

The second `<INPUT>` tag,

```
<INPUT TYPE = "button" VALUE = "Done"
       onClick = "check(this.form)">
```

creates a button labeled *Done*. The button also contains an event handler, **onClick**. When the user clicks a button, this event handler invokes the **check()** function to process the completed form. We pass a single parameter, **this.form**, to the **check()** function. The parameter makes the form's elements accessible to the JavaScript function.

The check() Function

Figure 14.6 contains the head of the *First Form* page. In addition to the usual `<TITLE>...</TITLE>` tags, the head also includes `<SCRIPT>...</SCRIPT>` tags. The JavaScript script contains the definition of the **check()** function that implements the **onClick** event handler.

Let's begin by examining the header of the **check()** function,

```
function check(form)
```

The header contains a parameter, **form**, that represents the form created in the body of the page. This lets us use the form elements inside the function.

The body of the function contains an **if** statement that acts like an error loop. The **if** statement compares the value in the 0th form element with a null string. A null string indicates that

```
<HTML>
<HEAD><TITLE>Forms</TITLE>
<SCRIPT LANGUAGE = "JavaScript">
<!--
  function check(form)
  {//validate a text form
  // if blank send an error message and ask to reenter
    if (form.elements[0].value == "") {
       alert("You didn't enter your  name.");
       form.yourName.focus();
       form.yourName.select();
       return;
    }
    document.write("Glad to meet you, " + form.yourName.value  + ".<BR><BR>");
  }
    //-->
</SCRIPT></HEAD>
```

Figure 14.6 The **check()** Function

the user didn't fill in the text field. If this is the case, we display an alert box with an error message. The statement that does this is

```
alert("You didn't enter your name.");
```

The user must click on the *OK* box to remove the alert box.

Next, we use the **focus()** and **select()** methods to place a blinking cursor in the *yourName* text field. The field is now ready to accept new user input.

Finally, we use a **return;** statement to terminate the **check()** function. The **document.write()** statement is not executed, because the user did not supply the correct information. The JavaScript script does not execute the **document.write()** statement until the user supplies non-null data. When the JavaScript script executes the **document.write()** statement, the message is not written on the current page. Instead, JavaScript opens a new blank page and places the message on this page. The appearance is often displeasing, and we examine an alternative in the next example.

A NUMERIC TEXT FIELD FORM

We can use text fields to obtain numeric data, and our next web page focuses on this application. After we finish creating this page, you will know how to do all of the following:

1. use a table to control the layout and appearance of form elements;
2. convert a text field's value to a number;
3. check form elements for missing data;
4. check form elements for nonnumeric data;
5. use a text field to display results;
6. use a *Clear* button to erase the text fields.

Using Tables to Control Layout and Appearance

HTML uses a default "flow layout" for form elements. A flow layout uses a left-to-right, top-to-bottom arrangement. This means that the first element is in the leftmost position. New elements are added to the right. A new row of elements is started when the right edge of the browser is reached. Figure 14.7 shows the *Numeric Form* page using the default layout.

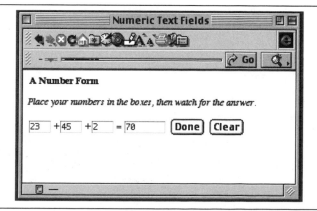

Figure 14.7 The *Numeric Form* Page With the Default Layout

Figure 14.8 shows the same page with a table layout. The *Done* and *Clear* buttons are now aligned with the first two text fields.

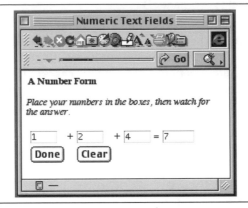

Figure 14.8 The *Numeric Form* Page With a Table Layout

Figure 14.9 contains the body of the *Numeric Form* page. The **<FORM>...</FORM>** tags create a container for the table that houses the form's elements. The first three text fields, *Number 1*, *Number 2*, and *Number 3*, hold the user-supplied input. The last text field, *Answer*, holds the sum of the three numbers supplied by the user. We place the text fields in a single row. The columns for the first and second numbers are followed by columns with a plus sign. The column for the third number is followed by a column with an equals sign. The *Done* and *Clear* buttons appear in a separate row. An empty column separates these two buttons, because we want to align the buttons with the first two text fields.

```
<BODY BGCOLOR = " white">
<B>A Number Form</B>
<P>
<I>Place your numbers in the boxes, then watch for the answer.</I>
<P>
<FORM NAME = "Numbers">
<TABLE>
<TR>
<TD><INPUT TYPE = "text" NAME = "Number 1" SIZE = "5"></TD><TD>+</TD>
<TD><INPUT TYPE = "text" NAME = "Number 2" SIZE = "5"></TD> <TD>+</TD>
<TD><INPUT TYPE = "text" NAME = "Number 3 " SIZE = "5"></TD> <TD>=</TD>
<TD><INPUT TYPE = "text" NAME = "Answer" SIZE = "6"></TD></TR>
<TR><TD><B>
<INPUT TYPE="button" NAME = "Done" VALUE = "Done"
       onClick = checkAll(this.form)></TD>
<TD></TD><!-- Skip plus field -->
<TD>
<INPUT TYPE = "button" NAME = "Clear"  VALUE = "Clear"
       onClick = "clean(this.form)">
</TD></TR>
</TABLE>
</FORM>
</BODY></HTML>
```

Figure 14.9 The Body of the *Numeric Form* Page

As Figure 14.9 indicates, each button contains an **onClick** event handler. The **check()** function implements the event handler for the *Done* button. The **clean()** function implements the event handler for the *Clear* button. Both functions pass the form as a parameter. A JavaScript script located in the head of the *Numeric Form* page contains the definitions of these functions.

Validating the Text Fields

We've already encountered the infamous *NaN* error several times. Form information is no less prone to this error. Prior to adding the three user-supplied numbers, we'll want to make sure that we have valid information.

Invalid numeric information comes in two flavors: null and nonnumeric. A null value occurs when the user clicks the *Done* button without filling in one or more of the text fields. A nonnumeric error occurs when the user places a nonnumeric character in a text field. Although it might be logical to assume that the **isNaN()** function would view null strings as nonnumeric data, this is not the case. This means that the **check()** function needs to check both for nonnumeric data and for null data.

Figure 14.10 shows the error traps that we are about to implement. In Figure 14.10(a), the user has forgotten to enter data in a text field. The **check()** function issues an alert box containing an error message and the name of the offending text field. This text field is brought into focus for the user. In Figure 14.10(b), the user has placed the letter *a* in the third text field. The **check()** function prints a different error message and brings this text field into focus.

(a) Missing Data   **(b) Non-numeric Data**

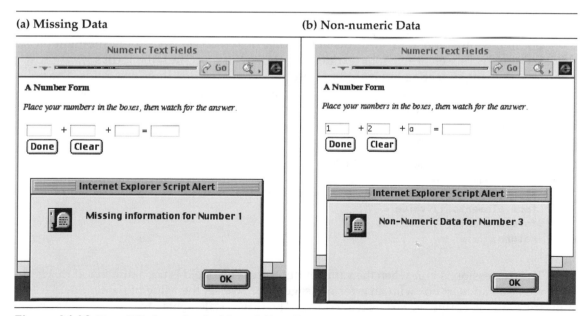

Figure 14.10 Error Windows for the *Numeric Form* Page

Figure 14.11 contains the definition of the **check()** function. Carefully examine the code. Try to determine why the **for** statement executes as long as *i* is less than *form.length-3*.

```
function check(form)
 { //Check all the text fields
 for (i= 0; i < form.length-3; i++) {
   if (isNaN(form.elements[i].value) )
   { //non-numeric data
       alert("Non-numeric data for "+ form.elements[i].name);
       form.elements[i].value = "";
       form.elements[i].focus();
       return;
   }
   if (form.elements[i].value == "")
   {//null data
       alert("Missing data for " + form.elements[i].name);
       form.elements[i].focus();
       return;
   }
 }
 //all fields contain numeric data
 var sum = 0;
 for (i = 0; i < form.length-3; i++)
   sum = sum + parseFloat(form.elements[i].value);
 form.Answer.value = sum;
}
```

Figure 14.11 The **check()** Function: *Numeric Form* Page

Count the number of form elements in the *Numeric Form* page. Your count should indicate that this form has six elements: four text fields and two buttons. Thus, the form's length is six. The **for** statement appearing in Figure 14.11 processes only the first three text fields. The valid indices for these text fields are 0, 1, and 2. The termination check for the **for** statement ensures that the *Answer* text field and the two buttons are not processed by the **for** statement, because *length-3 = 6-3 =3.*

Now let's consider the first **if** statement in the loop body:

```
if (isNaN(form.elements[i].value) )
{ //non-numeric data
  alert("Non-numeric data for "+ form.elements[i].name);
  form.elements[i].value = "";
  form.elements[i].focus();
  return;
}
```

The expression is *true* when the value of the current text field is not a number. If this is the case, we issue an alert box with an error message. Next, we set the value of the text field to the null string, and we bring the text field into focus. The **return** statement in the body of the **if** statement halts the execution of the **check()** function.

Now consider the second **if** statement,

```
if (form.elements[i].value == "")
{//null data
  alert("Missing data for " + form.elements[i].name);
  form.elements[i].focus();
  return;
}
```

The expression is *true* when the text field contains a null string. If this is the case, we issue an alert box with an error message, and we bring the offending text field into focus. We don't need to set the text field's value to null, because that value is what triggered the error. The **return** statement in the body of this **if** statement also halts execution of the **check()** function.

Finally, let's examine the code segment that calculates the sum when all of the text fields contain numeric data:

```
var sum = 0;
for (i = 0; i < form.length-3; i++)
    sum = sum + parseFloat(form.elements[i].value);
form.Answer.value = sum;
```

We begin the summation process by initializing *sum* to zero. A **for** statement successively adds each of the form elements to *sum*. These elements are strings, so we must use the **parseFloat()** function to transform them into their floating-point equivalents. After the **for** statement terminates, we place *sum* into the *Answer* text field.

Clearing a Form

We are now ready to examine the code that clears the form. Figure 14.12 shows the confirm window that appears when a user clicks the *Clear* button. Although we could simply clean all of the text fields, it's usually a good idea to warn a user before you remove all of the information. The user can stop the clearing by selecting the *Cancel* button. If the user chooses the *OK* button, we clean the page.

Figure 14.13 contains the HTML **<HEAD>...</HEAD>** tags with the script containing the **clean()** function.

The **clean()** function uses the *flag* variable to hold the user's response to the confirm window. We use this boolean variable to form the expression in the **if** statement. The body of the **if** statement is executed only if *flag* is *true*.

The body of the **if** statement contains a single **for** statement that we use to clean all of the text fields. The test expression in the **for** statement, **i < length-2**, cleans all four text fields, but it skips the two buttons at the end of the form, because we can't clear them. We use the **elements[]** array to set the value of each text field to the empty string. After the **for** statement terminates, we bring the first element into focus.

The Text Area Object

A text field can accommodate a single row of text. When a problem requires several lines of textual input, we use a text area. An **<INPUT>** tag is not used to create a text area; instead, HTML provides a special set of tags: **<TEXTAREA>** ... **</TEXTAREA>**. The space between these tags contains default text for the text area.

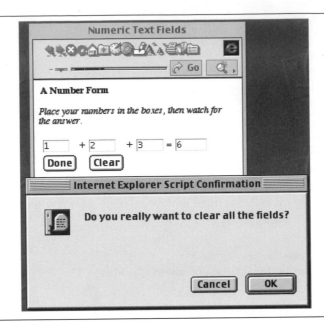

Figure 14.12 Clearing the *Numeric Form* Page

```
<TITLE>Text Form Validation</TITLE>
<SCRIPT LANGUAGE = "JavaScript">
<!--
// Put the check() function here
function clean(form)
{ //clean the text fields
   var flag = confirm("Do you really want to clear all the fields?");
   if (flag) { //user wants to clear
      for (i = 0; i < form.length-2; i++)
         form.elements[i].value = "";
      form.elements[0].focus();
   }
 }
//-->
</SCRIPT></HEAD>
```

Figure 14.13 The **clean()** Function: *Numeric Form* Page

The HTML **<TEXTAREA>** tag and its corresponding JavaScript object appear in Figure 14.14. Although the text area methods and event handlers are identical to the ones used for a text field, there are differences in the HTML attributes and JavaScript properties. The interpretation of the attributes and properties is as follows:

(a) HTML	**(b) The JavaScript textarea Object**

<pre><TEXTAREA NAME = "Text Area Name"
ROWS = "Number Of Rows"_{opt}
COLS = "Number Of Columns"_{opt}
WRAP = "off" | "physical" |
 "virtual"_{opt}
onBlur = "Event Handler"_{opt}
onFocus = "Event Handler"_{opt}
onChange = "Event Handler"_{opt}
onSelect = "Event Handler"_{opt}>
Place default text here
</TEXTAREA></pre>
	name **Properties**
	type
	defaultValue
	value
	blur() **Methods**
	focus ()
	select ()
	onBlur = **Event Handlers**
	onChange =
	onFocus =
	onSelect =

Figure 14.14 Text Areas

The NAME *Attribute.*   This attribute uniquely identifies the text area. We use the corresponding JavaScript **name** property to examine or change a text area's value.

The ROWS *Attribute.*   This attribute sets the number of rows in a text area. The ROWS attribute does not have a corresponding JavaScript property.

The COLS *Attribute.*   This attribute sets the number of columns in a text area. The COLS attribute is equivalent to the SIZE attribute in a text field. There is no corresponding JavaScript property for the COLS attribute.

The WRAP *Attribute.*   The WRAP attribute controls the text wrapping as follows:

1. WRAP = "OFF". Lack of wrapping is the default. This means that the text continues to scroll to the right, often extending beyond the boundaries of the text area. The user must press the *Enter* key to cause the text to wrap to the next line.

2. WRAP = "PHYSICAL". When a **PHYSICAL** wrap is used, text automatically wraps to the next line. The browser inserts hidden control characters which physically embed a new line into the text. These hidden characters are machine-specific. For example, Unix systems embed a new line character (**\n**), Macintoshes embed a carriage return (**\r**), and Windows embeds both a carriage return and a new line character (**\r\n**).

3. WRAP = "VIRTUAL". When the wrap style is **VIRTUAL**, text also automatically wraps to the next line. However, the browser does not insert control characters into the text.

   There is no corresponding JavaScript property for the WRAP attribute.

The type *Property.*   The **type** property is set to **textarea**. Be sure to notice the difference between the HTML and its corresponding JavaScript type.

The `value` *and* `defaultValue` *Properties.* Any text placed between the `<TEXTAREA>...</TEXTAREA>` tags is interpreted as a default value. JavaScript stores this default value in the `defaultValue` property. The text entered by the user is stored in the `value` property.

The *Text Area* Page

To illustrate text areas, we create a simple page with two text areas: an *Original* area and a *Selected Text* area. The user types text into the *Original* text area. When they press the *Copy* button, the browser copies the text from the *Original* area to the *Selected Text* area. If the user has a three-button mouse, they can also highlight text in the *Original* text area. Pressing the middle mouse copies only the selected text to the second text area. The *Text Area* page also includes a *Clear* button that lets the user clear both text areas. Figure 14.15 contains a sample page.

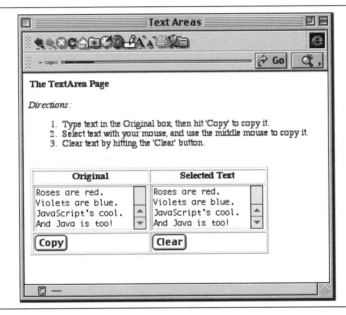

Figure 14.15 The *Text Area* Page

The Body of the *Text Area* Page

Construction of the *Text Area* page begins with the page's body. The body contains the HTML tags that create the two text areas and buttons. By beginning with the body, we can check the page's appearance before we develop the JavaScript script that processes this form. The event handler is not included until the form's appearance is acceptable.

Using Figure 14.15 as your guide, try to create the body of the *Text Area* page. Notice how a table controls the layout of the form's elements. When you're finished, examine the HTML contained in Figure 14.16. It contains the body of the *Text Area* page.

As Figure 14.16 indicates, we use a table to align the form's elements correctly. This table contains column headings for the *Original* and *Selected Text*. We place the two text areas in separate columns below their respective headings. Both text areas have a width of 20 columns and a height of four rows. We place the *Copy* and *Clear* buttons below the text areas. Each but-

```
<BODY BGCOLOR = "white">
<B>The Text area Page</B>
<P>
<I>Directions:</I>
<OL>
<LI>Type text in the Original box, then hit 'Copy' to copy it.
<LI> Select text with your mouse, and use the middle mouse to copy it.
<LI> Clear text by hitting the 'Clear' button.
</OL>
<P>
<FORM NAME = "formPage">
<TABLE BORDER = "1' CELLPADDING  = "3" >
<TR><TH>Original</TH> <TH>Selected Text</TH></TR>
<TR><TD>
<TEXTAREA NAME = "Original" ROWS = "4" COLS = "20"></TEXTAREA></TD>
<TD><TEXTAREA NAME = "Copy" ROWS = "4" COLS = "20"></TEXTAREA></TD>
</TR><TR>
<TD> <INPUT TYPE  = "button" VALUE = "Copy"
     onClick = "copy(this.form)"></TD>
<TD> <INPUT TYPE = "button" VALUE = "Clear"
     onClick = "clean(this.form)"></TD></TR>
</TR></TABLE>
</FORM>
</BODY>
```

Figure 14.16 The Body of the *Text Area* Page

ton has its own event handler. The *Copy* button uses the **copy()** function to implement the **onClick** event handler; the *Clear* button uses the **clean()** function to implement this event handler.

The Head of the *Text Area* Page

A script in the head of the *Text Area* page contains the definitions of the **copy()** and **clean()** functions that implement the two event handlers. The code for each of these functions is short and simple. Figure 14.17 contains the definition of the **copy()** function. The body of this function contains a single line of code that assigns the value in the *Original* text field to the *Copy* text field.

The **clean()** function sets the value of each text area to the empty string and brings the *Original* text area into focus. Figure 14.18 contains the definition of the **clean()** function and its enclosing script.

```
function copy(form)
{//copy from original to copy
   form.Copy.value = form.Original.value;
}
```

Figure 14.17 The **copy()** Function

```
<HEAD><TITLE>Text Areas</TITLE>
<SCRIPT LANGUAGE = "JavaScript">
<!--
 //put the copy() Function here

 function clean(form)
 {//clean the text areas
   form.Original.value = "";
   form.Copy.value ="";
   form.Original.focus();
 }
//-->
</SCRIPT> </HEAD>
```

Figure 14.18 The `clean()` Function

HTML BUTTON TYPES

We've used the HTML **button** type several times in our programs. In addition to these "push" buttons, HTML provides two additional types of buttons, as illustrated in Figure 14.19. The buttons in the row labeled *Ice Creams* are radio buttons. A user must not select more than one button in such a row. The buttons in the row labeled *Sodas* are check boxes. The user may select none, one, several, or all of the buttons in this row. The final row contains the familiar *Done* button. When the user presses this button, a script displays the selected ice cream, and the selected sodas, in the text area.

Our previous examples required information that was unique to the user. For example, the *Numeric Form* page let the user choose some numbers. We use radio buttons and check boxes

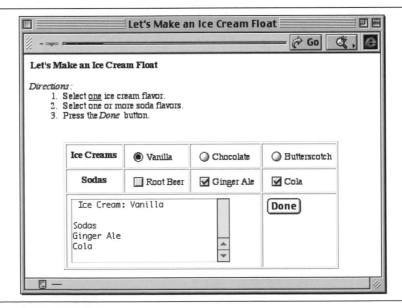

Figure 14.19 HTML Button Types

when we have short lists of predefined values. The ice creams and sodas displayed in Figure 14.19 fit into this category.

Radio buttons and checkboxes are easier for the end user to use than are text fields, because the former requires only a mouse click. They are also less error-prone, because we control the lists. We examine each of these form elements beginning with radio buttons.

Radio Buttons

Figure 14.20 contains the HTML tag that creates a radio button. The associated JavaScript *radio* object is also listed.

(a) HTML	(b) The JavaScript *radio* Object	

```<INPUT TYPE = "radio"```
 ```   NAME = "Button Group"```
 ```   VALUE = "Button Value"```opt
 ```   CHECKED```opt
 ```   onClick = "Event Handler"```opt ```>Label```
	```type```
	 ```ButtonGroup.length```
	 ```ButtonGroup[].value```
	 ```ButtonGroup[].defaultChecked```
	 ```ButtonGroup[].checked```
	
	 ```onClick =```
		Properties
		
		 Event
		
		 Handler

Figure 14.20 Radio Buttons

The meanings of the HTML attributes, the related JavaScript properties, and the event handler are as follows:

The **NAME** *Attribute.*   The **NAME** attribute creates a group of radio buttons. All of the buttons in the group have the same name. For example, all of the ice cream buttons share the same name, *"Ice Cream"*. Each group of radio buttons has an associated array that shares the same name as the value associated with the **NAME** attribute. Each element in the array is an object that holds the *value, defaultChecked,* and *checked* properties for the radio button in the indicated array positions. The radio buttons are placed in the array in the order in which they are created. The first radio button is in the 0th position, by JS counting.

The **TYPE** *Attribute.*   The **TYPE** attribute identifies the element as a **radio** button. JavaScript has a corresponding **type** property.

The **VALUE** *Attribute.*   Because all radio buttons in a group share the same name, it is the **VALUE** attribute that uniquely identifies a button within the group. The value becomes the name of a particular button in the group. This is useful if we want to print the name of the selected radio button.

The **CHECKED** *Attribute.*   The **CHECKED** attribute preselects a button. We can use the **CHECKED** attribute with no more than one radio button in a group. If we use this attribute, the user finds that a button has been checked before the filling in of the form. The **CHECKED** attribute is associated with the JavaScript **defaultChecked** property; the **checked** property holds the button selected by the user.

The **onClick** *Event Handler.*   The **onClick** event handler is invoked when the user selects a radio button. JavaScript also provides a **click()** method, but it does not work correctly.

The *Football* Page

To illustrate radio buttons, we create a *Football* page that incorporates several of the pages written in previous chapters plus two new pages. Figure 14.21 contains a sample page. The page uses a frame-based approach. The left frame contains a group of radio buttons that serve as navigational tools. When the user clicks one of these buttons, the browser loads the corresponding page into the right frame. In Figure 14.21, the user selected the *Standard Defense* button. A page illustrating the standard defensive line appears in the right frame.

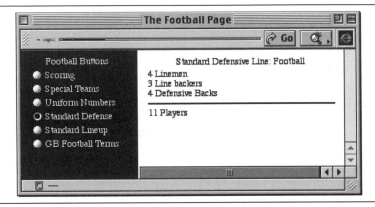

Figure 14.21 The *Football* Page

The Frame Layout

Since the *Football* page is frame-based, we'll take a quick tour of the frame layout. Figure 14.22 contains the `startPage.html` file that establishes the frame layout. The order of the frames is important.

```
<HTML>
<HEAD> <TITLE>The Football Page </TITLE></HEAD>
<FRAMESET COLS = "35%,*" BORDER = "0">
<FRAME SRC = "buttons.html" NORESIZE NAME = "menu">
<FRAME SRC = "football.html"  NORESIZE SCROLLING  = "yes"  NAME ="main">
</FRAMESET>
</BODY>
</HTML>
```

Figure 14.22 The Frame Set Page: `startPage.html`

The frameset page creates two frames. The first frame, which contains the buttons, is static. The second frame initially contains the *football.html* file. This file contains a simple set of directions. When the user selects a button, the browser loads the selected file into the second frame. Because we're using JavaScript to handle the button clicks, we'll also use JavaScript to load the file. This means that we must be able to access the second frame from within a JavaScript script. By design, the JavaScript **document** object contains **parent** and **frames[]** properties that let us access the frameset and its frames.

When we load a frame-based page into a browser, JavaScript stores the frameset page in the **parent** property of the **document** object. JavaScript also loads the frames into the **frames[]** array, using the order specified in the frameset. The **frames[]** array is a property of the **parent** object. Thus, the file listed in the first **<FRAME>** tag is stored in **frames[0]**, the file listed in the second **<FRAME>** tag is stored in **frames[1]**, and so on. Figure 14.23 shows the relation between the **parent** and **frames[]** properties of the *Football* page.

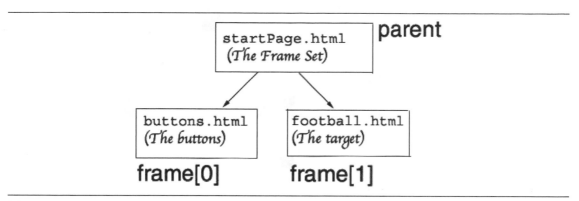

Figure 14.23 The Frame Layout for the *Football* Page

The *Label* and *URL* Arrays

The *buttons.html* file creates the form appearing in the left-hand frame and the JavaScript script that processes it. To facilitate creating the form and processing it, we use two arrays. The first array, *Label*, contains the radio-button labels appearing in Figure 14.21. The second array, *URL*, contains URLs that correspond to the button labels. Figure 14.24 contains the array declarations.

We place the *Label* and *URL* arrays in a JavaScript script located in the head of the *buttons* frame. This script also contains the definition of the event handler for button clicks.

```
var Label = new Array("Scoring",
    "Special Teams",
    "Uniform Numbers",
    "Standard Defense",
    "Standard Lineup",
    "GB Football Terms");
    var URL = new Array(
        "scoring.html",
        "specialTeam.html",
        "uniforms.html",
        "defense.html",
        "lineup.html",
        "gbterms.html");
```

Figure 14.24 The *Label* and *URL* Arrays for the *Football* Page

Creating the *Football* Form

The body of the *buttons* frame creates the football buttons, which appear as white buttons against a black background. A JavaScript script is used to create these buttons. Figure 14.25 contains the body of the *buttons* frame.

```
<BODY BGCOLOR = "black"  TEXT = "white">
<CENTER>Football Buttons</CENTER>
<FORM NAME = 'football'>
<SCRIPT LANGUAGE = "JavaScript">
<!--
   var i;
   for (i=0; i < Label.length; i++){
     document.write("<INPUT TYPE = 'radio' NAME = 'web'");
     document.write("onClick = 'getPage(this.form)'>");
     document.write(Label[i] + "<BR>");
   }
//-->
</SCRIPT>
</FORM></BODY>
```

Figure 14.25 The Body of the *buttons* Frame

The JS script uses a **for** statement to create the buttons. Let's examine each of the statements in the loop body. The first statement,

```
document.write("<INPUT TYPE = 'radio' NAME = 'web'");
```

begins the **<INPUT>** tag for the ith button. This statement indicates that the form element is a **radio** button and that the name of the button is *web*. All of the radio buttons share this name.

The second statement,

```
document.write("onClick = 'getPage(this.form)'>");
```

ends the **<INPUT>** tag for the ith button. This statement contains the event handler. All radio buttons use the same event handler: the **getPage()** function.

The last statement,

```
document.write(Label[i] + "<BR>");
```

places the button's label on the frame.

The getPage() Function

The **getPage()** function implements the event handler for radio button clicks. The function definition appears in Figure 14.26.

```
function getPage(form)
{ //get the page and jump to it
  var i;
  for (i=0; i < form.web.length; i++)
    if (form.web[i].checked)
        parent.frames[1].location.href = URL[i];
}
```

Figure 14.26 The **getPage()** Function

The **getPage()** function uses a **for** statement that examines each of the radio buttons. The body of the **for** statement contains an **if** statement that finds the selected button. Once we've found the selected button, we change the URL of the right frame. To do this, we access the **location** property of **frames[1]**. This property, which is an object in its own right, contains an **href** property. Changing the **href** property loads a new page into **frame[1]**. We use the *URL* array, which is coordinated with the *Label* array, to load the correct page.

Figure 14.27 contains the complete code for the *buttons* frame. The use of arrays shortens the code and creates an elegant, error-free approach to processing a group of radio buttons.

```
<HTML><HEAD>
<SCRIPT LANGUAGE = "JavaScript">
<!--
 //create arrays for the labels and urls
   var Label = new Array("Scoring","Special Teams",
       "Uniform Numbers","Standard Defense",
       "Standard Lineup","GB Football Terms");

   var URL = new Array("scoring.html", "specialTeam.html",
       "uniforms.html","defense.html",
       "lineup.html","gbterms.html");
function getPage(form)
{ //get the page and jump to it
  var i;
  for (i=0; i < form.web.length; i++)
    if (form.web[i].checked)
       parent.frames[1].location.href = URL[i];
}
//-->
</SCRIPT>
</HEAD>

<BODY BGCOLOR = "black"  TFXT = "white">
<CENTER>Football Buttons</CENTER>
<FORM NAME = 'football'>
<SCRIPT LANGUAGE = "JavaScript">
<!--
   var i;
   for (i=0; i < Label.length; i++){
     document.write("<INPUT TYPE = 'radio' NAME = 'web'");
     document.write("onClick = 'getPage(this.form)'>");
     document.write(Label[i] + "<BR>");
   }
//-->
</SCRIPT>
</FORM></BODY></HTML>
```

Figure 14.27 The *buttons* Frame

Checkboxes

We're now ready to examine the last of the HTML button types. Figure 14.28 contains the HTML tag that creates a checkbox and its corresponding JavaScript object.

The HTML tag that creates a checkbox resembles the tag used to create a radio button. There are a few subtle differences, however. The meanings of the HTML attributes, the related JavaScript properties, and the event handler are as follows:

(a) HTML	(b) The JavaScript checkbox Object

```<INPUT TYPE = "checkbox"```
   ```NAME = "Box Name"```
   ```VALUE = "Box Value"```opt
   ```CHECKED```opt
   ```onClick = "Event Handler"```opt```>``` **Label**
	`type` **Properties**
	`name`
	`value`
	`defaultChecked`
	`checked`
	`onClick =` **Event Handlers**

Figure 14.28 Checkboxes

The **NAME** *Attribute.* The **NAME** attribute identifies the checkbox. Unlike radio buttons, which use the same name, each checkbox has a different name. The JavaScript **name** property holds the name of the checkbox.

The **TYPE** *Attribute.* The **TYPE** attribute identifies the element as a **checkbox**. JavaScript has a corresponding **type** property.

The **VALUE** *Attribute.* The **VALUE** attribute typically is used only in server-side script processing.

The **CHECKED** *Attribute.* The **CHECKED** attribute preselects one or more checkboxes. When this property is used, the user sees a check mark in the box when the page is first loaded. The **CHECKED** attribute is associated with the JavaScript **defaultChecked** property; the **checked** property indicates that the box is currently checked.

The **onClick** *Event Handler.* The **onClick** event handler indicates the action taken when a box is checked. JavaScript also provides a **click()** method, but it does not work correctly.

The *Favorite Colors* Page

As our example of checkboxes, we create a *Favorite Colors* page. Figure 14.29 contains a sample page. The page contains a set of color checkboxes. The user may select as many boxes as is wished. When the user clicks the *Done* button, we display the selected colors in the text area.

The *Favorite Colors* page uses both checkboxes and a button. Although we could attach an event handler to each of the check boxes, we usually don't process the form until the user has completed the selections. By clicking the *Done* button, the user indicates that the filling out of the form has been finished.

Creation of the Checkboxes. Creating a set of checkboxes is similar to creating a set of radio buttons. We create an array of checkbox labels. This array is put into a JavaScript script located in the head of the page. The *Favorite Colors* page uses the **colors[]** array, which is defined as

```
var colors = new Array("red", "white", "blue", "green", "yellow", "orange",
   "violet", "pink");
```

Figure 14.30 contains the body of the *Favorite Colors* page. The script that creates the checkboxes is highlighted. As this figure indicates, the color form is put into a table, so that we can more easily control the layout of the checkboxes. The script places each checkbox in a table column. The **colors[]** array generates both the name and the label of the checkbox.

We create the *Output* text area and *Done* button, using standard HTML tags after the script terminates HTML. The text area contains a default value of *Your Favorite Colors*. The *Done* button uses the **process()** function located in the head of the page to implement the **onClick** event handler.

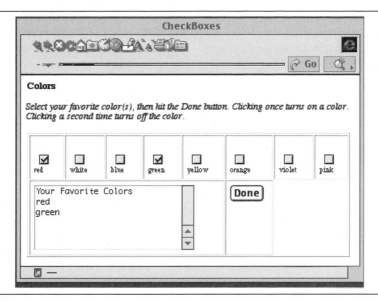

Figure 14.29 The *Favorite Colors* Page

```
<BODY BGCOLOR = "white">
<B>Colors</B><P>
<I>Select your favorite color(s), then hit the Done button. Clicking once turns on a color.
Clicking a second time turns off the color.</I>
<P>
<FORM NAME = "colorForm">
<TABLE  BORDER = '1' CELLPADDING ='5'>
<TR>
<SCRIPT LANGUAGE = "JavaScript">
<!--
   var i;
   for (i = 0; i < colors.length; i++) {
      document.write("<TD><INPUT TYPE = 'checkbox' Name = '");
      document.write(colors[i] + "'> ");
      document.write(colors[i] + "</TD>");
   }
//-->
</SCRIPT>
<TR><TD COLSPAN = "5"><TEXTAREA NAME = "Output" ROWS = "6"  COLS = "30">
Your favorite colors:
</TEXTAREA></TD>
<TD VALIGN = "top"><FONT SIZE = "2">
<INPUT TYPE = "button" VALUE = "Done" onClick = "process(this.form)">
</TD></TR></TABLE>
</FORM>
</BODY>
```

Figure 14.30 The Body of the *Favorite Colors* Page

*The Head of the **Favorite Colors** Page.*　　Now, let's examine the head of the *Favorite Colors* page. Figure 14.31 contains the code. In addition to creating the **colors[]** array, we also create a string variable, *outputString*, to preserve the original value in the text area. The **process()** function uses this string to initialize *Output's* **value** and **defaultValue** properties. The statement that accomplishes this is

```
form.Output.value = form.Output.defaultValue = outputString;
```

```
<HEAD><TITLE>CheckBoxes</TITLE>
<SCRIPT LANGUAGE = "JavaScript">
<!--
   var colors = new Array("red", "white", "blue", "green", "yellow", "orange", "violet", "pink");
   var outputString = "Your Favorite Colors";

   function process(form)
   {//find the checked buttons and add their names to the text area
      var i;
      form.output.value = form.Output.defaultValue = outputString;
      for (i = 0; i < colors.length; i++)
        if (form.elements[i].checked)
           form.Output.value = form.Output.value + "\r\n" + colors[i];
   }
//-->
</SCRIPT>
</HEAD>
```

Figure 14.31 Head of the *Favorite Colors* Page

The **process()** function uses a **for** statement to find the selected checkboxes. The **if** statement examines the **checked** property of each checkbox. If this property is *true*, we append a new line (**\n**), and the color name (**colors[i]**) to the text area's value.

SELECT LISTS

A select list can mimic either a group of radio buttons or a set of checkboxes. Select lists conserve space when the list of alternatives is long. Unlike check boxes or radio buttons, select lists require their own set of tags: **<SELECT>...</SELECT>**. These tags create a container that holds the select list. An **<OPTION>** tag generates each alternative appearing in the list. Figure 14.32 contains the HTML tags that create a select list and the corresponding JavaScript objects.

The meanings of the HTML attributes, the related JavaScript properties, and the event handler are as follows:

The **NAME** *Attribute.*　　The **NAME** attribute identifies the select list. JavaScript has a corresponding **name** attribute.

The **MULTIPLE** *Attribute.*　　The HTML **<SELECT>** tag creates a single select list. A single select list mimics a group of radio buttons, because the user can select only one option from the list.

(a) HTML	(b) JavaScript	
```<SELECT```	`type`	**Properties**
`NAME = "Select Name"`	`name`	
`SIZE = "List Size"`_{opt}	`length`	
`MULTIPLE`_{opt}	`selectedIndex`	
`onBlur = "Event Handler"`_{opt}	`options[i]`	
`onFocus ="Event Handler"`_{opt}	`options[i].defaultSelected`	
`onChange = "Event Handler`_{opt}`">`	`options[i].selected`	
`<OPTION VALUE = "Option Value"`_{opt}`>`**Label**	`options[i].text`	
`...`	`options[i].value`	
`<OPTION SELECTED`_{opt}`>`**Label**	`blur()`	**Methods**
`</SELECT>`	`focus()`	
	`onChange=`	**Event**
	`onBlur=`	**Handlers**
	`onFocus=`	

Figure 14.32 Select Lists

Figure 14.33(a) contains a select list of ice-cream toppings. Only one option is displayed. The displayed option is the first one in the list, if the user has not made a selection. If the user has selected an option, it is displayed. The small box to the right is a click box that activates a pull-down menu containing all of the options.

The **MULTIPLE** attribute creates a multiple select list. A multiple select list mimics a set of checkboxes, because the user can select none, one, several, or all of the options. Figure 14.33(b) contains a select list of colors. The default display is browser dependent. Netscape displays all of the options in the list; Internet Explorer displays only the first four options.

The **type** *Property.* JavaScript uses the **type** property to hold the select list's type. If the select list allows only a single selection, its type is **select-one**. If the select list allows multiple selections, its type is **select-multiple**.

(a) Single Select   (b) Multiple Select

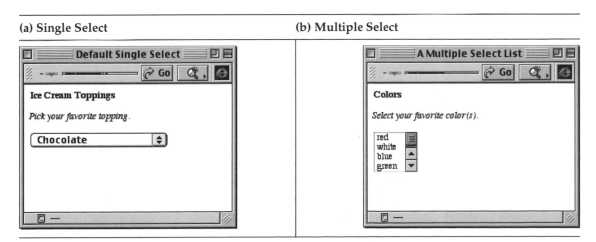

Figure 14.33 The **MULTIPLE** Attribute

The **SIZE** *Attribute.* The **SIZE** attribute changes the default display for select lists. Figure 14.34(a) uses **SIZE="8"** for the ice-cream toppings list. Figure 14.34(b) uses **SIZE="2"** for the colors list. Scrollbars are automatically displayed whenever the size is greater than one but less than the length of the list. There is no corresponding JavaScript property.

(a) SIZE = "8"   **(b) SIZE = "2"**

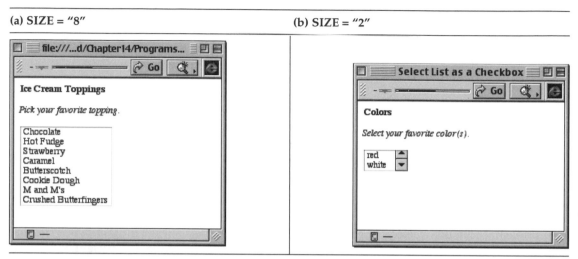

Figure 14.34 The **SIZE** Attribute

The **selectedIndex** *Property.* Java Script uses the **options[]** array to store information on each option. The **selectedIndex** property holds the index (subscript) of the selected option for a single select list.

The **options[]** *Array.* The **options[]** array contains properties associated with HTML **<OPTION>** tag attributes. These properties are:

1. **defaultSelected.** The **defaultSelected** property is *true* if the **<OPTION>** tag contains a **SELECTED** attribute. Otherwise it is *false.*

2. **selected.** The **selected** property is *true* if the user selected an option. Otherwise it is *false.*

3. **value.** The **value** attribute is set to **null** if the **VALUE** attribute is not used. Otherwise it contains the string assigned to the **VALUE** attribute in the **<OPTION>** tag.

4. **text.** The **text** property contains the text of the label that appears with the option.

The methods and event handlers used with select lists are the same ones used by text fields and text areas, **onFocus, onBlur, onChange,** and **onSelect.** Since these event handlers interact in unpredictable ways, we use a simple button to signal the completion of a form containing select lists.

The Shakespearean Quiz Page: Email Version

As our *select list* example, we create a short Shakespearean quiz. This quiz consists of five quotations. A select list of plays is presented for each question. The user finishes the quiz, then clicks the *Email Quiz* button. The quiz questions and the user's answers are emailed to the quiz's author. Figure 14.35 contains the email version of our *Shakespearean Quiz* page.

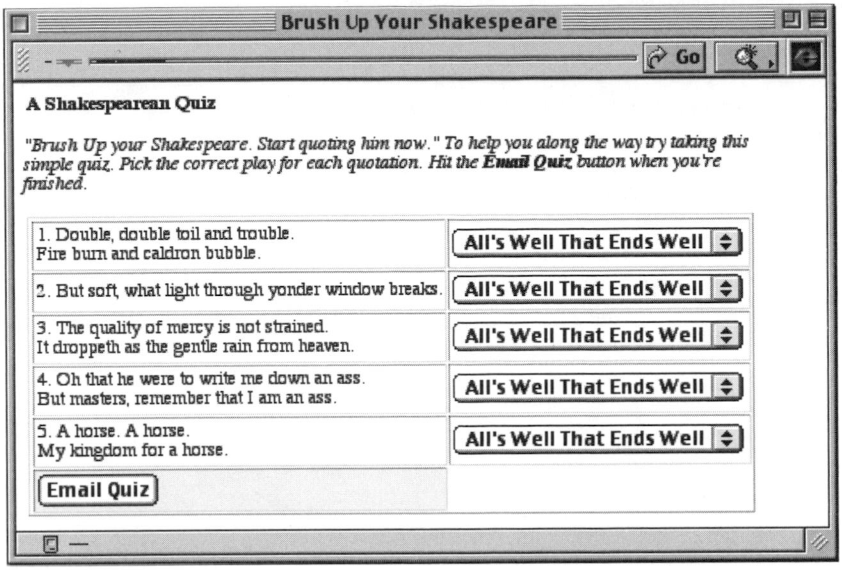

Figure 14.35 The *Shakespearean Quiz* Page, email version

The Head of the *Shakespearean Quiz* Page

A script in the head of the page contains arrays that are used to generate the question numbers, the questions, and the list of plays. This script is found in Figure 14.36.

Using arrays lets us easily add more questions to the quiz or add more Shakespearean plays to the select lists. An event handler is not necessary because this is the one case for which a *Submit* button works in JavaScript.

The <FORM> Tag

The <FORM> tag, which is located in the body of the script, contains the event handler for the *Submit* button, *Email Quiz*. To implement the event handler we must

- set the METHOD to POST;
- set the ACTION to an email address of the form, *name@server*; and
- set the ENCTYPE to text/plain, unless you like URLencoded data.

The form tag used in the Shakespearean page is found in Figure 14.37.

Plain text encryption uses the following format to email the form's data:

```
objects[0].name₀=objects[0].value₀
objects[1].name₁=objects[1].value₁
...
```

The Body of the *Shakespearean Quiz* Page

Figure 14.38 contains the body of the *Shakespearean Quiz* page. A script creates the select list for each question.

Unlike our previous examples, the JS script in the body of the page generates the table and the form elements that are encased in it. The nested **for** statements do most of the work, so we'll

```
<HEAD> <TITLE> Brush Up Your Shakespeare </TITLE>
<SCRIPT LANGUAGE = "JavaScript">
<!--
    var QNumber = new Array("1", "2", "3", "4", "5");
    var Questions = new Array(
    "Double, double toil and trouble.<BR> Fire burn and caldron bubble.",
    "But soft, what light through yonder window breaks.",
    "The quality of mercy is not strained. <BR>
     It droppeth as the gentle rain from heaven.",
    "Oh that he were to write me down an ass.<BR>
     But masters, remember that I am an ass.",
    "A horse. A horse. <BR>My kingdom for a horse.");

    var Plays = new Array("All's Well That Ends Well",
      "Hamlet",
      "Henry V",
      "Macbeth",
      "Measure for Measure",
      "Merchant of Venice",
      "Much Ado About Nothing",
      "Othello",
      "Richard II",
      "Ricard III",
      "Romeo and Juliet",
      "The Taming of the Shrew",
      "The Tempest");
//-->
</SCRIPT>
</HEAD>
```

Figure 14.36 Head of the *Shakespearean Quiz* Page

```
<FORM NAME = "brushUP"
 METHOD = "POST"
 ACTION = "mailto:yourname@server"
 ENCTYPE = "text/plain">
```

Figure 14.37 The **<FORM>** Tag for the *Shakespearean Quiz* Page, email version

focus our attention on them. We begin with an examination of the outer **for** statement. The crucial statements are these:

```
for (i=0; i< Questions.length; i++){//outer loop
    document.write("<TR><TD>");
    document.write(QNumber[i] + ". " + Questions[i]+ "</TD><TD>");
    document.write("<SELECT NAME = " + QNumber[i] +">");
            //inner loop begins here
    document.write("</SELECT></TD></TR>");
}
```

```
<BODY BGCOLOR = "white">
<B>A Shakespearean Quiz</B>
<P>
<I> "Brush Up your Shakespeare. Start quoting him now."  To help you along the way try taking this
simple quiz. Pick the correct play for each quotation. Hit the <B>Email Quiz</B> button when
you're finished.
<P>
<FORM NAME = "brushUP"
 METHOD = "POST"
 ACTION = "mailto:yourname@server"
 ENCTYPE = "text/plain">
<SCRIPT LANGUAGE = "JavaScript">
<!--
    var i,j;
    document.write("<TABLE BORDER = '1' CELLPADDING = '2'
                     BGCOLOR = 'white'");
    for (i=0; i< Questions.length; i++){//outer loop
      document.write("<TR><TD>");
      document.write(QNumber[i] + ". " + Questions[i]+ "</TD><TD>");
      document.write("<SELECT NAME = " + QNumber[i] +">");
      for (j = 0; j < Plays.length; j++) //inner loop
          document.write("<OPTION> " + Plays[j]);
      document.write("</SELECT></TD></TR>");
    }
    document.write("<TR><TD BGCOLOR = 'white'><B>");
    document.write("<INPUT TYPE = 'submit' VALUE = 'Email Quiz'>");
    document.write("</B></TD></TR></TABLE>");
//-->
</SCRIPT></FORM></BODY>
```

Figure 14.38 The Body of the *Shakespearean Quiz* Page, email version

The outer **for** statement prints the question number and the question for each quiz item. Because each question has its own select list, we also start the select list in the outer loop. The question number is the name of the list. For example, when $i = 0$, the JS script generates the following code:

```
<TR><TD>1. Double, double, toil and trouble.
         Fire burn and caldron bubble. </TD>
<TD><SELECT NAME = 1>
     //Inner loop generates the options
</SELECT> </TD></TR>
```

The options for each select list are identical; we use the same list of Shakespearean plays. The inner **for** statement generates the options:

```
for (j = 0; j < Plays.length; j++) //inner loop
    document.write("<OPTION> " + Plays[j]);
```

After the **for** statement terminates, we create the *Submit* button. The **INPUT** statement uses the **VALUE** attribute to display the label *Email Quiz* on the *Submit* button.

Figure 14.39 shows a sample email message produced by this script. We can easily identify the question number and the user's answer.

```
Date: Thu, 15 Jul 1999 12:30:13 -0500
From: Susan Anderson-Freed <myname@myserver
MIME-Version: 1.0
To: myname@myserverm
Subject: Form posted from Mozilla
Content-Disposition: inline; form-data

1=Hamlet
2=Measure for Measure
3=Othello
4=Ricard III
5=The Taming of the Shrew
```

Figure 14.39 The Email Message

The Shakespearean Quiz: Self-Correcting Version

The email version of the *Shakespearean Quiz* page does not use the JavaScript options properties. To illustrate these properties, we create a self-correcting version of this quiz. This version uses a confirm window to display the user's score along with an appropriate message. Figure 14.40 contains a sample page.

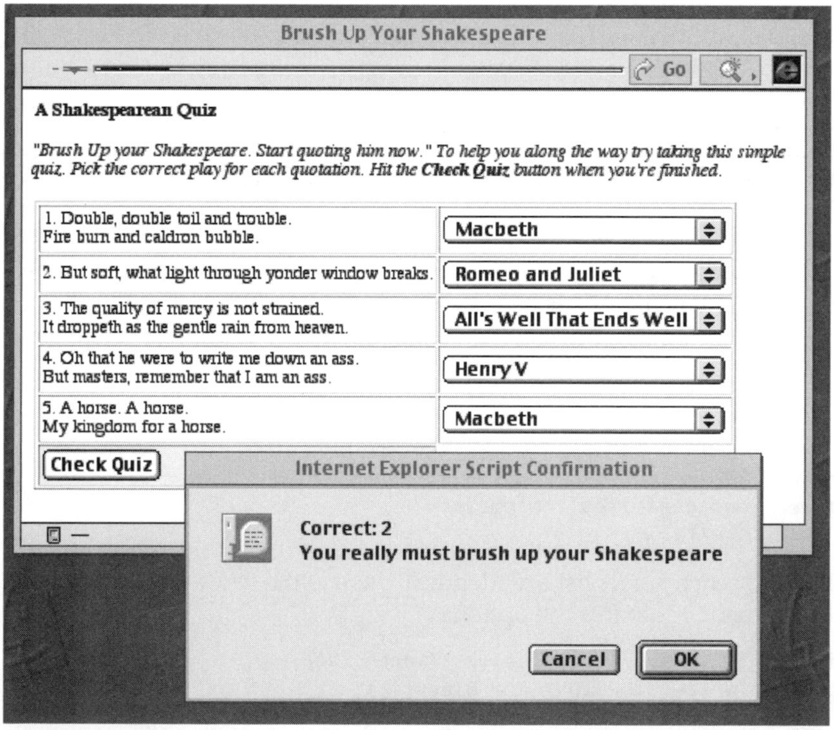

Figure 14.40 The *Shakespearean Quiz* Page, self-correcting version

Transforming the quiz into a self-correcting version requires two minor changes in the body of the original page:

1. We replace the **<FORM>** tag in the email version with the tag

   <FORM Name = "brushUP">

2. We replace the submit button in the email version with a regular button. This button uses an event handler that corrects the quiz. The new code is

   ```
   document.write("<INPUT TYPE = 'button' value = 'Check Quiz'
                   onClick = 'checkQuiz(this.form)'>");
   ```

The self-correcting version requires one additional array, **answers[]**, which contains the subscript number of the correct play for each question. This array and the event handler are found in the head of the page. The code is displayed in Figure 14.41.

```
<HEAD> <TITLE> Brush Up Your Shakespeare </TITLE>
<SCRIPT LANGUAGE = "JavaScript">
<!--
    // Put QNumber[] Array Here
    // Put Questions[] Array Here
    // Put Plays[] Array Here
    var answers = new Array(3,10,5,0,9);

    function checkQuiz(form)
    { //check the quiz and report the result
        var count = 0;
        for (i = 0; i < form.length-1; i++) //skip button
            if (form.elements[i].selectedIndex == answers[i])
                count++;
        var outString = "Correct: " + count;
        if (count == 5)
            confirm(outString + "\nCongratulations! A perfect score");
        if (count -- 4)
            confirm(outString + "\nGood job!");
        if (count == 3)
            confirm(outString + "\nAverage work");
        if (count < 3)
            confirm(outString + "\nYou really must brush up your Shakespeare");
    }
//-->
</SCRIPT></HEAD>
```

Figure 14.41 The Head of the *Shakespearean Quiz* Page, self-correcting version

The **checkQuiz()** function appearing in Figure 14.41 implements the **onClick** event handler. This function counts the number of correct answers and prints an appropriate message.

Counting the correct answers requires a **for** statement that loops through the select lists. Prior to the start of this loop, we set the count to zero. Let's examine the **for** statement:

```
for (i = 0; i < form.length-1; i++) //skip button
    if (form.elements[i].selectedIndex == answers[i])
        count++;
```

Notice the test expression used in the **for** statement header. We set this expression to `i < form.length-1` because we must skip the *Check Quiz* button at the end of the form. The body of the **for** statement contain an **if** statement that compares the **selectedIndex** for the current element with the corresponding element in the **answers[]** array. If a match occurs, we add one to the count of correct answers (*count*). After the **for** statement terminates, we print the number of correct answers. We use a set of **if** statements to append an appropriate message to the score. The message is placed in a confirm window.

THE *MUSKRAT MOUNDS SURVEY* PAGE

We conclude this chapter by developing a page that incorporates several form elements. This final example also includes form verification. Figure 14.42 contains a sample page. This page asks the user to enter first name, last name, and address. Two radio buttons are used to determine whether the user will attend the Muskrat Mounds Potluck. Attending users are asked to enter their favorite food and story. As Figure 14.42 indicates, the current user, Molly Muskrat, submitted the form without entering her address. An alert window asks her to enter her address.

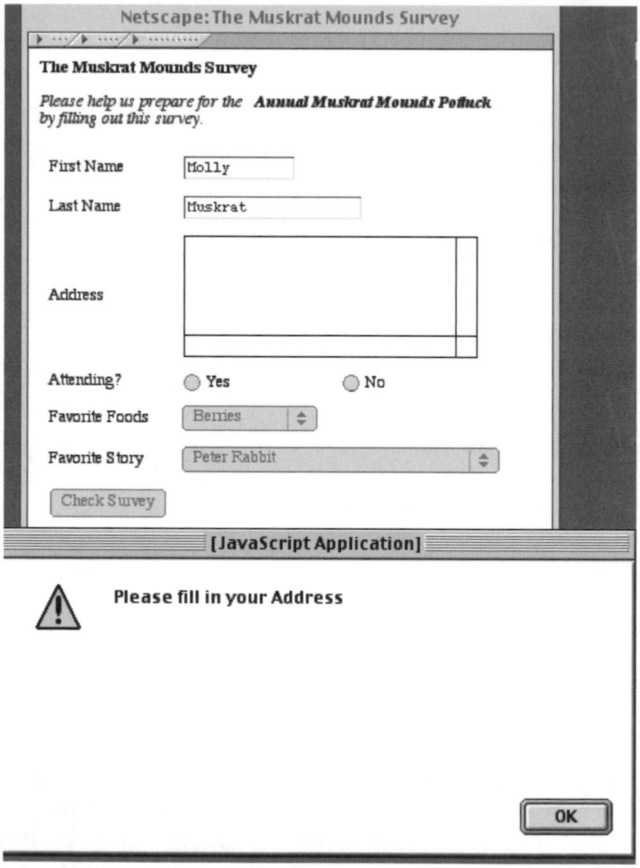

Figure 14.42 The *Muskrat Mounds Survey* Page, Data Entry

Figure 14.43 shows the survey results after three participants answered the questionnaire. The survey results are displayed in a separate window. Netscape Navigator adds new survey results to previous results. Internet Explorer displays the results for the last participant only.

```
                  Netscape: MM Survey Results

First Name: Molly
Last Name: Muskrat
Address: 654 Spillway St. Muskrat Mounds
Attending: Yes
Favorite Food: Salmon
Favorite Story: Mrs. Tiggie Winkle

First Name: Mary
Last Name: Muskrat
Address: 654 Spillway St. Muskrat Mounds
Attending: No

First Name: Milly
Last Name: Mouse
Address: 100 Spillway St. Muskrat Mounds
Attending: Yes
Favorite Food: Berries
Favorite Story: The Tale of the Two Bad Mice
```

Figure 14.43 The *Muskrat Mounds Survey* Page, Results

OPENING AND CLOSING WINDOWS

When a user loads the *Muskrat Mounds Survey* page into their browser, the page spawns a small window that displays the survey results. The window is closed when the user exits the survey page.

To open a window, we use the **window.open()** method. The syntax of this method is

```
Window = window.open("URL", "Window Name", "Window Features");
```

The *URL* parameter holds the URL of the page loaded into the window. This parameter can contain the URL of an existing page. For example, a weather page might open a window containing a page that converts Fahrenheit temperatures into their Celsius equivalents. An empty string can also be used for the URL. This opens an empty window that can be used to store information generated by the parent window.

The second parameter names the window. This parameter is useful only when the URL contains the name of an existing page. The window named in the second parameter is not editable. To create an editable window we place the call to the **open()** method on the right-hand side of an assignment statement. The variable named on the left-hand side of the assignment statement is the editable window.

The last parameter is a string containing the window's features. Figure 14.44 lists these features.

Feature	Explanation
toolbar	The toolbar contains the Back, Forward, Home, Edit buttons, and so on.
location	The *location* or *Netsite* window appears below the toolbar.
directories	The *directories* hold the *What's New* , *What's Cool* and related buttons.
status	The window's status line.
menubar	The File, Edit, View, pull-down menus
scrollbars	The scrollbars are displayed as necessary
resizable	The resize handles at the bottom right corner of the window
width = *number*	The width of the window in pixels.
height = *number*	The height of the window in pixels.

Figure 14.44 Window Features

To activate the auxiliary window when a page is loaded, we place an **onLoad** event handler in the **<BODY>** tag. The tag for the *Muskrat Mounds Survey* page is

```
<BODY BGCOLOR = "white"
            onLoad = "win = createWindow()"
            onUnload = "win.close()">
```

The **onLoad** event handler invokes the **createWindow()** function, which is located in a script in the head of the page, to create and return a new window. The window is called *win*. Figure 14.45 contains the definition of the **createWindow()** method.

```
function createWindow()
{
  win = open ("", "", "menubar,  scrollbars");
  win.document.write("<HEAD><TITLE>MM Survey Results</TITLE></HEAD>");
  win.document.write("<BODY BGCOLOR = 'white'>");
  return win;
}
```

Figure 14.45 The **createWindow()** Function

The function definition indicates that the spawned window will have a menu bar and scroll bars. The menu bar does not appear on a Macintosh, because Macintoshes use the system's menu bar. The scroll bars are visible only when they are needed.

The **onUnload** event handler closes the window when the user leaves the *Muskrat Mounds Survey* page.

The Body of the *Muskrat Mounds Survey* Page

The *Muskrat Mounds Survey* page uses two arrays located in the head of the page to furnish the options for the two select lists. The arrays are defined as follows:

```
var food = new Array("Berries", "Carrots", "Insects", "Salmon", "Salad", "Smelt",
"Trout");
var story = new Array("Peter Rabbit", "Molly's Adventure", "Jeremy Fisher",
"Mrs. TiggieWinkle", "The Tale of the Two Bad Mice",
"Toad's Great Adventure");
```

The survey form appears in the body of the *Muskrat Mounds Survey* page. Two small scripts generate the select lists for *Favorite Food* and *Favorite Story*. The remainder of the form is generated through HTML tags. Figure 14.46 contains the body of the *Muskrat Mounds Survey* page.

The Head of the *Muskrat Mounds Survey* Page

The *Muskrat Mounds Survey* page contains a *Check Survey* button. When the user clicks this button, the **onClick** event handler invokes the **checkSurvey()** function to check the survey information.

```
<BODY BGCOLOR = "white"
            onLoad = "win = createWindow()"
            onUnload = "win.close()">
<B>The Muskrat Mounds Survey</B><P>
<I>Please help us prepare for the <B>Annual Muskrat Mounds Potluck</B> by
filling out this survey.</I><P>
<TABLE CELLPADDING = "3">
<FORM NAME = "Survey">
<TR><TD>First Name</TD>
<TD COLSPAN = "3">
<INPUT TYPE = "text" NAME = "First Name" SIZE = "12" ></TD></TR>

<TR><TD>Last Name</TD>
<TD COLSPAN = "3">
<INPUT TYPE = "text" NAME = "Last Name" SIZE = "20"></TD></TR>

<TR><TD>Address</TD>
<TD COLSPAN = "3">
<TEXTAREA NAME = "Address" ROWS = "5" COLS = "30" WRAP = "Physical">
</TEXTAREA></TD></TR>

<TR><TD>Attending?</TD>
<TD> <INPUT TYPE = "radio" NAME = "Attending"  VALUE = "Yes">Yes</TD>
 <TD><INPUT TYPE = "radio" NAME = "Attending"  VALUE = "No">No</TD></TR>
<TR><TD>Favorite Foods</TD>
<TD COLSPAN = "3"><SELECT NAME = "Food">
<SCRIPT LANGUAGE = "JavaScript">
<!--
    for(var i=0; i< food.length; i++)
        document.write("<OPTION>" + food[i]);
//-->
</SCRIPT></SELECT></TD>
</TR>

<TR><TD>Favorite Story</TD>
<TD COLSPAN = "3"> <SELECT NAME = "Story">
<SCRIPT LANGUAGE = "JavaScript">
<!--
    for (var i = 0; i < story.length; i++)
        document.write("<OPTION>" + story[i]);
//-->
</SCRIPT></SELECT>
</TD></TR>

<TR> <TD><INPUT TYPE = 'button'  VALUE = 'Check Survey'
onClick  = "checkSurvey(this.form)"></TD></TR></FORM>
</TABLE></BODY>
```

Figure 14.46 The Body of the *Muskrat Mounds Survey* Page

The **checkSurvey()** function performs form validation for the first name, last name, address, and attendance fields. The two text fields and the text area use the same validation technique. The form element's value is compared to the null string. If a match occurs, an alert window displays an error message. The offending field is brought into focus. We use a **for** statement to check the text fields and area. The code is as follows:

```
for (var i=0;  i <=2; i++)
{//Check the text fields
    if (form.elements[i] .value == "") {
        alert("Please fill in your "+ form.elements[i].name);
        form.elements[i].focus();
        return;
    }
    outString = outString + form.elements[i].name + ": " +
            form.elements[i].value;
    outString += "<BR>";
}
```

When the user correctly fills in a text field or the text area, the form element's name and value is added to *outString*. This string is reinitialized to the empty string each time the **checkSurvey()** form is invoked. After the form is completed, the contents of *outString* is written to the spawned window, *win*.

Form validation of the attendance field consists of a simple **if** statement:

```
if (!form.Attending[0].checked && !form.Attending[1].checked)
{//didn't fill in attendance information
    alert("Please fill in the attendance information.");
    return;
}
```

The expression in the **if** statement is *true* when neither of the attendance buttons has been checked. If this is the case, we issue an alert window and return the user to the form.

We do not need to check either of the select lists, because the first option in the select list is automatically preselected by the browser. The selected options are added to *outString* only if the user plans to attend the potluck. The code that adds this information is the following:

```
if (form.Attending[0].checked) {
    outString += "Attending: Yes<BR>";
    var index = form.Food.selectedIndex;
    outString =  outString + "Favorite Food: "  + food[index] + "<BR>";
    index = form.Story.selectedIndex;
    outString = outString + "Favorite Story: " + story[index] + "<P>";
}
else
  outString += "Attending: No <P>";
```

Notice that we use the **selectedIndex** property to determine which option the user selected.

Figure 14.47 contains the head of the *Muskrat Mounds Survey* page. The last statement in the **checkSurvey()** function writes *outString* to the spawned window. This statement is

```
win.document.write(outString);
```

```
<HTML><HEAD><TITLE>The Muskrat Mounds Survey</TITLE>
<SCRIPT LANGUAGE = "JavaScript">
<!--
var food = new Array("Berries", "Carrots", "Insects", "Salmon", "Salad", "Smelt", "Trout");
var story = new Array("Peter Rabbit",  "Molly's Adventure",  "Jeremy Fisher",
"Mrs. TiggieWinkle", "The Tale of the Two Bad Mice", "Toad's Great Adventure");
function createWindow()
{
  win = open ("", "", "menubar, scrollbars");
  win.document.write("<HEAD><TITLE>MM Survey Results</TITLE></HEAD>");
  win.document.write("<BODY BGCOLOR = 'white'>");
  return win;
}
function checkSurvey(form)
{ //Check the form for complete information
   var outString = "";
   for (var i=0;  i <=2; i++)
   {//Check the text fields
       if (form.elements[i] .value == "") {
       alert("Please fill in your "+ form.elements[i].name);
       form.elements[i].focus();
       return;
       }
       outString = outString + form.elements[i].name + ": " +
                   form.elements[i].value;
       outString += "<BR>";
   }
   if (!form.Attending[0].checked && !form.Attending[1].checked)
   {//didn't fill in attendance information
      alert("Please fill in the attendance information.");
      return;
   }
   if (form.Attending[0].checked) {
      outString += "Attending: Yes<BR>";
      var index = form.Food.selectedIndex;
      outString =  outString + "Favorite Food: "  + food[index] + "<BR>";
      index = form.Story.selectedIndex;
      outString = outString + "Favorite Story: " + story[index] + "<P>";
   }
   else
      outString += "Attending: No <P>";
   win.document.write(outString);
}
//-->
</SCRIPT></HEAD></HTML>
```

Figure 14.47 The Head of the *Muskrat Mounds Survey* Page

> ## EXERCISES

1. **The *First Form* Page, Revisited.** Rewrite the *First Form* page (Figure 14.4) so that the results are displayed in a text field. Figure 14.48 shows a sample page.

Figure 14.48 The *First Form* Page, revisited

2. **The *Ice Cream Float* Page.** Implement the *Ice Cream Float* page found in Figure 14.19.

3. **The *Ice Cream* Page.** Create an *Ice Cream* page that asks the user to pick a favorite ice cream and favorite topping. Print the topping and ice cream in a text area. The user is not allowed to select more than one topping and one ice cream.

4. **The *Silly Sentences* Page.** Figure 14.49 contains a *Silly Sentences* page. The page contains buttons that let the user form very simple sentences that appear in a text field at the top of the page. A `clear` button lets the user start a new sentence. Implement this page.

5. **The *Extended Silly Sentences* Page.** Extend the *Silly Sentences* page by adding the following:
   - a separate row for indefinite articles—include *A, An, The*;
   - a separate for row for punctuation—include *. ? !*;
   - a new category (*adjectives*)—this lets the user write sentences like *The happy cat ate*;
   - a new category (*adverbs*)—now the user can write sentences like *A sad bird sang slowly*.

6. **More Silly Sentences.** Change the Silly Sentence display area to a text area. Add the parts of speech suggested in the previous exercises, but also add conjunctions (e.g., *and, or, but*).

7. **A *Picnic* Page.** Figure 14.50 contains a picnic questionnaire. Create a script that reproduces this page.

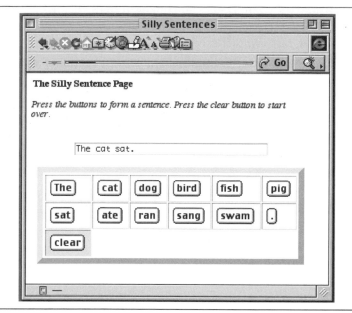

Figure 14.49 The *Silly Sentences* Page

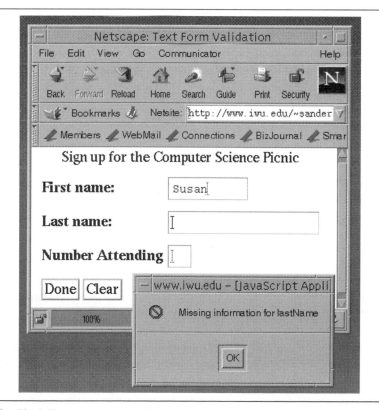

Figure 14.50 The *Picnic* Page

8. **Another *Picnic* Page.** Revise the questionnaire used in the last problem so that it contains a set of radio buttons of entry choices (e.g., hamburgers, pizza, tacos). Also, add a set of checkboxes that asks for the favorite soft drink.

9. **A Multiple-Choice Quiz, Email Version.** Figure 14.51 contains a sample multiple-choice test. Develop a JavaScript multiple-choice test that contains at least five questions. Email the answers to yourself.

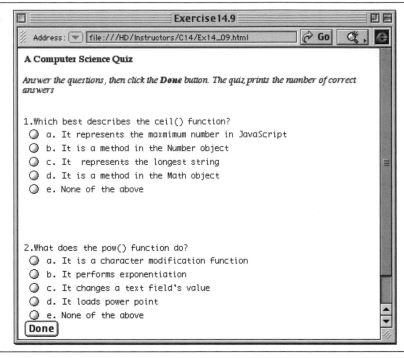

Figure 14.51 The *Multiple-Choice Test* Page

10. **A Multiple-Choice Quiz, Self-correcting Version.** Revise the previous exercise. Print the number of correct answers rather than emailing the answers.

11. **A True/False Quiz, Email Version.** Develop a true/false quiz on a subject of your choice. Email the answers to yourself.

12. **A True/False Quiz, Self-correcting Version.** Repeat the previous exercise, but check the answers, and report on the number of correct answers.

13. **A *Crossword Puzzle* Page.** Figure 14.52 contains a JavaScript crossword puzzle. The puzzle erases incorrect words and prints a message when the user correctly fills out the puzzle. Implement this page.

14. **A *Weather Links* Page.** Search the web for weather-related links. Create a *Weather Links* page, using the *Football* page model. The buttons should appear in the left-hand frame. When the user clicks a button, load the weather page into the right-hand frame.

15. **The *Football* Page, Revisited.** Implement the *Football* page using select lists. Place the select list in the top frame. When the user selects a button, load the selection in the bottom frame.

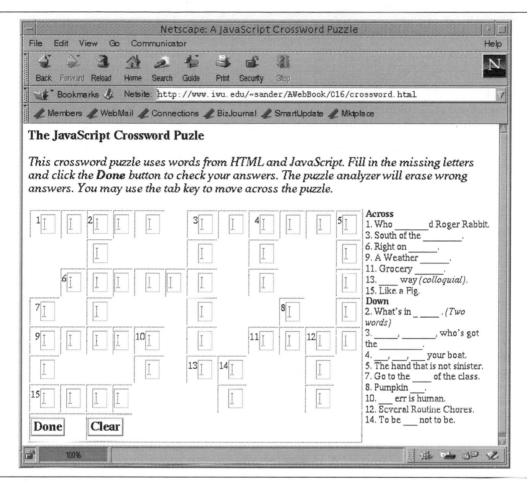

Figure 14.52 The *Crossword Puzzle* Page

16. **The *Weather Links* Page, Revisited.** Implement the *Weather Links* page using a single select list. Follow the model of the previous exercise.

17. **The *Favorite Colors* Page, Revisited.** Implement the *Favorite Colors* page (Figure 14.29) using a select list.

18. **A *Programming Languages* Page.** Develop a page that asks the user to select the programming languages that they know. The list should include HTML (Selected), JavaScript, Perl, Java, C, C++, Visual Basic, Fortran, Cobol, and Scheme. Count the languages selected by the user. Print the languages and the count. (Hint: Use the `options[i].selected` property.)

19. **The *Programming Languages* Page, Revisited.** Implement the previous page, but use checkboxes to present the language lists.

20. **The *User Address* Page.** Create a page that asks the user to enter their first and last name, address, city, and state. Use text fields for first and last name, address, and city. Use a single select list for the state. Include a *Done* button. When the user presses this button, print out the user's address in a text area.

➤ JAVASCRIPT AND HTML VOCABULARY

Button. A button is a form element that is available to JavaScript and Java programmers. The programmer may specify a button label and create an event handler for a button click.

Check box. Checkboxes are used to implement short lists of multiple selection items. The user may check none, one, or several of the checkboxes. Clicking once in a check box turns on the check box. Clicking a second time turns off the check box.

Form. The HTML `<FORM>` tag lets the programmer create interactive pages. Processing the script requires knowledge of a web programming language such as JavaScript, Perl, or Java.

Radio button. Radio buttons are used to implement short lists of single selection items, that is, a list in which the user may select only one item.

Reset button. The reset button is used to reset a form. This button is used in CGI processing and is not relevant to JavaScript form processing.

Select List. Select lists can be used to implement either radio buttons or checkboxes that have a large number of options. For example, suppose we want users to select the state of their birth. Creating fifty radio buttons would take a significant amount of space. A single-select list accomplishes the same task, while using very little space.

Submit Button. In CGI (Perl) script processing, the user presses a submit button to indicate that the form has been completed. In JavaScript, we use the submit button only to email form results to the form's creator.

Text Area. A text area is a form element that lets the user type in several lines of text.

Text Field. A text field is a form element that lets the user type in a single line of text.

15 The String, RegExp, and Date Objects

THE *STRING* OBJECT

We have used strings in many of our applications, but only as simple variables or literals. Strings, whether defined as variables or literals, are JavaScript objects and as such have a rich set of methods. The JavaScript 1.1 *String* class contained methods that duplicated HTML format tags. This version also contained a subset of methods found in the Java *String* class. JavaScript 1.2 introduced additional methods, many of which are derived from Perl. Figure 15.1 contains the string properties and the methods that mimic HTML tags.

String Properties		
	length	
	prototype	
Methods	**JavaScript**	**HTML Equivalent**
	big()	<BIG>..</BIG>
	small()	<SMALL>..</SMALL>
	bold()	<B>..</B>
	italics ()	<I>..</I>
	blink()	<BLINK>..</BLINK>
	strike()	<STRIKE></STRIKE>
	fixed()	<TT>..</TT>
	sub()	_{..}
	sup()	^{..}
	fontcolor('ColorName')	<FONT COLOR = 'ColorName'>..</FONT>
	fontsize(1..7)	<FONT SIZE = 1..7>..</FONT>

Figure 15.1 String Properties and HTML methods

As Figure 15.1 indicates, the JavaScript *String* object has two properties: **length** and **prototype**. The **length** property contains the number of characters in a string. For example, the following code creates a string variable and prints the number of characters in it:

```
var aString = "Hello";
document.write("String: " + aString + " Length: " + aString.length);
```

We can also use this property with literals, as the following code demonstrates:

```
document.write("String: Hello Length: " + "hello".length);
```

Both examples produce the same result on a web page: `String: Hello Length: 5`.

The **prototype** property creates new string methods or properties. These methods or properties apply to all strings created within a web page.

A *Bold Italic* Page

Figure 15.1 listed several string methods and their HTML counterparts. The string methods do not require a closing tag, and the methods can be used with both variables and literals. Figure 15.2 contains a simple page that prints text in bold, italics, or bold italics. The format of the word **be** changes according to the font style, while the word **bold** is always in **bold**, and the word `italics` is always in *italics*. Try writing this page in plain HTML, then rewrite it in JavaScript, using only `document.write()` statements.

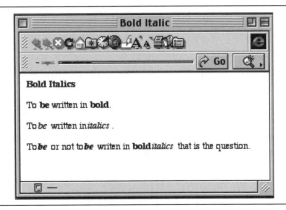

Figure 15.2 The *Bold Italic* Page

Figure 15.3(a) contains an HTML version of *Bold Italic* page. Figure 15.3(b) contains the equivalent JavaScript version. The two versions produce identical results, but the JavaScript version is obviously more tedious.

(a) HTML	To \<B\> be\</B\> written in \<B\>bold\</B\>.\<P\> To \<I\>be\</I\> written in \<I\>italics\</I\>.\<P\> To \<B\>\<I\>be\</I\>\</B\> or not to \<B\>\<I\>be\</B\>\</I\> written in \<B\>bold\</B\> \<I\>italics\</I\> that is the question.

(b) JavaScript Version 1	`<SCRIPT LANGUAGE = "JAVASCRIPT">`
	`<!--`
	`    document.write("To <B>be</B> written in <B>bold</B>. <P>");`
	`    document.write("To <I>be</I> written in <I>italics</I>. <P>");`
	`    document.write("To <B><I>be</I></B> or not to ");`
	`    document.write("<B><I>be</I></B> written in  ");`
	`    document.write("<B>bold</B> <I>italics</I> that is the question.");`
	`//-->`
	`</SCRIPT>`

Figure 15.3 HTML and JavaScript Versions of the *Bold Italic* Page

We can rewrite our page, using the JavaScript **bold()** and **italics()** methods. Since the words *bold* and *italics* are always written in their respective fonts, we can create string variables to represent each font:

```
var bold = "bold".bold();
var ital = "italics".italics();
```

The font styles are now permanently attached to the variables. The font style of the word *be* changes, so we do not create a variable representing this word. Instead, we attach the appropriate string method to the literal *"be"*. Figure 15.4 contains a script that implements the *Bold Italics* page with the JavaScript **String** methods.

```
<SCRIPT LANGUAGE = "JAVASCRIPT">
<!--
  var bold = "bold".bold();
  var ital = "italics".italics();
  document.write("To " + "be".bold() + " written in " +  bold + ".<P>");
  document.write("To " + "be".italics() + " written in " + ital +  ".<P>");
  document.write("To " + "be".bold().italics() + " or not to ");
  document.write("be".bold().italics() + " written in  ");
  document.write(bold + " " +  ital + " that is the question.");
//-->
</SCRIPT>
```

Figure 15.4 The *Bold Italic* Page: *String* Methods Version

The new version of the *Bold Italic* page is an improvement over the two original versions. We can now permanently assign font styles to variables rather than constantly encasing the same string in HTML tags. In addition, we avoid a frequent set of HTML errors: forgetting or mistyping a closing tag. The new version won't be a hit with the nontouch-typing crowd, because the JavaScript method names are rather long. We fix this problem by creating prototypes that rename the **bold()** and **italics()** methods, and we create a new method for bold italics.

The *String* **Prototype Property**

We created *Array* prototypes in Chapter 13. *String* prototypes use exactly the same two-step technique:

Step 1. Create a JavaScript Function.   We create a JavaScript function that implements the desired task. This function uses self-reference to refer to the current object. The object is explicitly converted to a string by using the **toString()** method. We append the style methods to this method and return the result. Figure 15.5 contains a function that returns a string in bold italics font.

Step 2. Create a String Prototype.   The prototype links the function to the *String* object. The general form of the prototype statement is:

```
String.prototype.Name = functionName
```

```
function boldItalics(){
  return this.toString().bold().italics();
}
```

Figure 15.5 The **boldItalics()** Function

The prototype for the **boldItalics()** function is

```
String.prototype.BI = boldItalics;
```

The prototype uses only two letters, so even nontouch-typers will find it easy to use. Figure 15.6 contains the definitions of the bold and italics prototypes, known as **B()** and **I()**, and the rewrite of the *Bold Italics* page using these methods.

```
<SCRIPT LANGUAGE = "JAVASCRIPT">
<!--
  function boldItalics(){
     return this.toString().bold().italics();}

   function B(){
     return this.toString().bold();}

   function I(){
     return this.toString().italics();}

  String.prototype.BI = boldItalics;
  String.prototype.B = B;
  String.prototype.I = I;

  var bold = "bold".B();
  var ital = "italics".I();
  document.write("To " + "be".B() + " written in " + bold + ".<P>");
  document.write("To " + "be".I() + " written in " + ital + ".<P>");
  document.write("To " + "be".BI() + " or not to ");
  document.write("be".BI() + " written in ");
  document.write(bold + " " + ital + " that is the question.");
//-->
</SCRIPT>
```

Figure 15.6 The *Bold Italic* Page: Prototype Version

Additional JavaScript 1.1 String Methods

JavaScript 1.1 incorporated several methods from the Java *String* class:

charAt(*index*). The **charAt()** method has a single numeric parameter, *index*. The method returns the character found at the position numbered *index*.

indexOf(*aString*). The **indexOf()** method has a single string parameter, *aString*. The method returns the index (position) of the first occurrence of the value of the parameter in a string, if the value is found. Otherwise, it returns a **-1**.

lastIndexOf(*aString*). As its name suggests, the **lastIndexOf()** method returns the last occurrence of the value of the parameter in the string, if the value is found. Otherwise, it returns a **-1**.

substring(*start, stop*). The **substring()** method creates a new string by extracting the characters between *start* and *stop-1*, inclusive. The method is almost identical to the string **slice()** method that was added in JavaScript 1.2.

toLowerCase(). The **toLowerCase()** method converts all of the characters in a string to lower case-letters.

toUpperCase(). The **toUpperCase()** method converts all of the characters in a string to upper-case letters.

    Figure 15.7 contains a short sample page that illustrates these methods. The JS script that produces this page contains a string variable, *message*, which is initialized to *All the world's a stage.* The page prints the string with index positions so that you can verify the results. A table of the methods and results is also printed.

Index	0	1	2	3	4	5	6	7	8	9	10	11	12	13	14	15	16	17	18	19	20	21	22	23
message=	A	l	l		t	h	e		w	o	r	l	d	'	s		a		s	t	a	g	e	.

Method	Example	Result
charAt()	document.write(message.charAt(6));	e
indexOf()	document.write(message.indexOf("a"));	16
lastIndexOf()	document.write(message.lastIndexOf("a"));	20
substring()	document.write(message.substring(4,8));	the
toUpperCase()	document.write(message.toUpperCase());	ALL THE WORLD'S A STAGE.
toLowerCase()	document.write(message.toLowerCase());	all the world's a stage.

Figure 15.7 String Methods

JavaScript 1.2 String Methods

JavaScript 1.2 introduced new string methods. Several of the methods require *RegExp* objects, which we will examine in the next section. The remaining methods are the following:

concat(*String*). The **concat()** method adds the string passed as a parameter to the end of the string invoking the method.

charCodeAt(*index*). The **charCodeAt()** method has a single numeric parameter, *index*. The method returns the character code associated with the character at the index position. The character code is the ASCII value on PC systems, the Unicode character on Macs.

String.fromCharCode(n_1, n_2...n_n). The **fromCharCode()** method contains one or more numeric parameters representing ASCII or Unicode characters. The method works only with the *String* object. It returns a string. For example, on IBM systems the letter 'A' has an ASCII value of 65 and the letter 'a' has an ASCII value of 97, so the statement

```
var word = String.fromCharCode(65,97);
```

creates a new string, *word*, containing "Aa".

substr(*start*, *length*_{optional}). The **substr()** method contains two parameters. The first parameter is a starting index. The second parameter is a length. The method creates a new string that begins at *start* and is *length* characters long. If the length isn't specified, the new string includes all characters from *start* to the end of the string.

slice(*start*, *last-1*_{optional}). The *String* **slice()** method is identical to the *Array* **slice()** method.

split(*delimiter*, *limit*_{optional}). The **split()** method splits a string into pieces. The pieces are automatically assigned to an array. The *delimiter* can be a character or a regular expression.

anchor(*ANameLabel*).   The **anchor()** method creates HTML anchor tags. For example, the following statements create an anchor:

```
var textBooks = "Course Text Books".anchor("book");
document.write(textBooks);
```

These statements are equivalent to the HTML statement

```
<A NAME = 'book'> Course Text Books</A>
```

link(*HREFaddress*).   The **link()** method creates an HTML **<A REF>** link tag. For example, the following statements put a link to my home page on the current page:

```
var homePage = "Home Page".link("http://www.iwu.edu/~sander/");
document.write(homePage);
```

These statements are equivalent to the HTML statement

```
<A HREF = "http://www.iwu.edu/~sander/"> Home Page </A>
```

Figure 15.8 contains a table illustrating these methods. The *message* variable is set to *All the world's a stage.*

Method	Example	Result
charCodeAt()	document.write(message.charCodeAt(5));	65
fromCharCode()	document.write(String.fromCharCode(97,98,99));	abc
concat()	document.write(message.concat(" Shakespeare"));	All the world's a stage. Shakespeare

split()	var words = message.split(" ")
	words.sort();
	for (i = 0; i < words.length; i++)
	document.write(words[i] + "
	");
		All
		a
		stage.
		the
		world's

slice()	document.write(message.slice(4));	the world's a stage.
substr()	document.write(message.substr(4,3));	the

Figure 15.8 JavaScript 1.2 *String* methods

The remaining string methods, **match()**, **replace()**, and **search()**, require regular expressions as parameters. Regular expressions, which are new to JavaScript 1.2, reflect Perl's influence on web programming.

REGULAR EXPRESSIONS

A regular expression is a vehicle for creating and checking patterns. Many operating systems provide elementary pattern-matching capabilities. For example, DOS lets users search for all HTML files by typing **dir *.htm**. The asterisk (*) is shorthand for *"match zero or more characters."* Regular expressions are created by combining characters and *meta-characters*. Meta-characters are symbols, such as the asterisk, that are part of the regular expression language. Figure 15.9 lists the meta-characters used by JavaScript.

Quantifier	Meaning	Construct	Meaning
*	Match zero or more times.	\d	Match digits
+	Match one or more times.	\D	Do not match digits
?	Match zero or one.	\w	Match Word: letters, digits, underscore
{n}	Match exactly n times.	\W	Do not match words
{n, }	Match at least n times.	\s	Match "white space" (space, \n, \t, \r, \f)
{n, m}	Match at least n times but	\S	Do not match white space
	no more than m times	\b	Match Word boundary (letters only)
( )	Override precedence		Do not Match Word boundary (letters only)
	Remember pattern	\B	
[ ]	Pattern set		
\Character	Match a meta character.		
^	Match at beginning		
$	Match at end		
.	Match any character except new line		
|	Match either character on left or on right.		

Figure 15.9 Regular Expression Meta-Characters

Figure 15.9 divides regular expression meta-characters into quantifiers and constructs. *Quantifiers* control pattern repetition or placement. For example, suppose we want to search for two **a** s. We could write the pattern as **/aa/** or as **/a{2}/**. Notice how the pattern is encased in slashes, **/ /**. *Constructs* are used to match larger groupings. For example, suppose we want to search for words that begin with *at*. We could write this as **/\bat/**, or we could use a quantifier, and write this as **/^at/**. Similarly, if we wish to search for words that end with *at*, we could write this as **/at\b/** or as **/at$/**.

Creating and using regular expressions in JavaScript can be confusing, because JavaScript has two types of regular expression objects: programmer-created regular expressions (*regexes*) and a single system **RegExp**. Each type of object has different properties. The system **RegExp** has no methods, while programmer-created regexes have three methods. Neither type of *regex* has any event handlers. Figure 15.10 shows the object definition for these two regular expression objects.

The single system regular expression, **RegExp**, stores information on the most recently invoked programmer-created *regex*. Programmer-created regular expressions furnish a pattern for checking. The properties of a programmer-created *regex* are *read-only*, that is, a programmer cannot modify them. The methods associated with a programmer-created *regex* check the *regex* against a string. The methods are **test()**, **exec()**, and **compile()**.

The test() Method

The **test()** method requires a string as a parameter. It returns a *true/false* answer. This method is equivalent to the string **match()** method. For example, suppose we have the following declarations:

```
var string = "perch catFish croppie angelFish";
var regex = /loach|perch/;
```

(a) Programmer RegExp		(b) System RegExp	
Properties			
source	// The regex	input	//test string
global	// Default: *true*	multiline	// Default: *false*
ignoreCase	// Default: *false*	lastMatch	// Match string
lastIndex	// last match index	lastParen	// Last parenthesis: character
		leftContext	// Pre-match string
		rightContext	// Post-match string
		RegExp.$1 to RegExp.$9	// Parenthesized expressions
Methods (for (a) only)			
RegExp(*regex*, "g"_{opt}"i"_{opt})		// Constructor for inputted Regex's	
exec(*String*)		// Execute regex	
compile(*String*, "gi"_{opt})		// Repeated executions	
test(*String*)		// test for match (*true*) or no match (*false*)	

Figure 15.10 JavaScript Regular Expression Objects

The regex indicates that we are searching for the word *loach* OR the word *perch*. We'd like to know whether either (or both) of these words appears in the string. Figure 15.11(a) uses the *regex* **test()** method to return a *true/false* answer; Figure 15.11(b) uses the string **match()** method. Both methods produce the same result: */loach/perch/ found in perch catFish croppie angelFish*.

The exec() Method

The **exec()** method also requires a string as a parameter. This method returns a combination array/object. Assume that we assign this array/object to the variable *result*; we can now access the information as follows:

result[0]. The first element in the array contains the *regex* if a match occurred; otherwise, it is undefined.

```
(a)    if (regex.test(string))
            document.write(regex + " found in " + string);
       else
            document.write(regex + " NOT found in " + string);
```

```
(b)    if (string.match(regex))
            document.write(regex + " found in " + string);
       else
            document.write(regex + " NOT found in " + string);
```

Figure 15.11 The **test()** and **match()** Methods

result.index.   The *index* property contains the index of the match start if a match occurred.

result.input.   The *input* property contains the input string.

The regex **exec()** method is roughly equivalent to the string **search()** method. For example, suppose we have the following string and regex:

```
string = "cat";
regex = /[aeiou]/;
```

The regex uses the set meta-characters **[]** to indicate that that we are searching for any lower-case vowel. Figure 15.12(a) uses the regex **exec()** method; Figure 15.12(b) uses the string **match()** method.

	Code	Results
(a)	`result = regex.exec(string);` `if (result){` `document.write(" Index: " + result.index);` `document.write(" Input: " + result.input);` `document.write(" [0]: " + result[0]);` `}`	`Index: 1` `Input: cat` `[0]: a`

(b)	`result2 = string.search(regex);`
	`document.write("<P>String Result(index):`
	    `" + result2);`
		`String Result(index): 1`

Figure 15.12 The **exec()** and **search()** Methods

Notice the use of an **if** statement in Figure 15.12(a). Since *result* is undefined (*false*) if the regular expression cannot be matched, printing *result* would produce "garbage." Therefore, we print *result*'s properties only if a match occurs.

The compile() Method

The **compile()** method is usually coupled with a **while** statement that repeatedly changes a regex and checks it against a string.

The *RegExp* Page

Figure 15.13 contains a page that lets us use the properties of the system **RegExp** object. As this figure indicates, the user enters a string and a pattern. The default modifier is *gi*, which signifies a global search that is case insensitive. The page returns the **Match**ed string if a match occurs. It also returns the strings that appear to the **Left** and the **Right** of the matched string. If the user's regular expression contains parenthesized expressions, the page prints the last parenthesized expression and the first two parenthesized expressions. Notice the regular expression used in the sample page. Its English translation is: *Find exactly two p's followed by zero or more characters of any type EXCEPT new line followed by exactly two g's.*

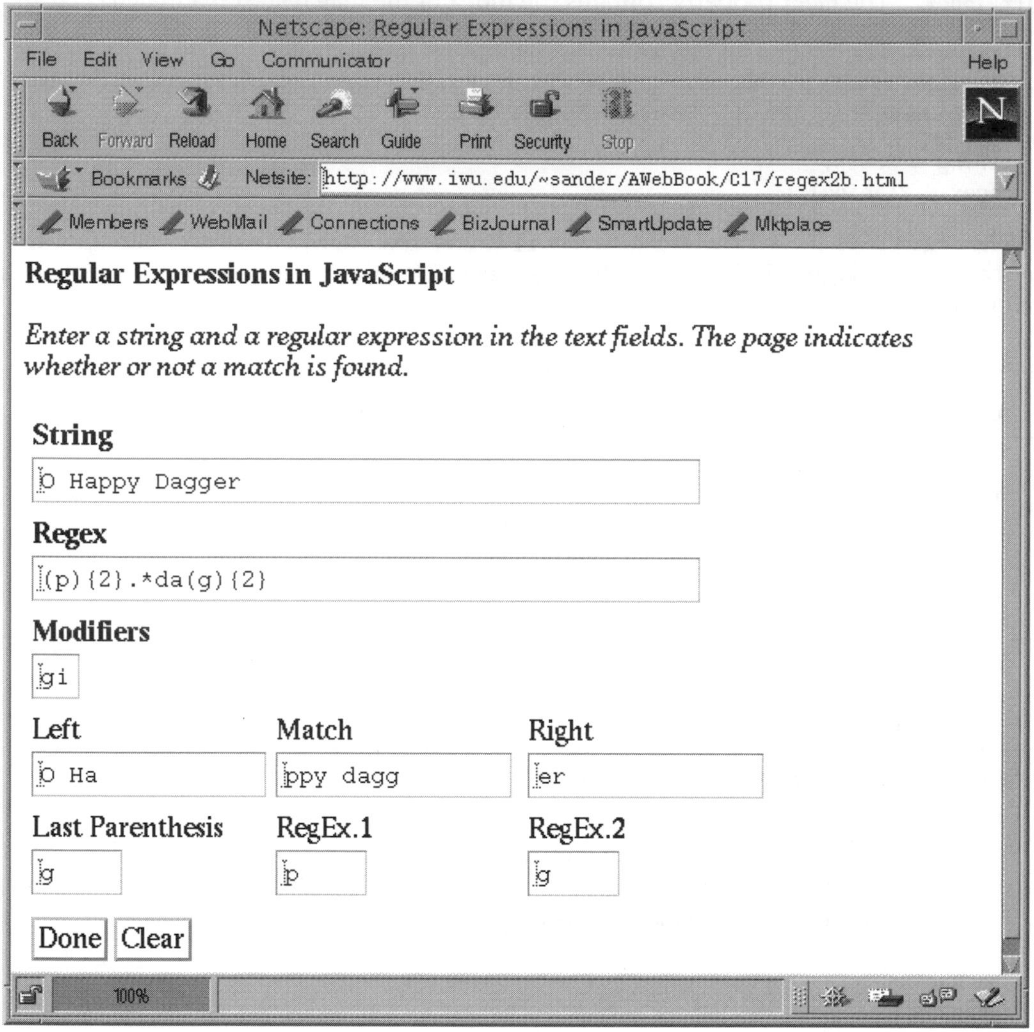

Figure 15.13 The *RegExp* Page

The form used in the *RegExp* page is created through HTML tags that appear in the body of the page. The code appears in Figure 15.14.

The clean() Function

The **clean()** function implements the event handler for the *Clear* button. This function is defined in a JS script located in the page's head. Figure 15.15 contains the function definition.

The **clean()** function uses a **for** statement to place a null string in every text field. It then sets the value and default value of the *modify* field to *gi*. Finally, the function puts the *string* text field into focus.

```
<BODY BGCOLOR = "white">
<B>Regular Expressions in JavaScript</B>
<P>
<I>Enter a string and a regular expression in the text fields.  The page indicates whether or not a
match is found.
<FORM NAME = "regex">
<TABLE>
<TR><TD COLSPAN = "3"><B>String</B><BR>
<INPUT TYPE = 'text' NAME = 'string' SIZE = "45"></TD></TR>
<TR><TD COLSPAN = "3"><B>Regex</B><BR>
<INPUT TYPE = 'text' NAME = 'regex' SIZE = "45"></TD>
</TR>
<TR><TD><B>Modifiers</B><BR>
<INPUT TYPE = 'text' NAME = 'modify' SIZE = "2 " VALUE = "gi"></TD>
</TR>
<TR><TD>Left<BR>
<INPUT TYPE = 'text'  NAME = 'left' SIZE = "15"></TD>
<TD>Match <BR>
<INPUT TYPE = 'text' NAME = 'result' SIZE = "15">
</TD>
<TD>Right<BR>
<INPUT TYPE = 'text' NAME = 'right' SIZE = "15"></TD></TR>
<TR><TD>Last Parenthesis<BR>
<INPUT TYPE = 'text' NAME = 'last' SIZE = "5"></TD>
<TD>RegEx.1<BR>
<INPUT TYPE = 'text' NAME = 'regex1' SIZE = "5"></TD>
<TD>RegEx.2<BR>
<INPUT TYPE = 'text' NAME = 'regex2' SIZE = "5"></TD>
<TR>
<TD> <INPUT TYPE  = "button" VALUE = "Done"
      onClick = "check(this.form)">
 <INPUT TYPE = "button" VALUE = "Clear"
      onClick =  "clean(this.form)"></TD>
</TR></Table></FORM>
</BODY>
```

Figure 15.14 The Body of the *RegExp* Page

```
function clean(form)
  {// clean the textfields
    for(i=0; i < form.length; i++)
      form.elements[i].value =  "";
    form.modify.value = form.modify.defaultValue = "gi";
    form.string.focus();
  }
```

Figure 15.15 The **clean()** Function: *RegExp* Page

The check() Function

The **check()** function constructs a new regular expression object from the *regex* and *modify* text fields. Since the *regex* is created from user input we must use the **RegExp** object constructor. The constructor uses the following form:

> *Variable* = new RegExp(*regex*, *gi*_{optional});

Although the constructor shares the same name as the system **RegExp**, the new object created is not the system **RegExp**. It's simply another programmer-created regex. Once it has been created, we use the **exec()** method to test the regex against the string. If a match occurs, we place the system **RegExp** properties in the form fields. Figure 15.16 contains the **check()** function and shows the placement of the **clean()** function developed earlier.

```
<HEAD><TITLE>Regular Expressions in JavaScript</TITLE>
<SCRIPT LANGUAGE = "JavaScript">
<!--
    function check(form)
    {//create a regex and check the string
    var string = form.string.value;
    var modifiers = form.modify.value;
    if (modifiers != "")
        regex = new RegExp(form.regex.value, modifiers);
     else
        regex = new RegExp(form.regex.value);
     var found = regex.exec(string)
     if (found) {
       form.left.value = RegExp.leftContext;
       form.right.value = RegExp.rightContext;
       form.result.value = found[0];
       form.last.value = RegExp.lastParen;
       form.regex1.value = RegExp.$1;
       form.regex2.value = RegExp.$2;
     }
     else
       form.result.value = "NO MATCH";
    }
    // The clean() Function goes here
//-->
</SCRIPT></HEAD>
```

Figure 15.16 The Head of the *RegExp* Page

The *String Methods* Page

As our next example of regular expressions, we create a page that lets the user experiment with string methods that are related to regular expressions. Figure 15.17 contains a sample page. The user enters a string, a regular expression, and possibly a replacement string, then selects a string method button. The results are placed in the *Result* text field.

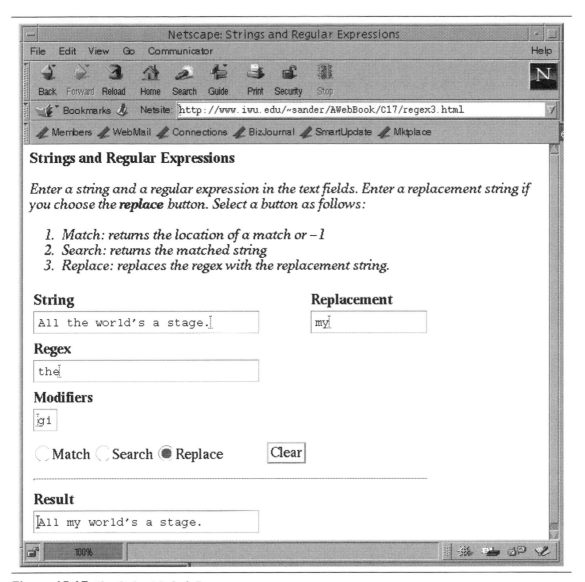

Figure 15.17 The *String Methods* Page

The body of the *String Methods* page uses HTML tags to create the form. The body appears in Figure 15.18. The field names and the event handlers are highlighted.

The *String Methods* and the *RegExp* pages use the same **clean()** function to implement the *Clear* button event handler. Both pages contain a **check()** method that constructs a *regex* object from the user's input. The differences in the two pages occur after the *regex* is created. The *String Method* page uses a **for** statement to find the clicked button. Once it has been found, a **switch** statement is used to invoke the appropriate string method. Figure 15.19 contains the code for the **check()** function.

```
<BODY BGCOLOR = 'white'>
<B>Strings and Regular Expressions</B>
<P>
<I>Enter a string and a regular expression in the text fields. Enter a replacement string if you
choose the <B>replace</B> button. Select a button as follows:
<OL> <LI>Match: returns the location of a match or -1
<LI>Search: returns the matched string
<LI>Replace: replaces the regex with the replacement string.
</OL>
<FORM NAME = "regex"><TABLE>

<TR><TD COLSPAN = "2"><B>String</B><BR>
<INPUT TYPE = 'text' NAME= 'string' SIZE = "30"></TD>
<TD><B>Replacement</B><BR>
<INPUT TYPE = 'text' NAME = 'sub' SIZE = "15"></TD></TR>
<TR><TD COLSPAN = "3"><B>Regex</B><BR>
<INPUT TYPE = 'text' NAME = 'regex' SIZE = "30"></TD>
</TR>
<TR><TD><B>Modifiers</B><BR>
<INPUT TYPE = 'text' NAME = 'modify' SIZE = "2" VALUE = "gi"></TD>
</TR>
<TR><TD><INPUT TYPE = "radio"  NAME = 'options'  VALUE = "match"
         onClick = "check(this.form)"> Match
<INPUT TYPE = "radio" NAME = 'options'  VALUE = "search"
       onClick = "check(this.form)"> Search
<INPUT TYPE = "radio"  NAME = 'options' VALUE = "replace"
       onClick = "check(this.form)"> Replace
 <TD> <INPUT TYPE = "button"  VALUE = "Clear"
       onClick = "clean(this.form)"></TD></TR>
<TR><TD COLSPAN = "3"> <HR></TD></TR>
<TR><TD><B>Result</B> <BR>
<INPUT TYPE = "text" NAME = 'result' SIZE = "30">
</TD></TR>
</TABLE></FORM>
</BODY>
```

Figure 15.18 The Body of the *String Methods* Page

We've touched only the surface of regular expressions. The two pages we created let you experiment with *regular expressions*. Beginning programmers often find regular expressions confusing; they frequently match a much wider range of strings than a beginner foresees. We'll see regular expressions again when we discuss Perl programming.

THE DATE OBJECT

The JavaScript *Date* object incorporates most of the methods found in the Java **Date** class. These methods let programmers *get* and *set* dates in a variety of ways. Figure 15.20 lists the JavaScript *Date* methods. The *Date* object has no programmer-accessible properties.

```
<HTML><HEAD><TITLE>Strings and Regular Expressions</TITLE>
<SCRIPT LANGUAGE = "JavaScript">
<!--
    function check(form)
    {//create a regex and check the string
        var string = form.string.value;
        var modifiers = form.modify.value;
        var sub = form.sub.value;
        if (modifiers != "")
            regex = new RegExp(form.regex.value, modifiers);
        else
            regex = new RegExp(form.regex.value);
        for (i = 0; i < form.options.length; i++)
          if(form.options[i].checked)
              break;
        switch(I) {
        case 0: form.result.value = string.match(regex);
                break;
        case 1: form.result.value = string.search(regex);
                break;
        case 2: form.result.value = string.replace(regex, sub);
        }
    }
    The  clean() Function goes here
//-->
</SCRIPT></HEAD>
```

Figure 15.19 The Head of the *String Methods* Page

Get **Methods**	*Set* **Methods**	*Other* **Methods**
getDate ()	setDate ()	Date()
getDay ()		setUTC ()
getMonth ()	setMonth (1..31)	getTimezoneOffset ()
getYear ()	setYear (0x..xx)	toLocaleString ()
getFullYear()	setFullYear(xxxx)	toGMTString ()
getTime()	setTime(0..)	Date.parse()
getHours ()	setHours (0..23)	Date.UTC()
getMinutes()	setMinutes(0..59)	
getSeconds()	setSeconds(0..59)	

Figure 15.20 *Date* Methods

The purpose of these methods is as follows:

getDate() *and* **setDate().**   The **getDate()** method returns a value between 1 and 31. This value corresponds to the day of the month. The **setDate()** method changes the day of the month. It has a single parameter, a number between 1 and 31.

getDay().   The **getDay()** method returns the weekday associated with a date. The weekday value returned is encoded as an integer, where 0 is equivalent to Sunday, 1 is equivalent to Monday, and so on. Programmers usually create a **switch** statement to convert this numeric value into a string.

getMonth() *and* **setMonth().**   The **getMonth()** method returns a numeric value between 0 and 11 that represents the month. January is encoded as a 0, February is encoded as a 1, and so on. The **setMonth()** method changes the month. It has a single parameter, a numeric value between 0 and 11. The **setMonth()** method uses the same numeric values as the **getMonth()** method. Programmers usually create a **switch** statement to convert this numeric value into a string, or *vice versa*.

getYear() *and* **setYear().**   The **getYear()** method returns the last two digits of the current year. It assumes that the current year is in the 20th century. The **setYear()** method changes the year. It has a single parameter that represents the last two digits of the year. The **getFullYear()** and **setFullYear()** are similar, but each uses a four-digit year.

getTime() *and* **setTime().**   The **getTime()** method returns the number of milliseconds that have passed since January 1, 1970 00:00:00 GMT (Greenwich Mean Time). The **setTime()** method changes what the program thinks is the number of milliseconds that have passed since January 1, 1970 00:00:00 GMT (Greenwich Mean Time).

getHours() *and* **setHours().**   The **getHours()** method returns the hour in Naval Time (0..23). The **setHours()** method sets the hours. It requires a single parameter, a numeric value between zero and 23.

getMinutes() *and* **setMinutes().**   The **getMinutes()** method returns the minutes as a number between zero and 59. The **setMinutes()** method changes the minutes.

getSeconds() *and* **setSeconds().**   The **getSeconds()** method returns the seconds as a number between zero and 59. The **setSeconds()** method changes the seconds.

Other Methods

The remaining methods perform various GMT conversions.

Creating a *Date* object requires a call to the **Date()** constructor. Figure 15.21 lists the various possibilities.

```
new Date()
new Date("Month dd, yyyy hh:mm:ss")
new Date("Month dd, yyyy")
new Date(yy, mm, dd, hh, mm, ss)
new Date(yy, mm, dd)
new Date(milliseconds)
```

Figure 15.21 The **Date()** Constructors

Dates in History

Figure 15.22 contains a simple illustration of the JavaScript *Date* object. The page asks the user to enter a month, a day, and a year. The page prints the weekday corresponding to the user's date.

The body of the *Dates in History* page uses HTML tags to create the history form. The code for the body appears in Figure 15.23. The field names and the event handlers are highlighted.

Figure 15.22 The *Dates in History* Page

```
<BODY BGCOLOR = 'white'>
<B>Dates in History</B>
<P>
<I>Enter a month, day, and year in the textfields.  The page prints the week day.
</I>
<P>
<FORM><TABLE>
<TR><TD>Month<BR>
<INPUT TYPE = 'text' NAME = 'month' SIZE = "15"></TD>
<TD>Day<BR>
<TNPUT TYPE = 'text' NAME = 'day' SIZE = "2"></TD>
<TD>Year<BR>
<INPUT Type = 'text' NAME = 'year' SIZE = "4" VALUE = "19"></TD></TR>
<TD>WeekDay<BR>
<INPUT TYPE = 'text' NAME = 'weekDay' SIZE= "10"></TD></TR>
<TR>
<TD> <INPUT TYPE  = "button" VALUE = "Done"
            onClick = "findDay(this.form)">
 <INPUT TYPE = "button" VALUE = "Clear"
        onClick = "clean(this.form)"></TD>
</TR></TABLE></FORM>
</BODY>
```

Figure 15.23 The Body of the *Dates in History* Page

The JS Script located in the head of the page defines the **findDay()** and **clean()** functions used to implement the event handlers for the *Done* and *Clear* buttons. The **clean()** function is similar to the ones used in previous examples. The **findDay()** function has several tasks:

Task 1. A string is constructed from the user's input. This string is of the form *Month Day, Year*.

Task 2. A new *Date* object is constructed that uses the string as a parameter to the constructor.

Task 3. The weekday is found and placed in the *weekDay* field. The **getDate()** method is used to find the numeric value of the weekday. An array, *weekDays*, contains the spellings. An assignment statement is used to place the weekday into the *weekDay* text field.

Figure 15.24 contains the head of the *Dates in History* page.

```
<HEAD><TITLE>Dates in History</TITLE>
<SCRIPT LANGUAGE = "JavaScript">
<!--
var weekDays = new Array("Sunday", "Monday", "Tuesday", "Wednesday",
    "Thursday", "Friday", "Saturday");
  function findDay(form)
  {// obtain the user's date and find the week day
    with (form){
      var dateString = elements[0].value + " ";
      dateString = dateString + elements[1].value+ ", ";
      dateString = dateString + elements[2].value;
    }
    var aDate = new Date(dateString);
    var day = aDate.getDay();
    form.elements[3].value = weekDays[day];
  }
  The clean() function goes here
//-->
</SCRIPT>
</HEAD>
```

Figure 15.24 Head of the *Dates in History* Page

SCRAMBLED WORDS AND A SHUFFLE FUNCTION

We conclude this chapter with an example that pushes JavaScript to its limits (perhaps even beyond its limits). This example uses the *String, Array,* and *Date* classes to create a *Scrambled Words* page. Figure 15.25 shows a sample page. The page presents the user with several scrambled words. The user must unscramble the words to find the JavaScript terms.

The developing of this page will be our most complicated JavaScript coding to date. The page creates a two-dimensional array representing the scrambled words—an interesting feat, in view of the fact that JavaScript provides only one-dimensional arrays. The page also uses two shuffle functions to rearrange the letters. The random shuffling uses the current seconds and minutes to seed the shuffling.

The JS script for the *Scrambled Words* page involves several functions; we use a hierarchical chart to display the page's components. The chart appears in Figure 15.26.

The functions depicted in the hierarchical chart are defined in a script located in the head of the page. A separate script located in the body of the page loads the scrambled words and text fields onto the page. We begin with the function definitions and variable declarations appearing in the head of the page.

The *Scrambled Words* page uses three arrays:

The words Array. This array of strings contains the spellings of the original unscrambled words. The declaration is

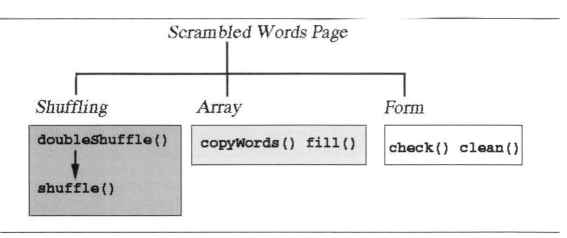

Figure 15.25 The *Scrambled Words* Page

Figure 15.26 Hierarchical Chart for the *Scrambled Words* Page

```
var words = new Array("method", "checkbox", "property","javascript", "select",
    "button");
```

The original Array.   To scramble the words, we must be able to access the individual characters. The *original* array is a two-dimensional array in which each row represents a word and each column represents a letter in a word. Remember that two-dimensional arrays are not implemented in JavaScript, at least not explicitly. However, we can implement them by creating an array whose elements are one-dimensional arrays—that is, we have an array of arrays. Figure 15.27 shows the structure of the *original* array.

Column (→) Row (↓)	[0]	[1]	[2]	[3]	[4]	[5]	[6]	[7]	[8]	[9]
[0]	m	e	t	h	o	d				
[1]	c	h	e	c	k	b	o	x		
[2]	p	r	o	p	e	r	t	y		
[3]	j	a	v	a	s	c	r	i	p	t
[4]	s	e	l	e	c	t				
[5]	b	u	t	t	o	n				

Figure 15.27 Two-Dimensional Representation of the *original* Array

The copyWords() Method

The **copyWords()** method handles the creation of the two-dimensional array. This method requires the array of strings as a parameter. It returns an array with the structure depicted in Figure 15.27. The code for the **copyWords()** method appears in Figure 15.28.

```
function copyWords(stringArray)
{//copy the strings into the 2D array
  for (i = 0; i < stringArray.length; i++){
    this[i] = new Array();
    for (j = 0; j < stringArray[i].length; j++)
      this[i][j] = stringArray[i].charAt(j);
  }
}
Array.prototype.copyWords = copyWords;
```

Figure 15.28 The **copyWords()** Method

The **copyWord()** function uses a set of nested **for** statements. The outer **for** statement controls the row subscripts. The statement

    this[i]=new Array();

tells JavaScript that the ith element of this array is a new array. Voila! We've just turned this array into a two-dimensional array. The inner **for** statement controls the column subscripts. The statement

    this[i][j] = stringArray[i].charAt(j);

tells JavaScript to find the jth character of the ith string. We place this character in position `[i][j]` of this array. The subscripts, `[i][j]`, are standard Perl and Java two-dimensional array notation. They work in JavaScript quite nicely, even though JavaScript does not officially have two-dimensional arrays.

Copying the *Original* Array

After we create the two-dimensional array of characters, we must copy this array to a second array, *scrambled*. The *scrambled* array will hold the scrambled words. It is tempting to use a simple assignment statement to copy the *original* array, as follows

```
var scrambled = new Array();
scrambled = original;
```

This technique makes *scrambled* a pseudonym for *original*—that is, we have two different names that refer to the same array. Now, the *scrambled* array must scramble the characters in the words without destroying or changing the *original* array, so we must physically copy each element of *original* into *scrambled*. Once all are copied, we can change *scrambled* to our heart's delight without affecting the *original* array. Figure 15.29 contains the definition of the **fill()** method.

```
function fill(anArray)
{//copy an array or words and shuffle the letters
   for (i = 0; i < anArray.length; i++){
     this[i] = new Array();
     for (j= 0; j < anArray[i].length; j++)
       this[i][j] = anArray[i][j];
   }
}
Array.prototype.fill = fill;
```

Figure 15.29 The **fill()** Method

Scrambling the *scrambled* Array

After we copy the two-dimensional array of characters into *scrambled*, we obviously need to scramble the letters in each word. Most of the words are short, so a single shuffle doesn't do much. The **doubleShuffle()** method shuffles the letters in a row twice. The first shuffle uses the current seconds to randomize the positions. The second shuffle uses the current minutes. Figure 15.30 contains the definition of the **doubleShuffle()** method.

The actual shuffle is handled by the **shuffle()** function. This function uses the shuffling algorithm appearing in Donald Knuth's *The Art of Computer Programming, Volume 2*. The algorithm requires a random seed, *U*. Programmers frequently use the current system time in either seconds or minutes as a random seed. The JavaScript interpretation of Knuth's shuffle algorithm appears in Figure 15.31.

```
function doubleShuffle()
{//shuffle twice to mix order
    var U;
    var i;
    var today = new Date();
    for (i = 0; i < this.length; i++){
       U = today.getSeconds()/60;
       Shuffle(this[i], U);
       U = today.getMinutes()/60;
      shuffle(this[i],U);
    }
}
Array.prototype.doubleShuffle = doubleShuffle;
```

Figure 15.30 The **doubleShuffle()** Method

```
function shuffle(aWord, U)
{//shuffle the word using Knuth's technique
    for(i = aWord.length-1; i > 0; i--){
       k = Math.floor(i*U)+1;
       temp = aWord[k];
       aWord[k] = aWord[i];
       aWord[i] = temp;
    }
}
```

Figure 15.31 The **shuffle()** Function

The **doubleShuffle()** method passes the **shuffle()** method a row (word) in the original array and the random seed. The **shuffle()** method uses the random seed to rearrange the characters in the word.

We have now assembled all the pieces necessary to scramble the words. All that's left is the creation of the functions that implement the event handlers. Figure 15.32 contains the definitions of the **check()** and **clean()** functions and shows the placement of the previously developed functions and methods.

The body of the *Scrambled Words* page contains a script that creates a table and a form holding the scrambled words and the text boxes for the user's unscrambled letters. A second table and form contains the *Done* and *Clear* buttons. The code for the body of the *Scrambled Words* page appears in Figure 15.33.

The *Scrambled Words* page illustrates the computing power of JavaScript. This page uses advanced programming techniques to create code that is easily changed. For example, we can easily modify the words to be scrambled by simply changing the *words* array, and changing this array is very easy.

```
<HEAD><TITLE>Scrambled Words</TITLE>
<SCRIPT LANGUAGE = "JavaScript">
<!--
// The    fill()   function goes here
// The    doubleShuffle()   function goes here
// The    shuffle()   function goes here
// The    copyWords()   function goes here
  Array.prototype.fill = fill;
  Array.prototype.doubleShuffle = doubleShuffle;
  Array.prototype.copyWords = copyWords;

   var words = new Array("method", "checkbox", "property", "javascript",
   "select", "button");
   var original = new Array();
   original.copyWords(words);

   var scrambled = new Array();
   scrambled.fill(original);
   scrambled.doubleShuffle();

  function check(form)
  {//check the users entries with the array of original words
     var i,j;
     var flag = true;
     for (i = 0; i < form.length-1; i++)
       for (j=0; j < form[i].elements.length; j++) {
            letter = form[i].elements[j].value;
            letter = letter.toLowerCase();
            if (original[i][j] != letter){
             //erase incorrect entries
               form[i].elements[j].value = "";
               flag = false;
            }
        }
     if (flag)
        confirm("Congratulations your answers were correct");
  }

function clean(form)
{ //clear the text fields
  var flag = confirm("Do you really want to clear all the fields?");
  if (flag) { //user wants to clear
     for (i=0; i < form.length-1; i++)
        for (j = 0; j < form[i].elements.length; j++)
            form[i].elements[j].value = "";
     form[0].elements[0].focus();
  }
}
//-->
</SCRIPT></HEAD>
```

Figure 15.32 The Head of the *Scrambled Words* Page

```
<BODY BGCOLOR = "white">
<CENTER><B>JavaScript Scrambled Words</B></CENTER>
<BR><BR>
<I>Directions: Each of the scrambled words represents a JavaScript term.  Unscramble the words.
Click the <I>Done</I> button to check your answers. Wrong letters are replaced with blanks.
</I>
<BR><BR>
<SCRIPT LANGUAGE = "Javascript">
<!--
for (i = 0; i < scrambled.length; i++){
 //each word has its own form
  document.write("<FORM><TABLE CELLPADDING = '1'><TR><TD ALIGN = 'left'>");
  aWord = scrambled[i];
  for(j= 0; j < aWord.length; j++)
     document.write(aWord[j]);
  document.write(" </TD>");

  for(j= 0; j < aWord.length; j++) {
       document.write("<TD><INPUT TYPE = 'Text' NAME = 'let1-"+ I + j + "'");
       document.write("SIZE = '1'> </TD>")
  }
  document.write("</TR></TABLE></TD>");
  document.write("</TR></FORM></TABLE>");
}
//-->
</SCRIPT>
<TABLE>
<TR><FORM NAME = "finish">
<TR><TD COLSPAN = "2">
<INPUT TYPE="Button" VALUE = "Done"
     onClick = "check(document.forms)">
</TD>
<TD COLSPAN = "2">
<INPUT TYPE="Button" VALUE = "Clear"
     onClick = "clean(document.forms)">
</TD></TR></FORM>
</TABLE>
</BODY>
```

Figure 15.33 The Body of the *Scrambled Words* Page

> ## EXERCISES

1. **The *big, blue, blinking* Page.** Modify the *Bold Italic* page so that the *be*'s are in a size 5, blue, blinking font. Use a string prototype.

2. **The *ASCII or Unicode* Page: Version 1.** Create a page that prints the ASCII (PC) or Unicode (Mac) value for all characters. Characters have numeric values between 0 and 255.

3. **The *ASCII or Unicode* Page: Version 2.** Create a form that lets a user enter a character or a number. Create two buttons. The first button transforms the character into its ASCII or Unicode equivalent. The second button transforms an ASCII or Unicode number into it character equivalent.

4. **The *Name* Page.** Create a form that asks the user to enter a full name in a single text field. Parse the text field into personal name, middle initial, and family name. Print the parsed information with appropriate labels in a text area.

5. **The *Phone Number* Page.** Create a regular expression that validates phone numbers. Phone numbers should be of the form *(ddd)ddd-dddd*, where *d* represents a digit.

6. **A *Date* Page.** Create a page in which you enter a date with all fields filled. That is, include the time section in the date. Use the **get** methods to retrieve each field. Print the information in a user-friendly manner. The month and weekday should be words. The hours should not be in naval time.

7. **The *Cryptograms* Page.** Cryptograms are words that are encoded. The simplest code is the Caesar cipher. A Caesar cipher takes each letter and replaces it with a letter that is K characters away. For example, if K−4, each letter would be replaced by the letter fourth following (See Figure 15.34.)

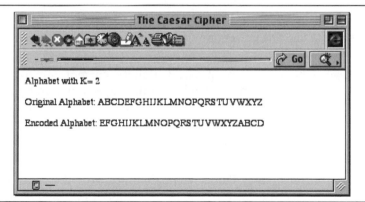

Figure 15.34 The Caesar Cipher, K=4 Page

Develop a cryptogram page that displays an encrypted message. Figure 15.35 shows a sample page.

8. **The *Daily Cryptograms* Page.** Modify the previous exercise so that you have a different K and a different message for each day of the week. Check the current day, and print the appropriate puzzle for that day.

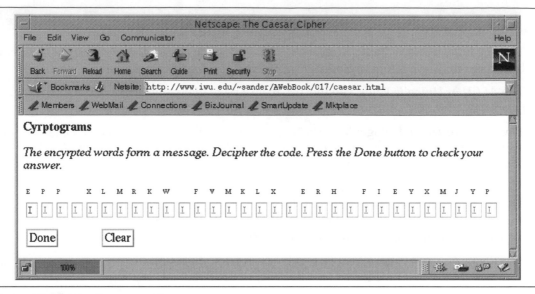

Figure 15.35 The *Cryptogram* Page

9. **The *Days in History* Page.** Use text fields to ask the user to enter a month, day, and year. Print the number of days that have passed between the user's date and the current date.

10. **The *Greetings* Page, Variation 1.** Obtain the current date and use it to print a message based in the following way on the current time:
    - If the current hour is between 12:00 A.M. and 11:59 A.M., print "Good Morning."
    - If the current hour is between 12:00 noon and 5:59 P.M., print "Good Afternoon."
    - If the current time is between 6:00 P.M. and 11:59 P.M., print "Good Evening."

    Also, print the message, "The current time is: "XX:XXam" or "XX:XXpm," depending on the current time.

11. **The *Holidays* Page.** Obtain the current date. Check the current date to determine whether it's a holiday. (Establish your own holiday list.) If the day is a holiday, print an appropriate message. For example, if the current day is October 31, print "Happy Halloween."

12. **The *Matrix Summation* Page.** Create a two-dimensional array of numbers. Find the row sums, the column sums, and the overall sum. Print the matrix and the sums. Figure 15.36 shows an example page.

13. **The *JavaScript Definitions* Page.** Find seven definitions from the JavaScript chapters. Create a `Date` object and place the current date in it. (JavaScript automatically sets the date to the current date.) Find the weekday, and print a different JavaScript definition for each day of the week.

14. **The *Array of Birthdays* Page.** Create an array of `Date` objects containing the birthdays of family members. Sort the `Date` objects by month (January is first) and date. Print out your sorted list.

15. **The *Card Shuffling* Page.** Simulate the shuffling and dealing of a hand of five cards. Use a double shuffle: one for the suit, one for the card. Print out the five cards.

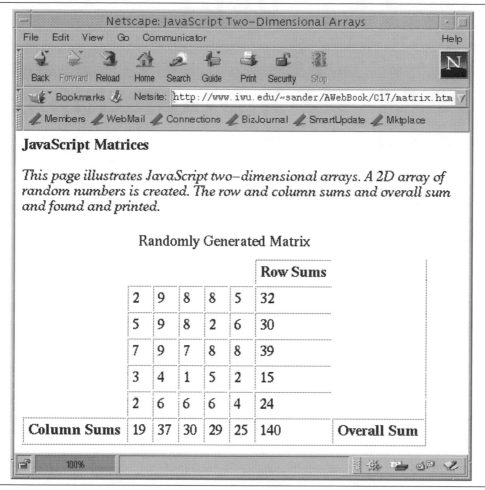

Figure 15.36 The *Matrix* Page

16. **The *Array of Person Objects* Page.** Create an array of *Person* objects. A person has a first name and a birthday. Create methods that let the user enter a new person or print all of the elements in the *Person* array.

➤ JAVASCRIPT VOCABULARY

Meta-character. A meta-character is a character that is part of the regular expression language and not part of the pattern that we seek to match.

Regular expression. We use regular expressions for pattern matching. A regular expression is composed of literals, quantifiers, and constructs. JavaScript 1.2 regular expressions are based heavily on Perl regular expressions. Currently, Netscape Navigator 4.0 or higher recognizes JavaScript regular expressions. Internet Explorer does not yet allow regular expressions.

PART III PERL

16 Introduction to Perl: Web Basics and Scalars

INTRODUCTION

Larry Wall created *Perl* (*P*ractical *E*xtraction and *R*eport *L*anguage) as a shell language for the UNIX operating system. As its name implies, Perl provides facilities for gathering Unix system statistics and generating reports from them. Since its introduction in 1987, Perl has grown in popularity, not only as a Unix language, but as a web programming language.

Perl's flexibility and ease of coding make it an excellent choice for server-side web programming. As its name implies, a *server-side* language executes a web script from a server on the programmer's side. The programmer has far greater capabilities, but there are also greater risks to system security. In contrast, HTML and JavaScript are *client-side* languages. A *client-side* web language runs on the user's machine. Client-side languages pose fewer risks for the page's creator, but such languages also have limited applications.

An inexperienced Perl programmer can open the server to a wide array of security threats from malicious or mischievous hackers. Most of the security threats arise from improper form handling. Therefore, our initial Perl pages will be static. That is, we will not ask the user for input until we learn how to properly screen the input against "hack attacks."

OBTAINING PERL

The Perl compiler is available on Unix, Linux, Windows, and Macintosh platforms. The Comprehensive Perl Archive Network (CPAN) contains zipped versions of the compiler. The URL is http://www.perl.com/CPAN/. (If you leave the last slash off the address, you will be sent to the closest mirror site to obtain your copy of Perl.) Perl is also typically included in the software package that comes with the Linux operating system.

To run Perl Web programs, you will also need an Internet server. The Linux operating system includes an option that lets you create an Internet server. The Apache server is another popular server. Both Linux and Apache are readily available. You can purchase them for a small fee, or you may download them from the Internet. If you have an Internet Service Provider, you must obtain CGI privileges prior to running Perl Web programs.

CGI (Common Gateway Interface) represents a machine-independent protocol. We must use this protocol when we create server-side forms. CGI access is not automatic. In fact, many Web masters prohibit CGI use. Those systems that allow CGI access require the following items:

- a special directory called *cgi-bin*. You must place all CGI programs in this directory. In other words, all Perl programs must be located in this directory. Because any server has only a single *cgi-bin* directory, many Web masters use the second approach instead.
- a *cgi* extension on all CGI programs. This approach offers greater flexibility; each programmer can place CGI programs in a directory of choice.

Check with your Web master to see which approach your server uses. If your Web master will not grant you CGI privileges, create your own server by downloading either the Linux operating system or the Apache web server.

A PERL WEB PAGE

As a first Perl programming exercise, we create the web page appearing in Figure 16.1.

Figure 16.2 contains the Perl code that produces the *Hello Web* page. Examine the code. Notice the use of double and single quotation marks as well as the placement of semicolons. Compare the Perl code with the JavaScript version of this page. (See Figure 8.2.)

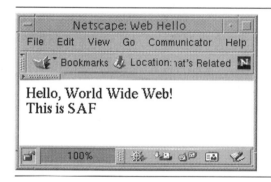

```
#!/usr/local/bin/perl
# File name: hello.pl.cgi
print "Content-type: text/html", "\n\n";
print "<HTML> <HEAD>", "\n";
print "<TTTLE> Web Hello</TITLE></HEAD>\n";
print "<BODY BGCOLOR = 'white'>\n";
print "Hello, World Wide Web!<BR>\n";
print "This is SAF\n";
print "</BODY></HTML>", "\n";
exit(0);
```

Figure 16.1 The *Hello Web* Page   **Figure 16.2** Perl Code for the *Hello Web* Page

The Perl code displayed in Figure 16.2 begins with two comment lines. Perl uses the pound (#) symbol to denote the start of a comment. A Perl comment can appear anywhere on a line and ends when the line ends. By convention, the first line of any Perl program is a comment indicating the location of the Perl compiler. Thus, the statement

```
#!/usr/local/bin/perl
```

indicates that the Perl compiler resides in the **/usr/local/bin** directory. This is the usual location for a Perl compiler in a Unix or Linux environment.

The statement

```
print "Content-type: text/html", "\n\n";
```

must appear before any other **print** statement in a Perl Web script. This statement indicates that the content of the script is written in HTML. The two new-line characters, **"\n\n"**, are part of the CGI protocol.

The remaining **print** statements contain the HTML code for the page. Each **print** statement should end with a new-line character, "**\n**". We can include this character within a print message, as in the statement

```
print "This is SAF\n";
```

Alternatively, we can write the new-line character as a separate message, as in the statement

```
print "<HTML> <HEAD>", "\n";
```

The last line in the Perl script, **exit(0);**—calls a built-in Perl function that terminates the Perl program. Passing a zero to the function indicates that the program terminated without errors. To ensure correct execution of a Perl program, the **exit()** function is always invoked at the end of a Perl script.

As Figure 16.2 indicates, all Perl statements are terminated with a semicolon.

CREATING AND RUNNING A PERL WEB SCRIPT

Creating a Perl Web page requires greater care than creating a comparable JavaScript page. The Web browser will not display a useful error message if we make a mistake in the Perl code. This means that we must ensure that the code is correct before we load it into a browser. We use the following steps to create and run the sample Perl Web script.

Step 1. Create the Perl Script. Using your favorite text editor, enter the code shown in Figure 16.2. Make sure that the file is written in plain text or ASCII. Save the file under the name **hello.pl.cgi**. Although this file appears to have two extensions, **.pl.cgi**, the true extension is **.cgi**. Including **.pl** as part of the file name identifies the file as a CGI script written in Perl.

Step 2. Run the Perl Script through the Perl Compiler. We run the script through the Perl compiler to check for syntax errors. In a browser any errors will trigger only a generic "server error", so we must make sure that the script is error free before we load it into a browser. Figure 16.3 shows the call to the Perl compiler and the output from the compiler. When the Perl code is error free, the compiler prints a listing of the code.

```
gallifrey% perl hello.pl.cgi
Content-type: text/html

<HTML> <HEAD>
<TITLE> Web Hello</TITLE></HEAD>
<BODY BGCOLOR = 'white'>
Hello, World Wide Web!<BR>
This is SAF
</BODY></HTML>
```

Figure 16.3 The *Hello Web* Page: Compiler Output

Step 3. Change Privileges. If it is appropriate for your system, make sure that everyone (Group, Others) has read and execute privileges for the script. Typically, Unix and Linux users must set the privileges.

Step 4. Load the Script into a Web Browser. To load a CGI program into a browser, place the script's name in the location or Netsite window of the browser.

HANDLING SYNTAX ERRORS

Figure 16.4 contains a revision of the *Hello Web* page. The new page contains a syntax error in the highlighted line. Try to determine the cause of the error. Compare this line with the other **print** statements.

The highlighted **print** statement in Figure 16.4 is missing the beginning quotation mark. Figure 16.5 shows what happens when this page is loaded into a browser. The error message conveys almost no useful information.

```
#!/usr/local/bin/perl
# File name: hello.pl.cgi
print "Content-type: text/html", "\n\n";
print <HTML> <HEAD>", "\n";
print "<TITLE> Web Hello</TITLE></HEAD>\n";
print "<BODY BGCOLOR = 'white'>\n";
print "Hello, World Wide Web!<BR>\n";
print "This is SAF\n";
print "</BODY></HTML>", "\n";
exit(0);
```

Figure 16.4 An Erroneous Perl Program

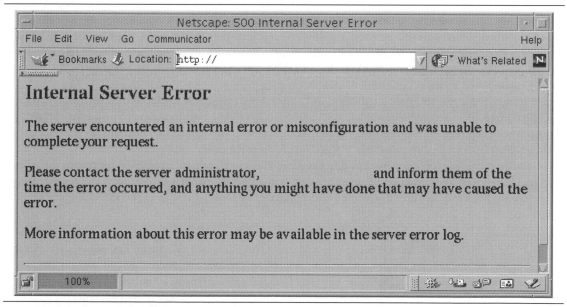

Figure 16.5 Netscape Error Page

Figure 16.6 shows the output of the erroneous program when the program is run through the Perl compiler. The highlighted line indicates the error source. The remaining errors are a "snowball effect" resulting from the first error. In other words, the first error makes Perl "think" that there are several other errors.

Although Perl error messages can be, and often are, obscure, they do convey more information than the Netscape error page displayed in Figure 16.5.

```
gallifrey% perl helloWrong.pl.cgi
syntax error at helloWrong.pl.cgi line 4, near "HEAD>"
Backslash found where operator expected at helloWrong.pl.cgi line 4, near "", "\"
String found where operator expected at helloWrong.pl.cgi line 5, near "print ""
  (Might be a runaway multi-line "" string starting on line 4)
Bare word found where operator expected at helloWrong.pl.cgi line 9, near "print "</BODY"
  (Might be a runaway multi-line // string starting on line 5)
String found where operator expected at helloWrong.pl.cgi line 9, near "</HTML>", ""
Backslash found where operator expected at helloWrong.pl.cgi line 9, near "", "\"
String found where operator expected at helloWrong.pl.cgi line 9, at end of line
Can't find string terminator '"' anywhere before EOF at helloWrong.pl.cgi line 9.
```

Figure 16.6 Perl Error Output

SCALAR VARIABLES IN PERL

We used the Perl **print** statement several times in the *Hello Web* page. In this first example, double quotation marks were used to encase the string literals.

Using double quotation marks within a **print** statement tells the Perl compiler that it should interpolate any scalar variables appearing inside the quotation marks. In this context, *interpolation* means that Perl should use the value associated with a variable.

In Perl, a scalar variable holds a single indivisible value. Perl has three scalar types: numbers, strings, and references. Perl uses the dollar sign, **$**, as a prefix for all scalar variable names. By convention, Perl variable names use lower-case letters, underscores, and numerals. Perl is case sensitive, and it follows C programming style in naming variables: C does not use capital letters in its variable names, and neither does Perl. Some examples of valid scalar variable names are: **$i, $sum, $my_answer**. Perl determines the appropriate scalar type for a variable from the context. Thus, if the code requires a number, Perl interprets the scalar variable as a number. If it cannot transform the variable's value into a number, it gives it a value of zero. Similarly, if the code requires a string, Perl interprets the value associated with a variable as a string. Perl's flexibility makes programming easy, but it also makes writing erroneous code easy.

To illustrate interpolation, we rewrite the *Hello Web* page, using variables to represent the page's title and background color and the programmer's first name. Figure 16.7 contains the revised page. Try to create the variables and the **print** statements before looking at the Perl code in Figure 16.8.

Figure 16.7 The *Hello Web* Page, version 2

```
#!/usr/local/bin/perl
$title = "My First Web Page";
$name = "Susan";
$background = "white";

print "Content-type: text/html", "\n\n";
print "<HTML> <HEAD>", "\n";
print "<TITLE>$title</TITLE></HEAD>\n";
print "<BODY BGCOLOR = $background>\n";
print "Hello, World Wide Web!<BR>\n";
print "This is $name!\n";
print "</BODY></HTML>", "\n";
exit(0);
```

Figure 16.8 Perl Code for the *Hello Web* Page, version 2

Figure 16.8 contains the Perl code for the second version of the *Hello Web* page. The code that creates and uses the scalar variables is highlighted.

SINGLE QUOTATION MARKS AND THE print STATEMENT

Using single quotation marks within a `print` statement indicates that the Perl compiler should not interpolate any variables. This means that the information between single quotation marks is printed exactly as it appears. For example, suppose we rewrite the *Hello Web* page as depicted in Figure 16.9. The two highlighted lines of code use single quotation marks to print the two messages in the browser's window.

```
#!/usr/local/bin/perl
$title = "My First Web Page";
$name = "Susan";
$background = "white";

print "Content-type: text/html", "\n\n";
print "<HTML> <HEAD>", "\n";
print "<TITLE>$title</TITLE></HEAD>\n";
print "<BODY BGCOLOR = $background>\n";
print 'Hello, World Wide Web!<BR>\n';
print 'This is $name!\n';
print "</BODY></HTML>", "\n";
exit(0);
```

Figure 16.9 Perl Code for *Hello Web* Page, version 3

Figure 16.10 contains the output of the *Hello Web* page, version 3. Neither the new-line (**\n**) characters nor the variable name (**$name**) are interpolated. If the other **print** statements had used single quotation marks, the browser would have crashed, because it would not have correctly interpreted the content types—nor would the browser have values for the title or the background color.

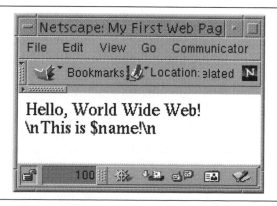

Figure 16.10 The *Hello Web* Page, version 3

A HERE DOCUMENT

Perl provides a compact method for printing several lines of text. This method, known as a *Here Document*, uses the syntax displayed in Figure 16.11. As this figure indicates, the **print** statement uses a label of the programmer's choice. The **print** statement prints text until it reaches the label. The spacing in the **print** statement is crucial. There should be a space between **print** and the angular brackets <<. There should not be a space anywhere else.

```
print <<"HereLabel";
These are the lines of text that I want printed.
A Here Document interpolates all variables,
and prints text until it reaches the HereLabel
which should be on a separate line.
HereLabel
```

Figure 16.11 Syntax for a Here Document

Figure 16.12 contains a fourth version of the *Hello Web* page. This script's output is identical to the Web page depicted in Figure 16.7. The Perl script uses a *Here Document* to create the page. The *content-type* statement appears outside of the *Here Document*. The remaining statements are contained within the *Here Document*.

```
#!/usr/local/bin/perl
$title = "My First Web Page";
$name = "Susan";
$background = "white";

#content type must go outside here document
print "Content-type: text/html", "\n\n";
print <<"DOC_END";

<HTML> <HEAD>\n
<TITLE>$title</TITLE></HEAD>\n
<BODY BGCOLOR = $background>\n
Hello, World Wide Web!<BR>\n
This is $name!\n
</BODY></HTML>\n

DOC_END
exit(0);
```

Figure 16.12 Perl Code for the *Hello Web* Page, version 4

QUOTATIONS FOR COMMAND INTERPRETATION

The final type of Perl quotation mark is potentially the most dangerous to system security. Perl provides a set of *back quotation* marks (`). (The back quotation mark is usually found with the tilde (~) on the computer keyboard. It looks like a French "grave" accent mark.) Back quotation marks are used to execute operating system commands. For example, Figure 16.13 contains a page that executes two Unix system commands, **echo** and **wc**. The **echo** command echoes (displays) the text

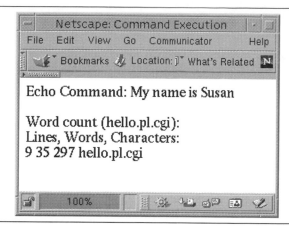

Figure 16.13 The *Unix Command* Page

that appears after it. The **wc** command (word count) displays the number of lines, words, and characters in a file.

Figure 16.14 contains the Perl script for the *Unix Command* page. The statements containing back quotation marks are highlighted. Notice the use of double *and* back quotation marks in the **print** statements. We can use more than one type of quotation mark, as long as we use commas to separate the different quotation fields. We can also encase single quotation marks within a double quotation field.

```perl
#!/usr/local/bin/perl
$title = "Command Execution";
$background = "white";

print "Content-type: text/html", "\n\n";
print "<HTML> <HEAD>", "\n";
print "<TITLE>$title</TITLE></HEAD>\n";
print "<BODY BGCOLOR = $background>\n";
print "Echo Command: ", `echo  My name is Susan`, "<P>\n";
print "Word count (hello.pl.cgi):<BR> Lines, Words, Characters:<BR>\n";
print `wc hello.pl.cgi`, "\n";
Print "</BODY></HTML>", "\n";
exit(0);
```

Figure 16.14 Perl Code for the *Unix Command* Page

Although the use of back quotation marks is "safe" in the *Unix Command* page, this facility poses severe security risks when Perl scripts are used to process Web forms. For example, suppose we create a form with a text field for the user's name. A malicious user might enter the name `rm *.*` This command would remove all the files in the current directory. With only a little more effort, a malicious user could remove all of the files from the hard drive or steal all of the passwords from the server. We can write Perl scripts that guard against malicious users, but doing so requires a strong foundation in Perl fundamentals, so we won't create our first interactive forms until Chapter 18.

NUMBERS IN PERL

Perl provides integers and floating-point numbers in decimal, hexadecimal, and octal representation. Figure 16.15 contains examples of Perl numeric variables.

```
$oct_num = 0123;
$hex_num = 0x2F;
$num = 45;
$num2 = 12.3456;
```

Figure 16.15 Perl Numeric Variables

Perl uses the same conventions as Java when determining a number's base: a prefix of zero indicates an octal number, a prefix of 0X or 0x indicates a hexadecimal number. Octal and hexadecimal numbers are automatically converted to decimal representation by the Perl **print** statement.

Perl provides several arithmetic operators. Figure 16.16 contains a list of the most commonly used operators, arranged in order of their precedence. (Appendix C contains a complete list of the Perl operators.)

Operator	Meaning
++	Increment
--	Decrement
-	Unary Minus (Negative number)
+	Unary Plus
**	Exponentiation
*	Multiplication
/	Division
%	Modulus
+	Addition
-	Subtraction
=	Assignment
**=	Assignment/Exponentiation
*=	Assignment/Multiplication
/=	Assignment/Division
%=	Assignment/Modulus
+=	Assignment/Addition
-=	Assignment/Subtraction

Figure 16.16 Common Perl Arithmetic Operators

The Perl arithmetic operators are almost identical to the arithmetic operators provided by JavaScript. The one exception is exponentiation: Perl provides an exponentiation operator, whereas JavaScript uses a built-in function. The Perl exponentiation operator returns powers or roots. For example, $x = 2**3; finds the third power of 2 and places the result in $x. Similarly, $y = 2 **0.50; finds the square root of 2 and places the result in $y.

Figure 16.17 contains a page that evaluates several simple arithmetic expressions. The page contains three scalar variables, $i, $j, and $x, with values of 10, 2, and 12.3456, respectively. The page prints the arithmetic expression and the result obtained by the expression. Try to write the Perl code for this web page before looking at the code in Figure 16.18.

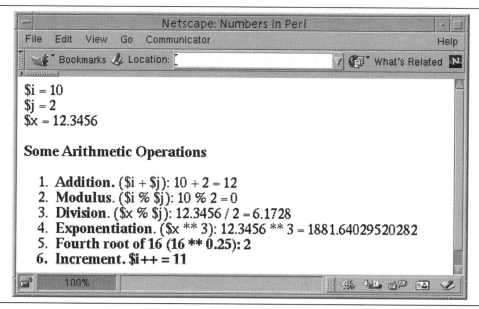

Figure 16.17 The *Arithmetic Expressions* Page

```perl
#!/usr/local/bin/perl
$i = 10;
$j = 2;
$x = 12.3456;
print "Content-type: text/html", "\n\n";
print "<HTML> <HEAD>", "\n";
print "<TITLE> Numbers in Perl</TITLE></HEAD>\n";
print "<BODY BGCOLOR = 'white'>\n";
print '$i = ', "$i\n";
print '<BR>$j = ', "$j\n";
print '<BR>$x = ', "$x<P>\n";
print "<B>Some Arithmetic Operations</B><BR>\n";
$answer = $i + $j;
print '<OL><LI><B>Addition.</B> ($i + $j): ', "$i + $j = $answer\n";
$answer = $i % $j;
print '<LI><B>Modulus</B>. ($I % $j): ', "$i % $j = $answer\n";
$answer = $x/$j;
print '<LI><B>Division</B>. ($x % $j): ', "$x / $j = $answer\n";
$answer = $x**3;
print '<LI><B>Exponentiation</B>. ($x ** 3): ', "$x ** 3 = $answer\n";
$answer = 16 ** 0.25;
print "<LI><B>Fourth root of 16 (16 ** 0.25): $answer\n";
$i++;
print '<LI><B>Increment</B>. $i++ = ', "$i\n";
print "</OL></BODY></HTML>", "\n";
exit(0);
```

Figure 16.18 Code for the *Arithmetic Expressions* Page

The Perl code for the *Arithmetic Expressions* page appears in Figure 16.18. The code uses the variable **$answer** to store the results of the arithmetic operation. The **print** statement that follows uses an uninterpolated string to print a **<LI>** tag followed by a parenthesized arithmetic expression. An interpolated string prints the contents of the variables.

PERL ARITHMETIC FUNCTIONS

Perl provides several arithmetic functions. Figure 16.19 lists these functions.

Function	Meaning
abs(x)	Return the absolute value of x.
atan2(x)	Return the arc tangent of x in radians.
chr(x)	Return the character whose ASCII value corresponds with x.
cos(x)	Return the cosine of x in radians.
exp(x)	Return e^x.
int(x)	Return the integer equivalent to x.
log(x)	Return $\log_e x$.
rand(x)	Return a fractional random number between 0 and x.
sin(x)	Return the sine of x in radians.
sqrt(x)	Return the square root of x.

Figure 16.19 Perl Arithmetic Functions

As an illustration of these functions, we rewrite the JavaScript *Sales Tax* page developed in Chapter 9. (See Figures 9.14 through 9.16.) Figure 16.20 contains the sample page. This page contains variables for the item's cost, tax rate, sales tax, and total amount. Try to rewrite the code for this page before examining the code in Figure 16.21.

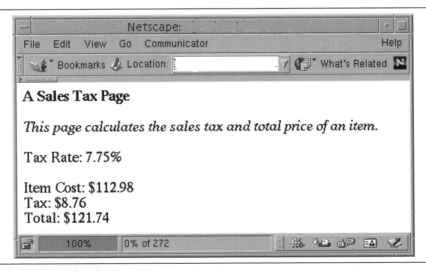

Figure 16.20 The *Sales Tax* Page, Perl version

The Perl version of the *Sales Tax* page uses a modification of the technique developed in the JavaScript version. We use the `int()` function with the parameter `int($tax*100+0.5)` to obtain the two digits to the right of the decimal point. We divide this result by 100 to produce the correct dollars-and-cents format.

Printing the leading dollar signs poses a slight problem, because Perl assumes that a dollar sign indicates a scalar variable. To print a dollar sign we use a back slash as a prefix: `\$`. (We can use the backslash to print other symbols—for example, `\'` or `\"`, prints single or double quotation marks in a string, respectively.)

Figure 6.21 contains the Perl code for the *Sales Tax* page. The statement that calls the `int()` function and the statements that print dollar signs are highlighted.

```perl
#!/usr/local/bin/perl
$tax_rate = 7.75;
$item_cost = 112.98;

print "Content-type: text/html", "\n\n";
print "<HTML> <HEAD>", "\n";
print "<TITLE> </TITLE></HEAD>\n";
print "<BODY BGCOLOR = 'white'>\n";
print "<B>A Sales Tax Page</B><P>\n";
print "<I>This page calculates the sales tax and";
print " total price of an item.</I><P>\n";
print "Tax Rate: $tax_rate%<P>\n";
print "Item Cost: \$$item_cost<BR>\n";
$tax = $item_cost * ($tax_rate/100);
$tax = int($tax*100+0.5)/100;
$total = $item_cost + $tax;
print "Tax: \$$tax<BR>\n";
print "Total: \$$total<BR>\n";
print "</BODY></HTML>", "\n";
exit(0);
```

Figure 16.21 Perl Code for the *Sales Tax* Page

STRINGS IN PERL

Unlike many other programming languages, Perl provides several string operators. Figure 16.22 lists these operators in order of their precedence. (Appendix C contains the complete Perl precedence hierarchy.)

Operator	Meaning
++	Increment
=~	Match
!~	Does not match
x	Repetition
.	Concatenation
=	Assignment
.=	Assignment/Concatenation
x=	Assignment/Repetition

Figure 16.22 Perl String Operators

Let's consider each of these operators separately, reserving a discussion of the matching operators for Chapter 18.

Assignment. We use the assignment operator to place a string literal, expression, or variable into a string variable. For example, `$word1 = "bird";` assigns the string literal *bird* to the scalar variable `$word1`. Similarly, the statement

```
$word2 = $word1;
```

would then assign the contents of `$word1` (*bird*) to `$word2`.

Concatenation. String concatenation, also known as string addition, creates a new string by appending one string to the end of a second string. The concatenation operator always returns a new string, so we must use concatenation in conjunction with the assignment operator. For example, the following statements assign a value of *"birdhouse"* to `$word1`:

```
$word1 = "bird";
$word1 = $word1."house";
```

Perl also provides a combined assignment/concatenation operator that lets us rewrite the *birdhouse* assignment statement as

```
$word1.="house";
```

Repetition. Concatenation creates longer strings from possibly distinct strings; the repetition operator creates longer strings from the *same* string. Because the repetition operator always returns a new string, we must use this operator in conjunction with an assignment operator. For example, the following statements assign a value of *catcat* to `$word`:

```
$word = "cat";
$word = $word x (2);
```

Perl also provides a combined assignment/repetition operator that lets us rewrite the *catcat* assignment statement as

```
$word x= 2;
```

The repetition number is enclosed in parentheses when the repetition operator is not part of a combined assignment/repetition operator.

Increment. The increment operator advances the last character in a string to the next ASCII character. Both prefix (`++$word`) and postfix (`$word++`) forms of this operator exist. For example, the following statements change the value in `$word` from *apple* to *applf*:

```
$word = "apple";
$word++;
```

Figure 16.23 contains a sample page illustrating the Perl string operators. Figure 6.24 contains the code for the *String Operators* page.

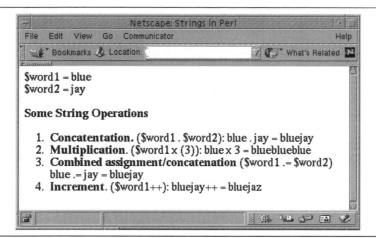

Figure 16.23 The *String Operators* Page

```
#!/usr/local/bin/perl
$word1 = "blue";
$word2 = "jay";
print "Content-type: text/html", "\n\n";
print "<HTML> <HEAD>", "\n";
print "<TITLE> Strings in Perl</TITLE></HEAD>\n";
print "<BODY BGCOLOR = 'white'>\n";
print '$word1 = ', "$word1\n";
print '<BR>$word2 = ', "$word2<P>\n";
print "<B>Some String Operations</B><BR>\n";

$answer = $word1 . $word2;
print '<OL><LI><B>Concatentation.</B> ($word1 . $word2): ', "\n";
print "$word1 . $word2 = $answer\n";

$answer = $word1 x (3);
print '<LI><B>Multiplication</B>. ($word1 x (3)): ', "$word1 x 3 = $answer\n";

$word1 .= $word2;
print '<LI><B>Combined assignment/concatenation</B> ($word1 .= $word2)', "\n";
print "blue .= jay = $word1\n";

$before = $word1++;
print '<LI><B>Increment</B>. ($word1++): ', "$before++ = $word1\n";
print "</OL></BODY></HTML>", "\n";
exit(0);
```

Figure 16.24 Perl Code for the *String Operators* Page

Perl String Functions

Perl provides several built-in string functions. Figure 16.25 contains a list of the simplest string functions. We examine several other string functions when we discuss pattern matching in Chapter 18. The functions listed in Figure 16.25 let us convert a string to all upper or lower case letters. We can also find the starting index of a sub-string within a string.

Function	Meaning
index(*string, substring*)	Return the starting index of a sub-string in a string. Return −1 if the sub-string is not in the string. Scan the string from the left.
lc(*expression*)	Return the expression in lowercase letters only.
lcfirst(*expression*)	Return the expression with the first letter in lowercase. The remaining letters are unchanged.
length(*expression*)	Return the number of characters in an expression.
ord(*string*)	Return the ASCII value of the first character in a string.
rindex(*string, substring*)	Return the starting index of a sub-string in a string. Return −1 if the sub-string is not in the string. Start the search from the **right** of the string.
uc(*expression*)	Return the expression in uppercase letters only.
ucfirst(*expression*)	Return the expression with the first character written in uppercase letters.

Figure 16.25 Simple String Functions

Figure 16.26 contains a *String Functions* page that illustrates several of the functions listed in Figure 16.25.

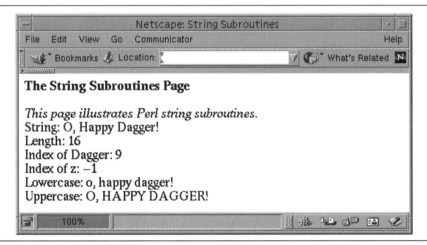

Figure 16.26 The *String Functions* Page

The *String Functions* page prints the length of the string. It searches for the string *Dagger* and *z*. Notice that *Dagger* has an index of 9, while *z* has an index of -1. Although *Dagger* starts at the 10th letter in *O, Happy Dagger!*, it has an index of 9, because Perl counts starting with zero. Figure 6.27 shows Perl's indexing method. The negative index associated with *z* indicates that it was not found in the string.

0	1	2	3	4	5	6	7	8	9	10	11	12	13	14	15
O	,		H	a	p	p	y		D	a	g	g	e	r	!

Figure 16.27 Index positions for `$string`

Figure 16.28 contains the Perl code for the *String Functions* page. The function calls are highlighted.

```
#!/usr/local/bin/perl
print "Content type: text/html", "\n\n",
print "<HTML> <HEAD>", "\n";
print "<TITLE> String Functions</TITLE></HEAD>\n";
print "<BODY BGCOLOR = 'white'>\n";
print "<B>The String Functions Page</B><P>\n";
print "<I>This page illustrates Perl string functions.</I><BR>\n";
$string = "O, Happy Dagger!";
print "String: $string<BR>\n";
$length = length($string);
print "Length: $length<BR>\n";
$index1 = index($string, "Dagger", 0);
print "Index of Dagger: $index1<BR>\n";
$index1 = index($string, "z");
print "Index of z: $index1<BR>\n";

$string = lc($string);
print "Lowercase: $string<BR>\n";
$string = uc($string);

print "Uppercase: $string<BR>\n";
print "</BODY></HTML>", "\n";
exit(0);
```

Figure 16.28 Perl Code for the *String Functions* Page

> ## EXERCISES

These exercises let you practice writing Web pages in Perl. Many exercises involve rewriting code previously created in HTML or JavaScript. Several of the JavaScript exercises ask for user data, but omit that portion of the exercise. Supply appropriate test data of your choice. The exercises are simple and should increase your familiarity with Perl syntax.

1. **The *Muskrat Mounds Tree Farm* Page.** Rewrite the *MM Tree Farm* page, Version 2, as a Perl script. (See Figure 1.21.)

2. **The *Logo Page*.** Create a logo of your choice using <HR> tags. Write your HTML code as a Perl script.

3. **The *Standard* Page.** Rewrite the *Standard Colors* page as a Perl script. (See Figure 2.13.)

4. **The *Animal Alphabet* Page.** Rewrite the *Animal Alphabet* page, Version 2, as a Perl script. (See Figure 3.22.)

5. **The *Special Teams* Page.** Rewrite the *Special Teams* page as a Perl script. (See Figure 4.17.)

6. **The *Link Colors* Page.** Rewrite the *Link Colors* page as a Perl script. (See Figure 5.3.)

7. **The *Simple Precedence* Page.** Rewrite the *Simple Precedence* page as a Perl script. (See Figure 9.6.)

8. **The *Circle* Page.** Rewrite the *Circle* page as a Perl script. (See Figure 9.17.) Create variables for the area, circumference, *pi*, and *r*. Make sure that you have test data.

9. **The *Quadratic Function* Page.** Rewrite the *Quadratic Function* page as a Perl script. (See Figure 9.18.) This page calculates the positive and negative roots of quadratic equations. Create variables for *a, b, c*, and the positive and negative roots. Make sure that the values for *a, b*, and *c* do not produce complex numbers or a division-by-zero error.

10. **The *Trapezoid* Page.** Rewrite the *Trapezoid* Page as a Perl script. (See Figure 9.22.) This page calculates the area of a trapezoid. Develop appropriate test values for the height and the two bases.

11. **The *Box* Page.** Rewrite the *Box* page as a Perl script. (See Figure 9.23.) This page calculates the perimeter and area of a box. Create variables for the length, width, perimeter, and area.

12. **The *Floor and Ceiling* Page.** Create a Perl script that translates the arithmetic expressions in Figure 9.29. This exercise asks you to implement floor and ceiling functions. *Hint: The* `int()` *function is similar to the JavaScript* `floor()` *function. The JavaScript* `ceil()` *function does not have a Perl equivalent, but you can develop comparable code by following the code in the Sales Tax page.*

13. **The *Exponentiation* Page.** Create a Perl script that translates the arithmetic expressions in Figure 9.30. Use the Perl exponentiation operator.

14. **The *String Concatenation* Page.** Create three string variables, `$word1`, `$word2`, and `$word3`, containing the string literals *ruby, throated*, and *hummingbird*, respectively. Experiment with the string repetition and concatenation operators. Minimally, your page should create a new string consisting of *ruby-throated hummingbird*.

15. **The *String Functions* Page.** Create a page that illustrates the use of the `lcfirst()` and `ucfirst()` string functions. Follow the example give in the *String Functions* page.

16. Create a page that illustrates the use of the `ord()` and `chr()` functions. These functions, which are also available in C and C++, convert a character to its ASCII equivalent, and *vice versa*.

17. Create a string of your choice. Use the `index()` and `rindex()` functions to search for the index position of the string starting from the left and the right, respectively.

➤ PERL TIPS AND VOCABULARY

CGI. CGI (Common Gateway Interface) is the protocol used to pass information from a user's form to a server-side script.

Client-Side. A client-side language, such as JavaScript, processes a script on the *client* (user's) machine. Client-side languages have fewer capabilities, but also pose fewer security risks, than server-side languages.

Interpolation. Interpolation refers to the translation of escape sequences, such as \n, and of variables. Variables placed inside a doubly quoted string are interpolated, that is, Perl replaces the variable names with the variables' values. Variables placed inside a singly quoted string are not interpolated.

Scalar. A scalar data type contains a single, indivisible value. Perl has three types of scalars: numbers, strings, and references.

Server-Side. A server-side language, such as Perl, processes a script from the programmer's machine on the server. Programmers must have *cgi-bin* privileges before they can write server-side scripts. Server-side languages pose greater security risks.

17 Arrays, References, Hashes, and Iteration

INTRODUCTION

In Chapter 11 we discussed JavaScript's iteration statements, and in Chapter 13 we examined arrays. In this chapter, we will focus on Perl's iteration statements and arrays. Many of the concepts discussed in the JavaScript chapters apply to Perl as well. In fact, the only new material that we cover is references and hashes. Therefore, we'll move through the preliminary material at a rapid pace.

ONE-DIMENSIONAL ARRAYS

Perl arrays are indexed with the same techniques employed by JavaScript and Java. The first subscript is always zero, and the array elements are accessed by position. Figure 17.1 contains the syntax for creating an array in Perl. Perl uses the *at* symbol (@) to identify a variable as an array. The parenthesized elements on the right-hand side of the assignment statement constitute a list in Perl.

```
@array_name = (element_0, element_1, ...., element_{n-1});
```

Figure 17.1 Array-Declaration Syntax in Perl

For example, suppose we want to create an array of barnyard animals. Initially, the list consists of *pig, ox, horse*, and *chicken*. The Perl code that creates this array is

```
@barnyard = ("pig", "ox", "horse", "chicken");
```

Because *barnyard* is an array of *strings*, each animal name must be enclosed in quotation marks. Either single quotation marks or double quotation marks can be used.

Unlike those in many programming languages, Perl arrays are dynamic. This means that the size of the array can grow or shrink as the program runs. To determine the current size of an array, we assign the array to a scalar variable. For example, the statement

```
$size = @barnyard;
```

creates a scalar variable, `$size`, that holds the number of elements currently in the *barnyard* array.

To access an individual element in an array, we use scalar notation. For example, to print the value in array position 1, we write

```
print "$barnyard[1]\n";
```

Similarly, to put *sheep* in the `$size` position of the *barnyard* array, we write

```
$barnyard[$size] = "sheep";
```

Perl arrays can contain elements of different types. For example, the following declaration creates an array with integers, floating-point numbers, and strings:

```
@mixed = (1, "one", 12.345, "two", 2);
```

ITERATION STATEMENTS

Processing all the elements in an array requires an iteration statement, and Perl offers four distinct iteration statements: `for`, `while`, `until`, and `foreach`. The first three iteration statements use expressions formed with relational and logical operators. Figure 17.2 lists Perl's relational and logical operators in order of precedence. (Appendix C contains the complete Perl precedence hierarchy.)

Numeric Relational Operator	String Relational Operator	Logical Operator	Description
		!	Logical Not
<	lt		Less than
<=	le		Less than/equal
>	gt		Greater than
>=	ge		Greater than/equal
==	eq		Equality
!=	ne		Inequality
<=>	cmp		Signed Comparison
		&&	Logical and
		| |	Logical or

Figure 17.2 Perl Relational and Logical Operators (Highest to Lowest Precedence)

As Figure 17.2 indicates, Perl provides two sets of relational operators. Perl's numeric relational operators are identical to JavaScript's relational operators; however, Perl adds a signed comparison operator (`<=>` or `cmp`). This operator compares two numbers or strings. It returns a negative one (`-1`) if the first number or string is less than the second, a zero if the two numbers or strings are the same, a positive one if the first number or string is greater than the second.

The Perl Iteration Statements

To illustrate the Perl iteration statements, we create a page that displays the array of barnyard animals. We'll write four versions of this page: one for each of the iteration statements. All versions display identical results in the browser. Figure 17.3 shows the browser display.

Figure 17.3 The *Barnyard Animals* Page

The **for** Statement

The Perl **for** statement is virtually identical to JavaScript's **for** statement. In fact, the only difference is Perl's requirement that the body of any iteration or selection statement include braces, **{}**. Figure 17.4(a) shows the syntax of Perl's **for** statement. The header of the **for** statement contains optional *initial*, *test*, and *change* expressions. The body of the **for** statement is executed as long as the test expression is *true*. Figure 17.4(b) contains the Perl script that produces the *Barnyard Animals* page illustrated in Figure 17.3

The **while** Statement

Figure 17.5(a) shows the syntax for the Perl **while** statement. As this figure indicates, the **while** statement contains a header with a parenthesized expression. The block of code in the body is executed as long as the expression is *true*. Figure 17.5(b) contains a revision of the *Barnyard Animal*

(a) The for Statement	**(b) Script for the *Barnyard Animals* Page**
| ```
for (initial_expression_opt;
    test_expression_opt;
    change_expression_opt)
{
    perl_statement;
    ...
    perl_statement;
}
``` | ```
#!/usr/local/bin/perl
@barnyard = ("pig", "ox", "horse", "chicken");
$size = @barnyard;
print "Content-type: text/html", "\n\n";
print "<HTML> <HEAD>", "\n";
print "<TITLE>The for Statement</TITLE></HEAD>\n";
print "<BODY BGCOLOR = 'white'>\n";
print "<B>Barnyard Animals</B><P>\n";
for ($i=0; $i<$size; $i++)
{ print "$barnyard[$i]<BR>\n";}
print "</BODY></HTML>", "\n";
exit(0);
``` |

Figure 17.4 The *Barnyard Animals* Page, **for** Version

(a) The `while` Statement	(b) Script for the *Barnyard Animals* Page
| ```perl
while(expression)
{
    perl_statement;
    ...
    perl_statement;
}
``` | ```perl
#!/usr/local/bin/perl
@barnyard = ("pig", "ox", "horse", "chicken");
$size = @barnyard;
print "Content-type: text/html", "\n\n";
print "<HTML> <HEAD>", "\n";
print "<TITLE>The for Statement</TITLE></HEAD>\n";
print "<BODY BGCOLOR = 'white'>\n";
print "<B>Barnyard Animals</B><P>\n";
$i = 0;
while ($i < $size){
    print "$barnyard[$i]<BR>\n";
    $i++;}
print "</BODY></HTML>", "\n";
exit(0 );
``` |

Figure 17.5 The *Barnyard Animals* Page, `while` Version

page that uses a `while` statement to print the *barnyard* array. The page's appearance is identical to that from the **for** statement version.

The `until` Statement

The **until** statement, which is unique to Perl, reverses the logic of a **while** statement. Figure 17.6(a) shows the syntax of the **until** statement. As this figure indicates, the header of the **until** statement contains a parenthesized expression. The code in the body of the **until** statement is executed *until* the expression becomes *true*. Figure 17.6(b) contains a new version of the *Barnyard Animal* page that uses an **until** statement to print the *barnyard* array.

(a) The until Statement	(b) Script for the *Barnyard Animals* Page
| ```perl
until(expression)
{
    perl_statement;
    ...
    perl_statement;
}
``` | ```perl
#!/usr/local/bin/perl
@barnyard = ("pig", "ox", "horse", "chicken");
[inicoB]$size = @barnyard;
print "Content-type: text/html", "\n\n";
print "<HTML> <HEAD>", "\n";
print "<TITLE>The for Statement</TITLE></HEAD>\n";
print "<BODY BGCOLOR = 'white'>\n";
print "<B>Barnyard Animals</B><P>\n";
$i=0;
until ($i == $size)
{ print "$barnyard[$i]<BR>\n";
    $i++;}
print "</BODY></HTML>", "\n";
exit(0);
``` |

Figure 17.6 The *Barnyard Animals* Page, **until** Version

Notice the expression used in the **until** statement header. The expression indicates that the loop is executed until *i* equals *size*.

The **foreach** Statement

The **foreach** statement, which is also unique to Perl, is designed to automate array processing. This statement processes all the elements in an array beginning with the element in the 0th position and continuing until it reaches the $n - 1^{th}$ position, where *n* represents the size of the array. Figure 17.7(a) summarizes the syntax of the **foreach** statement.

As this figure indicates, the **foreach** statement contains a header followed by a body enclosed in braces. The header contains a scalar variable that represents an element in the array. The scalar variable is followed by an array enclosed in parentheses. As this statement's name implies, the Perl compiler executes the statements in the body *for each* element in the array.

Figure 17.7(b) contains this last version of the *Barnyard Animal* page. The code for the **foreach** statement is highlighted. Notice the simplicity of this iteration statement. The **foreach** statement is clearly the preferred favorite whenever we need to process all of the elements in a one-dimensional array.

(a) The **foreach** Statement	(b) Script for the *Barnyard Animal* Page
`foreach $variable(@array)` `{` `    perl_statement;` `    ...` `    perl_statement;` `}`	`#!/usr/local/bin/perl` `@barnyard = ("pig", "ox", "horse", "chicken");` `print "Content-type: text/html", "\n\n";` `print "<HTML> <HEAD>", "\n";` `print "<TITLE>The for Statement</TITLE></HEAD>\n";` `print "<BODY BGCOLOR = 'white'>\n";` `print "<B>Barnyard Animals</B><P>\n";` `foreach $animal (@barnyard)` `{ print "$animal \n";}` `print "</BODY></HTML>", "\n";` `exit(0);`

Figure 17.7 The *Barnyard Animals* Page, **foreach** Version

BUILT-IN ARRAY FUNCTIONS

In Chapter 13, we discussed several JavaScript *Array* methods. JavaScript derived these methods from built-in Perl functions. Figure 17.8 displays the Perl array functions.

As Figure 17.8 indicates, Perl functions come in two varieties: functions that require a single parameter, and those that require more than one parameter. Only the latter functions require a parenthesized list of parameters. Parentheses are not necessary when a single parameter is passed.

The Perl array functions have the following interpretations:

The **sort** *Function.* This function sorts an array based on lexicographic order. The function returns an array of the sorted elements. We can change the sort order by placing a block, as denoted by braces, before the array. The block contains the new sort order. For example, to sort an array, *numbers*, in ascending order, we write

```
@sorted = sort {$a-$b} @numbers;
```

Perl Function	Description
@*sorted_name* = **sort** @*array*;	Sort an array using lexicographic order.
@*sorted_name* = **sort** {*order* } @*array*;	Sort using *order*.
@*reverse_name* = **reverse** @*array*;	Reverse an array.
@*array* = @*original*[*start..stop*];	Create a new array using *start..stop*.
@*array* = @*original*[*i, j, k*];	Create an array from *i, j, k*.
@*array* = **grep**(/*pattern*/, @*original*);	Create an array based on pattern-matching.
push(@*array*, *element*);	Add to right end (**[$size]**) of *array*.
unshift(@*array*, *element*);	Add to left end (**[0]**) of *array*.
$*variable* = **pop** @*array*;	Remove from right end (**[$size]**) of *array*.
$*variable* = **shift** @*array*;	Remove from left end (**[0]**) of *array*.

Figure 17.8 The Perl Array Functions

Similarly, to sort in descending order, we write

```
@sorted = sort{$b -$a} @numbers;
```

Here, **$a** and **$b** represent adjacent elements in the array, **$a** having the lower subscript.

The **reverse** *Function.*   As its name implies, this function returns an array that reverses the elements in the array passed as a parameter. For example, we reverse the *numbers* array with the statement

```
@reversed = reverse @numbers;
```

Slicing an Array.   Slicing an array creates a new array by extracting array elements from specific positions. We can extract the elements in a range denoted by *start..stop*, where *start* and *stop* are array positions. For example, we create a new array containing the first four elements of the *numbers* array with the statement

```
@first = @numbers[0..3];
```

We can also extract specific elements by using a comma-separated list. For example, the following statement creates a new array containing the elements in the first and third positions of the *numbers* array:

```
@odd = @numbers[1,3];
```

The **grep** *Function.*   The **grep** function uses a pattern to extract elements from an array. We discuss patterns in Chapter 18. However, as an example, assume that we want to extract all two-digit numbers from the *numbers* array. The statement that accomplishes this is

```
@two_digit = grep(/\d\d/, @numbers);
```

The pattern is enclosed in slash marks. In this example, **\d** indicates a digit from 0 to 9, inclusive.

The Array Functions Page

Figure 17.9 contains a sample page that illustrates the **sort**, **reverse**, and **grep** functions as well as array slices.

The *Array Functions* page creates a prefilled array of numbers. The statement that creates this array is

```
@numbers = (16, 31, 6, 11, 8, 13);
```

```
#!/usr/local/bin/perl
print "Content-type: text/html", "\n\n";
print "<HTML> <HEAD>", "\n";
print "<TITLE>Perl Array Functions</TITLE></HEAD>\n";
print "<BODY BGCOLOR = 'white'>\n";
print "<B>Array Functions in Perl</B><P>\n";
@numbers = (16, 31, 6, 11, 8, 13);
@lexicographic = sort @numbers;
@sorted = sort{$a - $b} @numbers;
print "Lexicographic sort:\n";
foreach $x(@lexicographic)
{ print "$x \n"; }
print "<P>Ascending Order: \n";
foreach $y(@sorted)
  { print "$y \n";}
@reverse = reverse @sorted;
print "<P>Sorted array (reversed): \n";
foreach $y(@reverse)
  { print "$y \n";}
@new_numbers = @numbers[0..2, 4];
print "<P>Slice: [0..1,4] \n";
foreach $y(@new_numbers)
  { print "$y \n";}
@two_digit = grep(/\d\d/, @numbers);
 print "<P>Two Digit: \n";
foreach $y(@two_digit)
  { print "$y \n";}
print "</BODY></HTML>\n";
exit(0);
```

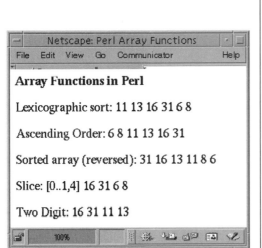

Figure 17.9 The *Array Functions* Page

Figure 17.10 Perl Code for the *Array Functions* Page

The *numbers* array is sorted first in lexicographic and then ascending order; reversing the sorted array next creates a new array that is sorted in descending order. The page also contains a new array that uses both slicing methods to extract elements from the *numbers* array. A final array containing only the two-digit numbers is created by invoking the **grep** function.

Figure 17.10 contains the Perl script for the *Array Functions* page. The function calls are highlighted. You might want to compare the Perl functions with their JavaScript counterparts. (See Chapter 13.)

The push, pop, shift, and unshift Functions

Figure 17.8 also contains Perl functions that add or remove elements from either the left or right ends of an array. We discussed the JavaScript versions of these functions in Chapter 13. (See Figures 13.7 through 13.9.)

As Figure 17.8 indicates, we use the **push** function to add an element to the right end of an array, the **unshift** function to add an element to the left end of an array. For either function, we place the array and the element we wish to add inside parentheses. The element may be a literal or a scalar variable.

The **pop** function removes the element at the right end of the array; the **shift** function removes the element at the left end of an array. Neither of these functions requires parentheses; we simply place the array after the function's name. Both functions return the removed element.

In Chapter 13, we created a *House Pets* page that illustrated JavaScript's version of these functions. (See Figures 13.7 through 13.9). Figure 17.11 contains the Perl version of the *House Pets* page.

Figure 17.12 contains the Perl code for the *House Pets* page. Originally, the *housepets* array contains only *cat* and *dog*. The first column of the table displays the original *housepets* array. The

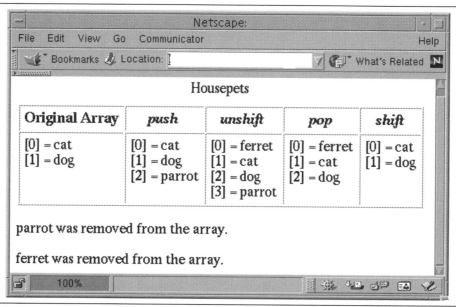

Figure 17.11 The *House Pets* Page, Perl version

second and third columns display the *housepets* array after the *push* and *unshift* operations, respectively. The size of the array is redefined prior to printing each of these columns. The fourth and fifth columns display the *housepets* array after the *pop* and *shift* operations, respectively. The array size is also redefined prior to printing each of these columns.

REFERENCES

We can also create two-dimensional arrays in Perl. However, creating such arrays requires references. A *reference* is a scalar variable that holds the address (or memory location) of another variable.

Creating and using references is easy. For example, assume that we have three scalar variables, **$x**, **$y**, and **$word**, containing 10, 12.345, and *cat*, respectively. We'd like to create three references, **$x_ref**, **$y_ref**, and **$word_ref**, that contain the addresses of **$x**, **$y**, and **$word**, respectively. Figure 17.13 shows the relation between **$x**, **$y**, and **$word** and **$x_ref**, **$y_ref**, and **$word_ref**.

In Figure 17.13, **$x**, **$y**, and **$word** contain the values 10, 12.345, and *cat*, respectively. The Perl compiler stores these variables in memory locations of its choosing. Assume that the Perl compiler placed **$x** in memory location 0xccb4c, **$y** in 0xccb70, and **$word** in 0xccb94. Notice how the three reference variables, **$x_ref**, **$y_ref**, and **$word_ref**, contain the addresses of the three scalar variables, **$x**, **$y**, and **$word** .

```perl
#!/usr/local/bin/perl
@housepets = ("cat", "dog");
print "Content-type: text/html", "\n\n";
print "<HTML> <HEAD>", "\n";
print "<TITLE></TITLE></HEAD>\n";
print "<BODY BGCOLOR = 'white'>\n";
print "<TABLE BORDER = '1' CELLPADDING = '5'>\n";
print "<CAPTION>Housepets</CAPTION>\n";
print "<TR><TH>Original Array</TH>\n";
print "<TH><I>push</I> </TH>\n";
print "<TH><I>unshift</I> </TH>\n";
print "<TH><I>pop</I></TH>\n";
print "<TH><I>shift</I></TH></TR>\n";
print "<TR><TD VALIGN = 'top'>\n";

$size = @housepets;
for ($i = 0; $i < $size; $i++) {
  print "[$i] = $housepets[$i]<BR>\n"; }
print "</TD><TD VALIGN = 'top'>\n";

push(@housepets, "parrot");
$size = @housepets;
for ($i = 0; $i < $size; $i++) {
  print "[$i] = $housepets[$i]<BR>\n"; }

print "</TD><TD VALIGN = 'top'>\n";
unshift(@housepets, "ferret");
$size = @housepets;
for ($i = 0; $i < $size; $i++) {
  print "[$i] = $housepets[$i]<BR>\n"; }

print "</TD><TD VALIGN = 'top'>\n";
$popped = pop @housepets;
$size = @housepets;
for ($i = 0; $i < $size; $i++) {
  print "[$i] = $housepets[$i]<BR>\n"; }

print "</TD><TD VALIGN = 'top'>\n";
$shifted = shift @housepets;
$size = @housepets;
for ($i = 0; $i < $size; $i++) {
  print "[$i] = $housepets[$i]<BR>\n"; }

print "</TD></TR></TABLE>\n";
print "<P>$popped was removed from the array.<BR>\n";
print "<BR>$shifted was removed from the array.\n";
print "</BODY></HTML>", "\n";
exit(0);
```

Figure 17.12 Perl Code for the *House Pets* Page

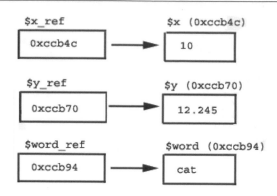

Figure 17.13 Variables and References

Figure 17.14 displays a page that shows the relation between the three scalar variables and their corresponding reference variables. The page prints the address of each scalar variable and the variable's value. Perl always prints references in the format SCALAR(0x....).

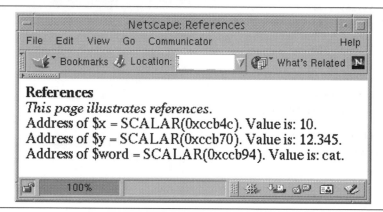

Figure 17.14 The *References* Page

Creating References

Figure 17.15 contains the syntax for creating a reference in Perl. As this figure indicates, reference are created by placing a backslash before the variable that appears on the right-hand side of the assignment statement.

```
$reference_variable = \$variable;
```

Figure 17.15 Syntax for a Reference

We create the three references to $x, $y, and $word with the following code:

```
$x_ref = \$x;
$y_ref = \$y;
$word_ref = \$word;
```

Dereferencing

After we have created references for $x, $y, and $word, we can use these references to obtain the contents of $x, $y, and $word. *Dereferencing* is the official term used to indicate that we do not want the address stored in a reference, but the contents stored at that address. For example, when we dereference $x_ref we are obtaining the 10 stored in address 0xccb4c. To dereference a reference, we use two dollar signs before the variable name instead of one. For example, to dereference $x_ref we write $$x_ref.

Figure 17.16 contains the Perl code for the *References* page. The statements that create the references and dereference them are highlighted.

```
#!/usr/local/bin/perl
print "Content-type: text/html", "\n\n";
print "<HTML> <HEAD>", "\n";
print "<TITLE>References</TITLE></HEAD>\n";
print "<BODY BGCOLOR = 'white'>\n";
print "<B>References</B><BR>\n";
print "<I>This page illustrates references. </I><BR>\n";
$x = 10;
$y - 12.345;
$word = "cat";
$x_ref = \$x;
$y_ref = \$y;
$word_ref = \$word;
print "Address of \$x = $x_ref. Value is: $$x_ref.<BR>\n";
print "Address of \$y = $y_ref. Value is: $$y_ref.<BR>\n";
print "Address of \$word = $word_ref. Value is: $$word_ref.<BR>\n";
print "</BODY></HTML>", "\n";
exit(0);
```

Figure 17.16 Perl Code for the *References* Page

TWO-DIMENSIONAL ARRAYS IN PERL

When we create a two-dimensional array in Perl, we create a one-dimensional array of references to one-dimensional arrays. Thus, we have an array of references to arrays. Each of the component arrays can have a different size, although it's easier to process the two-dimensional arrays when the component arrays are of the same size. Figure 17.17 contains a Web page that prints the contents of a two-dimensional array. We use this page to illustrate the basics of two-dimensional arrays.

As Figure 17.17 indicates, the matrix contains three rows. The arrays composing this matrix contain three, five, and two elements, respectively. Perl provides two basic techniques for prefilling a matrix. Both techniques use references. The first technique uses *anonymous references*; the second technique uses *named references*.

As its name implies, an anonymous reference does not have a named variable associated with it. Anonymous references do not exist independently of the array that contains them. By contrast, a named reference has an identifiable variable name, and we can access a named reference independently.

Figure 17.18 illustrates both techniques for prefilling a matrix. Figure 17.18(a) uses a list of anonymous references. With this technique, we create an array using the standard parentheses to encase the array elements. To create the anonymous references, we use brackets, rather than parentheses, to encase the elements of each of the one-dimensional arrays.

Figure 17.18 (b) uses named references to create the matrix. With this technique, we create a separate array for each of the matrix rows. We fill the matrix with references, denoted by the backslash (\), to these arrays.

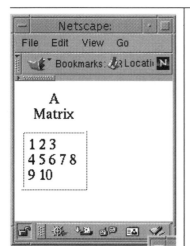

Figure 17.17 The *Basic Matrix* Page

(a) Anonymous References	(b) Named References
| ```
@matrix1 = (
  [1,2,3],
  [4,5,6,7,8],
  [9,10]);
``` | ```
@row0 = (1,2,3);
@row1 = (4,5,6,7,8);
@row2 = (9,10);
@matrix = (\@row0, \@row1, \@row2);
``` |

Figure 17.18 Prefilling Two-Dimensional Arrays in Perl

Accessing Matrix Elements

Accessing a particular cell in a matrix requires a row subscript and a column subscript. For example, to access the "2" that appears in row 0 and column 1, we write `$matrix[0][1]`. Similarly, to access the "7" that appears in the first row and the third column, we write `$matrix[1][3]`.

We can process a two-dimensional array by using either a **foreach** or a **for** statement. Figure 17.19 contains Perl code to print a matrix by using both techniques. The examples show an alternative method of creating the **for** and **foreach** statement headers. Rather than specifying the initial, test, and change expressions, we specify the lower and upper bounds for the loop. For example, let's consider the **foreach** statement appearing in Figure 17.19(a).

The outer **foreach** statement,

```
foreach $i (0..@{matrix})
```

indicates that the *i* subscripts start at zero and end with the last row in *matrix*. After each iteration of the outer loop, *i* is incremented.

The inner **foreach** statement,

```
foreach $j (0..@{$matrix[$i]})
```

indicates that the *j* subscripts start at 0 and end with the last column of the current row. After each iteration of the inner loop, *j* is incremented.

Figure 17.19(b) contains the **for** statement version for printing a matrix. This figure shows an alternative method for determining the last subscript in an array. The last subscript for a one-dimensional array of references is **$#matrix**. The last subscript for each of its constituent one-dimensional arrays is **$#{$matrix[$i]}**.

(a) The **foreach** Version	(b) The **for** Version

<pre>foreach $i (0..@{matrix}) {
  foreach $j (0..@{$matrix[$i]}){
    print "$matrix[$i][$j] \n";
  }
  print "
\n";
}</pre>
	<pre>for $i(0..$#matrix) {
	  for $j(0..$#{$matrix[$i]}){
	    print "$matrix[$i][$j]\n";
	  }
	  print "
\n";
	}</pre>

Figure 17.19 Printing a Matrix

Figure 17.20 contains the complete code for the *Basic Matrix* page. The page was created by using the technique illustrated in Figure 17.18(b).

```
#!/usr/local/bin/perl
#Create the matrix
 @row0 = (1,2,3);
 @row1 = (4,5,6,7,8);
 @row2 = (9,10);
 @matrix = (\@row0, \@row1, \@row2);
 @col_size = (3,5,2);
print "Content-type: text/html", "\n\n";
print "<HTML> <HEAD>", "\n";
print "<TITLE></TITLE></HEAD>\n";
print "<BODY BGCOLOR = 'white'>\n";
print "<TABLE BORDER = '1' CELLPADDING = '5'>\n";
print "<CAPTION>Matriz</CAPTION>\n";
print "<TR><TD>\n";
foreach $i (0..@{matrix})  {
    foreach $j (0..@{$matrix[$i]}){
      print "$matrix[$i][$j] \n";
    }
    print "<BR>\n";
}
print "</TD></TR></TABLE>\n";
print "</BODY></HTML>", "\n";
exit(0);
```

Figure 17.20 Perl Code for the *Basic Matrix* Page

HASHES

Perl's built-in data types include *hashes*, also known as *associative arrays*. The Perl arrays previously introduced use indices (or positions) to access information; a hash organizes data by using unique keys. Each key has a corresponding value. Perl uses a randomizing function called a *hash* function to place *key–value* pairs in the computer's memory, and information retrieval is very quick. Programmers often use hashes to implement "look-up tables" or "dictionaries" of information.

To illustrate hashes, we create a simple *English–German Animal Dictionary*. Figure 17.21 contains a sample page. Notice that each English animal name has associated its German counterpart.

Figure 17.21 The *English–German Animal Dictionary* Page

CREATING A HASH

Perl provides two alternative methods for declaring and prefilling a hash. Both methods use a percent sign as a prefix for a hash variable, and both methods place a key followed by its associated value in a list. Figure 17.22 illustrates both hash declaration methods.

(a) `%hash_variable = (key₁, value₁, ..., keyₙ, valueₙ);`

(b) `%hash_variable = (key₁=>value₁, ..., keyₙ=>valueₙ);`

Figure 17.22 Syntax for a Hash Declaration

As Figure 17.22(a) indicates, the first hash declaration method uses a comma-separated list in which a key is followed immediately by its corresponding value. The alternative method illustrated in Figure 17.22(b) provides a visual association between a key and its value: A key is linked to its associated value by use of the => operator. This method uses commas to separate the *key=>value* pairs from each other.

Applying Figure 17.22(a) to the *Animal Dictionary* page yields the following hash declaration.

```
%dictionary = ("cows", "K&uuml;he", "horses", "Pferde", "fish", "Fische","birds",
"V&ouml;gel", "cats", "Katzen", "dogs", "Hunde");
```

Because this is an *English–German* dictionary the *English* name is the key and the German counterpart is the value. This means that we can use the English keys to look up German animals, but we cannot go in the reverse direction—that is, we cannot find the English equivalent of a German animal; we would need a second hash variable to do this. (Several of the German names use HTML character entities to produce the correct umlauts.)

Unlike with standard arrays, we cannot easily determine the size of a hash. We cannot use the standard array "trick" of assigning the array to a scalar variable; this produces "garbage" when applied to a hash. This is not typically a problem, because Perl provides several built-in functions that let us extract all of the keys or values from a hash or specific key–value pairs. Perl also lets us add or remove key–value pairs from a hash.

The *English–German Animal Dictionary* page uses the **keys** function to print the English animal names, and it uses the **values** function to print the German counterparts. Figure 17.23 contains the syntax for these two functions.

(a) Extracting the keys from a hash	(b) Extracting the values from a hash
`foreach $key(keys %dictionary)` `{ print "$key \n";}`	`foreach $value(values %dictionary)` `{ print "$value \n";}`

Figure 17.23 The **keys** and **values** Functions

To extract either the keys or values from a hash, we use a **foreach** statement. Rather than placing an array variable as a parameter, we use **keys** *%hash* when we want to extract the keys, and we use **values** *%hash* when we want to extract the values. In the current example, the hash's name is *dictionary*.

Figure 17.24 contains the complete Perl code for the *English–German Animal Dictionary* page. The code that creates the hash and extracts the keys and values is highlighted.

Adding Key–Value Pairs to a Hash

Figure 17.25 contains a revision of the *English–German Animal Dictionary* page. The page now includes toads and turtles. The new animals were added after the original hash was created. The page also illustrates two look-ups: one for *Dogs*, which is a key in the hash table, and one for *Oxen*, which is not a key in the hash table. Notice the message printed with *Oxen*.

Figure 17.26(a) contains the syntax for adding a key–value pair to a hash. A new hash element is a scalar, so we use scalar notation. The new key, which can be either a literal or a variable, is encased in braces. The associated value, which also might be either a literal or a variable, appears on the right-hand side of the assignment operator.

Figure 17.26(b) contains the syntax for extracting a value from a hash table. The syntax is the reverse of adding a key–value pair. We place the scalar variable that will hold the value on the left-hand side of an assignment statement. We place the hash variable, with key enclosed in braces, on the right-hand side of the assignment statement. The key can be either a literal or a variable. Perl returns the value if the key exists in the hash table; otherwise, Perl returns the empty string. (Hence, the empty German equivalent for *Oxen*.)

```
#!/usr/local/bin/perl
%dictionary = ("cows", "K&uuml;he", "horses", "Pferde", "fish", "Fische","birds", "V&ouml;gel",
"cats", "Katzen", "dogs", "Hunde");

print "Content-type: text/html", "\n\n";
print "<HTML> <HEAD>", "\n";
print "<TITLE>Hashes</TITLE></HEAD>\n";
print "<BODY BGCOLOR = 'white'>\n";
print "<TABLE BORDER = '1' CELLPADDING = '5'>\n";
print "<CAPTION>English-German Animal Dictionary</CAPTION>\n";
print "<TR><TH>English</TH>\n";
print "<TH><I>Deutsch</I> </TH></TR>\n";
print "<TR><TD>\n";
foreach $key(keys %dictionary)
{ print "$key<BR>\n";}
print "</TD><TD>\n";
foreach $value(values %dictionary)
{ print "$value<BR>\n";}
print "</TD></TR></TABLE>\n";
print "</BODY></HTML>", "\n";
exit(0);
```

Figure 17.24 Perl Code for the *English–German Animal Dictionary* Page

Figure 17.25 Adding Animals to the *English–German Dictionary*

(a) Adding a Key-Value Pair	(b) Extracting a Value
$hash_variable{key} = value;	*$value = $hash_variable{key};*

Figure 17.26 Adding a Key–Value Pair

Figure 17.27 contains the Perl code for the revised version of the *English–German Animal Dictionary* page. In addition to adding key–value pairs for *turtles* and *toads* and looking up the values for *Dogs* and *Oxen*, this code also shows a new approach to handling the keys or values in a hash. The statements

```
@english = keys(%dictionary);
@deutsch = values(%dictionary);
```

place the keys into array named **@english** and the values into an array named **@german**. We use these arrays to print a table of the English words and their German counterparts.

```
#!/usr/local/bin/perl
%dictionary = ("cows", "K&uuml;he", "horses", "Pferde", "fish", "Fische","birds", "V&ouml;gel",
"cats", "Katzen", "dogs", "Hunde");

#add turtles and toads to the dictionary
$dictionary{"toads"} = "Kr&ouml;ten";
$new_key = "turtles";
$new_value = "Schildkr&ouml;ten";
$dictionary{$new_key} = $new_value;

@english = keys(%dictionary);
@deutsch = values(%dictionary);

print "Content-type: text/html", "\n\n";
print "<HTML> <HEAD>", "\n";
print "<TITLE>Hashes</TITLE></HEAD>\n";
print "<BODY BGCOLOR = 'white'>\n";
print "<TABLE BORDER = '1' CELLPADDING = '5'>\n";
print "<CAPTION>English-German Animal Dictionary</CAPTION>\n";
print "<TR><TH>English</TH>\n";
print "<TH><I>Deutsch</I> </TH></TR>\n";
print "<TR><TD>\n";
foreach $word(@english)
{ print "$word<BR>\n";}
print "</TD><TD>\n";
foreach $word(@deutsch)
{ print "$word<BR>\n";}
print "</TD></TR></TABLE>\n";
#lookup words
$lookup = $dictionary{"dogs"};
print "<P>Dogs is $lookup in German.<P>\n";
$lookup = $dictionary{"oxen"};
print "Oxen is $lookup in German.\n";
print "</BODY></HTML>", "\n";
exit(0);
```

Figure 17.27 Perl Code for the *English–German Animal Dictionary* Page, version 2

REMOVING KEY–VALUE PAIRS

The third (and our final) example of the *English–German Animal Dictionary* page appears in Figure 17.28. This version illustrates deletions of key–value pairs. We also use the **each** function to print the list after the deletions.

Figure 17.28 The *English–German Animal Dictionary* Page, version 3

Figure 17.29(a) contains the syntax for deleting a key–value pair from a hash. Figure 17.29(b) shows the Perl code that deletes toads and fish from the *English–German Animal Dictionary*.

As Figure 17.29 indicates, we delete a key–value pair by using the hash variable, represented as a scalar, with the key name enclosed in braces, as a parameter to the **delete** function. If the key exists, Perl removes the key–value pair; otherwise, it ignores the **delete** operation.

(a) Syntax for Deletion	(b) Deletion Examples

`delete $hash_variable{key};`	`delete $dictionary{"toads"};`
	`$name = "fish";`
	`delete $dictionary{$name};`

Figure 17.29 Hash Deletions

The each Function

In addition to the **foreach** statement, Perl provides an **each** statement that is specifically designed to extract key–value pairs from a hash. The **each** statement is usually coupled with a **while** statement, is shown in the syntax example given in Figure 17.30.

```
while (($key, $value) = each(%hash_variable)){
    Statements to process keys and values;
}
```

Figure 17.30 Syntax for the **each** statement

The use of parentheses in Figure 17.30 provides the clue to determining how the **each** statement works. The innermost parentheses,

> **($key, $value)** = **each(%hash_variable)**

indicate that Perl should extract *each* key–value pair. The first variable in the parenthesized list on the left-hand side of the assignment operator holds the key; the second variable holds the value.

The **while** statement executes the statements in the body as long as the variables holding the key and value are not empty. The **each** function returns empty strings when Perl has processed all the key–value pairs in a hash.

Figure 17.31 contains the Perl code for the final version of the *English–German Animal Dictionary* page.

```perl
#!/usr/local/bin/perl
%dictionary = ("cows", "K&uuml;he", "horses", "Pferde", "fish", "Fische","birds", "V&ouml;gel",
"cats", "Katzen", "dogs", "Hunde", "toads", "Kr&ouml;ten");

print "Content-type: text/html", "\n\n";
print "<HTML> <HEAD>", "\n";
print "<TITLE>Hashes</TITLE></HEAD>\n";
print "<BODY BGCOLOR = 'white'>\n";
print "<TABLE BORDER = '1' CELLPADDING = '5'>\n";
print "<CAPTION>English-German Animal Dictionary</CAPTION>\n";
print "<TR><TH>English</TH>\n";
print "<TH>Deutsch</TH>\n";
print "<TH> After Deletions</TH> </TR>\n";
print "<TR><TD VALIGN = 'top'>\n";
foreach $word(keys %dictionary)
{ print "$word<BR>\n";}
print "</TD><TD VALIGN = 'top'>\n";
foreach $word(values %dictionary)
{ print "$word<BR>\n";}
delete $dictionary{"toads"};
$name = "fish";
delete $dictionary{$name};
print "</TD><TD VALIGN = 'top'>";
while (($english, $german) = each(%dictionary))
{ print "$english = $german<BR>\n";}
print "</TD></TR></TABLE>\n";
print "</BODY></HTML>", "\n";
exit(0);
```

Figure 17.31 Perl Code for the *English–Animal Dictionary* Page, final version

The ENV Hash

As a last example of a simple hash, we examine the built-in ENV hash. The ENV hash contains information about the user's browser, including the server software and the CGI interface. Figure 17.32 contains a sample page. The keys appear in the left column; the values for the author's server appear in the right column.

At some point, you will want to obtain information for your server. The Perl code appearing in Figure 17.33 prints out each of the keys and associated values. Load the code into your browser and compare your results with those appearing in Figure 17.32.

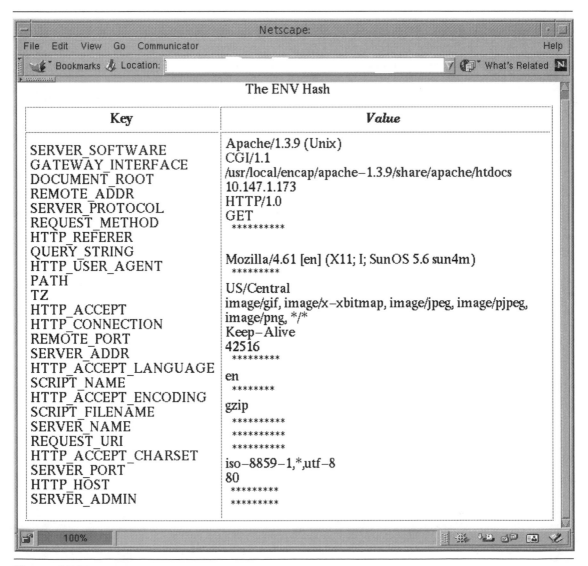

Figure 17.32 The *Environmental Hash* Page

```
#!/usr/local/bin/perl
print "Content-type: text/html", "\n\n";
print "<HTML><HEAD><TITLE></TITLE></HEAD>\n";
print "<BODY BGCOLOR = 'white'>\n";
@key = keys(%ENV);
@value = values(%ENV);

print "<TABLE BORDER = '1' CELLPADDING = '5'>\n";
print "<CAPTION>The ENV Hash</CAPTION>\n";
print "<TR><TH>Key</TH>\n";
print "<TH><I>Value</I> </TH></TR>\n";
print "<TR><TD>\n";
foreach $word(@key)
{ print "$word<BR>\n";}
print "</TD><TD>\n";
foreach $word(@value)
{ print "$word<BR>\n";}
print "</TD></TR></TABLE>\n";
print "<\BODY><\HTML>\n";
exit(0);
```

Figure 17.33 Perl Code for the *Environmental Hash* Page

ARRAYS OF HASHES

We conclude this chapter by creating two complex structures in Perl: an array of hashes, and a hash of hashes. Both examples involve multilanguage dictionaries. Figure 17.34 contains the first example: an array of hashes. The first column contains the Arabic representation of the numbers from 1 to 5. The second, third, and fourth columns contain the English, German, and Tibetan equivalents. The English and German are written equivalents; the Tibetan is a phonetic equivalent. A simple lookup for the English equivalent of "0" appears below the table. We could also conduct similar lookups for German and Tibetan numbers.

Figure 17.35 contains the Perl code that creates the array of hashes.

The declaration of the **@numbers** array uses parentheses to encase the list comprising the array components. Because each of the array components is a hash, we use braces **{}** to encase each array component. Perl always indexes arrays from zero, so the first set of braces contains the English and German equivalents for "0". The Tibetan equivalent is missing. Thus, the statement

```
{#0
    english => "zero",
    german => "null",},
```

indicates that **$numbers[0]** contains a hash with two keys, *english* and *german*. The *english* key has an associated value of *zero,* the *german* key has an associated value of *null.* The next set of braces contains the hash for **$numbers[1]**. This hash contains *english, german,* and *tibetan* keys with associated values of *one, eins,* and *chik,* respectively. The remaining indices follow a similar pattern. Notice the use of comments to highlight the indices.

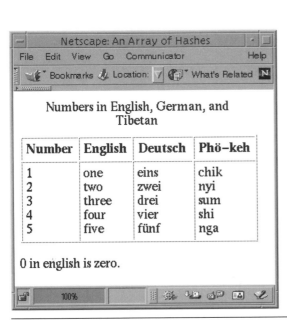

Figure 17.34 A *Multilanguage Counting Dictionary* Page

```
@numbers = (
   {#0
      english => "zero",
      german => "null",},
   {#1
      english => "one",
      german => "eins",
      tibetan => "chik", },
   {#2
      english => "two",
      german => "zwei",
      tibetan => "nyi", },
   {#3
      english => "three",
      german => "drei",
      tibetan => "sum", },
   {#4
      english => "four",
      german => "vier",
      tibetan => "shi", },
   {#5
      english => "five",
      german => "f&uuml;nf",
      tibetan => "nga", },);
```

Figure 17.35 The **numbers** Array

Accessing Elements in an Array of Hashes

To access an element in an array of hashes, we use both array and hash notation. Figure 17.36 contains the syntax for accessing an element.

$*array*[**index**]{*key*}

Figure 17.36 Access Method, Array of Hashes

As Figure 17.36 indicates, we use scalar notation, $*array*, to access an individual element, because individual elements are scalars. However, the underlying structure is an array, so we place the desired index after the variable name. The index can be either a literal or a variable. The hash key follows the index. The hash key can also be either a literal or a variable. For example, suppose we want to print the Tibetan equivalent of 5; the code that does this is

```
$number5 = $numbers[5]{tibetan};
print "5 is phonetically equivalent to $number5 in Tibetan.\n";
```

We use a **for** statement to print all of the language equivalents. For example, the following statements print the Tibetan equivalents of the numbers from 1 to 5:

```
for ($i= 1; $i < $size; $i++) {
  $tibetan = $numbers[$i]{tibetan};
  print "$tibetan<BR>\n"; }
```

Figure 17.37 contains the Perl code for the *Multilanguage Counting Dictionary* page.

```
#!/usr/local/bin/perl
#Put the declaration of @numbers HERE
print "Content-type: text/html", "\n\n";
print "<HTML> <HEAD>", "\n";
print "<TITLE>An Array of Hashes</TITLE></HEAD>\n";
print "<BODY BGCOLOR = 'white'>\n";
print "<TABLE BORDER = '1' CELLPADDING = '5'>\n";
print "<CAPTION>Numbers in English, German, and Tibetan</CAPTION>\n";
print "<TR><TH>Number</TH><TH>English</TH>\n";
print "<TH>Deutsch </TH>\n";
print "<TH> Ph&ouml;-keh</TH></TR>\n";
print "<TR><TD>\n";
$size = @numbers;
for ($i=1; $i < $size; $i++)
{ print "$i<BR>\n"; }
print "</TD><TD>\n";
for ($i= 1; $i < $size; $i++) {
  $english = $numbers[$i]{english};
  print "$english<BR>\n"; }
print "</TD><TD>\n";
for ($i= 1; $i < $size; $i++) {
  $german = $numbers[$i]{german};
  print "$german<BR>\n"; }
print "</TD><TD>\n";
for ($i= 1; $i < $size; $i++) {
  $tibetan = $numbers[$i]{tibetan};
  print "$tibetan<BR>\n"; }
print "</TD></TR></TABLE>\n";
print "</BODY></HTML>", "\n";

$zero = $numbers[0]{english};
print "<P> 0 in english is $zero.\n";
exit(0);
```

Figure 17.37 Perl Code for the *Multilanguage Counting Dictionary* Page

A Hash of Hashes

To illustrate a hash of hashes, we create a *Multilanguage Weekdays* page. This page lets users find the German and Tibetan (phonetic) equivalents of English weekdays. Figure 17.38 contains a sample page. The page illustrates both a German and Tibetan lookup. It would be pointless to print a complete lookup table, because the weekdays would be randomized by the Perl compiler.

Figure 17.39 contain the Perl code for the declaration of the *weekdays* hash.

The declaration of the *weekdays* hash uses parentheses to enclose the hashes. The first declaration—

```
'Monday' =>
  {
      german => "Montag",
      tibetan => "sa da wa",
  },
```

Figure 17.38 A *Multilanguage Weekdays* Page

```
%weekdays = (
    'Monday' =>
    {
       german => "Montag",
       tibetan => "sa da wa",
    },
    'Tuesday' =>
    {
       german => "Dienstag",
       tibetan => "sa mik ma",
    },
    'Wednesday' =>
    {
       german => "Mittwoch",
       tibetan => "sa lak pa",
    },
    'Thursday' =>
    {
       german => "Donnerstag",
       tibetan => "sa phu ba",
    },
    'Friday' =>
    {
       german => "Freitag",
       tibetan => "sa pa sahng",
    },
  );
```

Figure 17.39 The *weekdays* Hash

—indicates that *Monday* is a hash key whose associated value is a second hash,

```
{
        german => "Montag",
        tibetan => "sa da wa",
    },
```

The internal hash contains two keys, `german` and `tibetan`, with associated values of `Montag` and *sa da wa*, respectively.

The remaining hashes are created in a similar fashion.

Accessing Elements in a Hash of Hashes

Figure 17.40 contains the syntax for accessing an element in a hash of hashes.

`$hash_name{OuterHashKey}{InnerHashKey}`

Figure 17.40 Access Method: Hash of Hashes

As Figure 17.40 indicates, we use scalar notation to access an individual value in a hash of hashes. We place the two hash keys after the name of the hash. The outer hash key precedes the inner hash key. For example, to print the Tibetan phonetic equivalent of Wednesday, we would write

```
$tibetan = $weekdays{'Wednesday'}{tibetan};
print "Wednesday in Tibetan is $tibetan.\n";
```

Figure 17.41 contains the Perl code for the *Multilanguage Weekdays* page.

```
#!/usr/local/bin/perl
#Put the weekdays hash declaration HERE

print "Content-type: text/html", "\n\n";
print "<HTML> <HEAD>", "\n";
print "<TITLE>An Array of Hashes</TITLE></HEAD>\n";
print "<BODY BGCOLOR = 'white'>\n";

$german = $weekdays{'Monday'}{german};
print "Monday in German is $german.<BR>\n";
$tibetan = $weekdays{'Tuesday'}{tibetan};
print "Tuesday in Tibetan is $tibetan.\n";
print "</BODY></HTML>", "\n";
exit(0);
```

Figure 17.41 Perl Code for the *Multilanguage Weekdays* Page

A Final Note. We have created arrays of arrays, arrays of hashes, and hashes of hashes. Can we also create a hash of arrays? The answer is yes, and in Chapter 20 we use this structure to process multifield forms.

➤ ■ **EXERCISES**

1. **The *Arithmetic Mean* Page.** Create a Perl version of the *Arithmetic Mean* page. (See Figure 13.23.)

2. **The *Factorial* Page.** Modify the JavaScript *Factorial* page discussed in Chapter 11. (See Figures 11.10 through 11.13). Your new page should be written in Perl.

3. **The *Multiplication Table* Page.** Rewrite the *Multiplication Table* page (shown in Figures 11.14 through 11.19) as a Perl script. Write the multiplication table for the numbers from one to seven.

4. **The *Sequential Search* Page.** Create a Perl version of the *Sequential Search* page. (See Figure 13.14.)

5. **The *Harmonic Function* Page.** Rewrite the *Harmonic Function* page as a Perl script. Pick a value of your choice for *n*. (See Figure 11.32.)

6. **The *Alternating Series* Page.** Rewrite the *Alternating Series Function* page as a Perl script. Pick a value of your choice for *n*. (See Figure 11.33.)

7. **The *Kitchen Conversions* Page.** Rewrite the *Kitchen Conversions* page as a Perl script. Pick values of your choice for the lowest and highest liters. (See Figure 11.34.)

8. **The *Liquid Measures* Page.** Rewrite the *Liquid Measures* as a Perl script. Pick values of your choice for the lowest and highest cups. (See Figure 11.36.)

9. **The *Fahrenheit-to-Celsius Conversion* Page.** Rewrite the *Celsius-to-Fahrenheit* page as a Perl Script. (See Figure 11.2 through Figure 11.6). Use −20 as the lowest Celsius value and 40 as the highest. Print the temperatures at two-degree increments.

10. **The *Matrix Page*.** Create a Perl page that sums the rows and columns in a two-dimensional array. Print the matrix and the row and columns sums.

11. **The *Phone Number* Page.** Create a hash (associative array) with the names of your five best friends as the keys and their phone numbers as the values.

12. **The *Mailing List* Page.** Use a hash of hashes to create a mailing list. The person's name is the key; the street address, city, state, and zip are keys for the secondary hash tables.

13. **The *Thesaurus* Page.** Create a small thesaurus. Pick several of your favorite words as the keys. Make the list of similar words the values.

14. **The *Dictionary* Page.** Create a JavaScript dictionary. Use the terms appearing in Chapters 16 and 17 as the keys. Use the definitions as the values.

15. **The *HTML Tags Dictionary* Page.** Pick several HTML tags from Part I. Use the tags (without the angular brackets) as the keys. Use the definitions appearing in Part I as the values, or make up definitions of your own.

16. **The *??? -English Dictionary* Page.** Pick a language of your choice (other than German or Tibetan). Use words from that language as the keys. The values are to be the English counterparts.

17. **The *Multilanguage Counting* Page, Revisited.** Add Spanish and Japanese to the *Multi-Language Counting Dictionary* Page. (See Figures 17.34 through 17.37 and Figure 25.42.) The numbers from 1 to 5 in Spanish are uno, dos, tres, cuatro, cinco. The numbers from 1 to 5 in Japanese are ichi, ni, san, chi, go.

18. **The *Multilanguage Weekday* Page, Revisioted.** Create a table that prints the weekdays and the Tibetan and German equivalents. In what order are the weekdays listed?

19. **The *Multilanguage Weekdays* Page, Revisited Again.** Add another language of your choice to the *Multilanguage Weekdays* page.

20. **The *Multilanguage Greetings* Page.** Creating a hash of hashes of greetings. Use the greetings found in Figure 17.42, or add languages of your choice.

English	Spanish	Tibetan
Hello.	Hola.	Tashi deleh.
Good bye.	Adios.	Kah leh pe.

Figure 17.42 Greetings in Three Languages

21. **The *Pattern Matching* Page.** Create an array containing the names of ten friends or family members. Choose a two-letter pattern, such as *us*, that occurs in at least two names in your list. Use the **grep** function to create a new array that contains the names of the individuals who match your pattern.

➤ **PERL VOCABULARY**

Anonymous Reference. An anonymous reference is an unnamed reference. We typically use anonymous references when creating two-dimensional arrays. (See Figure 17.18(a).)

Associative Array. *Associative array* is another name for a hash.

Hash. A Perl structure that organizes information on randomly stored and accessed key–value pairs.

List. We create a Perl list by placing scalars in parentheses. We use commas to separate the scalars. Lists are typically found on the right-hand side of an assignment statement that creates an array or a hash.

Reference. A reference is a variable that holds the address of another variable.

18 URLencoding, Patterns, Text Fields, and Selection Statements

INTRODUCTION

This chapter covers several seemingly disparate subjects. We begin the chapter with a review of the HTML form tag in preparation for creating Perl scripts that process forms. Unlike JavaScript, which automatically "decodes" form information, a Perl script receives a URLencoded string. Before we can use the form's information, we must decode it. Decoding requires knowledge of Perl's pattern operators. We examine these operators gradually, reserving a complete discussion for the final section of this chapter. Perl's set of pattern operators is both complex and rich, so you might choose to ignore that final section until you need to decipher complex patterns. We also examine Perl's selection statements in this chapter, and we create frame-based pages that display both the user's completed form and the processed results.

THE HTML <FORM> TAG, REVISITED

Figure 18.1 shows the HTML **<FORM>** tag listed with its optional attributes. When we create a form that will be processed with a Perl script, we must use both the **ACTION** and the **METHOD** attributes. The **ACTION** attribute holds the URL of the Perl script that processes the form's data. The **METHOD** attribute holds the data transmission method used by the browser.

```
<FORM NAME = "form.name"opt
    ACTION = "URL"
    METHOD = "POST | GET"
    ENCTYPE = "mimeType"opt
    TARGET = "Target Page or Frame"opt
    onSubmit = "eventHandler"opt
    onReset = "eventHandler"opt>
    formElement1
        ....
    formElementn
</FORM>
```

Figure 18.1 The HTML <FORM> Tag

Browsers can submit data to a script by using either the **GET** or the **POST** method. The **GET** method requires a URLencoded string containing less than 256 characters. The browser truncates (chops off) the string at 255 characters. Thus, we use the **GET** method when we have small forms with only a few data fields. Search engines, which contain a single field for the search string, constitute the most common use of the **GET** method. We use the **POST** method when the URLencoded string exceeds 255 characters. We explore both transmission methods in this chapter.

URLENCODING

When a browser sends a completed form to a CGI script for processing, it uses URLencoding. Figure 18.2 shows the encoding scheme.

Encoding Symbol	Meaning
&	The ampersand separates the form's fields.
=	The assignment operator separates a field name from the user's response.
+	Plus signs are used to transmit spaces.
%	Hexadecimal notation is used to represent non-alphanumeric characters.

Figure 18.2 URLencoding

To illustrate URLencoding, we examine the form contained in Figure 18.3. This form asks the user to enter first and last names and Social Security Number. The form uses five input fields, two for the name and three for the Social Security Number (SSN). Arrows link the fields with the **<INPUT>** tags used to create them. Look at these **<INPUT>** tags, and then examine the *Netsite* window. The window shows the URLencoding for the completed form.

In addition to revealing the URLencoding, the *Netsite* window also reveals the data transmission method. This page uses the **GET** method to pass data to the script. The **GET** method always places the URLencoded data in the *Netsite* window. The script's name and a question mark, **?**,

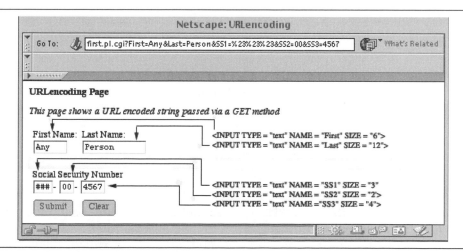

Figure 18.3 A Form with URLencoded Data

precede the URLencoded data. The **POST** method does not display the URLencoded data in the *Netsite* window.

Let's examine the URLencoded data more closely, beginning with the ampersand, **&**, symbol. The URLencoded string is

```
First=Any&Last=Person&SS1=%23%23%23&SS2=00&SS3=4567
```

Separating the string at the ampersands reveals the name–data pairs. Figure 18.4 contains these pairs.

Field Name=User Data
First=Any
Last=Person
SS1=%23%23%23
SS2=00
SS3=4567

Figure 18.4 The Field Name–User Data Pairs

Refer back to Figure 18.3. Notice the correspondence between these pairs and the field names in the **<INPUT>** tag and the user's data in the completed form. Notice also the user's data for the first Social Security Number, **SS1**. Because the pound sign is not an alphanumeric character, the browser uses the ASCII value for the pound symbol, represented as a hexadecimal number (**%23**).

Obviously, we must decode the URLencoded data before we can use it. We could opt to use one of the readily available packages that provide "automatic" decoding—for example, **cgi.pm**. Although these packages are helpful, it's quite easy to write your own decoding package. This chapter covers the basics of decoding, which we'll package into subroutines in the next chapter. By the time we're finished, you will have written your own decoding package. We will develop the decoding package in small, simple steps. The first forms focus on understanding the decoding process and the transmission methods.

The GET Method

Figure 18.5 contains a simple form that asks the user to enter a first name. The user has entered a "goofy" name. The name contains nonalphabetic characters, including several "suspicious" characters, that is, characters that a malicious user could use to wreak havoc on a server.

Figure 18.6 contains the HTML for the *First Name* page. The form elements are embedded in a borderless table. The HTML tags that create the form are highlighted.

The **<FORM>** tag used in the *First Name* page contains a **METHOD** attribute that specifies the **GET** method as the data transmission method. The **ACTION** attribute identifies the script that processes this form as *nameGet.pl.cgi*. The browser passes the form's data to the script when the user presses the *Submit Form!* button. The tag that creates this button is

```
<INPUT TYPE = "submit" VALUE = "Submit Form">
```

The **VALUE** attribute changes the default label, the submit button. If you prefer the default label, *Submit Query*, don't use the **VALUE** attribute.

The *First Name* page also contains a *Clear Form* button, created with the following tag:

```
<INPUT TYPE="reset" VALUE="Clear Form">
```

Figure 18.5 The *First Name* Page, **Get** Version

```
<HTML><HEAD><TITLE> Form Processing Using get</TITLE></HEAD>
<BODY BGCOLOR = 'white'>
<CENTER><TABLE>
<TR><TD><H1>What is your first name?</H1></TD></TR>
<TR><TD>
<FORM ACTION="nameGet.pl.cgi" METHOD = "GET">
<INPUT  TYPE="text" NAME="Name" SIZE="12"></TD></TR>
<TR><TD>
<INPUT TYPE="submit" VALUE="Submit Form!">
<INPUT TYPE="reset"  VALUE="Clear Form">
</FORM></TD></TR>
</TABLE></CENTER>
</BODY></HTML>
```

Figure 18.6 HTML for the *First Name Form*

The **VALUE** attribute changes the default label from *Reset* to *Clear Form*. As its name implies, this button restores the form to its original state.

Figure 18.7 contains the processed *First Name* page. The Perl script prints several key–value pairs from the **ENV** hash, as well as the URLencoded string and the processed name field. Normally, we would print only the processed fields, but, in these early stages, the **ENV** hash and the URLencoded string will provide us clues to the data-passing method and the URLencoding. Look at the values associated with the **ENV** keys. Only the **REQUEST_METHOD** and **QUERY_STRING** keys have nonempty values. The **REQUEST-METHOD** indicates that the **GET** method was used to transmit the data. When the form uses the **GET** method, the **QUERY_STRING** holds the URLencoded string.

Decoding the *First Name* Form: A Five-Step Approach

Decoding the *First Name* form requires five steps. Although each step translates into a single line of Perl code, the details are "gory." If you don't understand the details, don't worry. We'll look at several more forms in this chapter. You'll see the same set of steps and code used repeatedly.

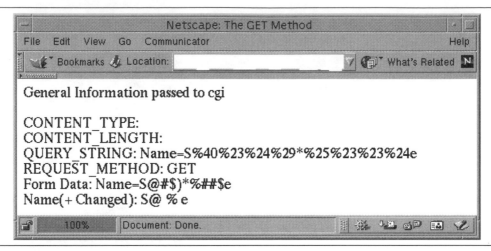

Figure 18.7 The "processed" *First Name* Page

We use the following steps to process the *First Name* page:

Step 1. Obtain the Form's Data. We obtain the form data by assigning the value associated with the **QUERY_STRING** key to a scalar variable. The following assignment statement accomplishes this task:

```
$form_data = $ENV{'QUERY_STRING'};
```

Step 2. Convert Hexadecimal Characters to Their ASCII Equivalents. The user entered several hexadecimal characters as part of the first name. We must convert these characters (%40, %23, %24, %29, and %25) back to their original character representations [@, #, $,), and %, respectively]. Conversion requires the Perl **pack()** function and the substitution (**s///**) and match/assignment operators (**=~**) operators. The code that handles the conversion is

```
$form_data =~ s/%([\dA-Fa-f][\dA-Fa-f])/pack ("C", hex ($1))/eg;
```

Let's examine the operators and **pack()** function separately, beginning with the match/assignment operator.

A. The match/assignment Operator. The match/assignment operator, **=~**, also called a binding operator, "binds" the pattern produced on the right-hand side of the operator to the variable appearing on the left-hand side of the operator. The current example indicates that we will bind the result of the substitution operator to the scalar variable **$form_data**.

B. The substitution Operator. We use the substitution operator to modify strings that do not have conflicting (or simultaneous) substitutions. When we have simultaneous substitutions, we use the transliteration operator discussed at the end of this chapter. For example, if we want to change all of the upper-case letters in a string to their lower-case equivalents, while also changing all of the lower-case letters to their upper-case equivalents, we have a simultaneous substitution. On the other hand, if we want to change the plus signs to spaces or hexadecimal characters to their ASCII equivalents, we have a nonsimultaneous substitution.

Figure 18.8 contains the syntax for the substitution operator and the valid options that we may use with it.

Substitution Operator Syntax	Options
s/_string_**/**_replacement pattern_**/**_options_	e: Evaluate the replacement as a pattern
	g: Global replacement (throughout string)
	i: Ignore case
	m: Treat strings as multi-lines

Figure 18.8 The Substitution Operator

As Figure 18.8 indicates, the substitution operator uses slashes to separate the string, replacement pattern, and options. The string represents the hexadecimal digits found in **$form_data**. Hexadecimal digits always have the pattern %XX, where X is a letter between A and F or between a and f or a number between zero and nine. The Perl version of this pattern is

%([\dA-Fa-f][\dA-Fa-f])

We represent this pattern as a regular expression. The regular expression begins with a percent sign. The parenthesized expression that follows the percent sign identifies the pattern that we will change. Perl uses scalar variables to number parenthesized expressions in a regular expression. The first parenthesized expression is **$1**, the second is **$2**, and so on up to **$9**. The parenthesized expression holds the pattern for two hexadecimal digits. The pattern, **[\dA-Fa-f]**, indicates that we are searching for a digit (**\d**), an upper-case letter between A and F, or a lower-case letter between a and f. This is the standard definition of one hexadecimal digit.

The replacement for a hexadecimal digit is the result returned by calling the **pack()** function. Finally, the substitution operator uses the _e_ and _g_ options. The _global_ option indicates that Perl should look for the pattern through the entire string, that is, the entire **$form_data** variable. The evaluate option indicates that it should evaluate any expressions.

C. The **pack()** *Function.*   The **pack()** function requires two parameters. The first parameter specifies the result type. In the current example, C indicates that we wish to replace the original hexadecimal characters (XX) with their ASCII character (C) equivalents. The second parameter specifies the current format of the data. In this example, **hex($1)**, indicates that the data is in hexadecimal format.

Step 3. Separate the Field Name from User Data.   The *First Name* page contains a single data field, so the next step is the separation of the field name from the user's data. (In a multifield form, we would have to separate the fields before we perform this step.) The browser sends the data to the script in _field name = data_ form. To separate the field name from the data, we use the **split()** function. This function uses a pattern to split a string into constituent parts. We can place these parts into scalar variables or into an array. The **split()** statement that we use to separate field name and data is

```
($field_name, $name) = split (/=/, $form_data);
```

This statement indicates that we are splitting **$form_data** at the equal sign. Anything to the left of the equal sign is placed in **$field_name**. Anything to the right of the equal sign is placed in **$name**. The equal sign is discarded. Thus, after Perl executes this statement, **$field_name** and **$name** contain _Name_ and _S@#$)*##$e_, respectively.

Step 4. Remove Suspicious Characters.   After the split operation, **$name** holds the user's data. Before processing the form further, we'll want to remove suspicious characters. Figure 18.9 contains a list of suspicious and suspect characters. The characters contained in Figure 18.9(a) are suspicious because they represent operators used in operating-system shell languages. We already know that text enclosed in back quotation marks executes Unix commands. The asterisk

(a) Suspicious Characters	(b) Suspect Characters
; < > & * ` |	( ) { } ! # : " ' \ $

Figure 18.9 Suspicious and Suspect Characters

and period are wild cards for pattern matching. Combining these operators would let a malicious user remove all of the files in the current directory with the command `rm *.*`.

Figure 18.9(b) contains characters that are not generally harmful when used alone, but form users should not need these characters to complete most Web forms, so we can remove them as well from the form data.

We use the substitution and match/assignment operators to remove the suspicious and suspect operators. The single statement that accomplishes this task is

```
$name =~ s/[;<>\(\)\{\}\*\|'`\&\$!#:"\\]/\ $1/g;
```

This statement contains the set, denoted by brackets, of symbols that we wish to replace. Several of these characters, most notably ( ) { } * & \, are part of the pattern-matching language, so we must denote them by escape sequences. (Remember an escape sequence is a character sequence that begins with a backslash.) The replacement pattern /\ $1/ indicates that we will replace every character in the set with a space. Everything that is not suspect is unchanged. (This is the significance of the $1.)

Step 5. Convert Plus Signs To Spaces. URLencoding replaces all spaces with plus signs, so, as our last step, we transform the plus signs back to spaces. We use a simple substitution to accomplish this task. The statement is

```
$name =~ s/+/\ $1/g;
```

Figure 18.10 contains the complete Perl code for the *First Name* page. The Perl code that decodes the data is highlighted.

```
#!/usr/local/bin/perl
print "Content-type: text/html", "\n\n";
print "<HTML><HEAD><TITLE>The GET Method</TITLE></HEAD>\n";

print "<BODY BGCOLOR = 'white'>\n";
$form_data = $ENV{'QUERY_STRING'}; #1
$form_data =~ s/%([\dA-Fa-f][\dA-Fa-f])/pack ("C", hex ($1))/eg; #2
print "General Information passed to cgi<P>\n";
print "CONTENT_TYPE:  $ENV{'CONTENT_TYPE'}<BR>\n";
print "CONTENT_LENGTH:  $ENV{'CONTENT_LENGTH'}<BR>\n";
print "QUERY_STRING: $ENV{'QUERY_STRING'}<BR>\n";
print "REQUEST_METHOD: $ENV{'REQUEST_METHOD'}<BR>\n";
print "Form Data:  $form_data<BR>\n";
($field_name, $name) = split (/=/, $form_data); #3
$name =~ s/[;<>\(\)\{\}\*\|'`\&\$!#:"\\]/\ $1/g; #4
$name =~ s/+/\ $1/g;   #5
print "Name(+ Changed): $name<BR>\n";
print "<\BODY><\HTML>\n";
exit (0);
```

Figure 18.10 Perl Code for the *nameGet.pl.cgi* Script

The POST Method

Figure 18.11 contains a modified version of the *First Name* page. The new version uses the POST method to past the user's data to the script. In short forms, we can use either the POST or the GET method. When the URLencoded string exceeds 255 characters, we must use the POST method, because the QUERY_STRING cannot hold more than 255 characters.

Figure 18.11 The *First Name* Page: POST version

As Figure 18.11 indicates, Netscape displays a *Security Warning* box whenever the POST method is used to transmit data. The user must press the *Continue Submission* button to submit the data to the script.

Figure 18.12 contains the HTML for the POST version of the *First Name* page. Only the values attached to the ACTION and the METHOD attributes of the <FORM> tag have been changed. The remainder of the code is identical to that for the GET version of this page. The METHOD attribute indicates that the POST method is used to transmit data to the script. The ACTION attribute contains the name of the new script, *namePost.pl.cgi*.

```
<HTML><HEAD><TITLE> Form Processing</TITLE></HEAD>
<BODY BGCOLOR = 'white'>
<CENTER><TABLE>
<TR><TD><H1>What is your first name?</H1></TD></TR>
<TR><TD><FORM ACTION="namePost.pl.cgi" METHOD = "POST">
<INPUT  TYPE="text" NAME="Name" SIZE="12"></TD></TR>
<TR><TD><INPUT TYPE="submit" VALUE="Submit Form!">
<INPUT TYPE="reset"  VALUE="Clear Form">
</FORM></TD></TR>
</TABLE></CENTER></BODY></HTML>
```

Figure 18.12 HTML for the *First Name* Page: POST version

Figure 18.13 contains the page produced by the *namePost.pl.cgi* script. This script prints several keys and their corresponding values from the **ENV** hash. Carefully compare the values appearing in Figure 18.13 with the values displayed in Figure 18.7. What differences do you notice in the values associated with the displayed keys from the **ENV** hash?

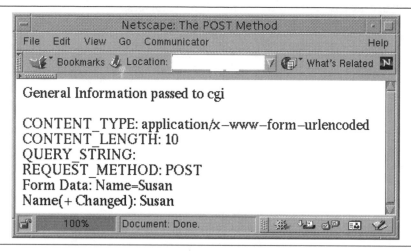

Figure 18.13 The Processed *First Name* Page: **POST** version

As Figure 18.13 indicates, when we use the **POST** method, the browser assigns values for the **CONTENT_TYPE** and **CONTENT_LENGTH** keys of the **ENV** hash. If you count the characters in the form data passed to the script (*Name=Susan*), you'll discover that this count matches the value associated with the **CONTENT_LENGTH** key. The content length is crucial, because the **POST** method reads the form's data from the standard input device. Without the content length, we would not know how many characters to read.

We're now ready to decode the **POST** version of the *First Name* page. We use the same five-step approach discussed with the **GET** method.

Decoding the *First Name* Form: POST Method

Step 1: Obtain the Form's Data. Obtaining the form data requires two lines of code when we use the **POST** method. We begin with an assignment statement that places the value associated with the **CONTENT_LENGTH** key into a scalar variable, *form_size*:

```
$form_size = $ENV{'CONTENT_LENGTH'};
```

Next, we use the Perl **read()** function to read the form's data from the standard input device. The **read()** function requires three parameters. The first parameter contains the name of the input device. The code calls for the standard input device, which Perl calls **STDIN**. The second parameter is a scalar variable that holds the string read from the standard input device. The last parameter contains the number of characters that we will read. The Perl statement that reads the form's data and places it in **$form_data** is

```
read (STDIN, $form_data, $form_size);
```

The **POST** and **GET** methods differ only in the first step. Steps 2 through 5 of the decoding process are identical for both methods. Each step requires a single line of code. Let's quickly review the remaining steps.

Step 2: Convert the Hexadecimal Character to Their ASCII Equivalents. Once we've obtained the form data, either through the standard input device in the **POST** method or the **QUERY_STRING** in the **GET** method, we will want to convert any hexadecimal characters back to their ASCII equivalents. We use the following line of code to accomplish this task:

```
$form_data =~ s/%([\dA-Fa-f][\dA-Fa-f])/pack ("C", hex ($1))/eg;
```

Step 3: Separate the Field Name from the User Data. If the form contains a single field, we can split the field name from the user's data at the equal sign. In more complex forms, we'll need to separate the fields at the ampersands before we separate the field names from the data. We use the same line of code that appeared in the **GET** method:

```
($field_name, $name) = split (/=/, $form_data);
```

After the split, **$field_name** holds the name specified in the **<INPUT>** tag, and **$name** holds the user's name.

Step 4: Remove Suspicious Characters. The next step removes both suspicious and suspect characters from the user's data. We use the same line of code that appeared in the **GET** method:

```
$name =~ s/[;<>\(\)\{\}\*\|'`\&\$!#:"\\]/\ $1/g;
```

Step 5: Convert Plus Signs to Spaces. The last step changes any plus signs back to spaces. Once again, we can copy the code that appeared in the **GET** method:

```
$name =~ s/+/\ $1/g;
```

Figure 18.14 contains the complete Perl code for the **POST** version of the *First Name* page. The steps are highlighted.

```
#!/usr/local/bin/perl
print "Content-type: text/html", "\n\n";
print "<HTML><HEAD><TITLE>The POST Method</TITLE></HEAD>\n";
print "<BODY BGCOLOR = 'white'>\n";
$form_size = $ENV{'CONTENT_LENGTH'}; #1
read (STDIN, $form_data, $form_size);
$form_data =~ s/%([\dA-Fa-f][\dA-Fa-f])/pack ("C", hex ($1))/eg; #2
print "General Information passed to cgi<P>\n";
print "CONTENT_TYPE: $ENV{'CONTENT_TYPE'}<BR>\n";
print "CONTENT_LENGTH:  $ENV{'CONTENT_LENGTH'}<BR>\n";
print "QUERY_STRING: $ENV{'QUERY_STRING'}<BR>\n";
print "REQUEST_METHOD: $ENV{'REQUEST_METHOD'}<BR>\n";
print "Form Data:  $form_data<BR>\n";
($field_name, $name) = split (/=/, $form_data); #3
$name =~ s/[;<>\(\)\{\}\*\|'`\&\$!#:"\\]/\ $1/g; #4
$name =~ s/+/\ $1/g; #5
print "Name(+ Changed): $name<BR>\n";
print "<\BODY><\HTML>\n";
exit(0);
```

Figure 18.14 Perl Code for the *First Name* Page: **POST** version

PERL SELECTION STATEMENTS

Processing a form often requires responding to the user's data. For example, consider the *Azalea* page we discussed in Chapter 10. (See Figure 10.7.) This page asked the user to enter a *pH* level. If the level was in the correct range for growing azaleas, the JavaScript script printed out a message indicating that the range was acceptable. Figure 18.15 contains the same *Azalea* page, but this time we process the form with a Perl script.

The Perl *Azalea* page uses a text field for the *pH* level and includes *Submit* and *Reset* buttons. Figure 18.16 contains the HTML that creates the page displayed in Figure 18.15.

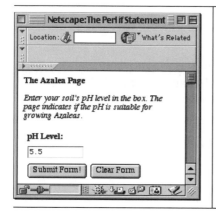

```
<HTML><HEAD><TITLE>The Perl if Statement </TITLE></HEAD>
<BODY BGCOLOR = 'white'>
<B>The Azalea Page</B><P>
<I> Enter your soil's pH level in the box. The page indicates
if the pH is suitable for growing Azaleas.
<TABLE><TR><TD><B>pH Level: </B></TD></TR>
<TR><TD><FORM ACTION="azaleaIf.pl.cgi" METHOD = "GET">
<INPUT  TYPE="text" NAME="Name" SIZE= "12"></TD></TR>
<TR><TD><INPUT TYPE="submit" VALUE="Submit Form!">
<INPUT TYPE="reset"  VALUE="Clear Form"></TD></TR>
</FORM></TABLE></BODY></HTML>
```

Figure 18.15 The *Azalea* Page: Perl version   **Figure 18.16** HTML for the *Azalea* Page: Perl version

Figure 18.17 shows the processed script for the form appearing in Figure 18.15. A *pH* of 5.5 is in the acceptable range, so the script prints a message indicating that the user can grow azaleas. If the *pH* had been higher than 5.5, the script would display the same message shown in Figure 10.7(b): *Sorry. Your pH is too high for Azaleas.*
When we processed the JavaScript version of this page, we used an **if...else** statement. Perl also provides an **if...else** statement, but Perl uses a slightly different syntax. Figure 18.18 contains the syntax for the Perl **if...else** statement.

The Perl **if** statement header begins with the word **if** followed by a parenthesized expression. The block of code after the expression is executed if the expression is *true*. The **elsif** and **else** clauses are optional. If the **elsif** (short for **else if**) clause is present, the expression in its header is evaluated. If this expression is *true*, the block of code after the expression is executed. If the expression is *false*, the next **elsif** expression is evaluated if one is present. Otherwise, the Perl compiler executes the block of code after the **else** clause. If an **else** clause is not present, Perl continues execution of the script.

Figure 18.19 contains the complete Perl code for the *Azalea* page. Notice the call to the **split()** function. This call splits **$form_data** into two variables, **$field_name** and **$ph**. The change in the field name, **$ph**, is the only modification to the five-step decoding process discussed earlier.

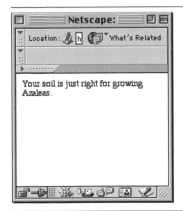

Figure 18.17 The Processed *Azalea* Form

```
if (expression)
   { statement₁;
       statementₙ; }
elsif (expression)optional
       { statement₁;
           statementₙ; }
elseoptional
{ statement₁;
       statementₙ; }
```

Figure 18.18 Syntax for the Perl
`if...else` statement

```
#!/usr/local/bin/perl
print "Content-type: text/html", "\n\n";
print "<HTML><HEAD><TITLE></TITLE></HEAD>\n";
print "<BODY BGCOLOR = 'white'>\n";
$form_data = $ENV{'QUERY_STRING'};
$form_data =~ s/%([\dA-Fa-f][\dA-Fa-f])/pack ("C", hex ($1))/eg;
($field_name, $ph) = split (/=/, $form_data);
$ph =~ s/[;<>\(\)\{\}\*\|'`\&\$!#:"\\]/\ $1/g;
$ph =~ s/+/\ $1/g;
if ($ph <= 5.5)
  { print "Your soil is just right for growing Azaleas.\n"}
else
   {print "Sorry. Your pH is too high for Azaleas.\n"}
print "<\BODY><\HTML>\n";
exit(0);
```

Figure 18.19 Perl Code for the *Azalea* Page

The *Test Score* Page

We developed a *Test Score* page in Chapter 9. You might want to review the JavaScript version of this page, because we're going to create a Perl version of this page. (See Figures 9.5 through 9.7.) The Perl version uses text fields to hold the number of correct answers and the number of total questions. We also use frames to place the completed information on the same Web page as the form. Figure 18.20 shows a sample page.

We use frames later in this chapter and in subsequent ones, so let's briefly consider the layout used to create this page. Figure 18.21 shows the directory structure for the *Test Score* page. Typically, it's easier to store all the files for one frame-based page in a directory dedicated to them alone.

The *grades* directory contains a `startTest.html` file that contains the frameset definition for the *Test Score* page. Figure 18.22 contains the HTML for this file.

The frameset divides the *Test Score* page into three frames. The leftmost frame, `testScore.html`, contains the form. A middle frame, `border.html`, creates a small black border that separates the form and the results. The `result.html` file is initially loaded into the third, or

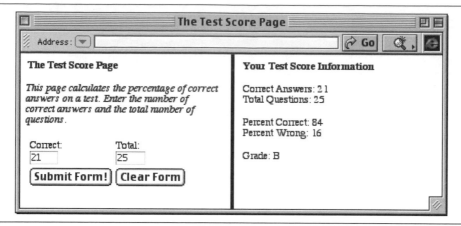

Figure 18.20 The *Test Score* Page: Perl version

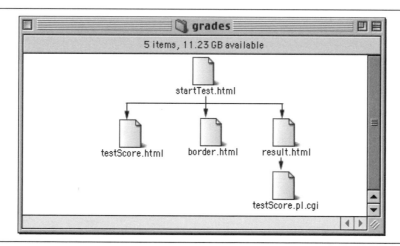

Figure 18.21 Directory Structure for the *Test Score* Page: Perl version

```
<HTML>
<HEAD> <TITLE> The Test Score Page</TITLE></HEAD>
<FRAMESET COLS = "50%, 1%,*"BORDER = "0">
  <FRAME SRC = "testScore.html" NAME ="main" NORESIZE SCROLLING = "no">
  <FRAME SRC = "border.html" NAME ="border" NORESIZE SCROLLING = "no">
  <FRAME SRC = "result.html" NAME  = "results" NORESIZE SCROLLING = "no" >
</FRAMESET>
</HTML>
```

Figure 18.22 The *Test Score Page, The Frameset*

rightmost, frame. This page displays a message indicating that the form results will be placed in this frame. When the user completes the form, the Perl script places the processed results in the rightmost frame, there by replacing the *result.html* file.

Figure 18.23(a) contains the *border.html* file; Figure 18.23(b) contains the *result.html* file.

(a) *border.html*	(b) *result.html*

```<HTML>```
```<HEAD><TITLE></TITLE></HEAD>```
```<BODY BGCOLOR = 'black'>```
```</BODY></HTML>```
	```<HTML>```
	```<HEAD><TITLE></TITLE></HEAD>```
	```<BODY BGCOLOR = "white">```
	```<I>This frame holds your query results.</I>```
	```</BODY></HTML>```

Figure 18.23 The *border* and *result* Files

Figure 18.24 contains the *testScore.html* file. This file contains the *Test Score* form. The form uses the **POST** method to pass information to the *testScore.pl.cgi* script. We've specified *results* as the target for the processed form.

```
<HTML><HEAD><TITLE> </TITLE></HEAD>
<BODY BGCOLOR = 'white'>
<B>The Test Score Page</B><P>
<I>This page calculates the percentage of correct answers on a test.
Enter the number of correct answers and the total number of questions.
</I><P>
<TABLE><TR><TD>
<FORM ACTION="testScore.pl.cgi" METHOD = "POST" TARGET = "results">
Correct: <BR><INPUT  TYPE="text" NAME="Correct" SIZE="5"></TD>
<TD>Total:<BR>
<INPUT TYPE = "text" NAME = "Total" SIZE = "5"></TD></TR>
<TR><TD><INPUT TYPE="submit" VALUE="Submit Form!"></TD>
<TD><INPUT TYPE="reset"  VALUE="Clear Form"></TD></TR>
</FORM></TABLE></BODY></HTML>
```

Figure 18.24 The *Test Score* Form

The *Test Score* form contains two text fields, one for the number of correct answers and a second for the total number of questions. The form also includes the usual *Submit* and *Reset* buttons.

Decoding Steps for a Multiple-Field Form

This form contains two text fields, so we must modify the decoding process slightly. The first two steps remain unchanged:

Step 1. Obtain the Form Data.

Step 2. Convert Hexadecimal Character to Their ASCII Equivalents.
We're using the **POST** method to pass the user's data to the script, so we use the code found in the *namePost* page. The code that handles the first two steps is

```
$form_size = $ENV{'CONTENT_LENGTH'};  #1
read (STDIN, $form_data, $form_size);
$form_data =~ s/%([\dA-Fa-f][\dA-Fa-f])/pack ("C", hex ($1))/eg; #2
```

After these steps, **$form_data** contains the string **Correct=21&Total=25**. Notice the ampersand, used to separate the two form fields. Before we can separate the field names from their associated data, we must separate the fields.

Step 3a. Separate the Form Fields.   To separate the fields, we once again rely upon the **split()** function. We split the form data at the ampersand, placing the results in an array. The code that accomplishes this step is

```
@fields = (split(/&/, $form_data));  #3a
$size = @fields;
```

This code creates the *fields* array and a *size* scalar that holds the number of elements in *fields*. Figure 18.25 shows the contents of the *fields* array and size.

Variable	Contents
$fields[0]	Correct=21
$fields[1]	Total=25
$size	2

Figure 18.25 The *fields* Array

We use a **for** statement to complete the decoding process. The remaining steps are as follows:

Step 3b. Separate the Field Names from the User Data.

Step 4. Remove Suspicious Characters.

Step 5. Convert Plus Signs to Spaces.

Step 6. Store the Field Name–User Data Pairs in a Hash.

Because the form data now contain multiple fields, we use a hash to store the form data. The field name as it appears in the **<INPUT>** tag becomes the key; the user's response is stored as the associated value. Using a hash, lets us quickly retrieve the user's information. The code that we develop for this example works for forms of every size, and it will work without modification for text areas, radio buttons, and single-select fields. Figure 18.26 contains the **for** statement that executes Steps 3b through 6.

```
for ($i=0; $i < $size; $i++){create hash of name value pairs
   ($key, $value) = (split /=/, $fields[$i]);  #3b
   $value =~ s/[;<>\(\)\{\}\*\|''`\&\$!#:"\\]/\ $1/g; #4
   $value =~ s/+/\ $1/g; #5
   $hash{$key} = $value; #6
}
```

Figure 18.26 Decoding a Multiple-Field Form: Steps 3b through 6

The **for** statement appearing in Figure 18.26 splits an element of the *fields* array on the equal sign. The field name appearing to the left of the equal sign is placed in **$key**, the user's response, which appears to the right of the equal sign, is placed in **$value**. Next, we remove the suspicious characters from **$value** and convert any plus signs back to spaces. The last step adds the **$key–$value** pair to *hash*.

After we've decoded the form, we can determine the percentage of correct and incorrect answers. We also use an **if...elsif...else** statement to determine the letter grade. Figure 18.27 contains the complete Perl code for the *Test Score* page.

```
#!/usr/local/bin/perl
print "Content-type: text/html", "\n\n";
print "<HTML><HEAD><TITLE>The POST Method</TITLE></HEAD>\n";
print "<BODY BGCOLOR = 'white'>\n";
$form_size = $ENV{'CONTENT_LENGTH'};   #1
read (STDIN, $form_data, $form_size);
$form_data =~ s/%([\dA-Fa-f][\dA-Fa-f])/pack ("C", hex ($1))/eg; #2
@fields = (split(/&/, $form_data));   #3a
$size = @fields;

for ($i=0; $i < $size; $i++){#4 create hash of name value pairs
   ($key, $value) = (split /=/, $fields[$i]);   #3b
    $value =~ s/[;<>\(\)\{\}\*\|'`\&\$!#:"\\]/\ $1/g; #4
    $value =~ s/+/\ $1/g; #5
    $hash{$key} = $value; #6
}
$correct = $hash{"Correct"};
$total = $hash{"Total"};
$per_correct = $correct/$total *100;
$per_wrong = 100 - $per_correct;
print "<B>Your Test Score Information</B><P>\n";
print "Correct Answers: $correct<BR>\n";
print "Total Questions: $total<P>\n";
print "Percent Correct: $per_correct<BR>\n";
print "Percent Wrong: $per_wrong<P>\n";
if ($per_correct >= 90 && $per_correct <= 100)
   {print "Grade: A<BR>\n"}
elsif ($per_correct >= 80 && $per_correct < 90)
 {print "Grade: B<BR>\n"}
elsif ($per_correct >= 70 && $per_correct < 80)
 {print "Grade: C<BR>\n"}
elsif ($per_correct >= 60 && $per_correct < 70)
 {print "Grade: D<BR>\n"}
else
 {print "Grade: F<BR>\n"}
print "<\BODY><\HTML>\n";
exit(0);
```

Figure 18.27 Perl Code for the *Test Score* Page

The unless Statement

Perl provides an **unless** statement that represents the inverse of an **if** statement without **elsif** or **else** clauses. Figure 18.28 contains the syntax for the **unless** statement.

```
unless (expression)
{ statement₁;
     . . .
     statementₙ; }
```

Figure 18.28 The **unless** Statement

The header for the **unless** statement contains a parenthesized expression. The block of code that comprises the body of the statement is executed *unless* the expression is *true*. In other words, Perl executes the statements in the body only if the expression is *false*.

To illustrate the **unless** statement, we modify the *Azalea* page. The new version prints a warning message only if the user's soil is unsuitable for growing Azaleas. The **unless** statement does not have an alternative clause, so, if the expression is *true*, nothing will be printed (when the user's soil *is* acceptable for growing azaleas). Figure 18.29 contains a sample page.

Figure 18.30 contains the HTML that creates the new *Azalea* page. The page is almost identical to the original version of this page. The changes are highlighted.

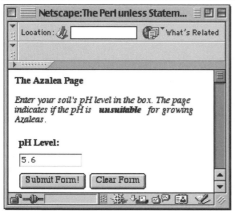

```
<HTML><HEAD><TITLE>The Perl unless Statement
</TITLE></HEAD>
<BODY BGCOLOR = 'white'>
<B>The Azalea Page</B><P>
<I> Enter your soil's pH level in the box. The page
indicates
if the pH is <B>unsuitable</B> for growing Azaleas.
<TABLE><TR><TD><B>pH Level: </B></TD></TR>
<TR><TD><FORM ACTION="azaleaUnless.pl.cgi" METHOD =
"GET">
<INPUT  TYPE="text" NAME="Name" SIZE= "12"></TD></TR>
<TR><TD><INPUT TYPE="submit" VALUE="Submit Form!">
<INPUT TYPE="reset"  VALUE="Clear Form"></TD></TR>
</FORM></TABLE></BODY></HTML>
```

Figure 18.29 The *Azalea* Page, **unless** version

Figure 18.30 HTML for the *Azalea* Page: **unless** version

Figure 18.31 shows the processed page corresponding to the form displayed in Figure 18.29. The *pH* level is too high, so the user cannot grow azaleas.

Figure 18.32 contains the complete Perl script that processes the *Azalea* page. Compare the five decoding steps with the original version of this page. The code in the decoding steps is unchanged; we've simply modified the processing that occurs after the decoding.

```perl
#!/usr/local/bin/perl
print "Content-type: text/html", "\n\n";
print "<HTML><HEAD><TITLE></TITLE></HEAD>\n";
print "<BODY BGCOLOR = 'white'>\n";
$form_data = $ENV{'QUERY_STRING'}; #1
$form_data =~ s/%([\dA-Fa-f][\dA-Fa-f])/pack
    ("C", hex ($1))/eg; #2
($field_name, $ph) = split (/=/, $form_data); #3
$ph =~ s/[;<>\(\)\{\}\*\|'`\&\$!#:"\\]/\ $1/g; #4
$ph =~ s/+/\ $1/g; #5
unless($ph <= 5.5)
    {print "Sorry. Your pH is too high for Azaleas.\n"}
print "<\BODY><\HTML>\n";
exit(0);
```

Figure 18.31 The Processed Page for the *Azalea* Form

Figure 18.32 Perl Code for the *Azalea* Page: **unless** version

Statement Modifiers

The Perl iteration and selection statements execute a block of code. Perl defines a block as any statements encased in braces **{}**. Perl also includes four statement modifiers that we use when we want to execute a single statement. The four modifiers appear in Figure 18.33.

Modifier	Example
statement if(expression);	print "Small #($n) \n" if ($n <= 100);
statement unless (expression);	print "Small #($n) \n" unless ($n > 100);
statement while (expression);	$n=10; print "Count $n \n" while ($n-- >0);
statement until (expression);	$n=10; print "Count $n \n" until ($n-- ==0);

Figure 18.33 Statement Modifiers in Perl

Try rewriting the Perl script in Figure 18.32 by replacing the **unless** statement with a modifier.

Unlike JavaScript, Perl does not have a **switch** statement. The absence of this statement does not diminish Perl's processing capabilities.

PERL PATTERNS AND REGULAR EXPRESSIONS

We briefly discussed regular expressions in Chapter 15. The current (optional) section covers regular expressions in Perl. Perl provides a rich set of operators that we can use to match or modify strings. We examine these operators by considering several small examples. The chapter concludes with a *RegEx* page that lets you experiment with these examples or create new patterns of your own. A separate set of regular-expression exercises is included at the end of the chapter.

Operators and Functions that use Regular Expressions

Figure 18.34 contains a list of the Perl operators and functions that use regular expressions.

Purpose	Syntax
Matching	$*scalar* =~ **m**/*regex*/*options* $*scalar* =~ /*regex*/*options*
Not Matching	$*scalar* !~ **m**/*regex*/*options* $*scalar* !~ /*regex*/*options*
Substitution	$*scalar* =~ **s**/*pattern*/*replacement*/*options*
Transliteration	$*scalar* =~ **tr**/*pattern*/*replacement*/*options* $*scalar* =~ **y**/*pattern*/*replacement*/*options*
Splitting	(*scalar list*) = **split**(/*pattern*/, $*scalar*); @*array* = **split**(/*pattern*/, $*scalar*);
Searching	@*array* = **grep**(/*pattern*/, @*array*);

Figure 18.34 Perl Operators and Functions That Use Regular Expressions

We've used several of the operators and both functions appearing in Figure 18.34. The substitution and transliteration operators (**s**, **tr**, and **y**) search for a pattern in the scalar variable that appears on the left-hand side of the binding operator, =~. These operators require two regular expressions: the first represents a pattern and the second represents a replacement. We use the substitution operator for nonsimultaneous substitution and the transliteration operator (either **tr** or **y**) for simultaneous substitutions. With any of these operators, the *replacement* regular expression is substituted for the *pattern* regular expression in the scalar variable on the left-hand side of the binding operator.

The **split()** and **grep()** functions use a single regular expression to represent a pattern. The **split()** function returns either a list of scalar variables, or an array, that hold the results of splitting a scalar variable on the pattern. The **grep()** function requires an array as a pattern. It returns an array containing the elements that matched the pattern.

Matching and Not-Matching Options

As Figure 18.34 indicates we can also use the matching operator, =~, and its complement, the nonmatching operator, !~, without the substitution or transliteration operators. When used this way, the =~ and !~ operators return a *true* or *false* answer, and they use a different set of options. Figure 18.35 contains these options.

OPTION	MEANING
i	Ignore case
g	Global search
m	Treat strings as multiple lines
s	Treat strings as a single line
o	Compile pattern once
x	Extended regular expressions Allow space as a separator

Figure 18.35 Options for the *Matches* and *Does Not Match* Operators

The most frequently used options are **i** and **g**. The **i** option ignores the case in the pattern. The **g** option indicates that the search should scan the entire string.

Using Quantifiers and the Matching Options

Perl contains several additional operators that we can use to construct regular expressions. Of these operators, *quantifiers* have the highest precedence although we can use parentheses to override precedence. Figure 18.36 contains the list of quantifiers available in Perl. (JavaScript 1.2 uses the same set of quantifiers.)

Let's consider two simple examples that use the quantifiers and options.

Regular Expressions, Example 1. Suppose we have a string variable created with the statement

```
$string = "Ca at";
```

We want to know whether the regular expression **/Cat*/** appears in this string. This regular expression indicates that we are searching for a *C* followed by an *a* followed by zero or more *t*s.

Quantifier	Meaning
*	Pattern appears zero or more times
+	Pattern appears one or more times
?	Pattern appears zero or one times
$\{n\}$	Pattern appears **exactly** n times
$\{n,\}$	Pattern appears **at least** n times
$\{n,m\}$	Pattern appears **at least** n times, but no more than m times

Figure 18.36 Perl Quantifiers

Figure 18.37 contains an **if...else** statement that uses the matching operator to form the expression. If the string matches the regular expression, we print a message indicating that a match was found. Otherwise, we print a message that indicates that a match did not occur.

```
if ($string =~ /Cat*/)
   {print "/Cat*/ found in $string.<BR>\n";}
else
   {print "/Cat*/ not found in $string.<BR>\n";}
```

Figure 18.37 Regular Expressions, example 1

In this example, the **else** clause is executed, because the regular expression does not appear in the string.

Regular Expressions, Example 2.   Suppose we modify the string with the statement

>   **$string = "cat";**

The new regular expression is **/Cat+/i**. This regular expression states that we are searching for a C (or c) followed by an a (or A) followed by at least one t (or T). Figure 18.38 contains a modified **if...else** statement. In this example, the **if** clause is executed, because the regular expression appears in the string.

```
if ($string =~ /cat+/i)
   {print "/Cat+/ found in $string.<BR>\n";}
else
   {print "/Cat+/ not found in $string.<BR>\n";}
```

Figure 18.38 Regular Expressions, example 2

Matching Constructs and Sets

Perl provides constructs that we can use to match character and digits sets. Each construct has an equivalent set representation. We can use either a construct or set notation. Figure 18.39 contains the constructs and their equivalent set notations.

Let's consider two examples using the matching constructs and equivalent sets.

Construct	Set Equivalent	Meaning
\d	[0-9]	Match digits
\D	!~ /[0-9]/	Match non-digits
\w	[a-zA-Z_]	Match word characters
\W	!~ /[a-aA-Z_]/	Match non-word characters
\s	[\n\r\f\t]	Match "white" space, that is, spaces, new lines, returns, form feeds and tabs
\S	!~ / [\n\r\f\t]/	Match non-white space

Figure 18.39 Matching Constructs and Sets

Regular Expressions, Example 3. Assume that we have a string defined as

```
$string = "CatDogFishBird";
```

We want to check this string for "white space." Figure 18.40(a) contains an **if...else** statement that uses the construct to check for white space, while Figure 18.40(b) uses the pattern set. In both examples, Perl executes the **print** statement in the **else** clause, because the string does not contain any white space.

```
(a)  if ($string =~ /\s/)
        {print "$string contains white space.<BR>\n";
     else
        {print "$string contains no white space.<BR>\n";}
```

```
(b)  if ($string =~ / \n\r\t\f/)
        {print "$string contains white space.<BR>\n";}
     else
        {print "$string contains no white space.<BR>\n";}
```

Figure 18.40 Regular Expressions, example 3: Checking for *white space*

Regular Expressions, Example 4. (Checking for Digits). Assume that we have a string defined as

```
$string = "CS 455";
```

We want to know if this string contains digits. Figure 18.41(a) contains an **if...else** statement that uses a construct to check for digits, while Figure 18.41(b) contains the equivalent statement using a set. In both cases, Perl executes the **print** statement in the **if** clause, because the string **does** contain digits.

```
(a)  if ($string =~ /\d/)
        {print "$string contains digits.<BR>\n";
     else
        {print "$string contains no digits.<BR>\n";}
```

```
(b)  if ($string =~ /[0-9]/)
        {print "$string contains digits.<BR>\n";}
     else
        {print "$string contains no digits.<BR>\n";}
```

Figure 18.41 Regular Expressions, example 4: Checking for Digits

Other Pattern Operators

Figure 18.42 contains a list of the remaining pattern operators.

Operator	Meaning
\c	Escape sequence to match a meta character.
^	Match occurs at the beginning of string or line.
$	Match occurs at the end of the string or line.
.	Match any single character except \n.
c|d	Match the character to the left of the pipe symbol | or to the right.

Figure 18.42 Other Pattern Operators.

Let's look at two examples that use these operators.

Regular Expressions, Example 5. Assume that we have a string defined as

```
$string = "Angelfish, Loach, clownfish";
```

We want to know whether this string ends with the word *Fish*. We don't care whether *fish* is written in lower-case or upper-case letters. Figure 18.43 contains an **if...else** statement that checks for this pattern. In this example, Perl executes the **print** statement in the **if** clause, because the string ends with the word *fish*.

```
if ($string =~ /(.*)Fish$/i)
    {print "$string ends with fish.<BR>\n";}
else
    {print "$string does not end with fish.<BR>\n";}
```

Figure 18.43 Regular Expressions, example 5

Regular Expressions, Example 6. Assume that we have a string defined as

```
$string = "Ca at";
```

We want to know whether this string begins with the word *cat*. We don't care whether *cat* is written in upper-case or lower-case letters. Figure 18.44 contains an **if...else** statement that checks for this pattern. In this example, Perl executes the **print** statement in the **else** clause, because the string does *not* begin with the word *cat*.

```
if ($string =~ /^Cat/i)
    {print "$string begins with cat.<BR>\n";}
else
    {print "$string does not begin with cat.<BR>\n";}
```

Figure 18.44 Regular Expressions, example 6

Status Variables

Perl contains several built-in variables that record the status of a pattern-matching, substitution, or transliteration operation. Figure 18.45 contains a list of these status variables.

Status Variable	Meaning
$_	Holds a string that can be used for matching, substitution, or transliteration.
$`	Holds the characters that appear to the left of a match.
$&	Holds that matched string
$'	Holds the character that appears to the right of a match.
$1 through $9	Holds the contents of the first through ninth parenthesized expressions

Figure 18.45 Perl Status Variable

The RegEx Page

We created a JavaScript *RegEx* page in Chapter 15. This page works well in Netscape, but it does not work in Internet Explorer. Figure 18.46 contains a Perl version of this page that works in both browsers. The form appearing in the left frame lets the user enter a string and a regular expression. The Perl script prints the pattern and string in the right frame. It also prints the match information and the contents of the parenthesized expressions. We can use this page to check any of the examples discussed earlier and any of the pattern-matching practice exercises.

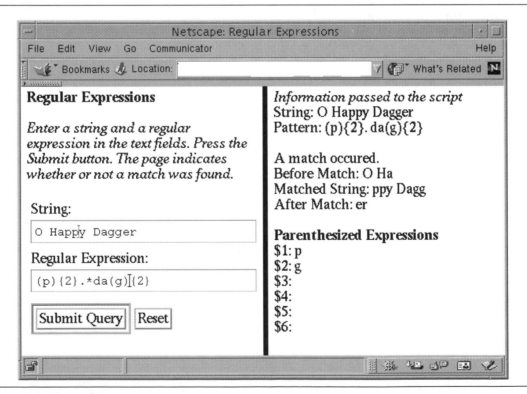

Figure 18.46 The *RegEx* Page, Perl version

Figure 18.47 contains the directory structure for the *RegEx* page. The *startReg.html* file contains the frameset for the page. The *regex.html* file contains the form that we place in the left frame. The *border.html* frame displays a small black border in the middle frame, and the *result.html* frame places an opening message in the right frame. After the user submits the form, the *regexp.pl.cgi* script places the results in the right frame.

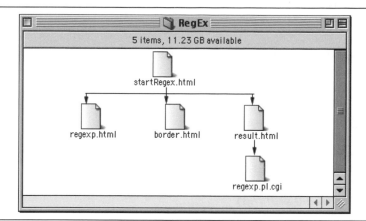

Figure 18.47 The *RegEx* Page Directory Structure

Figure 18.48 displays the contents of the *regexp.html* file.

```
<HTML><HEAD><TITLE> </TITLE></HEAD>
<BODY BGCOLOR = 'white'>
<B>Regular Expressions</B><P>
<I>Enter a string and a regular expression in the text fields. Press the Submit button. The page
indicates whether or not a match was found.
</I><P>
<TABLE><TR><TD>
<FORM ACTION="regexp.pl.cgi" METHOD = "POST" TARGET = "results">
String: <BR>
<INPUT  TYPE="text" NAME="string" SIZE="30"></TD></TR>
<TR><TD>Regular Expression:<BR>
<INPUT TYPE = "text" NAME = "expr" SIZE = "30"></TD></TR>
<TR><TD>
<INPUT TYPE="submit">
<INPUT TYPE="reset"></TD></TR>
</FORM></TABLE></BODY></HTML>
```

Figure 18.48 The *RegEx* Form

Figure 18.49 contains the Perl script that processes the *RegEx* page. This script uses the six-step process developed for the *Test Score* page. Step 4 has been modified so that only the suspicious characters are changed to spaces. Since many of the suspect characters are pattern-matching operators, removing them would have rendered the page useless.

```perl
#!/usr/local/bin/perl
print "Content-type: text/html", "\n\n";
print "<HTML><HEAD><TITLE>The POST Method</TITLE></HEAD>\n";
print "<BODY BGCOLOR = 'white'>\n";
$form_size = $ENV{'CONTENT_LENGTH'}; #1
read (STDIN, $form_data, $form_size);
$form_data =~ s/%([\dA-Fa-f][\dA-Fa-f])/pack ("C", hex ($1))/eg; #2
@fields = (split(/&/, $form_data)); #3a
$size = @fields;

for ($i=0; $i < $size; $i++){#create hash of name value pairs
   ($key, $value) = (split /=/, $fields[$i]); #3b
    $value =~ s/[;<>\*\|`]/\ $1/g;  #4Remove only suspicious characters
    $value =~ s/+/\ $1/g; #5
    $hash{$key} = $value; #6
}
print "<I>Information passed to the script</I><BR>\n";
print "String: $hash{'string'}<BR>\n";
print "Pattern: $hash{'expr'}<P>\n";

if ($hash{'string'} =~ /$hash{'expr'}/gi)
{ print "A match occured. <BR>\n";
  print "Before Match: $`<BR>\n";
  print "Matched String: $&<BR>\n";
  print "After Match: $'<P>\n";
}
  else {print "No match occured.<P>\n"; }
print  "<B>Parenthesized Expressions</B> <BR>\n";
print "\$1: $1<BR>\n";
print "\$2: $2<BR>\n";
print "\$3: $3<BR>\n";
print "\$4: $4<BR>\n";
print "\$5: $5<BR>\n";
print "\$6: $6<BR>\n";
print "<\BODY><\HTML>\n";
exit(0);
```

Figure 18.49 The *RegEx* Script

The *RegEx* script uses an **if...else** statement to determine whether the expression appears in the string. If a match occurs, we use the status variables to print the characters to the left of the match, the matched characters, and the characters to the right of the match. If a match does not occur, we print a message to that effect. The Perl script also uses status variables to print the first six parenthesized expressions.

Transliteration

We conclude the chapter by briefly discussing the transliteration operator. Figure 18.50 contains the syntax and the options for this operator.

Transliteration Syntax	Options
$*scalar* =~ **tr**/*pattern*/*replacement*/*options* $*scalar* =~ **y**/*pattern*/*replacement*/*options*	m: matches complement d: deletes character if there is not match s: removes repetitions, only one occurrence remains

Figure 18.50 Transliteration Syntax and Options

As Figure 18.50 indicates, Perl has two transliteration operators, **tr** and **y**. Of these two operators, **tr** is the more frequently used. We examine two examples that use the transliteration operator.

Transliteraion, Example 1.   Assume that we have a string defined as

```
$string = "Fish Bird Dog Ferret";
```

We want to change the upper-case letters to their lower-case counterparts, and *vice versa*. Figure 18.51 contains the Perl code that performs this task.

```
$string =~ tr/[A-Za-z]/[a-zA-Z]/;
print "$string<BR>\n";
```

Figure 18.51 Transliteration, example 1

Transliteration Example 2 (Counting Characters).   We can also use the transliteration operator to count characters. To do this, we place the string in the $_ status variable. We place the pattern that we wish to count in the pattern portion, and we leave the replacement blank. For example, suppose we have a string defined as

```
$string = "Bass Perch Pike";
```

We want to know the number of vowels that appear in this string. Figure 18.52 contains the Perl code that performs this task.

```
$string = "Bass Perch Pike";
$_ = $string;
$count = tr/aAeEiIoOuU//;
print "The number of vowels is: $count.<BR>\n";
```

Figure 18.52 Transliteration, example 2

➤ **EXERCISES**

For each of the following exercises, create both an HTML file containing the form and a Perl script that process-es the form. Experiment with using a frame-based page to display the form and the processed information.

1. **The** *Garden* **Page.** Create a page with a single text field for the **Hours of Shade**. Use the chart in Figure 10.31 to print the appropriate garden type for the appropriate hours of shade.

2. **The** *Wind Chill* **Page.** Create a page with a single text field for a temperature in Fahrenheit. Use the chart in Figure 10.32 to display the temperature and the wind chill effect correspon-ding to the temperature.

3. **The** *Hurricane* **Page.** Create a page with a single text field for the current wind speed. Print the wind speed, pressure, storm surge, damage, and hurricane classification for this wind speed. Use the chart displayed in Figure 10.34 as your guide.

4. **The** *Tornado* **Page.** Create a page with a single text field for the current wind speed. Print the wind speed, tornadic description, and F-scale rating. Use the chart displayed in Figure 10.35 as your guide.

5. **The** *Richter Scale* **Page.** Create a page with a single text for a Richter scale reading. Print out the Richter scale reading, the TNT equivalent, and the damage. Use Figure 10.36 as your guide.

6. **The** *Heat Index* **Page.** Create a page with a single text field, the current temperature. Print the temperature and the danger zone description. Use Figure 10.37 as your guide.

7. **The** *Person* **Page.** Create an HTML form and a Perl script that process the Web page depict-ed in Figure 18.3.

8. **The** *Celsius To Fahrenheit* **Page.** Create a Perl version of the *Celsius to Fahrenheit* page ap-pearing in Figure 11.2. Use text fields for the lowest and highest Celsius values and the de-gree change.

9. **The** *Multiplication* **Page.** Create a page with text fields representing the lowest and highest integer. Create a multiplication table that corresponds to the user's numbers. Use Figure 11.13 as your guide.

10. **The** *Tipping* **Chart.** Create a page with text fields for the minimum and maximum cost and the tip as a percentage. Print a table that prints the cost and the corresponding tip. Print the table for $1.00 increments, starting at $7.00.

11. **The** *Sales Tax* **Chart.** Create a page with text fields for the purchase amount and the tax rate as a percentage. Print a table that contains the purchase amount, the amount of tax, and the total cost. Print the table for $5.00 increments in the purchase price.

12. **The** *Addition* **Page.** Create a page with text fields for four numbers. Add the numbers and display the result.

13. **The** *Rectangle* **Page.** Create a page with text fields for the width and length. Print the width, length, area, and perimeter of the rectangle. (See Figure 9.23)

14. **The** *Trapezoid* **Page.** Create a page with text fields for two bases and a height. Print the bases, the height, and the area of the trapezoid. (See Figure 9.22.)

15. **The *Roots of the Quadratic Equation* Page.** Create a page with text fields for *a, b,* and *c.* Print the positive and negative roots of the quadratic equation. (See Figure 9.18.)

16. **The *Circle* Page.** Create a page with a text field for the radius. Print the radius, the area, and circumference of the circle. (See Figure 9.17.)

17. **The *Square and Cube Roots* Page.** Create a page with text fields for the lowest and highest number and the change value. Print a chart containing the numbers and their square and cube roots.

➤ PRACTICE EXERCISES FOR REGULAR EXPRESSIONS

The following exercises contain strings and regular expressions. Translate the regular expression into English. Determine whether the string contains the regular expression. Use the RegEx page to check your answers.

1. Assume **$string = "cat";**. Assume that the regular expression is **/Cat{1,}/**. Does the *regex* appear in **$string**? Why or why not?

2. Create a string of your choice. Create an **if..else** statement that checks the string for nondigits. Write both construct and set versions.

3. Create a string of your choice. Create an **if..else** statement that checks the string for word characters. Write both construct and set versions.

4. Create a string of your choice. Create an **if..else** statements that checks the string for vowels.

5. Create a string of your choice. Create an **if..else** statement that checks the string for arithmetic operators.

6. Create a string of your choice. Create an **if..else** statement that checks the string for from zero to three occurrences of the word *dog*.

7. Create a string of your choice. Create an **if..else** statement that checks the string for at least two occurrences of the word *fish*.

8. Create a string of your choice. Create an **if..else** statement that determines whether the string begins with *A*.

9. Create a string of your choice. Create an **if..else** statements that determines whether the string ends with a sentence punctuation mark—that is, a period, question mark, or exclamation point.

10. Create a string of your choice. Create an **if..else** statement that determines whether the string begins with a # or ends with a semi-colon.

11. Create a string of your choice. Create an **if..else** statement that determines whether the string begins with an alphabetical character, contains two *a*'s in the middle, and ends with a period.

12. Create a string of your choice. Create an `if..else` statement that determines whether the string contains the word *apple* or *pear*.

13. Create a transliteration that transforms all *a*'s to *z*'s, and *vice versa*.

14. Count the number of white-space characters that appear in a string.

15. Count the number of digits that appear in a string.

16. Count the number of nondigits that appear in a string.

17. Create a transliteration that shifts all alphabetical characters by two—For example, an *a* becomes a *c*, and a *z* becomes a *b*.

> ## PERL VOCABULARY

Block.   A Perl block is defined as any code encased in braces {}.

Escape Sequence.   An escape sequence is a character sequence beginning with a backslash.

Matching Construct.   A construct is a built-in escape sequence that matches character sets. Figure 18.39 contains a list of the Perl matching constructs and their equivalent set representations.

Meta-character.   A meta-character is a character that is part of the regular expression language. Meta-characters include quantifiers, parentheses, set notation, and the operators listed in Figure 18.42. We must represent meta-character by using an escape sequence.

Modifier.   Perl contains four statement modifiers: `if, unless, while`, and `until`. Figure 18.33 contains examples using the Perl statement modifiers.

Quantifier.   A quantifier determines the number of repetitions of a pattern. The quantifier follows the pattern. Figure 18.36 contains a list of the Perl quantifiers.

Status Variable.   Perl uses status variables to record search information. `$&` contains the matched string, `` $` `` contains the characters to the left of the match, and `$'` contains the characters to the right of the match. `$1` through `$9` hold the characters in the first through ninth parenthesized expressions.

White Space.   White space refers to the space character and to the escape sequences for a new line, form feed, return, or tab.

19 Subroutines, Text Areas, Radio Buttons, Checkboxes, and Select Lists

SUBROUTINE BASICS

Although Perl contains a rich set of built-in functions, at times we need to write our own functions. Programmer-created functions are called *subroutines* in Perl. In this chapter, we create subroutines that print HTML tags and process form data. We consider each of the form elements separately so that we can focus on the URLencoding for each form element.

Defining a Subroutine

Figure 19.1 contains the syntax for defining a Perl subroutine.

---

sub *name*
{#*Include a comment indicating the purpose of the subroutine*
        statement₁;
        . . .
        statementₙ;
}

Figure 19.1 Syntax for a Perl Subroutine

A Perl subroutine consists of a header followed by a block of code. The header begins with the word **sub** followed by the name of the subroutine. Unlike in JavaScript, the Perl subroutine header does not contain a parameter list. Perl uses the array @_ to hold the parameters passed in a call. We extract the individual parameters and place them in variables, a process that we will examine shortly.

The block of code that follows the header can contain variable declarations and executable statements. The scope of variables declared in a subroutine depends on the declaration statement. We will also examine variable declarations shortly.

When we create subroutines we include an **exit(0);** statement to terminate the main body of a Perl script. The subroutine definitions are placed after the **exit(0);** statement. If the **exit(0);** statement is missing, Perl attempts to execute the subroutine definitions, but the Perl compiler has no values for the parameters, so many error messages will result.

Calling a Subroutine

Perl uses an ampersand, **&**, to denote a subroutine call. For example, assume that we created a subroutine named **footer()**. The subroutine prints the **</BODY>** and **</HTML>** tags that close a Web page. We call this subroutine with the statement

```
&footer();
```

Perl also lets us call this subroutine like a built-in function. This means that we can remove the leading ampersand and, because this subroutine has no parameters, we can leave off the parentheses. We write this version of the call as

```
footer;
```

Simple Subroutines

As our first example, we create subroutines that print the opening and closing tags for a Web page. We name these subroutines **header()** and **footer()**, respectively. Figure 19.2 contains the definition of the **header()** subroutine.

```
sub header
{# print the header for the HTML page
    print "Content-type: text/html", "\n\n";
    print "<HTML><HEAD><TITLE></TITLE></HEAD>\n";
    print "<BODY BGCOLOR = 'white'>\n";
}
```

Figure 19.2 The **header()** Subroutine Definition

The body of the **header()** subroutine contains three **print** statements. The first statement prints the content-type, the second and third statements the **<HEAD>**, **<TITLE>**, and **<BODY>** tags. We use the default color *white* for the body and we omit the title. We can call the **header()** subroutine with the statement **&header;** or **&header();** or **header;**

Figure 19.3 contains the definition of the **footer()** subroutine. This subroutine contains a single **print** statement.

```
sub footer
{# print the footer for the html page
    print "</BODY></HTML>";
}
```

Figure 19.3 The **footer()** Subroutine Definition

Figure 19.4 contains a small test program for the **header()** and **footer()** subroutines. Once we've entered and tested this program, we can remove the **print** statement appearing between the subroutine calls. If we do this, we'll have a template that we can use in any program.

```
#!/usr/local/bin/perl
&header;
print "This is my first use of subroutines.<BR>\n";
&footer;
exit(0); #Don't forget the exit()

sub header
{# print the header for the HTML page
   print "Content-type: text/html", "\n\n";
   print "<HTML><HEAD><TITLE></TITLE></HEAD>\n";
   print "<BODY BGCOLOR = 'white'>\n";
}

sub footer
{# print the footer for the html page
   print "</BODY></HTML>";
}
```

Figure 19.4 A Sample Test Page

TEXT FIELDS AND TEXT AREAS

As our first example of form processing by the use of subroutines, we create a small *Mailing Label* page. The page contains text fields for the user's first and last names and a text area for the user's address. The page uses JavaScript to validate the form fields before invoking the Perl script that processes the page. Figure 19.5 illustrates form validation for the first name field. In this example, the user pressed the *Submit* button without filling in this field. An alert window indicates the cause of the error and asks the user to fill out the first name field. Similar alert windows appear if the user omits the last name or address fields.

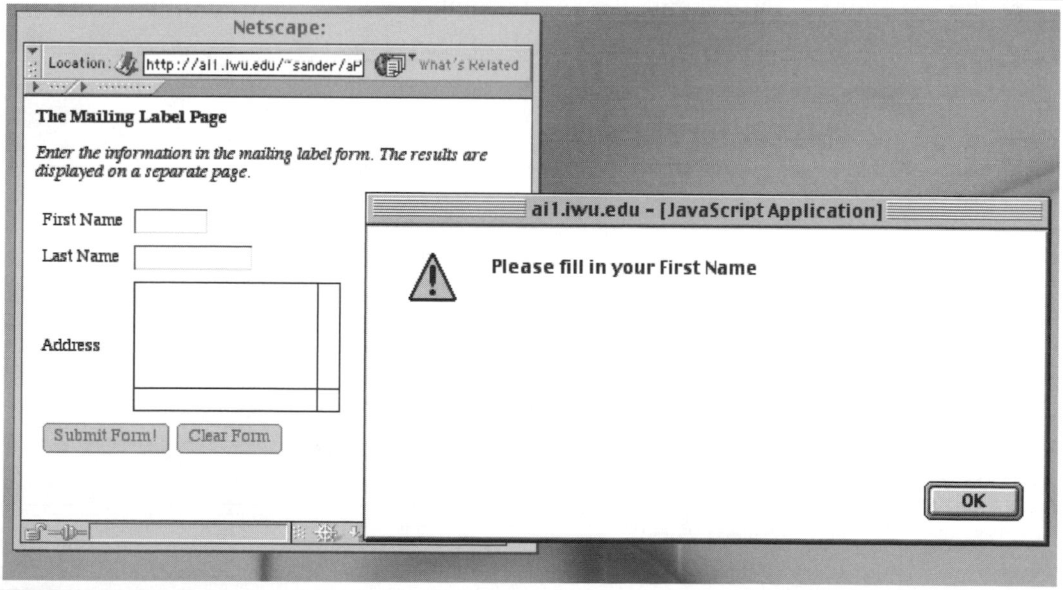

Figure 19.5 A *Mailing Label* Page With Form Validation

Figure 19.6 contains a completed mailing label. The form appears in the Figure 19.6(a), and the completed mailing label appears in Figure 19.6(b)

(a) The Mailing Label Form   **(b) The Completed Label**

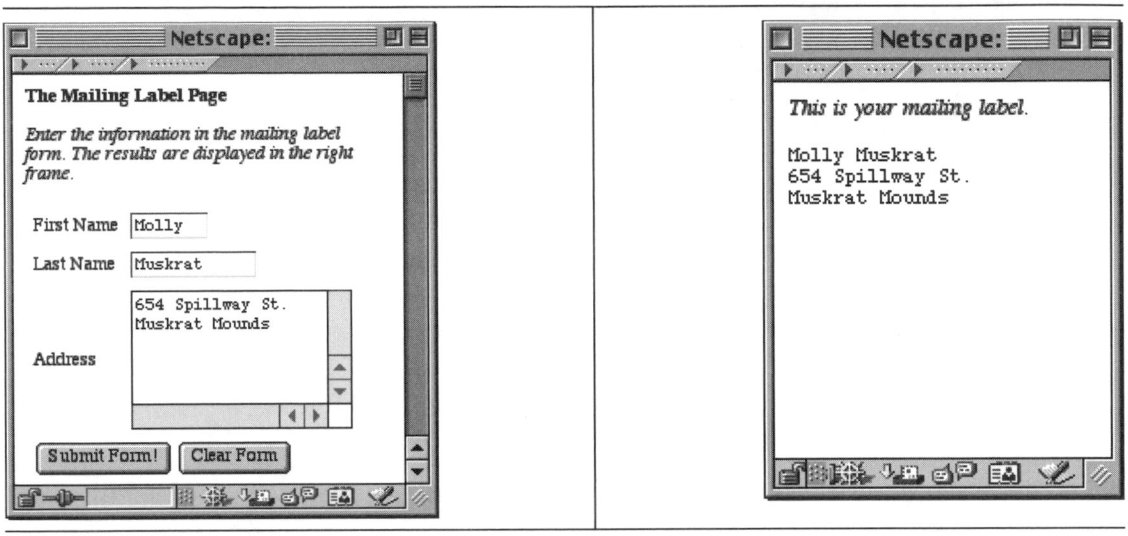

Figure 19.6 A Completed Mailing Label

The Body of the *Mailing Label* Page

Figure 19.7 contains the body of the *Mailing Label* page. The body contains the HTML statements that create the *Mailing Label* form. The form contains text fields for the first and last names and a text area for the address. The text area allows a maximum of 5 rows and 30 columns and uses a physical wrap style to preserve the new-line characters.

```
<BODY BGCOLOR = 'white'>
<B>The Mailing Label Page</B><P>
<I>Enter the information in the mailing label form. The results are displayed
in the right frame.
</I><P>
<TABLE><FORM  NAME = "Mailing" ACTION ="mLabel.pl.cgi" METHOD = "POST"
 onSubmit = "return checkLabel(Mailing)">
<TR><TD>First Name</TD>
<TD><INPUT  TYPE="text" NAME="First" SIZE="7"></TD></TR>
<TD>Last Name</TD>
<TD><INPUT TYPE = "text" NAME = "Last" SIZE = "12"></TD></TR>
<TR><TD>Address</TD>
<TD><TEXTAREA NAME = "Address" ROWS = "5" COLS = "18" WRAP = "PHYSICAL">
</TEXTAREA></TD></TR>
<TR><TD COLSPAN = "2">
<INPUT TYPE="submit" VALUE="Submit Form!">
<INPUT TYPE="reset"  VALUE="Clear Form"></TD></TR>
</FORM></TABLE></BODY></HTML>
```

Figure 19.7 The Body of the *Mailing Label* Page

Notice the <FORM> tag contained in Figure 19.7:

```
<FORM NAME = "Mailing" ACTION ="mLabel.pl.cgi" METHOD = "POST"
onSubmit = "return checkLabel(Mailing)">
```

This tag indicates that the data is passed to the *mLabel.pl.cgi* script by using the **POST** method. The <FORM> tag also includes an **onSubmit** event handler that invokes a **checkLabel()** function located in the head of the page. This function is invoked whenever the user presses the *Submit* button.

The checkLabel() Subroutine

The **checkLabel()** subroutine uses a **for** statement to check each of the fields for a null value. If a null value is encountered, the function uses an alert window to print an error message. The offending form element is brought into focus and the function returns a *false* value. The **checkLabel()** subroutine returns *true* when the user has filled in all of the form's fields. The data is passed to the Perl script only after the **checkLabel()** subroutine returns *true*. Figure 19.8 contains the head of the *Mailing Label* page. The head contains the definition of the **checkLabel()** subroutine.

```
<HTML>
<HEAD><TITLE> </TITLE>
<SCRIPT LANGUAGE = "JavaScript">
<!--
  function checkLabel(form)
  {
     for (var i= 0; i <= 2; i++)
        if (form.elements[i].value == "")
        { //check the text fields and area
           if (i < 2)
             alert("Please fill in your " + form.elements[i].name
                   + " Name");
           else
              alert("Please fill in your " + form.elements[i].name);
           form.elements[i].focus();
           return false;
        }
     return true;
  }
//-->
</SCRIPT></HEAD>
```

Figure 19.8 The **checkLabel()** Subroutine

The Perl Script that Processes the *Mailing Label* Page

The *mLabel.pl.cgi* script that we're about to develop uses the **header()** and **footer()** subroutines created in the previous section. We also develop **get_data()** and **label()** subroutines. The **get_data()** subroutine decodes the form data and places the results in a hash. The **label()** subroutine prints the mailing label that appears in Figure 19.6(b).

The get_data() Subroutine

Development of the **get_data()** subroutine begins with a consideration of URLencoding. We discussed URLencoding for text fields in the previous chapters. Remember that text fields are encoded as *name=value* pairs. This same encoding scheme also applies to text areas. Since the form element names must be unique, we can use a hash to store the decoded information. The *name* attribute in the HTML form becomes the hash key, while the user's data becomes the associated value.

Creating the hash in the subroutine body is easy. Passing the hash as a parameter is problematic, because Perl "flattens" any hash passed as a parameter. Flattening a hash transforms it into a list that must be reconstructed into a hash when it is returned. Flattening and restoring a hash take time. To preserve the hash's structure and to save time, we pass the hash as a reference. Assume that the hash is appropriately labeled *hash*. The call to the **get_data()** subroutine is

```
&get_data(\%hash);
```

The body of the **get_data()** subroutine uses the six-step decoding process developed in Chapter 18:

Step 1: Obtain the Form Data

Step 2: Convert Hexadecimal Characters to their ASCII equivalents

Step 3a: Separate the Form Fields

Step 3b: Separate the Field Names from the User Data

Step 4: Remove Suspicious Characters

Step 5: Convert Plus Signs to Spaces

Step 6: Store the Field Name–User Data Pairs in a Hash

The **get_data()** subroutine should handle both the **POST** and the **GET** method. To automatically obtain the form data for either transmission method, we create an **if...else** statement that determines the transmission method. Recall that the value associated with the **REQUEST_METHOD** key of the **ENV** hash holds the transmission method; we compare this value with *POST*. If a match occurs, we read the form data; otherwise, we get the form data from the **QUERY_STRING**. Figure 19.9 contains the **if...else** statement that obtains the form data.

```
if ($ENV{'REQUEST_METHOD'} eq "POST") { #1 -- POST
    $form_size = $ENV{'CONTENT_LENGTH'};
    read (STDIN, $form_data, $form_size);
  }
else
  {$form_data = $ENV{'QUERY_STRING'};} #1 -- GET
```

Figure 19.9 Obtaining the Form Data

The code for Steps 2 through 5 is identical to the code appearing in Figure 18.26 (or any other Perl programs that use the six-step decoding process). Figure 19.10 contains the Perl code for the **get_data()** subroutine.

The **get_data()** subroutine contains three **my()** statements. A **my()** statement creates variables that are local to the subroutine. Local variables have meaning only within the body of the subroutine. Creating local variables not only saves memory, it also lets us reuse variables names in subroutines or in the main Perl program. As Figure 19.10 demonstrates, we can use the **my()** function to declare variables and provide initial variables. The statements

```
my(@fields);
my($size, $form_size, $key, $value, $i);
```

```
sub get_data
{ #Use Steps 1 - 6 to get and decode the data
my(@fields);
  my($size, $form_size, $key, $value, $i, $form_data);
  my($hash) = @_;

  if ($ENV{'REQUEST_METHOD'} eq "POST") { #1 -- POST
    $form_size = $ENV{'CONTENT_LENGTH'};
    read (STDIN, $form_data, $form_size);
  }
  else
    {$form_data = $ENV{'QUERY_STRING'};} #1 -- GET
  $form_data =~ s/%([\dA-Fa-f][\dA-Fa-f])/pack ("C", hex ($1))/eg; #2
  @fields = (split(/&/, $form_data)); #3a
  $size = @fields;

  for ($i=0; $i < $size; $i++){
    ($key, $value) = (split /=/, $fields[$i]); #3b
    $value =~ s/[;<>\(\)\{\}\*\|'`\&\$!#:"\\]/\ $1/g; #4
    $value =~ s/+/\ $1/g;   #5
    $$hash{$key} = $value;    #6  Derefernce
  }
  $_[0] = $hash;
}
```

Figure 19.10 The **get_data()** Subroutine, *Mailing Label* Page

declare, but do not initialize, several local variables. By contrast, the statement

> `my($hash) = @_;`

creates a local variable, **$hash**, which is assigned the contents of the @_ array. This local variable is a reference to a hash. Because it is a reference, adding a new key–value pair requires a dereference. A slightly modified Step 6 handles the dereferencing. The modified Perl statement for Step 6 is

> `$$hash{$key} = $value;`

The last statement in the **get_data()** subroutine places the hash reference into the first position of the @_ array. The statement is

> `$_[0] = $hash;`

The label() Subroutine

The **label()** subroutine prints the mailing label. The current implementation of this subroutine requires the the first name, last name, and street as separate parameters. This lets us explore multiple parameters in Perl. The call to the **label()** subroutine is

> `&label($hash{'First'}, $hash{'Last'}, $hash{'Address'});`

Figure 19.11 contains the Perl code for the **label()** subroutine. This code uses the **local()** function to place the parameters into variables. The syntax for the **local()** function differs slightly from that of the **my()** function: The **local()** function places the assignment operator and value within the parentheses; the **my()** function places them outside the parentheses. The scopes, of these two functions also differ. Variables declared with a **my()** function have scope only within the declaring subroutine. By contrast, variables declared via a **local()** function have meaning within the

```
sub label
{ # print the mailing label
    local ($first_name = $_[0]);
    local ($last_name = $_[1]);
    local ($address = $_[2]);
    print "<I>This is your mailing label.<P></I>";
    print "<PRE>$first_name $last_name\n";
    print "$address</PRE>\n";
}
```

Figure 19.11 The `label()` Subroutine

declaring subroutine *and* within any subroutines called by the declaring subroutine. (Perl calls these *dynamically scoped variables*.) In most circumstances, the **my()** function is preferable; it prevents subtle, unintentional interactions between subroutines. Using **my()** is also quicker, because variables declared with **local()** are pushed and popped from a system stack as needed.

The three **local()** statements appearing in Figure 19.11 extract the three parameters from the @_ array. Each parameter is a scalar variable, so we use scalar notation. Thus, the statement

```
local ($first_name = $_[0]);
```

extracts the first parameter (**$_[0]**) and places it in the dynamically scoped variable **$first_name**. The remaining **local()** statements place the second (**$_[1]**) and third (**$_[2]**) parameters in **$last_name** and **$address**, respectively.

The **label()** subroutine uses **<PRE>...</PRE>** tags to print the mailing label. Although we created the text area with a physical wrap, the new-line characters (**\n**) are ignored by browsers. This means that the browser prints all of the text area's contents on a single line. The **<PRE>...</PRE>** tags preserve the original formatting.

We can preserve the original formatting of a text area without using **<PRE>...</PRE>** tags. Figure 19.12 contains a modification of the **for** statement used in the **get_data()** subroutine. The new **for** statement contains an **if** statement that searches for the text area *Address*. Once it has been found, we use the substitution operator to replace the new-line characters (**\n**) with **
** tags. Figure 19.13 contains the main program of the *mLabel.pl.cgi* script. All of the code resides in subroutines; the Perl code in the main program is short and simple.

```
for ($i=0; $i < $size; $i++){
    ($key, $value) = (split /=/, $fields[$i]);        #3b
    $value =~ s/[;<>\(\)\{\}\*\|'`\&\$!#:"\\]/\ $1/g; #4
    $value =~ s/+/\ $1/g;                              #5
    if ($key eq "Address")          #Replace \n with <BR>
    { $value =~ s/[\n]/<BR>$1/gi;}
    $$hash{$key}[0] = $value;   #6
}
```

Figure 19.12 An Alternate Approach for Processing a Text Area

```
#!/usr/local/bin/perl
&header;
&get_data(\%hash);
&label($hash{'First'}, $hash{'Last'}, $hash{'Address'});
&footer;
exit(0);

#Put the header() Subroutine Definition Here
#Put the footer() Subroutine Definition Here
#Put the get_data() Subroutine Definition Here
#Put the label() Subroutine Definition Here
```

Figure 19.13 The *mLabel.pl.cgi* Script

RADIO BUTTONS

Next, we consider radio buttons. To illustrate the decoding process, we create a simple *true-false* quiz. Figure 19.14 contains a sample page.

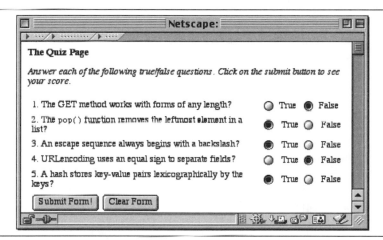

Figure 19.14 The *T/F Quiz* Page

Figure 19.15 shows the processed quiz. In this example, the user answered four out of the five questions correctly. The Perl script indicates the percentage of correct answers and a letter grade, in addition to the number of correct answers.

Figure 19.16 contains the HTML that generates the *T/F Quiz* form. The radio buttons are divided into five groups, named *q1* through *q5*, respectively. Each radio button group requires two **<INPUT>** tags. The first tag holds the *true* option, the second the *false* option.

The get_data() Subroutine

The *T/F Quiz* form uses the **POST** method to pass the completed form information to the *quiz.pl.cgi* script. When the user presses the *Submit Form!* button, the browser passes the URLencoded data to the script. The encoding for radio buttons is identical to that for text fields

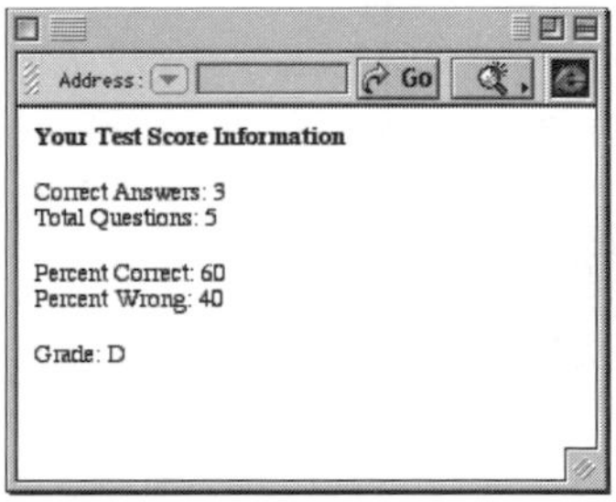

Figure 19.15
The Processed T/F Quiz

```
<HTML><HEAD><TITLE> </TITLE></HEAD>
<BODY BGCOLOR = 'white'>
<B>The Quiz Page</B><P>
<I>Answer each of the following true/false questions. Click on the
    submit button to see your score.</I><P>
<TABLE>
<FORM ACTION="quiz.pl.cgi" METHOD = "POST">
<TR><TD>1. The GET method works with forms of any length?</TD>
<TD><INPUT TYPE = "radio" NAME = "q1" VALUE = "true"> True</TD>
<TD><INPUT TYPE = "radio" NAME = "q1" VALUE =
    "false"> False</TD></TR>

<TR><TD>2. The <TT>pop()</TT> function removes the leftmost element
    in a list?</TD>
<TD><INPUT TYPE = "radio" NAME = "q2" VALUE = "true">
     True</TD>
<TD><INPUT TYPE = "radio" NAME = "q2" VALUE = "false"> 
    False</TD></TR>

<TR><TD>3. An escape sequence always begins with a backslash? </TD>
<TD><INPUT TYPE = "radio" NAME = "q3" VALUE = "true"> 
    True</TD>
<TD><INPUT TYPE = "radio" NAME = "q3" VALUE = "false"> 
    False</TD></TR>

<TR><TD>4. URLencoding uses a0n equal sign to separate fields?</TD>
<TD><INPUT TYPE = "radio" NAME = "q4" VALUE = "true">
     True</TD>
<TD><INPUT TYPE = "radio" NAME = "q4" VALUE = "false"> 
    False</TD></TR>

<TR><TD>5. A hash stores key-value pairs lexicographically by the
    keys?</TD>
<TD><INPUT TYPE = "radio" NAME = "q5" VALUE = "true"> 
    True</TD>
<TD><INPUT TYPE = "radio" NAME = "q5" VALUE = "false">
     False</TD></TR>

<TR><TD COLSPAN = "2">
<INPUT TYPE="submit" VALUE="Submit Form!">
<INPUT TYPE="reset"  VALUE="Clear Form"></TD></TR>
</FORM></TABLE></BODY></HTML>
```

Figure 19.16 HTML for the *T/F Quiz* Page

and text areas. That is, the browser passes each selection from a radio button group as a *name=value* pair. Thus, the form information appearing in Figure 19.14 is sent to the script as

```
q1=false&q2=true&q3=true&q4=false&q5=true
```

Although we can use a hash to store the decoded form, determining the user's score is easier if we store the form data in an array. Using an array requires only minor modifications to the **get_data()** subroutine. Figure 19.17 contains the new version of the **get_data()** subroutine. The changes are highlighted.

```
sub get_data
{ #Use Steps 1 -6 to get and decode the data
  my(@fields);
  my($size, $form_size, $key, $value, $i, $form_data);
  my($answers)= @_;

  if ($ENV{'REQUEST_METHOD'} eq "POST") {
    $form_size = $ENV{'CONTENT_LENGTH'};
    read (STDIN, $form_data, $form_size);
  }
  else
     {$form_data = $ENV{'QUERY_STRING'};}
  $form_data =~ s/%([\dA-Fa-f][\dA-Fa-f])/pack ("C", hex ($1))/eg;
  @fields = (split(/&/, $form_data));
  $size = @fields;

  for ($i=0; $i < $size; $i++){
     ($key, $value) = (split /=/, $fields[$i]);
     $value =~ s/[;<>\(\)\{\}\*\|'`\&\$!#:"\\]/\ $1/g;
     $value =~ s/+/\ $1/g;
     $$answers[$i] = $value;
  }
  @_= $answers;
}
```

Figure 19.17 The **get_data()** Subroutine, *T/F Quiz* Page

The **get_data()** subroutine uses a reference to an array rather than a reference to a hash as a parameter. The call is

> **&get_data(\@answers);**

You might wonder why we can't pass the array as a parameter because @_ holds an array. In most circumstances, if we have one array as the only parameter, we can simply pass the array rather than a reference to the array. Unfortunately, when we pass an array as a parameter, Perl lets us modify the array elements, but does not let us modify the array itself. Because the **@answers** array does not exist prior to the call to the **get_data()** subroutine, we must pass it as a reference:

The get_score() Subroutine

After the call to the **get_data()** subroutine, the **@answers** array contains the user's data. To determine the user's score, we create a **get_score()** subroutine. This subroutine has three parameters: a reference to **@answers**, the total number of questions (**$total**), and the number of correct answers (**$correct**). The call is

> **$total = 5; #total number of questions**
> **&get_score(\@answers, $total, $correct);**

The **get_score()** subroutine contains an auxiliary array, **@correct_answers**, that obviously holds the correct answers for the quiz. Figure 19.18 shows the relation between **@answers** and **@correct_answers**.

Index	@answers	@correct_answers
[0]	"false"	"false"
[1]	"true"	"false"
[2]	"true"	"true"
[3]	"false"	"false"
[4]	"true"	"false"

Figure 19.18 The **@answers** and **@correct_answers** Arrays

Compare the two arrays on an index-by-index basis. You should be able to determine the user's score easily. Storing the form data in an array lets us use a **for** statement to determine the number of correct answers. Figure 19.19 contains the definition of the **get_score()** subroutine.

```
sub get_score
{
my($answers, $size, $correct) = @_;
my(i,$correct);
my(@correct_answers);
@correct_answers = ("false", "false", "true", "false", "false");
$correct = 0;
for ($i = 0; $i < $size; $i++){
   if($answers->[$i] eq $correct_answers[$i])
   { $correct++};
 }
 $_[2] = $correct;
}
```

Figure 19.19 The **get_score()** Subroutine

The **get_score()** subroutine uses a **my()** statement to place the three parameters into **$answers**, **$size**, and **$correct**. Additional **my()** statements create the scalar variables **$i** and **$correct** and the array **@correct_answers**. We initialize **$correct** to zero prior to the start of the **for** loop. The **for** statement compares each element in the two arrays. We increment **$correct** for each match. Notice the **if** statement that compares the array elements:

    if ($answers->[$i] eq $correct_answers[$i])

Because *answers* is a reference to an array, we must dereference it. The dereference (**$answers->[$i]**) uses the arrow operator. We could also dereference the array by using the **$** operator (**$$answers[$i]**).

After the **for** statement terminates, we place the number of correct answers (**$correct**) into the third parameter, **$_[2]**.

The **print_results()** Subroutine

The **print_results()** subroutine prints the test score results. We pass the number of correct and total answers as parameters. The subroutine call is

    &print_results($correct,$total);

The `print_results()` subroutine contains two variables, **$correct** and **$total**, which we extract from the @_ array with the statement

> `my($correct, $total) = @_;`

We create two additional variables with the statement

> `my ($per_correct, $per_wrong);`

The body of the **print_results()** subroutine follows the code developed for the *Test Score* page. (See Figure 18.27.) We calculate the percentage of correct and erroneous answers. We print a count of correct answers and total questions, and we print the percentages of correct and incorrect answers. We use a set of **if...elsif...else** statements to determine the user's letter grade.

Figure 19.20 contains the definition of the **print_results()** subroutine.

```
sub print_results
{#print the scores and grade
  my($correct, $total) = @_;
  my ($per_correct, $per_wrong);
  $per_correct = $correct/$total *100;
  $per_wrong = 100 - $per_correct;
  print "<B>Your Test Score Information</B><P>\n";
  print "Correct Answers: $correct<BR>\n";
  print "Total Questions: $total<P>\n";
  print "Percent Correct: $per_correct<BR>\n";
  print "Percent Wrong: $per_wrong<P>\n";
  if ($per_correct >= 90 && $per_correct <= 100)
    {print "Grade: A<BR>\n"}
  elsif ($per_correct >= 80 && $per_correct < 90)
    {print "Grade: B<BR>\n"}
  elsif ($per_correct >= 70 && $per_correct < 80)
    {print "Grade: C<BR>\n"}
  elsif ($per_correct >= 60 && $per_correct < 70)
    {print "Grade: D<BR>\n"}
  else
    {print "Grade: F<BR>\n"}
}
```

Figure 19.20 The `print_results()` Subroutine

Figure 19.21 contains the main Perl program for the *T/F Quiz*. As usual, most of the code resides in the subroutines.

CHECKBOXES

To illustrate check boxes, we create a *Web Languages* page. Figure 19.22(a) contains the *Web Languages* form, and Figure 19.22(b) contains a processed form.

Figure 19.23 contains the HTML that creates the *Web Languages* form appearing in Figure 19.22(a). Notice the **<INPUT>** tag used to create the C++ checkbox. The name for this checkbox is CPP rather than C++ because of the peculiarities of URLencoding: Spaces are encoded as plus signs, so the script would not be able to differentiate "C" from "C++" had we named this check box "C++".

```
#!/usr/local/bin/perl
$total = 5; #total number of questions
&header;
&get_data(\@answers);
&get_score(\@answers, $total, $correct);
&print_results($correct,$total);
&footer;
exit(0);

#put the print_results() subroutine definition here
#put the get_score() subroutine definition here
#put the get_data() subroutine definition here
#put the header() subroutine definition here
#put the footer() subroutine definition here
```

Figure 19.21 Perl Code for the *T/F Quiz* Page

(a) The Web Languages Form

(b) The Processed Form

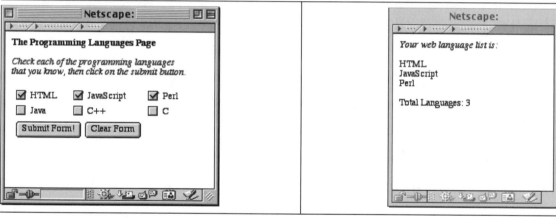

Figure 19.22 The *Web Languages* Page

```
<HTML><HEAD><TITLE> </TITLE></HEAD>
<BODY BGCOLOR = 'white'>
<B>The Programming Languages Page</B><P>
<I>Check each of the programming languages that you know, then click on the submit button.</I><P>
<TABLE>
<FORM ACTION="checkB.pl.cgi" METHOD = "POST" TARGET = "results">
<TR><TD><INPUT TYPE = "checkbox" NAME = "HTML">HTML</TD>
<TD><INPUT TYPE = "checkbox" NAME = "JavaScript">JavaScript</TD>
<TD><INPUT TYPE = "checkbox" NAME = "Perl">Perl</TD></TR>
<TR><TD><INPUT TYPE = "checkbox" NAME = "Java">Java</TD>
<TD><INPUT TYPE = "checkbox" NAME = "CPP">C++</TD>
<TD><INPUT TYPE = "checkbox" NAME = "C">C</TD></TR>
<TR><TD COLSPAN = "2">
<INPUT TYPE="submit" VALUE="Submit Form!">
<INPUT TYPE="reset"  VALUE="Clear Form"></TD></TR>
</FORM></TABLE></BODY></HTML>
```

Figure 19.23 The *Web Languages* Form

The get_data() Subroutine

Unlike radio buttons, check boxes allow multiple selections. Because each check box has a different name, the URLencoding scheme used for check boxes differs from that used by text fields, text areas, and radio buttons in two respects. First, the browser ignores all unchecked boxes. Thus, the script receives information only about the boxes that were checked. Second, checkboxes are encoded as *name=on* pairs. This means that the relevant information appears in the *name*. Although we could store the *name=on* pairs as *Key–Value* pairs in a hash, an array of check box names is easier to use. The get_data() subroutine passes a reference to an array as a parameter. The call is

```
&get_data(\@languages);
```

The get_data() subroutine contains a my() statement that assigns the @_ array to $languages. We also use my() statements to create a local array, *fields*, and the local scalar variables used to process the form data. The statements are

```
my(@fields);
my($size, $form_size, $key, $value, $i, $form_data);
my($languages) = @_;
```

We use the six-step decoding process to create the array of selected languages. Ordinarily, the last step creates a new hash entry with the form *name* field as the key and the user's data as the value. In the current example, we place the key into the *languages* array. The statement is

```
$$languages[$i] = $key;
```

Notice that we must dereference *languages*, because it is associated with the reference to an array that we passed as a parameter.

We assign *languages* to $_[0] at the end of the get_data() subroutine. Figure 19.24 contains the definition of the get_data() subroutine.

```
sub get_data
{ #Use Steps 1 -6 to get and decode the data
  my(@fields);
  my($size, $form_size, $key, $value, $i, $form_data);
  my($languages) = @_;
  if ($ENV{'REQUEST_METHOD'} eq "POST") {#1 -- POST
    $form_size = $ENV{'CONTENT_LENGTH'};
    read (STDIN, $form_data, $form_size);
  }
  else
     {$form_data = $ENV{'QUERY_STRING'};} #1 -- GET
  $form_data =~ s/%([\dA-Fa-f][\dA-Fa-f])/pack ("C", hex ($1))/eg; #2
  @fields = (split(/&/, $form_data));                              #3a
  $size = @fields;

  for ($i=0; $i < $size; $i++){
    ($key, $value) = (split /=/, $fields[$i]);          #3b
     $value =~ s/[;<>\(\)\{\}\*\|'`\&\$!#:"\\]/\ $1/g;   #4
     $value =~ s/+/\ $1/g;                              #5
     $$languages[$i] = $key;   #6 Modified--Place the key in languages
  }
  $_[0]= $languages;
}
```

Figure 19.24 The get_data() Subroutine, *Web Languages* Page

The count() Subroutine

Once we've obtained the array of checked languages, we pass this array to the **count()** subroutine. This subroutine prints and counts the languages. The call to this subroutine is

&count(@languages);

The **count()** subroutine uses a **foreach** statement to process the *languages* array. The **foreach** statement contains an **if...else** statement that checks the element's name. If the name is *CPP*, we print "C++"; otherwise, we print the element's name. Figure 19.25 contains the definition of the **count()** subroutine.

Figure 19.26 contains the Perl script for the *Web Languages* page. The main program contains very little code, because we've used subroutines to divide the program into small, simple tasks.

```
sub count
{
 my(@languages) = @_;
 my($size) =0;
 my($element);
 print "<I>Your web language list is: <P></I>\n";
 foreach $element(@languages)
 {  if ($element eq "CPP")
     { print "C++<BR>\n"; }
    else
       {print "$element<BR>\n";}
    $size++;
 }
  print "<BR>Total Languages: $size<BR>\n";
}
```

Figure 19.25 The **count()** Subroutine for the *Web Languages* Page

```
#!/usr/local/bin/perl
&header;
&get_data(\@languages);
&count(@languages);
&footer;
exit(0);

#Put the count() subroutine definition here
#Put the get_data() subroutine definition here
#Put the header() subroutine definition here
#Put the footer() subroutine definition here
```

Figure 19.26 The Main Program for the *Web Languages* Page

MULTIPLE-SELECT LISTS

Multiple-select lists provide an alternative to checkboxes when we have long lists of items. Figure 19.27 contains a *Programming Language* page. The form appearing in Figure 19.27(a) asks users to check all of the languages that they know. Only the first eight languages in the list of 16 languages are displayed. The processed form appearing in Figure 19.27(b) includes the list of selected languages and a count of the languages.

(a) The Programming Languages Form

(b) The Processed Form

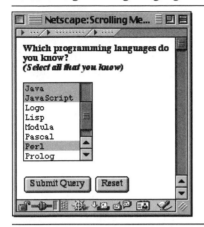

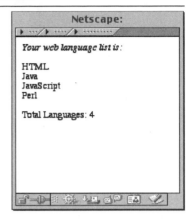

Figure 19.27 The *Programming Languages* Page

The language list is long, so we rely upon JavaScript to create the **<OPTION>** tags. A script in the head of the page creates an array of language names; a script in the body of the page fills the **<OPTION>** tags. Figure 19.28 contains the HTML that creates the *Programming Languages* form.

```
<HTML><HEAD> <TITLE> Scrolling Menus </TITLE>
<SCRIPT LANGUAGE = "JavaScript">
<!--
  var list = new Array("Ada", "Algol", "C", "C++", "Fortran", "HTML",
  "Java", "JavaScript", "Logo", "Lisp", "Modula", "Pascal", "Perl",
  "Prolog", "Scheme", "Snobool");
//-->
</SCRIPT></HEAD>
<BODY BGCOLOR = "white">
<FORM ACTION = "selectLang.pl.cgi" METHOD = "POST" TARGET = "results">
<B>Which programming languages do you know?<BR>
<I>(Select all that you know)</I></B>
<BR><BR>
<SELECT NAME = "Languages" SIZE = "8"  MULTIPLE>
<SCRIPT LANGUAGE = "JavaScript">
<!--
  for (var i=0; i < list.length; i++) {
    if (list[i] == "C++")
      document.write("<OPTION VALUE = 'CPP'>");
    else if (list[i] == "HTML")
        document.write("<OPTION SELECTED>");
    else document.write("<OPTION>");
    document.write(list[i]);
    }
//-->
</SCRIPT></SELECT>
<P>
<INPUT TYPE = "SUBMIT"> <INPUT TYPE = "RESET">
</FORM></BODY></HTML>
```

Figure 19.28 HTML for the *Programming Languages* Form

The JavaScript script that creates the **<OPTION>** tags includes **if...else** statements that create a **VALUE** of *CPP* for the C++ option and selects the *HTML* option.

Processing the Form Data

The URLencoding for multiple-select lists presents another variation from the previous encoding schemes. The browser sends only the selected options to the script. These options are sent as *Select List Name=Option* pairs. For example, if the user selected Perl, Java, and JavaScript, the URLencoding would be

> `Languages=Perl&Languages=Java&Langauges=JavaScript`

Obviously, we cannot use a hash to store a multiple-select list, because each selected option has the same name. Thus, the hash would store only the last *Select_List_Name=Option* pair.

The **get_data()** subroutine that processes the multiple select list uses an array to hold the selected options. This page is similar to the *Web Languages* page, and the calls to the **get_data()** subroutine are identical. Thus, we call the **get_data()** subroutine with the statement

> **&get_data(\@languages);**

The **get_data()** subroutine used in the *Programming Languages* page is virtually identical to the **get_data()** subroutine used in the *Web Languages* page. In fact, only a single line differentiates the two subroutines. Figure 19.29 shows the difference in these two form elements.

Web Languages **Page** (Checkbox)	*Programming Languages* **Page** (Multiple Select List)
`$$languages[$i] = $key;`	`$$languages[$i] = $value;`

Figure 19.29 Decoding Checkboxes and Multiple Select Lists

As Figure 19.29 indicates, we place the *key* field in the array when using a checkbox. When using a multiple-select list, we place the *value* field in the array.

The *Programming Languages* script uses the same **count()** subroutine and the same main program as the *Web Languages* page.

SINGLE-SELECT LISTS

The last simple form uses a single select-list. Figure 19.30 contains a sample page that shows the user how to find the current time in Tibetan. We use a frame-based approach so that the user can view both the English and Tibetan times. The left frame asks *What time is it?* This question is followed by *It is _____ o'clock.* A single select list lets the user pick an hour between 1 and 12. The right frame repeats the question in Tibetan (phonetically) and then provides the Tibetan response for the time selected in the left frame.

The *Telling Time* form uses a JavaScript script to generate the select list options. The HTML file that creates the *Telling Time* form appears in Figure 19.31.

The *Telling Time* form uses the **POST** method to transmit data to the script, `time.pl.cgi`. The form contains a single select list. We use HTML to create the opening tag for the list. A JavaScript script generates the hours used for the list options. After the script terminates, we use the **</SELECT>** tag to close the list. HTML tags are also used to create the *submit* and *reset* buttons.

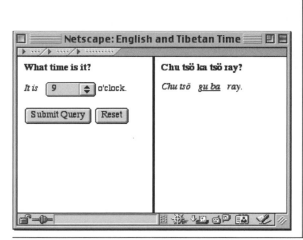

Figure 19.30 The *Telling Time* Page

```
<HTML><HEAD> <TITLE> </TITLE> </HEAD>
<BODY BGCOLOR = "white">
<B>What time is it?</B>
<P>
<FORM ACTION = "time.pl.cgi" METHOD = "POST"
    TARGET = "results">
<I>It is</I>
<SELECT NAME = "Hours" SIZE = "1">
<SCRIPT LANGUAGE = "JavaScript">
<!--
    for (var i=1; i<=12; i++)
        document.write("<OPTION>" + i);
//-->
</SCRIPT> </SELECT>
o'clock.
<P>
<INPUT TYPE = "SUBMIT"> <INPUT TYPE = "RESET">
</FORM></BODY></HTML>
```

Figure 19.31 HTML for the *Telling Time* Form

The get_data() Subroutine

A *single select* list uses the same encoding scheme as text fields, text areas, and radio buttons. The browser transmits the user's selection as a *name=value* pair. In the current example, the script receives

```
time=9
```

The form contains only a single *name–value* pair, so we don't need to create a hash to store the form information. Of course, we could opt to use the same **get_data()** subroutine appearing in the *Mailing Label* page. (See Figure 19.10.) However, we instead modify the **get_data()** subroutine, to illustrate the **return** statement. The Perl **return** statement returns a scalar, hash, or array. The syntax of the **return** statement is

```
return expression;
```

where *expression* is anything that produces a value. Figure 19.32 contains the new version of the **get_data()** subroutine. Only the highlighted line differs from the **get_data()** subroutine used in the *Mailing Label* page appearing in Figure 19.10.

The new **get_data()** subroutine returns a value, and we use an assignment statement to preserve that value. The call to the **get_data()** subroutine is

```
$time = &get_data;
```

The print_time() Subroutine

The **print_time()** subroutine prints the Tibetan time. The subroutine contains an array of Tibetan hours, **@tibetan_hour**, that contains the Tibetan phonetic equivalents of the hours from 1 to 12. Perl array subscripts start from zero and times start from one, so the 0th position of this array has the value *"undefined"*. The array declaration is

```
@tibetan_counts = ("undefined", "chik ba", "nyi ba",
"sum ba", "shi ba","nga ba", "trook ba",
"d&uuml;n ba", "ge ba", "gu ba", "chu ba",
"chu chik ba","chu nyi ba");
```

We pass the English time as a parameter to the **print_time()** subroutine. The call is

```
&print_time($time);
```

```
sub get_data
{ #Use Steps 1 -6 to get and decode the data
 my(@fields);
 my($size, $form_size, $key, $value, $i,$form_data);
 my (%hash);
 if ($ENV{'REQUEST_METHOD'} eq "POST") { #1-- POST
    $form_size = $ENV{'CONTENT_LENGTH'};
    read (STDIN, $form_data, $form_size);
 }
 else
    {$form_data = $ENV{'QUERY_STRING'};} #1 -- GET
 $form_data =~ s/%([\dA-Fa-f][\dA-Fa-f])/pack ("C", hex ($1))/eg; #2
 @fields = (split(/&/, $form_data)); #3a
 $size = @fields;
 for ($i=0; $i < $size; $i++){
    ($key, $value) = (split /=/, $fields[$i]); #3b
     $value =~ s/[;<>\(\)\{\}\*\|'`\&\$!#:"\\]/\ $1/g; #4
     $value =~ s/+/\ $1/g; #5
 }
 return $value;
}
```

Figure 19.32 The **get_data()** Subroutine, *Telling Time* Page

The **print_time()** subroutine contains a **my()** statement that extracts the parameter and places it in **$time**. The remainder of the code consists of two **print** statements. The first **print** statement prints the Tibetan phonetic equivalent of *What time is it?* The second statement prints the Tibetan time. To obtain the correct Tibetan time, we use **$time** as an index to the **$tibetan_hour** array. Figure 19.33 contains the definition of the **print_time()** subroutine.

Figure 19.34 contains the Perl script for the *Telling Time* page.

```
sub print_time
{#print the question and the time in Tibetan
  my($time) = $_[0];
  my(@tibetan_hour) = ("undefined", "chik ba", "nyi ba", "sum ba",
  "shi ba", "nga ba", "trook ba", "d&uuml;n ba", "ge ba", "gu ba",
  "chu ba", "chu chik ba","chu nyi ba");
  print "<B>Chu ts&ouml; ka ts&ouml; ray?</B><P>\n";
  print "<I>Chu ts&ouml; <U>$tibetan_hour[$time]</U> ray.</I><BR>\n";
}
```

Figure 19.33 The **print_time()** Subroutine

```
#!/usr/local/bin/perl
&header;
$time = &get_data;
&print_time($time);
&footer;
exit(0);
#Put the print_time() subroutine definition here
#Put the header() subroutine definition here
#Put the footer() subroutine definition here
#Put the get_data() subroutine definition here
```

Figure 19.34 The *Telling Time* Script

SUMMARY OF FORM ELEMENTS

With the exception of on the *Mailing Label* page, we examined the HTML form elements in isolation. The encoding scheme used for the various form elements does not follow a consistent pattern. Figure 19.35 summarizes the encoding schemes and the solutions developed in this chapter. In Chapter 20, we will develop a structure that provides a consistent approach to accessing the various types of form elements. When we've finished, we will have a single **get_data()** subroutine that works with any type of form element.

Form Element	Encoding	Storage
Text Field	*name=value*	Hash
Text Area	*name=value*	Hash
Radio Button	*name=value*	Hash
Checkbox	*name=on*	Array of *Names*
Single Select List	*name=value*	Hash
Multiple Select List	*name=value$_1$*	Array of *Values*
	....	
	name=value$_n$	

Figure 19.35 HTML Form Elements and Perl Storage Possibilities

➤ EXERCISES

These exercises create simple forms with only a few form elements. Create frame-based versions of these pages.

1. **The label() Subroutine, Revisited.** Modify the label() subroutine so that the parameter is a reference to a hash.

2. **The get_data() Subroutine, Revisited.** Modify the get_data() subroutine displayed in Figure 19.10 so that the new-line characters in the text area are replaced with <BR> tags.

3. **The *Favorite Football Team* Page.** Create a radio button page that lists the names of the NFL teams. Ask the user to select a favorite team. Print an appropriate message that indicates whether you agree with the user's choice.

4. **The *Favorite Sports* Page.** Create a radio button page that lists several popular sports. Ask the user to select a favorite sport. Print the name of the sport and an appropriate message.

5. **The *Favorite Team* Page, Select List Version.** Rewrite the *Favorite Team* page. Use a single-select list.

6. **The *Favorite Sports* Page.** Rewrite the favorite sports page. Let the user select as many sports as desired. Use a checkbox.

7. **The *Computer Science Quiz* Page.** Rewrite the *Computer Science Quiz* page as a Perl script. (See Figure 14.51.)

8. **The *Favorite Quotation* Page.** Create a text area that holds the user's favorite quotation. Print the quotation in a bold, italic font.

9. **The *Favorite Ice Creams* Page.** Create a page that asks the user to select a favorite ice-cream flavor. Use radio buttons.

10. **The *Favorite Ice Cream* Page, Single-Select List.** Rewrite the *Favorite Ice Cream* page, using a single-select list.

11. **The *Favorite Colors* Page.** Create a page that lets the user select a favorite primary color (red, blue, yellow) and a favorite secondary color (yellow, orange, purple). Use radio buttons. Print the user's selections.

12. **The *Pizzas and Toppings* Page.** Create a page that lets the user select a favorite style of pizza (deep-dish or thin), a favorite sauce (Marinara, Alfredo, etc.), and favorite toppings. The pizza style and sauces should be radio buttons. The toppings should be a checkbox.

13. **The *Pizza and Toppings* Page, Version 2.** Rewrite the *Pizza* page. Use single-select lists for the pizza style and sauce; use a multiple-select list for the toppings.

14. **The *Favorite Food Groups* Page.** Create radio buttons for each of the major food groups (fruits, vegetables, meat or meat alternative, and grains). Ask the user to select a favorite from each list.

15. **The *Favorite Food Groups* Page, Version 2.** Rewrite the *Food Groups* page. Use single-select lists for each of the food groups.

16. **The *Picnic* Page.** Rewrite the *Picnic* page as a Perl Script. (See Figure 14.50. Don't worry about form verification.)

17. **The *Crossword Puzzle* Page.** Rewrite the *Crossword Puzzle* page as a Perl script. (See Figure 4.51.)

18. **The *Favorite Book* Page.** Create a set of radio buttons with a list of authors. Ask the user to select a favorite author. Print a list of books written by that author.

19. **The *Favorite Composer* Page.** Create a multiple-select list that contains a list of composers (either classical or contemporary). Print the composers and the name of a composition written by each composer.

20. **The *Favorite Composer* Page, Version 2.** Rewrite the *Favorite Composer* page. The user may select as many composers as desired. Print a list of compositions written by the composers. The composers should be listed in alphabetical order.

21. **The *Favorite Household Pet* Page.** Create a page with household pets. Let the user select as many pets as desired.

22. **The *Favorite Dog and Cat Breeds* Page.** Create a page with lists of dog and cat breeds. Ask the user to select a favorite dog breed and a favorite cat breed. Print the breeds and a message of your choice.

23. **The *Favorite Vacation Spots* Page.** Create a page of favorite vacation spots. Ask the user to select his or her favorite spot. Create a list of URLs that link to the vacation spots. When the user selects the favorite spot, link to the URL for that vacation spot.

24. **The *Perl Vocabulary* Page.** Create a page that lists Perl vocabulary from the previous chapters. When the user selects a vocabulary word, the right frame should display the definition.

25. **The *HTML Tags* Page.** Create a page that lists HTML tags. When the user selects a tag, the right frame should display the tag's syntax. Review the tag summaries that appear at the ends of Chapters one through seven.

20 Multiple-Field Forms, Email, Files, and CGI.pm

INTRODUCTION

We concluded the last chapter with a comparison of the URLencoding for form elements and a discussion of the storage possibilities for the decoded elements. Because text fields, text areas, radio buttons, and single-select lists use a *name=value* encoding scheme, a hash works well for these form elements. By contrast, an array works well for checkboxes and multiple-select lists. We can combine these two storage techniques to create a consistent decoding scheme for form elements. The new technique uses a hash of arrays.

THE *COMPUTER SURVEY* PAGE——INTRODUCTION

To illustrate this technique, we create a *Computer Survey* page. The page contains at least one example of each of the form elements that we have studied. Figure 20.1 contains a sample page. The *Computer Survey* displayed in Figure 20.1 contains radio buttons, checkboxes, text fields, a text area, a single-select list, and a multiple-select list.

Figure 20.2 shows the processed page. The user's name and address are placed above the computer experience.

The *Computer Survey* Page——Head and Body

The *Computer Survey* page uses JavaScript and HTML to generate the form. The head of the page contains a JavaScript script that creates arrays for the title (*honorific*), computer system (*system*), language list (*list*), and experience (*years*). Figure 20.3 contains the head of the *Computer Survey* page.

The body of the *Computer Survey* page creates the HTML form. The form is placed within a borderless table to control the alignment of the form elements. The first name, last name, and address fields and the *submit* and *reset* buttons are created with HTML tags. The title, computer

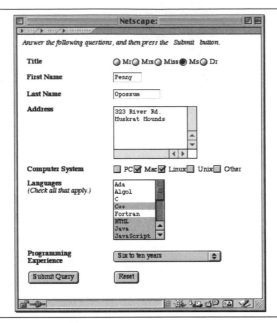

Figure 20.1 The *Computer Survey* Page

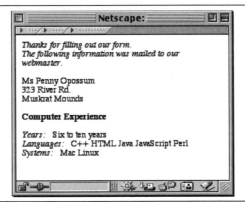

Figure 20.2 A Processed *Computer Survey* Form

```
<HTML><HEAD><TITLE> </TITLE>
<SCRIPT LANGUAGE = "JavaScript">
<!--
  var honorific = new Array("Mr","Mrs", "Miss","Ms", "Dr");
  var system = new Array("PC", "Mac", "Linux", "Unix", "Other");
  var list = new Array("Ada", "Algol", "C", "C++", "Fortran", "HTML",
  "Java", "JavaScript", "Logo", "Lisp", "Modula", "Pascal", "Perl",
  "Prolog", "Scheme", "Snobool", "Other");
  var years =  new Array("Less than one year", "One to five years",
  "Six to ten years", "More than ten years");
//-->
</SCRIPT></HEAD>
```

Figure 20.3 The Head of the *Computer Survey* Page

system, programming language, and programming experience fields are created with JavaScript scripts. For example, the JavaScript script that generates the radio buttons for the title options is

```
<SCRIPT LANGUAGE = "JavaScript">
<!--
    for (var i=0; i< honorific.length; i++) {
      document.write("<INPUT TYPE = 'radio'
          NAME = 'title' VALUE = '");
      document.write(honorific[i] + "'>" + honorific[i]);
    }
//-->
</SCRIPT>
```

Figure 20.4 contains the body of the *Computer Survey* page. The code that generates the form elements is highlighted.

```
<BODY BGCOLOR = 'white'>
<I>Answer the following questions, and then press the <I>Submit</I>
button.</I>
<TABLE CELLPADDING = "3">
<FORM ACTION="computer.pl.cgi" METHOD = "POST">
<TR><TD><B>Title </B></TD>
<TD>
<SCRIPT LANGUAGE = "JavaScript">
<!--
    for (var i=0; i< honorific.length; i++) {
      document.write("<INPUT TYPE = 'radio' NAME = 'title' VALUE = '");
      document.write(honorific[i] + "'>" + honorific[i]);
    }
//-->
</SCRIPT>
</TD></TR>
<TR><TD><B>First Name </B></TD>
<TD><INPUT  TYPE="text" NAME="First" SIZE="7" ></TD></TR>

<TR><TD><B>Last Name </B></TD>
<TD><INPUT  TYPE="text" NAME="Last" SIZE="12"></TD></TR>

<TR><TD VALIGN = "top"><B>Address</B></TD>
<TD><TEXTAREA NAME = "Address" ROWS = "5" COLS = "18" WRAP = "PHYSICAL">
</TEXTAREA></TD></TR>

<TR><TD><B> Computer System</B></TD>
<TD><SCRIPT LANGUAGE = "JavaScript">
<!--
  for (var i=0;   i < system.length; i++){
    document.write("<INPUT TYPE = 'checkbox'");
    document.write("NAME = '" + system[i] + "'>" + system[i]);
  }
//-->
</SCRIPT></TD></TR>
<TR>
<TD VALIGN = "top"><B>Languages</B><BR>
```

Figure 20.4 The Body of the *Computer Survey* Page   *(continues)*

```
<I>(Check all that apply.)</I></TD><TD>
<SELECT NAME = "languages" SIZE = "8"  MULTIPLE>
<SCRIPT LANGUAGE = "JavaScript">
<!--
 for (var i=0; i < list.length; i++) {
   if (list[i] == "C++")
     document.write("<OPTION VALUE = 'CPP'>");
   else if (list[i] == "HTML")
      document.write("<OPTION SELECTED>");
   else document.write("<OPTION>");
   document.write(list[i]);
   }
//-->
</SCRIPT></SELECT></TD></TR>
<TR><TD> <B>Programming Experience</B></TD>
<TD><SELECT NAME = "years" SIZE = "1">
<SCRIPT LANGUAGE = "JavaScript">
<!--
  var i;
  for(i=0; i < years.length; i++)
       document.write("<OPTION>" + years[i]);
//-->
</SCRIPT>
</SELECT></TD></TR>
<TR><TD> <INPUT TYPE="submit"> </TD>
<TD> <INPUT TYPE="reset"> </TD></TR>
</FORM></TABLE></BODY></HTML>
```

Figure 20.4 *(continued)*

The Encoded Form Data and Its Decoded Representation

Examine the completed form appearing Figure 20.2. When Penny Opossum presses the *Submit* button, the browser sends the following URLencoded information to the script:

> `title=Ms&First=Penny&Last=Opossum&Address=323+River+Rd.\nMuskrat+Mounds&Mac=on&Lin`
> `ux=on&languages=CPP&languages=HTML&languages=Java&languages=JavaScript&languages =`
> `Perl&years=Six+to+ten+years`

Notice the encoding used for computer systems and programming languages. The two checked operating systems are encoded as *name=on* pairs, while the selected computer languages all share the same field name. Figure 20.5(a) isolates the encoded *name=value* pairs. Figure 20.5(b) shows the structure of the hash of arrays that we're about to create.

Let's consider the structure illustrated in Figure 20.5(b). The hash keys correspond to the **NAME** attribute of the HTML tag that generated the form element. This is true for every form element except the checkboxes. For checkboxes, we use the name of the JavaScript array, `system`, that generated the checkboxes. Because text fields, text areas, radio buttons and single-select list always pass a *name=value* pair to the script, we use the *name* as the hash key. We place the *value* in the 0th array position.

(a) Encoded Fields	(b) Storage Representation
title=Ms	$hash{'title'}[0]="Ms";
First=Penny	$hash{'First'}[0]="Penny";
Last=Opossum	$hash{'Last'}[0]="Opossum";
Address=323+River+Rd.\n Muskrat+Mounds	$hash{'Address'}[0]="323 River Rd. Muskrat Mounds";
Mac=on Linux=on	$hash{'system'}[0]="Mac"; $hash{'system'}[1]="Linux";
languages=Perl language=CPP languages=HTML languages=Java languages=JavaScript years=Six+to+ten+years	$hash{'languages'}[0]="Perl"; $hash{'languages'}[1]="C++"; $hash{'languages'}[2]="HTML"; $hash{'languages'}[3]="Java"; $hash{'languages'}[4]="JavaScript"; $hash{'years'}[0]="Six to ten years";

Figure 20.5 Encoded Fields and Their Storage Representation

The URLencoding for checkboxes and multiple-select lists deviates from the standard encoding. Check boxes are passed to the script as *name=on* pairs. We use the name of the JavaScript array, *system*, as the key. We add the *name* of each selected checkbox to the array associated with *system*.

The selected options in the multiple-select list all share the same name. The information is passed to the script as *languages=selectedOption* pairs. In this case, the relevant information resides in the *selectedOption*. Thus, we add each *selectedOption* to the array. The key is *languages*.

The get_data() Subroutine

Prior to creating the **get_data()** subroutine, let's review the six-step process that we've used to decode form data:

Step 1. Obtain the Form Data.

Step 2. Convert the Hexadecimal Characters to Their ASCII Equivalents.

Step 3a. Separate the Form Fields.

Step 3b. Separate the Field Names from the User Data.

Step 4. Remove the Suspicious Characters.

Step 5. Convert Plus Signs to Spaces.

Step 6. Store the Field Name–User Data Pairs in a Hash.

Examine these steps. Which steps are affected by the shift to a hash of arrays? Clearly, Steps 1 through 5 are not affected by the shift in storage representations. Thus, we can use the code we previously developed for these steps. Figure 20.6 contains a stub of the **get_data()** subroutine that shows the first five steps of the decoding process. The only modification of the code is the use of **my()** statements to create two arrays, *languages* and *system*. The *languages* array creates the list of selected programming languages. The *system* array creates the list of selected operating systems. The highlighted comments in Figure 20.6 outline the new code that we must add to the **get_data()**

```
sub get_data
{ #Use Steps 1 -6 to get and decode the data
  my($size, $form_size, $key, $value, $i, $form_data);
  my($hash) = @_;
  my(@languages);
  my (@system);
  if ($ENV{'REQUEST_METHOD'} eq "POST") {#1 -- Post Method
    $form_size = $ENV{'CONTENT_LENGTH'};
    read (STDIN, $form_data, $form_size);
  }
  else                                    #1 -- Get Method
     {$form_data = $ENV{'QUERY_STRING'};}
  $form_data =~ s/%([\dA-Fa-f][\dA-Fa-f])/pack ("C", hex ($1))/eg; #2
  @fields = (split(/&/, $form_data));                            #3a
  $size = @fields;
  for ($i=0; $i < size; $i++){
    ($key, $value) = (split /=/, $fields[$i]);                   #3b
    $value =~ s/[;<>\(\)\{\}\*\|'`\&\$!#:"\\]/\ $1/g;            #4
    $value =~ s/+/\ $1/g;                                        #5
    #if statement to handle the text area
    #if...elseif...else statement for languages, system
    # and every thing else
  }
  #Put @language array into the hash
  #Put @system array into the hash
  $_[0] = $hash;
}
```

Figure 20.6 The **get_data()** Subroutine, *Computer Survey* Page: Initial Version

subroutine. As the comments indicate, the first task singles out the text area. It contains multiple lines of code with a physical wrap, so we must replace the **\n** used to terminate lines with **
** tags. The **if** statement compares the current key name with *Address*. If they match, we use the substitution operator to replace the new line characters with **
** tags. The code is

```
if ($key eq "Address")
{ $value =~ s/[\n]/<BR>$1/gi;}
```

We use the **if...elsif...else** statement to determine whether the *key* matches *languages* or one of checkbox names. If the *key* matches *languages* we push the *value* onto the *languages* array. The code is

```
if ($key eq "languages") #Multiple Select List
    { if ($value eq "CPP")
         {$value = "C++";}
       push (@languages, $value); }
```

Notice that we also determine whether *value* matches *"CPP"*. If a match occurs, we change *value* to *"C++"*.

We use the **elsif** clause to determine whether the *key* matches one of the checkbox names. If it does, we push the *key* onto the *system* array. The code is

```
elsif ($key eq "PC" | $key eq "Mac" | $key eq "Linux" |
        $key eq "Unix" | $key eq "Other") #Checkbox
    { push (@system, $key);}
```

The **else** clause handles all of the remaining form elements. Because these elements contain a single *key–value* pair, we add the *key–value* pair to the hash. The **value** resides in the 0th position of the array. The code is

```
else   #Anything else
   {$$hash{$key}[0] = $value;}
```

Notice that we must dereference the hash.

Figure 20.7 contains the complete code for the **if...elsif...else** statement.

```
if ($key eq "languages") #Multiple Select List
   { if ($value eq "CPP")
        {$value = "C++";}
     push (@languages, $value); }
elsif ($key eq "PC" | $key eq "Mac" | $key eq "Linux" |
        $key eq "Unix" | $key eq "Other") #Checkbox
   { push (@system, $key);}
else                          #Anything else
   {$$hash{$key}[0] = $value; }
```

Figure 20.7 Creating the Hash of Arrays

After the **for** statement terminates, we create the hash entries for the multiple-select list and the checkboxes. We create the hash entry for the multiple-select list with the following statement:

```
$$hash{"languages"} = [@languages];
```

The statement dereferences the hash. The new key is *languages*. The value is the *languages* array. Notice the notation. We must use the brackets to assign the entire array as the value.

We create the hash entry for the check boxes in a similar fashion. The statement is

```
$$hash{"system"} = [@system];
```

This statement creates a new key, *system*. The value is the *system* array.

We've developed the **get_data()** subroutine in pieces; now, it will be helpful to see the entire method. Figure 20.8 contains the complete code for the **get_data()** subroutine.

The **print_field()** Subroutine

The **print_field()** subroutine displays the array associated with a key. This subroutine requires two parameters: the key's name, and a reference to the hash. For example, to print the values associated with the *languages* key, we use the statement

```
&print_field("languages", \%hash);
```

The **print_field()** subroutine contains a **my()** statement that places the contents of the **@_** array into the variables *key* and *hash_ref*. We also use a **my()** statement to create the variable *name*. This variable is the index for the **foreach** statement that extracts the array.

The code for the **foreach** statement is

```
foreach $name (keys %$hash_ref){
   if ($name eq $key)
        {print "@{$$hash_ref{$name}}\n";}
}
```

```
sub get_data
{ #Use Steps 1 -6 to get and decode the data
  my($size, $form_size, $key, $value, $i, $form_data);
  my($hash) = @_;
  my(@languages);
  my (@system);
  if ($ENV{'REQUEST_METHOD'} eq "POST") {#1 -- Post Method
    $form_size = $ENV{'CONTENT_LENGTH'};
    read (STDIN, $form_data, $form_size);
  }
  else                                   #1 -- Get Method
    {$form_data = $ENV{'QUERY_STRING'};}
  $form_data =~ s/%([\dA-Fa-f][\dA-Fa-f])/pack ("C", hex ($1))/eg; #2
  @fields = (split(/&/, $form_data));                         #3a
  $size = @fields;
  for ($i=0; $i < $size; $i++){
    ($key, $value) = (split /=/, $fields[$i]);                #3b
    $value =~ s/[;<>\(\)\{\}\*\|'`\&\$!#:"\\]/\ $1/g;         #4
    $value =~ s/+/\ $1/g;                            #5
    if ($key eq "Address")
    { $value =~ s/[\n]/<BR>$1/gi;}
    if ($key eq "languages")
     { if ($value eq "CPP")
        {$value = "C++";}
       push (@languages, $value); }
    elsif ($key eq "PC" | $key eq "Mac" | $key eq "Linux" |
      $key eq "Unix" | $key eq "Other")
    { push (@system, $key);}
    else
     {$$hash{$key}[0] = $value;}
  }
  $$hash{"languages"} = [@languages];
  $$hash{"system"} = [@system];
  $_[0] = $hash;
}
```

Figure 20.8 The **get_data()** Subroutine, *Computer Survey* Page

Notice the header of the **foreach** statement. Because *hash_ref* is passed as a reference, we must place the hash prefix, **%**, before the variable name, **$hash_ref**. The body of the **foreach** statement contains an **if** statement that compares the name passed as a parameter with the current key. If a match occurs, the array associated with the name is printed. To access this array, we dereference the hash by using double dollar signs: **$$hash_ref**. Next, we use block notation to create an array from the values:

> **@{$$hash_ref{$name}}**

The **print** statement prints the complete array. Figure 20.9 contains the definition of the **print_field()** subroutine.

```
sub print_field
{ # print a value
  my($key,$hash_ref) = @_;
  my ($name);
  foreach $name (keys %$hash_ref){
    if ($name eq $key)
      {print "@{$$hash_ref{$name}}\n";}
  }
}
```

Figure 20.9 The `print_field()` Subroutine, *Computer Survey* Page

Figure 20.10 contains the Perl code for the *Computer Survey* page. It uses a combination of **print** and **print_field()** statements to control the appearance of the information displayed in Figure 20.2

```
#!/usr/local/bin/perl
&header;
&get_data(\%hash);
print "<I>Thanks for filling out our form.<BR>\n";
print "This is your form information.</I><P>\n";
&print_field("title",\%hash);
&print_field("First", \%hash);
&print_field("Last", \%hash);
print "<BR>\n";
&print_field("Address", \%hash);
print "<P><B>Computer Experience</B><P>\n";
print "<I>Years:</I> ";
&print_field("years", \%hash);
print "<BR><I>Languages:</I> ";
&print_field("languages", \%hash);
print "<BR><I>Systems:</I> \n";
&print_field("system", \%hash);
&footer;
exit(0);
#Put the get_data() Subroutine Definition Here
#Put the print_field() Subroutine Definition Here
#Put the header() Subroutine Definition Here
#Put the footer() Subroutine Definition Here
```

Figure 20.10 The Perl Code for the *Computer Survey* Page

The *Computer Survey* Page: Email Version

The *Computer Survey* page displays the processed information as a Web page. Suppose we also want to email the results to someone. We can email the survey results by adding one subroutine to the Perl code for the *Computer Survey* page. Figure 20.11 contains a sample email message. The email contains the keys and their associated values.

```
Delivered-To: Recipient@Email.address
Date Fri, 13 Oct 2000 10:52:59 -0500
From: Sender@Email.address
Mime-Version: 1.0
```

The completed form information is:

```
Ms Penny Opossum
323 River Rd.
Muskrat Mounds
```

```
Years of Experience: Six to ten years
Language Knowledge: C++ HTML Java
JavaScript Perl
System Experience: Mac Linux
```

Figure 20.11 Email Message for the *Computer Survey* Page

Email Basics

Emailing form information requires knowledge of file handling. The previous Perl scripts used the standard input and output devices, known as **STDIN** and **STDOUT**, respectively. These device names are called *file handles*.

Perl assumes that **read** statements read from **STDIN** and **print** statements write to **STDOUT**. Therefore, we can omit the file handle from **read** and **print** statements when we use **STDIN** or **STDOUT**. When we email information, we instead write to the email device handler for our system.

We use a three-step technique to write information to email form data.

Step 1. Open a File Handle.   The syntax for opening a file handle is

open (File Handle, "Device Name");

As the syntax indicates, the **open()** function requires a handle name and a device name as parameters. For example, suppose Molly Muskrat is the email recipient. Her name is **mmusk** and her address is **musk.rat.com**. The statement that opens the **MAIL** handle is

open(MAIL, "|mail mmusk\@musk.rat.com");

The handle name is **MAIL**. The string literal indicates that Molly's address is piped (|) to the standard mail server (**mail** on most machines).

Step 2. Print the Information to the File.   The **print** statement has an alternative form that includes a file handle. To change the file handle, we pass the file handle and the string as parameters to the **print** statement. For example, to print the string *My name is Penny Opossum* to the email file, we write

print MAIL, "My name is Penny Opossum\n";

(When writing to any file, we use the new-line character to terminate lines.)

Step 3. Close the File.   When we've finished using a file, we close it. To accomplish this task, we call the **close()** function using the file handle as a parameter. For example, we close the mail file with the statement

close(MAIL);

Figure 20.12 contains the definition of the **print_all_mail()** subroutine. We pass a reference to the hash as a parameter. The following statement illustrates the call:

&print_all_mail(\%hash,);

The **print_all_mail()** subroutine opens a mail handle for Molly Muskrat. (Of course, you'll want to substitute your own email address to test the page.) The subroutine contains a series of **print**

```
sub print_all_mail
{ #print all of the arrays
  my($hash_ref) = @_;
  my ($value);
  open(MAIL, "|mail mmusk\@musk.rat.com");
  print MAIL "The completed form information is:\n\n";
  print MAIL "$$hash_ref{'title'}[0] $$hash_ref{'First'}[0] $$hash_ref{'Last'}[0]\n";
  $value = $$hash_ref{'Address'}[0];
  $value =~ s/<BR>/\n$1/gi;
  print MAIL "$value\n\n";
  print MAIL "Years of Experience: $$hash_ref{'years'}[0]\n";
  print MAIL "Language Knowledge: @{$$hash_ref{'languages'}}\n";
  print MAIL "\nSystem Experience: @{$$hash_ref{'system'}}\n";
  close(MAIL);
}
```

Figure 20.12 The `print_all_mail()` Subroutine

statements that create the email message. The information is stored in random order in the hash, but we extract it in a manner that conveys meaning. Thus, the user's name and address are printed first. The **
** tags in the address are converted to new-line characters prior to the printing the address. The computer experience is printed after the mailing information.

Figure 20.13 contains the Perl script that creates the email version of the *Computer Survey* page. The highlighted lines show the modifications made to the original version of this page.

```
#!/usr/local/bin/perl
&header;
&get_data(\%hash);

print "<I>Thanks for filling out our form.<BR>\n";
print "The following information was mailed to our webmaster.</I><P>\n";
&print_field("title", \%hash);
&print_field("First", \%hash);
&print_field("Last", \%hash);
print "<BR>\n";
&print_field("Address", \%hash,);
print "<P><B>Computer Experience</B><P>\n";
print "<I>Years:</I> ";
&print_field("years", \%hash);
print "<BR><I>Languages:</I> ";
&print_field("languages", \%hash);
print "<BR><I>Systems:</I> \n";
&print_field("system", \%hash);
&print_all_mail(\%hash);
&footer;
exit(0);
#put print_all_mail() subroutine definition here
#put print_field() subroutine definition here
#put get_data() subroutine definition here
#put header() subroutine definition here
#put footer() subroutine definition here
```

Figure 20.13 The Script for the *Computer Survey* Page, email version

Reading Disk Files

We now turn our attention to disk files. We begin with a page that reads the information from a disk file. Retrieving this information is an easy task in Perl. The first step is the creation of a sample disk file. Figure 20.14 contains a small verse. Using your favorite text editor, retype the verse, or pick a poem of your choice. Save the file in ASCII or in plain text format. Name the file **poem.txt**.

```
Roses are Red.
Violets are Blue.
JavaScript's Cool.
And Perl is too.
```

Figure 20.14 The **poem.txt** File

Once we've created the file, we're ready to create a Web page that displays it. Figure 20.15 contains the desired Web page.

Creating the page shown in Figure 20.15 requires two Perl subroutines in addition to the "usual" **header()** and **footer()** subroutines. The first subroutine reads the disk file; the second prints the file's contents onto a Web page.

The read_file() Subroutine

We use a three-step procedure to read a text file.

Step 1. Open the File.   We open a file for reading by using the technique used to open a file for email. We call the **open()** function, passing the file handle and the disk file name as parameters. The statement that opens the file is

```
open(FILE, $name);
```

This statement opens a file handle, **FILE**, that is an alias for the disk file contained in **$name**.

Step 2. Read the File.   We use the file-reading operator, <>, to load the file's contents into an array. The statement that reads the file and places it in the array is

```
@FileInfo = <FILE>;
```

The operator <> encloses the file handle. The read operator is placed on the right-hand side of an assignment statement. The array that holds the file's contents is placed on the left-hand side of the assignment operator.

Step 3. Close the file.   After we've read the file, we close it, by means of the statement

```
close(FILE);
```

Figure 20.16 contains the definition of the **read_file()** subroutine. The **read_file()** subroutine contains a **my()** statement that extracts the file's name from the parameter. The statement is

```
my($name) = @_;
```

The subroutine contains a second **my()** statement that creates a local array, *FileInfo*. This array will hold the extracted file information.

The **read_file()** subroutine uses the three-step process to extract the file information. After we've extracted the information, we return the array containing this information. We call the **read_file()** subroutine with the statement

```
@contents = read_file("poem.txt");
```

We pass the file **poem.txt** as the parameter. The subroutine returns an array that we assign to **@contents**.

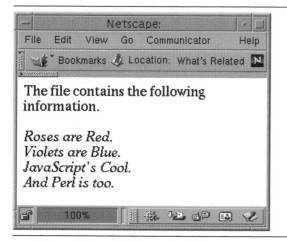

Figure 20.15 The *Read File* Page

```
sub read_file{
    #read the information from the file
    my($name) = @_;
    my (@FileInfo);
    open(FILE, $name);   #1
    @FileInfo = <FILE>;  #2
    close(FILE);         #3
    return @FileInfo;
}
```

Figure 20.16 The **read_file()** Subroutine

The print_file() Subroutine.

The **print_file()** subroutine prints the array onto the Web page. We pass an array with the file's contents as a parameter. We use a **my()** statement to extract the array. The statement is

    my(@contents) = @_;

    The **print_file()** subroutine contains a **foreach** statement that prints the *contents* array. The body of this statement prints the current poem line, **$element**, followed by a **
** tag. Figure 20.17 contains the definition of the **print_file()** subroutine.

```
sub print_file
{
  #print the contents of the file
  my(@contents) = @_;
  my($element);
  print "The file contains the following information.<P><I>\n";
  foreach $element(@contents)
     {print "$element<BR>";}
  print "</I>\n";
}
```

Figure 20.17 The **print_file()** Subroutine

    Figure 20.18 contains the Perl code for the *Read File* page. The main program contain four subroutine calls and a call to the **exit()** function.

THE *SUGGESTION BOX* PAGE

To illustrate writing to a file, we create an online suggestion box for the Muskrat Mounds Tree Farm. Figure 20.19 contains a sample page. The left frame contains the suggestion box. The right frame shows the current suggestions. The suggestions are printed in reverse order of submission, with the most recent suggestion appearing at the front of the list.

```perl
#!/usr/local/bin/perl
&header;
@contents = read_file("poem.txt");
&print_file(@contents);
&footer;
exit(0);
#Put the read_file() Subroutine definition here
#Put the print_file() Subroutine definition here
#Put the header() Subroutine definition here
#Put the footer() Subroutine definition here
```

Figure 20.18 Perl Code for the *Read File* Page

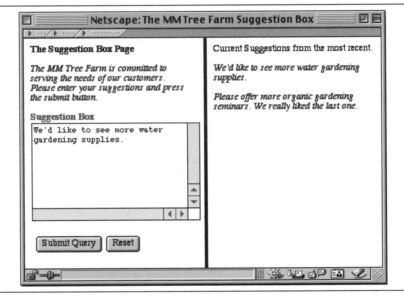

Figure 20.19 The *Suggestion Box* Page

Figure 20.20 contains the HTML for the *Suggestion Box* page. The form uses a single text area to obtain the user's suggestions.

The Perl Script for the *Suggestion Box* Page

When the user presses the *Submit* button, the browser passes the single field to the Perl script. The Perl script uses the **read_file()** and **print_file()** subroutines developed in the last section. The **print_file()** subroutine contains a minor change in the opening message.

Although we can use the **get_data()** subroutine from the previous section, it's easier to use a simplified version of this subroutine. The simplified version extracts the single field and returns it the main Perl program. Figure 20.21 contains the code for the **print_file()** and **get_data()** subroutines.

Completing the Perl script for the *Suggestion* Box page requires a subroutine that writes the suggestions to a file.

```
<HTML><HEAD><TITLE> </TITLE></HEAD>
<BODY BGCOLOR = 'white'>
<B>The Suggestion Box Page</B><P>
<I>The MM Tree Farm is committed to serving the needs of our customers. Please enter your
suggestions and press the submit button.</I>
</I><P>
<FORM NAME = "Suggestions" ACTION ="suggest.pl.cgi" METHOD = "POST"
TARGET = "results">
<FONT COLOR = "green"><B>Suggestion Box</B></FONT>
<TEXTAREA NAME = "Suggest" ROWS = "8" COLS = "30" WRAP = "PHYSICAL">
</TEXTAREA>
<TABLE><TR><TD COLSPAN = "2">
<INPUT TYPE="submit">
<INPUT TYPE="reset"></TD></TR>
</FORM></TABLE></BODY></HTML>
```

Figure 20.20 The *Suggestion Box* Form

```
sub print_file
{
  #print the contents of the file
  my(@contents) = @_;
  my($element);
  print "Current Suggestions from the most recent.<P><I>\n";
  foreach $element(@contents)
  {print "$element";}
  print "</I>\n";
}
sub get_data
{ #Simplified decoding to obtain the text area
  my($form_data, $form_size, $key, $value);
  $form_size = $ENV{'CONTENT_LENGTH'};
  read (STDIN, $form_data, $form_size);
  $form_data =~ s/%([\dA-Fa-f][\dA-Fa-f])/pack ("C", hex ($1))/eg;
  ($key, $value) = (split /=/, $form_data);
   $value =~ s/[+;<>\(\)\{\}\*\|`\&\$!#:"\\]/\ $1/g;
   $value =~ s/[\n]/<BR>$1/gi;
   $value = $value . "<P>";
   return $value;
}
```

Figure 20.21 The **print_file()** and **get_data()** Subroutines, *Suggestion Box* Page

The write_file() Subroutine

Prior to developing the **write_file()** subroutine, we must create the **address.txt** file. Initially, this file contains nothing. If doing so is appropriate for your system, set the privileges so that everyone has read, execute, *and write* privileges. The file must exist, because we call the **read_file()** subroutine before the **write_file()** subroutine. Perl will read an empty file, but it won't read a nonexistent file!

Writing to a disk file is similar, but not identical, to sending an email message. We use a three-step approach.

Step 1. Open the File. When we open a file for writing, we can choose either to write a new file or to append to an existing file. Writing to a new file destroys any previously existing file with the same name. Appending to a file adds the data to the end of the file without destroying the file's original contents. To create a new file for writing, we use the statement

```
open(FILE, ">$file_name");
```

This statement creates a new file handle, **FILE**, linked to the name contained in **$file_name**.

Step 2. Write to the File. We use **print** statements with the file handle as a parameter to write to the file.

Step 3. Close the File. We use the **close()** function with the file handle as a parameter to close the file.

Figure 20.22 contains the definition of the **write_file()** subroutine.

```
sub write_file {
#write addreses to file
  my($file_name, $contents_ref)= @_;
  my($line);
  open(FILE, ">$file_name");
  foreach $line (@$contents_ref)
  { print FILE $line; }
    close(FILE);
}
```

Figure 20.22 The **write_file()** Subroutine

Notice the **foreach** statement used to print the lines to the file. Because we passed the *contents* array as a reference, we must indicate that the scalar **$contents_ref** is a reference to an array; hence, we use **@$contents_ref**.

The Perl Script for the *Suggestion Box* Page

Figure 20.23 shows the Perl code for the *Suggestion Box* page. Notice the highlighted statements in Figure 20.23. The first statement,

```
$suggestion = &get_data();
```

calls the **get_data()** subroutine. The modified version of this subroutine returns the contents of the text area.

The second statement,

```
@contents = read_file("suggest.txt");
```

invokes the **read_file()** subroutine. This subroutine returns the array of suggestions.
The last statement,

```
unshift (@contents, $suggestion);
```

uses the **unshift()** function to place the latest suggestion at the front of the *contents* array. We then call the **write_file()** subroutine to write the *contents* array to the disk file. The statement is

```perl
#!/usr/local/bin/perl
&header;
$suggestion = &get_data();
@contents = read_file("suggest.txt");
unshift (@contents, $suggestion);
&write_file("suggest.txt", \@contents);
&print_file(@contents);
&footer;
exit(0);
#put the print_file() Subroutine Here
#put the get_data() Subroutine Here
#put the write_file() Subroutine Here
#Put the header() Subroutine Here
#Put the footer() Subroutine Here
#Put the read_file() Subroutine Here
```

Figure 20.23 Perl Code for the *Suggestion Box* Page

```perl
&write_file("suggest.txt", \@contents);
```

After we've written the information to the file, we call the **print_file()** subroutine to print the file. The statement is

```perl
&print_file(@contents);
```

THE CGI.pm MODULE

Lincoln Stein developed the **CGI.pm** module to facilitate creating and processing Web forms. The module is standard equipment on Perl 5.004 and later versions. To illustrate **CGI.pm**, we rewrite the *Computer Survey* page using this module. The final product's appearance will be identical to the *Computer Survey* page displayed in Figure 20.1. However, we generate this product by using only Perl scripts.

Processing the Computer Survey Form with CGI.pm

We may use either of two techniques to access **CGI.pm** and its methods. Figure 20.24 lists both techniques.

(a) Methods Group Approach	(b) Object-Oriented Approach

`use CGI qw/`*methods group*`/;`
`$title = param("title");`
	`use CGI;`
	`$form = CGI::new();`
	`$title = $form->param("title");`

Figure 20.24 Accessing the **CGI.pm** Module

The *Methods Group Approach*, listed in Figure 20.24(a), lets us load parts of the **CGI.pm** module. We use the *quote words* (**qw**) operator to select the methods group. We place the desired methods group between the slashes. Figure 20.25 lists several commonly used methods groups.

Method Group	Purpose
:all	Complete package
:cgi	CGI methods
:form	HTML form methods
:html	All HTML methods
:html2	All HTML 2.0 methods
:html3	All HTML 3.0 methods
:netscape	All Netscape Extensions
:standard	HTML 2.0, Form, and CGI methods

Figure 20.25 Commonly Used Method Groups

Once we've loaded a methods group, we can call methods in that group. Figure 20.24(a) contains a call to the **param()** method. This method contains a single parameter that represents the name of a form element. The method returns the value associated with the form element. In our example, we call the method with *title*. **CGI.pm** returns the value that the user selected (that is, Mr., Mrs., Miss., Ms., or Dr.).

The Object-Oriented Approach

Figure 20.24(b) illustrates the object-oriented approach. With this approach, we load the **CGI.pm** module with the statement

```
use CGI;
```

Next, we use a constructor to create a new CGI object. In our example, the new object is called *form*. The statement that constructs it is

```
$form = CGI::new();
```

Once we've created the object, we can access any of the CGI methods. For example, to obtain the value associated with the *First* field of the *Computer Survey* form, we write

```
$name = $form->param('First');
```

When we use the object-oriented approach, we must dereference the method; hence, we use the -> operator.

Processing the *Computer Survey* Page by Using CGI.pm

Figure 20.26 contains a new version of the script that uses **CGI.pm** to process the *Computer Survey* form. The calls to the **param()** method are highlighted.

Figure 20.27 contains the page produced by the Perl code appearing in Figure 20.26. This page is comparable to the *Computer Survey* results page appearing in Figure 20.2. Compare Figure 20.27 and Figure 20.2. Which page looks better? Why?

The page appearing in Figure 20.27 has several flaws that detract from the page's appearance:

Address.　Penny's address is contained on a single line, although she wrote it on two lines when she filled out the form in Figure 20.1. Of course, we know that the new-line characters used in the text area are ignored by browsers. To fix this problem, we need to replace the new-line characters with **
** tags. The statement that does this is

```
$street =~  s/[\n]/<BR>$1/gi; #Change newlines to <BR>
```

Computer Languages.　**CGI.pm** places values associated with a multiple-select list into an array. The **print** statement,

```
print param("languages");
```

```
#!/usr/local/bin/perl
use CGI qw/:standard/;
&header;
print "<I>Thanks for filling out our form.<BR>\n";
print "This is your form information.</I><P>\n";
print param("title");
print param("First");
print " ";
print param("Last");
print "<BR>";
print param("Address");
print "<P><B>Computer Experience</B><P>");
print "<I>Years: </I> ";
print param("years");
print "<BR><I>Languages: </I>";
print param("languages");
print "<BR><I>Systems: </I>";
@systems = ("PC", "Mac", "Linux", "Unix", "Other");
foreach $element (@systems)
{  print param($element);}
&footer;
exit(0);
#Put the header() subroutine definition here
#Put the footer() subroutine definition here
```

Figure 20.26 The *Computer Survey* Form, **CGI.pm**, version 1

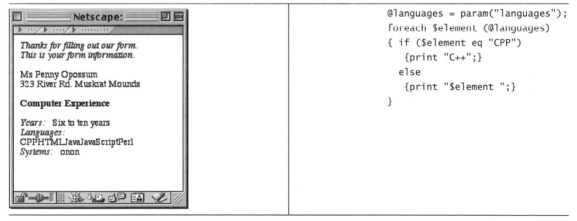

Figure 20.27 Page Produced by Perl
Code in Figure 20.26

```
@languages = param("languages");
foreach $element (@languages)
{ if ($element eq "CPP")
    {print "C++";}
  else
    {print "$element ";}
}
```

Figure 20.28 Printing Multiple-Select Lists with
CGI.pm

prints the entire array. However, the array elements are printed without spacing. In addition, the value **CPP** is printed rather than the label "C++". To solve these problems, we use the code contained in Figure 20.28.

Checkbox Elements. The checkbox elements win the prize for the most obscure output. The page prints *on* twice, to indicate that the user selected two operating systems—but which two were selected? To solve this problem, we create a **foreach** statement that cycles through each of the checkbox names. We call the **param()** method with each of the names. The **param()** function returns *false* for nonexistent elements, so we can use an **if** statement to place the names of selected elements (only) into a string. Figure 20.29 contains the statements that create a string of selected checkboxes.

```
$os =  "<BR><I>Systems: </I>";
@systems = ("PC", "Mac", "Linux", "Unix", "Other");
foreach $element (@systems)
{  if (param($element))
   {$os .= $element." ";}}
print "$os";
```

Figure 20.29 Creating a String of Selected Checkboxes

Figure 20.30 contains a revised version of the Perl code for the *Computer Survey* page. The code in this page uses **CGI.pm**. The code results are identical to the page displayed in Figure 20.2.

```
#!/usr/local/bin/perl
use CGI qw/:standard/;
&header;
print "<I>Thanks for filling out our form.<BR>\n";
print "This is your form information.</I><P>\n";
print param("title");
print param("First");
print " ";
print param("Last");
print "<BR>";
$street = param("Address");
$street =~  s/[\n]/<BR>$1/gi; #break on spaces
print "$street";
print "<P><B>Computer Experience</B><P>";
print "<I>Years: </I> ";
print param("years");
print "<BR><I>Languages: </I>";
@languages = param("languages");
foreach $element (@languages){
    if ($element eq "CPP")
      {print "C++";}
    else
     {print "$element ";}
}
$os =  "<BR><I>Systems: </I>";
@systems = ("PC", "Mac", "Linux", "Unix", "Other");
foreach $element (@systems)
{  if (param($element))
   {$os .= $element." ";}}
print "$os";
&footer;
exit(0);
#Put the header() Subroutine Definition Here
#Put the footer() Subroutine Definition Here
```

Figure 20.30 Perl Code for the *Computer Survey* Page: **CGI.pm**, user-friendly version

Creating The *Computer Survey* Form with CGI.pm

Creating a form with **CGI.pm** is substantially more complicated than merely processing a form with it. Each form element has its own method. The methods include parameters for each of the HTML attributes, including the event handlers. There are also methods that mimic the **<FORM>** and **</FORM>** tags, as is shown in Figure 20.31.

```
startform(-name=>'form name',
-method=>'GET' | 'POST',
-action=>'script name',
-target=>'frame name',
-encoding=>'encoding scheme');
```
Put the form elements here
```
endform();
```

Figure 20.31 CGI.pm Methods that Create a Form

The **start_form()** method contains named parameters that correspond to each of the HTML **<FORM>** tag attributes. A named parameter uses a dash as a prefix to the parameter name. Thus, programmers can identify parameters by their names rather than by their position. We use the following statement to create the form for the *Computer Survey* page:

```
print $form->startform(-action=>'compCgi.pl.cgi',
       -method=>'POST', -target=>'results');
```

This statement indicates that the browser should use the **POST** method to transmit the form data to the *compCgi.pl.cgi* script.

Text Fields and Text Area Methods

Figure 20.32 contains the text field and text area methods. Only the commonly used named parameters are included in this table. Most of the parameter names match their corresponding HTML tag attributes. The only deviation appears in the **-default** parameter. This parameter, which specifies a default value, corresponds to the HTML **VALUE** attribute.

(a) Text Field	(b) Text Area

`textfield(-name=>'name',`
` -default =>'value',`
` -size=>'number',`
`    ...`
` -onChange=>'function',`
` -onFocus=>'function'`
` -onBlur=>'function'`
` -onSelect=>'function');`
	`textarea(-name=>'name',`
	` -default =>'value',`
	` -rows=>'number',`
	` -columns=>'number',`
	` -wrap=>'wrap style',`
	` -onChange=>'function',`
	` -onFocus=>'function'`
	` -onBlur=>'function'`
	` -onSelect=>'function');`

Figure 20.32 Text Field and Text Areas Methods: CGI.pm

(a) HTML	(b) `CGI.pm`

`<INPUT  TYPE="text"`
`        NAME="First"`
`        SIZE="7">`
	`print $form->textfield(`
	`    -name=>'First',`
	`    -size=>'7');`

`<INPUT  TYPE="text"`
`        NAME="Last"`
`        SIZE="12">`
	`print $form->textfield(`
	`    -name=>'Last',`
	`    -size=>'12');`

`<TEXTAREA`
`  NAME = "Address"`
`  ROWS = "5"`
`  COLS = "18"`
`  WRAP = "PHYSICAL">`
`</TEXTAREA>`
	`print $form->textarea(`
	`    -name=>'street',`
	`    -rows=>'5',`
	`    -cols=>'18',`
	`    -wrap=>'physical');`

Figure 20.33 HTML Tags and Their `CGI.pm` equivalents

The *Computer Survey* page uses text fields for the person's first and last names and a text area for the address. Figure 20.33(a) shows the HTML tags used in the initial version of the *Computer Survey* page. Figure 20.33(b) shows the `CGI.pm` equivalents.

Radio Buttons and Checkboxes

Figure 20.34 contains the `CGI.pm` methods that create checkboxes and radio buttons.

(a) Radio Buttons	(b) Checkboxes

`radio_group(-name=>'`*name*`',`
`  -values=>\@`*values*`,`
`  -default=>'`*selected value*`',`
`  -labels=>\%`*hash*`);`
	`checkbox(-name=>'`*name*`',`
	`  -checked=>'`*checked value*`',`
	`  -value=>'`*value*`',`
	`  -label=>'`*label name*`');`

Figure 20.34 Radio Buttons and Check Boxes: `CGI.pm`

The checkbox method closely resembles its HTML equivalent. `CGI.pm` uses the **radio_group()** method to create a set of radio buttons. The elements in the **radio_group()** share a common name. An array furnishes the values and labels for the buttons. We can change the labels by using a hash with the value as the key and the label as its value. Figure 20.35 shows the `CGI.pm` methods that create the *title* radio buttons and the *system* checkboxes. Compare this code with the HTML appearing in Figure 20.2.

The *title* Radio Buttons	The *system* Checkboxes

`@honorific = ("Mr","Mrs", "Miss","Ms", "Dr");`
 	
`print $form->radio_group(`
`   -name =>'title',`
`   -values=>\@honorific);`
	`@system = ("PC", "Mac", "Linux", "Unix", "Other");`
	
	`foreach $element(@system)`
	`{ print $form->checkbox(`
	`    -name=>$element,`
	`    -label=>$element); }`

Figure 20.35 The *title* and *system* Form Elements

Buttons and Select Lists

CGI.pm also contains methods that create JavaScript-style buttons as well as the standard *Submit* and *Reset* buttons. Figure 20.36(a) contains the "buttons" methods. Figure 20.36(b) contains the description of the **scrolling_list()** method. The latter method creates single- or multiple-select lists.

(a) Buttons	(b) Select lists

button(-name=>'*name*',
  -value=>'*button label*',
  -onClick=>'*function*');
 	
submit();
 	
reset();
	scrolling_list(-name=>'*name*',
	  -values=>\@*option names*,
	  -default=>'*selected option*',
	  -size=>'*number*',
	  -multiple=>'*true*',
	  -labels=>\%*label names*,
	  -onFocus=>'*function*'
	  -onBlur=>'*function*'
	  -onSelect=>'*function*');

Figure 20.36 Buttons and Select Lists: CGI.pm

The **scrolling_list()** method includes a **-multiple** parameter. Setting this parameter to *true* creates a multiple-select list. Omitting this parameter creates a single-select list. The **-values** parameter creates the option values and labels for the list, using the array passed as a parameter. The **-labels** parameter changes some or all of the labels by passing a reference to a hash as a parameter. The value is the key, and the label is its associated value.

Figure 20.37 contains the CGI.pm method calls that create the *languages* multiple-select list and the *years* single-select list.

(a) The *language* List	(b) The *years* List

`@language_list =("Ada", "Algol",`
`"C", "CPP", "Fortran", "HTML",`
`"Java", "JavaScript", "Logo",`
`"Lisp", "Modula", "Pascal", "Perl",`
`"Prolog", "Scheme", "Snobol",`
`"Other");`
 	
`$label{"CPP"} = "C++";`
 	
`print $form->scrolling_list(`
`  -name=>'languages',`
`  -values=>\@language_list,`
`  -size=>'8',`
`  -multiple=>'true',`
`  -labels=>\%label,`
`  -default=>"HTML");`
	`@years =  ("Less than one year",`
	`"One to five years",`
	`"Six to ten years",`
	`"More than ten years");`
	
	`print $form->scrolling_list(`
	`    -name=>'years',`
	`    -values=>\@years);`

Figure 20.37 Multiple- and Single-Select Lists

We create the *language* list in Figure 20.37(a) with the help of an auxiliary array, **@language_list**, and a hash, **%label**. The hash contains a single key–value pair that creates the "C++" label. The **-default** parameter selects the HTML option.

Figure 20.38 contains the Perl code that creates the *Computer Survey* form by using **CGI.pm** methods. The form's appearance is identical to that of the form displayed in Figure 20.1.

```perl
#!/usr/local/bin/perl
use CGI;
$form = CGI::new();

&header;
print "<I>Answer the following questions, and then press\n";
print " the <I>Submit</I>button.</I>\n";
print "<TABLE>";
print $form->startform(-action=>'compCgi.pl.cgi', -method=>'POST',
-target=>'results');
@honorific = ("Mr","Mrs", "Miss","Ms", "Dr");
print "<TR><TD><B>Title</B></TD><TD>";
print $form->radio_group(-name =>'title', -values=>\@honorific);
print "</TD></TR>";
print "<TR><TD><B>First Name</B></TD><TD>";
print $form->textfield(-name=>'First', -size=>'7');
print "</TD><TR><TD><B>Last Name</B></TD><TD> ";
print $form->textfield(-name=>'Last', -size=>'12');
print "</TD></TR><TD VALIGN = 'top'><B>Address</B></TD><TD>";
print $form->textarea(-name =>'street', -rows=>'5',
      -cols=>'18', -wrap=>'physical');
print "</TD></TR><TR><TD VALIGN = 'top'>";
print "<B>Computer Systems</B></TD><TD>";

@system = ("PC", "Mac", "Linux", "Unix", "Other");
foreach $element(@system)
{ print $form->checkbox(-name=>$element, -label=>$element); }
print "</TD></TR><TR><TD VALIGN = 'top'>";
print "<B>Languages</B><BR><I>Check all that apply.</I></TD><TD>";

@language_list =("Ada", "Algol", "C", "CPP", "Fortran", "HTML",
  "Java", "JavaScript", "Logo", "Lisp", "Modula", "Pascal", "Perl",
  "Prolog", "Scheme", "Snobool", "Other");
$label{"CPP"} = "C++";
print $form->scrolling_list(-name=>'languages',-values=>\@language_list, -size=>'8', -
multiple=>'true', -labels=>\%label, -default=>"HTML");
 print "</TD></TR><TR><TD VALIGN = 'top'>";

 @years =  ("Less than one year", "One to five years",
  "Six to ten years", "More than ten years");
print "</TD></TR><TR><TD><B>Experience</B></TD><TD>";
print $form->scrolling_list(-name=>'years',-values=>\@years);
print "</TD></TR><TR><TD>";
print $form->submit();
print $form->reset();
print $form->endform();
print "</TD></TR></TABLE>";
&footer;
exit(0);
```

Figure 20.38 The *Computer Survey* Form Created with **CGI.pm**

THE OPINION POLL PAGE

We conclude our excursion into Perl programming with a page that integrates many of the concepts learned in previous chapters. As our example, we create and process an opinion poll for the fictitious *Holiday Gazette*. Figure 20.39 displays the opening page for the opinion poll. As this figure indicates, the user can either fill out a survey or examine the survey results.

Figure 20.40 contains the HTML for the Opinion Poll's opening page.

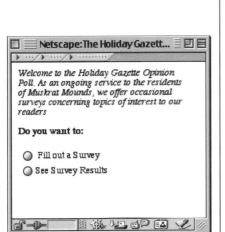

```
<HTML><HEAD> <TITLE> The Holiday Gazette Opinion
     Poll</TITLE></HEAD>
<BODY BGCOLOR = "white">
<I> Welcome to the Holiday Gazette Opinion Poll. As an
     ongoing service
to the residents of Muskrat Mounds, we offer occasional
     survey concerning topics of interest to our readers</I>
<P><B> Do you want to:
<P>
<TABLE><FORM NAME = "Poll">
<TR><TD><INPUT TYPE _ "radio" NAME = "Opening" VALUE =
     "Take"
onClick = "window.open('FillOut.html')"> Fill out a
     Survey</TD></TR>
<TR><TD><INPUT TYPE = "radio" NAME = "Opening" VALUE = "See"
onClick = "window.open('pollResults.pl.cgi')">See Survey
     Results</TD></TR>
</FORM></TABLE></HTML>
```

Figure 20.39 The *Splash* Page for the MM Opinion Poll

Figure 20.40 HTML for the Opinion Poll's opening Page

The opening page contains a form with two radio buttons. Each radio button includes an **onClick** event handler. The first radio button uses the **onClick** event handler to open the form page. The statement is

```
<INPUT TYPE = "radio" NAME = "Opening" VALUE = "Take"
onClick = "window.open('FillOut.html')"> Fill out a Survey
```

The second radio button uses the **onClick** event handler to load the Perl script that displays the survey results. The statement is

```
<INPUT TYPE = "radio" NAME = "Opening" VALUE = "See"
onClick = "window.open('pollResults.pl.cgi')">See Survey Results
```

The *Holiday Gazette* Opinion Poll

Figure 20.41 displays the *Opinion Poll* form that appears when the user selects the *Fill out a Survey* button. The poll contains two demographic questions and three opinion questions.

Figure 20.42 contains the HTML that creates the opinion poll form. The form uses only HTML tags.

When the user presses the *Submit* button in the opinion poll form, the browser passes the form data to the *pollSubmit.pl.cgi* script. This script adds the completed form information to a

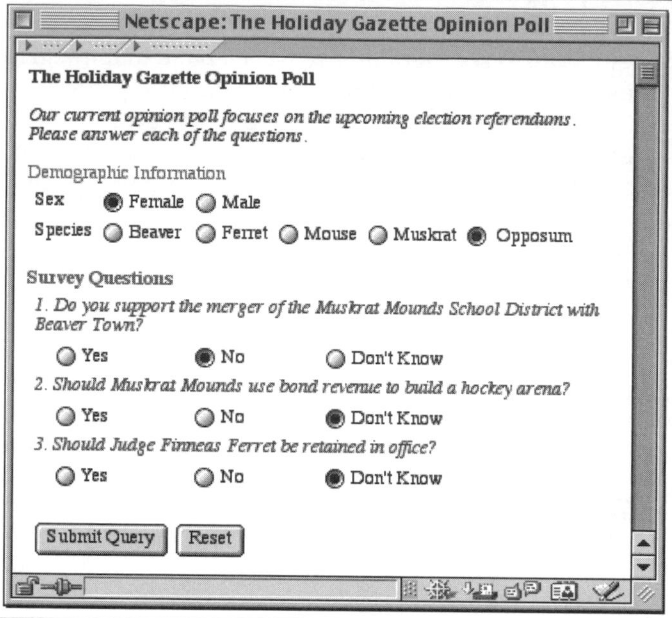

Figure 20.41 The *Opinion Poll* Form

file. A separate script displays the survey results when the user presses the *See Survey Results* button in the opening page.

Placing multifield form data into a file requires an encoding scheme. The encoding scheme must preserve each individual's responses so that we can extract and summarize the form data. For example, the encoding scheme for the opinion poll data should let us easily calculate summary statistics. Thus, we should be able to determine how many males and how many females filled out the survey. We should also be able to determine how many respondents favored merging the school districts or voted to retain Judge Finneas Ferret. Since users can ask to see the survey results at any given point in time, we must be able to update the results continuously. Fortunately, we already have a ready-made encoding scheme. Since we've used URLencoding extensively, we simply append the URLencoded data into the poll file. Figure 20.43 contains the Perl script that appends the form information to the *poll.txt* file.

As Figure 20.43 indicates, we use the **read()** function to obtain the form data and place it in **$form_data**. Next, we open the file for appending. Notice the call to the **open()** function:

```
open(FILE, ">>poll.txt");
```

The double angular brackets, **>>**, indicate that text is added to the end of the file. The file's previous contents are preserved. The two **print** statements,

```
print FILE $form_data;
print FILE "\n";
```

```
<HTML><HEAD><TITLE>The Holiday Gazette Opinion Poll </TITLE></HEAD>
<BODY BGCOLOR = 'white'>
<B>The Holiday Gazette Opinion Poll</B>
<P>
<I>Our current opinion poll focuses on the upcoming election referendums. Please answer each of
the questions.
</I><P>
<FORM ACTION ="pollSubmit.pl.cgi" METHOD = "POST">
<FONT COLOR = "green"<B>Demographic Information</B> </FONT>
<TABLE>
<TR><TD>Sex</TD>
<TD><INPUT  TYPE="radio" NAME="Sex" VALUE = "Female">Female</TD>
<TD><INPUT  TYPE="radio" NAME="Sex" VALUE = "Male">Male</TD></TR>
<TR HEIGHT = 80><TD>Species</TD>
<TD><INPUT TYPE = "radio" NAME = "Species" VALUE = "Beaver">Beaver</TD>
<TD><INPUT TYPE = "radio" NAME = "Species" VALUE = "Ferret">Ferret</TD>
<TD><INPUT TYPE = "radio" NAME = "Species" VALUE = "Mouse">Mouse</TD>
<TD><INPUT TYPE = "radio" NAME = "Species" VALUE = "Muskrat">Muskrat</TD>
<TD><INPUT TYPE = "radio" NAME = "Species" VALUE = "Opposum"> Opposum</TD>
</TR> </TABLE>
<P>
<FONT COLOR = "green"><B>Survey Questions</B></FONT>
<TABLE>
<TR><TD COLSPAN = "4"><FONT COLOR = "blue">
<I>1. Do you support the merger of the Muskrat Mounds School District with Beaver
Town?</FONT></I></TD></TR>
<TR><TD></TD><TD><INPUT  TYPE="radio" NAME="Q1" VALUE = "Yes">Yes</TD>
<TD><INPUT  TYPE="radio" NAME="Q1" VALUE = "No">No</TD>
<TD><INPUT  TYPE="radio" NAME="Q1" VALUE = "DK">Don't Know</TD></TR>

<TR><TD COLSPAN = "4"><FONT COLOR = "blue">
<I>2.Should Muskrat Mounds use bond revenue to build a hockey arena?</I></FONT></TD></TR>
<TR><TD></TD><TD><INPUT  TYPE="radio" NAME="Q2" VALUE = "Yes">Yes</TD>
<TD><INPUT  TYPE="radio" NAME="Q2" VALUE = "No">No</TD>
<TD><INPUT  TYPE="radio" NAME="Q2" VALUE = "DK">Don't Know</TD></TR>

<TR><TD COLSPAN = "4"><FONT COLOR = "blue">
<I>3. Should Judge Finneas Ferret be retained in office?</I>
</FONT></TD></TR>
<TR><TD></TD><TD><INPUT  TYPE="radio" NAME="Q3" VALUE = "Yes">Yes</TD>
<TD><INPUT  TYPE="radio" NAME="Q3" VALUE = "No">No</TD>
<TD><INPUT  TYPE="radio" NAME="Q3" VALUE = "DK">Don't Know</TD></TR></TABLE>
<P>
<TABLE>
<TR><TD COLSPAN = "2">
<INPUT TYPE="submit">
<INPUT TYPE="reset" ></TD></TR>
</FORM></TABLE></BODY></HTML>
```

Figure 20.42 HTML for the *Opinion Poll* Form

```
#!/usr/local/bin/perl
&header;
#get the form data as a string
$form_size = $ENV{'CONTENT_LENGTH'};
read (STDIN, $form_data, $form_size);
open(FILE, ">>poll.txt");
print FILE $form_data;
print FILE "\n";
close(FILE);
print "Thank you for filling out the latest Holiday Gazette opinion poll.\n";
&footer;
exit(0);
#Put the header() Subroutine Here
#Put the footer() Subroutine Here
```

Figure 20.43 Perl Script to Process the *Opinion Poll* Form

append the form data and a new-line character to the end of the file. The file is then closed. The new-line characters separate the survey's respondents. Figure 20.44 displays the contents of the *poll.txt* file after thirteen respondents had filled out the survey. Notice the URLencoding.

```
Sex=Female&Species=Beaver&Q1=Yes&Q2=No&Q3=No

Sex=Male&Species=Beaver&Q1=Yes&Q2=Yes&Q3=No

Sex=Female&Species=Ferret&Q1=Yes&Q2=No&Q3=No

Sex=Female&Species=Muskrat&Q1=Yes&Q2=No&Q3=No

Sex=Male&Species=Ferret&Q1=No&Q2=Yes&Q3=No

Sex=Male&Species=Muskrat&Q1=Yes&Q2=Yes&Q3=No

Sex=Female&Species=Beaver&Q1=Yes&Q2=No&Q3=No

Sex=Male&Species=Ferret&Q1=No&Q2=No&Q3=No

Sex=Female&Species=Mouse&Q1=Yes&Q2=Yes&Q3=No

Sex=Male&Species=Mouse&Q1=DK&Q2=No&Q3=No

Sex=Female&Species=Ferret&Q1=Yes&Q2=No&Q3=No

Sex=Male&Species=Ferret&Q1=No&Q2=No&Q3=No

Sex=Female&Species=Opposum&Q1=No&Q2=DK&Q3=DK
```

Figure 20.44 The *poll.txt* File

The *Survey Results* Page

Figure 20.45 displays a simple page of summary statistics for the opinion poll. The page shows the demographic breakdown of the respondents and the straw-poll votes on the three survey questions.

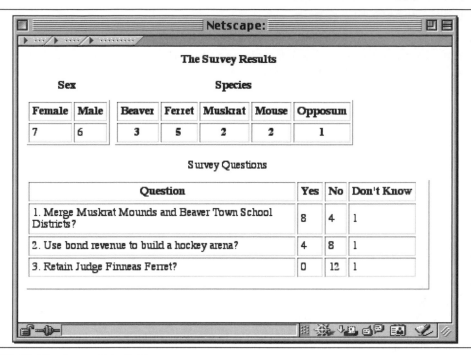

Figure 20.45 The *Survey Results* Page

Figure 20.46 contains the Perl script for the *Survey Results* page. The main program of the script reads the *poll.txt* file into an array of strings, **@file_info**. This array is passed to the **get_data()** subroutine. The **get_data()** subroutine not only decodes **@file_info**, it changes this array of strings to an array of hashes. Each respondent represents an array position. The respondent's information is stored as a hash. The modified **@file_info** array is passed to the **print_results()** subroutine. This subroutine creates the tables appearing in Figure 20.45.

```
#!/usr/local/bin/perl
&header;
open(FILE, "poll.txt");
@file_info = <FILE>;
close(FILE);
&get_data(@file_info);
&print_results(@file_info);
&footer;
exit(0);
#Put the header() Subroutine Here
#Put the footer() Subroutine Here
```

Figure 20.46 The Perl Script for the *Opinion Poll Results* Page

The get_data() Subroutine

When we developed the **get_data()** subroutine, we used a six-step decoding process to extract the form data. In previous examples, we processed the data for only one individual. In the current example, we must extract the information for n individuals, where n represents the number of survey respondents. Figure 20.47 contains the code for the **get_data()** subroutine.

```
sub get_data
{ #Use Steps 1 -6 to get and decode the data
  #Create an array of hashes for each respondent
  my($size, $form_size, $key, $value, $i, $j, $element);
  my(@fields);
  my(@file_info) = @_;
  $i = 0;
  foreach $element(@file_info)
  {#parse the data --> create an array of hashes
    $element =~ s/%([\dA-Fa-f][\dA-Fa-f])/pack ("C", hex ($1))/eg; #2
    @fields = (split(/&/, $element));                   #3a
    $hash_size = @fields;
    for ($j=0; $j < $hash_size; $j++){
      ($key, $value) = (split /=/, $fields[$j]);        #3b
      $value =~ s/[;<>\(\)\{\}\*\|'`\&\$!#:"\\]/\ $1/g; #4
      $value =~ s/+/\ $1/g;                             #5
      chomp($value);
      $file_info[$i]{$key} = $value;                    #6
    }
    $i++;
  }
  @_ = @file_info;
}
```

Figure 20.47 The **get_data()** Subroutine, *Survey Results* Page

The **get_data()** subroutine for the *Survey Results* page uses a **foreach** statement to extract the data for each respondent. An inner **for** statement creates the hash for each respondent by using Steps 2 through 6 of the decoding process. Let's examine the **for** statement:

```
for ($j=0; $j < $hash_size; $j++){
  ($key, $value) = (split /=/, $fields[$j]);        #3b
  $value =~ s/[;<>\(\)\{\}\*\|'`\&\$!#:"\\]/\ $1/g; #4
  $value =~ s/+/\ $1/g;                             #5
  chomp($value);
  $file_info[$i]{$key} = $value;                    #6
}
```

The loop index, **$j**, processes each element in the **@fields** array. This array contains the *name=value* pairs for the current respondent, **$i**. The *name–value* pairs are split on the equal sign, the suspect and suspicious characters are removed, and the plus signs are changed to spaces. (All this occurs in steps 3b through 5 of the decoding process.) Prior to creating the hash for the ith respondent, we call the **chomp()** function. This function removes any new-line characters in **$value**. Removing the new-line characters is crucial, because Question 3 *always* contain a new-line character. For example, if the respondent answered *Yes*, the *name–value* pair for Question 3 is *Q3=Yes\n*. To develop a consistent technique for processing the survey results, we must remove the new-line character. After we've chomped the new-line character, we create the hash entry for the current *key–value* pair.

The `print_results()` Subroutine

The **print_results()** subroutine creates the tables of summary statistics. This subroutine relies upon several arrays to reduce the code's length. The array declarations are as follows:

```
my(@species_name) = ("Beaver", "Ferret", "Muskrat", "Mouse", "Opposum");
my(@qresponse) = ("Yes", "No", "DK");
my(@qn) = ("Q1", "Q2", "Q3");
my(@species_count) = (0,0,0,0,0);
my(@qcount) = ([0,0,0], [0,0,0],[0,0,0]);
my(@qlabel) = ("1. Merge Muskrat Mounds and Beaver Town School Districts?","2. Use
bond revenue to build a hockey arena?","3. Retain Judge Finneas Ferret?");
```

The arrays automate the calculation of the statistics. For example, consider the **foreach** statement that counts the number of respondents in each species:

```
foreach $j(0..$#species_name)
{ #count the species
  $species_count[$j]++
      if($file_info[$i]{'Species'} eq $species_name[$j]);
}
```

This statement loops through the *species_name* array. The **if** statement compares the value associated with the *Species* key for the ith respondent with the value in **$species_name[$j]**. If a match occurs, **$species_count[$j]** is incremented.

Tabulating the results for the opinion questions requires a two-dimensional array. The questions occupy the row positions, and the *Yes, No,* and *DK* responses occupy the 0th, 1st, and 2nd column positions, respectively. The nested **foreach** statement that tabulates the opinion questions is

```
foreach $j(0..$#qn)
{#count each opinion, put in matrix
   foreach $k(0..$#qresponse) {
      $qcount[$j][$k]++
          if ($file_info[$i]{$qn[$j]} eq $qresponse[$k]);
   }
}
```

After the results are tabulated, we create a table for each of the demographic questions and a table that combines all of the opinion questions. Figure 20.48 contains the definition of the **print_results()** subroutine.

The *Opinion Poll* page clearly displays Perl's ability to process and summarize complex forms. Without knowledge of URLencoding, processing this form would be difficult; we would need to develop an encoding scheme to store the information in a text file.

```perl
sub print_results
{ #tabulate the survey results
  my(@file_info) = @_;
  my($i, $j, $k,  $species, $male,$female);
  my(@species_name) = ("Beaver", "Ferret", "Muskrat", "Mouse", "Opposum");
  my(@qresponse) = ("Yes", "No", "DK");
  my(@qn) = ("Q1", "Q2", "Q3");
  my(@species_count) = (0,0,0,0,0);
  my(@qcount) = ([0,0,0], [0,0,0],[0,0,0]);

  my(@qlabel) = ("1. Merge Muskrat Mounds and Beaver Town School Districts?",
  "2. Use bond revenue to build a hockey arena?",
  "3. Retain Judge Finneas Ferret?");
  foreach $i(0..$#file_info)
  { #print the summary statistics for each hash key
     $female++  if ($file_info[$i]{'Sex'} eq "Female");
     $male++    if ($file_info[$i]{'Sex'} eq "Male");
     foreach $j(0..$#species_name)
     { #count the species
        $species_count[$j]++
           if($file_info[$i]{'Species'} eq $species_name[$j]);
     }
     foreach $j(0..$#qn)
     {#count each opinion, put in matrix
        foreach $k(0..$#qresponse) {
          $qcount[$j][$k]++
              if ($file_info[$i]{$qn[$j]} eq $qresponse[$k]);
        }
     }
  }
  print "<CENTER><B>The Survey Results</B></CENTER><P>\n";
  print "<TABLE BORDER =  '1' CELLPADDING = '3' ALIGN = 'LEFT'>\n";
  print "<CAPTION> <B>Sex</B></CAPTION>\n";
  print "<TR><TH>Female</TH><TH>Male</TH></TR>\n";
  print "<TR><TD> $female </TD><TD>  $male</TD></TR></TABLE><P>\n";

  print "<TABLE BORDER = '1' CELLPADDING = '3'>\n";
  print "<CAPTION> <B>Species</B></CAPTION><TR>\n";
  foreach $i(0..$#species_name){
  print "<TH>$species_name[$i]</TH>\n";}
  print "</TR><TR>\n";
  foreach $i(0..$#species_name){
        print "<TH>$species_count[$i]</TH>\n";}
   print "</TR></TABLE><P>\n";

  print "<TABLE BORDER = '1' CELLPADDING = '3'><CAPTION> Survey Questions</CAPTION>\n";
  print "<TR><TH>Question</TH><TH>Yes</TH><TH>No</TH><TH>Don't Know</TH></TR>\n";
  foreach $i(0..@{qcount})
  { #print the matrix of opinion questions and responses
    print "<TR><TD>$qlabel[$i]</TD>\n";
    foreach $j(0..@{$qcount[$i]})
    {print "<TD>$qcount[$i][$j]</TD>\n";}
    print "</TR>\n";
  }
  print "</TABLE>\n";
}
```

Figure 20.48 The **print_results()** Function, *Opinion Poll* Page

➤   **EXERCISES**

1. **The *Mailing Label* Page: email version.** Modify the *Mailing Label* page so that the user's data is emailed to you. Email the fields as they appear in the form, not as they appear in the hash. (See Figure 19.5.)

2. **The *Mailing Label* Page: CGI.pm.** Process the mailing label form using **CGI.pm**. The form results should be identical to those displayed in Figure 20.1.

3. **The *Mailing Label* Page: CGI.pm.** Use **CGI.pm** to create the mailing label form. The form results should be identical to those displayed in Figure 20.1

4. **The *Guest Book* Page.** Create a guest book page that asks users to enter their names and comments. Include a checkbox that lets the user see the contents of the guest book. Write the user's information to a file.

5. **The *Picnic* Page.** Modify the picnic page so that the user's information is emailed to you. See Figure 14.50.

6. **The *Picnic* Page: file version.** Modify the picnic page so that each completed form is added to a text file. Create a second page that prints the names of everyone who's signed up for the picnic and prints a count of the number attending.

7. **The *T/F Quiz* Page, revisited.** Modify the T/F quiz appearing in Chapter 19 by emailing the results to yourself. (See Figure 19.14.)

8. **The *Multiple Choice Quiz* Page.** Create a multiple-choice quiz, following the model used in Figure 14.51. Use the hash-of-arrays approach to process the quiz.

9. **The Multiple Choice Quiz CGI.pm version.** Process the multiple-choice quiz by using **CGI.pm**.

10. **The *Multiple Choice Quiz* Page: CGI.pm version.** Create the multiple-choice quiz form with **CGI.pm**.

11. **The *Multiple Choice Quiz* Page: file version.** Modify the *Multiple Choice* page. Add text fields for the user's first and last name. Create a file that contains the form information for everyone who answers the quiz. Create a separate file that prints the file information.

12. **The *Shakespearean Quiz* Page.** Rewrite the Shakespearean Quiz. Use a hash of arrays to process the form. Print the user's score. Email the results to yourself. (See Figure 14.35.)

13. **The *Shakespearean Quiz* Page: CGI.pm version.** Rewrite the Shakespearean Quiz. Use **CGI.pm** to create the form and to process it.

14. **The *Temperature Conversion* Page.** Create a page that contains radio buttons for Celsius and Fahrenheit and a text field for the temperature. If the user selects the Celsius button, convert the temperature to Fahrenheit. If the user selects the Fahrenheit button, convert the temperature to Celsius. Display the Fahrenheit and Celsius temperatures. Use a hash of arrays to store the data.

15. **The *Temperature Conversion* Page: CGI.pm version.** Use **CGI.pm** to create the temperature conversion form and to process it.

16. **The *Regular Expressions* Page: CGI.pm version.** Use CGI.pm to create the *Regular Expressions* page and to process it. (See Figure 18.46.)

17. **The *Weekday Lookup* Page.** Modify the *Weekday Lookup* Page. (See Figure 17.38). Your new page should let the user select the language: German, Tibetan, and any other languages you might wish to include. You should also let the user pick the weekday. The user must select only a single language and a single weekday. Print the weekday in English and in the chosen language. Use a hash of arrays to store the form data.

18. **The *Weekday Lookup* Page: CGI.pm version.** Use CGI.pm to create the *Weekday Lookup* form and to process the script.

19. **The *Mailing Label* Page.** Modify the *Mailing Label* page to create a file of mailing labels. Add the new mailing labels to the end of the file. Figure 20.49 shows a sample page.

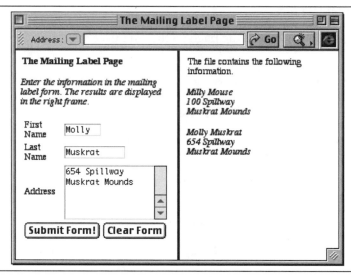

Figure 20.49 *Mailing Label Modification* Page

20. **The *Opinion Poll* Page, revisited.** Modify the *Survey Results* page of the opinion poll page. The new page should print cross-tabulated results for males and females—that is, create a table that displays the number of males and females that voted *yes*, *no*, and *don't know* on each of the three opinion questions.

21. **The *Opinion Poll* Page, revisited.** Modify the *Survey Results* page so that percentages are printed instead of raw numbers. Be sure to include the total number of respondents, so that individuals can reconstruct the raw data.

22. **The *Opinion Poll* Page, revisted.** Add three more opinion questions to the opinion poll page. Add these questions to the results page.

23. **The *Sales Tax* Page.** Create a *Sales Tax* page. The page should have text fields for the total item cost and the tax rate as a percentage. Print the item cost, tax rate, total amount of tax, and total cost of the item. Use a hash of arrays to store the form data.

24. **The *Sales Tax* Page: CGI.pm version.** Use CGI.pm to create the *Sales Tax* form and to process the results.

PART IV JAVA

21 Introduction to Java: Applets, Primitive Data Types, and Text Fields and Areas

INTRODUCTION TO JAVA

In Part II, we covered JavaScript. In Part IV, we turn our attention to Java. Java was developed by Sun MicroSystems, which also played a major role in the development of JavaScript. Although the two languages use the same selection and iteration statements, there are substantial differences between Java and JavaScript. Unlike JavaScript, Java is a strongly typed language. This means that we must declare all variables and constants before we use them. The declaration includes a specification of the variable or constant's type. Java also fully embodies the principles of object-oriented programming. It is impossible to create even the simplest Java program without using the built-in class libraries.

Unlike many programming languages, Java is machine-independent. This means that Java programs are portable across different platforms. For example, the Java programs used in this book were originally written on a Unix platform and tested on Java's Applet Viewer and Hot Java browser. The programs were ported to a Mac and retested on Internet Explorer. The Java classes worked consistently across platforms.

Java uses a unique translation system to obtain machine-independence. The Java compiler, *javac*, translates a Java program into *byte-code*. *Byte-code* is an intermediate translation that omits machine-specific details. To run byte-code, we either use the Java interpreter, *java*, or we run the byte-code on a Java-enabled browser. When we use the Java interpreter, the program is called an *application*. When we use a Java-enabled browser, the program is called an *applet*. In this book, we concentrate on writing applets.

Java Development

Java is a language in transition. When Sun released Java 1.0, it used a single event handler embodied in the **action()** method that responded to all events. Typical events might include clicking a mouse button, using a scroll bar, filling in a text field or text area, checking a box, or clicking a radio button. Java 1.1 replaced this single event handler with event handlers geared toward specific types of objects. For example, the mouse has two event handlers: one handler responds to mouse clicks, the second handler to mouse drags. Similarly, scroll bars require an event handler different from that for text areas. Java 1.2, also known as Platform 2, added a 2D graphics

493

package and lightweight components (Swing), while retaining the AWT (Abstract Windowing Toolkit) available in Java 1.1.

Obtaining Java

Java is freely available from Sun MicroSystems at http://java.sun.com. At the time of this writing, one could download Java 1.2 for Unix, Linux, and PC platforms. A Macintosh version was anticipated, but not released. (Code Warrior offers Java 1.2 in its professional package, which also includes C, C++, and Perl compilers.)

THE FIRST APPLET

We've written a *Hello* program in HTML, JavaScript, and Perl. Figure 21.1 contains a Java version of this program. The bold text at the top of the page was written with HTML tags. The applet's text follows the HTML text.

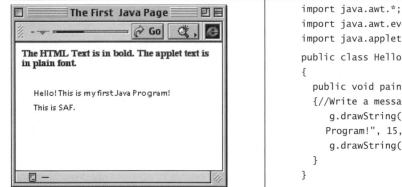

```
import java.awt.*;
import java.awt.event.*;
import java.applet.*;

public class Hello extends Applet
{
  public void paint(Graphics g)
  {//Write a message on the page
      g.drawString("Hello! This is my first Java
      Program!", 15, 20);
      g.drawString("This is SAF.", 15,38);
  }
}
```

Figure 21.1 The *Hello* Page: Java Version   **Figure 21.2** The *Hello* Applet

We use the following steps to create and run a Java applet:

Step 1. Create the Java Program File.   Using an editor of your choice, type the code appearing in Figure 21.2. Don't worry about what the code means; we examine it in detail shortly. Save the program under the name *Hello.java*. Make sure that you save the program in ASCII or in plain text.

Step 2. The Java Compiler.   To create the byte-code for this program, type *javac Hello.java* in a terminal window on Unix or Linux systems, or select the compile option if using an integrated environment. If the program compiles successfully, you should see a new file named *Hello.class*. This is the byte-code version of the program. If the program does not compile successfully, the Java compiler displays error messages with the offending lines. Carefully compare these lines with the code appearing in Figure 21.2.

Step 3. Change Class Privileges.   If relevant for your platform, change the privileges on the *Hello.class* program so that everyone has read and execute privileges. (Typically, you need to change privileges on a Unix platform.)

Step 4. Create an HTML Program.   Once the Java program compiles successfully, you must create an HTML page that holds the applet. HTML provides **<APPLET>...</APPLET>** tags to load your applet. (Strictly speaking, HTML 4.0 does not allow **<APPLET>...</APPLET>** tags. It prefers the generic **<OBJECT> ... </OBJECT>** tags.)

Figure 21.3 contains the syntax for the **<APPLET>** tag.

```
<APPLET ALT = "Alternate text"
        ALIGN = "LEFT" | "CENTER" | "RIGHT" | "TOP" | "BOTTOM"
        CODE = "Java Class"
        CODEBASE = "Applet directory"
        HEIGHT = "Pixels"
        HSPACE = "Pixels"
        VSPACE = "Pixels"
        WIDTH = "Pixels">
        <PARAM NAME = "Name" VALUE = "Value">
        ...
        <PARAM NAME = "Name" VALUE = "Value">
</APPLET>
```

Figure 21.3 The <APPLET>...</APPLET> Tags

The **<APPLET>** tag contains several attributes, many of which are optional. The crucial attributes are highlighted. The meaning of the attributes is as follows:

The **ALT** *Attribute.*   The **ALT** attribute displays a message if the browser is not Java-enabled. We can also place alternative text between the **<APPLET>** and **</APPLET>** tags.

The **ALIGN** *Attribute.*   The **ALIGN** attribute specifies the position of the applet on the page. By default, applets are left-aligned.

The **CODE** *Attribute.*   The **CODE** tag contains the name of the Java class. In the current example, the Java class is *Hello.class*.

The **CODEBASE** *Attribute.*   The browser assumes that the Java code is located in the current directory. We use the **CODEBASE** attribute when the Java class is in a different directory. For example, the original version of the *Hello* program resided on a Unix machine, where the HTML and Java class files were in the same directory, and so a **CODEBASE** attribute was not necessary. When the program was tested on a Macintosh by using Code Warrior, the Java class file was placed in a separate directory. The **CODEBASE** attribute was then needed to specify the location of the Java class file.

The **HEIGHT** *and* **WIDTH** *Attributes.*   The **HEIGHT** and **WIDTH** attributes specify the number of vertical and horizontal pixels, respectively. The numbers chosen for these attributes determine the location of objects within the applet. The overall appearance of an applet can change dramatically when the **HEIGHT** and **WIDTH** attributes are changed.

The **VSPACE** *and* **HSPACE** *Attributes.*   The **VSPACE** and **HSPACE** attributes specify the size of the "gutter" around the applet. The gutter is an invisible border that separates the applet from the HTML that surrounds it.

An applet can also include optional **<PARAM>** tags, short for parameters, that are used to pass information from the HTML program to the applet. The parameter **NAME** is recognized within the Java program.

Figure 21.4 contains the HTML program that produces the *Hello* page depicted in Figure 21.1. Type in the code and save it as a plain text or ASCII file.

```
<HTML><HEAD><TITLE>The First Java Page</TITLE></HEAD>
<BODY BGCOLOR = "white">
<B>The HTML Text is in bold. The applet text is in plain font.</B>
<P>
<APPLET CODE = "Hello.class"
  WIDTH = 200 HEIGHT = 100>
</APPLET>
</BODY></HTML>
```

Figure 21.4 HTML for the *Hello* Page: Java Version

Step 5. Load the Page into a Browser. As the final step in creating an applet, we load the HTML page into a Java-enabled browser.

JAVA LANGUAGE CHARACTERISTICS

The *Hello* program illustrates many features of Java programming. After dissecting this program, you should begin to grasp these features.

Packages. Java includes extensive class libraries. These libraries reside in packages that we must import before we can use the classes. The *Hello* program loaded three packages, **awt**, **event**, and **applet**, by means of the following statements:

```
import java.awt.*;
import java.awt.event.*;
import java.applet.*;
```

The first statement loads the entire Abstract Windowing Toolkit (**awt.***). The second statement loads all the event handlers (**event.***). We don't actually need the event handlers for the *Hello* program, but these import statements form a trilogy that we'll routinely use for all Java programs. The last statement loads the applet package.

Classes. We write Java applets by extending the *Applet* class. This is evident in the following statements:

```
public class Hello extends Applet
{
  // New class definition goes here
}
```

The first statement illustrates several features of Java programming. Let's begin with the class name, *Hello*. By convention, Java programmers always capitalize the first letter of every word appearing in the class name. Our small program creates one class, *Hello*, and uses two built-in classes, *Applet* and *Graphics*. Our next program will use seven classes: *Label*, *Applet*, *ActionListener*, *TextField*, *ActionEvent*, *String*, and *Graphics*. Notice how easily we can identify the classes, thanks to Java's naming conventions.

Fields and Methods. A Java class definition can contain variable or constant definitions and function definitions. We refer to variables and constants as *class fields* and functions as *class methods*.

By convention, Java programmers capitalize the first letter of the second, and subsequent, words in a variable or method definition. The first letter of the first word is not capitalized. A constant's name is entirely in uppercase. The *Hello* program contains a single class method: `paint()`.

Visibility Modifiers. The `Hello` class declaration indicates that the class has *public* access. This means that anyone can use the class. Java provides four visibility modifiers:

- `private`. Typically, we use `private` when we declare variables and constants in a class definition. This means that only elements in the same class can see these elements.

- `protected`. Protected visibility lets a subclass "see" the protected element. The elements in the class itself also have access to the protected element.

- `public`. Public visibility, as its name implies, means that everyone has access to this element. Notice that the `Hello` class and the `paint()` method have public access. Classes and methods generally have public access.

- `package`. Package visibility lets elements within the same class, or classes within the same package, access the element. We won't be creating our own packages, so we won't worry about this visibility modifier.

Class Hierarchy. Java contains an extensive hierarchy of classes in which subclasses inherit methods from their ancestors. Figure 21.5 shows the lineage of the *Hello* class.

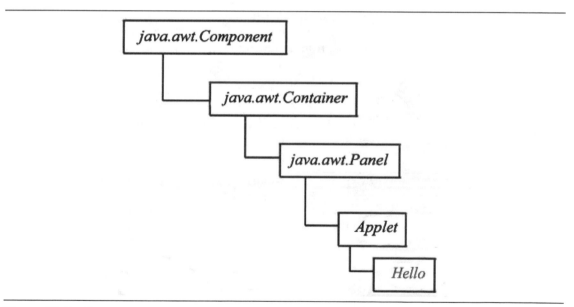

Figure 21.5 The Class Hierarchy for the *Hello* Class

As Figure 21.5 indicates, the `Hello` class inherits fields and methods from the `Applet` class. The `Applet` class inherits fields and methods from the `Panel` class. The `Panel` class, in turn, inherits from the `Container` class, which inherits from the `Component` class. The `paint()` method that we used in the `Hello` class is part of the `Component` class definition. We may use methods found in any of these ancestral classes.

THE paint() METHOD

Although the *Hello* class inherits the **paint()** method from the *Component* class, we can (and, here, must) rewrite this method to suit our needs. The browser automatically runs the **paint()** method when the applet is initially loaded into the browser and whenever the user reloads the page. The modified version of this method appears in Figure 21.6.

```
public void paint(Graphics g)
  {//Write a message on the page
     g.drawString("Hello! This is my first Java Program!", 15, 20);
     g.drawString("This is SAF.", 15,38);
  }
```

Figure 21.6 The **paint()** Method for the *Hello* Class

The **paint()** method should have public access so that the browser can invoke it. The **void** appearing in the method header denotes the return type. It indicates that the **paint()** method returns nothing to the caller. The **paint()** method always contains a single parameter, which is a *Graphics* object. We use the *Graphics* method **drawString()** to write information onto the web page. The **drawString()** method requires three parameters: a string, and x (column) and y (row) coordinates. The (x, y) coordinates are represented in pixels. The pixel coordinates of the top left corner of the applet are (0,0).

The first call to the **drawString()** method writes the message, *Hello! This is my first Java Program*, from a starting location of column 15 and row 20. The second call to the **drawString()** method writes the message, *This is SAF.*, from a starting location of column 15 and row 38.

THE *FIRST NAME* PAGE: JAVA VERSION

We've written a *First Name* page in JavaScript and Perl. Figure 21.7 contains the Java version of this page.

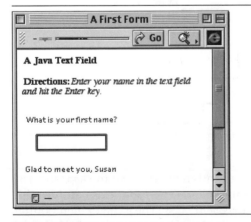

```
<HTML><HEAD><TITLE>A First Form</TITLE></HEAD>
<BODY BGCOLOR = "white">
<B>A Java Text Field</B><P>
<B>Directions: </B><I>Enter your name in the
    text field and hit the Enter key.</I><P>
<APPLET CODE = "FirstForm.class"
  WIDTH = 120 HEIGHT = 180>
</APPLET></BODY></HTML>
```

Figure 21.7 The *First Name* Page: Java Version

Figure 21.8 HTML for the *First Name* Page

Figure 21.8 contains the HTML that loads the applet. The **WIDTH** and **HEIGHT** attributes are crucial in determining the applet's appearance on the page.

All applets use the *FlowLayout* manager as the default layout manager. This manager places the applet's elements in a left-to-right and top-to-bottom layout. Often an applet's appearance is improved by changing the **WIDTH** and **HEIGHT**.

Labels and Text Fields

To create the *First Form* class that implements the *First. Name* page, we must use the *Label* and *TextField* classes. Both classes are descendents of the *Component* class, as Figure 21.9 indicates. The *Label* class is a direct descendent of the *Component* class. The *TextField* and *TextArea* classes have the *Component* and *TextComponent* classes as ancestors.

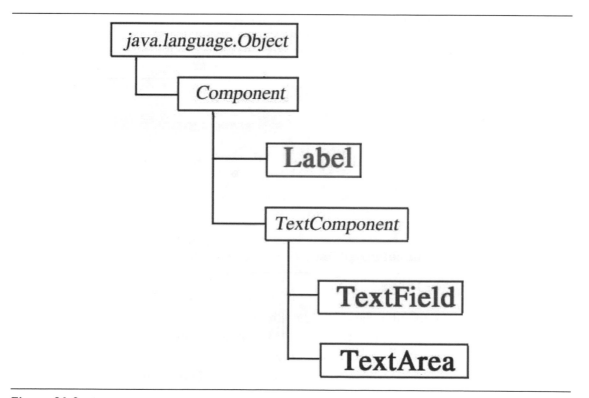

Figure 21.9 The *Label* and *TextField* Class Hierarchy

The Label Class

The *Hello* applet used the **drawString()** method to place strings on a page, but this method requires pixel coordinates, so it is cumbersome. We can also place messages on the page by creating and adding *Label* components. The message *What is your first name?* appearing in Figure 21.8 was produced in this manner. Figure 21.10(a) contains the syntax for creating a **Label** object. Figure 21.10(b) lists the **Label** methods.

(a) **Label** Syntax	(b) **Label** Methods

`Label name = new Label(String s);`	`String name.getText();`
	`void name.setText(String s);`
	`int name.getAlignment();`
	`name.setAlignment(int align);`

Figure 21.10 The *Label* Class

THE SYNTAX OF JAVA METHODS: UNRAVELED

Figure 21.10(b) uses standard Java notation to illustrate class methods. This notation probably looks strange to a beginning programmer. The syntax is designed to provide readers with a shorthand (and therefore cryptic) explanation of the value returned by the method and the parameters required by the method. You should not interpret these method summaries literally. For example, let's consider the **setText()** method. This method returns a **void** value and requires a single string as a parameter. Figure 21.11 shows the relation between the syntax given in Figure 21.10(b) and a typical method call.

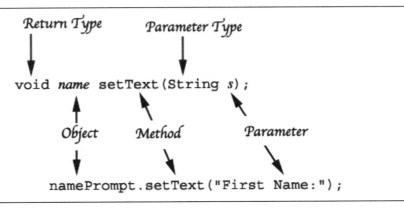

Figure 21.11 Interpreting Method Syntax

Examine the method call in Figure 2.11. The return and parameter types do not appear in the call. The type information appears in the syntax diagrams so that programmers can call the method correctly.

Examples of *Label* Method Calls

Now let's return to the methods listed in Figure 21.10. The *Label* syntax illustrated in Figure 21.10(a) includes an assignment statement. The type (*Label*) and variable name appear on the left-hand side of the assignment operator (=). The right-hand side of the assignment statement constructs a new *Label* object. The *Label* constructor requires a string as a parameter. For example, the label appearing in the *First Name* page was created with the statement

```
private Label namePrompt = new Label("What is your first name?");
```

The parameter is a string literal as denoted by double quotation marks. Notice the use of the **private** visibility modifier for the *namePrompt* variable. This prevents any accidental or malicious use of this variable by the user.

The *Label* class includes methods to get and set the text and alignment. The *Label* class definition contains three alignment constants: **LEFT**, **CENTER**, and **RIGHT**. For example, we center text for the *namePrompt* variable with the statement

```
namePrompt.setAlignment(Label.CENTER);
```

Similarly, we change *namePrompt's* text to *First Name:* with the statement

```
namePrompt.setText("First Name: ");
```

The TextField Class

The *First Form* class page also uses the *TextField* class. Figure 21.12 contains the syntax for creating a new *TextField* object.

```
TextField name = new TextField(int size);
```

Figure 21.12 Constructing a *TextField* Object

The *TextField* constructor contains a single parameter that determines the size of the text field. For example, the statement that creates the *nameField* text field is

```
private TextField nameField = new TextField(12);
```

This text field provides twelve columns for the user's name.

The *FirstForm* Class Definition

We're now ready to look at the *FirstForm* class definition. Figure 21.13 contains the code. Comments, denoted by **//**, show the placement of the **init()** and **actionPerformed()** methods, which we will examine shortly.

```
import java.awt.*;
import java.awt.event.*;
import java.applet.*;

public class FirstForm extends Applet implements ActionListener
{ //Create a text box for the user's name
  private Label namePrompt = new Label("What is your first name?");
  private TextField nameField = new TextField(12);
  private String message = " ";
 //Put the init() Method here
 // Put the actionPerformed() Method here
  public void paint(Graphics g)
  {//paint the message on the screen
    g.drawString(message, 1,80);
  }
}
```

Figure 21.13 The *FirstForm* Class Definition

Notice the *FirstForm* class header. Because the page prints a message containing the user's name, we must implement an event handler to "listen" for changes in the text field. The *ActionListener* event handler listens for the *Return* or *Enter* key. Whenever the user presses this key, the action listener calls the **actionPerformed()** method to respond to the event.

The *FirstForm* class definition contains a **paint()** method that writes the *message* string on the page beginning in the first column and the 80th row. Notice the statement that creates the *message* string:

```
private String message = " ";
```

Unlike *TextField* and *Label* objects, *String* objects are created without using **new** to construct the object. In the current example, *message* initially contains a single space. Because the **paint()** method is always invoked when the page is loaded, we must give *message* an initial value to avoid a *Null Pointer Exception* error.

The init() Method

The *ActionListener* does not listen for text field events automatically. To make it listen, we must add an action listener to these objects. We add event handlers to text field objects and we add form elements to the page in the **init()** method. The **init()** method is automatically invoked when the browser loads the page for the first time. Figure 21.14 contains the **init()** method for the *FirstForm* class.

```
public void init()
  { //init is used to initialize the web page
    add(namePrompt);
    add(nameField);
    nameField.addActionListener(this);
  }
```

Figure 21.14 The **init()** Method: *FirstForm* Class

The **init()** method uses the **add()** method from the *Component* class to place the label and text field in the applet. We haven't specified a layout manager, so the applet uses the default flow layout manager. The narrowness of the applet causes the label to appear above the text field. Ordinarily, the label would appear to the left of the text field.

We add the action listener to the text field by using the **addActionListener()** method of the *TextField* class. This method contains a single parameter, which is an *ActionListener* object. We pass a reference (**this**) to the current *ActionListener* as a parameter.

The actionPerformed() Method

When the user presses the *Enter* or *Return* key in the *nameField* text field, the action listener invokes the **actionPerformed()** method. We will now write a new version of this method to respond to the text field event. Figure 21.15 contains that new **actionPerformed()** method for the *FirstForm* class.

Let's examine each of the lines in this method, beginning with the method header,

```
public void actionPerformed(ActionEvent e)
```

```
public void actionPerformed(ActionEvent e)
{ //process the text field response
   String name = nameField.getText();
   message = "Glad to meet you, " + name;
   nameField.setText(" ");
   repaint();
}
```

Figure 21.15 The **actionPerformed()** Method: *FirstForm* Class

The method header gives public access to the **actionPerformed()** method. The method has a **void** return type and a single parameter that is an *ActionEvent* object.

The first line of the body,

String name = nameField.getText();

creates a local string variable, *name*. We do not use a visibility modifier inside method definitions. The **private** visibility modifier is used only when we create class fields.

The string definition uses the **getText()** method to obtain the contents of the *nameField* text field.

Once we've obtained the user's name, we use the string concatenation operator (+) to re-define the *message* string as *Glad to meet you,* followed by the user's name. We then use the **setText()** method to replace the user's name in the text field with a space. This lets another user enter a name without the hassle of erasing the previous user's name.

The final statement in the **actionPerformed()** method calls the **repaint()** method. This method removes anything drawn on the page. After the page is cleaned, **repaint()** automatically calls the **paint()** method. Because *message* starts as a space, the **paint()** method replaces this "empty" string with the new string.

PRIMITIVE DATA TYPES IN JAVA

The *FirstForm* class used a text field to obtain the user's name. A text field always stores information as a Java string. We can use text fields to obtain numbers, characters, or Boolean (true/false) information; however, we must convert this information from a string to its appropriate type. Figure 21.16 lists the elementary data types available in Java. If you're familiar with C or C++, the Java primitive data types will come as no surprise; Java "borrowed" all of the primitive data types of C/C++. Java also added a **boolean** type. The type name appears in the left column. The middle column contains the value range for the type. The right column contains the object wrapper for the type. The object wrapper contains conversion methods that let a programmer change between data types.

The data types appearing in Figure 21.16 are arranged from the smallest to the largest. We can divide these elementary types into four groups: character, boolean, integral, and floating point. We use the **boolean** type when we have true/false data. We use the **char** type when our information contains a single character. For example, we can use a character to represent an answer to a multiple-choice question or the middle initial in a person's name. The four integral types, **byte**, **short**, **int**, and **long**, provide integers (counting numbers) of various sizes. For most applications

Type	Encoding	Wrapper Class
boolean	*true*, *false*	Boolean
byte	8-bit signed integer (−128 to 127)	Byte
char	16-bit unsigned integer in Unicode Characters	Character
short	16-bit signed integer (−32,768 to 32,767)	Short
int	32-bit signed integer ($\approx \pm 2$ Billion)	Integer
long	64-bit signed integer ($\approx \pm 1.8447e19$)	Long
float	32-bit in IEEE 754 standard (≈ 6 digits of precision to the right of the decimal point)	Float
double	64-bit in IEEE 754 standard (≈ 12 digits of precision to the right of the decimal point)	Double

Figure 21.16 Java's Primitive Data Types

requiring an integer, we'll use the **int** type. The two floating-point types, **float** and **double**, differ in precision. The **float** type retains approximately six digits of precision to the right of the decimal point; the **double** type "doubles" the precision.

Java also provides three additional numeric classes. Two of these classes, **BigInteger** and **BigDecimal**, extend the size of the integral types and the precision of the floating-point types. Thus, we can create objects that have a greater range than **long** or greater floating point precision than **double**. The remaining class, **Math**, contains methods that implement trigonometric and other common mathematical functions, including exponentiation, floors, and ceilings.

ARITHMETIC OPERATORS

The Java arithmetic operators are identical to the JavaScript operators. Figure 21.17 contains these operators listed in order of precedence. (Appendix D contains the complete Java operator hierarchy.)

Symbol	Meaning	
++	Increment	**Highest Precedence**
--	Decrement	
+	Unary plus	
-	Unary minus	
*	Multiplication	
/	Division	
%	Modulus	
+	Addition	
-	Subtraction	
=	Assignment	**Lowest Precedence**
+=	Assignment/Addition	
-=	Assignment/Subtraction	
*=	Assignment/Multiplication	
/=	Assignment/Division	
%=	Assignment/Modulus	

Figure 21.17 Java's Arithmetic Operators

We've written many JavaScript programs that use mathematical operators. Therefore, our next Java programs focus on obtaining and converting information from Java text fields. Java stores all text field information as a string, so we must be able to convert a string into each of the primitive types, and *vice versa*. Unfortunately, Java does not provide a consistent technique for these conversions. For example, the technique used to convert a string to one of the integral types will not work when we want to convert a string to a character or a boolean. These conversions are crucial if we want to use any data type, so we must closely examine each of the conversion techniques. When we've finished, we will have an arsenal of techniques that we can use for any type of data.

The Integral Types

Converting a string to one of the integral types is relatively painless. Each of the object wrappers contains a method that automatically converts a string to the desired type. Figure 21.18 lists the conversion method for each of the integral types.

Primitive Type	Conversion Method
byte	byte Byte.parseByte(String *s*);
short	short Short.parseShort(String *s*);
int	int Integer.parseInt(String *s*);
long	long Long.parseLong(String *s*);

Figure 21.18 Integral Conversion Methods

Notice that each of the wrapper classes contains a "parse" method that requires a string parameter and returns a value of the primitive type. The integral types all use much the same conversion technique, so we will use only the **int** type to illustrate the conversion process. Figure 21.19 contains an *Integer Conversion* page. The user places an integer into the integer text field and presses the "Enter" key. The sum text field contains the current sum. We also print the input sequence that produced the sum on the page.

To conserve space, we won't examine the complete HTML code for this and subsequent pages. (The accompanying CD contains the complete HTML.) Instead, we will focus on the applet tags. Pay particular attention to the **WIDTH** and **HEIGHT** attributes. Try changing these attributes, and then notice the effect this has on the labels and text fields. The **<APPLET>** tag used for the *Integer Conversion* page is

```
<APPLET CODE ="ConvertInt.class"
    WIDTH ="220" HEIGHT = "180">
</APPLET>
```

A width of 220 pixels easily accommodates all the labels and text fields, so the default flow layout manager displays all these objects in a single row.

The ConvertInt Class Definition

Figure 21.20 contains the *ConvertInt* class definition. This definition contains labels and text fields for the integer and sum. The definition also contains a string to hold the input sequence and an integer, *sum*, to hold the sum.

The *ConvertInt* class definition requires **init()**, **paint()**, and **actionPerformed()** methods. The **paint()** method appears in Figure 21.20. This method writes the *message* string on the page beginning at column 1 and row 60.

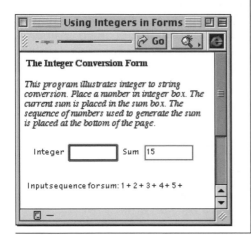

Figure 21.19 The *Integer Conversion* Page

```
import java.awt.*;
import java.awt.event.*;
import java.applet.*;

public class ConvertInt extends Applet implements
ActionListener
{ //Create a text boxes for the integer and the sum
  private Label intLabel =  new Label("Integer");
  private Label intSumLabel =  new Label("Sum");
  private TextField intField =  new TextField(8);
  private TextField intSumField =  new TextField(16);
  private int sum = 0;
  private String message = "Input sequence for sum: ";
  //Put the init() Method here
 public void paint(Graphics g)
 { //write the numbers used to create the sum on the
applet
   g .drawString(message, 1, 60);
 }
 //Put the actionPerformed() Method Here
}
```

Figure 21.20 The *ConvertInt* Class Definition

The init() Method.

Figure 21.21 contains the definition of the **init()** method. This method adds the labels and text fields to the applet. We add an action listener to the *intField* text field. We don't want the user to change the sum, so we use the **setEditable()** method with the parameter *false* to indicate that the *sumField* text field cannot be modified by the user.

The actionPerformed() Method.

The definition of the **actionPerformed()** method appears in Figure 21.22. Notice the multi-line comment that appears in the body of this method. Multi-line comments begin with **/*** and end with ***/**.

The body of the **actionPerformed()** method contains five lines of code. The first line,

```
sum += Integer.parseInt(intField.getText());
```

```
public void init()
{ //place the labels and text fields in the
    applet
  add(intLabel);
  add(intField);
  intField.addActionListener(this);

  add(intSumLabel);
  add(intSumField);
  intSumField.setEditable(false);
}
```

Figure 21.21 The **init()** Method:
ConvertInt Class

```
public void actionPerformed(ActionEvent e)
{ /*calculate the sum and place in sum text field
    Add integer to the message string */
  sum += Integer.parseInt(intField.getText());
  intSumField.setText(Integer.toString(sum));
  message = message + intField.getText() + " + ";
  intField.setText("");
  repaint();
}
```

Figure 21.22 The **actionPerformed()** Method:
ConvertInt Class

uses the **parseInt()** method from the *Integer* wrapper object to convert the user's data into an integer. The integer is converted and added to the sum in this single line of code. The second statement,

```
intSumField.setText(Integer.toString(sum));
```

places the new sum into the sum text field. Because the sum is an integer, we must convert it back to a string. The **Integer.toString()** method handles the conversion.

We also modify the *message* string to contain the new number followed by a plus sign. Next, we set the integer text field to the empty string, so that the user will be able to enter the next number easily. Finally, we call the **repaint()** method to rewrite the *message* string.

CHARACTER CONVERSIONS

Obtaining a character from a text field requires a second conversion technique. To illustrate this technique, we create a page that asks the user to enter a lower-case letter. We display the upper-case counterpart in a second, uneditable text field.

Figure 21.23 contains the *Character Conversion* page.

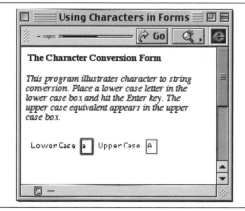

Figure 21.23 The *Character Conversion* Page

The applet tag creates a 170 × 200 rectangle for the applet. The tag is

```
<APPLET CODE = "ConvertChar.class" WIDTH = "170" HEIGHT = "200">
</APPLET>
```

The *ConvertChar* Class Definition

The text fields and labels used in the *Character Conversion* page follow the format used in the *Integer Conversion* page. Figure 21.24 contains the definition of the *ConvertChar* class.

The *ConvertChar* class definition contains text fields and labels for the upper- and lower-case letters. Notice the size of the text fields. Each is set to one column, which is just enough space to hold a single letter. This single letter is a string of size one and not a character. The variable *letter* holds the user's letter after we've converted it to a character.

The *actionPerformed()* Method

The **actionPerformed()** method handles the string-to-character conversions. We uses the **charAt()** method from the *String* class to obtain the character. The syntax of this method is

```
char String.charAt(int position);
```

```
import java.awt.*;
import java.awt.event.*;
import java.applet.*;

public class ConvertChar extends Applet implements ActionListener
{ //Convert lower case to its upper case equivalents
  private Label lowerLabel =  new Label("Lower Case");
  private Label upperLabel =  new Label("Upper Case");
  private TextField lowerField =  new TextField(1);
  private TextField upperField =  new TextField(1);
  private char letter;

public void init()
{ //place the labels and text fields in the applet
  add(lowerLabel);
  add(lowerField);
  lowerField.addActionListener(this);

  add(upperLabel);
  add(upperField);
  upperField.setEditable(false);
}
//Put the actionPerformed() Method Here
}
```

Figure 21.24 The *ConvertChar* Class Definition

As the syntax indicates, the **charAt()** method returns the character located at the position passed as a parameter. String positions use a starting index of zero. For example, suppose we want to find the first character in the string literal *Hello*. The code is

```
char ch = "Hello".charAt(0);
```

Notice that we do not need to use the class name, *String*, to invoke the **charAt()** method.

Now let's consider the conversion needed in the **actionPerformed()** method. We know that this method is invoked when the user presses the *Enter* key while focus is in the lower-case text field. We must use the **getText()** method to obtain the user's selection. We then use the **charAt()** method to obtain the character in the 0th position. We can combine the two tasks in one statement:

```
char letter  = (lowerField.getText()).charAt(0);
```

The parentheses encasing **lowerField.getText()** indicate that we obtain the string and then pass it to the **charAt()** method.

After we obtain the letter, we use the **toUpperCase()** method of the *Character* class to produce the upper-case counterpart. This method returns the upper-case version of the character passed as a parameter. If an upper-case counterpart does not exist, the method returns the original value of the parameter. The statement that transforms *letter* into its upper-case version is

```
letter = Character.toUpperCase(letter);
```

Next, we convert *letter* to a string, so that we can place it in the upper-case text field. Unfortunately, conversion requires the creation of a *Character* object, because the **toString()**

method does not work with the elementary **char** type. (This is just one of Java's current inconsistencies.) We construct the *Character* object with the statement

```
Character upLetter = new Character(letter);
```

Now we can use the **toString()** method of the *Character* class to convert the upper-case letter into a string. We can combine the conversion and placement into the upper case text field. The statement that accomplishes these tasks is

```
upperField.setText(upLetter.toString());
```

We use the call to the **toString()** method as the parameter to the **setText()** method. The **toString()** method is invoked first, then the result is used as the parameter in the outher method.

Figure 21.25 contains the definition of the **actionPerformed()** method. The conversion techniques used in this method can easily be applied whenever we need character data.

```
public void actionPerformed(ActionEvent e)
{ /*Get the character, convert it to upper case
   Place in upper box */
   char letter = (lowerField.getText()).charAt(0);
   letter = Character.toUpperCase(letter);
   Character upLetter = new Character(letter);
   upperField.setText(upLetter.toString());
}
```

Figure 21.25 The **actionPerformed()** Method: *ConvertChar* Class

FLOATING-POINT CONVERSIONS

Java 1.1 provided "parse" methods for the integral types, but not for the floating-point types. Java 1.2 introduced "parse" methods for the floating-point types. Figure 21.26 contains the syntax for these new methods.

(a) float	float Float.parseFloat(String s);
(b) double	double Double.parseDouble (String s);

Figure 21.26 Parse Methods for Floating-Points: Java 1.2

The new methods are consistent with the integral parse methods displayed in Figure 21.18. Currently, these methods compile successfully on Java 1.2 compilers; however, the resulting applets will not load into the current browsers. We can use a more cumbersome conversion technique until the browsers catch up with the Java compilers. The *Float Conversion* page appearing in Figure 21.27 illustrates the conversion process.

The *Float Conversion* page uses a format similar to the *Integer Conversion* page. The HTML creates a 300 × 250 rectangle for the applet. The tag is

```
<APPLET CODE = "ConvertFloat.class" WIDTH = "300" HEIGHT = "250">
</APPLET>
```

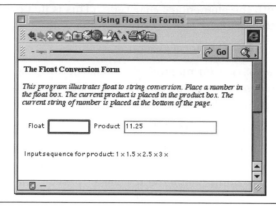

Figure 21.27 The *Float Conversion* Page

The *ConvertFloat* Class Definition

As Figure 21.27 indicates, the *Float Conversion* page displays a floating-point text field. A second, noneditable text field holds the product. We display the input sequence below the two text fields. Reexamine the code for the *Integer Conversion* page, then try to write the class definition for the *Float Conversion* page. You should be able to write the class definition and the **init()** and **paint()** methods. When you have finished, examine Figure 21.28. It contains the *ConvertFloat* class definition.

```
import java.applet.Applet;
import java.awt.*;
import java.awt.event.*;
public class ConvertFloat extends Applet implements ActionListener
{ //Create a text boxes for the float and the product
  private Label floatLabel =  new Label("Float");
  private Label ProductLabel =  new Label("Product");
  private TextField floatField =  new TextField(8);
  private TextField ProductField =  new TextField(20);
  private float number;
  private float product = 1.0f;
  private String message = "Input sequence for product: ";
public void init()
{ //place the labels and text fields in the applet
  add(floatLabel);
  add(floatField);
  floatField.addActionListener(this);
  add(ProductLabel);
  add(ProductField);
  ProductField.setEditable(false);
}
public void paint(Graphics g)
{ //write the numbers used to create the sum on the applet
    g.drawString(message, 1,60);
}
// Put the actionPerformed() Methodhere
}
```

Figure 21.28 The *ConvertFloat* Class Definition

The *ConvertFloat* class definition contains labels and text fields for the floating-point number and product. The definition also contains two floating-point variables, *number* and *product*. We give *product* an initial value of 1.0. The statement that does this is

```
private float product = 1.0f;
```

Notice that we use the suffix **f** to indicate that 1.0 is a *float* literal. If we forget to append the **f**, as in

```
private float  product = 1.0;
```

the Java compiler reports a type error, because 1.0 is a *double* literal and not a *float* literal.

The **init()** and **actionPeformed()** method of the *ConvertFloat* class parallel their counterparts in the *ConvertInt* class.

Converting Strings to Floating-Point Numbers

Although the sample page focuses on the **float** type, the conversion technique also works for **doubles**. Figure 21.29(a) shows the string-to-float conversion technique; Figure 21.29(b) shows the string-to-double conversion technique.

```
(a) float      Float fNum = new Float(String s);
               float number = fNum.floatValue();

(b) double     Double dNum = new Double(String s);
               double number = dNum.doubleValue();
```

Figure 21.29 String-to-Floating-Point Conversion Techniques

Converting a string to a **float** or a **double** requires two lines of code. The first line creates a new **Float** or **Double** object. We pass the string as a parameter. Once we've constructed the new object, we use either the **floatValue()** or the **doubleValue()** method to create the **float** or **double** number. For example, we obtain and convert the value in the floating-point text field with the following statements:

```
Float fNum = new Float (floatField.getText());
float number = fNum.floatValue();
```

Converting Floating-Point Numbers to Strings

To display a floating-point number on the page, we must convert it to a string. Figure 21.30(a) shows the float-to-string conversion; Figure 21.30(b) shows the double-to-string conversion. These conversions use the **toString()** method found in each of the wrapper objects.

```
(a) float      textField.setText(Float.toString(float x));
(b) double     textField.setText(Double.toString(double x));
```

Figure 21.30 Floating-Point-to-String Conversion Techniques

The **actionPerformed()** Method

Figure 21.31 contains the definition of the **actionPerformed()** method. This method uses the **float** conversion technique illustrated in Figure 21.29(a) to obtain the user's number. We multiply this number into the old product. We convert the new product to a string by using the conversion technique illustrated in Figure 21.30(a). The conversions are highlighted.

```
public void actionPerformed(ActionEvent e)
{ /*calculate the product and place in product text field
    Add float to the message string */
    Float fNum = new Float (floatField.getText());
    float number = fNum.floatValue();
    product *= number;
    ProductField.setText(Float.toString(product));
    message = message + floatField.getText() + " x ";
    floatField.setText("");
    repaint();
}
```

Figure 21.31 The **actionPerformed()** Method: *ConvertFloat* Class

Before reading further, try to create a *ConvertDouble* class. This class requires simple modifications of the *ConvertFloat* class. Pick a new arithmetic operation of your choice.

BOOLEAN CONVERSIONS

Our final conversion technique here focuses on boolean values. Figure 21.32 contains a sample page. The user enters a *true* or *false* value in the Boolean text field. The negation is printed in the second, noneditable text field.

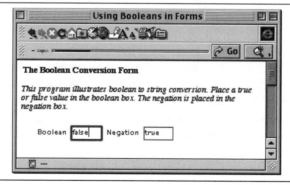

Figure 21.32 The *Boolean Conversion* Page

The *Boolean Conversion* page uses the same structure as the *Character Conversion* page. You might want to try creating a *BooleanConv* class definition, using the *Character Conversion* page as your model. You should be able to create the text fields and labels and the **init()** method. The **<APPLET>** tag that loads the applet is

```
<APPLET CODE = "BooleanConv.class" WIDTH = "230" HEIGHT = "300">
</APPLET>
```

The *BooleanConv* Class Definition

The *BooleanConv* class definition contains labels and text fields for the boolean and its negation. The **init()** method adds the labels and text fields to the applet. We add an action listener to the boolean text field, *booleanField*. We use the **setEditable()** method to make the negation text field, *NotField*, uneditable. Figure 21.33 contains the *BooleanConv* class definition.

```
import java.awt.*;
import java.awt.event.*;
import java.applet.*;

public class BooleanConv extends Applet implements ActionListener
{ //Negate a boolean
  private Label booleanLabel =  new Label("Boolean");
  private Label NotLabel =  new Label("Negation");
  private TextField booleanField =  new TextField(5);
  private TextField NotField =  new TextField(5);
public void init()
{ //place the labels and text fields in the applet
  add(booleanLabel);
  add(booleanField);
  booleanField.addActionListener(this);

  add(NotLabel);
  add(NotField);
  NotField.setEditable(false);
}
//Put the actionPerformed() Method here
}
```

Figure 21.33 The *BooleanConv* Class Definition

The `actionPreformed()` Method

The *BooleanConv* class definition does not contain a **boolean** variable declaration. Instead, we create two **Boolean** objects in the **actionPerformed()** method. The first object contains the converted text-field value. The second object contains the negation. Figure 21.34 contains the definition of the **actionPerformed()** method.

```
public void actionPerformed(ActionEvent e)
{ /*calculate the product and place in product text field
    Add boolean to the message string */
    Boolean BoolFlag = new Boolean(booleanField.getText());
    Boolean NotFlag = new Boolean(!BoolFlag.booleanValue());
    NotField.setText(NotFlag.toString());
}
```

Figure 21.34 The **actionPerfomed()** Method: *BooleanConv* Class

The **actionPerfomed()** method illustrates the two *Boolean* object constructors. These constructors create new *Boolean* objects by passing either a string or a boolean value as a parameter. We create the **BoolFlag** object by passing the text-field data to the constructor. We construct the **NotFlag** object by passing a boolean value. The statement

    Boolean NotFlag = new Boolean(!BoolFlag.booleanValue());

uses the **booleanValue()** method to obtain the primitive boolean value. The negation operator, **!**, reverses the value. This cumbersome conversion process clearly shows that a wrapper object (*Boolean*) is not the same as its corresponding primitive type (*boolean*).

    The final statement in the **actionPerformed()** method converts the boolean value in the **NotFlag** object to a string, which we display in the *NotField* text field.

THE *TEXTCOMPONENT* **CLASS**

We've used text fields in our initial Java programs. Now we examine text fields and their closely related cousins, text areas, more closely. Both classes are descendents of the *TextComponent* class, which provides several methods that the *TextField* and *TextArea* classes inherit. Figure 21.35 lists the most frequently used methods.

Method	Description
`int getCaretPosition();`	Returns position of text caret (cursor).
`String getSelectedText();`	Returns the highlighted string.
`int getSelectionStart();`	Returns beginning position of highlighted text.
`int getSelectionEnd();`	Returns the end position of highlighted text.
`String getText();`	Returns text string.
`void select(int `*start*`, int `*end*`);`	Highlights the text between *start* and *end*.
`void selectAll();`	Highlights all text.
`void setCaretPosition(int `*size*`);`	Changes caret size to *size*.
`void setEditable(boolean `*isEditable*`);`	Editable = *true*. Not editable = *false*.
`void setText(String `*text*`);`	Places *text* in the text component.
`boolean isEditable();`	Returns *true* if editable. Returns *false* if not.

Figure 21.35 *TextComponent* Methods

The *Caret* Page

Our previous Java programs used the **getText()**, **setText()**, and **setEditable()** methods. We explore additional methods from the *TextComponent* class in the next example. Figure 21.36 contains a Web page that reports the starting, ending, and caret (cursor) position of a selected piece of text.

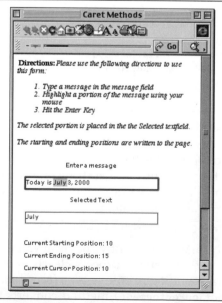

Figure 21.36 The *Caret* Page

The *Caret* page contains two text fields. The first text field holds the user's string. The second field holds the highlighted text. The page displays the beginning and ending positions of the highlighted text and the current caret position.

The **<APPLET>** tag creates a 230 × 300 rectangle for the applet. The HTML code is

```
<APPLET CODE = "Caret.class" WIDTH = "230" HEIGHT   = "300">
</APPLET>
```

The Caret Class Definition

The *Caret* class definition contains labels and text fields for the message and the selected text. The definition also contains integers to hold the positional information and a string to hold the selected text. Figure 21.37 contains the definition of the *Caret* class.

```
import java.awt.*;
import java.awt.event.*;
import java.applet.*;

public class Caret extends Applet implements ActionListener
{ //Create a text box for the user's message
  private static final int Y_POS = 140; // starting row for output

  private Label messagePrompt = new Label("Enter a message");
  private TextField messageField = new TextField(30);
  private Label selectPrompt = new Label("Selected Text");
  private TextField selectField = new TextField(30);
  private int start = -1;
  private int end = -1;
  private int caret = -1;
public void init()
{ //add prompt, textfield, and actionListener
  add(messagePrompt);
  add(messageField);
  messageField.addActionListener(this);
  add(selectPrompt);
  selectField.setEditable(false);
  add(selectField);
}
public void paint(Graphics g)
{ //write the positional information
  g.drawString("Current Starting Position: " + start, 10 ,Y_POS);
  g.drawString( "Current Ending Position: " + end, 10, Y_POS+20);
  g.drawString("Current Cursor Position: " + caret, 10, Y_POS+40);
}
}
```

Figure 21.37 The *Caret* Class Definition

The *Caret* class definition contains our first example of a constant definition. By convention, a Java constant's name contains only upper-case letters and underscores. The constant definition

```
private static final int Y_POS = 140;
```

holds the starting *y* position used in the **drawString()** method calls. Now, Java constants are *static*, so they must be declared in the class definition. They cannot be defined in methods, because then every call would redefine the constant, and, because a *static* object can be defined only once, the redefinitions would then trigger a Java error.

The `actionPerformed()` Method

The **actionPerformed()** method definition contains several examples of *TextComponent* method calls. Specifically, the **getSelectedText()** method obtains the highlighted text. The **getSelectionStart()**, **getSelectionEnd()**, and **getCaretPosition()** methods retrieve the positional information. Figure 21.38 contains the definition of the **actionPerformed()** method.

```
public void actionPerformed(ActionEvent e)
{ //process the text field response
    String selected = messageField.getSelectedText();
    selectField.setText(selected);
    start = messageField.getSelectionStart();
    end = messageField.getSelectionEnd();
    caret = messageField.getCaretPosition();
    repaint();
}
```

Figure 21.38 The **actionPerformed()** method: *Caret* Class

TEXT AREAS

We've created and processed text areas in JavaScript and Perl; now, we examine the Java *TextArea* class. Java text areas differ from text fields in two respects. First, text areas extend beyond a single line. Second, text areas do not have an action listener. Java provides a *TextListener* that we can use either with text areas or with text fields. In most circumstances, the *TextListener* is of little practical value, because it responds to all text changes—it is invoked each time the user presses a key.

The *TextArea* class contains the five constructors listed in Figure 21.39.

As Figure 21.39 indicates, we can create a text area containing a default string. We can also specify the rows and columns as well as the scroll-bar style in the definition. If we choose not to specify the rows, columns, and scroll-bar style, Java uses its default, a very large text area with horizontal and vertical scroll bars.

```
TextArea name = new TextArea();
TextArea name = new TextArea(String s);
TextArea name = new TextArea(int rows, int cols);
TextArea name = new TextArea(String s, int rows, int cols);
TextArea name = new TextArea(String s, int rows, int cols, int scrollbars);
```

Figure 21.39 The *TextArea* Constructors

To specify a scroll-bar style, we use one of the constants contained in Figure 21.40.

```
TextArea.SCROLLBARS_BOTH (default)
TextArea.SCROLLBARS_HORIZONTAL_ONLY
TextArea.SCROLLBARS_VERTICAL_ONLY
TextArea.SCROLLBARS_NONE
```

Figure 21.40 The Scroll-Bar Constants

The *TextArea* Methods

In addition to the methods inherited from the *TextComponent* class, the *TextArea* class contains three methods that are unique to it. Figure 21.41 lists these methods.

Method	Description
append(String s);	Add the string at the end of the text area.
insert(String s, int pos);	Insert the string at the indicated position.

replaceRange
  (String s, int start, int end);
	Replace text between *start* and *end*
	  with the string.

Figure 21.41 *TextArea* Methods

As Figure 21.41 indicates, we can add a string to the end of a text area, insert a string into a text area, or replace a portion of the text area with a new string.

The *InsertText* Page

As an illustration of text areas, we develop a page that inserts text into a text area. Figure 21.42(a) shows a sample page. The message in the text area contains an obvious mistake, because the user entered only *How are today?*. Figure 21.42(b) shows the page after the user corrected the error. The text field contains *you*, which was placed in the appropriate position in the text area.

The **<APPLET>** tag creates a 230 × 400 rectangle for the applet. The HTML is

```
<APPLET CODE = "TextAreaInsert.class" WIDTH = 230 HEIGHT = 400>
</APPLET>
```

(a) Text Area: Grammatical Error

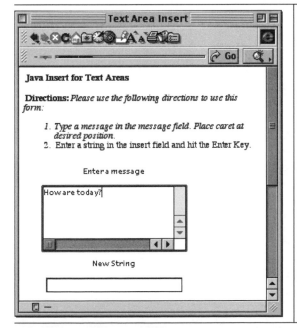

(b) Corrected Text Area

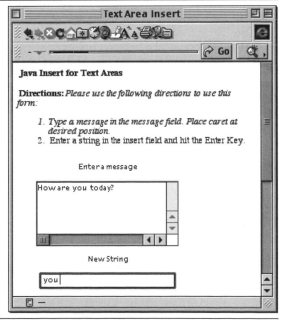

Figure 21.42 The *Insert Text* Page

The *TextAreaInsert* Class Definition

The *TextAreaInsert* class creates a 5 × 25 text area that contains the user's message. A corresponding 25-column text field holds the string that the user wishes to insert. An action listener added to the text field responds to events.

The *TextAreaInsert* class also defines a string, *insertStr*, which holds the text string data, and an integer, *caretPos*, which holds the cursor position in the text area. When the user presses the *Enter* key in the text field, the applet inserts the string at the cursor position.

Figure 21.43 contains the definition of the *TextAreaInsert* class.

```java
import java.awt.*;
import java.awt.event.*;
import java.applet.*;

public class TextAreaInsert extends Applet implements ActionListener
{ //Use a text area and text field to illustrate an insert operation
  private Label messagePrompt = new Label("Enter a message");
  private TextArea messageField = new TextArea(5, 25);
  private Label insertPrompt = new Label("New String");
  private TextField insertField = new TextField(25);

  private String insertStr;
  private int caretPos;

public void init()
{ //add prompt, textfield, and actionListener
  add(messagePrompt);
  add(messageField);
  //add actionListener to the text field.
  add(insertPrompt);
  add(insertField);
  insertField.addActionListener(this);
}
//Put the actionPerformed() Method here
}
```

Figure 21.43 The *TextAreaInsert* Class Definition

The actionPerformed() Method

The **actionPerformed()** method requires only three lines of code. The first line obtains the new string from the text field. The second line gets the caret position from the text area. The last line calls the **insert()** method to place the string in the text area at the cursor's position. Figure 21.44 contains the code.

```java
public void actionPerformed(ActionEvent e)
{ //insert string and caret position
    insertStr = insertField.getText();
    caretPos = messageField.getCaretPosition();
    messageField.insert(insertStr, caretPos);
}
```

Figure 21.44 The **actionPerformed()** Method: *TextAreaInsert* Class

THE MATH CLASS

In Chapter 9, we examined the JavaScript *Math* object. We conclude this chapter with an examination of the Java *Math* class. Figure 21.45 contains the constants and methods available in the Java *Math* class. You might want to compare the Java Math class and the JavaScript *Math* object. (See Figure 9.10.) A comparison shows that the Java Math class and JavaScript *Math* object provide exactly the same methods. The do differ in the number of constants: The Java *Math* class provides constants for **PI** and **E**; the JavaScript *Math* object provides constants for **PI**, **E**, **LOG10E**, **LOG2**, **SQRT1_2**, **SQRT2**, **LN2**, and **LN10**. The absence of the last six constants does not affect Java's computational powers.

Constants		Math Methods		Trig Methods	
Name	Meaning	Method	Meaning	Method	Meaning
E	2.718281828459045	ceil(x)	Integer above	cos(x)	Cosine
PI	3.141592653589793	floor(x)	Integer below	sin(x)	Sine
		round(x)	Round	tan(x)	Tangent
		abs(x)	Absolute value	acos(x)	Arc cosine
		sqrt(x)	Square root	asin(x)	Arc sine
		min(x,y)	Minimum	atan(x)	Arc tangent
		max(x,y) pow(x,y)	Maximum x^y		

Figure 21.45 The Java *Math* Class

The *Powers* Page

To illustrate the Java *Math* class, we create a *Powers* page. Figure 21.46 displays a sample page. The page contains *x* and *y* text fields. When the user presses the *Enter* key in either text field, the applet calls the **pow()** method to calculate x^y. The applet displays *x*, *y*, and x^y on the page.
The **<APPLET>** tag creates a 220 × 100 rectangle for the applet. The HTML is

```
<APPLET CODE = "Powers.class" WIDTH = "220" HEIGHT = "100">
</APPLET>
```

The *Powers* Class Definition

The *Powers* class definition contains labels and text fields for *x* and *y*. We also create a *message* string that is drawn on the page after the user presses the *Enter* key. Initially, *message* contains a single space. This prevents an error when the page loads. Figure 21.47 contains the *Powers* class definition.

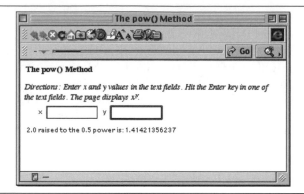

Figure 21.46 The *Powers* Page

The variable declarations and **init()** and **paint()** methods rely upon techniques developed earlier in the chapter.

```
import java.awt.*;
import java.awt.event.*;
import java.applet.*;
public class Powers extends Applet  implements ActionListener
{ //Create a text boxes for the doubles and the exponent
  private Label xLabel =  new Label("x");
  private Label yLabel =  new Label("y");
  private TextField xField =  new TextField(10);
  private TextField yField =  new TextField(10);
  private String message = " ";
public void init()
{ //place the labels and text fields in the applet
  add(xLabel);
  add(xField);
  xField.addActionListener(this);
  add(yLabel);
  add(yField);
  yField.addActionListener(this);
}
public void paint(Graphics g)
{// write the result on the page
  g.drawString(message, 1,45);
}
//Put the actionPerformed() Method Definition Here

}
```

Figure 21.47 The *Powers* Class Definition

The `actionPerformed()` Method

The **actionPerformed()** method creates two *Double* objects, one for each text field. We pass the text fields' contents to the constructors. Once we've constructed the objects, we use the **doubleValue()** method to construct the primitive **double** variables. We pass these variables to the **pow()** method. We convert the values back to strings as we create the *message* string. Figure 21.48 contains the definition of the **actionPerformed()** method.

```
public void actionPerformed(ActionEvent e)
{ /*calculate the product and place in product text field
   Add float to the message string */
   Double xNum = new Double(xField.getText());
   double x = xNum.doubleValue();
   Double yNum = new Double(yField.getText());
   double y = yNum.doubleValue();
   double pow  = Math.pow(x,y);
   message = Double.toString(x) + " raised to the " +
   Double.toString(y) + " power is: " + Double.toString(pow);
   xField.setText("");
   yField.setText("");
   repaint();
}
```

Figure 21.48 The **actionPerformed()** Method: *Powers* Class

Your knowledge of the JavaScript *Math* object will let you easily create applets that use the equivalent Java *Math* class methods.

➤ EXERCISES

The initial exercises ask you to extend your repertoire of conversion techniques. Many of the remaining exercises ask you to create Java versions of JavaScript exercises or programs developed in Chapter 9. Use text fields to obtain the information from the user.

1. **The *Byte Conversion* Page.** Using the *Integer Conversion* page as your model, create a byte conversion page.

2. **The *Short Conversion* Page.** Using the *Integer Conversion* page as your model, create a short conversion page.

3. **The *Long Conversion* Page.** Using the *Integer Conversion* page as your model, create a long conversion page.

4. **The *Fat Grams* Page.** Create a Java version of the *Fat Grams* page. Use text fields to obtain the grams of fat and the total calories. Use the **drawString()** method to display the grams of fat, total calories, and percentage of fat calories. Figure 21.49 contains the formula.

5. **The *Pass Percentage* Page.** Create a Java page that asks the user to enter the number of completed (football) passes and the number of total passes. Print the numbers of completed passes and of total passes and the percentage of complete passes. The formula appears in Figure 21.50.

$$\frac{\text{Fat grams} \cdot 9}{\text{Total Calories}} \cdot 100 \qquad\qquad \frac{\text{Completed passes}}{\text{Total Passes}} \cdot 100$$

Figure 21.49 Percentage of Fat Calories   **Figure 21.50** Percentage of Completed Passes

6. **The *Number* Page.** Figure 14.7 contains a simple numeric page. Create a Java version of this page. You don't need *Done* or *Clear* buttons. Make the first number an integer, the second a float, the third a double. Print the sum, stored as a double, in a noneditable text field.

7. **The *Circle* Page.** Create a page that calculates the area and circumference of a circle. Ask the user to enter the radius. Print out the radius, the area, and the circumference. (See Figure 9.17.)

8. **The *Roots of the Quadratic Function* Page.** Create a page that calculates the positive and negative roots of the quadratic equation. The user should enter the values for *a, b, c*. Print out these values and the two roots. Use only a test data set that produces two roots. (See Figure 9.18.)

9. **The *Parallelogram* Page.** Create a page that calculates and displays the area of a parallelogram. Obtain the width and height of the parallelogram. Your page should display the width, height, and area, with appropriate messages. (See Figure 9.19.)

10. **The *Triangle* Page.** Create a page that calculates and displays the area of a triangle. Obtain the base and height of the triangle. (See Figure 9.20.)

11. **The *Trapezoid* Page.** Create a page that calculates and displays the area of a trapezoid. Obtain the two bases and the height. Print the user's data and the area. (See Figure 9.22.)

12. **The *Box* Page.** Create a page that calculates the area and perimeter of a box. Obtain the length and width. Display the length, width, area, and perimeter. (See Figure 9.23.)

13. **The *Monetary Conversion* Page.** Find the monetary conversion rates in your local paper (or try the New York Times). Ask the user to enter an amount in US dollars. Convert this amount to the foreign currencies listed in the NY Times.

14. **A *Formula* Page.** Create a page that calculates the formula depicted in Figure 9.26.

15. **A *Formula* Page.** Create a page that calculates the formula depicted in Figure 9.27.

16. **A *Formula* Page.** Create a page that calculates the formula depicted in Figure 9.28.

17. **A *Formula* Page.** Create a page that calculates the formula depicted in Figure 9.29.

18. **A *Formula* Page.** Create a page that calculates the formula depicted in Figure 9.30.

19. **The *Let's Make Change* Page.** Create a Java version of the *Let's Make Change* page. (See Figures 9.11 through 9.13.)

20. **The *TextAppend* Page.** Create a *TextAppend* page using the model given in the *TextInsert* page. This page should display a text area and a text field. When the user presses the *Enter* key in the text field, append the string to the text area.

22 Selection and Iteration Statements, Buttons, and Arrays

INTRODUCTION

We begin this chapter by examining Java's selection and iterations statements. You'll grasp these statements easily, because Java and JavaScript use the same set of statements. For example, Java provides **if...else** and **switch** statements for selection and **for**, **do**, and **do...while** statements for iteration. The syntax of each of the Java statements is identical to that of the corresponding JavaScript statement.

SELECTION STATEMENTS

The **if** Statement

Figure 22.1 contains the syntax for the **if...else** statement. As this figure indicates, we use an expression to select between alternative pieces of code. If the expression is *true*, Java executes the statement after the expression. If the expression is *false*, Java executes the statement in the **else** clause, if an **else** clause is present. Java assumes that any **if** or **else** clause contains a single statement. Multiple statements in either clause are handled by creating a compound statement. Like its JavaScript counterpart, a compound statement is simply a set of statements encased in braces.

We create an expression in Java by using relational, logical, or boolean operators. Figure 22.2 lists these operators in order of precedence.

```
if (Boolean Expression)
    true statement;
else
    false statement;
```

Figure 22.1 Syntax of the Java **if** Statement

523

Operator	Meaning
!	Logical not
<	Less than
<=	Less than or equal
>	Greater than
>=	Greater than or equal
==	Equal
!=	Not Equal
&	Boolean and
^	Boolean xor
|	Boolean or
&&	Logical and
||	Logical or

Figure 22.2 Java Relational and Logical Operators

As Figure 22.2 demonstrates, Java provides all the relational and logical operators of JavaScipt; however, Java also introduces three boolean operators: *and* (**&**), *exclusive or* (^), and *or* (|). For most applications, the standard relational and logical operators will suffice.

The *Wind Chill* Page

As a "warm-up" exercise in selection statements, we create a *Wind Chill* page. The page asks the user to enter a wind chill. The frostbite risk is displayed on the page. Figure 22.3 contains a sample page.

Figure 22.3 The *Wind Chill* Page

The HTML applet tag creates a 230 × 200 rectangle to hold the applet. The tag is

```
<APPLETCODE = "WindChill.class" WIDTH = "230" HEIGHT = "200">
</APPLET>
```

The `WindChill` Class Definition

The *WindChill* class definition contains a label and text field for the user's input. We also include two strings in the definition. The first string contains the frostbite risk for the user's temperature. The second string contains an informational message indicating how long it takes flesh to freeze at the user's temperature. We also create an integer to hold the converted temperature supplied by the user. Figure 22.4 contains the WindChill class definition.

```java
import java.awt.*;
import java.awt.event.*;
import java.applet.*;

public class WindChill extends Applet implements ActionListener
{ //Create a text boxes for the current wind chill

  private Label windChillLabel =  new Label("Wind Chill");
  private TextField windChillField =  new TextField(16);
  private int windChill;
  private String effect = "Frostbite Risk: ";
  private String extraEffect = " ";

public void init()
{ //place the wind chill label and text field in the applet
  add(windChillLabel);
  add(windChillField);
  windChillField.addActionListener(this);
}

public void paint(Graphics g)
{ //write the effect message and extra message to the screen
  int yPos = 60;
  g.drawString(effect, 1, yPos);
  g.drawString(extraEffect, 1, yPos+20);
}

//Put the actionPerformed() Method Here
}
```

Figure 22.4 The *WindChill* Class Definition

The actionPerformed() Method

The **actionPerformed()** method uses the **parseInt()** method to convert the user's response into an integer. The **if...else** statement uses the wind chill chart appearing in Figure 10.32 to place the appropriate messages in the *effect* and *extraEffect* strings. We call the **repaint()** method to write the two strings on the page. Figure 22.5 contains the definition of the **actionPerformed()** method.

Buttons and the switch Statement

Figure 22.6 contains the syntax for the Java **switch** statement. Unlike its JavaScript counterpart, the Java **switch** statement requires an *ordinal* variable in the **switch** header and ordinal values in the **case** statements. An *ordinal* is any type that contains an obvious predecessor and successor for each value. All of the integral types and characters are ordinal. The floating-point types and strings are not.

The **switch** statement requires unique ordinal values for the **case** tags. Braces are not needed to group the statements associated with a **case** tag or tags.

```
public void actionPerformed(ActionEvent e)
{ /*Get the wind chill and create message string */
    windChill = Integer.parseInt(windChillField.getText());
    if ((windChill <= 9) && (windChill >= -10)) {
        effect = "Frostbite Risk: Little";
        extraEffect = "You might feel unpleasant";
    }
    else if ((windChill <= -11) && (windChill >= -25)) {
        effect = "Frostbite Risk: Possible";
        extraEffect = "It takes more than a minute to freeze flesh.";
    }
    else if ((windChill <= -26) && (windChill >= -65)) {
        effect = "Frostbite Risk: DANGER";
        extraEffect = "It takes less than a minute to freeze flesh.";
    }
    else if (windChill <= -66) {
        effect = "Frosbite Risk: WARNING";
        extraEffect = "It takes less than 30 seconds to freeze flesh.";
    }
    else {
        effect = "There is no danger of frosbite";
        extraEffect = "Enjoy the weather.";
    }
    repaint();
}
```

Figure 22.5 The **actionPerformed()** Method: *WindChill* Class

```
switch (Ordinal Variable) {
    case Ordinal Value : Statement(s)
            break; optional
  case Ordinal Value: ...case Ordinal Value: Statement(s)
            break; optional
  default: Statement(s)optional
}
```

Figure 22.6 Syntax of the Java **switch** Statement

Evaluation of the **switch** statement follows three simple rules.

Rule 1. Java evaluates **case** statements from top to bottom. When a **case** value matches the ordinal variable's value, all statements below the **case** value are executed.

Rule 2. A **break** statement halts execution of the statements.

Rule 3. The optional **default** statement creates code that executes when the ordinal variable's value does not match any of the **case** values.

Button Basics

Because the **switch** statement involves no new concepts, we combine the demonstration of it with Java buttons. We've created many JavaScript buttons, so the transition to Java buttons is an easy one. Figure 22.7 contains a summary of the Java **Button** class.

Description	Syntax
Button Constructor	`Button name = new Button();` `Button name = new Button(String s);`
Event Handler	`ActionListener`

Methods	`String name.getLabel();`
	`name.setLabel(String s);`
	`name.addActionListener(this);`

Event Processor	`void actionPerformed(ActionEvent e);`

Figure 22.7 The Java *Button* Class

As Figure 22.7 indicates, two *Button* constructors are available. The first constructor creates a button without a "face" label. The second constructor uses a *String* parameter to create a "labeled" button. The *Button* class includes methods that change (**setLabel()**) or obtain (**getLabel()**) a button's label. Both *TextField* and *Button* objects use an *ActionListener*. The **addActionListener()** method adds the action listener to a button. The **actionPerformed()** method responds to button clicks.

The Hurricane Page

To illustrate the **switch** statement, we create a *Hurricane* page. Figure 22.8 contains a sample page. This page uses Java buttons to provide the user interface. When the user clicks a hurricane button, the page prints the relevant information for the hurricane category. In Figure 22.8, the user selected the Category **2** button.

The HTML creates a 320 × 300 rectangle to hold the applet. The tag is

```
<APPLET CODE = "Hurricane.class" WIDTH = "320" HEIGHT = "300">
</APPLET>
```

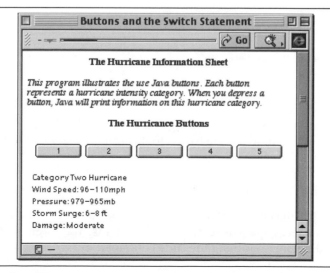

Figure 22.8 The *Hurricane* Page

The *Hurricane* Class Definition

Figure 22.9 contains the *Hurricane* class definition. The class fields include five buttons, one for each hurricane category. The definition also includes five strings, one for each of the hurricane messages. Initially, the message strings contain the message labels. This precaution avoids a *Null Pointer Exception* error when the browser loads the page.

```java
import java.awt.*;
import java.awt.event.*;
import java.applet.*;

public class Hurricane extends Applet implements ActionListener
{ /*Create buttons for the hurricane categories
    Use a switch statement to print our hurricane information */
    private Button Category1 = new Button("1");
    private Button Category2 = new Button("2");
    private Button Category3 = new Button("3");
    private Button Category4 = new Button("4");
    private Button Category5 = new Button("5");
    private String hurricane = "Category ";
    private String pressure = "Pressure: ";
    private String windSpeed = "Wind Speed: ";
    private String stormSurge = "Storm Surge: ";
    private String damage = "Damage: ";

// Put the init() Method Here

public void paint(Graphics g)
{//write the hurricane messages on the applet
    int yPos = 50;
    int change = 15;
    g.drawString(hurricane, 1, yPos);
    g.drawString(windSpeed, 1, yPos+change);
    g.drawString(pressure, 1, yPos+2*change);
    g.drawString(stormSurge, 1, yPos+3*change);
    g.drawString(damage, 1, yPos+4*change);
}

//Put the actionPerformed() Method Here
}
```

Figure 22.9 The *Hurricane* Class Definition

The **paint()** method draws the five strings on the page. We haven't yet discussed the **for** statement, so this **paint()** method uses five calls to the **drawString()** method. The code is easy to understand, but tedious.

The init() Method

The **init()** method adds the action listeners to the buttons and adds the buttons to the applet. The code uses the same techniques developed for text fields. You might want to write the code for the **init()** method before examining the code contained in Figure 22.10.

```
public void init()
{ /*place the buttons in the applet
    add an actionListener for each button */
    add(Category1);
    Category1.addActionListener(this);
    add(Category2);
    Category2.addActionListener(this);
    add(Category3);
    Category3.addActionListener(this);
    add(Category4);
    Category4.addActionListener(this);
    add(Category5);
    Category5.addActionListener(this);
}
```

Figure 22.10 The `init()` Method: *Hurricane* Class

The `actionPerformed()` Method

The *ActionListener* invokes the **actionPerformed()** method when the user clicks a button. The code in this method must first determine which button the user selected. By design, the *ActionEvent* object passed as a parameter contains a method, **getActionCommand()**, that lets us extract the selected button's label. Figure 22.11 contains the syntax for this method.

```
String ActionEvent.getActionCommand();
```

Figure 22.11 The **getActionCommand()** Method

As Figure 22.11 suggests, the **getActionCommand()** method returns a string that represents the label of the selected button. Assume that we named the *ActionEvent* object *e*, the statement that obtains the selected button is

```
String eventString = e.getActionCommand();
```

Because the button labels are numbers, we can use the **parseInt()** method to obtain the integer equivalents. The statement is

```
int buttonNum = Integer.parseInt(eventString);
```

We use *buttonNum* to control the **switch** statement. This statement provides a **case** label for each of the hurricane categories. The statements associated with the **case** labels construct the appropriate hurricane information strings for the selected hurricane category. Once we've created these strings, we call the **repaint()** method to place them in the applet.

Figure 22.12 contains the code for the **actionPerformed()** method.

```java
public void actionPerformed(ActionEvent e)
{ /*find the depressed button,  Create a message string */
 String eventString = e.getActionCommand();
 int buttonNum = Integer.parseInt(eventString);
 switch (buttonNum)
 {
    case 1: hurricane = "Category One Hurricane";
            windSpeed = "Wind Speed 74-95mph";
            pressure =   "Pressure: Above 980mb";
            stormSurge = "Storm Surge: 4-5 ft";
            damage = "Damage: Minimal";
            break;
    case 2: hurricane = "Category Two Hurricane";
            windSpeed = "Wind Speed: 96-110mph";
            pressure =   "Pressure: 979-965mb";
            stormSurge = "Storm Surge: 6-8 ft";
            damage = "Damage: Moderate";
            break;
    case 3: hurricane = "Category Three Hurricane";
            windSpeed = "Wind Speed: 111-130mph";
            pressure =   "Pressure: 964-945mb";
            stormSurge = "Storm Surge: 9-12 ft";
            damage = "Damage: Extensive";
            break;
    case 4: hurricane = "Category Four Hurricane";
            windSpeed = "Wind Speed: 131-155mph";
            pressure =   "Pressure: 944-920mb";
            stormSurge = "Storm Surge: 13-18ft";
            damage = "Damage: Extreme";
            break;
    case 5: hurricane = "Category Five Hurricane";
            windSpeed = "Wind Speed: Above 155 mph";
            pressure =   "Pressure: Below 920";
            stormSurge = "Storm Surge: Above 18 ft";
            damage = "Damage: Catastophic";
            break;
 }
 repaint();
}
```

Figure 22.12 The **actionPerfomed()** Method: *Hurricane* Class

ITERATION STATEMENTS

The for Statement

We begin our excursion into Java's iteration statements by examining the **for** statement. Figure 22.13 reviews the syntax of this statement, which is identical to that of its JavaScript counterpart.

---

for(*Initial Expression*;_{opt} *Test Expression*;_{opt} *Change Expression*_{opt}) *statement*;

Figure 22.13 The Java **for** statement

The **for** statement contains a header with three optional expressions. The first expression provides an initial value for the **for** statement index. The second expression tests for termination. We form this expression from the logical and relational operators listed in Figure 22.2. The last expression modifies the index variable so that the **for** statement eventually terminates.

The **for** statement executes the code in the loop's body as long as the test expression is *true*. If the test expression is initially *false*, the body of the **for** statement is never executed. The body of the **for** statement can consist of a single statement or a compound statement.

The Decimal To Binary, Octal, and Hexadecimal Page

Computer scientists often must convert numbers from the decimal system that we humans prefer to one of the binary-based systems that computers prefer. To illustrate the **for** statement, we create a page that displays a range of decimal numbers and their binary, octal (base-8), and hexadecimal (base-16) equivalents. Text fields let the user enter the starting and ending numbers for the range. Figure 22.14 contains a sample page.

The HTML creates a 400 × 600 rectangle to hold the applet. The tag is

```
<APPLET CODE = "IntToHex.class" WIDTH = "400" HEIGHT = "600">
</APPLET>
```

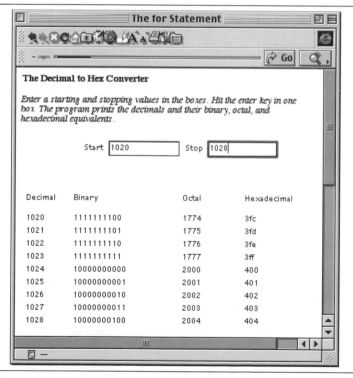

Figure 22.14 The *Decimal Conversion* Page

The *IntToHex* Class Definition

The *IntToHex* class definition creates a label, text field, and integer to represent the starting value for the range. A second label, text field, and integer represent the ending value. Four constants specify the column locations for the decimal, binary, octal, and hexadecimal rapresentations of the number. Figure 22.15 contains the class definition. The constants are highlighted.

```java
import java.awt.*;
import java.awt.event.*;
import java.applet.*;

public class IntToHex extends Applet implements ActionListener
{ //Implement an Decimal to Hex Converter
  //Define column contants for table placement
  private static final int DECIMAL_COL = 5;
  private static final int BINARY_COL = 65;
  private static final int OCTAL_COL = 200;
  private static final int HEX_COL = 280;

  private Label startPrompt = new Label("Start");
  private TextField startField = new TextField(12);
  private Label stopPrompt = new Label("Stop");
  private TextField stopField = new TextField(12);
  private int start = 0, stop= 0;

public void init()
{ //add the prompts and text fields
  add(startPrompt);
  add(startField);
  startField.addActionListener(this);
  add(stopPrompt);
  stopField.addActionListener(this);
  add(stopField);
}

//Put the paint() Method Here

public void actionPerformed(ActionEvent e)
{ //process the text field response
  start = Integer.parseInt(startField.getText());
  stop = Integer.parseInt(stopField.getText());
  repaint();
}
}
```

Figure 22.15 The *IntToHex* Class Definition

The **init()** method for the *IntToHex* class adds an action listener to each text field. The method also adds the labels and text fields to the applet. The **actionPerformed()** method obtains and converts the values in the text fields.

The **paint()** Method

The **paint()** method uses a **for** statement to create the columns of decimal, binary, octal, and hexadecimal numbers. Creation of the latter three columns requires a conversion of the decimal number. These conversions would be an onerous task if we had to do them manually, but the *Integer* class sensibly contains methods that handle the conversions automatically. Figure 22.16 contains the syntax for the conversion methods.

Method	Description
`String Integer.ToBinaryString(int i);`	Return binary equivalent of *i*.
`String Integer.ToOctalString(int i);`	Return octal equivalent of *i*.
`String Integer.ToHexString(int i);`	Return hexadecimal equivalent of *i*.

Figure 22.16 Integer Conversion Methods

As Figure 22.16 indicates, each of the conversion methods requires an integer parameter. The method returns a string containing the binary, octal, or hexadecimal equivalent of the decimal representation. Because the methods return strings, we can use them directly in the **drawString()** method calls.

Figure 22.17 contains the definition of the **paint()** method. The **for** statement that generates the conversion table is highlighted. Notice the use of the *yPos* variable to change the row positions. The constants we created in the class definition determine the column positions.

```
public void paint(Graphics g)
{ //Convert the number to hex, octal and binary
//draw the number on the page
  int yPos = 80; //row position
  int i;
  g.drawString("Decimal", DECIMAL_COL, yPos);
  g.drawString("Octal", OCTAL_COl, yPos);
  g.drawString("Hexadecimal", HEX_COL, yPos);
  g.drawString("Binary", BINARY_COL, yPos);
  yPos += 25;

  for (i=start; i<= stop; i++) {
    g.drawString(i+" ", DECIMAL_COL, yPos);
    g.drawString(Integer.toOctalString(i), OCTAL_COL, yPos);
    g.drawString(Integer.toHexString(i), HEX_COL, yPos);
    g.drawString(Integer.toBinaryString(i), BINARY_COL, yPos);
    yPos += 16;
  }
}
```

Figure 22.17 The **paint()** Method: *IntToHex* Class

The while Statement

Next, we turn our attention to Java's **while** statement. Figure 22.18 reviews the syntax for this statement.

```
while(expression)
    statement;
```

Figure 22.18 The Java **while** Statement

Java's **while** statement, like its JavaScript counterpart, contains a header with a parenthesized expression. We create this expression by using the relational and logical operators appearing in Figure 22.2. The statement in the loop body can be a single statement or a compound statement. The statement is executed as long as the expression is *true*. If the expression is initially *false*, the statement in the body is ignored.

The Fahrenheit-To-Celsius Page

To illustrate the **while** statement, we create a page that displays Fahrenheit temperatures and their Celsius equivalents. The page lets the user specify the starting and stopping temperature and the Fahrenheit increment. Figure 22.19 contains a sample page. In this example, the user selected starting and stopping values of 95 and 70 and a five-degree increment.

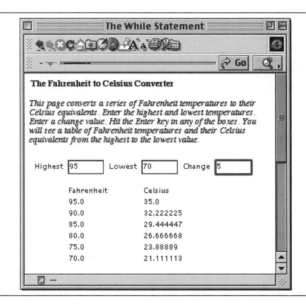

Figure 22.19 The *Fahrenheit To Celsius* Page

The HTML creates a 300 × 400 rectangle to hold the applet. The tag is

```
<APPLET CODE = "FtoC.class" WIDTH = "300" HEIGHT = "400">
</APPLET>
```

The *FtoC* Class Definition

The *FtoC* class definition creates three sets of labels, text fields, and floats to represent the starting, stopping, and temperature-change values. It also contains constants to specify the column positions for the Fahrenheit and Celsius temperatures. Figure 22.20 contains the class definition.

The *FtoC* class definition follows the same model as the *IntToHex* class. The **init()** method adds an action listener to each text field and adds the labels and text fields to the applet. The **actionPerformed()** method obtains and converts the values in the text fields.

The paint() Method

Figure 22.21 contains the definition of the **paint()** method. When the page loads, the **paint()** method places only the *Fahrenheit* and *Celsius* titles on the page. We do not want the **while** state-

```java
import java.awt.*;
import java.awt.event.*;
import java.applet.*;

public class FtoC extends Applet implements ActionListener
{ //Create a converion table for Fahrenheit to Celsius
  private static final int X1_POS = 50;
  private static final int X2_POS = 150;
  private Label startPrompt = new Label("Highest");
  private TextField startField = new TextField(6);
  private Label stopPrompt = new Label("Lowest");
  private TextField stopField = new TextField(6);
  private Label changePrompt = new Label("Change");
  private TextField changeField = new TextField (6);
  //set values to prevent while loop from executing when page loads
  private float highest = -1;
  private float lowest = 0;
  private float change = 0;
  public void init()
  { //add the labels and textboxes to the applet
    add(startPrompt);
    add(startField);
    startField.addActionListener(this);
    add(stopPrompt);
    stopField.addActionListener(this);
    add(stopField);
    add(changePrompt);
    add(changeField);
    changeField.addActionListener(this);
  }
  //Put the paint() Method Here
public void actionPerformed(ActionEvent e)
  { //Obtain the Floats from the text fields
   Float highestF = new Float(startField.getText());
   Float lowestF = new Float(stopField.getText());
   Float changeF = new Float(changeField.getText());

   highest = highestF.floatValue();
   lowest = lowestF.floatValue();
   change = changeF.floatValue();
   repaint();
  }
}
```

Figure 22.20 The *FtoC* Class Definition

ment to execute until the user enters values. To accomplish this, we provide initial values for *highest* (-1) and *lowest* (0) that create a *false* expression.

The **while** statement converts the Fahrenheit temperatures to their Celsius equivalents. The conversion formula uses floating-point literals, denoted by the suffix **f**. After the conversion, we call the **drawString()** method to write both temperatures on the page. Finally, we decrement *fahrenheit* and increment the row position (*yPos*).

We could easily write the *Fahrenheit To Celsius* page by using a **for** statement to print the temperature chart. In fact, Figure 22.21 labels each of the expressions, to facilitate this translation.

```
public void paint(Graphics g)
  { //get the parameters, then print the Fahrenheit-Celsius table
     float celsius, fahrenheit;
     int yPos = 50;
     g.drawString("Fahrenheit", X1_POS, yPos);
     g.drawString("Celsius", X2_POS, yPos);
     yPos += 15;
     fahrenheit = highest;     //initialize fahrenheit
     while (fahrenheit >= lowest) { //test expression
       celsius = 5.0f/9.0f*(fahrenheit - 32.0f);
       g.drawString(Float.toString(fahrenheit), X1_POS, yPos);
       g.drawString(Float.toString(celsius), X2_POS, yPos);
       fahrenheit -= change; // change expression
       yPos += 15;
     }
  }
```

Figure 22.21 The **paint()** Method: *FtoC* Class

The do...while Statement

The last of Java's iteration statements is also the least frequently used. Figure 22.22 reviews the syntax of Java's **do...while** statement. This statement is identical to its JavaScript counterpart.

Unlike the **while** statement, the **do...while** statement places the test expression at the end of the loop. We form the expression with the logical and relational operators listed in Figure 22.2. The body of the **do...while** statement can contain a single statement or a compound statement. This statement (single or compound) is executed as long as the expression is *true*. The test for termination appears at the end of the loop, so the statement in the loop's body is always executed *at least one time*.

```
do
     statement;
while(TestExpr);
```

Figure 22.22 The Java **do...while** Statement

The *Celsius to Fahrenheit* Page

We've previously created a page to convert Fahrenheit temperatures to their Celsius equivalents; we now reverse this process. The illustration of the **do...while** statement creates a table of Celsius temperatures and their Fahrenheit equivalents. The page uses the same model as the *Fahrenheit To Celsius* page.

Figure 22.23(a) shows the *Celsius to Fahrenheit* page that is initially displayed. The initial page contains a sample conversion chart, which indicates that $0°$ C $\approx 32°$ F. The initial values for *highest* (0), *lowest* (1), and *change* (1) force the **do...while** loop to execute only once. Figure 22.23(b) displays the page after the user has selected *highest*, *lowest*, and *change* values of 5, -1, and 1, respectively.

The HTML page creates a 300×400 rectangle to hold the applet. The tag is

```
<APPLET CODE = "CtoF.class" WIDTH = "300" HEIGHT = "400">
</APPLET>
```

(a) Starting Page

(b) After User Enters Values

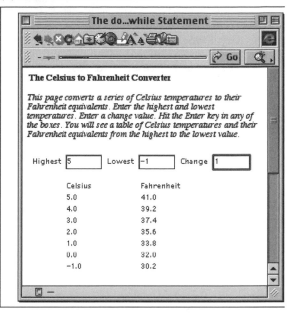

Figure 22.23 The *Celsius To Fahrenheit* Page

The *CtoF* Class Definition

Figure 22.24 contains the *CtoF* class definition. The code is virtually identical to that of the *FtoC* class definition. In fact, the only differences appear in the initial values assigned to *highest*, *lowest*, and *change* and in the definition of the **paint()** method.

```
import java.awt.*;
import java.awt.event.*;
import java.applet.*;

public class CtoF extends Applet implements ActionListener
{ //Create a Celsius to Fahrenheit conversion table
  //Use class fields from FtoC class
  private float highest = 0;
  private float lowest = 1;
  private float change = 0;

  //Same init() method as FtoC class
  //Put the paint() method Here
  //Same actionPerformed() method as the FtoC class
}
```

Figure 22.24 The *CtoF* Class Definition

The paint() Method

Figure 22.25 contains the definition of the **paint()** method. The code largely follows the model developed for the *FtoC* class, except that we use a **do...while** statement to print the temperature table.

```
public void paint(Graphics g)
  { //get the parameters, then print the Celsius-Fahrenheit table
    float celsius, fahrenheit;
    int yPos = 100;
    g.drawString("Celsius", X1_POS, yPos);
    g.drawString("Fahrenheit", X2_POS, yPos);
    yPos += 15;
    celsius = highest;
    do {
      fahrenheit = 9.0f/5.0f* celsius + 32.0f;
      g.drawString(Float.toString(celsius), X1_POS, yPos);
      g.drawString(Float.toString(fahrenheit), X2_POS, yPos);
      celsius -= change;
      yPos += 15;
    } while(celsius >= lowest);
}
```

Figure 22.25 The **paint()** Method: *CtoF* Class

ARRAY BASICS

The underlying concept of an array is shared by many programming languages. An array is defined as a group of objects that share a common name and are accessed by some organized scheme—usually position. In most programming languages, the objects must be chosen from the same type; we can create an array of integers or of characters or of floats, but we cannot create an array that contains both characters and floats. This is true of Java and JavaScript. Perl is an exception to this rule; it allows "mixed" lists.

We use brackets, [], to denote array subscripts. The first subscript in a Java array is zero; the last subscript is the size of the array minus one. We can create an array with predefined values. For example, the following statement creates an array of animal names:

```
private static final String [] animalNames = {"cat", "dog", "bird", "fish", "horse"};
```

This statement indicates that we are creating a constant (**static final**) string array, **String[]**, that contains the five strings appearing in the list on the right-hand side of the assignment statement. Java uses braces, **{ }**, to enclose the array elements. Figure 22.26 shows the array elements and their corresponding subscripts.

Subscript	Contents
animalNames[0]	"cat"
animalNames[1]	"dog"
animalNames[2]	"bird"
animalNames[3]	"fish"
animalNames[4]	"horse"

Figure 22.26 The *animalNames* Array

Declaring the *animalNames* array as a constant prevents accidental modification of the array's elements or the size of the array.

We can also create arrays with mutable elements. For example, the following statement creates an array of buttons:

```
private Button[] animals = new Button[animalNames.length];
```

The *animalNames* and *animal* arrays are of the same size, because we use the *length* field of *animalNames* to set the size of the *animals* array. All Java arrays have a *length* field that contains a number telling how many elements there are in the array.

Let's consider another declaration. The following statements also create an array of buttons:

```
private static int MAX_BUTTONS = 12;
private Button[]  numbers = new Button[MAX_BUTTONS];
```

These statements create an array, *numbers*, with subscripts numbered from zero to eleven. The array elements are currently undefined, because we have not assigned any values to them.

The *Array Buttons* Page

As a preview of things to come, we create a page of buttons, using the *numbers* and *animalNames* arrays. Figure 22.27 contains a sample page. The buttons in this page are for appearance only; they don't actually do anything.

The HTML page creates a 300 × 300 rectangle to hold the applet. The tag is

```
<APPLET CODE = "OneDArrays.class" WIDTH = "300" HEIGHT = "300">
</APPLET>
```

The *horse* button appears in the middle of the page, because the default flow layout manager uses a center alignment.

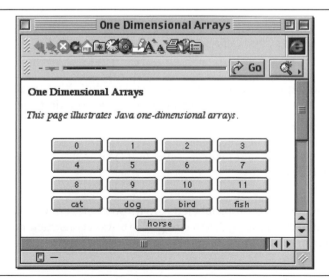

Figure 22.27 The *Array Buttons* Page

The *OneDArrays* Class Definition

The definition of the *OneDArrays* class appears in Figure 22.28. The class definition contains the string and button arrays discussed earlier. The definition contains only an **init()** method, because the buttons are for display purposes only.

```java
import java.awt.*;
import java.awt.event.*;
import java.applet.*;

public class OneDArrays extends Applet
{//Create an array of buttons
   private static int MAX_BUTTONS = 12;
   private Button[]  numbers = new Button[MAX_BUTTONS];

   private static final String [] animalNames = {"cat", "dog", "bird", "fish", "horse"};
   private Button[]  animals = new Button[animalNames.length];

public void init()
{//Place the labels on the panel
   int i;
   for (i = 0; i < MAX_BUTTONS; i++)
   {//create new buttons from integers
      numbers[i] = new Button(Integer.toString(i));
      add(numbers[i]);
   }

   //create new buttons from string of names
   for (i=0; i< animalNames.length; i++){
      animals[i] = new Button(animalNames[i]);
      add(animals[i]);
   }
}
}
```

Figure 22.28 The *OneDarrays* Class Defintion

The **init()** method appearing in the *OneDarrays* class definition uses **for** statements to construct the buttons and place them on the page. Let's consider the first **for** statement:

```java
for (i = 0; i < MAX_BUTTONS; i++)
{//create new buttons from integers
   numbers[i] = new Button(Integer.toString(i));
   add(numbers[i]);
}
```

This statement creates the buttons labeled zero through eleven. We produce the button label by converting the **for** statement index, i, to a string. The button constructor appearing on the right-hand side of the assignment statement creates the new button for the ith element of the *numbers* array. The array declaration—

```java
private Button[]  numbers = new Button[MAX_BUTTONS];
```

—constructs only a new array. Buttons are objects in their own right, so we must also use a constructor to create each of the individual buttons. After we've created a new button, we add it to the applet.

Now, let's examine the second **for** statement:

```
for (i=0; i< animalNames.length; i++)
{
    animals[i] = new Button(animalNames[i]);
    add(animals[i]);
}
```

This statement constructs the *animals* buttons using the *animalNames* array to furnish the labels. After the button is constructed, we add it to the applet.

Using arrays to create multiple applet objects reduces the code and creates a consistent interface. Try rewriting the Hurricane page, using an array to create and load the buttons.

Two-Dimensional Arrays

Java provides two- (and higher-) dimensional arrays. Java implements these multiple-dimensional arrays by defining an array whose elements are arrays. Thus, a two-dimensional array is simply a one-dimensional array in which each of the elements is a one-dimensional array.

We can prefill a two-dimensional array by placing the constituent one-dimensional arrays in the definition of the two-dimensional array. For example, the following statement creates a two-dimensional array *String* array:

```
private static final String [][] matrixNames = {
        {"[0][0]", "[0][1]", "[0][2]", "[0][3]", "[0][4]"},
        {"[1][0]", "[1][1]", "[1][2]", "[1][3]", "[1][4]"},
        {"[2][0]", "[2][1]", "[2][2]", "[2][3]", "[2][4]"},
        {"[3][0]", "[3][1]", "[3][2]", "[3][3]", "[3][4]"}};
```

The array contains four rows and four columns; the array elements are strings representing the matrix's subscripts.

The *Matrix Sums* Page

As an example of two-dimensional arrays, we create a matrix of randomly generated numbers. The new class, *Matrix2*, prints the matrix, the row and column sums, and the grand total. Figure 22.29 contains a sample page. Although the user selects the matrix size, a default size of five rows and five columns is suggested.

The HTML creates a 300 $\times$ 300 rectangle to hold the applet. The tag is

```
<APPLET CODE = "Matrix2.class" WIDTH = "300" HEIGHT = "300">
</APPLET>
```

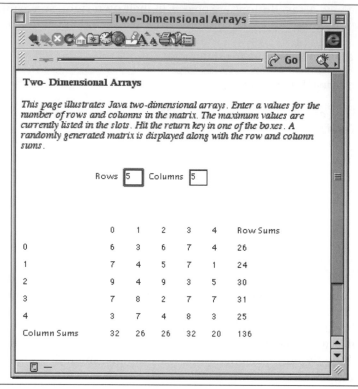

Figure 22.29 The *Matrix Sums* Page

The *Matrix2* Class Definition

The *Matrix2* class definition contains labels and text fields for the user-entered rows and columns. An integer array, *matrix*, stores the two-dimensional array. The array declaration

```
private int [][] matrix = new int[MAX_ROWS][MAX_COLS];
```

creates a matrix that is MAX_ROWS × MAX_COLS. We also create variables, *rows* and *columns*, that hold the user's choices. These variables are initially undefined, so we also include a boolean variable, *paintFlag*, that is initially set to *false*. This variable is changed to *true* in the **actionPerformed()** method. The **paint()** method contains an **if** statement that prints the matrix only when *paintFlag* is *true*. Figure 22.30 contains the definition of the *Matrix2* class.

The **init()** method of the *Matrix2* class adds the labels and text fields to the applet. The **setText()** method places the maximum row and column sizes in the text fields. The user accepts the default sizes by pressing the *Enter* key in either of the text fields. Otherwise, the user can change either or both of the text fields. Pressing the *Enter* key records the changes.

The **actionPerformed()** method obtains the row and column sizes. The **createMatrix()** method generates the matrix of random numbers. This method is not a member of any built-in class; it's unique to the *Matrix2* class. After the matrix is created, we call **repaint()** to draw it on the applet.

```
import java.awt.*;
import java.awt.event.*;
import java.applet.*;

public class Matrix2 extends Applet implements ActionListener
{ //Create an array of buttons
    private static int MAX_ROWS = 5;
    private static int MAX_COLS = 5;
    private static int COL_CHANGE = 30; //used by drawString() for column placement
    private static int COL_START = 100;
    private Label rowLabel = new Label("Rows");
    private Label colLabel = new Label("Columns");
    private TextField rowField = new TextField(2);
    private TextField colField = new TextField(2);
    private int rows, columns;
    private int [][] matrix = new int[MAX_ROWS][MAX_COLS];
    private boolean paintFlag = false;   //paint matrix if flag is true
public void init()
{//place labels and textfields in the panel
    add(rowLabel);
    rowField.setText(Integer.toString(MAX_ROWS));
    rowField.addActionListener(this);
    add(rowField);
    add(colLabel);
    colField.setText(Integer.toString(MAX_COLS));
    colField.addActionListener(this);
    add(colField);
}
public void actionPerformed(ActionEvent e)
{ //process the text field response
  rows = Integer.parseInt(rowField.getText());
  columns = Integer.parseInt(colField.getText());
  paintFlag = true;
  createMatrix();
  repaint();
}
//Put the createMatrix() Method Here
//Put the paint() Method Here
}
```

Figure 22.30 The Matrix2 Class Definition

CREATING NEW CLASS METHODS

Adding new methods to a class is easy in Java. Java provides (the same) syntax for rewriting such built-in class methods as **paint()**, **actionPerformed()**, and **init()** and for creating new methods. Figure 22.31 reviews this syntax.

As Figure 22.31 indicates, we place the access specifier (usually **public**) and the return type to the left of the method name. The parameter list is placed inside the parentheses that appear to the right of the method name. A compound statement, as denoted by the braces, forms the body of the method.

```
Access-Specifier Return-Type Method-Name (Parameter-List)
{
    //Body of the method
}
```

Figure 22.31 Syntax for Defining a New Method

When we use a built-in method, the *return type* and the *parameter list* are predetermined. We cannot add new parameters or change the return type. When we create a new method, we select the return type and the parameter list. In Java, we can use any previously defined types for a return type or parameter. Java determines the parameter-passing method from the parameter's type. Arrays and objects are always passed by reference. Any thing else is passed by value. (See the *JavaScript Vocabulary* section in Chapter 12 if you need to review parameter-passing.)

The createMatrix() Method

The **createMatrix()** method has **public** access (so that we can use it). It has a **void** return type and an empty parameter list. The header is

```
public void createMatrix()
```

The body of **createMatrix()** introduces the **rand()** method found in the *Math* class. This method is similar to its JavaScript counterpart. Both methods generate a pseudo-random **double** between zero and one. In the current example, we want to create integers between zero and nine, so that we can check the page for logical errors. (That is, are the sums correct?)

Obtaining integers in the correct range requires doing the following:

- multiplying the value returned by **rand()** by the desired maximum value, to generate a **double** between zero and one less than the maximum, inclusive;

- *casting* the result type to create an integer.

Figure 22.32 contains the definition of the **createMatrix()** method. The method contains a nested **for** statement that generates a matrix of random numbers, using the row and column sizes provided by the user.

The paint() Method

The **paint()** method contains an **if** statement that prints the matrix only after the user has selected the number of rows and columns. A **for** statement prints the column labels. A nested **for** state-

```
public void createMatrix()
{//create a matrix of randomly generated numbers between 0 and 9
    int i, j;
    for (i = 0; i < rows; i++)
      for (j = 0; j < columns; j++)
        matrix[i][j] = (int) (Math.random() * 10);
}
```

Figure 22.32 The **createMatrix()** Method

ment calculates the row and column sums. This **for** statement also prints the matrix and the row sums. A second nested **for** statement calculates and prints the column sums and the grand total. Figure 22.33 contains the definition of the **paint()** method. Highlighted comments denote the start of each of the **for** statements.

```
public void paint(Graphics g)
{//write the matrix to the panel
  int y = 100;
  int x = COL_START;
  int rowSum, columnSum, grandSum;
  int i, j;
  if (paintFlag) {
    //create column labels
    for (i = 0; i < columns; i++) {
      g.drawString(Integer.toString(i), x, 80);
      x+= COL_CHANGE;
  }
    g.drawString("Row Sums", x, 80);

    //print the matrix, calculate and print the row sums
    x = COL_START;
    for (i = 0; i < rows; i++) {
      rowSum = 0;
      g.drawString(Integer.toString(i), 0, y); //row label
      for (j=0; j < columns; j++) {
        g.drawString(Integer.toString(matrix[i][j]), x, y);
        x += COL_CHANGE;
        rowSum += matrix[i][j];
      }
      g.drawString(Integer.toString(rowSum), x, y);
      x = COL_START;
      y+= 20;
    }
    //determine column sums and grand total
    x = COL_START;
    g.drawString("Column Sums", 0, y);
    grandSum = 0;
    for (j = 0; j < columns; j++) {
      columnSum = 0;
      for (i=0; i< rows; i++)
        columnSum += matrix[i][j];
      g.drawString(Integer.toString(columnSum), x, y);
      x += COL_CHANGE;
      grandSum += columnSum;
    }
    g.drawString(Integer.toString(grandSum), x, y);
  }
}
```

Figure 22.33 The **paint()** Method: *Matrix2* Class

➤ **EXERCISES**

The exercises draw upon the JavaScript programs and exercises discussed earlier in the book. I've selected several exercises, but there are many more that you can use for practice. You could choose additional exercises from Chapters 10, 11, and 13 and from the first part of Chapter 14. Compare the JavaScript versions with their Java counterparts.

1. **The *Azalea* Page: Java version.** Create a Java version of the *Azalea* page shown in Figure 10.9.

2. **The *Primary Colors* Page.** Create a Java version of the *Primary Colors* page shown in Figure 10.24.

3. **The *Freshwater Aquarium* Page.** Create a Java version of the *Freshwater Aquarium* page. Ask the user to enter the *pH* level, nitrate level, and current temperature. Print a message for each variable to indicate whether the level is acceptable. (See Figure 10.30.)

4. **The *Garden* Page.** Create a page that indicates what type of garden a user should plant. Ask the user to enter the number of hours of shade. Use the chart in Figure 10.31 to display the appropriate type of garden.

5. **The *Breeze Classification* Page.** Figure 10.33 contains the *Beaufort* Scale for breeze classification. Create a Java version of this program. As the user to enter the wind speed in kilometers. Print the classification.

6. **The *Tornado* Page.** Figure 10.35 contains the Fujita Scale for tornado classification. Create a page that lets the user enter a wind speed. Print the wind speed, its description, and the tornado classification. Use arrays to store the information.

7. **The *Richter Scale* Page.** Figure 10.36 contains the Richter Scale for earthquake classification. Ask the user to enter the magnitude. Print the magnitude, TNT equivalent, and damage. Use arrays to store the information.

8. **The *Heat Index* Page.** Figure 10.37 contains the Heat Index. Ask the user to enter the current heat index. Print out the heat index and the risk level.

9. **The *Light Classification* Page.** Scientists classify light according to its wavelength, as measured in microns (μ). (See Figure 10.39.) Create a page that asks a user to enter the light type. Display that light type and the micron range for that type.

10. **The *Quadratic Roots* Page.** Finding the roots of the quadratic equation depends on the values of *a*, *b*, and *c*. Figure 10.40 shows the rules. Create a page that asks the user to enter the values of *a*, *b*, and *c*. Print out the values and the appropriate rule and message. You do not have to calculate the roots.

11. **The *Multiplication* Page.** Figure 11.13 contains a *Multiplication Table* page. Create a Java version of this page. Explain the differences between the JavaScript and Java versions.

12. **The *Fibonacci Numbers* Page.** Figure 11.30 contains the Fibonacci formula. Create a page that asks the user to enter a value for *n*. Print *n* and Fib(n).

13. **The *Harmonic Function* Page.** Figure 11.32 contains the mathematical formula for the harmonic function. Create a page that asks the user to enter a value for *n*. Print *n* and H(n).

14. **The *Football Statistics* Page.** Figure 13.18 contains a *Football Statistics* page. Write a Java version of this page. Use predefined arrays.

15. **Medians.** Figure 13.33 contains the formula for medians. Modify the *Football Statistics* page so that it calculates and prints the mean and the median.

16. **The *Silly Sentences* Page.** Create a Java version of the *Silly Sentences* page displayed in Figure 14.49.

17. **The *Text Area* Page.** Figure 14.15 contains a *Text Area* page. Create a Java version of this page.

18. **The *Scrambled Words* Page.** Create a Java version of the *Scrambled Words* page. (See Figures 15.25 through 15.33.)

23 Layouts

JAVA'S LAYOUT MANAGERS

Java provides five distinct layout managers, including the default *FlowLayout* manager. Figure 23.1 contains a summary of these layout managers. The layout managers are arranged from the simplest to the hardest.

    The `Panel` class is listed separately (in gray) because it's not a layout manager *per se*. A *panel* is a container into which we place other components. All panels default to a *FlowLayout* layout manager. We can change a panel's layout manager to any of the layout managers listed in Figure 23.1. We can also create sophisticated user interfaces by combining panels and layout managers. We examine some of the combinations in this chapter.

Class	Description
`FlowLayout`	Left to Right, Top to Bottom Arrangement of Components
`GridLayout`	Grid of rows and columns.
`BorderLayout`	Compass Points Arrangement: NORTH, SOUTH, EAST, WEST, CENTER.
`CardLayout`	Components arranged like a deck of cards. Only top card can be seen.
`GridBagLayout`	Customized arrangement of components
`Panel`	A component with a default *FlowLayout* Manager.

Figure 23.1 The Java Layout Managers

THE *FLOWLAYOUT* MANAGER

Our previous pages used the default layout *FlowLayout* manager. To make the transition to the layout managers, we examine the alignment options for the *FlowLayout* manager. Figure 23.2 contains a page with ten buttons created with the default flow layout. The buttons were loaded into the page in numeric order. Thus, *Button 0* was loaded first and *Button 9* was loaded last. The *FlowLayout* manager loads the buttons from left to right, placing as many buttons in a row as the applet's width permits. Once a row is filled, the *FlowLayout* manager begins a second row. This

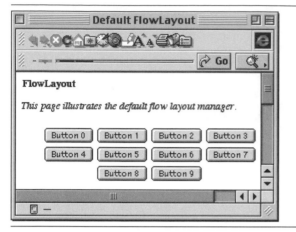

Figure 23.2 The Default *FlowLayout* Manager

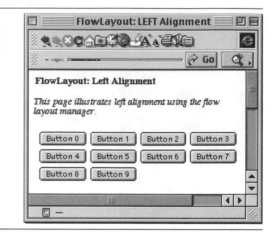

Figure 23.3 The *Left-Aligned Buttons* Page

process continues until all of the components are placed in the applet. If there is extra room in a row, the components are centered. This is evident in the placement of *Buttons 8* and *9*.

Figure 23.3 shows the same page of buttons, but this example uses a left alignment. Notice the placement of *Buttons 8* and *9*.

Figure 23.4 lists the three alignment options available for the *FlowLayout* manager. The options are constants within the *FlowLayout* class.

```
FlowLayout.LEFT
FlowLayout.CENTER (default)
FlowLayout.RIGHT
```

Figure 23.4 The *FlowLayout* Constants

Changing the default alignment (**CENTER**) to either a **LEFT** or **RIGHT** alignment requires a call to the **setLayout()** method. This method, which is part of the *Container* class, changes the layout manager. The syntax for this method is

> **void setLayout(*LayoutManager*);**

The **setLayout()** method requires a layout manager as a parameter. We can use a previously constructed layout manager or we can create an anonymous layout manager in the **setLayout()** call.

USING AN ANONYMOUS LAYOUT MANAGER

Figure 23.5 implements the *Left-Aligned Buttons* page by using an anonymous layout manager. The highlighted line in the **init()** method contains the call

> **setLayout(new FlowLayout(FlowLayout.LEFT));**

The establishing of the new layout manager must occur before components are added to the applet. The **add()** method calls used with a left-aligned flow layout do not differ from the **add()** method calls used in previous applets.

```
import java.awt.*;
import java.awt.event.*;
import java.applet.*;
public class FlowLeft extends Applet
{//Create an array of buttons
  private static int MAX_BUTTONS = 10;
  private Button [] buttons = new Button[MAX_BUTTONS];
  public void init()
  {// Create 10 buttons. LEFT alignment
   setLayout(new FlowLayout(FlowLayout.LEFT));
   int i;
   for (i = 0; i < MAX_BUTTONS; i++)
   {// create a new button
     buttons[i] = new Button("Button " + i);
     add(buttons[i]);
   }
  }
}
```

Figure 23.5 Using an Anonymous Layout Manager

USING A NAMED LAYOUT MANAGER

Figure 23.6 implements the *Left-Aligned Buttons* page by using a named layout manager. The new layout component is defined as a class field with the following statement:

> private FlowLayout flowLeft = new FlowLayout(FlowLayout.LEFT);

The layout manager is changed to *flowLeft* in the **init()** method with the statement

> setLayout(flowLeft);

```
import java.awt.*;
import java.awt.event.*;
import java.applet.*;
public class FlowName extends Applet
{//Create an array of buttons
  private static int MAX_BUTTONS = 10;
  private Button [] buttons = new Button[MAX_BUTTONS];
  private FlowLayout flowLeft = new        FlowLayout(FlowLayout.LEFT);
  public void init()
  {// Create 10 buttons. LEFT alignment
   setLayout(flowLeft);
   int i;
   for (i = 0; i < MAX_BUTTONS; i++)
   {// create a new button
     buttons[i] = new Button("Button " + i);
     add(buttons[i]);
   }
  }
}
```

Figure 23.6 Using a Named Layout Manager

Regardless of whether an anonymous or a named layout manager is used, the components are added to the applet in exactly the same way. Both techniques for changing a layout manager apply to all of Java's layout managers, so you're probably wondering which of the two techniques is preferable. All layout managers provide methods in addition to the constructor. If you plan to use these methods, you must create a named layout manager. If you're not going to use any of the layout methods, use an anonymous layout manager.

THE *FLOWLAYOUT* CLASS METHODS

Figure 23.7 contains the methods provided by the *FlowLayout* class. Similar methods are available in each of the other layout managers.

Method	Description
void setHgap(int *gap*);	Set the horizontal distance between components.
void setVgap(int *gap*);	Set the vertical distance between components.
int getHgap();	Return the horizontal distance.
int getVgap();	Return the vertical distance.

Figure 23.7 The *FlowLayout* Class Methods

Figure 23.7 indicates, the *FlowLayout* class contains methods that set or get the vertical or horizontal spacing between components. The *set* methods are rarely used, because an alternate constructor contains parameters to set the gaps. The syntax for this constructor is

```
new FlowLayout(int align, int hGap, int vGap);
```

THE *GRIDLAYOUT* MANAGER

As its name suggests, the *GridLayout* manager divides the applet into cells of equal height and width. The dimensions of the grid cells result from the interplay of three factors:

1. The applet's **WIDTH** and **HEIGHT**, as supplied by the **<APPLET>** tag.
2. The number of grid rows and columns, as specified by the *GridLayout* constructor.
3. The horizontal and vertical gap between cells, if any, as specified by the *GridLayout* constructor—the default is a horizontal and vertical gap of zero.

Figure 23.8 contains a sample page that uses a *GridLayout* to arrange twelve buttons into four rows and three columns. The vertical and horizontal gap is zero.

The HTML creates a 150 × 150 rectangle to hold the applet. This means that each cell in the grid is 50 pixels wide (150/3) and approximately 37 pixels high (150/4). The tag is

```
<APPLET CODE = "GridDefault.class" WIDTH = "150" HEIGHT = "150">
</APPLET>
```

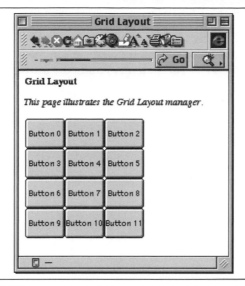

Figure 23.8 A *GridLayout* Page

The *GridLayout* Constructors and Methods

The *GridLayout* class provides the constructors listed in Figure 23.9. The first constructor creates a *GridLayout* manager, using the defaults for the rows, columns, and horizontal and vertical gaps. The second and third constructors contain parameters for the rows and columns. The third constructor adds parameters for the horizontal and vertical gaps.

```
new GridLayout()
new GridLayout(int rows, int columns)
new GridLayout(int rows, int columns, int hGap, int vGap)
```

Figure 23.9 The *GridLayout* Constructors

The *GridLayout* class includes the same "gap" methods listed in Figure 23.7. The additional methods listed in Figure 23.10 set the rows or columns. Remember that if we want to use any of the *set* or *get* methods, we must have a named layout manager.

Method	Description
void setRows(int *rows*);	Set the number of rows.
void setColumns(int *columns*);	Set the number of columns.
int getRows();	Return the number of rows.
int getColumns();	Return the number of columns.

Figure 23.10 Additional *GridLayout* Methods

The *GridDefault* Class Definition

Figure 23.11 contains the definition of the *GridDefault* class used to generate the *GridLayout* page displayed in Figure 23.8. The **setLayout()** method creates an anonymous grid layout consisting of four rows and three columns. The **for** statement adds the buttons to the layout manager.

```java
import java.awt.*;
import java.awt.event.*;
import java.applet.*;

public class GridDefault extends Applet
{//Create an array of buttons
    private static int MAX_BUTTONS = 12;
    private Button [] button = new Button[MAX_BUTTONS];

    public void init()
    {
        int i;
        //create a layout with 4 rows and 3 columns
        setLayout(new GridLayout(4,3));
        for (i = 0; i < MAX_BUTTONS; i++)
        {//Each region can hold a single button
            button[i] = new Button("Button " + i);
            add(button[i]);
        }
    }
}
```

Figure 23.11 The *GridDefault* Class Definition

Although the *GridLayout* manager frequently produces a cleaner appearance than the equivalent *FlowLayout* manager, the *GridLayout* manager is not flawless. First, we cannot control directly the size of the cells or their contents. We control the size by picking appropriate values for the applet's width and height, the number of rows and columns in the grid, and the gaps between the cells. We control the contents by arranging the components in sequential order, because the **add()** method places the components in the order it receives them. Second, each cell in a grid layout must contain a single component—for example, one button or text field or label. We can get around this *"One Cell Per Component"* rule by using panels.

PANELS

Figure 23.12 contains the Java version of the *Sales Tax* page. Notice the relation between the labels and their associated text fields. This page uses a flow layout; however, the labels appear above the text fields. A normal flow layout would place the labels to the left of the text fields.

The HTML creates a 280 × 200 rectangle for the applet. The tag is

```html
<APPLET CODE = "SalesTax.class" WIDTH = "280" HEIGHT = "200">
</APPLET>
```

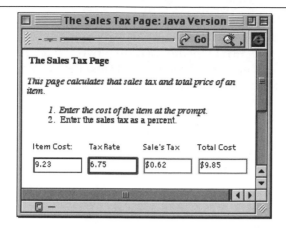

Figure 23.12 The *Sales Tax* Page, Java version

The *Sales Tax* page has a neat and orderly appearance because we create a panel for each label and its associated text field. Each panel uses a 2 × 1 grid layout. We use a flow layout to place the panels in the applet. Figure 23.13 contains a diagram of the layout. Notice the array of panels.

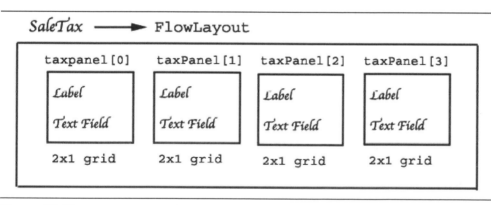

Figure 23.13 Layout Diagram for the *SalesTax* Class

The *Panel* class includes both the *Component* and *Container* classes as its ancestors. Thus, a panel is a container into which we place other containers or components. The *Panel* class has only constructors; it inherits its methods from the *Component* and *Container* classes. We can use either of two constructors to create a new panel. Figure 23.14 lists these constructors.

Constructor	Description
new Panel()	Create a new panel without a layout manager.
new Panel(LayoutManager *layout*);	Create a new panel with the layout manager specified by *layout*.

Figure 23.14 The *Panel* Constructors

THE *SALESTAX* CLASS DEFINITION

The *SalesTax* class definition follows our standard technique. We use arrays of strings and text fields to reduce the code in the **init()** method. The first two text fields hold the item cost and tax rate as specified by the user. The last two, noneditable text fields hold the amount of tax and the total cost. We create an array of panels to hold each label and its associated text field. Figure 23.15 contains the definition of the *SalesTax* class.

```
import java.awt.*;
import java.awt.event.*;
import java.applet.*;

public class SalesTax extends Applet implements ActionListener
{ //Ask user for cost ans tax rate. Calculate tax and totalcost
   private static final int INPUT_SIZE = 2;
   private static final String [] taxString = {"Item Cost: ",
      " Tax Rate" , "Sale's Tax", "Total Cost"};
   private TextField [] taxField = new TextField[taxString.length];
   private Panel [] taxPanel = new Panel[taxString.length];
   private float itemCost, taxRate, amountTax, totalCost;

 //Put the init() Method Here
 //Put the round() Method Here
 //Put the actionPerformed() Method Here
}
```

Figure 23.15 The *SalesTax* Class Definition

THE init() METHOD

The **init()** method constructs the labels and text fields and adds them to the panels. We use a three-step technique to add components to panels:

Step 1. Create a Panel. In the current example, each of the panels uses a 2×1 grid layout. Because the panels reside in an array, we use a **for** statement to create the panels. To create the ith panel we use the statement

```
taxPanel[i] = new Panel(new GridLayout(2,1));
```

where *i* is the current index value of the **for** statement.

Step 2. Add the Components to the Panel. In the current example, each panel holds a label and a text field. To add these components to a panel, we use the panel name with the **add()** method. Thus, we add the ith label and text field with the following statements:

```
taxPanel[i].add(new Label(taxString[i]));
taxPanel[i].add(taxField[i]);
```

An applet could contain several panels, so we must use the panel name as a prefix to the **add()** method. The dot operator that separates the panel name from the method simply indicates that we are using the particular **add()** method for that panel component.

Step 3. Add the Panels to the Applet.   Finally, we add the panels to the applet. We use the **add()** method without a component prefix to accomplish this task. In the current example, we add the panels with the statement

>   add(taxPanel[i]);

Incidentally, this statement is really a shorthand form of

>   this.add(taxPanel[i]);

We can abbreviate the **add()** call when we add components to the applet, but not when we add components to a panel.

Figure 23.16 contains the definition of the **init()** method. Notice the **if..else** statement. This statement compares the current index, *i*, with the constant, **INPUT_SIZE**, which has the value 2. If *i* is less than **INPUT_SIZE**, we add an action listener to the text field; otherwise, we make the text field noneditable because the first two text fields hold the user's information but the last two text fields hold the results.

```
public void init()
{ //add the labels and textboxes to the applet
    int i;
    for (i = 0; i < taxString.length; i++){
      taxField[i] = new TextField(8);
      taxPanel[i] = new Panel(new GridLayout(2,1));
      taxPanel[i].add(new Label(taxString[i]));
      taxPanel[i].add(taxField[i]);
      if (i < INPUT_SIZE)
        taxField[i].addActionListener(this);
      else
        taxField[i].setEditable(false);
     this.add(taxPanel[i]);
    }
}
```

Figure 23.16 The **init()** Method, *SalesTax* Class

The actionPerformed() Method

The **actionPerformed()** method is invoked when the user presses the *Enter* key in either of the first two text fields. The **getText()** method obtains the data in these fields. We use the float conversion technique discussed in Chapter 21 to transform the data into the **float** variables *itemCost* and *taxRate*. Next, we calculate the amount of tax and the total cost. These formulas sometimes yield a result not having exactly two digits of precision, so we create a **roundPlaces()** method to convert these numbers to "dollars and cents" notation. We place the rounded results, *amountTax* and *totalCost*, in the last two text fields. Figure 23.17 contains the definition of the **actionPerformed()** method.

```
public void actionPerformed(ActionEvent e)
{ //Obtain the FLoats from the text fields
   Float costF = new Float(taxField[0].getText());
   Float taxF = new Float(taxField[1].getText());
   itemCost = costF.floatValue();
   taxRate = taxF.floatValue()/100.0f;
   amountTax = roundPlaces(itemCost * taxRate, 2);
   totalCost = roundPlaces(itemCost + amountTax, 2);
   taxField[2].setText("$" + Float.toString(amountTax));
   taxField[3].setText("$" + Float.toString(totalCost));
}
```

Figure 23.17 The **actionPerformed()** Method, *SalesTax* Class

The roundPlaces() Method

Figure 23.18 contains the definition of the **roundPlaces()** method. This method is a modification of the JavaScript method developed in Figures 12.6 through 12.8.

```
public float roundPlaces(float number, int places)
{ // round the number to the desired decimal places
  return (float)(Math.round(number *
      Math.pow(10, places))/Math.pow(10,places));
}
```

Figure 23.18 The **roundPlaces()** Method

THE *BORDERLAYOUT* MANAGER

The *BorderLayout* manager uses compass points, as denoted by constants, to specify the location of a component. Figure 23.19 lists these constants.

As our first example of the border layout manager, we create a page that places a button in each of the locations specified by the border layout constants. The button's label bears the name of the constant. Figure 22.20 contains a sample page.

The HTML creates a 200 × 100 rectangle for the applet. The tag is

```
<APPLET CODE = "BorderDefault.class" WIDTH = "200" HEIGHT = "100">
</APPLET>
```

The *BorderLayout* Constructors

Creating the *BorderLayout* page begins with the choice of a constructor. Figure 23.21 lists the two constructors available for this class. As the figure demonstrates, we can create a *BorderLayout* manager with or without horizontal and vertical gaps.

The page displayed in Figure 23.20 uses the first constructor. The statement that changes the layout manager is

```
setLayout(new BorderLayout());
```

```
BorderLayout.NORTH
BorderLayout.SOUTH
BorderLayout.EAST
BorderLayout.WEST
BorderLayout.CENTER
```

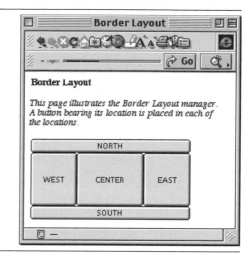

Figure 23.19 The *Border Layout* Constants

Figure 23.20 The *Border Layout* Page

```
new BorderLayout()
new BorderLayout(int hGap, int vGap)
```

Figure 23.21 The *BorderLayout* Constructors

To place the buttons on the page, we create arrays of button names and buttons in the class definition. A **for** statement in the **init()** method constructs the buttons and adds a button to the location specified by its label.

To add a component to a *BorderLayout*, we must pass both the component and the location to the **add()** method. The syntax is

add(Component c, **int** *location*);

The location refers to one of the *BorderLayout* constants contained in Figure 23.19.

Figure 23.22 contains the definition of the *BorderDefault* class. A **switch** statement places the buttons in the correct locations.

The *BorderLayout* manager provides only five locations into which we can place components. Each location can hold only a single component. We overcome this limitation by using panels. Although *BorderLayout* contains five locations, we don't need to use all of the locations. We can choose locations that match the needs of our program.

THE CARDLAYOUT MANAGER

The *CardLayout* manager arranges components as you would arrange a deck of cards. At any given time, only the top card on the deck is visible. A page using a card layout inevitably requires panels. One panel displays the top card. A second panel contains buttons that change the top card. Figure 23.23 contains a simplified page that illustrates the card layout. The top panel contains four buttons that let the user select from the first or last card in the deck or the previous or

```
import java.awt.*;
import java.awt.event.*;
import java.applet.*;
public class BorderDefault extends Applet
{ //Create an array of button
   private static final String [] buttonLabels = {"NORTH", "SOUTH",
 "EAST", "WEST" , "CENTER"};
  private Button []  button = new Button[buttonLabels.length];
   public void init()
   {
      int i;
      setLayout(new BorderLayout());
      for (i = 0; i < buttonLabels.length; i++)
      {//Each region can hold a single button
         button[i] = new Button(buttonLabels[i]);
         switch(i) {
         case 0: add(button[i], BorderLayout.NORTH);
                 break;
         case 1: add(button[i], BorderLayout.SOUTH);
                 break;
         case 2: add(button[i], BorderLayout.EAST);
                 break;
         case 3: add(button[i], BorderLayout.WEST);
                 break;
         case 4: add(button[i], BorderLayout.CENTER);
         }
      }
   }
}
```

Figure 23.22 The *BorderDefault* Class Definition

next card. The bottom panel displays the selected card. The current example uses four cards. Each card contains a label that identifies it. In Figure 23.23, the *Second Card* is currently on top.

The HTML creates a 300 × 200 rectangle for the applet. The tag is

```
<APPLET CODE = "CardDefault.class" WIDTH = "300" HEIGHT = "200">
</APPLET>
```

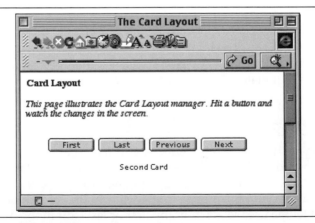

Figure 23.23 The *CardLayout* Page

The *CardDefault* Class Definition

Creating a card layout begins with a constructor. Figure 23.24 lists the two constructors available for the *CardLayout* manager. These constructors use the same syntax as constructors available for *BorderLayout*; however, the meaning attached to the horizontal and vertical gaps differs. Thus, we can create a *CardLayout* component with or without horizontal and vertical gaps, but "gap" in this context refers to the space between the card and the container that holds it.

```
new CardLayout()
new CardLayout(int hGap, int vGap)
```

Figure 23.24 The *CardLayout* Constructors

Figure 23.25 contains the definition of the *CardDefault* class. This class contains two panels: one for the buttons, and a second for the cards. The class also contains a named layout manager, *cardLayout*, because we need the layout manager's name to move between the cards in the deck.

```
import java.awt.*;
import java.awt.event.*;
import java.applet.*;

public class CardDefault extends Applet implements ActionListener
{ //Create an array of buttons
    private Panel buttonPanel = new Panel();
    private Panel cardPanel = new Panel();
    private CardLayout cardLayout = new CardLayout();
    private Button first = new Button("First");
    private Button last = new Button("Last");
    private Button previous = new Button("Previous");
    private Button next = new Button("Next");

  //Put the init() Method Here
  //Put the actionPerformed() Method Here
}
```

Figure 23.25 The *CardDefault* Class Definition

The init() Method

The **init()** method performs several routine tasks. We use this method to add the action listeners to the buttons and the buttons to the button panel. In addition, we must change the layout manager of the *cardPanel*. The statement that does this is

    cardPanel.setLayout(cardLayout);

Once we've switched layout managers, we add the cards. The **add()** method for the card layout requires two parameters. The first parameter specifies the component being placed in the card. The second parameter is a string that identifies the card. For example, the first card is added to the card panel with the statement

    cardPanel.add(new Label("First Card"), "One");

This statement creates a card containing the label *First Card*. The card's name is *"One"*.

Figure 23.26 contains the definition of the init() method.

```
public void init()
   { //add listeners for the buttons
      first.addActionListener(this);
      last.addActionListener(this);
      next.addActionListener(this);
      previous.addActionListener(this);

      //put buttons in the button Panel
      buttonPanel.add(first);
      buttonPanel.add(last);
      buttonPanel.add(previous);
      buttonPanel.add(next);

      //create the card Layout
      cardPanel.setLayout(cardLayout);
      cardPanel.add(new Label("First Card"), "One");
      cardPanel.add(new Label ("Second Card"), "Two");
      cardPanel.add(new Label("Third Card"), "Three");
      cardPanel.add(new Label ("Fourth Screen"), "Four");

      //Place both panels in the default layout manager
      add(buttonPanel);
      add(cardPanel);
   }
```

Figure 23.26 The **init()** Method, *CardDefault* Class

Notice that we finish the **init()** method by adding the two panels to the applet. Frequently, programmers place the components into the panels but forget to add the panels to the applet. The telltale sign of this error is an empty page.

CardLayout Methods

Figure 23.27 contains the *CardLayout* methods. These methods let us move between the cards. The *CardLayout* class also includes methods that set or get the vertical and horizontal gap. Used in this context, "gap" refers to the space between a card and the component that contains it.

Method	Description
void *card*.previous(Component *c*);	Display the previous card.
void *card*.next(Component *c*);	Display the next card.
void*card* .first(Component*c*);	Display the first card.
void *card*.last(Component *c*);	Display the last card.
void *card*.show(Component *C*, String *card*);	Display the card specified by *cd*.

Figure 23.27 The *CardLayout* Methods

As Figure 23.27 indicates, each of the *CardLayout* methods requires a component as a parameter. The component is typically the panel that holds the card layout. In the current example, the card layout manager is named *cardLayout*. The component that contains this layout manager is *cardPanel*.

Suppose we want to switch to the previous card. The statement that accomplishes this task is

```
cardLayout.previous(cardPanel);
```

Notice the **show()** method. It requires both a component and a string as parameters. The string identifies the card by name. Thus, this method places a specific card on the top of the deck. For example, suppose we want to place the second card on the top of the deck. The statement that accomplishes this is

```
cardLayout.show(cardPanel, "Two");
```

The actionPerformed() Method

Figure 23.28 contains the definition of the **actionPerformed()** class. We use this method to find the selected button. A series of **if...else if...else** statements compare the selected button's label with the set of button labels. When we find a match, we execute the method that corresponds to the button's label.

```
public void actionPerformed(ActionEvent e)
   { // get the button name and perform action based on it
     String buttonName = e.getActionCommand();
     if (buttonName.equals("Previous"))
        cardLayout.previous(cardPanel);
     else if (buttonName.equals("Next"))
        cardLayout.next(cardPanel);
     else if (buttonName.equals("First"))
        cardLayout.first(cardPanel);
     else if (buttonName.equals("Last"))
        cardLayout.last(cardPanel);
     else
        cardLayout.show(cardPanel, (String)buttonName);
   }
```

Figure 23.28 The **actionPerformed()** Method, *CardDefault* Class

COMBINING LAYOUTS: THE HURRICANE PAGE

The *Sales Tax* page provided a simple illustration of combined layouts. That page used a flow layout manager to place panels on the applet. Each panel used a 2×1 grid layout manager. The next example uses the grid, card, and border layout managers to create a new version of the *Hurricane* page. Review the original *Hurricane* page displayed in Figure 22.8. Now, examine the new version displayed in Figure 23.29. Both versions contain hurricane intensity buttons which, when pressed, reveal the information for the selected hurricane category. The new version, however, also contains buttons that let us move forward or backward through the hurricane categories. This version also has a "cleaner" appearance.

Picking the appropriate width and height for the applet is the first step in developing the new version of the *Hurricane* page. In this example, the HTML creates a 275×120 rectangle for the applet. The tag is

```
<APPLET CODE = "HurricaneCards.class" WIDTH = "275" HEIGHT = "120">
</APPLET>
```

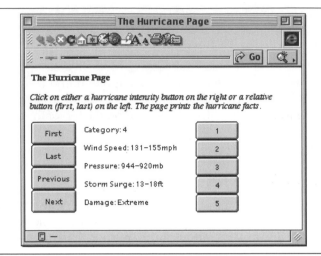

Figure 23.29 The *Hurricane* Page, multiple-layout version

Planning the Layout

Combining layout managers to produce a pleasing page requires planning and practice. We begin by creating a template for the page. This *paper and pencil* exercise provides a visual reference that we can use to code the class. Figure 23.30 contains the template for the *Hurricane* page. Not only does this figure reveal the page's layout; it also contains the field names that we will use in the class definition.

HurricaneCards ➡ BorderLayout

WEST   CENTER   EAST

buttonPanel   *cardPanel* ➡ CardLayout   *hurricanePanel*

messagePanel [i]

Category
Wind Speed
Pressure
Storm Surge
Damage

5x1 grid

1
2
3
4
5

4x1grid   5x1grid

Figure 23.30 Layout Template for the *HurricaneCards* Class

As Figure 23.30 indicates, the *HurricaneCards* class uses an overall border layout. The west and east location contain the *Movement* and *Hurricane Category* buttons, respectively. Each location can hold only a single component, so we place the buttons in panels. The *buttonPanel* uses a 4 × 1 grid layout manager, because we have four *Movement* buttons. The *hurricanePanel* uses a 5 × 1 grid layout manager, because we have five *Hurricane Category* buttons.

The center location uses a card layout manager to store the hurricane category information. Each hurricane card contains a separate label for the category, wind speed, pressure, storm surge, and damage level. Because a card cannot contain more than one component, we create a panel with a 5 × 1 grid layout manager for each card.

The *HurricaneCards* Class Definition

Figure 23.31 contains the definition of the *HurricaneCards* class. The definition relies heavily upon arrays to reduce the coding effort. Thus, we use arrays to store the names for the *Movement* and *Hurricane Category* buttons and for the hurricane card labels. We also create arrays to store the two sets of buttons and the message panel for the card layout.

```java
import java.awt.*;
import java.awt.event.*;
import java.applet.*;

public class HurricaneCards extends Applet implements ActionListener
{ //Create an array of buttons
    private Panel buttonPanel = new Panel();
    private Panel hurricanePanel = new Panel();
    private Panel cardPanel = new Panel();

    private CardLayout cardLayout = new CardLayout();

    private static final String [] cardLabel  = {"First","Last","Previous","Next"};
    private Button [] cardButton = new Button [cardLabel.length];

    private static final String [] category = {"Category: 1", "Category: 2", "Category: 3",
"Category: 4", "Category: 5"};

    private static final String [] windSpeed = {"Wind Speed: 74-95mph","Wind Speed: 96-110mph",
"Wind Speed: 111-130mph", "Wind Speed: 131-155mph", "Wind Speed: Above 155mph"};

    private static final String [] pressure = {"Pressure: Above 980m","Pressure: 979-
965mb","Pressure: 964-945mb","Pressure: 944-920mb","Pressure: Below 920mb"};

    private static final String [] stormSurge = {"Storm Surge: 4-5ft","Storm Surge: 6-8ft", "Storm
Surge: 9-12ft", "Storm Surge: 13-18ft", "Storm Surge: Above 18ft"};
    private String [] damage = {"Damage: Minimal","Damage: Moderate",
    "Damage: Extensive", "Damage: Extreme", "Damage: Catastrophic"};

    private static final String [] hurricaneLabel = {"1", "2","3", "4", "5"};
    private Button [] hurricaneButton = new Button [hurricaneLabel.length] ;
    private Panel [] messagePanel = new Panel [5];
  //Put the init() Method Here
  // Use the actionPerformed() method from the CardDefault class

}
```

Figure 23.31 The *HurricaneCards* Class Definition

The *HurricaneCards* definition contains a named card layout manager, appropriately called *cardLayout*. We must use a named manager so that we can access the display methods in the `actionPerformed()` method. The code for the `actionPerformed()` method is identical to that for the *cardDefault* class. Thus, we need only write the `init()` method to complete the page.

The `init()` Method

Coding the `init()` method is best accomplished by using a stepwise approach; the code is complex, so there are many opportunities to forget a piece of this puzzle. The task list is as follows:

Step 1. Create the Button Panel.   The button panel holds the *Movement* buttons that appear in the west location. We begin by setting the layout for this panel. The following statement creates a 4 × 1 grid layout manager. Notice that we use the length of the *cardLabel* array to create the grid.

```
buttonPanel.setLayout(new GridLayout(cardLabel.length,1));
```

Once we've established the layout manager, we use a **for** statement to create the buttons, add action listeners to them, and add the buttons to the panel. The **for** statement is

```
for (i = 0; i < cardLabel.length; i++){
  cardButton[i] = new Button(cardLabel[i]);
  cardButton[i].addActionListener(this);
  buttonPanel.add(cardButton[i]);
}
```

Step 2. Create the Card and Hurricane Panels.   We can create the card and hurricane button panels simultaneously, because each uses a 5 × 1 grid layout manager. Thus, we can fill both panels using a single **for** statement. First, we establish the layout manager for each panel with the following statements:

```
cardPanel.setLayout(cardLayout);
hurricanePanel.setLayout(new GridLayout(hurricaneLabel.length,1));
```

Next, we use a **for** statement to fill the panels. The code for the card panel is substantially more complicated, because we must create and fill the individual message panels for each card. Figure 23.32 contains the statements necessary to create the cards.

```
for(i=0; i < 5; i++)
{
  messagePanel[i] = new Panel();
  messagePanel[i].setLayout(new GridLayout(5,1));
  messagePanel[i].add(new Label(category[i]));
  messagePanel[i].add(new Label(windSpeed[i]));
  messagePanel[i].add(new Label(pressure[i]));
  messagePanel[i].add(new Label(stormSurge[i]));
  messagePanel[i].add(new Label(damage[i]));
  cardPanel.add(messagePanel[i], hurricaneLabel[i]);

  //Continue with the hurricane buttons
}
```

Figure 23.32 Creating the Hurricane Card Panel

As Figure 23.32 indicates, we construct a new panel for each element of the *messagePanel* array. All panels use a 5 × 1 grid layout manager. After we've established the layout manager, we create the information labels by using the strings contained in the *HurricaneCards* class definition. Because the labels are unnamed, we can create and add them to the message panel in one statement. Finally, we add the message panel to the card. Each card uses the hurricane label as the card identifier.

We finish the **for** statement by creating the hurricane intensity buttons, using the *hurricaneLabels* arrays. We add an action listener to each button, and we add the buttons to the hurricane panel. The statements that accomplish these tasks are the following:

```
hurricaneButton[i] = new Button(hurricaneLabel[i]);
hurricaneButton[i].addActionListener(this);
hurricanePanel.add(hurricaneButton[i]);
```

Step 3. Add the Panels to the Applet.   The final step is the easiest: We create the border layout for the applet, and we add the three panels to it. The following statements accomplish these tasks:

```
setLayout(new BorderLayout(10,1));
add(buttonPanel, BorderLayout.WEST);
add(cardPanel, BorderLayout.CENTER);
add(hurricanePanel, BorderLayout.EAST);
```

Notice the border layout constructor. It creates a horizontal gap of ten pixels and a vertical gap of one pixel between the components. The vertical gap is unnecessary, because we are not using the north and south locations.

Figure 23.33 contains the definition of the **init()** method.

```
public void init()
  { //add listeners for the buttons
    int i;
    buttonPanel.setLayout(new GridLayout(cardLabel.length,1));
    for (i = 0; i < cardLabel.length; i++){
     cardButton[i] = new Button(cardLabel[i]);
     cardButton[i].addActionListener(this);
     buttonPanel.add(cardButton[i]);
    }
   //create the card Layout
   cardPanel.setLayout(cardLayout);
   hurricanePanel.setLayout(new GridLayout(hurricaneLabel.length,1));
   for (i = 0; i < 5; i++){
     messagePanel[i] = new Panel();
     messagePanel[i].setLayout(new GridLayout(5,1));
     messagePanel[i].add(new Label(category[i]));
     messagePanel[i].add(new Label(windSpeed[i]));
     messagePanel[i].add(new Label(pressure[i]));
     messagePanel[i].add(new Label(stormSurge[i]));
     messagePanel[i].add(new Label(damage[i]));
     cardPanel.add(messagePanel[i], hurricaneLabel[i]);

     hurricaneButton[i] = new Button(hurricaneLabel[i]);
     hurricaneButton[i].addActionListener(this);
     hurricanePanel.add(hurricaneButton[i]);
   }
   setLayout(new BorderLayout(10,1));
   this.add(buttonPanel, BorderLayout.WEST);
   this.add(cardPanel, BorderLayout.CENTER);
   this.add(hurricanePanel, BorderLayout.EAST);
  }
```

Figure 23.33 The **init()** Method, *HurricaneCards* Class

The border layout manager uses only the west, center, and east locations, you might wonder whether this manager is even necessary. Couldn't we just use the default flow layout manager to load the three panels into the applet? The answer is *no*. Switching to a flow layout manager distorts the cards: the first label appears above the buttons, and the last label appears below the buttons. It is not a pretty sight! The border layout manager forces the three panels to share the same vertical space.

THE GRIDBAG LAYOUT MANAGER

The *GridBag* layout manager uses an (*x, y*) coordinate system or a more detailed compass-point system to place components into an applet or panel. This layout manager is clearly the most complicated of the Java layout managers. In fact, implementing a grid bag layout requires three Java classes:

The GridBagLayout Class. The constructor from this class creates a new grid bag layout manager.

The GridBagConstraints Class. This class contains the constants and fields that determine a component's position and appearance within the grid bag layout.

The Insets Class. The constructor from this class sets the top, left, bottom, and right pixel space that surrounds a component.

The *Herb Garden* Page

As our first example of a grid bag layout, we create an *Herb Garden* page. Figure 23.34 contains a sample page. The page contains three columns of buttons. When the user selects an herb button, a panel to the right of the buttons displays the herb's English and botanical name and the typical cooking uses for the herb.

The HTML creates a 500 × 110 rectangle for the applet. The tag is

```
<APPLET CODE  = "HerbGarden.class" WIDTH = "500" HEIGHT = "110">
</APPLET>
```

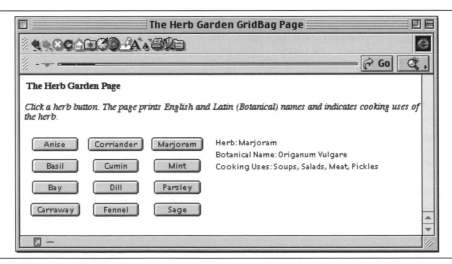

Figure 23.34 The *Herb Garden* Page

Preparing The GridBag

Creating a grid bag layout also begins with paper and pencil because we must establish the constraints used to place each component into the grid bag. We use a five-step approach to determine these constraints. To illustrate this approach, we reconstruct the *Herb Garden* grid bag layout.

Step 1. Determine the (x, y) Coordinates for Each Component.   With paper and pencil in hand, redraw the components on the *Herb Garden* page. That is, write the button names on the paper. Leave an area to the right to display the English and Latin names and the cooking uses of the selected herb. Next, draw vertical and horizontal lines to separate the components. Once finished, you should have a grid. Starting in the leftmost corner of your grid, number the columns beginning with zero. The columns are the *x* coordinates. Repeat this exercise for the rows. The rows are the *y* coordinates. Write the (x, y) coordinates inside each cell, using the notation **{x,y}**. For example, the coordinates for the *Anise* button are **{0,0}**; those for the *Fennel* button are **{3,1}**.

Step 2. Determine the Height and Width of Each Component.   Next, determine the dimensions of each component. The only crucial issue in the current example is the size of the drawing panel. Each of the buttons should have both a width and a height of one. The drawing panel has an arbitrary height and width of four.

When you've finished with the first two steps, you should have a grid that resembles the one displayed in Figure 23.35.

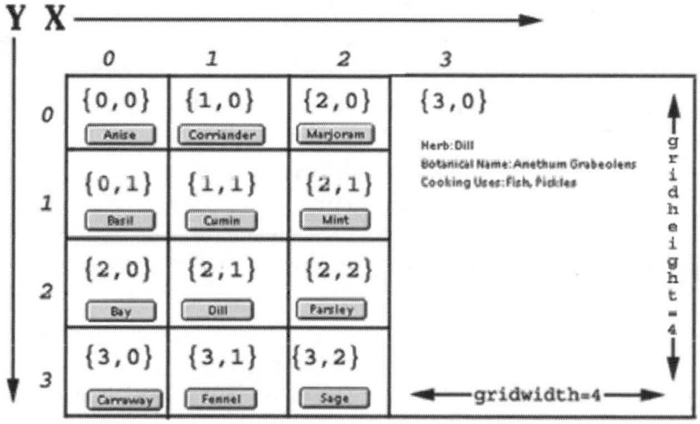

Figure 23.35 Component Layout for the *Herb Garden* Page

Step 3. Determine the Component Spacing.   The **GridBagConstraints** class uses a default gap of zero pixels between each of the components in a grid bag. We set the top, left, bottom, and right gap for each component with the **Insets** constructor. The *Herb Garden* page uses a five-pixel gap for each component.

Step 4. Determine the Fill Factor for Each Component.   Notice the herb buttons in the *Herb Garden* page. These buttons are not the same size. The fill factor lets us decide how we will fill any leftover space. For example, you should notice that the *Mint* button uses less space than the *Marjoram* button. We can choose how this button fills its extra space by selecting one of the following constants.

NONE.   This is the default fill factor. It indicates that component should not expand to fill any extra space.

HORIZONTAL. As its name implies, this fill factor expands the component horizontally, but not vertically.

VERTICAL. This fill factor expands the component vertically, but not horizontally.

BOTH. This fill factor expands the component both vertically and horizontally.

We use the default fill factor for the buttons. The drawing panel has a fill factor of **BOTH**.

Step 5. Determine the Weight For Each Component. We can give a vertical and horizontal weight to each component. Generally, we use the default, zero, for both in each component; however, we can let one component consume any leftover applet space by setting this component's weights to one. The buttons in the *Herb Garden* page use the default weights. The drawing panel's weights were set to one so that it can consume any extra applet space.

Once we've finished this five-step process, we can create the constraints for the grid bag. Figure 23.36 contains the set of constraints available in the *GridBagConstraints* class.

Field	Description	Defaults
anchor	Anchor constraints, if any.	CENTER
fill	Fill constraints for a component.	NONE
gridheight	Height of a component.	1
gridwidth	Width of a component.	1
gridx	Starting column of a component.	RELATIVE
gridy	Starting row of a component.	RELATIVE
insets	Spacing around a component (top, left, bottom, right).	new Insets(0,0,0,0)
ipadx	Internal column padding of a component.	0
ipady	Internal row padding of a component.	0
weightx	Column weight for a component.	0
weighty	Row weight for a component.	0

Figure 23.36 The *GridBagConstraints* Fields

We interpret these fields as follows:

The gridx and gridy fields. These fields correspond to the *x* and *y* coordinates that we created for each component in Step 1.

The gridwidth and gridheight fields. These fields correspond to the height and width of the cells. We determined these fields in Step 2.

The insets field. We determined the insets in Step 3. As indicated, we surround each component with a five-pixel gutter.

The fill field. We considered the fill factor in Step 4. The buttons use the default fill factor **NONE**. The drawing panel has the fill factor **BOTH**.

The weightx and weighty fields. We considered the weights in Step 5. The buttons use the default weights. We set the weights of the drawing panel to one so that it consumes any extra applet space.

The ipadx and ipady fields. These fields control a component's internal padding. We usually accept the default values.

The *GridBagConstraints* class also contains several constants, which are listed in Figure 23.37. We'll use the anchor constants in the next example. We typically use the **RELATIVE** default constant for all components. The **REMAINDER** constant lets the last component in a row fill any extra horizontal or vertical space.

Size	Fill	Anchor
RELATIVE	BOTH	NORTH
REMAINDER	VERTICAL	NORTHEAST
	HORIZONTAL	EAST
	NONE	SOUTHEAST
		SOUTH
		SOUTHWEST
		WEST
		NORTHWEST
		CENTER

Figure 23.37 The *GridBag* Constants (by type)

The *HerbGarden* Class Definition

Figure 23.38 contains the definition of the *HerbGarden* class. In addition to the usual arrays of button labels and buttons, the definition contains a predefined two-dimensional array, **xyConstraints[][]**, that contains the (*x, y*) coordinates for each button. We use this array to set the **gridx** and **gridy** fields for each button.

```java
import java.awt.*;
import java.awt.event.*;
import java.applet.*;

public class HerbGarden extends Applet implements ActionListener
{
  private static final String [] herbName = ["Anise", "Basil",
  "Bay", "Carraway", "Corriander","Cumin", "Dill", "Fennel",
  "Marjoram", "Mint", "Parsley", "Sage"};
  private static final String [] botanical = {"Pimpinella Anisum",
"Ociumum Basilicum","Laurus Nobilis", "Carum Carul", "Coriandrum", "Cuminum Cyminum", "Anethum
Grabeolens","Foeniculum vulgaris", "Origanum Vulgare", "Mentha Aquatica", "Pettroselinum Crispum",
"Salvia Officinalis"};
  private static final String [] cookingUses = {"Pickles, Preserves, Bread, Liquer", "Soups,
Tomato sauces, Salads", "Soups, Wine, Stew", "Bread, Cabbage, Liquer", "Curry powder, Bread,
Pickles, Hot Dogs",
  "Chicken, Chili, Curry Powder, Bread", "Fish, Pickles", "Seeds: Sausage, Bread, Pickles",
"Soups, Salads, Meat, Pickles", "Tea, Jelly, Sauces, Candy", "Soups, Stews, Garnishes", "Chicken,
Meat Pies"};
  private static final int [][] xyConstraints = {{0,0},{0,1}, {0,2}, {0,3}, {1,0}, {1,1}, {1,2},
{1,3}, {2,0}, {2,1}, {2,2}, {2,3}};
  private Label [] herbLabel = new Label[herbName.length];

 private Button [] herbButton = new Button[herbName.length];
 private GridBagLayout herbGrid = new GridBagLayout();
 private MessagePanel rightBox = new MessagePanel();
 private String [] outString =  {"Herb Name: ", "Botanical Name: ", "Cooking Uses"};

 //Put the init() Method Here
 //Put the actionPerformed() Method Here
}

//Put Message Panel Here
```

Figure 23.38 The *HerbGarden* Class Definition

The *HerbGarden* class also contains a named grid bag layout manager that we create with the statement

```
private GridBagLayout herbGrid = new GridBagLayout();
```

Notice the definition of the *rightBox* panel in the *HerbGarden* class definition:

```
private MessagePanel rightBox = new MessagePanel();
```

The definition indicates that *rightBox*, which is the display panel for the selected herb, is a *MessagePanel* object. *MessagePanel* is not a built-in Java class; it's a new class that we'll create for this page.

The *MessagePanel* Class Definition

The *MessagePanel* class will be an extension of the *Panel* class. The class definition contains two **public** methods, **paint()** and **draw()**. The **draw()** method is the interface that lets us pass information from the *HerbGarden* class to the *MessagePanel* class. In the current example, we want to pass the selected herb's English and botanical name and its cooking uses. We can use three parameters, or we can pass an array of strings. We will use the latter approach in this program.

We use the **paint()** method to draw the three strings onto the panel. The *x* and *y* coordinates used by the **drawString()** method are relative to the panel. In other words, the (0,0) position is the top-left corner of the panel (not of the applet, as it would normally be).

The complete definition of the *MessagePanel* class appears in Figure 23.39. We place this definition after the definition of the *HerbGarden* class.

```
public class MessagePanel extends Panel
{//Extend the panel class to create a new drawing panel
  String herbName = "";
  String botanical = "";
  String uses = "";

public void paint(Graphics g)
{//draw the herb information in the panel
 g.drawString(herbName, 5,10);
  g.drawString(botanical, 5, 25);
  g.drawString(uses,5,40);
}

public void draw(String [] input)
{//interface to the drawing program
  herbName = input[0];
  botanical = input[1];
  uses = input[2];
  repaint();
}
```

Figure 23.39 The *MessagePanel* Class Definition

The init() Method

We're now ready to continue our examination of the *HerbGarden* class. The **init()** method has several tasks, the first of which is the creation of the grid bag layout manager and its associated constraints class. We use the following statements to create the manager and its constraints:

```
setLayout(herbGrid);    //Use a gridbag layout
GridBagConstraints constraints = new GridBagConstraints();
```

Next, we create the insets. All of the components use the same insets, so we can use a single statement to establish the insets. The statement is

constraints.insets = new Insets(5,5,5,5);

We use a **for** statement to create the herb buttons and their action listeners. The **for** statement also sets the constraints for each button and adds the button to the applet. Figure 23.40 contains the code for the **for** statement.

```
for (i=0; i < herbName.length; i++)
{//Create the Herb buttons and their constraints
    herbButton[i] = new Button(herbName[i]);
    herbButton[i].addActionListener(this);
    constraints.gridx = xyConstraints[i][0];
    constraints.gridy = xyConstraints[i][1];
    add(herbButton[i], constraints);
}
```

Figure 23.40 Creating the Herb Buttons

Notice the last statement in Figure 23.40:

add(herbButton[i], constraints);

Because each component in a grid bag layout has its own set of constraints, the **add()** method for the grid bag layout requires two parameters: the component and its constraints.

We add the drawing panel to the applet after we've created the buttons. The code is highlighted in Figure 23.41. This figure contains the definition of the **init()** method.

```
public void init()
{ //put buttons in grid
    int i;
    setLayout(herbGrid);    //Use a gridbag layout
    GridBagConstraints constraints - new GridBagConstraints();
    constraints.insets = new Insets(5,5,5,5);
    for (i=0; i < herbName.length; i++)
    {//Create the Herb buttons and their constraints
        herbButton[i] = new Button(herbName[i]);
        herbButton[i].addActionListener(this);
        constraints.gridx = xyConstraints[i][0];
        constraints.gridy = xyConstraints[i][1];
        add(herbButton[i], constraints);
    }
    //Create the constraints for the drawing panel
    constraints.gridx = 3;
    constraints.gridy = 0;
    constraints.gridheight = 4;
    constraints.gridwidth = 4;
    constraints.fill = GridBagConstraints.BOTH;
    constraints.weightx = constraints.weighty = 1; //take up slack
    add(rightBox, constraints);
}
```

Figure 23.41 The **init()** Method, *HerbGarden* Class

The `actionPerformed()` Method

The **actionPeformed()** method is activated when the user selects an herb button. A **for** statement is used to determine which button the user picked. Once we've found the button, we construct the string array *outString*. This array contains the selected herb's English and botanical name and the cooking uses. We pass the array as a parameter to the **draw()** method. Figure 23.42 contains the definition of the **actionPerformed()** method.

```
public void actionPerformed(ActionEvent e)
{
  int i;
  String picked = e.getActionCommand();
  for (i = 0; i < herbName.length; i++)
    if (picked.equals(herbName[i])) {
      outString[0]= "Herb: " + herbName[i];
      outString[1] ="Botanical Name: " + botanical[i];
      outString[2]= "Cooking Uses: " + cookingUses[i];
      rightBox.draw(outString);
      break;
    }
}
```

Figure 23.42 The **actionPerformed()** Method, *HerbGarden* Class

The *GridBag* Layout Manager: Compass Points

We conclude this chapter with a second illustration of the Grid Bag layout manager. This example uses compass points to create a moving button. Figure 23.43 contains a sample page. The page has a button for each of the compass-point constants listed in Figure 23.37. Because the center button occupies all extra applet space, it has a large area in which it roams. The button shifts its position in respond to the button clicks: the **NORTHWEST** button was clicked in Figure 23.43, so the center button is located in the northwest corner of its space.

The HTML creates a 500 × 200 rectangle for the applet. The tag is

```
<APPLET CODE = "CompassPoints.class" WIDTH = "500" HEIGHT = "200">
</APPLET>
```

The *CompassPoints* Class Defintion

The *CompassPoints* class definition contains prefilled arrays that hold the compass-point names and their associated anchor constants. We also create a prefilled two-dimensional array, *xyConstraints*, that contains the (*x*, *y*) coordinates for each button. We use a one-dimensional array to store the buttons. Figure 23.44 contains the class definition.

The *CompassPoints* class contains our first example of a component. Notice the statement

```
private Component center;
```

The *center* object created by this statement will hold the center button. Using a component to hold the button is crucial when creating a moving button.

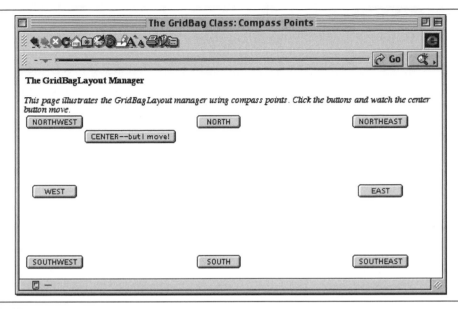

Figure 23.43 The *Compass Points* Page

```
import java.awt.*;
import java.awt.event.*;
import java.applet.*;

public class CompassPoints extends Applet implements ActionListener
{
  private String [] compassName = {"NORTH", "NORTHEAST", "EAST","SOUTHEAST",
   "SOUTH", "SOUTHWEST", "WEST", "NORTHWEST", "CENTER--but I move!"};
  private static final int [] anchorConstraints = {GridBagConstraints.NORTH,
  GridBagConstraints.NORTHEAST,
  GridBagConstraints.EAST,
  GridBagConstraints.SOUTHEAST,
  GridBagConstraints.SOUTH,
  GridBagConstraints.SOUTHWEST,
  GridBagConstraints.WEST,
  GridBagConstraints.NORTHWEST,
  GridBagConstraints.CENTER};

  private int [][] xyConstraints = {{1,0}, {2,0}, {2,1}, {2,2},
  {1,2}, {0,2}, {0,1}, {0,0}, {1,1}};
  private Label [] compassLabel = new Label[compassName.length];

  private Button [] compassButton = new Button[compassName.length];
  private GridBagLayout compass = new GridBagLayout();
  private Component center;
  //Put the init() Method Here
  //Put the actionPerformed() Method Here
}
```

Figure 23.44 The *CompassPoints* Class Definition

The init() Method

The **init()** method creates the buttons, adds an action listener to each one, and places the buttons in the applet. Because we use most of the default constraints for each button, we have relatively little code to write. Figure 23.45 contains the definition of the **init()** method.

```
public void init()
{ //put label and textfield in grid
    int i;
    setLayout(compass);    //Use a gridbag layout
    GridBagConstraints constraints = new GridBagConstraints();
    constraints.insets = new Insets(1,1,1,1);

    for (i=0; i < compassName.length; i++)
    {//Create the constraints for each object
        compassButton[i] = new Button(compassName[i]);
        compassButton[i].addActionListener(this);
        constraints.gridx = xyConstraints[i][0];
        constraints.gridy = xyConstraints[i][1];
        if (i == compassName.length-1)
          constraints.weightx = constraints.weighty = 1;
        add(compassButton[i], constraints);
    }
    center = compassButton[compassName.length-1];
}
```

Figure 23.45 The **init()** Method, *CompassPoints* Class

As Figure 23.45 indicates, all of the buttons use a gutter of one pixel. This lets the "roving" center button move close to the other buttons. The **for** statement uses the *xyConstraints* array to fill the grid fields for each button. We use an **if** statement to change the weights of the center button to one. This lets the center button consume all of the extra applet space. The final statement in the **init()** method assigns the center button to the *center* component.

The actionPerformed() Method

The **actionPerformed()** method changes the anchor of the center button in response to the user's button clicks. We didn't change the *anchor* field when we created the buttons, so each buttons is anchored to the center of its grid space. We gave the center button a lot of roaming space so that we can watch what happens when we change its anchor. To change the anchor, we must first obtain the grid bag constraints for the center component. The statement that accomplishes this task is

```
GridBagConstraints centerConstraints = compass.getConstraints(center);
```

This statement creates a new *GridBagConstraints* object named *centerConstraints*. We use the **getConstaints()** method to obtain the constraints. This method requires a single parameter, which must be a component.

Once we've obtained the constraints, we use a **for** statement to find the selected button. When we find this button, we change the anchor constraint of the center component. Changing the anchor constraint is a four-step procedure:

Step 1. Change the Anchor. We change the anchor with a simple assignment statement:

```
centerConstraints.anchor = anchorConstraints[i];
```

In this statement, *i* is the index of the selected button. The *anchorConstraints* array contains the anchor constraints.

Step 2. Set the Constraints.   Although we changed the anchor constraint, we must also set the new constraint. We use the **setConstraints()** method to accomplish this task. The **setConstraints()** method requires two parameters: a component, and a *GridBagConstraints* object. In our example, *center* is the component and *centerConstraints* is the *GridBagConstraints* object. The statement that sets the new constraints is:

```
compass.setConstraints(center, centerConstraints);
```

Step 3. Invalidate the Old Layout.   To display the center component with its new anchor, we must invalidate the current layout. The statement that does this is

```
invalidate();
```

Step 4. Validate the New Layout.   Finally, we call the **validate()** method to display the new layout, by means of the following statement

```
validate();
```

Figure 23.46 contains the definition of the **actionPerformed()** method.

```
public void actionPerformed(ActionEvent e)
{//find the selected button
 // Change the anchor constraint to match the selected button
  int i;
  GridBagConstraints centerConstraints =
compass.getConstraints(center);
  String picked = e.getActionCommand();
  for (i = 0; i < compassName.length; i++)
     if (picked.equals(compassName[i])) {
        centerConstraints.anchor = anchorConstraints[i];
        compass.setConstraints(center, centerConstraints);
        invalidate();
        validate();
     }
 }
```

Figure 23.46 The **actionPerformed()** Method, *CompassPoints* Class

➤ **EXERCISES**

1. **The *Sales Tax* Page.** Rewrite the *Sales Tax* page, using a flow layout without panels. Compare this page to the example appearing in Figure 23.12.
2. **The *Array Buttons* Page.** Rewrite the *Array Buttons* page. Use a grid layout of your choosing. (See Figure 22.27.)
3. **The *Matrix Sums* Page.** Rewrite the *Matrix Sums* page. Use a grid layout to place the matrix on the page. You may omit the row and column labels. (See Figure 22.29.)
4. **The *Float Conversion* Page.** Rewrite the *Float Conversion* page. Use panels to place the labels above the text fields. (See Figure 21.27.)

5. **The *Text Area Insert* Page.** Rewrite the *Text Area Insert* page. Use panels to place the labels above the text fields. (See Figure 21.42.)

6. **The *Silly Sentences* Page.** Rewrite the *Silly Sentences* page. Use combined layouts of your choice to create a pleasing appearance. (See Figure 14.49.)

7. **The *Wind Chill* Page.** Rewrite the *Wind Chill* page. Use a layout of your choice, but extend the panel class and write the results in this class. (See Figure 22.3.)

8. **The *Fahrenheit to Celsius* Page.** Rewrite the *Fahrenheit to Celsius* page. Extend the panel class to create a drawing surface to print the Fahrenheit-to-Celsius table. Use a border layout. Put the text fields and their associated labels in panels, and place the panels in the NORTH location. Put the drawing panel in the CENTER location. (See Figure 22.19.)

9. **The *Decimal Conversion* Page.** Rewrite the *Decimal Conversion* page, following the guidelines in the previous exercise. (See Figure 22.14.)

10. **The *Multiplication* Page.** Rewrite the *Multiplication* page. Extend the panel class to create a drawing surface for the table. Use a grid bag layout to arrange the components. (See Figure 11.13.)

11. **The *Cheese Head Survey* Page.** Figure 4.21 contains a *Cheese Head Survey* page written in HTML. Rewrite this page, using a *Grid Bag* Layout.

12. **The *Card Shuffle* Page.** Create a page that contains arrays of face values and suit values for a deck of cards. Create two card layouts, one for the face value, the other for the suit value. Put a shuffle button on the page. When the user selects this button, shuffle the cards. To shuffle, generate a random number that ranges over the size of each array.

13. **The *Herb Shuffle* Page.** Rewrite the *Herb Garden* page so that the herbs use a card layout.

14. **The *Football Player* Page.** Create a simplified deck of football-player "trading cards." Your deck should contain at least five cards.

15. **The *Pick a Sport* Page.** Pick a sport of your choice other than football. Create a deck of cards that represent the relevant statistics for your players.

16. **The *Football Player* Page, grid version.** Modify the *Football Player* page. Place the "cards" in a grid. Which arrangement do you prefer? Why?

17. **The *State Flora and Fauna* Page.** Create a GridBag version of the *State Flora and Fauna* page appearing in Figure 4.35. Create buttons for each statement. When the user presses a button, display the state information on the page. Follow the model used in the *Herb Garden* page.

18. **The *Birder's Checklist* Page.** Create a GridBag version of the *Birder's Checklist* page appearing in Figure 6.23. Use buttons for the bird categories. When the user presses a button, display the bird information on the page. Follow the model used in the *Herb Garden* Page.

24 Colors and Fonts

INTRODUCTION

In our previous Java applets, we relied upon the default colors and fonts when designing pages. In this chapter, we learn to change the foreground and background colors, and we explore the various font styles available in Java.

COLOR BASICS

The Java *Color* class provides thirteen color constants. Figure 24.1 contains a page that displays each of these colors. The colors are placed in panels arranged in a 4 × 4 grid. The background of each panel is set to the color constant named in the panel. (Notice that the color constant names violate Java's naming conventions; they resemble field names, not constant names.)

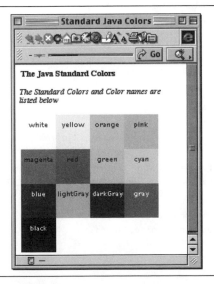

Figure 24.1 The Java *Color Constants* Page

The HTML creates a 200 × 200 rectangle for the applet. The tag is

```
<APPLET CODE = "ColorBasic.class" WIDTH = "200" HEIGHT = "200">
</APPLET>
```

The *Component* Class Color Methods

The *Component* class contains four methods that set or get the foreground or background color of any component or descendant of a component. Most classes in the AWT descend from the *Component* class, so we should be able to change the foreground and background colors of any object. Unfortunately, some browsers ignore some color requests. At the time of this writing, Netscape accepts all color requests, but Internet Explorer accepts only requests to change the background or foreground of an applet or of panels within it. Internet Explorer ignores requests to change the foreground or background of buttons, text fields, and text areas. Obviously, it's important to view applets on both major browsers before releasing them to the public.

Figure 24.2 lists the *Component* methods that *set* or *get* the foreground and background color of objects.

Method	Definition
`void setForeground(Color c);`	Change the foreground (text) color.
`void setBackground(Color c);`	Change the background color.
`Color getForeground();`	Return the foreground color.
`Color getBackground();`	Return the background color.

Figure 24.2 The *Component* Class Color Methods

The *ColorBasic* Class Definition

The *ColorBasic* class definition, which produced the applet displayed in Figure 24.1, relies upon arrays of color names and constants. Figure 24.3 contains the class definition. The array containing the color constants is highlighted.

```
import java.awt.*;
import java.awt.event.*;
import java.applet.*;

public class ColorBasic extends Applet
{//display the Java Standard Colors
 private static final String [] colorNames = {"white", "yellow", "orange", "pink", "magenta",
"red", "green", "cyan", "blue", "lightGray", "darkGray", "gray", "black"};
 private Color [] color = {Color.white, Color.yellow, Color.orange, Color.pink, Color.magenta,
Color.red, Color.green, Color.cyan, Color.blue, Color.lightGray, Color.darkGray, Color.gray,
Color.black};

private Label [] colorLabel = new Label[color.length];
private Panel [] colorPanel = new Panel[color.length];

//put the init() Method Here
}
```

Figure 24.3 The *ColorBasic* Class Definition

As Figure 24.3 indicates, the *ColorBasic* class definition also includes arrays of labels and panels. The **init()** method places the color names into the labels and the labels into the panels. The **init()** method also changes the background color of the panel to reflect the Java color constant. We change the foreground color of the gray, dark gray, blue, and black panels to white so that we can read the constant's name. Figure 24.4 contains the definition of the **init()** method. The code relies upon familiar techniques. The statements that change the background and foreground colors are highlighted.

```
public void init()
{ //put label in panel
  //change background of panel
    int i;
    setLayout(new GridLayout(4,4));
    for (i = 0; i < color.length; i++) {
        colorPanel[i] = new Panel();
        colorPanel[i].add(new Label(colorNames[i]));
        colorPanel[i].setBackground(color[i]);
        if ((i == 8) || (i > 9))
        //too dark to read color name switch to white
          colorPanel[i].setForeground(Color.white);
        add(colorPanel[i]);
    }
}
```

Figure 24.4 The **init()** Method, *ColorBasic* Class

Notice the **if** statement appearing in the **init()** method. When the loop index, *i*, equals eight or is greater than nine, the foreground color is changed to white. The corresponding colors are so dark that we wouldn't be able to read the color names if the foreground were black.

The *Graphics* Class Color Methods

The *Graphics* class contains its own set of methods that get or set the foreground color for drawing. Because the *Graphics* class draws within a container, which is a form of component, we can set the background color by using the *Component* class method. Figure 24.5 lists the two *Graphics* methods.

Method	Description
`void setColor(Color c);`	Set the foreground color.
`Color getColor();`	Return the foreground color.

Figure 24.5 The *Graphics* Class Color Methods

To illustrate the **setColor()** method, we create a page that writes a message in each of the built-in colors except white. Figure 24.6 contains a sample page.

The HTML creates a 400 × 300 rectangle for the applet. The tag is

```
<APPLET CODE = "GraphicsColors.class" WIDTH = "400" HEIGHT = "300">
</APPLET>
```

Figure 24.6 The *Graphics Colors* Page

Figure 24.7 contains the definition of the *GraphicsColors* class. The class uses the same string and color arrays as the previous example. The arrays omit *white*, because we wouldn't be able to see white text against a white background. The class definition requires only a **paint()** method. The statement that changes the foreground color is highlighted.

```
import java.awt.*;
import java.awt.event.*;
import java.applet.*;

public class GraphicsColors extends Applet
{
 private static final String [] colorNames = { "yellow", "orange", "pink", "magenta", "red",
"green", "cyan", "blue", "lightGray", "darkGray", "gray", "black"};
 private Color [] color = {Color.yellow, Color.orange, Color.pink, Color.magenta, Color.red,
Color.green, Color.cyan, Color.blue, Color.lightGray, Color.darkGray, Color.gray, Color.black};

public void paint(Graphics g)
{// Write a string in each built-in color
  int i;
  int yPos = 20;
  for (i=0; i < colorNames.length; i++) {
    g.setColor(color[i]);
    g.drawString("This line is written in " + colorNames[i] + ".", 10, yPos);
    yPos += 18;
  }
 }
}
```

Figure 24.7 The *GraphicsColors* Class Definition

The **setColor()** method of the *Graphics* class works with any of the *draw* methods. In Chapter 26, we'll use this method to change the foreground (drawing) color of lines, rectangles, ovals, poly lines, and polygons.

Custom Colors

Java also provides a *Color* constructor that lets us create custom colors. Figure 24.8 contains the definition of this constructor. (Two other constructors are available, but they are more specialized.)

```
new Color(int red, int green, int blue);
```

Figure 24.8 The *Color* Constructor

The *Color* constructor requires three integer parameters corresponding to the red, green, and blue (RGB) values of the color. We can pass either decimal or hexadecimal values for the parameters. If we pass decimal values, each parameter must be between 0 and 255; if we pass hexadecimal values, each parameter must be between 0x00 and 0xFF.

THE HTML COLORS PAGE

As an example of custom colors, we create a page that uses several of the built-in HTML colors. When we discussed colors in Chapter 2, we briefly examined the 100+ named colors available in HTML. Figure 24.9 contains six of these colors. Examine the RGB decimal and hex values for these colors. What is wrong with this set of HTML custom colors?

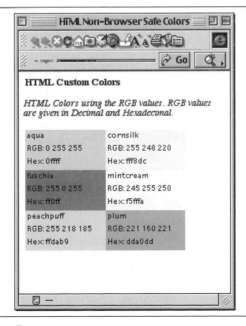

Figure 24.9 The *HTML Colors* Page

When we investigated colors in Chapter 2, we emphasized browser-safe colors. That palette of 216 colors presents the same "look" on any platform. To create these colors, we combine only 0x00, 0x33, 0x66, 0x99, 0xCC, and 0xFF when forming an RGB hex triplet. In Figure 24.9, only two of the HTML custom colors are browser safe: aqua (00 FF FF) and fuchsia (FF 00 FF). In fact, few of the 100+ named HTML colors are browser safe.

The *ColorHTML* Class Definition

Figure 24.10 contains the definition of the *ColorHTML* class. The definition has an array of color names that corresponds to the HTML custom colors. We also create a prefilled two-dimensional array of RGB triplets. The rows in this array represent a distinct color, while the columns are the red, green, and blue hexadecimal numbers for the color. The code that creates the two-dimensional array is highlighted.

```
import java.awt.*;
import java.awt.event.*;
import java.applet.*;

public class ColorHTML extends Applet {
//Create Some HTML colors using their hex RGB values
  private static final String [] colorNames = {" aqua", " cornsilk", " fuchsia", " mintcream", " peachpuff", " plum"};

  private static final int [][] hexValue = {
    {0x00,0xFF, 0xFF}, {0xFF, 0xF8, 0xDC},
    {0xFF, 0x00,0xFF}, {0xF5, 0xFF, 0xFA},
    {0xFF, 0xda, 0xb9}, {0xdd, 0xa0, 0xdd}};
  private Color [] color = new Color [colorNames.length];
  private Panel [] colorPanel = new Panel[colorNames.length];
}
```

Figure 24.10 The *ColorHTML* Class Definition

As Figure 24.10 indicates, the *ColorHTML* class also contains arrays of color names, colors, and panels. The *colorNames* array holds the names for the labels that we create in the **init()** method. Each panel holds a color, an RGB decimal label, and a hex label. We construct the RGB decimal and hex labels in the **init()** method by using the *hexValue* array. We also use this two-dimensional array to fill the *color* array with the HTML colors. Figure 24.11 contains the definition of the **init()** method.

As Figure 24.11 indicates, the *ColorHTML* class contains two grid layouts. We use a 3×2 grid layout to place the color panels on the page. Each color panel has a 3×1 grid layout that places the three labels in a single column. We use a **for** statement to construct the new colors. The statement

```
color[i] = new Color(hexValue[i][0], hexValue[i][1], hexValue[i][2]);
```

creates the ith color from the *hexValue* array. The 0th column contains the red value; the 1st column contains the green value; the 2nd column contains the blue value. The **for** statement also creates the color label, using the *colorNames* array. After we construct a color panel, we place the three labels into it. We use *decString* to construct the decimal representation of the RGB value from the *hexValue* array. We use *hexString* to construct the hexadecimal representation. We construct a

```
public void init()
{ /*General layout is a grid
   *Each panel has its own layout: grid layout 3 rows, 1 column
   *Colors are generated from the Hex rgb values
   *Decimal(default) rgb value is printed
   *Hex RGB values are printed using toHexString() */

   int i;
   String decString; //RGB value in base 10
   String hexString; //RGB value in base 16
   setLayout(new GridLayout(3,2));

   for (i = 0; i < colorNames.length; i++) {
   /* create a new color, color label and panel
    * place the name label, decimal value label, and hex value label
    * in the panel. Set the background color of the panel.
    * Add the panel to the Applet */

      color[i] = new Color(hexValue[i][0], hexValue[i][1],
               hexValue[i][2]);
      colorPanel[i] = new Panel();
      colorPanel[i].setLayout(new GridLayout(3,1));
      colorPanel[i].add(new Label(colorNames[i]));

      decString = " RGB: " + hexValue[i][0] + " ";
      decString += hexValue[i][1] + " ";
      decString += hexValue[i][2];
      colorPanel[i].add(new Label(decString));

      hexString = " Hex: " + Integer.toHexString(hexValue[i][0]);
      hexString += Integer.toHexString(hexValue[i][1]);
      hexString += Integer.toHexString(hexValue[i][2]);
      colorPanel[i].add(new Label(hexString));

      colorPanel[i].setBackground(color[i]);
      add(colorPanel[i]);
   }
}
```

Figure 24.11 The **init()** Method, *ColorHTML* Class

new, unnamed label for each string and place the labels in the panel. Notice that we must use the **Integer.toHexString()** method to create *hexString,* even though the *hexValues* array uses hexadecimal numbers. Remember that Java uses decimal representation for integers regardless of the base we used to create them.

JAVA FONTS

In Chapter 2, we learned how to change the face, style, and size of a font. We used the **<FONT>** tag to change the face and size, and we used the **<B>...</B>** and **<I>...</I>** tags to choose bold or italic styles. When we changed the size in HTML, we picked a number between 1 and 7, where 1 was the smallest font size and 7 was the largest. From a typographical viewpoint, the HTML fonts, while easy to use, aren't very sophisticated. Java's approach to fonts follows standard typographical conventions.

Java provides two font-related classes: *Font* and *FontMetrics*. The *Font* class contains a constructor that creates new fonts using a variety of font faces, styles, and point sizes. This class also contains methods that return font information. The *FontMetrics* class contains methods that return the typographical statistics (metrics) for the current font.

Font Metrics

Return for a moment to second grade, and recall your first experiences with printing. Your teacher furnished you with lined paper that resembles the "tablet" displayed in Figure 24.12. Each line on your tablet was divided into three solid lines. A dashed line separated the lines of print. You began forming your letters on the middle line. Typographically, this is the *baseline*. Certain letters, notably *g, j, p,* and *q,* descended into the lower line. These letters are *descenders*, and the gap from the baseline to the bottom of the letter is called the *descent*. Other letters, notably *b, d, f,* and *l,* ascend into the upper line. These letters are *ascenders*, and the gap from the baseline to the tip of the letter is called the *ascent*. The *leading* is the gap between the *descenders* of one row and the *ascenders* of the row that follows it. The *height* of a font is the *maximum ascent + maximum descent + leading*, where the *maximum ascent* is the *ascent* of the "tallest" letter, and the *maximum descent* is the *descent* of the "lowest" letter.

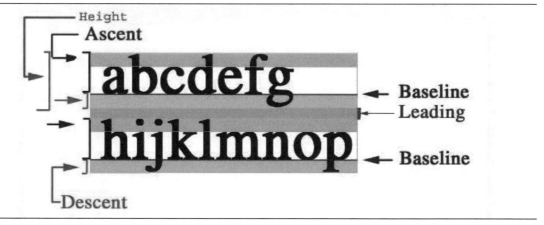

Figure 24.12 Typographical Metrics

We use the method calls listed in Figure 24.13 to obtain the font metrics for the current font.

```
FontMetrics Toolkit.getDefaultToolkit().getFontMetrics(Font f);
```

Figure 24.13 Obtaining the Font Metrics

Obtaining the font metrics begins with a call to the **getDefaultToolkit()** method. This method returns a *Toolkit* containing the platform-specific information for the current browser and computer system. We then invoke the **getFontMetrics()** method to return the font metrics for the font passed as a parameter. We learn how to construct a new font in the next section. For now, assume that we have a *Font* object named *currentFont*. We create a *FontMetrics* object, *fm*, containing the metrics for *currentFont* by using the statement

```
FontMetrics fm = Toolkit.getDefaultToolkit().getFontMetrics(currentFont);
```

Once we've created a *FontMetrics* object, we can use the methods listed in Figure 24.14. The method names parallel the typographical terminology displayed in Figure 24.12.

Method	Description
`int getAscent();`	Returns the font's ascent in pixels.
`int getDescent();`	Returns the font's descent in pixels.
`int getHeight();`	Returns the length of the longest character (includes leading) in pixels.
`int getLeading();`	Returns the font's leading.
`int getMaxAscent();`	Returns the maximum ascent for the font.
`int getMaxDescent();`	Returns the maximum descent for the font.
`int getMaxAdvance();`	Returns the width of the widest character in pixels.
`int charWidth(char ch);`	Returns the width of the character passed as a parameter (in pixels).
`int stringWidth(String s);`	Returns the width of the string passed as a parameter (in pixels).

Figure 24.14 The *FontMetrics* Methods

Later in the chapter, we use several of the methods listed in Figure 24.14 to align numbers in columns and to determine the correct spacing between lines of information.

Font Basics

Open your favorite word processor and find the *Font* menu. Examine the face names provided by your word processor. Most word processors offer a variety of font faces, including Times Roman, Courier, Helvetica, and Arial. As our first excursion into fonts, we create a page that lists the default font faces available on the user's platform. Figure 24.15 contains two sample pages. Figure 24.15(a) displays the **complete** list of fonts available on a Unix system. Figure 24.15(b) displays a partial list of the fonts available on the Macintosh system. Obviously, the Macintosh system offers many more possibilities than the Unix system.

The HTML used for this applet creates a 400 × 800 rectangle for the applet. The applet's height of 800 pixels provides more than ample space for the Unix fonts, while the Macintosh font list seems interminable. The tag is

```
<APPLET CODE  = "JavaFonts.class" WIDTH = "400" HEIGHT = "800">
</APPLET>
```

The *JavaFonts* Class Definition

To obtain the system-specific font list, we once again rely upon the **getToolkit()** method to return the current toolkit. The *Toolkit* class contains a **getFontList()** method that returns an array of strings containing the font faces available for the current system. The statement that retrieves the font list is

```
private String [] fontName = getToolkit().getFontList();
```

The *JavaFonts* class definition appears in Figure 24.16. The definition creates the *fontName* array and a *Font* variable, *currentFont*. We use *currentFont* in the **paint()** method to construct new fonts from the face names supplied by the *fontName* array.

(a) Unix Fonts

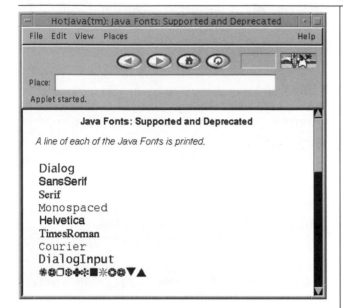

(b) Macintosh Fonts

Figure 24.15 Platform-Specific Font Faces

```
import java.awt.*;
import java.awt.event.*;
import java.applet.*;

public class JavaFonts extends Applet
{ //Display all the fonts available on the system
  private String [] fontName = getToolkit().getFontList();
  private Font currentFont;

//Put the paint() Method Here

}
```

Figure 24.16 The *JavaFonts* Class Definition

Constructing New Fonts

Figure 24.17 contains the syntax used to construct a new font.

```
Font fontName = new Font(String face/family, int STYLE, int point);
```

Figure 24.17 The *Font* Constructor

As Figure 24.17 indicates, creating a new font requires three parameters. The first parameter contains the face or family name of the font. The second parameter contains a font style constant. Figure 24.18 displays the style constants. The last style creates a bold italic font.

```
Font.PLAIN
Font.BOLD
Font.ITALIC
Font.BOLD |  Font.ITALIC
```

Figure 24.18 The *Font* Style Constants

The third parameter contains the point size. In typography, a point is 1/72 of an inch. Thus, smaller point sizes produce smaller fonts. Most textbooks use a point size of 10 or 12.

The paint() Method

The **paint()** method uses a **for** statement to create a new font from each of the names in *fontName* array. Each font is written in a plain style with a point size of 18. We use the following statement to create a new font:

```
currentFont = new Font(fontName[i], Font.PLAIN, 18);
```

After we create a new font, we use the **setFont()** method in the *Graphics* class to change the font. We pass the font as a parameter. Figure 24.19 contains the definition of the **paint()** method. The call to the **setFont()** method is highlighted.

```
public void paint(Graphics g)
{//Display each font  in 18 point
   int yPos = 25;
   int i;
   for(i=0; i < fontName.length; i++) {
        currentFont = new Font(fontName[i], Font.PLAIN,18);
        g.setFont(currentFont);
        g.drawString(fontName[i], 5, yPos);
        yPos+= 20;
   }
}
```

Figure 24.19 The **paint()** Method, *JavaFonts* Class

Logical Font Families and Components

Although we can create new fonts by using face names, Java discourages this practice, because the face names are platform-dependent. Instead, Java suggests that programmers use *logical* names to create fonts. Java currently recognizes five logical font families: Serif, SansSerif, Monospaced, Dialog, and DialogInput. These names describe a class of fonts rather than a specific font face. The first three logical names are well known in typography. A *serif* font adds small "squiggles," called serifs, to the ends of letters. A *sans serif* font is one that is literally without serif s. A monospaced font uses the same spacing for all characters in the font. Using a logical font rather than a specific font face lets the browser choose a font face from the logical family that fits any user's platform.

To illustrate the logical font families, we create a page that contains a button corresponding to each of the logical font names. The button's label is written in the logical family name. For example, the *Serif* button is written in a serif font. When the user presses a button, a message identifying the font, and written in the font, is printed on the page. Figure 24.20 shows a sample page. Notice the fonts displayed in the buttons.

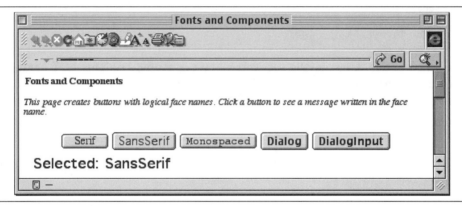

Figure 24.20 The Logical Font Families and Components

The HTML creates a 500 × 100 rectangle that holds the applet. The tag is

```
<APPLET CODE = "ButtonFonts.class" WIDTH = "500" HEIGHT = "100">
</APPLET>
```

The *ButtonFonts* Class Definition

The *ButtonFonts* class definition contains a prefilled *String* array containing the logical font names and an array of buttons. We use two strings to create the message drawn on the applet after the user selects a font button. Initially, the *message* string contains only *Selected.* Since this string is painted on the page when it is initially loaded, we want to avoid the *Null Pointer Exception* error that would result from an undefined string. When the user selects a font, we construct a new string that concatenates *Selected* and the selected font's name. The **actionPerformed()** method handles this task and then calls the **repaint()** method to write the message on the applet. Figure 24.21 contains the definition of the *ButtonFonts* class.

The **paint()** method in the *ButtonFonts* class relies upon familiar techniques. First, we create a new font, using the name selected by the user. We use the **setFont()** method of the *Graphics* class to change the font, and we use the **drawString()** method to write the message on the applet. The *y* coordinate in the **drawString()** method places the message below the button panel.

```
import java.awt.*;
import java.awt.event.*;
import java.applet.*;
public class ButtonFonts extends Applet implements ActionListener
{
    private static final String [] logicalNames = {"Serif", "SansSerif", "Monospaced", "Dialog",
"DialogInput"};
    private Button [] fontButtons = new Button[logicalNames.length];
    private String message  = "Selected: ";
    private String selected;
    private Panel input = new Panel();

    //Put the init() Method Here

    public void paint(Graphics g)
    {//write the message in the selected font
        Font currentFont = new Font(selected, Font.PLAIN, 18);
        g.setFont(currentFont);
        g.drawString(message, 10,50);

    }
  public void actionPerformed(ActionEvent e)
  { // get the button name and perform action based on it
     selected = e.getActionCommand();
     message = "Selected: " + selected;
     repaint();
  }
}
```

Figure 24.21 The *ButtonFonts* Class Definition

The init() Method

Although the *Component* and *Graphics* classes use different methods to set the foreground color, they use the same method, **setFont()**, to set the font. Thus, we use the **setFont()** method in the **paint()** method to change the font used to draw strings. We use the **setFont()** method in the **init()** method to change a component's font. Figure 24.22 contains the definition of the **init()** method for the *ButtonFonts* class.

```
public void init()
{//add the buttons, set the font
  int i;
  for (i=0; i < logicalNames.length; i++) {
    fontButtons[i] = new Button(logicalNames[i]);
    fontButtons[i].setFont(new Font(logicalNames[i], Font.PLAIN, 14));
    fontButtons[i].addActionListener(this);
    input.add(fontButtons[i]);
  }
  add(input);
}
```

Figure 24.22 The **init()** method, *ButtonFonts* Class

As Figure 24.22 indicates, all of the coding takes place within a single **for** statement. The **for** statement begins with the construction of a button containing a logical font name. Next, we use the **setFont()** method to change the button's font. We set each font button by passing an anonymous font to the **setFont()** method. The string at the ith index of the *logicalNames* array furnishes the face name. All the fonts use a plain style and are set at 14 points. The statement is

```
fontButtons[i].setFont(new Font(logicalNames[i], Font.PLAIN, 14));
```

We add an action listener to each button, and we add the buttons to the *input* panel. After the **for** statement terminates, we add the *input* panel to the applet.

UNICODE CHARACTERS

Most programming languages use ASCII to translate characters into the numeric equivalents recognized by a computer. The standard ASCII character set consists of 128 characters. The extended ASCII set, which includes European language characters, consists of 256 characters. Java represents characters with a much richer character set, referred to a Unicode. The Unicode character set is 65K (65,536) characters. A Unicode character is represented by four hexadecimal digits and is written as **'\uXXXX'**, where **\u** is the Unicode prefix and X denotes a hexadecimal digit.

The Unicode character set contains many language sets. You can view these sets at the Unicode web site, http://www.unicode.org. Figure 24.23 contains a small sampling of the languages available in Unicode. Unfortunately, while you can view the language sets at the Unicode web site, your system will not recognize a language set unless you purchase it.

Unicode	Language
\u0100 - \u017F	Latin Extended-A
\u0180 - \u024F	Latin Extended-B
\u0370 - \u03FF	Hebrew
\u0F20 - \u0F29	Tibetan
\u0370 - \u03FF	Greek
\u0E00 - \u0E7F	Thai

Figure 24.23 Some Unicode Language Sets

The *European Language* Set

The first 256 Unicode digits correspond to the extended ASCII character set, so we can use at least these characters in our applications. As our first Unicode example, we create a table of Unicode characters ranging from **'\u0070'** to **'\u00FF'**. Figure 24.24 contains a sample page.

As Figure 24.24 indicates, the first row of the Unicode table contains lower-case alphabetical characters. The following two rows are filled with question marks. The question marks indicate that these characters are currently unused or unrecognized by the browser. The row beginning with **'\u00A0'** contains the international monetary symbols. The European character sets follow. Notice the neat alignment of the characters into rows and columns. Because creating and printing Unicode characters is an easy task, we will use this page to apply the font metric methods discussed earlier in this chapter.

The *Unicode* Class Definition

Figure 24.25 contains the definition of the *Unicode* class. The class definition contains two one-dimensional arrays, *columnHeading* and *rowHeading,* that produce the labels running across and

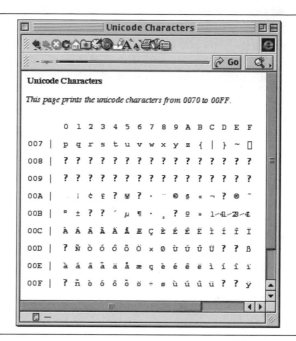

Figure 24.24 The *Unicode* Page

down the page, respectively. The two-dimensional array *unicode* contains the Unicode characters that populate the table.

```
import java.awt.*;
import java.awt.event.*;
import java.applet.*;
public class Unicode extends Applet
{
   private Font currentFont = new Font("Monospaced", Font.PLAIN, 12);
   private  FontMetrics fm = Toolkit.getDefaultToolkit().getFontMetrics(currentFont);
   private static final String [] columnHeading = {"0", "1", "2", "3", "4", "5", "6", "7","8", "9",
"A", "B", "C", "D", "E", "F"};
   private static final String [] rowHeading = {"007 | ","008 | ","009 | ","00A | ","00B | ","00C |
","00D | ", "00E | ","00F | "};
   private char [][] unicode = {
    {'\u0070', '\u0071', '\u0072', '\u0073','\u0074', '\u0075', '\u0076', '\u0077', '\u0078',
'\u0079', '\u007A', '\u007B', '\u007C', '\u007D', '\u007E', '\u007F'},
//Continue with 008, 009, 00A, 00B, 00C, 00D, 00E
{'\u00F0', '\u00F1', '\u00F2', '\u00F3', '\u00F4', '\u00F5', '\u00F6', '\u00F7', '\u00F8',
'\u00F9', '\u00FA', '\u00FB', '\u00FC', '\u00FD', '\u00FE', '\u00FF'}};
//Put the paint() method here
}
```

Figure 24.25 The *Unicode* Class Definition

As Figure 24.25 indicates, the *Unicode* class definition creates a monospaced plain font at 12 points that we use to print the table. We use the font metrics, *fm,* to create the column and row spacing.

The paint() Method

The **paint()** method generates the Unicode table. Figure 24.26 contains the code for this method. Examine the code and familiarize yourself with the variable names. Review the highlighted method calls. We'll dissect this method after you've had a chance to inspect the code.

```
public void paint(Graphics g)
{//write the unicode characters in the table
   int yPos = 20;
   int xPos;
   int i,j;
   g.setFont(currentFont);
    xPos =  (fm.stringWidth(rowHeading[0]) + 1);
    for (i = 0; i < columnHeading.length; i++)
    { //Write the column headings
        g.drawString( " " + columnHeading[i] , xPos, yPos);
        xPos += fm.getMaxAdvance() + fm.charWidth(' ');
    }
    for (i=0; i < unicode.length; i++)
    { //write the row headings
       xPos = 1;
       yPos = yPos + 2*fm.getHeight();
       g.drawString(rowHeading[i], xPos, yPos);
       xPos =  (fm.stringWidth(rowHeading[0]) + 1);
       for (j = 0; j< unicode[i].length; j++)
       {//write the unicode characters for the row
         g.drawString( " "+unicode[i][j], xPos, yPos);
         xPos += fm.getMaxAdvance() + fm.charWidth(' ');
       }
    }
 }
```

Figure 24.26 The **paint()** Method, *Unicode* Class

Printing the Column Labels.   The first task we confront in the **paint()** method is the creation of the column headings. To create these headings, we must set the column coordinate, *xPos*, so that we allow enough space to print the row headings on subsequent rows. We use the **stringWidth()** method to determine this distance. We establish the starting position for the column headings, and for each row of Unicode characters, with the statement

> **xPos = (fm.stringWidth(rowHeading[0]) + 1);**

The **stringWidth()** method determines the gap needed for the row headings. All the row headings are the same size, so it doesn't make any difference which one we use. Therefore, the current example uses the 0th row heading to determine the gap. We add one to *xPos* to leave one extra space between the row headings and the column headings or Unicode rows.

Once we've established the correct gap, we use a **for** statement to print the headings. Let's reconsider the code, which is reproduced in Figure 24.27.

```
for (i = 0; i < columnHeading.length; i++)
{ //Write the column headings
    g.drawString( " " + columnHeading[i] , xPos, yPos);
    xPos += fm.getMaxAdvance() + fm.charWidth(' ');
}
```

Figure 24.27 Printing the Column Headings

The **for** statement in Figure 24.27 calls the **drawString()** method to print the current heading. The **getMaxAdvance()** method returns the length of the widest character in the current font. The call to the **charWidth()** method returns the width of a space. We add the maximum advance and the width of a space to the current value of *xPos*. This gives us the *x* coordinate of the next column heading.

Printing the Row Headings and the Unicode Rows. Printing the row headings and the Unicode rows requires a nested **for** statement, as shown in Figure 24.28. The outer **for** statement prints the row headings, and the inner **for** statement prints the Unicode characters.

```
for (i=0; i < unicode.length; i++)
{ //write the row headings
    xPos = 1;
    yPos = yPos + 2*fm.getHeight();
    g.drawString(rowHeading[i], xPos, yPos);
    xPos =  (fm.stringWidth(rowHeading[0]) + 1);
    for (j = 0; j< unicode[i].length; j++)
    {//write the unicode characters for the row
        g.drawString( " "+unicode[i][j], xPos, yPos);
        xPos += fm.getMaxAdvance() + fm.charWidth(' ');
    }
}
```

Figure 24.28 Printing the Row Headings and Unicode Rows

Let's examine the outer **for** statement first. The outer **for** statement must set the row and column alignment. Because we print the row heading in the first column, *xPos* is reset to 1 at the beginning each row. The rows are double-spaced, so we add two times the height of the font to the current *yPos* value to obtain the position of the next row. The statement is

yPos = yPos + 2*fm.getHeight();

The row heading is printed after the row and column alignment is set. A row of Unicode characters follows the heading. The inner **for** statement prints a complete row of characters. The body of the inner **for** statement calls the **drawString()** method to print the current Unicode character. An assignment statement advances *xPos* to the next column.

The *German Sentences* Page

As a second Unicode example, we recreate the *German Sentences* page developed in Chapter 2. (See Figure 2.26.) Figure 24.29 contains the Java version. The German sentences, which are written in a plain font, contain Unicode characters. English counterparts are written in italics. We use double spacing to separate each set of sentences. Try to develop the class definition. It uses the same techniques developed in the *Unicode* class definition.

The HTML creates a 400 × 300 rectangle for the applet. The tag is

```
<APPLET CODE = "German1.class" WIDTH = "400" HEIGHT = "300">
</APPLET>
```

Figure 24.29 The *German Sentences* Page, Java version

The *German1* Class Definition

Figure 24.30 contains the *German1* class definition. A predefined array, *germanPhrase*, creates the German phrases. Notice how easily we intersperse the Unicode and characters to create these strings. A second array, *englishPhrase*, contains the English counterparts.

```
import java.awt.*;
import java.awt.event.*;
import java.applet.*;
public class German1 extends Applet
{
  private Font plainFont = new Font("Serif", Font.PLAIN, 12);
  private Font italicFont = new Font("Serif", Font.ITALIC, 12);
  private  FontMetrics fm = Toolkit.getDefaultToolkit().getFontMetrics(plainFont);
  private static final String [] germanPhrase =
  {"Das M\u00E4dchen i\u00DFt die Kartoffel!",
   "\u00D6ffnet die T\u00FCr!",
   "Gr\u00FC\u00DF Gott."};
private static final String [] englishPhrase =
    {"The girl eats the potato!", "Open the door!", "Hello."};
 //Put the paint() Method Here
}
```

Figure 24.30 The *German1* Class Definition

The paint() Method

Figure 24.31 contains the definition of the **paint()** method used in the *German1* class definition.

```
public void paint(Graphics g)
{ //write the strings on the applet
  int i;
  int x = 10;
  int y = 20;
  for (i=0; i< germanPhrase.length; i++)
  {
    g.setFont(plainFont);
    g.drawString(germanPhrase[i],x,y);
    y += fm.getHeight();

    g.setFont(italicFont);
    g.drawString(englishPhrase[i],x,y);
    y = y + 2*fm.getHeight();
  }
}
```

Figure 24.31 The **paint()** Method, *German1* Class

The **paint()** method uses a **for** statement to print the German phrases and English counterparts. We begin each iteration of the **for** statement by changing to the plain font used for the German phrases. We write the German phrase, then change the *y* coordinate. We will use single spacing between the German phrase and its English counterpart, so the statement that changes the *y* coordinate will be

```
y += fm.getHeight();
```

Once the German phrase is printed, we switch the font to the italic font used for the English phrases. We write the English phrase on the applet and change the *y* coordinate. We will use double spacing between each set of phrases, so the statement that changes the *y* coordinate this time will be

```
y = y + 2*fm.getHeight();
```

The *Degrees To Radians* Page

Our last font example corrects flaws that appeared in earlier pages. To illustrate these flaws, examine the *Degrees to Radians* page displayed in Figure 24.32. This page is not a pretty sight. The columns of degrees and radians are not right-aligned. In addition, the radians in the second column do not use the same precision to the right of the decimal point.

Now examine the *Degrees to Radians* page displayed in Figure 24.33. All of the numeric data are right-aligned, and all the radians use the same degree of precision. In addition, the new version does not use as much white space between the rows of numbers.

The *DegToRad* Class Definition

The *Degrees to Radians* page integrates many of the Java programming techniques we developed in the previous chapters. Panels with 2 × 1 grid layouts are used to place the labels above their associated text fields. The labels, text fields, and panels are stored in one-dimensional arrays to

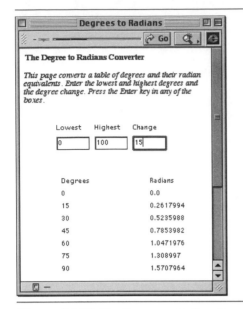

Figure 24.32 The *Degrees to Radians* Page, unformatted version

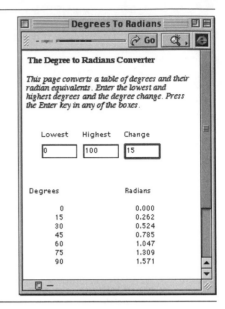

Figure 24.33 The *Degrees To Radians* Page, formatted version

ease the programming. You should be able to create the fields used by this class. Take a few minutes to outline these fields, then examine the class definition contained in Figure 24.34.

```
import java.awt.*;
import java.awt.event.*;
import java.applet.*;
public class DegToRad extends Applet implements ActionListener
{
  private static final int FIELD_SIZE = 6;
  private static final int X1 = 50;
  private static final int X2 = 180;
  private static final String [] inputString = {"Lowest", "Highest", "Change"};
  private TextField [] inputField = new TextField[inputString.length];
  private Panel [] inputPanel = new Panel[inputString.length];
  private Panel userPanel = new Panel();
  private int lowest, highest, change;
  private boolean paintFlag = false;
  private Font currentFont = new Font("Monospaced", Font.PLAIN, 12);
  private FontMetrics fm = Toolkit.getDefaultToolkit().getFontMetrics(currentFont);
//Put the init() Method Here
//Put the paint() Method Here
//put the roundPlaces() Method Here
//Put the checkPrecision() Method Here
//Put the actionPerformed() Method Here
}
```

Figure 24.34 The *DegToRad* Class Definition

In addition to the one-dimensional arrays, the *DegToRad* class definition includes three constants: **FIELD_SIZE**, **X1**, and **X2**. The first constant sets the field size of the text fields. The remaining constants establish the base column for the degrees and radians.

We use three integers, *lowest*, *highest*, and *change*, to store the user's data. We also use a boolean, *paintFlag*, to suppress printing the table before the user enters values. The final class fields create the font (*currentFont*) and font metrics (*fm*) used to generate the *Degrees to Radians* table.

The init() Method

The **init()** method uses a **for** statement to construct the input panels. Each panel uses a 2 × 1 grid layout. We construct the label and text field and add them to an input panel. We also add an action listener to the text field, and we add the panel to the user panel. We create this extra panel to force the applet to load the three input panels as a group. Figure 24.35 contains the definition of the **init()** method.

```
public void init()
{ //create panels, text fields and labels
  int i;
  for (i=0; i< inputString.length; i++) {
    inputPanel[i] = new Panel();
    inputPanel[i].setLayout(new GridLayout(2,1));
    inputField[i] = new TextField(FIELD_SIZE);
    inputPanel[i].add(new Label(inputString[i]));
    inputPanel[i].add(inputField[i]);
    inputField[i].addActionListener(this);
    userPanel.add(inputPanel[i]);
  }
  add(userPanel);
}
```

Figure 24.35 The **init()** Method, *DegToRad* Class

The actionPerformed() Method

The **actionPerformed()** method uses the **parseInt()** method to convert each of the text fields to its integer equivalent. We set *paintFlag* to *true* and call the **repaint()** method to generate the table. Writing the code for this method is a piece of cake. Figure 24.36 contains the definition.

```
public void actionPerformed(ActionEvent e)
{ //process the text field response
  lowest = Integer.parseInt(inputField[0].getText());
  highest = Integer.parseInt(inputField[1].getText());
  change = Integer.parseInt(inputField[2].getText());
  paintFlag = true;
  repaint();
}
```

Figure 24.36 The **actionPerfomed()** Method, *DegToRad* Class

The roundPlaces() and checkPrecision() Methods

Aligning the radians requires two methods. The **roundPlaces()** method developed previously is used to round the radians to three digits to the right of the decimal point. The **checkPrecision()** method will add zeros to radians that have a precision of less than three. To check the precision, we convert a radian to its string equivalent. Once it has been converted, we use the **indexOf()** method to find the decimal point. (Appendix E contains the definition of this method.)

We calculate the current precision by subtracting the index of the decimal point from the total length of the string. A **while** statement is used to add zeros to the string until the precision is three. Figure 24.37 contains the definitions of the **roundPlaces()** and **checkPrecision()** methods.

```
public float roundPlaces(float number, int places)
 { // round the number to the desired decimal places
    return (float)((Math.round(number * Math.pow(10, places))/Math.pow(10,places)));
 }
public String checkPrecision(float number, int precision)
  {
     String numString = Float.toString(number);
     int index = numString.indexOf('.');
     int currentPrecision = numString.length() - index;
     while (currentPrecision <= precision) {
         numString += "0";
         currentPrecision++;
     }
     return numString;
 }
```

Figure 24.37 The **roundPlaces()** and **checkPrecision()** Methods, *DegToRad* Class

The paint() Method

The **paint()** method uses **X1** and **X2** as the base columns for the degrees and radians, respectively. We determine the placement of the column labels by subtracting the width of the headings from the column constants. The two statements that create the column alignments are the following:

```
x1 = X1  - fm.stringWidth("Degrees");
x2 = X2 - fm.stringWidth("Radians");
```

We print the column headings with the two following statements:

```
g.drawString("Degrees", x1, yPos);
g.drawString("Radians", x2, yPos);
```

where *yPos* has an initial value of 100.

Once we've created the headings, we use a **for** statement to print the columns of degrees and their associated radians. Figure 24.38 contains the code for this statement.

```
for (degrees = lowest; degrees <= highest; degrees += change)
 { //Convert degrees to radian, align columns
     radians = roundPlaces(degrees * (float)Math.PI/180, 3);
     degString = Integer.toString(degrees);
     radString = checkPrecision(radians, 3);
     x1 = X1  - fm.stringWidth(degString);
     g.drawString(degString,x1, yPos);
     x2 = X2 - fm.stringWidth(radString);
     g.drawString(radString,x2, yPos);
     yPos = yPos + fm.getHeight();
 }
```

Figure 24.38 Aligning the Degrees and Radians Columns

The **for** statement converts the radians and degrees to their string equivalents and stores them in *degString* and *radString*, respectively. We determine the *x1* coordinate used for the degrees by subtracting the width of *degString* from **X1**. We use a similar technique to find the *x2* coordinate used for the radians. In this case, we subtract the width of *radString* from **X2**. The **drawString()** method prints the degrees and then the radians. The two calls use the same *yPos* coordinate. The *yPos* coordinate is changed before the next row in the table is printed. Figure 24.39 contains the code for the **paint()** method.

```java
public void paint(Graphics g)
{
  int degrees;
  float radians;
  String degString;
  String radString;
  int x1, x2;
  int yPos = 100;

  if (paintFlag)
  {//don't paint when page is loaded
    x1 = X1 - fm.stringWidth("Degrees");
    x2 = X2 - fm.stringWidth("Radians");
    g.drawString("Degrees", x1, yPos);
    g.drawString("Radians", x2, yPos);
    yPos = yPos + 2*fm.getHeight();
    for (degrees = lowest; degrees <= highest; degrees += change)
    { //Convert degrees to radian, align columns
      radians = roundPlaces(degrees * (float)Math.PI/180, 3);
      degString = Integer.toString(degrees);
      radString = checkPrecision(radians, 3);
      x1 = X1 - fm.stringWidth(degString);
      g.drawString(degString,x1, yPos);
      x2 = X2 - fm.stringWidth(radString);
      g.drawString(radString,x2, yPos);
      yPos = yPos + fm.getHeight();

    }
  }
}
```

Figure 24.39 The **paint()** Method, *DegToRad* Class

ADDENDUM

The *Font* class contains several methods that return characteristics of the current font. You might never need to use these methods; however, if you want to experiment with them, they are listed in Figure 24.40.

Method	Description
`String getName();`	Returns the font name.
`int getSize();`	Returns the font size.
`int getStyle();`	Returns the font style.
`Font getFont();`	Returns the font.
`boolean isBold();`	Returns *true* if the font is bold. Returns *false* otherwise.
`boolean isItalic();`	Returns *true* if the font is italic. Returns *false* otherwise.
`boolean isPlain();`	Returns *true* if the font is plain. Returns *false* otherwise.

Figure 24.40 Font Class Methods

➤ EXERCISES

1. **The *Color Grid Bag* Page.** Figure 24.41 contains a page with the thirteen built-in Java colors. The page uses a grid bag layout manager. When the user clicks a button, the background color of the page changes to reflect the user's choice. Implement this page.

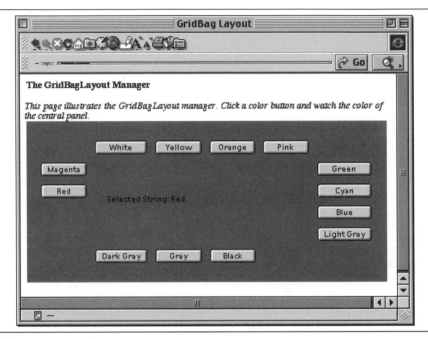

Figure 24.41 The *Color Grid* Page

2. **The *Color Grid Bag* Page, version 2.** Create a new version of the page illustrated in Figure 24.41. Your new page should contain a 6 × 2 grid of browser-safe colors of your choice. Place a drawing panel below the page. When the user clicks a button, change the color of the panel to reflect the user's choice.

3. **The *HTML Colors* Page.** Modify the HTML Colors page appearing in Figure 24.9. Use the **paint()** method to draw the information in the appropriate foreground color on the page.

4. **The *Character Entities* Page.** Create a Java version of the *Character Entities* page that appears in Figure 2.38.

5. **The *German Conversation* Page.** Create a Java version of the *German Conversation* page that appears in Figure 2.39.

6. **The *German Grammar* Page.** Create a Java version of the *German Grammar* page that appears in Figure 2.43.

7. **The *Multilanguage Counting* Page.** Create a Java version of the *Multilanguage Counting* page. Use arrays to store the Arabic, English, Tibetan, and German numbers. Print the numbers in columns. (See Figure 17.34.)

8. **The *Multilanguage Weekdays* Page.** Create a Java version of the *Weekdays* page. Use arrays to store the weekdays. Print the English, German, and Tibetan weekdays, using a Monday-through-Friday order. (See Figure 17.38.)

9. **The *Fahrenheit to Celsius* Page.** Modify the *Fahrenheit to Celsius* page so that the numbers are right-aligned. Use a **for** statement to create the tables. (See Figure 22.19.)

10. **The *Tipping Chart* Page.** Create a tipping chart page. Ask the user to enter the lowest and highest values and the change rate. Also ask the user to enter the tipping percentage. Create a table that prints the monetary value and the appropriate tip. The number should be right-aligned, and you should use leading dollar signs.

11. **The *Multiplication Table* Page.** Create a Java version of the *Multiplication* page appearing in Figure 11.13. The numbers should be right-aligned.

12. **The *Multiplication Table* Page, version 2.** Modify the previous exercise by allowing the user to enter the starting and ending values for the multiplication table.

13. **The *Font Metrics Information* Page.** Pick a logical font of your choice. Print the font information, using the methods displayed in Figure 24.14.

14. **The *Sales Tax* Page.** Create a *Sales Tax Table*. The page should ask the user to enter the lowest and highest values, the change rate, and the sales tax. The numbers should be right-aligned.

15. **The *Fibonacci Numbers* Page.** Create a *Fibonacci Numbers page*. Ask the user to enter the value of n. Print all of the Fibonacci numbers between 0 and n. Use two columns. The first column should contain the values of n. The second column should contain the corresponding Fibonacci number. The columns should be right-aligned. (See Figure 11.30.)

25 AWT Form Elements

INTRODUCTION

We've used the *TextField*, *TextArea*, and *Button* classes in previous chapters. In this chapter, we examine AWT's (Abstract Windowing Toolkit) remaining form-related classes. In Chapters 27 and 28, we explore Swing's form-related classes. Of the two packages, AWT is the older. Swing is unique to Java 1.2, and is actually a superset of AWT. This means that Swing contains additional classes that are not available in AWT. Each package has advantages and disadvantages. Therefore, it's worthwhile learning both of them.

CHECKBOXES

We begin our discussion of form elements with checkboxes. As a sample page, we create a set of seasonal checkboxes. The page asks users to select their favorite seasons of the year. Users can select none, one, several, or all of the seasons. When the current user presses a seasonal button, we update a tally sheet of seasonal counts. Figure 25.1 contains a sample page. As this page indicates, *Winter* is the clear favorite, with a count of 16.

The HTML tag creates a 280 × 100 rectangle for the applet. The tag is

```
<APPLET CODE = "CheckSeason.class" WIDTH = "280" HEIGHT = "100">
</APPLET>
```

The *Checkbox* Constructor

Figure 25.2 lists the three constructors used to create a new *Checkbox* object. As this figure indicates, we can create a new checkbox with or without a label, or with a label and a default state. The label specifies the text that appears to the right of the checkbox. For example, the labels used for the checkboxes in the *Seasons* page were *Spring*, *Summer*, *Fall*, and *Winter*. The default state for a checkbox is *false*, which means that the check box has not been selected. The third constructor lets us change this state to *true*, which means that the check box is already checked when the applet is loaded.

Figure 25.1 The *Favorite Seasons* Page

Constructor	Meaning
Checkbox();	Create a checkbox with no label
Checkbox(String s);	Create a checkbox with label s.
Checkbox(String s, boolean *state*);	Create a checkbox with label s, and boolean *state*.

Figure 25.2 The *Checkbox* Constructors

The Checkbox Methods

It makes little difference which constructor we use because the *Checkbox* class contains methods that set the label or the state of a check box. In most applications, we use the middle constructor; a checkbox without a label is of little value. Figure 25.3 contains a list of the most frequently used *Checkbox* methods.

Method	Description
String getLabel();	Returns the check box's label.
void setLabel(String s);	Change the check box's label.
boolean getState();	Return *true* if the check box is selected. Return *false* otherwise.
void setState (boolean *state*);	Change the check box's state. Use *true* to select the box. Use *false* to deselect it.
Object [] getSelectedObjects();	Return an array of the selected check boxes.
addItemListener(ItemListener *il*);	Add an item listener to a check box.

Figure 25.3 Frequently Used *Checkbox* Methods

Figure 25.3 illustrates several interesting features of checkboxes. The most important feature is the event handler. Unlike text fields and buttons, checkboxes do not use an action listener: they use an item listener. To activate the item listener, we must add an item listener to the checkbox. The *Checkbox* class also provides *get* methods that return a checkbox's label or state or an array of selected checkboxes.

Creating the Seasonal Check Boxes

We're now ready to create the *CheckSeason* class definition that implements the *Favorite Seasons* page. This definition appears in Figure 25.4.

```
import java.awt.*;
import java.awt.event.*;
import java.applet.*;

public class CheckSeason extends Applet implements ItemListener
{
    private static final Label seasonHeader = new Label("Seasons");
    private static final String [] seasonLabel = {"Spring", "Summer", "Fall", "Winter"};
    private Checkbox [] seasonBox = new Checkbox[seasonLabel.length];
    private int [] seasonCount = new int[seasonLabel.length];
    private Label [] countLabel = new Label [seasonLabel.length];
    private Panel seasonPanel = new Panel();
    private Panel countPanel = new Panel();

    //Put the init()   method Here
    //Put the itemStateChanged() method Here
}
```

Figure 25.4 The *CheckSeason* Class Definition

The *CheckSeason* class uses several arrays. A constant string array, *seasonLabel*, contains the checkbox labels. The size of this array determines the sizes of the remaining three arrays: *seasonBox*, *countLabel*, and *seasonCount*. We use the latter two arrays to create the tally sheet for the results.

The *CheckSeason* class definition also contains two panels: *seasonPanel* and *countPanel*. The *seasonPanel* holds the checkboxes; the *countPanel* holds the count labels.

The init() Method

The **init()** method has a large task list, but most of the tasks involve things that we've already learned. The first task is the establishment of the layout manager. We use a border layout that places the tally sheet panel in the center position and the checkbox panel in the south position. We set the background for the checkbox panel to yellow to make the checkboxes stand out.

After we've specified the layout manager, we create the checkboxes and the tally labels, and we add them to the appropriate panels. A **for** statement accomplishes these tasks, as is illustrated in Figure 25.5.

```
for (i = 0; i < seasonLabel.length; i++)
{// create new checkboxes and labels for the counts
    seasonBox[i] = new Checkbox(seasonLabel[i]);
    seasonBox[i].addItemListener(this);
    seasonPanel.add(seasonBox[i]);
    seasonCount[i] = 0;
    countLabel[i] =
    new Label(seasonLabel[i] + ":                " + seasonCount[i]);
    countPanel.add(countLabel[i]);
}
```

Figure 25.5 Creating the Checkboxes and Tally Labels

The body of the **for** statement in Figure 25.5 begins with the creation of the checkboxes. Next, an item listener is added to each checkbox, and the checkbox is placed in the season panel. We also initialize each of the season counts to zero. Finally, we create the season labels that will hold the tallies, and we add these labels to the count panel. Notice the constructor for the season label:

```
new Label(seasonLabel[i] + ":                    " + seasonCount[i])
```

We append a string containing several spaces to the season label. We do this to force the layout manager to leave enough space to store the counts. Although the *Component* class has a **setSize()** method, which theoretically sets the size of the components, the layout manager can, and usually does, ignore any **setSize()** method calls that are contained in an applet.

Figure 25.6 contains the definition of the **init()** method. Notice the constructor for the *Season Counts* label that appears in the north region. We use a prefix of several spaces to move this label toward the middle of the applet.

```
public void init()
{ /* Border layout is used. We put the check boxes in the SOUTH
    and the counts in the CENTER. The Season header is in the NORTH.*/
  int i;
  setLayout(new BorderLayout());
  seasonPanel.setBackground(Color.yellow);
  seasonPanel.add(new Label("Seasons"));
  for (i = 0; i <seasonLabel.length; i++)
  {// create new checkboxes and labels for the counts
      seasonBox[i] = new Checkbox(seasonLabel[i]);
      seasonBox[i].addItemListener(this);
      seasonPanel.add(seasonBox[i]);
      seasonCount[i] = 0;
      countLabel[i] =
          new Label(seasonLabel[i] + ":                    " + seasonCount[i]);
      countPanel.add(countLabel[i]);
  }
  add(seasonPanel, BorderLayout.SOUTH);
  add(new
      Label("                    Current Season Counts"),
      BorderLayout.NORTH);
  add(countPanel, BorderLayout.CENTER);
}
```

Figure 25.6 The **init()** Method, *CheckSeason* Class

The itemStateChanged() Method

When a user presses one of the checkboxes, the item listener invokes the **itemStateChanged()** method to handle the event. This method has a single parameter, which is an *ItemEvent* object. Figure 25.7 contains the definition of the **itemStateChanged()** method. The body of the **itemStateChanged()** method contains a **for** statement. An **if** statement within the body of the **for** statement finds the selected checkbox(es) by invoking the **getState()** method. This method returns *true* when a checkbox is selected. We increment the season count for each selected checkbox, then reset that checkbox's state to *false*. The body of the **for** statement also updates the season labels.

```
public void itemStateChanged(ItemEvent e)
{ //find the checked boxes and increment the counts
   int i;
   for (i= 0; i < seasonLabel.length; i++){
     if (seasonBox[i].getState()) {
        seasonCount[i]++;
        seasonBox[i].setState(false); //reset
      }
     countLabel[i].setText(seasonLabel[i] + ": " + seasonCount[i]);
   }
}
```

Figure 25.7 The **itemStateChanged()** Method, *CheckSeason* Class

The *CheckboxGroup* Class

In addition to checkboxes, AWT contains a *CheckboxGroup* class. A *CheckboxGroup* object looks and acts exactly like a set of HTML radio buttons as Figure 25.8 clearly indicates. This figure contains the *Favorite Foods* page that we're about to create.

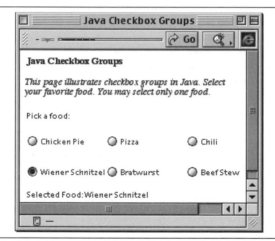

Figure 25.8 The *Favorite Foods* Page

The HTML tag creates a 300 × 120 rectangle for the applet. The tag is

```
<APPLET CODE = "CheckFood.class" WIDTH = "300" HEIGHT = "120">
</APPLET>
```

The *CheckboxGroup* Constructors and Methods

All of the *Checkbox* constructors and methods apply to *CheckboxGroup* objects. However, creating and processing *CheckboxGroup* objects requires additional constructors and methods. Figure 25.9 lists the new constructors and methods for *CheckboxGroup* objects.

As Figure 25.9 indicates, checkbox groups require two sets of constructors. The **CheckboxGroup()** constructor creates a new checkbox group. Because the constituent components in a checkbox group are checkboxes, we must also use the *Checkbox* constructor to create these boxes. We can create the checkboxes with the constructors appearing in Figure 25.3. If we do this, we must use the **setCheckboxGroup()** method to attach the checkbox to a group. Usually, it's easier to create the con-

Method	Description
CheckboxGroup();	**Constructor**
Checkbox (String *s*, boolean *state*, CheckboxGroup *cg*);	Construct check box as part of a check box group.
Checkbox(String *s*, CheckboxGroup *cg*, boolean *state*);	Construct check box as part of a check box group.
CheckboxGroup getCheckboxGroup();	Return the check box group.
void setCheckboxGroup(CheckboxGroup *cg*);	Set the check box group.
void setSelectedCheckbox(Checkbox *c*);	Set a checkbox in the group. This deselects a previously selected box.
Checkbox getSelectedCheckbox();	Return the selected check box.

Figure 25.9 The *CheckboxGroup* Methods

stituent checkboxes with either of the constructors listed in Figure 25.9. Both constructors require three parameters: a string containing the checkbox's label, the state of the checkbox, and the group to which the checkbox belongs. The two constructors differ only in the order of the parameters.

The *CheckboxGroup* class also contains methods that preselect one of the boxes in the group (**setSelectedCheckbox()**) or determine which box the user selected (**getSelectedCheckbox()**).

The *CheckFood* Class Definition

Let's examine the definition of the *CheckFood* class that implements the *Favorite Food* page. The definition appears in Figure 25.10. The statements that create the checkbox group and the array of checkboxes are highlighted. The *CheckFood* class definition contains an array of foods, *foodLabel*, that furnishes the labels for the checkboxes. The size of this array sets the size of the checkbox array. We create a panel, *foodPanel*, to hold the checkboxes. We also create a label to hold the name of the selected food. Notice the statement that creates this label:

```
private Label messageLabel =
    new Label("Selected Food: Wiener Schnitzel ");
```

```
import java.awt.*;
import java.awt.event.*;
import java.applet.*;

public class CheckFood extends Applet  implements ItemListener
{
   //Labels for the food boxes
    private static final String [] foodLabel = {"Chicken Pie", "Pizza", "Chili", "Wiener
Schnitzel", "Bratwurst", "Beef Stew"};

    private CheckboxGroup foodGroups = new CheckboxGroup();
    private Checkbox [] foodBox = new Checkbox[foodLabel.length];

    private Panel foodPanel = new Panel();
    private Label messageLabel =
            new Label("Selected Food: Wiener Schnitzel ");
    //Put the init() method here
    //Put the itemStateChanged() method here
}
```

Figure 25.10 The *CheckFood* Class Definition

We're sure that *everyone* loves Wiener Schnitzel, so we're going to preselect this box when we create the checkboxes.

The init() Method

Now let's examine the **init()** method for the *CheckFoods* class. Figure 25.11 contains the definition of this method.

```
public void init()
{ /* The food panel containing the checkbox group is placed in the
    CENTER. The food panel uses a grid of 2 rows and 3 columns.
    The selected food is displayed in the SOUTH region */
  int i;
  setLayout(new BorderLayout());
  foodPanel.setLayout(new GridLayout(2, 3));

  /*create the new checkboxes. Check the Wiener Schnitzel box */
  for (i = 0; i < foodLabel.length; i++){
      if (foodLabel[i].equals("Wiener Schnitzel"))
          foodBox[i] = new Checkbox(foodLabel[i], foodGroups, true);
      else
          foodBox[i] = new Checkbox(foodLabel[i], foodGroups, false);
      foodBox[i].addItemListener(this);
      foodPanel.add(foodBox[i]);
  }
  add(new Label("Pick a food: "), BorderLayout.NORTH);
  add(foodPanel, BorderLayout.CENTER);
  add(messageLabel, BorderLayout.SOUTH);
}
```

Figure 25.11 The **init()** Method, *CheckFood* Class

We begin the **init()** method by creating the layout managers. We use a border layout for the applet. The north region contains the *Pick a food* label. The center region contains the panel holding the checkbox group. This panel uses a 2 × 3 grid layout to place the six food boxes. The south region contains the label displaying the user's favorite food.

The **init()** method contains a **for** statement that constructs the individual checkboxes. Notice the **if...else** statement:

```
if (foodLabel[i].equals("Wiener Schnitzel"))
    foodBox[i] = new Checkbox(foodLabel[i], foodGroups, true);
else
    foodBox[i] = new Checkbox(foodLabel[i], foodGroups, false);
```

The expression uses the *String* **equals()** method to compare the current food label with *Wiener Schnitzel*. If they match, the check box is preselected. (Appendix E contains a definition of the **equals()** method.)

The itemStateChanged() Method

When the user presses one of the food buttons, the item listener invokes the **itemStateChanged()** method to handle this event. The code for this method is very simple. We use the **getSelectedCheckbox()** method to find the selected checkbox. Next, we use the **getLabel()** method to obtain the checkbox's label. We concatenate *Food Selected* and the label to form the text for the *message* label. Figure 25.12 contains the definition of the **itemStateChanged()** method.

```
public void itemStateChanged(ItemEvent e)
{ //find the checked box and change the message label
    Checkbox picked = foodGroups.getSelectedCheckbox();
    String pickedName = picked.getLabel();
    messageLabel.setText("Food Selected: " + pickedName);
}
```

Figure 25.12 The **itemStateChanged()** Method, *CheckFood* Class

CHOICE AND LIST CLASSES

In the next two sections, we cover Java classes that are equivalent to HTML select lists. Figure 25.13 illustrates these two classes. We can use either the *Choice* or the *List* class to implement single-select lists. Recall that a single-select list provides an alternative to radio buttons when we have a long list of options. The user must select only one option from the list.

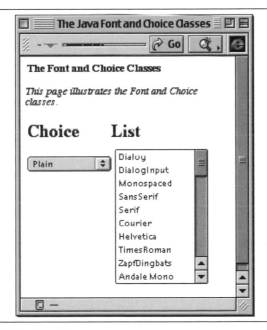

Figure 25.13 The *Font* and *Choice* Classes

As Figure 25.13 indicates, the *Choice* object displays a single option. The displayed option is the first option in the list, if the user hasn't selected an option, or the option selected by the user. In contrast, the *List* object displays all of the options in the list. Scrollbars are automatically added if the applet's height will not accommodate the complete list.

The *List* class also implements multiple-select lists. Recall that a multiple-select list provides an alternative to checkboxes when we have long lists of options. The user may select none, one, several, or all of the options in the list.

The *Choice* and *List* classes share many methods. It's easier to process a *Choice* object, so we will begin with that.

The *Choice* Class

Figure 25.14 contains a small *English–German* phrase book. When the user selects an English phrase, we display a German counterpart in the label at the bottom of the page.

The HTML tag creates a 280 × 100 rectangle for the applet. The tag is

```
<APPLET CODE = "GermanPhrases.class" WIDTH = "280" HEIGHT = "100">
</APPLET>
```

Figure 25.14 The *German Phrases* Page

The *GermanPhrases* Class Definition

Creating the *GermanPhrases* class definition begins with the header. Because *Choice* objects use an item listener like their *CheckboxGroup* counterparts, the header is

```
public class GermanPhrases extends Applet implements  ItemListener
```

We implement the English phrases and their German counterparts as arrays of strings. The German phrases present a slight complication: they contain umlauts. We handle this problem by using the appropriate Unicode characters. Figure 25.15 contains the definition of the *GermanPhrases* class.

As this figure indicates, the *GermanPhrases* class definition contains a new *Choice* object created with the statement

```
private Choice phraseChoice = new Choice();
```

We also create a panel, *phrasePanel*, that will hold the prompt and the choice object.

The *Choice* and *List* Methods

The *Choice* and *List* classes share many methods. These methods add items to or remove items from a list or determine which option(s) a user selected. We'll need to use several of these methods to implement the **init()** and **itemStateChanged()** methods. Figure 25.16 contains the *Choice* and *List* methods. We can use the **insert()** method only with the *Choice* class. The remaining methods work with either class.

```
import java.awt.*;
import java.awt.event.*;
import java.applet.*;

public class GermanPhrases extends Applet implements ItemListener
{
 private static final String [] englishPhrase = {"Good Day. (German)",
 "Good Day (Bavarian, Austrian)",
  "It is a beautiful day!",
  "Where is the subway?",
  "Do you like vanilla ice cream?"};

 private static final String [] germanPhrase = {"Guten Tag.",
 "Gr\u00FC\u00DF Gott.",
 "Es ist ein sch\u00F6ner Tag heute.",
 "Wo ist die U-Bahn?",
 "M\u00F6gen Sie Vanille-Eis?"};
 private Label phrasePrompt = new Label("English Phrase");
 private Choice phraseChoice = new Choice();
 private Panel phrasePanel = new Panel();
 private Label germanAnswer = new Label();
//Put the init() method here
//Put the itemStateChanged() method here
}
```

Figure 25.15 The *GermanPhrases* Class Definition

Method	Description
void add(String s);	Add an item.
void addItemListener(ItemListener il);	Add an item listener.
String getItem(int index);	Return the item at the *index* position.
int getSelectedIndex();	Return index of the selected item.
String getSelectedItem();	Return name of the selected item.
int getItemCount();	Return the number of items in the choice list.
Object [] getSelectedObjects();	Return the selected item. Use position [0]
void insert(String s, int index);	Insert an item at the *index* position.
void select(String s | int index);	Select an item. Use either the name or the index.
void remove(String s | int index);	Remove an item. Use either the name or the index.
void removeAll();	Remove all items.

Figure 25.16 The *Choice* and *List* Class Methods

Let's briefly examine the methods contained in Figure 25.16. We can group these methods into four categories:

Category 1. The add Methods. The **add()** method adds an item to a *Choice* or *List* object. The items are added in sequential order. The first item resides in the 0th position, the second item resides in the 1st position, and so on. All items are represented as strings. The **insert()** method of the *Choice* class puts an item into the position specified by *index*. The items with positions greater than or equal to *index* are shifted one position to the right.

The *Choice* and *List* classes include an **addItemListener()** method that activates the event handler. This method invokes the **itemStateChanged()** method to process the event.

Category 2. The remove Methods. The **removeAll()** method removes all of the items in a *Choice* or *List* object. This method is typically used to create dynamic lists whose contents change as the applet runs. The **remove()** method lets us remove a specific item from a *Choice* or *List* object. We can specify the item by name or position. The items to the right of the removed item are shifted to the left by one. For example, if we remove the 4th item in a list, the 5th item is moved into the 4th position, and so on.

Category 3. The get Methods. The *get* methods determine which item(s) a user selected. The **getSelectedItem()** returns the string representing the selected item; the **getSelectedIndex()** method returns the position of the selected item. The **getSelectedObjects()** method serves a dual purpose. For a *Choice* or a single-select *List*, the 0th position of the returned array contains the selected item. For a multiple-select list, an array of selected items is returned. In either case, the items are identified by their strings.

Category 4. Other Methods. The *Choice* and *List* classes also include methods that return an item in a specific position (**getItem()**) or return the number of items in the list (**getItemCount()**).

The init() Method

We're now ready to tackle the **init()** method. We begin by adding the items to the *Choice* object. We use a **for** statement and the **add()** method to add each string in the *englishPhrase* array to the *phraseChoice* object. The code is

```
for (i = 0; i < englishPhrase.length; i++)
        phraseChoice.add(englishPhrase[i]);
```

After we add the items, we add an item listener to *phraseChoice*. The code that accomplishes this is

```
phraseChoice.addItemListener(this);
```

The remaining tasks are simple. We create a 2×1 grid layout for the *phrase* panel. We place *phrasePrompt* and *phraseChoice* in the panel. We create a border layout for the applet. We put the *phrase* panel in the north and the *germanSentence* label in the south. Figure 25.17 contains the definition of **init()** method.

```
public void init()
{//initialize the English phrase list
  int i;
    for (i = 0; i < englishPhrase.length; i++)
      phraseChoice.add(englishPhrase[i]);
    phraseChoice.addItemListener(this);
    phrasePanel.setLayout(new GridLayout(2,1));
    phrasePanel.add(phrasePrompt);
    phrasePanel.add(phraseChoice);
    setLayout(new BorderLayout());
    add(phrasePanel, BorderLayout.NORTH);
    add(germanAnswer, BorderLayout.CENTER);
}
```

Figure 25.17 The **init()** Method, *GermanPhrases* Class

The `itemStateChanged()` Method

The **`itemStateChanged()`** method calls the **`getSelectedIndex()`** method to find the index of the selected English phrase. We paired the English and German strings when we created their respective arrays, so we can use the English string as an index to find the corresponding German string. We create a new string by concatenating *Deutsch*: and the German string. This string is placed in the *germanAnswer* label. Figure 25.18 contains the definition of the **`itemStateChanged()`** method.

```
public void itemStateChanged(ItemEvent e)
{//Get the index of the selected English Phrase
 // Find the corresponding German Phrase
  int selectedIndex = phraseChoice.getSelectedIndex();
  String germanString = "Deutsch: " + germanPhrase[selectedIndex];
  germanAnswer.setText(germanString);
}
```

Figure 25.18 The **`itemStateChanged()`** Method, *GermanPhrases* Class

The *List* Class

As our first example of the *List* class, we rewrite the *German Phrase* page, using a list to implement the English phrases. This lets us compare the appearance, creation, and processing of these two classes. Figure 25.19 contains the *German List* page. As this figure indicates, the list displays the first four English phrases. The selected phrase is highlighted by the browser. A German counterpart appears after the list.

Figure 25.19 The *German List* Page

The *List* Constructors

The *Choice* class has but a single constructor; the *List* class contains the three constructors displayed in Figure 25.20.

Constructor	Meaning
List();	Create a list with 4 rows visible (default) and a single select list (default).
List(int *visible*);	Create a list with *visible* rows displayed.
List (int *visible*, boolean *multiple*);	Create a list with *visible* rows displayed. Set *multiple* to *true* for a multiple selection list. Otherwise, use *false*.

Figure 25.20 The *List* Constructors

The first constructor, **List()**, creates a single-select list that displays four list items in Internet Explorer and the complete list in Netscape Navigator. The second constructor, **List(int)**, changes the number of displayed items. For example, the statement

```
List phraseList = new List(2);
```

creates a new *List*, *phraseList*, which displays the first two items in the list, if the user has *not* selected an item, or the selected item and the item below or above it, if the user *has* selected an item.

The last constructor, **List(int,boolean)**, creates multiple-select lists. For example, the statement

```
List phraseList = new List(2,true);
```

creates a new *List*, which displays two list items. Passing *true* as the second parameter creates the multiple-select list.

The *GermanList* Class Definition

We're now ready to create the *GermanList* class definition. You should be able to create the header and the class fields by examining the *GermanPhrase* class definition appearing in Figure 25.15. The changes for the list version are trivial. Try to write the new class definition. Don't worry about creating the **init()** or **itemStateChanged()** methods; we will examine these methods shortly.

When we implement the *German Phrase* page as a list, we change the class name in the header. The new class header is

```
public class GermanList extends Applet implements  ItemListener
```

We also replace the statement that creates the *Choice* object, *phraseChoice*, with a statement that creates the *List* object. The new statement is

```
private List phraseList = new List();
```

No other changes are required in the definition of the class fields.

The init() Method

The **init()** method used in the *GermanList* class is virtually identical to the method used in the *GermanPhrase* class. In fact, the only change is the replacement of the *phraseChoice* object with the *phraseList* object. Figure 25.21 contains the definition of the **init()** method. The changes are highlighted.

```
public void init()
{//initialize the English phrase list
  int i;
  for (i = 0; i < englishPhrase.length; i++)
    phraseList.add(englishPhrase[i]);
  phraseList.addItemListener(this);
  phrasePanel.setLayout(new GridLayout(2,1));
  phrasePanel.add(phrasePrompt);
  phrasePanel.add(phraseList);
  setLayout(new BorderLayout());
  add(phrasePanel, BorderLayout.NORTH);
  add(germanAnswer, BorderLayout.CENTER);
}
```

Figure 25.21 The **init()** Method, *GermanList* Class

The itemStateChanged() Method

Implementation of the **itemStateChanged()** method involves one minor modification of the method used in the *GermanPhrase* class. The new method appears in Figure 25.22. The change is highlighted.

```
public void itemStateChanged(ItemEvent e)
{//Get the index of the selected English Phrase
 // Find the corresponding German Phrase
  int selectedIndex = phraseList.getSelectedIndex();
  String germanString = "Deutsch: " + germanPhrase[selectedIndex];
  germanAnswer.setText(germanString);
}
```

Figure 25.22 The **itemStateChanged()** Method, *GermanList* Class

Now that we've implemented the *German Phrase* page by using *List* and *Choice* classes, it should be obvious that the two classes differ only in appearance and constructors. Both classes use the same **init()** and **itemStateChanged()** methods. When implementing a single-select list, we can use either a *List* or a *Choice* object. Pick the one that appeals to you.

The *Programming Language* Page

We've discussed two different techniques for implementing single-select lists in Java. In our next example, we use the *List* class to implement both single- and multiple-select lists of programming languages. The multiple-select list queries the user about their knowledge of programming languages. The single-select list asks the user to pick a favorite language. We assume that all users know HTML. We also assume that a user must be able to program in their favorite language. Therefore, the single-select list contains only the languages selected from the multiple-select list. This means that the list of favorite languages grows and shrinks as the user selects or deselects languages from the multiple-select list.

Figure 25.23 shows the *Programming Language* page as it appears when it is first loaded into the browser. We have preselected the HTML item from the *Knowledge* list. This is the only item that appears in the *Favorite* list. A text area displays the user's choices. This area is initially empty.

Figure 25.23 The *Programming Language* Page, before selections

Figure 25.24 shows the *Programming Language* page after the user has made selections. In this example, the user indicated ability to program in *HTML*, *JavaScript*, *Perl*, and *Java*. Only these languages appear in the *Favorite* list. The user has also chosen *Java* as the favorite language. The languages selected from the *Knowledge* and *Favorites* list appear in the text area.

Figure 25.24 The *Programming Language* Page, after selections

The HTML tag creates a 330 × 220 rectangle for the applet. The tag is

```
<APPLET CODE = "Programming.class" WIDTH = "330" HEIGHT = "220">
</APPLET>
```

The *Programming Class* Definition

Figure 25.25 contains the definition of the *Programming* class that implements the *Programming Language* page. The definition contains several arrays. We use the *language* array to create the *Knowledge* list. The remaining arrays create the panels, labels, and lists. Components related to the *Knowledge* list always reside in the 0th array position; components related to the *Favorite* list reside in the 1st position. Using arrays lets us remove redundant code and, thereby, reduce the code required to create this page by about one-half. The text area is unique, so we create it and its label and panel separately.

```
import java.awt.*;
import java.awt.event.*;
import java.applet.*;

public class Programming extends Applet implements  ItemListener
{
    private static final String [] language = {"Ada", "C", "C++", "ForTran", "HTML", "Lisp",
    "JavaScript", "Java", "ML", "Pascal", "Perl", "Prolog","Scheme",  "SQL", "tcl"};
    private String [] header = {"Knowledge", "Favorite"};
    private Label [] listLabel = new Label[header.length];
    private List [] languageList =new List[header.length];
    private Panel [] languagePanel = new Panel[header.length];
    private TextArea  outputArea = new TextArea(10,20);
    private Panel outputPanel = new Panel();
 //Put the init() method here
 //Put the itemStateChanged() method here
}
```

Figure 25.25 The *Programming* Class Definition

The *Programming Language* page uses a multiple-border layout. The easiest way to explain the layout, as well as the arrays appearing in the class definition, is by means of a picture. Figure 25.26 contains the layout diagram for the *Programming Language* page.

As Figure 25.26 indicates, the applet uses a border layout. The *Knowledge* panel resides in the west region, the *Favorite* panel in the center region, and the *User's Choice* panel in the east region. Each of the three panels also uses a border layout. The panel's label resides in the north region of its panel. The *Knowledge* and *Favorite* lists reside in the center regions of the **languagePanel[0]** and **languagePanel[1]** panels, respectively. The text area, *outputArea*, resides in the center region of the *outputPanel*.

The init() Method

The **init()** method handles the creation of the lists and the placement of the components into the applet. The language lists are created with the following statements:

```
languageList[0] = new List(0, true);  //multiple -- knowledge
languageList[1] =  new List();         //single -- favorite
```

The first statement creates the multiple-select list. When we set the first parameter to zero, we force the browser to display the default number of rows. When we set the second parameter to *true*, we create a multiple-select list. The second statement creates the *Favorite* list.

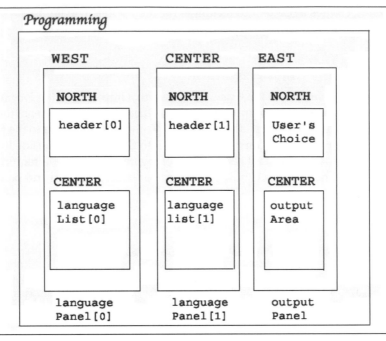

Figure 25.26 The Layout Diagram: *Programming* Class

After creating the two lists, we use a **for** statement to fill the *Knowledge* array. The code for the **for** statement follows (with the list method calls highlighted):

```
for (i = 0; i < language.length; i++){
//add the items to the list
    languageList[0].add(language[i]);
    if (language[i].equals("HTML")) {
       languageList[0].select(i);
       languageList[1].add(language[i]);
     }
  }
```

A second **for** statement adds an item listener to each list. The **for** statement also creates the list panels and list labels and adds the labels and lists to the panels. The **for** statement that accomplishes this is

```
for(i= 0;i < header.length; i++)
{//create the two sets of labels, lists, and text area
    languageList[i].addItemListener(this);
    languagePanel[i] = new Panel(new BorderLayout());
    languagePanel[i].add(new Label(header[i]), BorderLayout.NORTH);
    languagePanel[i].add(languageList[i], BorderLayout.CENTER);
}
```

To complete the **init()** method, we add the panels to the applet. We also add the label and text area to the output panel, and we add this panel to the applet. Figure 25.27 contains the definition of the **init()** method.

```
public void init()
{//initialize the language list
   int i;
   languageList[0] = new List(0, true);  //multiple -- knowledge
   languageList[1] =  new List();         //single --favorite
   for (i = 0; i < language.length; i++){
   //add the items to the list
      languageList[0].add(language[i]);
      if (language[i].equals("HTML")) {
         languageList[0].select(i);
         languageList[1].add(language[i]);
      }
   }
   setBackground(Color.white);
   setLayout(new BorderLayout());
   for(i= 0;i < header.length; i++)
   {//create the two sets of labels, lists, and text area
      languageList[i].addItemListener(this);
      languagePanel[i] = new Panel(new BorderLayout());
      languagePanel[i].add(new Label(header[i]), BorderLayout.NORTH);
      languagePanel[i].add(languageList[i], BorderLayout.CENTER);
   }
   add(languagePanel[0], BorderLayout.WEST);
   add(languagePanel[1], BorderLayout.CENTER);
   outputPanel.setLayout(new BorderLayout());
   outputPanel.add(new Label("User's Choices"), BorderLayout.NORTH);
   outputPanel.add(outputArea, BorderLayout.CENTER);
   add(outputPanel, BorderLayout.EAST);
}
```

Figure 25.27 The `init()` Method, *Programming* Class

Methods Unique to the *List* Class

Although the *List* and *Choice* classes share many methods, the *List* class contains additional methods that are unique to it. Figure 25.28 contains these methods.

Methods	Description
`int [] getSelectedIndexes();`	Return the indexes of selected items.
`String [] getSelectedItems();`	Return the names of selected items.
`int getRows();`	Return the number of visible rows.
`boolean isItemSelected(int index);`	Return *true* if the item at *index* is selected. Return *false* otherwise.
`boolean isMultipleMode();`	Return *true* for a multiple selection list. Return *false* otherwise.
`void replaceItem(String s, int index);`	Replace the item at *index* with *s*.
`void setMultipleMode(boolean state);`	Use *true* for multiple selection. Use *false* otherwise.
`void deselect(int index);`	Deselect the item at *index*.

Figure 25.28 Methods Unique to the *List* Class

Several of the methods listed in Figure 25.28 return information needed for multiple-select lists. The **getSelectedIndexes()** and **getSelectedItems()** methods return an array of the items selected from a multiple select list. The **getSelectedIndexes()** method returns an array of positions; the **getSelectedItems()** method returns an array of names. The **setMultipleMode()** and **isMultipleMode()** methods change the list's selection mode and determine whether the list is a multiple-select list, respectively. The remaining methods replace items (**replaceItem()**), deselect them (**deselect()**), and determine whether a particular item has been selected (**isItemSelected()**).

The itemStateChanged() Method

The item listener invokes the **itemStateChanged()** method when the user selects an item from either the *Programming* list or the *Favorite* list. This method obtains the selected items for the *Programming* list and the selected item from the *Favorite* list. We use the **getSelectedItems()** method to obtain the names of the items selected in the *Knowledge* list. The statement is

```
String [] selectAll = languageList[0].getSelectedItems();
```

This statement creates a string array, *selectAll*, that contains the names of the selected items. If the user has deselected all of the languages in the *Knowledge* list, *selectAll* will have a length of zero.

The **getSelectedItem()** method obtains the name of the item selected in the *Favorite* list. The statement is

```
String selectOne = languageList[1].getSelectedItem();
```

If the user has not yet selected a favorite language, this method returns a *null* string.

We also create a string, *outputText*, that contains the languages selected from each list. This string is placed into the text area. This string is initially set to the *null* string.

Once we've obtained the items selected from the lists, we use an **if** statement to construct the *Favorite* list from the selected items in the *Knowledge* list. We also add the selected languages to *outputText*. The **if** statement is:

```
if (selectAll.length > 0)
{//User has selected from the Knowledge list
   outputText = "Language Knowledge\n\n";
   languageList[1].removeAll();
   for (i = 0; i < selectAll.length; i++)
   {//Add to output area and the favorite list
      languageList[1].add(selectAll[i]);
      outputText = outputText + selectAll[i] + "\n";
   }
   outputText = outputText + "Total Languages: " +
               selectAll.length +"\n\n";
}
```

The expression in the **if** statement ensures that the *Knowledge* list contains at least one selected item. If this is the case, we place a label in the *outputText* string. We also remove all of the items from the *Favorite* list. We use a **for** statement to reconstruct the *Favorite* list, using only the items selected from the knowledge list. The **for** statement also adds the name of the selected item to the *outputText* string. When the **for** statement terminates, we add the count of the selected languages to *outputText*.

The **itemStateChanged()** method contains a second **if** statement:

```
if (selectOne != null)
   outputText = outputText + "Favorite Language:\n" + selectOne;
```

This statement adds the user's favorite language to the *outputText* string if the user has selected a favorite language. The last statement in the `itemStateChanged()` method uses the `setText()` method to put *outputText* into the text area.

Figure 25.29 contains the definition of the `itemStateChanged()` method. Notice the calls to the `invalidate()` and `validate()` methods. These calls ensure that the *Favorite* list is updated.

```
public void itemStateChanged(ItemEvent e)
{//record information about the event
  int i;
  String [] selectAll = languageList[0].getSelectedItems();
  String selectOne = languageList[1].getSelectedItem();
  String outputText= "";
  if (selectAll.length > 0)
  {//User has selected from the Knowledge list
    outputText = "Language Knowledge\n\n";
    languageList[1].removeAll();
    for (i = 0; i < selectAll.length; i++)
    {//Add to output area and the favorite list
      languageList[1].add(selectAll[i]);
      outputText = outputText + selectAll[i] + "\n";
    }
    outputText = outputText + "Total Languages: " +
      selectAll.length +"\n\n";
  }
  if (selectOne != null)
    outputText = outputText + "Favorite Language:\n" + selectOne;
  outputArea.setText(outputText);
  invalidate();
  validate();
}
```

Figure 25.29 The `itemStateChanged()` Method, *Programming* Class

SCROLL BARS

As our last example of AWT form-related classes, we examine scroll bars. Of course, we've seen many examples of scroll bars in our Web pages; the browser automatically adds them when a page does not fit into the browser's boundaries. We use these scroll bars to move around the page. When scroll bars are used to control movement, Java calls them *Scroll Panes*. We examine this type of scroll bar in Chapter 28.

Java also provides a second type of scroll bar, one that offers an alternative to *Choice* or single-select lists when the items are positive integers. Java uses the *Scrollbar* class to implement this second type of scroll bar.

Scroll-Bar Basics

The *Scrollbar* class contains three constructors that we use to create new *Scrollbar* objects. Figure 25.30 contains these constructors.

```
Scrollbar();
Scrollbar(int ORIENTATION);
Scrollbar(int ORIENTATION, int value, int visible, int min, int max);
```

Figure 25.30 The *Scrollbar* Class Constructors

The first *Scrollbar* constructor creates a *Scrollbar* object having the default parameters. These defaults create a vertical scroll bar with a range of 0 to 100. The size of the slider is set to 10, and the slider is aligned with the minimum value.

The second *Scrollbar* constructor uses all of the default parameters except *orientation*. We pass an *orientation* constant to change the scroll bar's alignment. The orientation constants are **Scrollbar.HORIZONTAL** and **Scrollbar.VERTICAL**.

The last constructor changes all of the scroll-bar parameters. The *orientation* parameter determines the scroll bar's alignment. The *min* and *max* parameters determine the scroll bar's range. The *value* parameter determines the initial location of the slider, and the *visible* parameter determines the size of the slider. The three scroll bars appearing in Figure 25.31 illustrate the scroll-bar parameters.

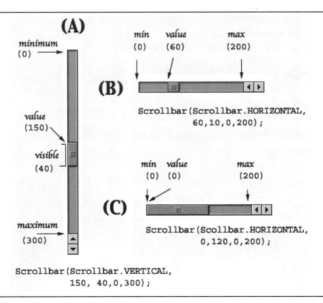

Figure 25.31 Scroll-Bar Basics

Scroll bar (A) is a vertical scroll bar. This scroll bar has a range of from 0 to 300. The *value* parameter (150) places the slider in the middle of the scroll bar; *visible* is set to 40, so that we have a long slider.

Scroll bars (B) and (C) are horizontal scroll bars with a range of from 0 to 200. Scroll bar (B) uses a slider of 10 pixels that is located at the 60th position. The slider for scroll bar (C) is located at the minimum position. Scroll bar (C) has a very wide slider. In fact, at 120 pixels, the slider occupies more than half of the scroll bar.

The *Scroll-Bar* Methods

In addition to the constructors, the *Scrollbar* class contains methods that change each of the scroll bar parameters individually or as a group. Figure 25.32 contains the most frequently used scroll-bar methods.

Method	Description
void addAdjustmentListener (AdjustementListenter al);	Add an adjustment listener.
int getMaximum();	Return the maximum value.
int getMinimum();	Return the minimum value.
int getOrientation();	Return the *ORIENTATION*.
int getValue();	Return the slider's position.
int getVisibleAmount();	Return the size of the slider.
void setMinimum(int *min*);	Change the minimum value to *min*.
void setMaximum(int *max*);	Change the maximum value to *max*.
void setOrientation(int *ORIENTATION*);	Change the orientation.
void setValue(int *value*);	Change the slider's position.
void setValues(int *value*, int *visible*, int *min*, int *max*);	Change all of scroll bar parameters except *ORIENTATION*.
void setVisibleAmount(int *visible*);	Change the slider's size.

Figure 25.32 Frequently Used Methods of the *Scrollbar* Class

Notice the first method listed in Figure 25.32:

```
void addAdjustmentListener(AdjustmentListenter al);
```

As this method indicates, scroll bars use an adjustment listener. When the user moves the slider, the adjustment listener calls the **adjustmentValueChanged()** method to respond to the event.

The *RGB Scroll-Bar* Page

Now that we've covered the basics, we're ready to create a page that uses scroll bars. Figure 25.33 contains a sample page. This page contains three scroll bars, labeled *Red*, *Green*, and *Blue*. Each scroll bar has a value range of from 0 to 256. The scroll bar's current value appears to the right of the scroll bar. Moving a scroll bar not only changes the scroll bar's value, it also changes the page's background color.

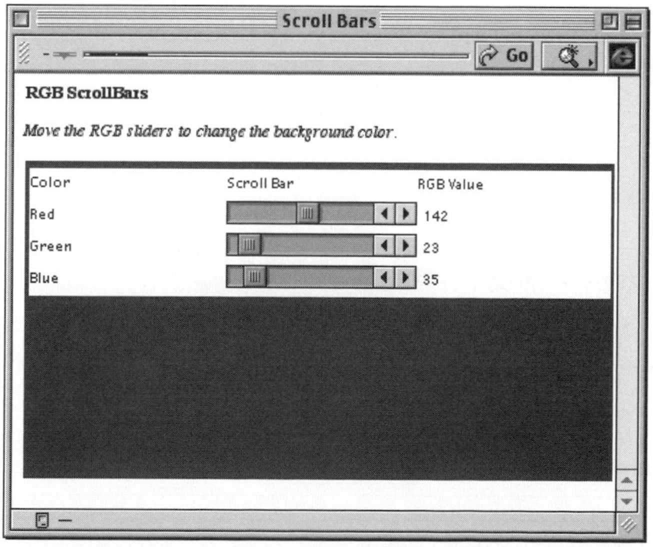

Figure 25.33 The *RGB Scroll-Bar* Page

The HTML tag creates a 410×220 rectangle for the applet. The tag is

```
<APPLET CODE = "RGBScrollbar.class" WIDTH = "410" HEIGHT = "220">
</APPLET>
```

The *RGBScrollBar* Class Definition

The creation of the *RGBScrollBar* class begins with the header. Scroll bars use an adjustment listener, so the header is

```
public class RGBScrollBar extends Applet implements AdjustmentListener
```

The body of the definition contains several arrays, as well as **init()**, **paint()**, and **adjustmentValueChanged()** methods. We use an array, *header*, to create the strings for the column headings. Its declaration is

```
private static final String [] header = {"Color",
"Scroll Bar                                   ",
"RGB Value"};
```

Notice the string that begins with *Scroll Bar* and continues with 45 spaces. Browsers have an obnoxious tendency to shrink scroll bars to the minimum possible size. At their minimum, scroll bars contain only the arrows. Here, the scroll bars are placed in the same column as the *Scroll Bar* label, and so we've forced the browser to extend the scroll bar to the size of the label: the more spaces in the label, the longer the scroll bar.

We use the remaining arrays in the *RGBScrollBar* class definition to create the strings for the scroll bar labels (*color*), the scrollbars (*rgbBar*), the scroll bar values (*rgbValue*), and the RGB color triplet (*RGB*). Figure 25.34 contains the definition of the *RGBScrollBar* class.

```
import java.awt.*;
import java.awt.event.*;
import java.applet.*;

public class RGBScrollBar extends Applet implements AdjustmentListener
{/* Create arrays for the headings, color names, rgb values, and the
    scrollbars. */
    private static final String [] header = {"Color",
    "Scroll Bar                                   ",
    "RGB Value"};
    private static final String [] color = {"Red", "Green", "Blue"};
    private Scrollbar [] rgbBar = new Scrollbar[color.length];
    private Label [] rgbValue = new Label[color.length];
    private int [] RGB = new int[color.length];
    private Color bgColor = new Color(0xFF,0xFF,0xFF); //set to white
    private Panel inputPanel = new Panel();

  //Put the init() Method here
  //Put the paint()  Method here
  // Put the adjustmentValueChanged() Method here
}
```

Figure 25.34 The *RGBScrollBar* Class Definition

The init() Method

The code for the **init()** method create a 4 × 3 grid layout for *inputPanel*. This panel contains both the headers and the scrollbars with their color and value labels. We use a **for** statement to place the headers in the first row of the panel:

```
for (i=0; i< header.length; i++)
    inputPanel.add(new Label(header[i]));
```

A second **for** statement places a color label, a scroll bar, and a value label in each of the remaining rows. An adjustment listener is also added to each scroll bar. The code is

```
for (i = 0; i < color.length; i++)
    {//Create the labels, scrollbars, and integer array
     //Add each to the panel
        RGB[i] = 0;
        inputPanel.add(new Label(color[i]));
        rgbBar[i] = new Scrollbar(Scrollbar.HORIZONTAL, 0, 0, 0, 256);
        rgbBar[i].addAdjustmentListener(this);
        inputPanel.add(rgbBar[i]);
        rgbValue[i] = new Label("     ");
        inputPanel.add(rgbValue[i]);
    }
```

The last statement in the **init()** method adds *inputPanel* to the applet.
Figure 25.35 contains the definition of the **init()** method.

```
public void init()
{ //add the labels and scrollbars in layout
  int i;
  inputPanel.setBackground(Color.white);
  inputPanel.setLayout(new GridLayout(4,3));
  for (i=0; i< header.length; i++)
     inputPanel.add(new Label(header[i]));

  for (i = 0; i < color.length; i++)
  {//Create the labels, scrollbars, and integer array
   //Add each to the panel
     RGB[i] = 0;
     inputPanel.add(new Label(color[i]));
     rgbBar[i] = new Scrollbar(Scrollbar.HORIZONTAL, 0, 0, 0, 256);
     rgbBar[i].addAdjustmentListener(this);
     inputPanel.add(rgbBar[i]);
     rgbValue[i] = new Label("     ");
     inputPanel.add(rgbValue[i]);
  }
  add(inputPanel);
}
```

Figure 25.35 The **init()** Method, *RGBScrollBar* Class

The adjustmentValueChanged() and paint() Method

The **adjustmentValueChanged()** method responds to slider movement. This method has a single parameter, which is an *AdjustmentEvent* object. The header for the **adjustmentValueChanged()** method is:

```
public void adjustmentValueChanged(AdjustmentEvent e)
```

The body of this method contains a **for** statement that obtains the current value of each of the sliders:

```
for (i = 0; i < color.length; i++) {
    RGB[i] = rgbBar[i].getValue();
    rgbValue[i].setText("  " + RGB[i]);
}
```

The *RGB* array holds the slider values, which are arranged in *red-green-blue* order—that is, the 0th subscript holds the *red* value, the 1st subscript holds the *green* value, and the last subscript holds the *blue* value. The *rgbValues* array contains the labels that display the current value for each slider. This array also is arranged in *red, green, and blue* order.

After the **for** statement terminates, we construct a new color by using the *RGB* array:

```
bgColor = new Color(RGB[0], RGB[1], RGB[2]);
```

We end the **adjustmentValueChanged()** method with a call to **repaint()**. The **repaint()** method invokes the **paint()** method, which changes the background color of the page. Figure 25.36 contains the definitions of the **paint()** and **adjustmentValueChanged()** methods.

The **paint()** method sets the background color to *bgColor*, which was created in the **adjustmentValueChanged()** method. The background color of the label panel is set to white.

```
public void paint(Graphics g)
{//change the background color
  setBackground(bgColor);
  labelPanel.setBackground(Color.white);
}
public void adjustmentValueChanged(AdjustmentEvent e)
{ //Scroll bar moved change the background color
  int i;
  //get the scroll bar values and change RGB labels
  for (i = 0; i < color.length; i++) {
    RGB[i] = rgbBar[i].getValue();
    rgbValue[i].setText("  " + RGB[i]);
  }
  //create the new color and change the background
  bgColor = new Color(RGB[0], RGB[1], RGB[2]);
  repaint();
}
```

Figure 25.36 The **paint()** and **adjustmentValueChanged()** Methods, *RGBScrollBar* Class

➤ EXERCISES

1. **The *Favorite Seasons* Page, revisited.** Modify the *Favorite Seasons* page appearing in Figure 25.1. Add a *Done* button to the page. When the user clicks this button, count all of the checked buttons and reset their states to *false*.

2. **The *Font Choice* Page.** Implement the *Font Choice* page displayed in Figure 25.37. Write the user's message in the selected font on the page. The message is stored in a label. Do not use the **paint()** method.

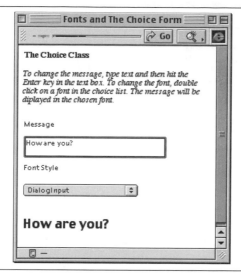

Figure 25.37 The *Font Choice* Page

3. **The *Ice-Cream Float* Page: Java version.** Implement the *Ice-Cream Float* page appearing in Figure 14.19.

4. **The *Favorite Colors* Page.** Create a Java version of the *Favorite Colors* page appearing in Figure 14.29.

5. **The *Fonts* Page.** Create a page that follows the model listed in Figure 25.38. The user may select any of the font options, but only one color. Include a text box for the user's message. After the user has selected the options, print the message, using the font and color information.

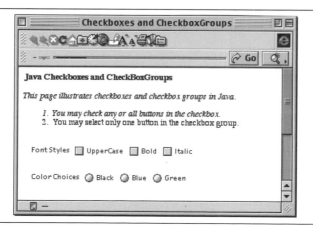

Figure 25.38 The *Fonts* Page

6. **The *Animal* Page.** Implement the *Animal* page appearing in Figure 25.39. The page should display the German name for the selected animal. Use the **drawString()** method to write the English name and its German counterpart.

Figure 25.40 contains the English animal names and their German counterparts.

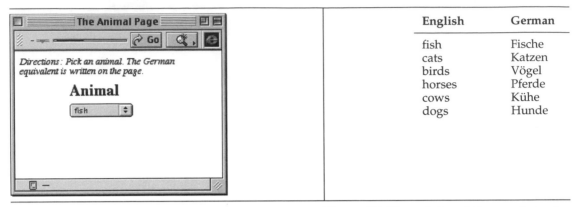

Figure 25.39 The *Animal* Page

Figure 25.40 English and German Animals

English	German
fish	Fische
cats	Katzen
birds	Vögel
horses	Pferde
cows	Kühe
dogs	Hunde

7. **The *Multilanguage Counting* Page, List version.** Implement the *Multilanguage Counting* page displayed in Figure 25.41.

Create a label that identifies the language and writes the number in that language. For example, if the user selects "1" and *Tibetan*, the label should be *English: 1 Tibetan: chik*. Figure 25.42 contains a language summary.

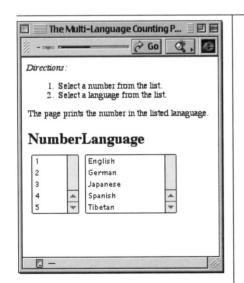

Figure 25.41 The *Multilanguage Counting* Page

Figure 25.42 English, German, Japanese, Spanish, and Tibetan Numbers

Arabic	English	German	Japanese	Spanish	Tibetan
1	one	eins	ichi	uno	chik
2	two	zwei	ni	dos	nyi
3	three	drei	san	tres	sum
4	four	vier	shi	cuatro	shi
5	five	fünf	go	cinco	nga

8. **The *Multilanguage Counting* Page, Choice version.** Implement the *Multilanguage Counting* page by using a *Choice* object.

9. **The *Multilanguage Weekdays* Page.** Implement the *Multilanguage Weekdays* page appearing in Figure 25.43.

The user may select more than one language. Place the English weekday and the equivalents in the selected languages in a text area. Figure 25.44 contains a list of English days and their equivalents in German, Spanish, and Tibetan.

English	German	Spanish	Tibetan
Sunday	Sonntag	domingo	sa nyi ma
Monday	Montag	lunes	sa da wa
Tuesday	Dienstag	martes	sa mik ma
Wednesday	Mittwoch	miércoles	sa lak pa
Thursday	Donnerstag	jueves	sa pu ba
Friday	Freitag	viernes	sa pa sang
Saturday	Samstag	sábado	sa pen ba

Figure 25.43 The *Multilanguage Weekdays* Page

Figure 25.44 English, German, Spanish, and Tibetan Weekdays

10. **The *Shakespearean Quiz*: Java version.** Rewrite the Shakespearean Quiz. (See Figure 14.40.) Report the user's score in a noneditable checkbox.

11. **The *Books* Page.** Create a list of books. Ask the user to indicate which books he or she has read. Construct a second list from the books selected in the first list. Ask the user to pick a favorite book from the second list. (We of course assume that users must have read their favorite books.)

12. **The *Movies* Page.** Repeat the last exercise, but develop a list of movies.

13. **The *Scrollbar Warm-up* Page.** Figure 25.45 contains a simple page that illustrates vertical and horizontal scroll bars. When the user moves a scroll bar, we display the current value. Implement this page.

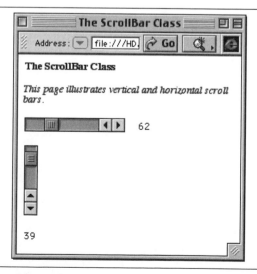

Figure 25.45 The *Scroll-Bar Warm-up* Page

14. **The *Computer Science Quiz.*** Create a Java version of the *Computer Science Quiz* page displayed in Figure 14.51.

15. **The *Survey* Page.** Create an opinion poll containing at least five questions. Give the user a 7-point scale, where 1 is "strongly agree" and 7 is "strongly disagree". Use scroll bars to record the user's opinions.

16. **The *MM Survey* Page.** Create a Java version of the *Muskrat Mounds Survey* page appearing in Figure 14.46.

17. **The *Telling Time in Tibetan* Page.** Create a Java version of the *Telling Time* page. (See Figure 19.31.)

18. **The *Telling Time in Tibetan* Page, Scroll-bar version.** Repeat the previous exercise, but use a scroll bar to obtain the hour.

19. **The *Computer Survey* Page.** Create a Java Version of the *Computer Survey* page appearing in Figure 20.1.

20. **The *Multilanguage Greeting* Page.** Figure 17.42 contains English, Tibetan, and Spanish greetings. Add more "Hello" and "Good bye" greetings, in languages of your choice. Create radio buttons for "Hello" and "Goodbye". Create a list of the languages. The user may select as many languages as desired. Print the English greeting and print the corresponding greetings in the languages selected by the user.

26 Mouse Events and Graphics

INTRODUCTION

In this chapter, we explore the drawing methods available in the *Graphics* class. We're familiar with one of these methods, **drawString()**. The *Graphics* class also contains methods that draw lines, rectangles, ovals, arcs, polygons, and polylines. Most methods come in two flavors: a *draw* method that creates an outline of the desired shape, and a *fill* method that creates a solid version of the shape. We begin with simple pages that illustrate these methods. Once we've learned the basics, we'll add mouse listeners to control the placement of shapes.

LINES

The simplest shape that we can draw in Java is a line. The **drawLine()** method requires four parameters. The parameters specify the starting ($x1$, $y1$) and ending ($x2$, $y2$) coordinates of a line. Figure 26.1 contains a diagram that shows the relation between these parameters.

The syntax for the **drawLine()** method is

```
g.drawLine(int x1, int y1, int x2, int y2);
```

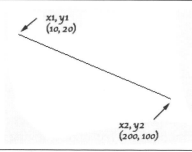

Figure 26.1 Illustration of the **drawLine()** Parameters

As this syntax indicates, we pass the first set of (x, y) coordinates, then the second set of (x, y) coordinates.

Figure 26.2 contains a simple illustration of the **drawLine()** method. Figure 26.2(a) contains the *Line* page; Figure 26.2(b) contains the definition of the *Line* class used to create this page. You might want to change the parameters in the **drawLine()** call and observe the location and size of the new line.

(a) The *Line* Page	**(b) The *Line* Applet**
| 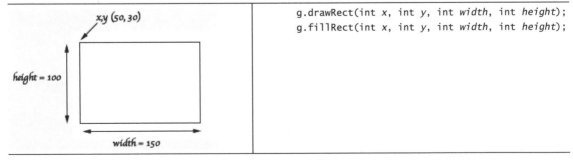 | ```java
import java.awt.*;
import java.awt.event.*;
import java.applet.*;

public class Line extends Applet
{
  public void paint(Graphics g){
    g.drawLine(10,20, 200, 100);
  }
}
``` |

Figure 26.2 The *Line* Page

RECTANGLES

The *Graphics* class provides two methods for drawing rectangles: the **drawRect()** method draws the outline of a rectangle; the **fillRect()** method draws a solid (filled) rectangle. Both methods require four parameters: the (x, y) coordinates for the top left corner of the rectangle, and the *width* and *height* of the rectangle. Figure 26.3 shows the relation between these parameters.

Figure 26.4 contains the syntax for the **drawRect()** and **fillRect()** methods. We pass the (x, y) coordinates, then the width, and then the height of the rectangle.

| *x,y* (50, 30)<br><br>*height* = 100<br><br>*width* = 150 | ```java
g.drawRect(int x, int y, int width, int height);
g.fillRect(int x, int y, int width, int height);
``` |

Figure 26.3 Illustration of the Rectangle Drawing Parameters   **Figure 26.4** The Rectangle Drawing Methods

Figure 26.5 contains an illustration of the rectangle drawing methods. Figure 26.5(a) contains the *Rectangles* page. Figure 26.5(b) contains the definition of the *Rectangles* applet that creates this page. Try modifying the parameters used in the calls, and observe the new rectangles.

(a) The *Rectangles* Page	(b) The *Rectangles* Applet

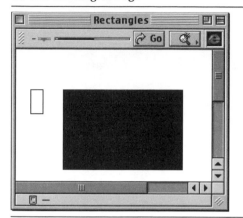	```import java.awt.*;```
	 ```import java.awt.event.*;```
	 ```import java.applet.*;```
	
	 ```public class Rectangles```
	 ```extends Applet {```
	
	 ```public void paint(Graphics g)```
	 ```{```
	 ``` g.drawRect(10,30, 15, 30);```
	 ``` g.fillRect(50,30, 150,100);```
	 ```}```
	 ```}```

Figure 26.5 The *Rectangles* Page

OVALS

The line and rectangle drawing methods are easy to understand, because we can see the relation between the parameters and the object that Java draws. Java's approach to ovals is not as intuitive to lay persons, although Java uses a familiar, albeit primitive, technique from computer graphics. Java creates ovals and arcs by using a *bounding rectangle*. To envision this technique, draw an oval on a piece of paper. Draw a rectangle around the oval so that the rectangle touches the oval. You should have an image resembling the one displayed in Figure 26.6.

Parameter names have been added to the bounding rectangle displayed in Figure 26.6. These names match the names used in the rectangle drawing methods. Thus, to draw an oval, we pass the parameters of its bounding rectangle.

Figure 26.7 contains the syntax for the oval methods. The **drawOval()** method draws the outline of the oval; the **fillOval()** method creates a solid oval.

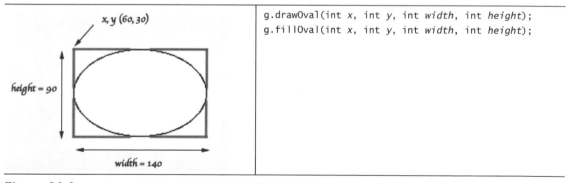

```
g.drawOval(int x, int y, int width, int height);
g.fillOval(int x, int y, int width, int height);
```

Figure 26.6 An Oval with its Bounding Rectangle

Figure 26.7 The Oval Drawing Methods

Figure 26.8 contains a simple illustration of the oval drawing methods. Figure 26.8(a) contains the *Oval* page; Figure 26.8(b) contains the definition of the *Oval* applet that produces this

(a) The *Oval* Page	(b) The *Oval* Applet

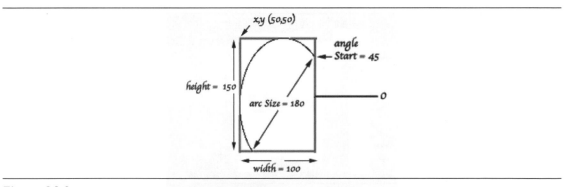

Figure 26.8 at left shows the window titled "Ovals" with an oval outline and a filled black oval.

```
import java.awt.*;
import java.awt.event.*;
import java.applet.*;

public class Oval extends Applet
{
  public void paint(Graphics g) {
     g.drawOval(10,30,  30,50);
     g.fillOval(60,30,  140,90);
  }
}
```

Figure 26.8 The *Oval* Page

page. Try changing the parameters. Observe the new ovals. Draw the bounding rectangles around the ovals. This will help you to visualize Java's drawing method.

ARCS

Java also uses bounding rectangles to draw arcs. To visualize this technique, draw an arc on a piece of paper. Draw lines from the cusp points and from the beginning and end of the arc. You should have a bounding rectangle when you're finished. Your bounding rectangle will have (x, y) coordinates for the top left corner, a width, and a height. We pass the (x, y) coordinates and the width and height of the bounding rectangle as the first four parameters to the arc-drawing methods. The arc methods require two additional parameters: the start of the angle and the size of the arc. Both parameters are measured in degrees. Figure 26.9 contains an illustration of the arc-drawing parameters.

Figure 26.9 An Arc with its Bounding Rectangle

Figure 26.9 contains a line labeled zero that extends from the 3:00 (three o'clock) position of the bounding rectangle. Starting angles have a 360-degree range, which is measured from zero degrees (3:00 position) to 359 degrees. The sign of the arc size determines the direction of the arc:

when the arc size is positive, Java follows a counter-clockwise direction; when the arc size is negative, Java follows a clockwise direction.

Figure 26.10 contains the syntax for the **drawArc()** and **fillArc()** methods. The **drawArc()** method draws the outline of the arc; the **fillArc()** method creates a solid arc.

```
g.drawArc(int x, int y, int width, int height, int startAngle, int arcSize);
g.fillArc(int x, int y, int width, int height, int startAngle, int arcSize);
```

Figure 26.10 The Arc-Drawing Methods

Figure 26.11 contains a simple illustration of the arc-drawing methods. Figure 26.11(a) contains the *Arcs* page; Figure 26.11(b) contains the applet that produces this page.

(a) The *Arcs* Page	(b) The *Arcs* Applet

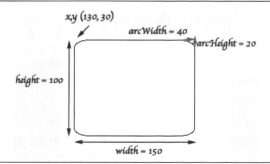	```
	import java.awt.*;
	import java.awt.event.*;
	import java.applet.*;
	
	public class Arcs extends Applet
	{
	  public void paint(Graphics g){
	    g.drawArc(0,30,140,160, 90,45);
	    g.fillArc(80,30, 200,150, 0,180);
	  }
	
	}
	``

Figure 26.11 The *Arcs* Page

ROUNDED RECTANGLES

In addition to the *plain* rectangles displayed in Figure 26.5, Java also provides methods that create rectangles with rounded corners. Creating rounded rectangles begins with the standard rectangle parameters. We add two additional parameters that determine the width and height of the arc used to create the rounded edge. Figure 26.12 contains an illustration of the parameters for drawing rounded rectangle.

Figure 26.12 Illustration of the Rounded-Rectangle Parameters

We use the **drawRoundRect()** method to create the outline of a rounded rectangle. We use the **fillRoundRect()** method to create a solid rounded rectangle. Figure 26.13 contains the syntax for these methods.

```
g.drawRoundRect(int x, int y, int width, int height, int angleWidth, int angleHeight);
g.fillRoundRect(int x, int y, int width, int height, int angleWidth, int angleHeight);
```

Figure 26.13 The Rounded-Rectangle Methods

Figure 26.14 contains a simple illustration of the rounded-rectangle methods. Figure 26.14(a) contains the *RoundRect* page; Figure 26.14(b) contains the applet used to create this page. Try changing the angle parameters. Notice the effect this has on the rectangle's corners.

(a) The *RoundRect* Page   **(b) The *RoundRect* Applet**

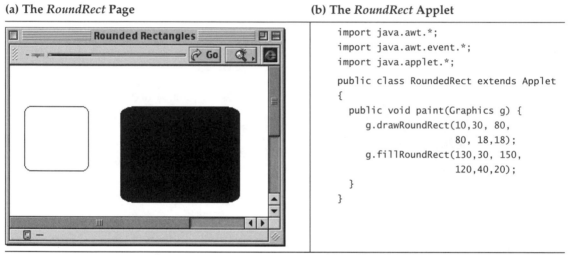

```
import java.awt.*;
import java.awt.event.*;
import java.applet.*;

public class RoundedRect extends Applet
{
    public void paint(Graphics g) {
        g.drawRoundRect(10,30, 80,
                             80, 18,18);
        g.fillRoundRect(130,30, 150,
                             120,40,20);
    }
}
```

Figure 26.14 The *Rounded Rectangle* Page

IMAGES

We use the **drawImage()** method of the *Graphics* class to paint an image on the page. The images must be stored in *jpeg* or *gif* format. Before we use this method, however, we must make the image accessible to the applet. To do this, we create an *Image* field in the class definition. For example, suppose that we have a file named *angels.jpeg*; then we can create the *Image* field with the statement

Image angels;

The **init()** method of the class definition uses the **getImage()** method to load the image file. The syntax of this method is

Image getImage(URL *url*, String *name*);

The **getImage()** method requires the full URL of the folder containing the applet and the name of the image file. We obtain the URL by calling the **getDocumentBase()** method. The syntax of this method is

URL getDocumentBase();

The **getDocumentBase()** method requires no parameters. It returns the URL of the document base.

Although the process looks complicated, it takes only one line of code. Thus, we load the *angels.jpeg* file into the *angels* image with the statement

```
angels = this.getImage(this.getDocumentBase(),"angels.jpeg");
```

Once we've loaded the image, we use the **drawImage()** method to paint the image on the page. The syntax of this method is

```
g.drawImage(Image img, int x, int y, ImageObserver IO);
```

This method requires four parameters: an image, the (x, y) coordinates for the top left corner, and an image observer. For example, suppose we want to place the *angels* image at the top left corner of the applet. The (x, y) coordinates are (0,0). The statement that paints the image is

```
g.drawImage(angels, 0, 0, this);
```

Notice that the image observer is only a self-reference.

Figure 26.15 contains the *Images* page. Figure 26.15(a) contains the image as it is displayed in the browser. Figure 26.15(b) contains the definition of the *Images* class.

(a) The *Images* Page	(b) The *Images* Applet
	```import java.awt.*;``` ```import java.awt.event.*;``` ```import java.applet.*;``` ```public class Images extends Applet``` ```{``` ``` private Image angels;``` ``` public void init()``` ``` {``` ``` angels =``` ``` this.getImage(``` ``` this.getDocumentBase(),``` ``` "angels.jpeg");``` ``` }``` ``` public void paint(Graphics g)``` ``` {``` ``` g.drawImage(angels, 0,``` ``` 0,this);``` ``` }``` ```}```

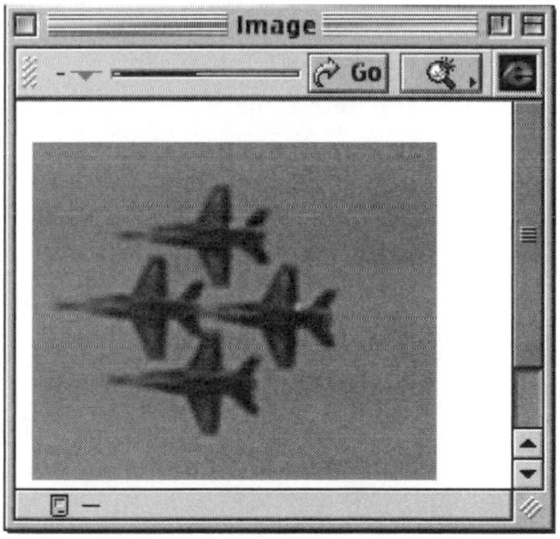

Figure 26.15 The *Images* Page

POLYGONS

In addition to such simple shapes as rectangles and ovals, the *Graphics* class contains methods that draw polygons and polylines. Figure 26.16 shows the syntax for the polygon methods. We will examine the polyline method in the next section.

```
g.drawPolygon(int [] xCoord, int [] yCoord, int sides);
g.fillPolygon(int [] xCoord, int [] yCoord, int sides);
```

Figure 26.16 The Polygon Drawing Methods

The **drawPolygon()** method creates an outline of a polygon; the **fillPolygon()** method creates a solid polygon. Both methods require three parameters. The *xCoord* and *yCoord* parameters are arrays that specify the (x, y) coordinates for each point in the polygon. The *sides* parameter specifies the number of sides in the polygon.

To illustrate the **drawPolygon()** method, we create a simple pentagon. Figure 26.17 contains the finished product.

Figure 26.18 contains the definition of the *FirstPoly* class. This definition contains several constants that we use to create the pentagon. The **CENTER_X** and **CENTER_Y** constants contain the center point, (100,100), of the polygon. The **SIZE** and **SIDES** constants contain the length (100 pixels) and number of sides (5) in the polygon.

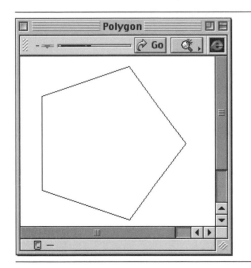

```java
import java.awt.*;
import java.awt.event.*;
import java.applet.*;
public class FirstPoly extends Applet {
    private static final int CENTER_X = 100;
    private static final int CENTER_Y = 100;
    private static final int SIDES = 5;
    private static final int SIZE = 100;
    private int [] xCoord = new int [SIDES+1];
    private int [] yCoord = new int [SIDES+1];
    //Put the init() Method Here
    //Put the paint() Method Here
}
```

Figure 26.17 The *Polygon* Page   **Figure 26.18** The *FirstPoly* Class Definition

The *FirstPoly* class definition also contains the two integer arrays, *xCoord* and *yCoord*, that hold the polygon's points. We want the polygon to close, so the size of the arrays is one greater than the number of points in the polygon because the last point has the same coordinates as the first.

The init() Method

The **init()** method fills the *xCoord* and *yCoord* arrays. We use elementary trigonometry to determine the (x, y) coordinates for each point. Figure 26.19 contains the trigonometric formulas. The x coordinate uses the cosine of the current angle, θ. The y coordinate uses the sine of the current angle, θ. The angle θ is measured in radians. Figure 26.20 contains the definition of the **init()** method.

(a) *x* Coordinate	(b) *y* Coordinate
x_i = CENTER_X + SIZE · cos(θ)	y_i = CENTER_Y - SIZE · sin(θ)

Figure 26.19 Trigonometric Formulas for Polygon Points

```
public void init()
{//create the coordinate arrays
   int i;
   double angle;
   for (i = 0; i <= SIDES; i++) {
      angle = (double)i/SIDES *2*Math.PI;
      xCoord[i] = (int) (CENTER_X + SIZE * Math.cos(angle));
      yCoord[i] = (int) (CENTER_Y - SIZE * Math.sin(angle));
   }
   setBackground(Color.white);
}
```

Figure 26.20 The **init()** Method: *FirstPoly* Class

As Figure 26.20 indicates, we use a **for** statement to calculate the current angle, and then we use the trigonometric formulas to calculate the points. Notice that we use a type cast to round the coordinates to their integer equivalents.

Although the **for** statement uses standard trigonometry to generate the points, it's hard to visualize the pentagon's points. Figure 26.21 contains an annotated version of the pentagon. A table of angles and of (*x*, *y*) coordinates appears to the left of the diagram. The diagram on the right contains the pentagon with its coordinate labels. Notice that the first and last coordinates are identical, that is, *xCoord[0]* == *xCoord[5]* and *yCoord[0]* == *yCoord[5]*. The starting and ending coordinates must be identical to ensure that the polygon closes.

Subscript	Angle	x Coord	y Coord
[0]	0	200	100
[1]	1.26	131	5
[2]	2.51	19	41
[3]	3.77	19	141
[4]	5.02	130	195
[5]	6.28	200	100

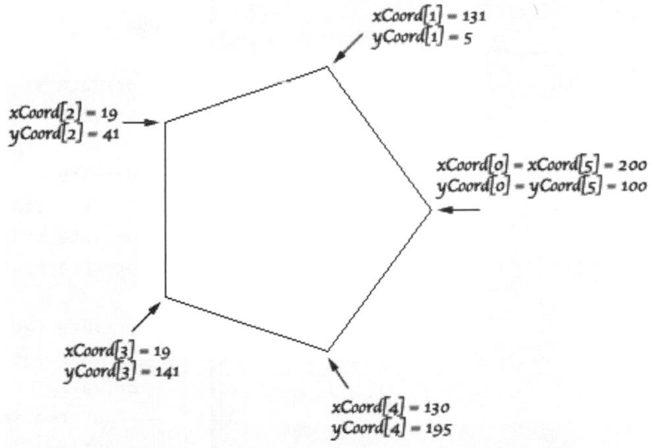

Figure 26.21 Illustration of Polygon Coordinates

The `paint()` Method

The `paint()` method contains a single line of code that invokes the **drawPolygon()** method to create the pentagon. Figure 26.22 contains the definition of the `paint()` method.

```
public void paint(Graphics g)
{ //create a filled polygon from the coordinate arrays
    g.drawPolygon(xCoord, yCoord, SIDES);
}
```

Figure 26.22 The `paint()` Method: *FirstPoly* Class

POLYLINES

At the beginning of this chapter, we created a page that drew a simple line. We now turn our attention to *polylines*. A polyline is simply a line composed of other lines. We draw polylines with the **drawPolyline()** method. The syntax of this method is

    g.drawPolyline(int [] *xCoord*, int [] *yCoord*, int *nPoints*);

Notice that the **drawPolyline()** and **drawPolygon()** methods have similar parameters. Each method requires arrays of *x* and *y* coordinates. The third parameter in the **drawPolyline()** method specifies the number of points in the polyline. (This will be the number of constituent lines plus one.)

To illustrate polylines, we will create a pentagonal spiral. Figure 26.23 contains the sample page. Figure 26.24 contains the definition of the *FirstPolyline* class that implements our *Polyline* page. The definition contains the same **CENTER_X**, **CENTER_Y**, and **SIDES** constants used in the *Polygon* page.

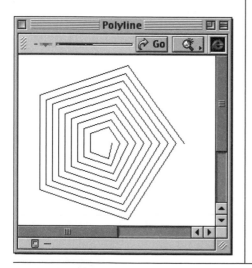

Figure 26.23 The *Polyline* Page

```
import java.awt.*;
import java.awt.event.*;
import java.applet.*;
public class FirstPolyline extends Applet
{
  private static final int CENTER_X = 100;
  private static final int CENTER_Y = 100;
  private static final int SIDES = 5;
  private static final int START_SIZE = 100;
  private static final int END_SIZE = 10;
  private static final int DECREMENT = 10;
  private static final int N_LINES =
                 (START_SIZE-END_SIZE)/DECREMENT*SIDES+1;
  private int [] xCoord = new int [N_LINES];
  private int [] yCoord = new int [N_LINES];
  private int size;
  //Put the init() Method Here
  //Put the paint() Method Here
}
```

Figure 26.24 The *FirstPolyline* Class Definition

The *FirstPolyline* class definition also includes three constants and a variable that determine the length of a side. The **START_SIZE** and **END_SIZE** constants contain the length of the longest and shortest lines, respectively. The variable *size* contains the current line length. The **DECREMENT** constant contains the length reduction. We use these constants to determine the number of lines (**N_LINES**) in the spiral polyline.

The init() Method

Figure 26.25 contains the definition of the **init()** method. Compare this method with its counterpart in the *FirstPolygon* class definition. What differences do you notice?

```
public void init()
   {//create the coordinate arrays
      int i;
      double angle;
      size = START_SIZE;
      for (i = 0; i < N_LINES; i++) {
         angle = (double)i/SIDES *2*Math.PI;
         xCoord[i] = (int) (CENTER_X + size * Math.cos(angle));
         yCoord[i] = (int) (CENTER_Y - size * Math.sin(angle));
         if ((i%SIDES) == (SIDES-1)) //reduce size
            size -= DECREMENT;
      }
      setBackground(Color.white);
}
```

Figure 26.25 The **init()** Method: *FirstPolyline* Class

The **init()** method uses a **for** statement to create the (x, y) coordinates for each point in the polyline. Because the lengths of the lines vary, we use the variable *size* to calculate the coordinates. Prior to the start of the **for** statement, we initialize *size* to **START_SIZE**. An **if** statement is used to reduce the line length just *before* the polyline would close to form a polygon. In the current example, the line length is reduced prior to creating the 5th, 10th, 15th, and so on, set of coordinates (counting the initial set as being the zeroth).

The paint() Method

Figure 26.26 contains the definition of the **paint()** method. The definition contains a single line of code that invokes the **drawPolyline()** method to draw the spiral polyline on the applet.

```
public void paint(Graphics g)
{ //create a filled polygon from the coordinate arrays
    g.drawPolyline(xCoord, yCoord, N_LINES);
}
```

Figure 26.26 The **paint()** Method: *FirstPolyline* Class

MOUSE EVENTS

Java includes a *MouseEvent* class that records information on mouse clicks. We can access this information by using one of the *MouseEvent* methods listed in Figure 26.27. As this figure indicates, we can obtain the x and y coordinates of the mouse separately by using the **getX()** and **getY()** methods, or we can obtain the current mouse position as a point.

MouseEvent Methods	Description
`int getClickCount();`	Return the number of mouse clicks at this position.
`int getX();`	Return the x coordinate of the mouse click.
`int getY();`	Return the y coordinate of the mouse click.
`Point getPoint();`	Return the x, y coordinates as a point.

Figure 26.27 The *MouseEvent* Methods

Mouse events occur when the user clicks a mouse button or drags the mouse. Each event has its own listener. When we want the applet to respond to mouse *clicks*, we add a mouse listener. When we want the applet to respond to mouse *movement*, we add a mouse *motion* listener.

The Mouse Listener

We created a page that draws a pentagon at fixed coordinates. We're now going to modify this page so that it draws the pentagon by using mouse coordinates. Figure 26.28 contains a sample page. The figure is static, so it's not obvious that a mouse click determines the pentagon's location.

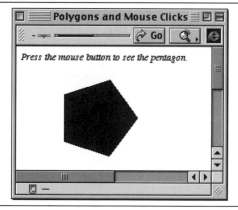

Figure 26.28 The *PolyMouse* Page

We cannot add a mouse listener to an applet in the same way that we previously added action or item listeners. We add a mouse listener by creating an inner class that extends the *MouseAdapter* class. An *inner* class is simply a class that is completely contained within another class. In our example, the *MouseAdapter* class is completely contained within the *PolyMouse* class.

This *MouseAdapter* class contains the methods listed in Figure 26.29. We add whichever methods we need to the inner class.

Two methods, **mouseEntered()** and **mouseExited()**, are activated when the mouse enters or leaves the boundaries of a component. All form objects are components, so we could use these

MouseAdapter **Methods**	Description
void mouseClicked(MouseEvent e);	Activated when a mouse button is clicked.
void mousePressed(MouseEvent e);	Activated when a mouse button is pressed.
void mouseReleased(MouseEvent e);	Activated when a mouse button is released.
void mouseEntered(MouseEvent e);	Activated when the mouse enters the boundaries of a component.
void mouseExited(MouseEvent e);	Activated when the mouse leaves the boundaries of a component.

Figure 26.29 The *MouseAdapter* Methods

methods to record information on the component. Typically, however, we use the three methods related to button clicks. As its name suggests, the **mousePressed()** method is activated when the user presses a mouse button. This method always precedes a mouse release event; a user must press a button before being able to release it. The **mouseClicked()** method is activated when the user clicks a button. A click occurs when the user presses and then releases a button.

The *PolyMouse* Class Definition

The *PolyMouse* class definition creates the applet that draws a pentagon when the user presses a mouse button. We draw the pentagon at the mouse's coordinates. Figure 26.30 contains the definition of the *PolyMouse* class.

```
import java.awt.*;
import java.awt.event.*;
import java.applet.*;

public class PolyMouse extends Applet
{
  private static final int SIDES = 5;
  private static final int SIZE = 50;
  protected int x, y;
  boolean paintFlag = false;
  private int [] xCoord = new int [SIDES+1];
  private int [] yCoord = new int [SIDES+1];

  //Put the init() Method Here
  //put the MouseListener Class Here
  //put the paint() Method Here
}
```

Figure 26.30 The *PolyMouse* Class Definition

The *PolyMouse* class contains constants that determine the length (**SIZE**) and number of sides (**SIDES**) in the polygon. We also create arrays, *xCoord* and *yCoord*, that contain the coordinates for each point on the polygon. Previously, we used the constants **X_CENTER** and **Y_CENTER** to denote the center point of the polygon. In this example, we use the mouse coordinates, (x, y), for the polygon's center point. Notice the variable declaration:

protected int x,y;

We declare x and y as protected so that the inner *MouseListener* class that we're about to create will have access to them.

The *MouseListener* Class

The *MouseListener* class contains a single method, **mousePressed()**. To create this class, we extend the *MouseAdapter* class. Figure 26.31 contains the definition of the *MouseListener* class.

```
class MouseListener extends MouseAdapter
{
 public void mousePressed(MouseEvent e)
 {
    x = e.getX();
    y = e.getY();
    paintFlag = true;
    repaint();
 }
} //end of MouseListener
```

Figure 26.31 The *MouseListener* Class: *PolyMouse* Class

The **mousePressed()** method obtains the mouse's *x* and *y* coordinates. These variables are protected, and so we can access them in both the **mousePressed()** method of the *MouseListener* class and the **paint()** method of the *PolyMouse* class. After obtaining the coordinates, we set the *paintFlag* to *true*. We initialized *paintFlag* to *false* in the *PolyMouse* class definition. We use an **if** statement in the **paint()** method to draw the polygon only when *paintFlag* is *true*. This prevents the applet from drawing a polygon before the user has pressed a mouse button. We call the **repaint()** method to paint the polygon on the applet.

The init() Method

Figure 26.32 contains the definition of the **init()** method. This method contains a single line of code that adds a mouse listener to the applet.

The **addMouseListener()** method requires a *MouseAdapter* object as parameter. Notice that we invoke the *MouseListener* constructor to create the new *MouseAdapter* object.

```
public void init()
{ //Create the mouse listener
    addMouseListener(new MouseListener());
}
```

Figure 26.32 The **init()** Method: *PolyMouse* class

The paint() Method

The **paint()** method uses an **if** statement that creates the polygon's coordinates and draws the polygon only when *paintFlag* is *true*. The **for** statement that fills the *xCoord* and *yCoord* arrays is similar to the statement used in the *FirstPoly* class definition. We simply replace the constants for the center point by the mouse coordinates, *x* and *y*. Once we've created the points, we call the **fillPolygon()** method to draw the polygon. Figure 26.33 contains the definition of the **paint()** method.

```
public void paint(Graphics g)
{//Draw a pentagon at the mouse coordinates
    int i;
    double angle;
    if (paintFlag){
        for (i = 0; i <= SIDES; i++)
        {//determine the pentagon's coordinates
            angle = (double)i/SIDES *2*Math.PI;
            xCoord[i] = (int) (x + SIZE * Math.cos(angle));
            yCoord[i] = (int) (y - SIZE * Math.sin(angle));
        }
        g.fillPolygon(xCoord,yCoord,SIDES);
    }
}
```

Figure 26.33 The `paint()` Method: *PolyMouse* Class

The Mouse Motion Adapter

We can also develop applets that respond to mouse movement. This requires the creation of an inner class that extends the *MouseMotionAdapter* class. This class contains the two methods listed in Figure 26.34.

MouseMotionAdapter **Methods**	Description
void mouseDragged(MouseEvent *e*);	Activated when the user drags the mouse.
void mouseMoved(MouseEvent *e*);	Activated when the user moves the mouse.

Figure 26.34 The *MouseMotionAdapter* Methods

The **mouseDragged()** method is activated when the user moves the mouse *while holding down a mouse button*. The **mouseMoved()** method is activated when the user moves the mouse but is not pressing a mouse button.

The *Drawing Mouse* Page

To illustrate the *MouseMotionAdapter*, we create a page that draws lines wherever the user drags the mouse. Figure 26.35 shows a sample page.

The *MouseDraw1* Class Definition

Figure 26.36 contains the definition of the *MouseDraw1* class that implements the *Drawing Mouse* page. The class definition contains three protected variables, *x, y,* and *start*. Notice that the applet contains only an **init()** method and the inner *MouseMotionListener* class.

The *MouseMotionListener* Class Definition

The *MouseMotionListener* implements the **mouseDragged()** method. This method draws lines wherever the user drags the mouse. The **mouseDragged()** method uses a technique for drawing lines that we have not yet covered. In the previous graphics pages, the class definition contained a **paint()** method that we accessed by calling the **repaint()** method. The **repaint()** method calls

<table>
<tr><td>

```
import java.awt.*;
import java.awt.event.*;
import java.applet.*;

public class MouseDraw1 extends Applet
{ //make protected so that mouse can use
    protected int x, y,start;
    //Put the MouseMotionListener Class Here
    //Put the init() Method Here
}
```

</td></tr>
</table>

Figure 26.35 The *Drawing Mouse* Page   **Figure 26.36** The *MouseDraw1* Class Definition

the **update()** method, which erases the drawing surface, and then calls the **paint()** method. Here, we don't want to erase the drawing surface, so we cannot use the **paint()** and **repaint()** methods. Instead, we use the **getGraphics()** method to return the *Graphics* object *g* to the **mouseDragged()** method. The statement is

    Graphics g = getGraphics();

By obtaining the *Graphics* object, we preserve the previously drawn lines.

The **mouseDragged()** method uses the **drawLine()** method to draw a line between the current and previous mouse coordinates. We use *x* and *y* to store the previous mouse coordinates and *newX* and *newY* to store the current mouse coordinates. Thus, to draw a line, we use the statement

    g.drawLine(x,y,newX,newY);

There is one minor problem with this approach: there are no previous coordinates when the user starts to drag the mouse. We use *start* to handle this problem. The **init()** method initializes *start* to zero. We increment *start* each time we invoke the **mouseDragged()** method. We know that we have two sets of line coordinates when *start* has a value greater than one.

We conclude the **mouseDragged()** method by assigning *newX* to *x* and *newY* to *y*. Thus, the current coordinates become the previous coordinates for the next mouse drag. Figure 26.37 contains the definition of the *MouseMotionListener* class.

The init() Method

The **init()** method contains two lines of code. The first line initializes *x*, *y*, and *start* to zero. The second line adds the mouse motion listener to the applet. We add the mouse motion listener with the statement

    addMouseMotionListener(new MouseMotionListener());

The parameter to this method is a *MouseMotionAdapter* object that we create by calling the *MouseMotionListener* constructor. Figure 26.38 contains the definition of the **init()** method.

```
class MouseMotionListener extends MouseMotionAdapter
{
 public void mouseDragged(MouseEvent e)
 {
   Graphics g = getGraphics();
   int newX = e.getX();
   int newY = e.getY();
   start++;
   if (start > 1)
     g.drawLine(x,y,newX,newY);
   x = newX;
   y = newY;
 }
}//end MouseMotionListener
```

Figure 26.37 The *MouseMotionListener* Class: *MouseDraw1* Class

```
public void init()
   {
     x = y = start = 0;
     addMouseMotionListener(new MouseMotionListener());
}
```

Figure 26.38 The **init()** Method: *MouseDraw1* Class

The *Star Polygon* Page

We've examined several simple graphics pages in this chapter. We conclude with two examples that combine many of the concepts that we've learned in previous chapters. As our first example, we create a *Star Polygons* page. Figure 26.39 contains a sample page.

The *Star Polygons* page contains text fields that let the user select the size and number of sides in a polygon. Although the sample page shows star polygons, the page draws both regular and star polygons. The *increment* field determines the type of polygon. Regular polygons, like the pentagon displayed in Figure 26.17, have a total turning angle of 360° (6.28 radians). A star polygon has a total turning angle that is a multiple of 360°. Creating star polygons involves a simple modification of the trigonometric formulas uses to create the x and y coordinates for each point in the polygon.

The *StarPolygons* Class Definition

Figure 26.40 contains the definition of the *StarPolygons* class. The definition uses arrays for the labels, text fields, and panels. We include three protected variables, *size*, *sides*, and *increment*, that will hold the values obtained from the text fields.

The *StarPolygons* class definition contains **init()** and **actionPerformed()** methods. The **init()** method creates the text fields and panels. It also adds the mouse listener. We use the **actionPerformed()** method to obtain the values from the text fields. The inner *MouseListener* class contains a **mousePressed()** method that obtains the current mouse coordinates. We draw the star (or regular) polygon at these coordinates.

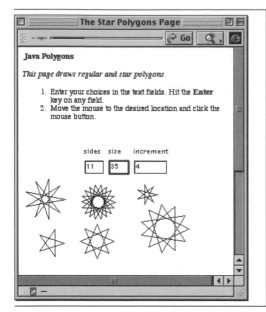

Figure 26.39 The *Star Polygon* Page

```
import java.awt.*;
import java.awt.event.*;
import java.applet.*;

public class StarPolygons extends Applet implements
ActionListener
{// Draw Polygons starting at x,y, with user
    determined sides and size.
    private String [] paramName = {"sides", "size",
"increment"};
    private TextField [] paramField = new
TextField[paramName.length];
    private Panel [] paramPanel = new Panel
      [paramName.length];
    private Panel inputPanel = new Panel();
    protected int sides, size, increment;

  //Put init() Method Here
  //Put MouseListener Class Here
  //Put actionPerformed() Method Here
}
```

Figure 26.40 The *StarPolygons* Class Definition

The init() Method

Figure 26.41 contains a layout diagram for the *Star Polygons* page. The diagram helps explain the code used in the **init()** method. As this figure indicates, the *Star Polygon* page contains an array of three panels, *paramPanel*. Each panel uses a 2 × 1 grid layout. The first row in the grid contains a label that identifies the text field. The second row in the grid contains the text field. We create the labels by using the *paramName* array. We create the text fields by using the *paramField* array. Each text field has an action listener. We're using arrays, so we use a **for** statement in the **init()** method to construct the text fields, labels, and panels and to add the text fields and labels to the panels. The **for** statement also adds each parameter panel to *inputPanel*. When the **for** statement terminates, we add *inputPanel* to the page, and we add a mouse listener to the applet. Figure 26.42 contains the definition of the **init()** method.

The actionPerformed() Method

The **actionPerformed()** method obtains the contents of each text field and converts the contents to its integer equivalent. Figure 26.43 contains the definition of the **actionPerformed()** method.

The *MouseListener* Class

The *MouseListener* class contains the definition of the **mousePressed()** method. This method uses the **getX()** and **getY()** methods to obtain the current mouse position. The statements are:

```
int x = e.getX();
int y = e.getY();
```

Notice that we declare *x* and *y* within the **mousePressed()** method. Since this method handles all of the drawing, we do not need to declare these variables in the *StarPoly* class definition.

We also create variables to represent the arrays of coordinates and the current angle. The statements are:

```
int [] xCoord = new int [sides+1];
```

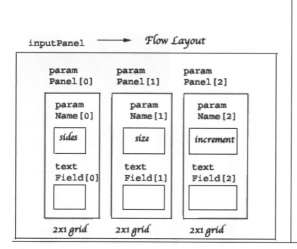

Figure 26.41 The *Star Polygon* Layout

```
public void init()
{
    int i;
    setBackground(Color.white);
    for (i = 0; i < paramName.length; i++)
    { //add the labels and textfields to a panel
        paramPanel[i] = new Panel();
        paramPanel[i].setLayout(new GridLayout(2,1));
        paramPanel[i].add(new Label(paramName[i]));
        paramField[i] = new TextField(3);
        paramField[i].addActionListener(this);
        paramPanel[i].add(paramField[i]);
        inputPanel.add(paramPanel[i]);
    }
    add(inputPanel);
    addMouseListener(new MouseListener());
}
```

Figure 26.42 The **init()** Method: *StarPolygons* Class

```
public void actionPerformed(ActionEvent e)
{ //Translate the paramField to integers and redraw canvas
    sides = Integer.parseInt(paramField[0].getText());
    size = Integer.parseInt(paramField[1].getText());
    increment = Integer.parseInt(paramField[2].getText());
}
```

Figure 26.43 The **actionPerformed()** Method: *StarPolygons* Class

```
int [] yCoord = new int [sides+1];
double angle;
```

Since we want to display several star polygons on a page, we use the **getGraphics()** method to obtain the current *Graphics* object. The statement is:

```
Graphics g = getGraphics();
```

The **mousePressed()** method uses a **for** statement to generate the x and y coordinates for each point on the polygon. The **for** statement is

```
for (j = 0; j <= sides; j++){
    angle = 2 * Math.PI * j / sides;
    xCoord[j] = (int) (x + size * Math.cos(increment*angle));
    yCoord[j] = (int) (y - size * Math.sin(increment*angle));
}
```

Notice the calls to the **sin()** and **cos()** methods. To create a star polygon, we pass the product of the angle by the increment.

Once we've generated the points, we call the **drawPolygon()** method to draw the polygon. If the total turning angle is simply 360°, the page displays a regular polygon. If the total turning angle is a higher multiple of 360°, the page displays a star polygon. Figure 26.44 contains the definition of the *MouseListener* class.

Figure 26.45 contains examples of *sides* and *increment* combinations that produce star polygons. Pick whatever size you wish. A size of 15 to 30 works well for most polygons.

```
class MouseListener extends MouseAdapter {
//Create a new mouse motion listener
   public void mousePressed(MouseEvent e)
   {
     int j;
     int x = e.getX();
     int y = e.getY();
     int [] xCoord = new int [sides+1];
     int [] yCoord = new int [sides+1];
     double angle;
     Graphics g = getGraphics();
      //create the x,y points for the polygon
      for (j = 0; j <= sides; j++){
         angle = 2 * Math.PI * j / sides;
         xCoord[j] = (int) (x + size * Math.cos(increment*angle));
         yCoord[j] = (int) (y - size * Math.sin(increment*angle));
      }
      g.drawPolygon(xCoord, yCoord, sides);
      }
}
```

Figure 26.44 The *MouseListener* Class: *StarPolygons* Class

Sides	Increment
5	3
7	4
8	3
9	4
11	4
18	7

Figure 26.45 Star Polygon Parameters

THE *PIE CHART* PAGE

As our last graphics example, we create a page that generates pie charts. A *pie chart* is a pictorial representation of statistical information. For example, government agencies frequently use pie charts to show the percentage of government monies spent on various social programs. Naturally, for *our* pie chart page, we'll pick a more interesting example. We're going to create a pie chart of America's favorite pies. (The data are fictitious.) This page combines several different layout managers as well as different form elements. Figure 26.46 contains a sample pie chart.

The *Pie Chart* page has several features that contribute to the complexity of the design. The features are:

The Pie Chart Caption. The *Pie Chart* page contains a text field that lets the user enter an optional caption for the pie chart. If the user provides a caption, we center it at the top of the drawing panel.

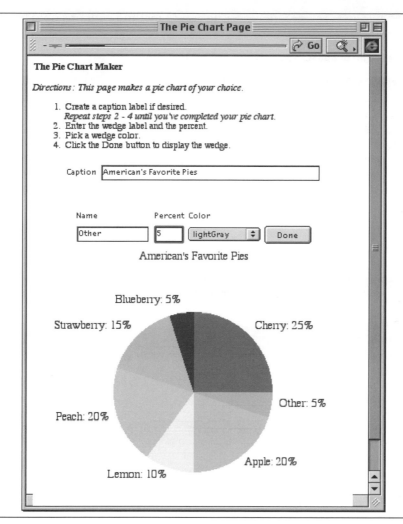

Figure 26.46 The *Pie Chart* Page

Pie Wedge Inputs. We use two text fields to obtain a pie wedge name and the percentage occupied by the wedge. We use a *Choice* object to obtain the wedge color. When the user presses the *Done* button, we create the pie wedge and its corresponding label. The label includes the wedge name and the percentage of the total pie.

Wedge Labels. We display the wedge labels at the midpoint of the wedge. We must move the wedges on the left-hand side of the pie to prevent them from sliding into the wedge.

The *PiePanel* Class

Creation of the *Pie Chart* page begins with the definition of the *PiePanel* class. This class contains the drawing surface for pie wedges and labels. The *PiePanel* class declaration contains two methods, **draw()** and **printLabel()**. The **draw()** method requires six parameters that correspond to the parameters used by the **fillArc()** method. The **draw()** method contains only two lines of code. The first line,

```
Graphics g = getGraphics();
```

calls the **getGraphics()** method to obtain the *Graphics* object *g*. The second line invokes the **fillArc()** method to create the wedge.

We use the **printLabel()** method to print the caption and wedge labels. This method requires three parameters which correspond to the parameters used by the **drawString()** method. The **printLabel()** method obtains the current *Graphics* object by calling the **getGraphics()** method. Once we've obtained the *Graphics* object, we use the **drawString()** method to print the caption or label. Figure 26.47 contains the definition of the *PiePanel* class.

```
public class PiePanel extends Panel
{//Create the PiePanel for drawing the pie
 public void draw(int x, int y, int width, int height, int startAngle, int angleSize)
 {//interface to the drawing program
  Graphics g = getGraphics();
  g.fillArc(x, y, width, height, startAngle, angleSize);
}
public void printLabel(String message, int x, int y)
{
  Graphics g = getGraphics();
  g.drawString(message, x,y);
 }
} //end of the Pie Panel Definition
```

Figure 26.47 The *PiePanel* Class

The *GenericPie* Class Definition

The *GenericPie* class implements the *Pie Chart* page appearing in Figure 26.46. The class definition includes a *PiePanel* object created with the statement

```
private PiePanel pie = new PiePanel();
```

Because *pie* is a panel in its own right, we can change its foreground and background color. We can also call the **draw()** and **printLabel()** methods to create the pie wedges and labels.

We also create four constants that correspond to the first four parameters used by the **fillArc()** method. The constants, which form the parameters for the arc's bounding rectangle, are created as follows:

```
private static final int START_X = 100;
private static final int START_Y = 75;
private static final int HEIGHT = 200;
private static final int WIDTH = 200;
```

The remaining arc parameters reflect the user's information, so we will determine these parameters in the **actionPerformed()** method.

We use two additional constants to find the midpoints of the arcs. These constants are

```
private static final int CENTER_X = START_X + WIDTH/2;
```

and

```
        private static final int CENTER_Y = START_Y + HEIGHT/2;
```

The *GenericPie* class definition contains arrays for the panels, text fields, and captions. Figure 26.48 contains the definition of the *GenericPie* class. Notice that we place the definition of the *PiePanel* class after the definition of the *GenericPie* class.

```
import java.awt.*;
import java.awt.event.*;
import java.applet.*;
public class GenericPie extends Applet  implements ActionListener, ItemListener
{// create a generic Pie chart maker
    private static final int START_X = 100;
    private static final int START_Y = 75;
    private static final int HEIGHT = 200;
    private static final int WIDTH = 200;
    private static final int CENTER_X = START_X + WIDTH/2;
    private static final int CENTER_Y = START_Y + HEIGHT/2;
    private static final String inputName [] = {"Name",
                      "Percent","Color", " "};
    private Panel [] inputPanel = new Panel[inputName.length];
    private Panel captionPanel = new Panel();
    private Panel allPanel = new Panel();
    private Panel northPanel = new Panel();
    private TextField captionField = new TextField(40);
    private PiePanel pie = new PiePanel();
    private TextField [] inputField = new TextField[2];
    private static final int [] FIELD_SIZE = {12,2};
    private Choice colorChoice = new Choice();
    private Button doneButton = new Button("Done");

    private Font currentFont = new Font("Serif", Font.PLAIN, 14);
    private FontMetrics fm =
       Toolkit.getDefaultToolkit().getFontMetrics(currentFont);
    private String  captionName;
    private int arcBegin, lastBegin, lastSize;

    private static final Color [] pieColor = {Color.white,
    Color.yellow, Color.orange,
    Color.pink,  Color.magenta, Color.red, Color.green,
    Color.cyan, Color.blue, Color.lightGray,
    Color.darkGray, Color.gray, Color.black};

    private static final String [] colorName = {"white", "yellow",
    "orange", "pink", "magenta", "red", "green", "cyan", "blue",
    "lightGray", "darkGray", "gray",  "black"};
 //Put init() Method Here
 //Put actionPerformed() Method Here
 //Put itemStateChanged() Method Here
} //end of Generic Pie Definition
//Put PiePanel class definition here
```

Figure 26.48 The *GenericPie* Class Definition

The `init()` Method

The *GenericPie* page uses a complex layout that we create in the **init()** method. The layout is best explained through a diagram. Figure 26.49 contains the layout diagram for the *GenericPie* page. We created the class fields in the class definition; now we use the **init()** method to construct text fields, labels, and panels and to place the text fields in the panels.

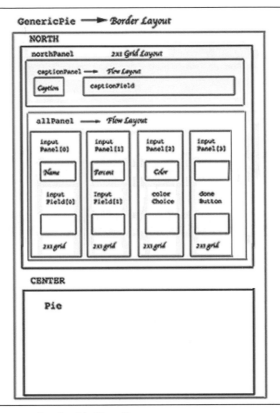

Figure 26.49 Layout Diagram for the *Pie Chart* Page

As Figure 26.49 indicates, the *GenericPie* class uses a border layout. We place *northPanel*, which contains all of the user input panels, in the north region and *pie* in the center region; *northPanel* uses a 2 × 1 grid layout. We place *captionPanel*, which contains the label and text field for the caption, in the first row of the grid. We place *allPanel* in the second row; *allPanel* contains four panels for the pie wedge information. Each panel uses a 2 × 1 grid layout. The first two panels contain the labels and text fields for the wedge name and percentage. The third panel contains the *Choice* object for the wedge color. The last panel contains the *Done* button.

The **init()** method uses a **for** statement to create each *inputPanel* serially. We construct each panel, and then add a label by using the *inputName* array. Each of the four panels holds different components, so we use a **switch** statement to create the correct components. Figure 26.50 contains the definition of the **init()** method.

Notice the **switch** statement contained in the **for** loop. When *i* is zero or one, we create a new text field object and we add it to the ith panel. When *i* is two we create the *Choice* object that holds

```
public void init()
{//create the applet
  int i,j;
  northPanel.setLayout(new GridLayout(2,1));
  for (i = 0; i < inputName.length; i++)
  {//create the input components and panel, add to allPanel
     inputPanel[i] = new Panel(new GridLayout(2,1));
     inputPanel[i].add(new Label(inputName[i]));
     switch(i)
     {
         case 0: case 1: inputField[i] = new TextField(FIELD_SIZE[i]);
                 inputPanel[i].add(inputField[i]);
                 break;
         case 2: for (j =0; j < colorName.length; j++)
                       colorChoice.addItem(colorName[j]);
                    colorChoice.addItemListener(this);
                    inputPanel[i].add(colorChoice);
                    break;
         case 3: inputPanel[i].add(doneButton);
                 doneButton.addActionListener(this);
     }
     allPanel.add(inputPanel[i]);
  }
  setBackground(Color.white);
  setLayout(new BorderLayout(5,5));
  captionPanel.add(new Label("Caption"));
  captionPanel.add(captionField);
  northPanel.add(captionPanel);
  northPanel.add(allPanel);
  add(northPanel, BorderLayout.NORTH);
  pie.setSize(380,250);
  pie.setFont(currentFont);
  add(pie, BorderLayout.CENTER);
  //first angle begins at 0
  arcBegin = lastBegin = lastSize = 0;
 }
```

Figure 26.50 The **init()** Method: *GenericPie* Class

the color names and we add it to the ith input panel. We also add an item listener to the *Choice* object. When *i* is three, we add the *Done* button to the ith panel, and we add an action listener to the button.

The itemStateChanged() Method

The item listener invokes the **itemStateChanged()** method when the user selects a wedge color. We use the **getSelectedIndex()** method to obtain the index of the selected color. Since the indices in the *Choice* object correspond to the colors in the *pieColor* array, we use this index to change the foreground color of the *pie* panel. This means that the wedge will be drawn in the selected color. Figure 26.51 contains the definition of the **itemStateChanged()** method.

```
public void itemStateChanged(ItemEvent e)
{// find the color and change the foreground
    int index = colorChoice.getSelectedIndex();
    pie.setForeground(pieColor[index]);
}
```

Figure 26.51 The **itemStateChanged()** Method: *GenericPie* Class

The actionPerformed() Method

The action listener invokes the **actionPerformed()** method when the user presses the *Done* button. As our first task, we obtain the wedge name and percent from the text fields. The statements that accomplish this are the following:

```
String wedgeName = inputField[0].getText();
int percent = Integer.parseInt(inputField[1].getText());
```

We add the percentage to *wedgeName* with the statement

```
wedgeName = wedgeName + ": " + percent + "%";
```

Next, we must determine the beginning angle for the wedge and the size of the wedge. To determine the size of the wedge, we translate the percentage, which is based on a scale running from 0 to 100, into an angle, which is based on a scale running from 0 to 360. The statement that converts the percentage to an angle is

```
int arcSize = (int) Math.round(360 * percent/100.0);
```

Determining the beginning angle of the arc is more complicated, because the starting angle of the current pie wedge is based on the cumulative angles of the previous wedges. We use the following statement to determine the angle start:

```
int arcBegin = lastBegin + lastSize;
```

As this statement indicates, we obtain the starting angle for the current wedge by adding the starting angle and the size of the previous wedge. We initialize *lastBegin* and *lastSize* to zero in the *GenericPie* definition. The **actionPerformed()** method updates these variables after we add each wedge.

Once we've determined the remaining arc coordinates, we call the **pie.draw()** method to draw the pie wedge. The statement is

```
pie.draw(START_X, START_Y, WIDTH, HEIGHT, arcBegin, arcSize);
```

After we create the pie wedge, we create its label. To do this, we first find the midpoint of the wedge, with the statement

```
int midPoint = 360 - (arcBegin + arcSize/2);
```

Next, we determine the *x* and *y* coordinates for the label, with the following statements:

```
x = CENTER_X + (int)Math.round(
               (WIDTH/2+10) * Math.cos(radians));
y = CENTER_Y + (int)Math.round(
               (HEIGHT/2+12) * Math.sin(radians));
```

If the midpoint of the wedge lies in the left half of the pie, we must move the *x* coordinate to the left. We use the font metrics methods to determine the distance we need to adjust *x*. The statement that moves the label to the left is

```
if ((midPoint > 90) && (midPoint < 270))
    x = x -  fm.stringWidth(wedgeName);
```

We also use the font metrics methods to center the caption if the user entered one. The statements used to place the caption on the page are as follows:

```
captionName = captionField.getText();
if (captionName.length() > 0) {
    x = pie.getBounds().width/2 -
        fm.stringWidth(captionName)/2;
    pie.printLabel(captionName, x, 10);
}
```

Notice that the we use the **pie.getBounds()** method to obtains the width of the *pie* panel. The **init()** method used the **setSize()** method to suggest a size for the *pie* panel. Although the browser can ignore this request, by using the **setSize()** method, we can obtain the actual bounds of the *pie* panel.

Figure 26.52 contains the definition of the **actionPerformed()** method.

```
public void actionPerformed(ActionEvent e)
 {//draw the pie chart and put the labels on the page
    String wedgeName = inputField[0].getText();
    int percent = Integer.parseInt(inputField[1].getText());
    wedgeName = wedgeName + ": " + percent + "%";
    int arcSize = (int) Math.round(360 * percent/100.0);
    int arcBegin = lastBegin + lastSize;
    int midPoint = 360 - (arcBegin + arcSize/2);
    int x,y;
    lastBegin = arcBegin;
    lastSize = arcSize;
    pie.draw(START_X, START_Y, WIDTH, HEIGHT, arcBegin, arcSize);
    double radians = 3.14159/180 *midPoint;
    x = CENTER_X + (int)Math.round((WIDTH/2+10) * Math.cos(radians));

    //angles for labels revolve in opposite direction, 90 is at bottom
    //adjust for left half of pie
    if ((midPoint > 90) && (midPoint < 270))
       x = x -  fm.stringWidth(wedgeName);
    y = CENTER_Y + (int)Math.round((HEIGHT/2+12) * Math.sin(radians));
    pie.setForeground(Color.black);
    pie.printLabel(wedgeName, x, y);
 //center the title on the page
 captionName = captionField.getText();
 if (captionName.length() > 0) {
   x = pie.getBounds().width/2 - fm.stringWidth(captionName)/2;
   pie.printLabel(captionName, x, 10);
 }
 }
}
```

Figure 26.52 The **actionPerformed()** Method: *GenericPie* Class

➤ ◼ **EXERCISES**

1. **The *Simple Shapes* Page.** Figure 26.53 contains an example of each of the basic drawing methods. Create a page like the one displayed in Figure 26.53. Your page does not need to duplicate the one displayed in Figure 26.53.

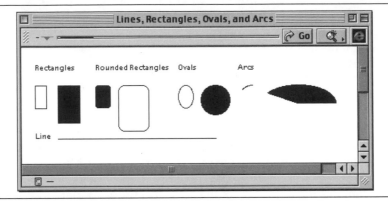

Figure 26.53 The *Simple Shapes* Page

2. **The *Simple Image* Page.** Figure 26.54 contains a page that loads a simple image into the browser, using a 2 × 2 grid. You will find the image in the CD that accompanies this text (*star.jpeg*).

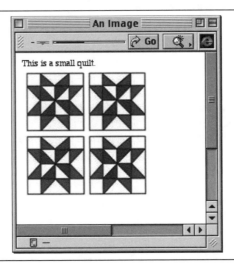

Figure 26.54 The *Simple Image* Page

(*Hint*: The *Image* class contains **getHeight()** and **getWidth()** methods, which return the height and width of the image. Figure 26.55 displays the syntax for these methods.)

`int getHeight();`	Return the height of an image in pixels.
`int getWidth();`	Return the width of an image in pixels.

Figure 26.55 *Image* Methods

3. **The *Simple Line* Page.** Figure 26.56 contains a line demonstration page. Reproduce this page.

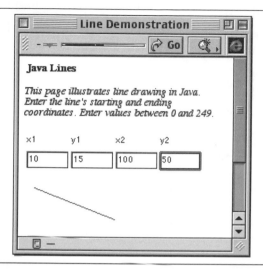

Figure 26.56 The *Simple Line* Page

4. **The *Simple Rectangle* Page.** Figure 26.57 contains a simple rectangle demonstration page. The page draw a single rectangle, using the user's input. Reproduce this page.

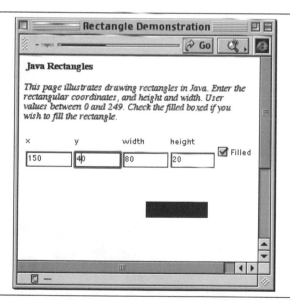

Figure 26.57 The *Simple Rectangle* Page

5. **The *Multiple Line Demonstration* Page.** Figure 26.58 contains a *Multiple Line Demonstration* page. Reproduce this page.

6. **The *Multiple Rectangle Demonstration* Page.** Figure 26.59 contains a *Multiple Rectangle Demonstration* page. Reproduce this page.

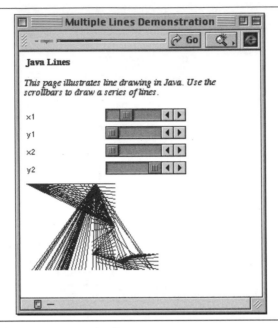

Figure 26.58 The *Multiple Line Demonstration* Page

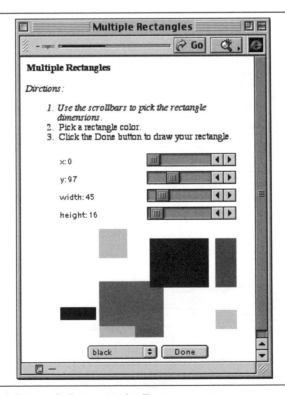

Figure 26.59 The *Multiple Rectangle Demonstration* Page

7. **The *Multiple Oval Demonstration* Page.** Figure 26.60 contains a *Multiple Oval Demonstration* page. Reproduce this page.

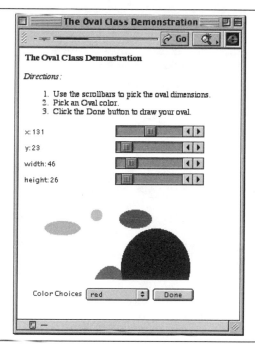

Figure 26.60 The *Multiple Oval Demonstration* Page

8. **The *Multiple Arc Demonstration* Page.** Figure 26.61 contains a *Multiple Arc Demonstration* page. Reproduce this page.

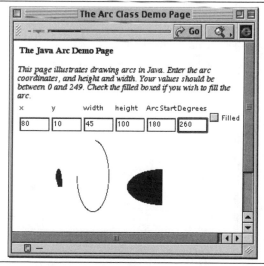

Figure 26.61 The *Multiple Arc Demonstration* Page

9. **The *PolyLine* Page.** Figure 26.62 contains a *Polyline* page. When the user clicks the mouse, the page creates a line between the previous mouse point and the current mouse point. Reproduce this page.

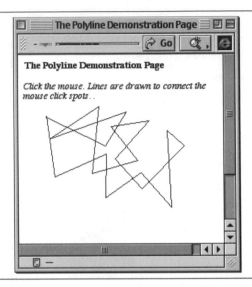

Figure 26.62 The *Polyline Demonstration* Page

10. **The *Polygon Demonstration* Page.** Figure 26.63 contains a *Polygon Demonstration* page. Reproduce this page.

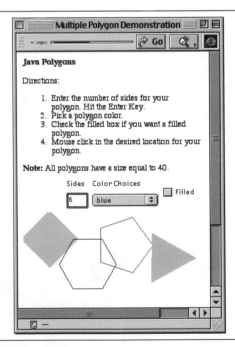

Figure 26.63 The *Polygon Demonstration* Page

11. **The *Doodling Mouse* Page.** Figure 26.64 contains a *Doodling Mouse* page. The page draws the selected shape when the user drags the mouse. The selected shapes are *Line, Open Rectangle, Filled Rectangle, Open Oval,* and *Filled Oval.*

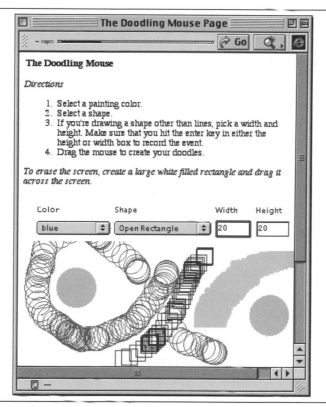

Figure 26.64 The *Doodling Mouse* Page

12. **The *Doodling Mouse* Page, version 2.** The first version of the *Doodling Mouse* page draws continuously. Remove the *mouse drag* and change the page to a *mouse click* version. The page should draw the shape at the clicked region.

13. **The *Shape Identification* Page.** Create a *Shape Identification* page for elementary school children. Use a `Choice` object to display the elementary shapes, from triangles to decagons. Use a second `Choice` object to display a list of colors. Add a *Done* button. Draw the shape in the selected color. Print an appropriate message, such as *The triangle is yellow.*

14. **The *Arc Demo* Page, revisited.** Modify the *Arc Demo* page so that it uses scroll bars for the width, height, arc beginning, and arc size. Add a `Choice` object for the colors and a *Done* button. When the user clicks the mouse, draw the arc.

15. **The *Multiple Rectangle* Page, revisited.** Modify the *Multiple Rectangle* page. Use the mouse to determine the *x* and *y* coordinates.

16. **The *Multiple Oval* Page, revisited.** Modify the *Multiple Oval* page. Use the mouse to determine the *x* and *y* coordinates.

17. **The *Rounded Rectangle* Page.** Create a *Rounded Rectangle* Page. Use scrollbars for the width, height, arc width, and arc height. Use the mouse to determine the *x* and *y* coordinates. Include a *Choice* object containing the standard colors.

18. **The *Twirling Polylines* Page.** Figure 26.65 contains a *Twirling Polylines* page. Implement this page.

    (*Hint:* Modify the *Polylines* page. Use *angle + angleChange* as a parameter to the **sin()** and **cos()** calls. Add a radian to the angle change at the end of the **for** statement.

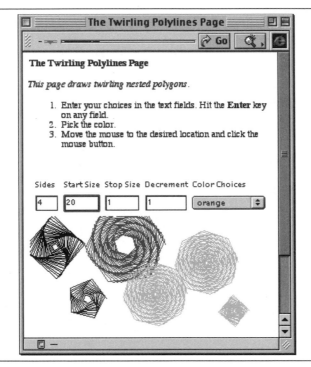

Figure 26.65 The *Twirling Polylines* Page

27 Swing Basics

INTRODUCTION

In Chapter 25, we used AWT (Abstract Windowing Toolkit) components to create interactive forms. In the remaining two chapters, we cover Swing. This chapter introduces Swing basics. The following chapter discusses Swing form elements.

SWING CHARACTERISTICS

Although Swing is a superset of AWT, Swing uses a different design philosophy. AWT relies upon *heavyweight* components; Swing uses *lightweight* components. An examination of the AWT class libraries shows that every component has a *peer*. For example, the TextField class has a peer, TextFieldPeer. The peer contains the platform-dependent information. When we create a TextField object, Java relies upon the peer to create the object on a specific platform. This means that the appearance of a text field can vary across browsers. The hidden peer makes the AWT components *heavyweight*.

Swing components do not have peers; hence, they are called *lightweight*. In addition, Swing components have a consistent look and feel. They are not platform-specific. The default "look and feel" is *Metal*, which is what we'll use in the next two chapters. Swing also provides *Motif* and *Windows* "look and feel," if you prefer those styles.

A Comparison of Swing with AWT

Swing and AWT applets differ in further respects:

ContentPane. In AWT, we add components directly to the applet. In Swing, we add components to *ContentPane*; we cannot add them directly to the applet. Each class definition contains a *Container* that holds the content pane. We obtain the content pane with the statement

```
Container contentPane = getContentPane();
```

Default Layout Manager. The default layout manager for AWT applets is *FlowLayout*. The default layout manager for Swing applets is *BorderLayout*.

The `repaint()` *Method.*   AWT applets always invoke the `update()` method prior to each call to the `paint()` method. The `update()` method erases the drawing surface, so that we start with a clean slate. Swing applets do *not* invoke the `update()` method. This means that the drawing surface is "dirty" after each call to the `repaint()` method.

Component Style.   The default style for Swing components is a gray background with a blue foreground and no borders. The background or foreground color of any component can be changed. In addition, Swing supports several border classes that let us choose the best border for each component.

Layout Managers.   Swing supports all of the layout managers available in AWT. Swing also includes four new layout managers: *BoxLayout, ScrollPaneLayout, OverlayLayout*, and *ViewPortLayout*. Here, we will cover only the *BoxLayout* manager.

Image Icons.   Swing contains an `ImageIcon` class. Many of the component constructors support icons. The use of icons makes our applets much more appealing visually.

Swing Components.   All Swing components use the prefix **J**, to differentiate Swing components from their AWT counterparts. Although we can include both Swing and AWT components in the same applet, this practice is generally discouraged. Because AWT components are heavyweight, they tend to overlay the lightweight Swing components. Generally, there is no need to combine Swing and AWT components because Swing contains equivalents to all of the AWT components.

A Comparison between Swing and AWT Components

We can compare Swing components to AWT components, as follows:

Identical or Nearly Identical Swing and AWT Components.   Swing provides *JTextField, JTextArea, JLabel, JButton, JList, JPanel*, and *JApplet* components that are virtually identical to their AWT counterparts.

Swing Components with Slightly Different Names.   The Swing `JScrollBar` class is equivalent to the AWT `Scrollbar` class. The Swing `JCheckBox` class is equivalent to the AWT `Checkbox` class.

Swing Components that are Similar to AWT Components.   Swing does not support the `CheckboxGroup` or `Choice` components. The Swing `RadioButton` class is similar to the AWT `CheckboxGroup` class; the Swing `ComboBox` class is similar to the AWT `Choice` class.

New Components.   Swing contains several new components. We examine the `JToggleButton`, `JOptionPane`, `JSlider`, and border classes.

Swing Setup

Swing is a superset of AWT that is included with the Java 1.2 release. Swing applets will run on Netscape Navigator, Versions 4.04 and greater, and on Internet Explorer, Version 4.00 or greater. In either case, you will need to change the system **CLASSPATH** variable so that it includes the location of the Swing jar files.

DIALOG BOXES

When we created our first JavaScript pages in Chapter 8, we relied upon the **alert()**, **prompt()**, and **confirm()** methods of the *Windows* object to obtain or pass information to a user. Swing has resurrected these small pop-up windows in its *JOptionPane* class. Figure 27.1 contains the *JOptionPane* methods that create these windows.

```
String showInputDialog(Object contents);

int showConfirmDialog(Component parent, Object contents);

void showMessageDialog(Component parent, Object contents, String title, int WINDOW_TYPE);
```

Figure 27.1 The *JOptionPane* Methods

All of the *JOptionPane* methods require an object that holds the contents of the pop-up window. In the case of the **showDialogInput()** and **showConfirmDialog()** methods, the object contains the prompt to the user. The object passed to the **showMessageDialog()** method could be anything. Passing an object as the parameter to these methods gives us greater flexibility. For example, we could pass strings, text areas, or icons to these methods.

The **showDialogInput()** method contains only the object as a parameter. In contrast, the **showConfirmDialog()** method requires the parent component and the window's contents as parameters. In most cases, we use *null* for the parent. The **showMessageDialog()** method requires two parameters in addition to the parent and the window's contents. The additional parameters let us put a title at the top of the window and specify the window's type. Figure 27.2 contains the *JOptionPane* constants that we use with the **showMessageDialog()** method.

```
JOptionPane.ERROR_MESSAGE
JOptionPane.INFORMATION_MESSAGE
JOptionPane.PLAIN_MESSAGE
JOptionPane.QUESTION_MESSAGE
JOptionPane.WARNING_MESSAGE
```

Figure 27.2 *JOptionPane* Constants

We create two simple pages to illustrate the *JOptionPane* methods. These pages are also our first introduction to Swing.

The *First Name* Page

As our first example of a Swing *JApplet*, we rewrite the *First Name* page appearing in Chapter 8. (See Figure 8.16.) Figure 27.3 displays the prompt window generated by the **showInputDialog()** method. This method places the *Input* title at the top of the window. It also places a question-mark icon, a text field for the user's response, and *OK* and *Cancel* buttons inside the window. The parameter passed to the method determines the prompt.

Figure 27.4 displays the response window generated by the **showMessageDialog()** method. This method places the information icon and the *OK* button inside the window. We supply the window's title and contents.

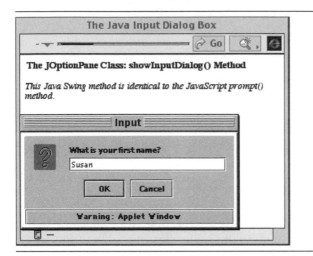

Figure 27.3 The *First Name* Page, Swing version   **Figure 27.4** The Processed *First Name* Page

The *PromptBox* Class Definition

A *Swing* applet begins with statements that load the Java packages. Swing applets use the same AWT packages; however, we add the Swing package to this list. The necessary **import** statements are the following:

```
import java.awt.*;
import java.awt.event.*;
import java.applet.*;
import javax.swing.*;
```

As is obvious from these statements, the Swing components are not in the *java* package but the *javax* package.

The header of a Swing class definition also differs from its AWT counterpart, because we must extend the *JApplet* class. The header for the *PromptBox* class definition that implements the *First Name* page is

```
public class PromptBox extends JApplet
```

The body of the *PromptBox* class contains calls to the **showInputDialog()** and **showMessageDialog()** methods. Because we are not creating components that reside on the applet, we don't need to worry about creating a content pane in these first examples.

Figure 27.5 contains the *PromptBox* class definition. The calls to the *JOptionPane* methods are highlighted. You might want to compare these calls to their JavaScript counterparts.

The *Confirm Window* Page

As our second example of the *JOptionPane* methods, we create a page that uses a confirm window. Figure 27.6 shows a sample page. The **showConfirmDialog()** method places the title *Select an Option*

```
import java.awt.*;
import java.awt.event.*;
import java.applet.*;
import javax.swing.*;
public class PromptBox extends JApplet
{
  public void init()
  {//check each of the Dialog boxes
  String name =
      JOptionPane.showInputDialog("What is your first name?");
  String result = "Glad to meet you, " + name + "!";
  JOptionPane.showMessageDialog(null,
      result,"Information",JOptionPane.INFORMATION_MESSAGE);
 }
}
```

Figure 27.5 The *PromptBox* Class Definition

at the top of the window. The method also places the question-mark icon and the *Yes, No,* and *Cancel* buttons inside the window. We pass the component's parent (which is usually *null*), and the window's contents as parameters.

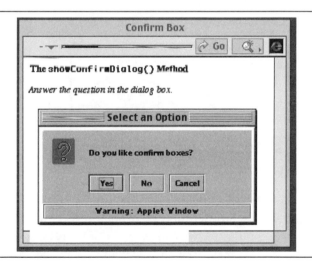

Figure 27.6 The *Confirm Window* Page

The Swing version of a confirm window differs from its JavaScript counterpart. The JavaScript version contains only *OK* and *Cancel* buttons. Because there are only two buttons, JavaScript returns *true* when the user selects the *OK* button, *false* when the user selects the *Cancel* button. As is evident from Figure 27.6, the Swing version of the confirm window contains three buttons. Swing returns a zero when the user selects the *Yes* button, a one when the user selects the *No* button, a two when the user selects the *Cancel* button. We use this three-valued approach to illustrate the plain, error, and question windows available in the **showMessageDialog()** method. We leave the warning window as an exercise.

Figure 27.7(a) shows the plain window displayed when the user selects the *Yes* button; Figure 27.7(b) shows the error window displayed when the user selects the *No* button; Figure 27.7(c) shows the question window displayed when the user selects the *Cancel* button. Each window contains a single *OK* button. The *JOptionPane* constant determines the icon displayed in the window.

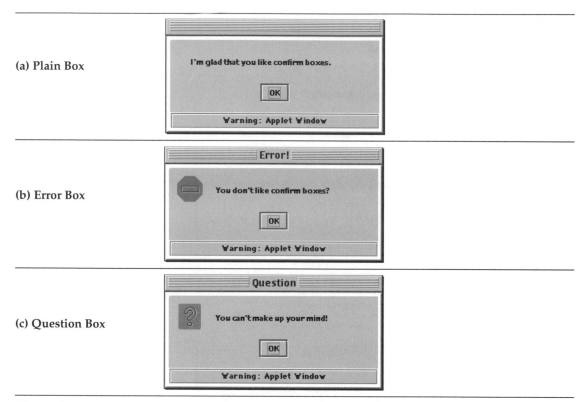

(a) Plain Box

(b) Error Box

(c) Question Box

Figure 27.7 Output from the *Confirm Window* Page

Figure 27.8 contains the definition of the *ConfirmBox* class. The *JOptionPane* method calls are highlighted. As this figure indicates, we call the **showConfirmDialog()** method and place the result in the *confirm* variable. The **switch** statement creates a message based on the value stored in *confirm*.

BORDERS

Each AWT component comes with a border style that varies according to the component. Although we can change a component's background and foreground color, we cannot change its border style. Swing has solved this problem by offering several different border styles. By default, Swing components are displayed without a border. To change the default, we use the **setBorder()**

```
import java.awt.*;
import java.awt.event.*;
import java.applet.*;
import javax.swing.*;
public class ConfirmBox extends JApplet
{
 public void init()
 {
    int confirm = JOptionPane.showConfirmDialog(null,
          "Do you like confirm boxes?");
    switch(confirm)
    {
    case 0:   JOptionPane.showMessageDialog(null,
                "I'm glad that you like confirm boxes.",
                "", JOptionPane.PLAIN_MESSAGE);
              break;
    case 1:  JOptionPane.showMessageDialog(null,
                "You don't like confirm boxes?",
                "Error!", JOptionPane.ERROR_MESSAGE);
              break;
    case 2:  JOptionPane.showMessageDialog(null,
                "You can't make up your mind!",
                "Question", JOptionPane.QUESTION_MESSAGE);
    }
 }
}
```

Figure 27.8 The *ConfirmBox* Class Definition

method, passing one of Swing's border classes as the parameter. The Swing border classes are found in their own package, which we load by means of the statement

  import javax.swing.border.*;

We now create several small pages, each of which illustrates one or more of the border classes. Although we use labels to show the border styles, we can use the **setBorder()** method with all of the Swing components. As we examine these pages, you might want to compare the labels that we create with the single label style available in AWT.

Line Borders

The first border page uses the *LineBorder, MatteBorder,* and *EtchedBorder* classes. Figure 27.9 contains a sample page. The label's text identifies the border.

As its name implies, the *LineBorder* class creates a line border. Figure 27.10(a) contains the *LineBorder* constructors. The first constructor creates a one-pixel border in the color passed as a parameter. The second constructor creates an *n*-pixel border in the color passed as a parameter.

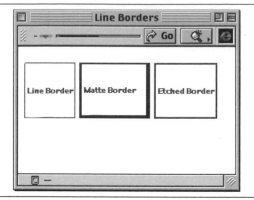

Figure 27.9 The *Line Borders* Page

Figure 27.10(b) contains the *MatteBorder* constructors. A matte border is "cut" to match the object. We specify different line sizes for the top, left, right, and bottom borders. We can pass these sizes individually or as an *Insets* object. We also pass the border color as a parameter. The *LineBorder* and *MatteBorder* classes produce the same border when the matte border uses the same size for the top, left, bottom, and right borders.

Figure 27.10(c) contains the constructors for *EtchedBorder*. This border produces a three-dimensional effect, because we pass a constant reflecting an apparent light source. The **EtchedBorder.RAISED** constant simulates an imaginary light source at the top left corner. The first constructor uses grays for the highlight and shadow. The second constructor uses the first color for the highlight and the second color for the shadow. The **EtchedBorder.LOWERED** constant simulates an imaginary light source at the bottom right corner. The second constructor uses the first color for the shadow and the second color for the highlight.

<table>
<tr><td>**(a)**</td><td>

```
LineBorder(Color lineColor);
LineBorder(Color lineColor, int n);
```
</td></tr>
<tr><td>**(b)**</td><td>

```
MatteBorder(Insets insets, Color borderColor);
MatteBorder(int top, int left, int bottom, int right, Color borderColor);
```
</td></tr>
<tr><td>**(c)**</td><td>

```
EtchedBorder(int TYPE);
EtchedBorder(int TYPE, Color firstColor, Color secondcolor);
```
</td></tr>
</table>

Figure 27.10 The *LineBorder, MatteBorder,* and *EtchedBorder* Constructors

The *LineBorderDemo* Class Definition

The *LineBorderDemo* class creates a container for the content pane. We also create a label for each of the border examples. The field declarations are as follows:

```
private Container contentPane = getContentPane();
private JLabel lineLabel = new JLabel(" Line Border ");
private JLabel matteLabel = new JLabel(" Matte Border ");
private JLabel etchedLabel = new JLabel(" Etched Border ");
```

Notice that we use the *JLabel* class to construct each of the labels.

The **init()** method sets the content panel's background color to white. We also define a new border layout with a horizontal and vertical gap of five pixels. We use the **setBorder()** method to create a new border for each of the labels. The statements that set the borders are the following:

```
lineLabel.setBorder(new LineBorder(Color.blue));
matteLabel.setBorder(new MatteBorder(2,3,4,5, Color.blue));
etchedLabel.setBorder(new
    EtchedBorder(EtchedBorder.LOWERED, Color.black,
    Color.red));
```

We also add each label to the content pane. Figure 27.11 contains the definition of the **init()** method. Try modifying the border constructors. Change the colors and the size of the lines.

```
import java.awt.*;
import java.awt.event.*;
import java.applet.*;
import javax.swing.*;
import javax.swing.border.*;
public class LineBorderDemo extends JApplet
{
  private Container contentPane = getContentPane();
  private JLabel lineLabel = new JLabel(" Line Border ");
  private JLabel matteLabel = new JLabel(" Matte Border ");
  private JLabel etchedLabel = new JLabel(" Etched Border ");
  public void init()
  {
    contentPane.setLayout(new BorderLayout(5,5));
    contentPane.setBackground(Color.white);
    lineLabel.setBorder(new LineBorder(Color.blue));
    contentPane.add(lineLabel,BorderLayout.WEST);
    matteLabel.setBorder(new MatteBorder(2,3,4,5, Color.blue));
    contentPane.add(matteLabel,BorderLayout.CENTER);
    etchedLabel.setBorder(new EtchedBorder(EtchedBorder.LOWERED,
        Color.black, Color.red));
    contentPane.add(etchedLabel, BorderLayout.EAST);
  }
}
```

Figure 27.11 The *LineBorderDemo* Class Definition

Bevel Borders

Swing provides two types of bevel borders: a bevel border and a soft bevel border. Both border styles produce a three-dimensional effect. Figure 27.12 contains a *Bevel Borders* page that illustrates these two styles.

Beveled borders are similar to etched borders. Both border styles use **RAISED** and **LOWERED** constants to simulate the effects of an imaginary light source. The constructors also contain parameters for the highlight and shadow colors. However, each of the beveled borders contains an additional constructor, which lets us specify outer and inner highlight colors and outer and inner shadow colors. Figure 27.13 contains the definitions of the beveled border constructors.

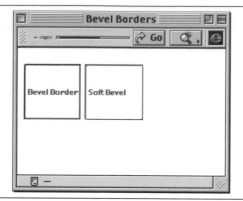

Figure 27.12 The *Bevel Borders* Page

```
BevelBorder(int TYPE, Color firstColor, Color secondColor);
SoftBevelBorder(int TYPE, Color firstColor, Color secondColor);

BevelBorder(int TYPE, Color firstColorOuter, Color firstColorInner, Color secondColorOuter,
  Color secondColorInner);

SoftBevelBorder(int TYPE, Color firstColorOuter, Color firstColorInner, Color secondColorOuter,
  Color secondColorInner);
```

Figure 27.13 The *BevelBorder* and *SoftBevelBorder* Constructors

The *BevelBorderDemo* class implements the *Bevel Border* page. The class definition has a container for the content pane and a label for each of the border styles. The labels are defined as follows:

```
private JLabel bevelLabel = new JLabel(" Bevel Border ");
private JLabel softLabel = new JLabel(" Soft Bevel ");
```

The **init()** method calls the **setBorder()** method to create a new border style for each of the labels. We create and set the border for *bevelLabel* with the statement

```
bevelLabel.setBorder(new BevelBorder(BevelBorder.RAISED,
Color.blue, Color.red));
```

Because *bevelLabel* has a raised border, the first color (blue) is the highlight, and the second color (red) is the shadow.

We create and set the border for *softLabel* with the statement

```
softLabel.setBorder(new
SoftBevelBorder(SoftBevelBorder.LOWERED,
Color.blue, Color.red));
```

Because *softLabel* has a lowered border, the first color (blue) is the shadow and the second color (red) is the highlight.

Figure 27.14 contains the definition of the *BevelBorderDemo* class. Try modifying the colors, and try using the four-color constructors.

```
import java.awt.*;
import java.awt.event.*;
import java.applet.*;
import javax.swing.*;
import javax.swing.border.*;
public class BevelBorderDemo extends JApplet
{
 private Container contentPane = getContentPane();
 private JLabel bevelLabel = new JLabel(" Bevel Border ");
 private JLabel softLabel = new JLabel(" Soft Bevel ");
 public void init()
 {
    contentPane.setLayout(new BorderLayout(5,5));
    contentPane.setBackground(Color.white);
    bevelLabel.setBorder(new BevelBorder(BevelBorder.RAISED,
      Color.blue, Color.red));
    contentPane.add(bevelLabel, BorderLayout.WEST);
    softLabel.setBorder(new SoftBevelBorder(SoftBevelBorder.LOWERED,
      Color.blue, Color.red));
    contentPane.add(softLabel, BorderLayout.CENTER);
  }
}
```

Figure 27.14 The *BevelBorderDemo* Class Definition

Titled Borders

Many of our previous applets used arrays of labels, components, and panels. We used the labels to identify the components. Swing provides titled borders that frequently eliminate the need to create component labels. Figure 27.15 contains a *Titled Border* page that illustrates these border styles. The first label uses the default title style. This style places the title in the upper left-hand corner. Notice the gray background for the title. The second label places the title at the bottom center position. The title is in a red, Monospaced, bold, 14-point font.

Figure 27.16 contains the *TitledBorder* constructors. Each of the constructors requires a *Border* object as the first parameter, which means that we can create titled borders under any of the border styles. The second parameter of each constructor is a string representing the page's title.

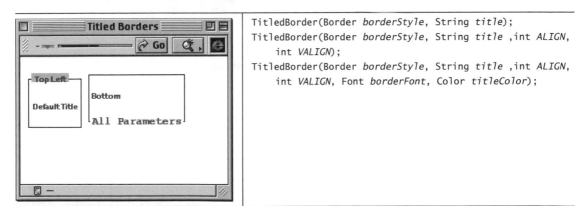

```
TitledBorder(Border borderStyle, String title);
TitledBorder(Border borderStyle, String title ,int ALIGN,
       int VALIGN);
TitledBorder(Border borderStyle, String title ,int ALIGN,
       int VALIGN, Font borderFont, Color titleColor);
```

Figure 27.15 The *Titled Borders* Page   **Figure 27.16** The *TitledBorder* Constructors

The first *TitledBorder* constructor creates a titled border with the title placed in the upper left-hand corner. The second and third constructors contain horizontal and vertical alignment parameters that let us change the title's location. Figure 27.17 contains the alignment constants. The last constructor also contains parameters that let us change the title's font and color.

Horizontal ALIGNment Constants	Vertical ALIGNment Constants
LEFT (default)	ABOVE_TOP
CENTER	TOP (default)
RIGHT	BELOW_TOP
	ABOVE_BOTTOM
	BOTTOM
	BELOW_BOTTOM

Figure 27.17 The *TitledBorder* Constants

The *TitleBorderDemo* Class

The *TitleBorderDemo* class implements the *Titled Border* page. The definition contains labels for each of the border styles. The statements that create the labels are the following:

```
private JLabel topTitle = new JLabel(" Default Title ");
private JLabel bottomTitle = new JLabel("Bottom ");
```

We also create a new font for the bottom title with the statement

```
private Font titleFont = new Font("MonoSpaced",
Font.BOLD, 14);
```

The **init()** method uses the **setBorder()** method to create a titled border for each label. The *topTitle* label uses the default title alignment. We create this border with the statement

```
topTitle.setBorder(new TitledBorder (
new LineBorder(Color.black, 1),
" Top Left "));
```

Creating the *bottomTitle* border requires two statements. The first statement sets the background color to white. The second statement uses the **setBorder()** statement to create the new titled border. The statements are the following:

```
bottomTitle.setBackground(Color.white);
bottomTitle.setBorder(new TitledBorder(
    new LineBorder(Color.black, 1), "All Parameters",
    TitledBorder.CENTER, TitledBorder.BOTTOM,
    titleFont,Color.red));
```

Figure 27.18 contains the definition of the *TitleBorderDemo* class. Try changing the border styles passed as the first parameter.

Other Border Styles

The two remaining border styles create empty and compound borders. The empty border is the default border style. A compound border contains two border styles. Figure 27.19 contains a page that illustrates these border styles.

```java
import java.awt.*;
import java.awt.event.*;
import java.applet.*;
import javax.swing.*;
import javax.swing.border.*;
public class TitleBorderDemo extends JApplet
{
  private Container contentPane = getContentPane();
  private JLabel topTitle = new JLabel(" Default Title ");
  private JLabel bottomTitle = new JLabel("Bottom ");
  private Font titleFont = new Font("MonoSpaced", Font.BOLD, 14);

  public void init()
  {
    contentPane.setBackground(Color.white);
    contentPane.setLayout(new BorderLayout(5,5));
    topTitle.setBorder(new TitledBorder
            (new LineBorder(Color.black, 1), " Top Left "));
    contentPane.add(topTitle, BorderLayout.WEST);
    bottomTitle.setBackground(Color.white);
    bottomTitle.setBorder(new TitledBorder(
      new LineBorder(Color.black, 1), "All Parameters",
      TitledBorder.CENTER, TitledBorder.BOTTOM,
      titleFont,Color.red));
    contentPane.add(bottomTitle, BorderLayout.CENTER);
  }
}
```

Figure 27.18 The *TitledBorderDemo* Class Definition

Figure 27.20 contains the definitions of *EmptyBorder* and *CompoundBorder* constructors. We use the *EmptyBorder* constructor to specify the spacing between a border and its component. We can pass an *Insets* object or integers representing the top, left, bottom, and right spacing in pixels. The *CompoundBorder* constructor requires two parameters, each representing a border style. The compound border displayed in Figure 27.19 is composed of three border styles. We can produce these more complex borders by nesting compound borders.

Figure 27.19 The *Other Border Styles* Page

(a) EmptyBorder(Insets *insets*);
        EmptyBorder(int *top*, int *left*, int *bottom*,
            int *right*);

(b) CompoundBorder(Border *outerBorder*, Border
            innerBorder);

Figure 27.20 The *EmptyBorder* and
CompoundBorder Constructors

The *OtherBorderDemo* Page

The *OtherBorderDemo* page creates labels for each of the border styles. The labels are defined as follows:

```
private JLabel emptyLabel = new JLabel(" Empty Border ");
private JLabel compoundLabel = new JLabel(" Bevel + Empty + Etched ");
```

The compound border style is complex, so we create a class field to represent it. The statement that creates this border style is

```
private CompoundBorder compound = new CompoundBorder(
    new CompoundBorder(
    new BevelBorder(BevelBorder.RAISED, Color.black,
        Color.gray),
    new EmptyBorder(2,2,2,2)),
    new EtchedBorder(10, Color.red, Color.black));
```

Notice that the first parameter in the *CompoundBorder* constructor is a call to the *CompoundBorder* constructor. The inner compound border constructor creates an outer bevel border and an inner empty border of two pixels. The empty border separates the beveled and etched borders. The first parameter becomes the outer border for the label. The inner border is the etched border that we pass as the second parameter.

The **init()** method uses the **setBorder()** method to create the two border styles. The statements are as follows:

```
emptyLabel.setBorder(new EmptyBorder(5,5,5,5));
compoundLabel.setBorder(compound);
```

Figure 27.21 contains the definition of the *OtherBorderDemo* class. Try changing the border styles used in the compound border. Try creating a compound border composed of four border styles.

```
import java.awt.*;
import java.awt.event.*;
import java.applet.*;
import javax.swing.*;
import javax.swing.border.*;
public class OtherBorderDemo extends JApplet
{
 private Container contentPane = getContentPane();
 private JLabel emptyLabel = new JLabel(" Empty Border ");
 private JLabel compoundLabel = new JLabel(" Bevel + Empty + Etched ");
 private CompoundBorder compound = new CompoundBorder(
        new CompoundBorder(
        new BevelBorder(BevelBorder.RAISED, Color.black, Color.gray),
        new EmptyBorder(2,2,2,2)),
        new EtchedBorder(10, Color.red, Color.black));
 public void init()
 {
    contentPane.setLayout(new BorderLayout(5,5));
    contentPane.setBackground(Color.white);
    emptyLabel.setBorder(new EmptyBorder(5,5,5,5));
    contentPane.add(emptyLabel, BorderLayout.WEST);
    compoundLabel.setBorder(compound);
    contentPane.add(compoundLabel, BorderLayout.CENTER);
  }
}
```

Figure 27.21 The *OtherBorderDemo* Class Definition

TEXT FIELDS AND TEXT AREAS

The Swing *JTextField* and *JTextArea* classes are virtually identical to their AWT counterparts. Swing *JTextField* and *JTextArea* components use the same methods and listeners as their AWT counterparts. The constructors use the same parameters, but we must remember to put the *J* prefix in front of the Swing constructors.

To illustrate the *Swing JTextField* and *JTextArea* classes, we rewrite the *Insert Text* page appearing in Figures 21.42 through 21.44. The new version of this page appears in Figure 27.22.

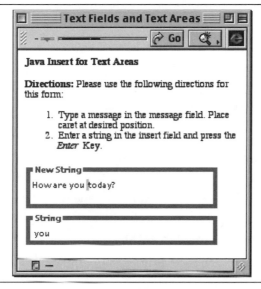

Figure 27.22 The *Insert Text* Page, Swing version

The Swing version of *InsertText* uses titled borders to create the captions. This page also uses a *BoxLayout* manager to place the components on the content pane.

The *TextExample* Class Definition

Figure 27.23 contains the definition of the *TextExample* class, which implements the *Insert Text* page. The class fields are virtually identical to their counterparts in the AWT version. The changes are highlighted. The **actionPerformed()** method is identical to its counterpart in the AWT version.

The init() Method

The **init()** method creates a box layout manager for the content pane. The *BoxLayout* constructor requires two parameters. The first parameter represents the component, and the second represents the orientation. We specify the orientation using the following *BoxLayout* constants:

```
BoxLayout.X_AXIS
BoxLayout.Y_AXIS
```

We use **X_AXIS** to align components horizontally; we use **Y_AXIS** to align components vertically. The definition of the constructor is

```
BoxLayout(Component comp, int ORIENTATION);
```

```
import java.awt.*;
import java.awt.event.*;
import java.applet.*;
import javax.swing.*;
import javax.swing.border.*;

public class TextExample extends JApplet implements ActionListener
{ //Use a text area and text field to illustrate an insert operation
  private Container contentPane = getContentPane();
  private JTextArea messageField = new JTextArea(5, 25);
  private JTextField insertField = new JTextField(25);
  private String insertStr;
  private int caretPos;
 //Put the init() Method Here
public void actionPerformed(ActionEvent e)
{ //Obtain find/replace strings and lengths
    insertStr = insertField.getText();
    caretPos = messageField.getCaretPosition();
    messageField.insert(insertStr, caretPos);
}
}
```

Figure 27.23 The *TextExample* Class Definition

We create and set the *BoxLayout* for the content pane with the statement

```
contentPane.setLayout(new
BoxLayout(contentPane, BoxLayout.Y_AXIS));
```

Notice that we pass the content pane as the first parameter. The second parameter aligns the text area and text field vertically.

Both components use a titled border with a five-pixel gray line border. We create and set the borders with the following statements:

```
messageField.setBorder( new TitledBorder(
    new LineBorder(Color.gray, 5), "New String"));
insertField.setBorder(new TitledBorder(
    new LineBorder(Color.gray, 5), "String")););
```

We conclude the **init()** method by adding the components to the content pane. We also add an action listener to the text field. Figure 27.24 contains the definition of the **init()** method.

```
public void init()
{ //add prompt, textfield, and actionListener
    contentPane.setLayout(new BoxLayout(contentPane, BoxLayout.Y_AXIS));
    messageField.setBorder( new TitledBorder(
        new LineBorder(Color.gray, 5), "New String"));
    insertField.setBorder(new TitledBorder(
        new LineBorder(Color.gray, 5), "String"));
    contentPane.add(messageField);
    contentPane.add(insertField);
    insertField.addActionListener(this);
}
```

Figure 27.24 The **init()** Method: *TextExample* Class

BUTTON AND LABEL ICONS

We've used labels to demonstrate Swing's border styles. In each of the examples, we created a simple label by passing a string as a parameter. Swing offers additional constructors that create labels by using combinations of strings and icons. We can do the same thing with buttons. The next example illustrates these features. Figure 27.25 contains a *Hummingbird* button and a *Cardinal* label. Pressing the *Hummingbird* button activates a pop-up window that lists the Latin name, favorite foods, and clutch size of Ruby-throated Hummingbirds. The gray border surrounding the button indicates that the button has been pressed. The button returns to its borderless default when the user presses the *OK* button in the pop-up window. The *Cardinal* label contains a red titled border.

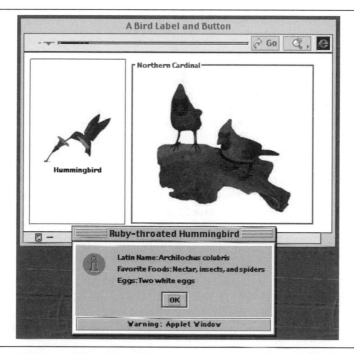

Figure 27.25 The *Bird Label* IPage

Figure 27.26 contains the constructors for the *JLabel* and *JButton* classes. The shaded areas show the new constructors available in Swing. As this figure indicates, we can create labels and buttons by using strings only, image icons only, or both strings and image icons.

JLabel Constructors	*JButton* Constructors
JLabel();	JButton();
JLabel(ImageIcon *icon*);	JButton(ImageIcon *icon*);
JLabel(String *s*);	JButton(String *s*);
JLabel(ImageIcon *icon*, int *ALIGN*);	JButton(ImageIcon *icon*, String *s*);
JLabel(String *s*, int *ALIGN*);	
JLabel(String *s*, ImageIcon *icon*, int *ALIGN*);	

Figure 27.26 The *JButton* and *JLabel* Constructors

The *JLabel* and *AbstractButton* Methods and Constants

The *Hummingbird* button appearing in Figure 27.25 contains both an icon and a string. Notice the placement of the string. The word *Hummingbird* is at the center and bottom of the button. By default, Swing places text in the middle right position of a label or button. In addition, buttons and labels do not contain borders. Swing provides a set of methods that lets us change these defaults. The methods apply to both the *JLabel* and the *AbstractButton* class. The *AbstractButton* class is the ancestor of the `JButton, JCheckBox, JToggleButton,` and `JRadioButton` classes. (We examine the latter three classes in Chapter 28.) This means that we can use these methods with any of the descendant classes. Figure 27.27 lists these methods.

```
void setHorizontalAlignment(int ALIGN);

void setHorizontalTextPosition(int ALIGN);

void setVerticalAlignment(int ALIGN);

void setVerticalTextPosition(int ALIGN);

void setBorderPainted(boolean painted);
```

Figure 27.27 The `JLabel` and `AbstractButton` Methods

The **setBorderPainted()** method contains a single *boolean* parameter. Passing a value of *true* creates a one-pixel black line border around the label or button. The **setHorizontal-TextPosition()** and **setVerticalTextPosition()** methods determine the placement of the string representing the label or button's text. The **setHorizontalAlignment()** and **setVertical-Alignment()** methods determine the placement of all components in a label or button. Figure 27.28(a) lists the horizontal placement constants; Figure 27.28(b) lists the vertical placement constants.

(a) Horizontal ALIGNment Constants	(b) Vertical ALIGNment Constants
SwingConstants.LEFT (default)	SwingConstants.TOP (default)
SwingConstants.CENTER	SwingConstants.MIDDLE
SwingConstants.RIGHT	SwingConstants.BOTTOM

Figure 27.28 Horizontal and Vertical Alignment Constants

The *BirdLabel* Class Definition

The *BirdLabel* class definition creates the *contentPane* class field and the fields for the label and button. The **init()** method creates the image icons and constructs the label and button.

The *BirdLabel* class definition also contains an **actionPeformed()** method. *ActionListener* invokes this method when we press the *Hummingbird* button. Figure 27.29 contains the definition of the *BirdLabel* class.

```
import java.awt.*;
import java.awt.event.*;
import java.applet.*;
import javax.swing.*;
import javax.swing.border.*;
public class BirdLabel extends JApplet implements ActionListener
{
  private JButton hummerButton;
  private JLabel cardinalLabel;
  private Container contentPane = getContentPane();
  //Put the init() Method Here
 //Put the actionPerformed() Method Here
}
```

Figure 27.29 The *BirdLabel* Class Definition

The init() Method

The **init()** method changes the content pane's layout to a border layout with a five-pixel horizontal gap and a one-pixel vertical gap. We construct the *Hummingbird* button with the statement

```
hummerButton = new JButton("Hummingbird",
    new ImageIcon
    (this.getImage(this.getDocumentBase(),"hummingbird.jpeg")));
```

We pass the string literal *Hummingbird* as the first parameter. The second parameter is the *ImageIcon* object that represents the picture. The *ImageIcon* constructor requires a single parameter that represents the image. We use the **getImage()** method to obtain the image. Recall that this method requires two parameters. The first parameter is the URL of the folder containing the image. We use the **getDocumentBase()** method to retrieve the URL. The second parameter is the name of the image file.

Once we've constructed the button, we use the alignment constants to place the *Hummingbird* label in the center bottom position of the label. We also set the button's background to white, and we add an action listener to the button. The statements that accomplish this are the following:

```
hummerButton.setBackground(Color.white);

hummerButton.setVerticalTextPosition(SwingConstants.BOTTOM);

hummerButton.setHorizontalTextPosition(SwingConstants.CENTER);

hummerButton.addActionListener(this);
```

We construct the *Cardinal* label without using more than an image icon as the parameter. We're using a titled border, so we don't need to pass a string identifying the label. We construct the *Cardinal* label and set its border with the following statements:

```
cardinalLabel = new JLabel(new ImageIcon(
    this.getImage(this.getDocumentBase(),
    "cardinal.jpeg")) );
```

```
    cardinalLabel.setBorder(new TitledBorder(
        new LineBorder(Color.red,2),
        "Northern Cardinal"));
```

We also set the background of the *Cardinal* label to white.

We conclude the **init()** method by adding the label and button to the content pane. Figure 27.30 contains the definition of the **init()** method.

```
public void init()
{//Load the image
    contentPane.setLayout(new BorderLayout(5,1));
    hummerButton = new JButton(
      "Hummingbird", new ImageIcon(this.getImage
       (this.getDocumentBase(),"hummingbird.jpeg")));
    hummerButton.setBackground(Color.white);
    hummerButton.setVerticalTextPosition(SwingConstants.BOTTOM);
    hummerButton.setHorizontalTextPosition(SwingConstants.CENTER);
    hummerButton.addActionListener(this);

    cardinalLabel = new JLabel(new ImageIcon(this.getImage(
          this.getDocumentBase(), "cardinal.jpeg")) );
    cardinalLabel.setBorder(new TitledBorder(
      new LineBorder(Color.red,2),
      "Northern Cardinal"));
    cardinalLabel.setBackground(Color.white);
    contentPane.setBackground(Color.white);
    contentPane.add(hummerButton,BorderLayout.WEST);
    contentPane.add(cardinalLabel,BorderLayout.CENTER);
}
```

Figure 27.30 The **init()** Method, *BirdLabel* Class

The **actionPerformed()** Method

The **actionPerformed()** method constructs a string that contains the *Latin name*, *Favorite Food*, and *Eggs*. We call the **showMessageDialog()** method to display this information. Figure 27.31 contains the definition of the **actionPerformed()** method.

```
public void actionPerformed(ActionEvent e)
{
  String hummerInfo = "Latin Name: Archilochus colubris\n" +
      "Favorite Foods: Nectar, insects, and spiders\n" +
      "Eggs: Two white eggs";
  JOptionPane.showMessageDialog(null, hummerInfo,
      "Ruby-throated Hummingbird",
       JOptionPane.INFORMATION_MESSAGE);
  }
```

Figure 27.31 The **actionPerformed()** Method, *BirdLabel* Class

➤ ▌ EXERCISES

1. **The *Warning Window* Page.** Create a page that displays a warning window.

2. **The *First Name* Page, validated version.** Create a Swing version of the *First Name* page appearing in Figure 14.4.

3. **The *Numeric Form* Page, Swing version.** Create a Swing version of the *Numeric Form* appearing in Figure 14.7.

4. **The *Mailing Label* Page, Swing version.** Create a Swing version of the *Mailing Label* page appearing in Figure 19.5. Use the pop-up windows to perform form validation.

5. **The *Text Area* Page, Swing version.** Create a Swing version of the *Text Area* page appearing in Figure 14.15.

6. **The *Text Field* Page, Swing version.** Create a Swing version of the *Text Field* page appearing in Figure 14.48. Validate the first name field.

7. **The *Sales Tax* Page, Swing version.** Create a Swing version of the *Sales Tax* page. Use form validation to ensure that the total cost and the sales tax are greater than zero. (See Figure 12.9.)

8. **The *Test Grade* Page, Swing version.** Create a Swing version of the *Test Grade* page. Use form validation to ensure that both the number of correct answers and the number of total questions are greater than zero. Also verify that the total number of questions is at least as great as the number of correct answers. (See Figure 10.19.)

9. **The *Factorial* Page, Swing version.** Create a Swing version of the *Factorial* page. Use form validation to ensure that n is greater than or equal to zero. (See Figure 11.12.)

10. **The *Titled Border Demonstration* Page.** Create a page that displays several titled borders. Alter the title's location and the border used to construct the titled border.

11. **The *Borders Demonstration* Page.** Create a *Borders Demonstration* page, following the model displayed in Figure 27.32.

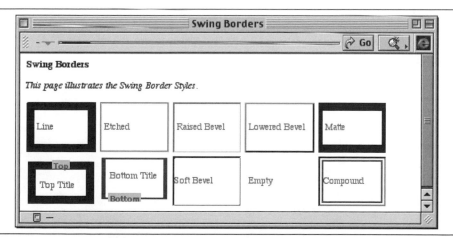

Figure 27.32 The *Borders Demonstration* Page

12. **The *Bird Buttons* Page.** The *CD* contains several bird images in the Chapter 28 folder. Create a set of bird buttons. When the user clicks on a button, display information similar to information displayed in the *Bird Label* page. (See Figure 27.25.)

13. **The *Bird Labels* Page.** Create a set of bird labels that combine the bird's name and image.

14. **The *Sports Buttons* Page.** Create icon buttons for sports. When the user clicks on a button, display information related to the button. For example, you might want to create baseball, basketball, football, and soccer icons. When the user clicks on a button, open a pop-up window that displays information on the sport.

15. **The *Flower Buttons* Page.** Repeat the previous exercise but create a set of flower buttons.

28 Swing Form Elements

INTRODUCTION

In Chapter 27, we explored the Swing *JButton* class. Swing provides three additional button classes: toggle buttons, radio buttons, and checkboxes. All these button classes are descendents of the *AbstractButton* class, so they all inherit the alignment methods listed in Figure 27.27.

TOGGLE BUTTONS

Toggle Buttons are new in Swing. These buttons act like on/off switches. Pressing the button once turns it on. Pressing a second time turns the button off. Figure 28.1 contains the *Bird Toggle* page. In this example, the *Blue Bird* button is on, while the *Chickadee* button is off. Notice the

Figure 28.1 The *Bird Toggle* Page

difference in appearance between these two buttons. When the user turns a toggle button "on," the page displays a pop-up *fact sheet* for the bird.

JToggleButton Constructors and Methods

The *JToggleButton* class has a rich set of constructors. We can create a toggle button by using an icon only, a string only, or both an icon and a string. We can also create a toggle button that starts toggled to the *on* position. Figure 28.2 contains the list of toggle button constructors. Passing a *true* to the constructors with the *boolean* parameter toggles the button to the *on* position. The default position is *off*.

```
JToggleButton();
JToggleButton(ImageIcon icon);
JToggleButton(String s);
JToggleButton(ImageIcon icon, boolean state);
JToggleButton(String s, boolean state);
JToggleButton(String s, ImageIcon icon, boolean state);
```

Figure 28.2 The *JToggleButton* Class Constructors

The *JToggleButton* class uses an *ItemListener,* as do the *JCheckBox* and *JRadioButton* classes. The **addItemListener()** method adds an item listener to a button. The item listener invokes the **itemStatechanged()** method to respond to item events. All of these button classes use the **isSelected()** method to determine whether a button is on or off. This method returns *true* when the button is on, *false* when it is off.

The *BirdToggle* Class Definition

The *BirdToggle* class relies upon arrays to reduce the code. We create arrays of bird names, bird file names, bird icons, and toggle buttons. Figure 28.3 contains the definition of the *BirdToggle* class.

```
import java.awt.*;
import java.awt.event.*;
import java.applet.*;
import javax.swing.*;
public class BirdToggle extends JApplet implements ItemListener
{
 private Container contentPane = getContentPane();
  private static final String [] birdName =
       {"Blue Bird", "Chickadee"};
  private static final String [] birdFile =
       {"bluebird.jpeg","chickadee.jpeg"};
  private ImageIcon [] birdIcon = new ImageIcon[birdName.length];
  private JToggleButton [] birdButton =
        new JToggleButton[birdName.length];
  private JPanel birdPanel = new JPanel();
  //Put the init() Method Here
  //Put the itemStateChanged() Method Here
}
```

Figure 28.3 The *BirdToggle* Class Definition

The init() Method

Each of the toggle buttons has a similar appearance, so we can use a **for** statement to create the toggle buttons and set their style. We begin by constructing the bird icons by means of the statement:

```
birdIcon[i] = new ImageIcon(this.getImage(this.getDocumentBase(), birdFile[i]));
```

Once we've constructed the icon, we construct the toggle button by means of the statement

```
birdButton[i] = new JToggleButton(birdName[i], birdIcon[i]);
```

Notice that each toggle button contains a label and an image. We place the label in the bottom center position by means of the following statements:

```
birdButton[i].setVerticalTextPosition(SwingConstants.BOTTOM);
birdButton[i].setHorizontalTextPosition(SwingConstants.CENTER);
```

We also set the background of the toggle buttons to white, and we add a border to each button:

```
birdButton[i].setBorderPainted(true);
birdButton[i].setBackground(Color.white);
```

The **for** statement concludes with statements that add an item listener to each button and add the button to the *bird* panel. When the **for** statement terminates, we add the *bird* panel to the content pane. Figure 28.4 contains the definition of the init() method.

```
public void init()
 {
  birdPanel.setBackground(Color.white);
  for (int i=0; i< birdName.length; i++)
  {
      birdIcon[i] = new ImageIcon(
         this.getImage(this.getDocumentBase(), birdFile[i]));
      birdButton[i] = new JToggleButton(birdName[i], birdIcon[i]);
      birdButton[i].setBorderPainted(true);
      birdButton[i].setBackground(Color.white);
      birdButton[i].setVerticalTextPosition(SwingConstants.BOTTOM);
      birdButton[i].setHorizontalTextPosition
            (SwingConstants.CENTER);
      birdButton[i].addItemListener(this);
      birdPanel.add(birdButton[i]);
  }
  contentPane.add(birdPanel, BorderLayout.NORTH);
 }
```

Figure 28.4 The init() Method, *BirdToggle* Class

The itemStateChanged() Method

Each of the toggle buttons could be on, so we use separate **if** statements to check each button. If the button is on, we construct a string containing information about the bird. We use the **showMessageDialog()** method to display the string in an information window. The window's title is the bird's name. If both buttons are on, the *Bluebird* window is displayed first. The *Chickadee* window is displayed after the user closes the *Bluebird* window. Figure 28.5 contains the definition of the **itemStateChanged()** method.

```
public void itemStateChanged(ItemEvent e)
{
 String birdInfo;
 if (birdButton[0].isSelected()){
    birdInfo = "This bird is approximately 6 1/2 inches.\n " +
      "The incubation period is 12  to 18 days.\n" +
      "The fledging period is approximately 16-21 days.";
    JOptionPane.showMessageDialog(null, birdInfo,
        "Eastern Bluebird",
        JOptionPane.INFORMATION_MESSAGE);
 }
 if (birdButton[1].isSelected()){
    birdInfo = "This bird is approximately 5 1/2 inches.\n " +
      "The incubation period is approximately 12 days.\n" +
      "The fledging period is 16 days.";
    JOptionPane.showMessageDialog(null, birdInfo,
        "Black-capped Chickadee",
        JOptionPane.INFORMATION_MESSAGE);
 }
}
```

Figure 28.5 The `itemStateChanged()` Method, *BirdToggle* Class

CHECKBOXES

Swing checkboxes are more versatile than their AWT counterparts because we can construct checkboxes with icons and strings. The `JCheckBox` constructors mimic the `JToggleButton` constructors appearing in Figure 28.2. We need only change the class name. The same applies to the `JRadioButton` constructors that we examine in the next section.

As our checkbox example, we create a simple *Duck Spotters* page. The page displays four checkboxes with duck images. We ask users to select all of the ducks that they have spotted. We print a list of the ducks observed by the current user. Figure 28.6 contains a sample page. As the figure indicates, the user has observed two ducks, a Mallard and a Pintail.

The *CheckDucks* Class Definition

The *CheckDucks* class implements the *Duck Spotters* page. The class definition contains arrays that hold the duck names, image file names, image icons, and duck checkboxes. We also create a panel to hold the checkboxes and a text area to display the list of ducks observed by the user. Figure 28.7 contains the definition of the *CheckDucks* class.

The init() Method

The **init()** method constructs the duck checkboxes by using the arrays created in the class definition. A **for** statement handles most of the code. Prior to the start of the **for** statement, we set the layout of the *duck* panel to a 2 × 2 grid layout. The body of the **for** statement begins with a statement that creates the image icons for the ducks:

```
duckImage[i] = new
ImageIcon(this.getImage(this.getDocumentBase(),
duckFile[i]));
```

Once we've created an image icon, we use it to construct the duck button, by means of the following statement

```
duckBox[i] = new JCheckBox(duckName[i], duckImage[i]);
```

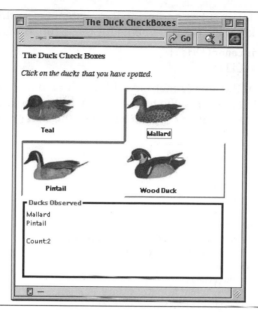

Figure 28.6 The *Duck Spotters* Page

```
import java.awt.*;
import java.awt.event.*;
import java.applet.*;
import javax.swing.*;
import javax.swing.event.*;
import javax.swing.border.*;

public class CheckDucks extends JApplet implements ItemListener
{
   private Container contentPane = getContentPane();
  private static final String [] duckName = {"Teal", "Mallard",
        "Pintail", "Wood Duck"};
  private static final String [] duckFile = {"greenTeal.jpeg",
     "mallard.jpeg", "pinTail.jpeg","woodDuck.jpeg"};
  private ImageIcon [] duckImage = new ImageIcon[duckName.length];
  private JCheckBox [] duckBox = new JCheckBox[duckName.length];
  private JTextArea outputArea = new JTextArea(10,30);
  private JPanel duckPanel = new JPanel();
  //Put the init() Method Here
  //Put the itemStateChanged() Method Here
}
```

Figure 28.7 The *CheckDucks* Class Definition

All of the duck buttons have a white background and a painted border. They also have the duck name positioned in the bottom center location. We use the following statements to create this style:

```
duckBox[i].setBackground(Color.white);
duckBox[i].setBorderPainted(true);
duckBox[i].setVerticalTextPosition(SwingConstants.BOTTOM);
duckBox[i].setHorizontalTextPosition(SwingConstants.CENTER);
```

We conclude the **for** statement by adding an item listener to each duck button. We also add the duck button to the duck panel. The statements for these functions are as follows:

```
duckBox[i].addItemListener(this);
duckPanel.add(duckBox[i]);
```

The final statements of the **init()** method add the duck panel to the north position of the content pane. We add a titled border to the text area and add the text area to the center position of the content pane. Figure 28.8 contains the definition of the **init()** method.

```
public void init()
{//Create the duck check boxes
  duckPanel.setLayout(new GridLayout(2,2));
  for (int i=0; i< duckName.length; i++)
  {
     duckImage[i] = new ImageIcon(
           this.getImage(this.getDocumentBase(), duckFile[i]));
     duckBox[i] = new JCheckBox(duckName[i], duckImage[i]);
     duckBox[i].setBackground(Color.white);
     duckBox[i].setBorderPainted(true);
     duckBox[i].setVerticalTextPosition(SwingConstants.BOTTOM);
     duckBox[i].setHorizontalTextPosition(SwingConstants.CENTER);
     duckBox[i].addItemListener(this);
     duckPanel.add(duckBox[i]);
  }
  contentPane.add(duckPanel, BorderLayout.NORTH);
  outputArea.setBorder(new TitledBorder(new
     LineBorder(Color.black, 3),"Ducks Observed"));
  contentPane.add(outputArea, BorderLayout.CENTER);
}
```

Figure 28.8 The **init()** Method, *CheckDucks* Class

The itemStateChanged() Method

The **itemStateChanged()** method definition contains an integer that holds the count of selected ducks and a string, *outString*, that holds the names of the selected ducks and the count. We use a **for** statement with an embedded **if** statement to determine which ducks the user selected:

```
for(int i=0 ; i < duckName.length; i++)
   if (duckBox[i].isSelected()) {
      outString = outString + duckBox[i].getLabel() + "\n";
      count ++;
   }
```

The **isSelected()** method used in the **if** expression returns a *true* when the checkbox is selected. We use the **getLabel()** method to add the name of the selected duck to *outString*. We also increment the count for each duck selected. After the **for** statement terminates, we add the count of selected ducks to *outString*, and we use the **setText()** method to place *outString* in the text area. Figure 28.9 contains the definition of the **itemStateChanged()** method.

Compare the *BirdToggle* and *CheckDucks* class definitions. You will discover that toggle buttons and checkboxes are very similar. If you attain mastery of one of these classes, you have also attained mastery of the other. In fact, you have also mastered the radio buttons that we will examine in the next section; all of these classes use the same constructors and methods. Only the class name changes.

```
public void itemStateChanged(ItemEvent e)
{ //find the checked boxes and increment the counts
   int count = 0;
   String outString = "";
   for(int i=0 ; i < duckName.length; i++)
     if(duckBox[i].isSelected()) {
       outString  = outString + duckBox[i].getLabel() + "\n";
       count ++;
     }
   outString = outString + "\nCount:" + count;
   outputArea.setText(outString);
}
```

Figure 28.9 The `itemStateChanged()` Method, *CheckDucks* Class

RADIO BUTTONS

To illustrate radio buttons, we create a *Bird Quiz* page. The page contains five quiz questions, which we display in a text area at the top of the page. The remainder of the page contains six bird radio buttons. Figure 28.10 shows the *Bird Quiz* page with the first quiz question displayed in the text area. The user selects a quiz answer by pressing one of the bird buttons. The page advances to the next question after the user selects a button.

After the user completes the quiz, we change the text area's title to *Your Score*, and we print the user's score in the text area. Figure 28.11 contains a completed quiz page.

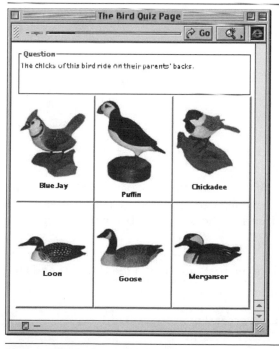

Figure 28.10 The *Bird Quiz* Page

Figure 28.11 A Completed *Bird Quiz* Page

The *BirdQuiz* Class Definition

The *BirdQuiz* class definition is lengthy, but the code is not difficult. The definition contains arrays of bird names, bird file names, bird icons, bird radio buttons, and bird questions. We also create an integer array that contains the index of the correct bird name for each question. Figure 28.12 contains the definition of the *BirdQuiz* class.

```
import java.awt.*;
import java.awt.event.*;
import java.applet.*;
import javax.swing.*;
import javax.swing.border.*;
public class BirdQuiz extends JApplet implements ItemListener
{
  private Container contentPane = getContentPane();
  private static final String [] birdName = {"Blue Jay",  "Puffin",
    "Chickadee", "Loon", "Goose", "Merganser"};
  private static final String [] birdFile = {"bluejay.jpeg",
    "puffin.jpeg", "chickadee.jpeg", "loon.jpeg",
    "goose.jpeg","merganser.jpeg"};
  private ImageIcon [] birdIcon = new ImageIcon[birdName.length];
  private JRadioButton [] birdButton =
      new JRadioButton[birdName.length];
  private static final String [] birdQuestion = {
  "The chicks of this bird ride on their parents' backs.",
  "This bird loves peanuts in the shell.\n The male and female build the nest.",
  "The female lays 6-8 eggs." +
  "The eggs are 0.6 inches in size.\n They are white with reddish streaks.\n",
   "The female lays a single white egg with pale lilac markings.\n" +
   "The adult birds like squid. The chicks eat fish.",
   "This bird winters in Mexico.\n" +
   "The female lays 10-12 white eggs." + "\nThis bird likes fish."};
  private static final int [] answers = {3,0,2,1,5};
  private JTextArea question = new JTextArea(5,30);
  private JPanel birdPanel = new JPanel();
  private int qNumber = 0;
  private int correct = 0;
  //Put the init() Method Here
  //Put the itemStateChanged() Method Here
}
```

Figure 28.12 The *BirdQuiz* Class Definition

As Figure 28.12 indicates, the *BirdQuiz* class definition also contains a panel for the bird buttons and a text area for the questions. We also create two integers. The first integer, *qNumber*, is the index of the current quiz question; the second integer, *correct*, holds the number of correct answers.

The init() Method

The **init()** method begins with statements that place the first question in the text area and create a titled border for the text area:

```
question.setText(birdQuestion[0]);
question.setBorder(new TitledBorder(new LineBorder(Color.black,1),
   "Question"));
```

We also create a 2×3 grid layout for the bird panel by means of the statement

```
birdPanel.setLayout(new GridLayout(2,3));
```

The **init()** method contains a **for** statement that creates the bird radio buttons and adds them to the bird panel. The body of this statement is virtually identical to what was used in the *CheckDucks* **init()** method. Compare the **for** statements used in these two **init()** methods. You will notice only minor differences between them.

After the **for** statement terminates, we add the *question* text area to the north position of the content pane, and we add the bird panel to the center position. Figure 28.13 contains the definition of the **init()** method.

```
public void init()
{
  question.setText(birdQuestion[0]);
  question.setBorder(new TitledBorder(new LineBorder(Color.black,1),
      "Question"));
  birdPanel.setLayout(new GridLayout(2,3));
  for (int i=0; i< birdName.length; i++)
  {//Create the bird radio buttons
      birdIcon[i] = new ImageIcon(this.getImage(
          this.getDocumentBase(), birdFile[i]));
      birdButton[i] = new JRadioButton(birdName[i], birdIcon[i]);
      birdButton[i].setBorderPainted(true);
      birdButton[i].setBackground(Color.white);
      birdButton[i].setVerticalTextPosition(SwingConstants.BOTTOM);
      birdButton[i].setHorizontalTextPosition(SwingConstants.CENTER);
      birdButton[i].addItemListener(this);
      birdPanel.add(birdButton[i]);
  }
  contentPane.add(question, BorderLayout.NORTH);
  contentPane.add(birdPanel, BorderLayout.CENTER);
}
```

Figure 28.13 The **init()** Method, *BirdQuiz* Class

The itemStateChanged() Method

We use an **if...else** statement in the **itemStateChanged()** method to determine when the user has finished the quiz. The **if** portion of this statement reads as follows:

```
if (qNumber < birdQuestion.length-1){
    if (birdButton[answers[qNumber]].isSelected())
        correct++;
    qNumber++;
    question.setText(birdQuestion[qNumber]);
}
```

The expression in the **if** header compares the current question number with the number of questions. If the question number is less than *birdQuestion.length*-1, that is, less than four, the user has not finished the quiz.

Notice the **if** statement contained in the body of the **if** statement. The expression in this inner **if** statement uses the index of the correct answer as the bird button index. The correct answer is in **answer[qNumber]**. If the user selected this bird, we increment the count of correct answers. After we've checked the answer, we increment the question number and place the next question in the text area.

The **else** clause handles the last question. The code is as follows:

```
else
{// get the last answer and report the score
    if (birdButton[answers[qNumber-1]].isSelected()) //
        correct++;
    String score = "Your bird quiz score is: " + correct;
    question.setBorder(new TitledBorder(
        new LineBorder(Color.black,1), "Your Score"));
    question.setText(score);
}
```

The user will not select any more buttons after answering the last quiz question, so the **else** clause must check the last answer. If the user answered correctly, we increment the count of correct answers. Once we've processed the last question, we create a string that contains the user's score. We change the text area's title to *Your Score*, and we put the score in the text area. Figure 28.14 contains the definition of the **itemStateChanged()** method.

```
public void itemStateChanged(ItemEvent e)
{
  if (qNumber < birdQuestion.length-1){
    if (birdButton[answers[qNumber]].isSelected())
        correct++;
    qNumber++;
    question.setText(birdQuestion[qNumber]);
  }
  else
  {// get the last answer and report score
    if (birdButton[answers[qNumber-1]].isSelected())
        correct++;
    String score = "Your bird quiz score is: " + correct;
    question.setBorder(new TitledBorder(new LineBorder(Color.black,1), "Your Score"));
    question.setText(score);
  }
}
```

Figure 28.14 The **itemStateChanged()** Method, *BirdQuiz* Class

SLIDERS

Swing contains a *JScrollBar* class that is virtually identical to AWT's *Scrollbar* class. The Swing class uses the same constructors and methods as its AWT counterpart. We're not going to discuss this class, because Swing provides a *JSlider* class that is a new, and greatly improved, version of the *Scrollbar* class. Figure 28.15 contains a page that illustrates the Swing sliders. As this figure indicates, we can create horizontal and vertical sliders. The default horizontal slider places the minimum slider value at the left corner and the maximum value at the right end. The default vertical slider places the minimum value at the top of the slider and the maximum value at the bottom. We can invert either of these sliders.

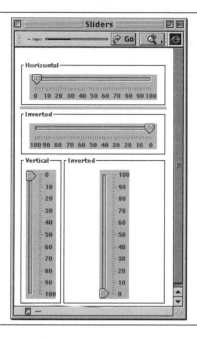

Figure 28.15 Sliders

Default sliders have neither tick marks nor numbers, but, as Figure 28.15 indicates, we can easily add them. We can also replace the numbers with icons.

The *JSlider* Constructors and Methods

Figure 28.16 lists the *JSlider* constructors.

```
JSlider();
JSlider(int ORIENTATION);
JSlider(int min, int max);
JSlider(int min, int max, int value);
JSlider(int ORIENTATION, int min, int max, int value);
```

Figure 28.16 The *JSlider* Constructors

The *JSlider* constructors resemble the *Scrollbar* and *JScrollBar* constructors. The default constructor, **JSlider()**, creates a horizontal slider with a minimum value of 0 and a maximum value of 100. The remaining constructors change the minimum and maximum values, the orientation, and/or the slider's initial value. To change the orientation, we use either of the following constants:

JSlider.HORIZONTAL
JSlider.VERTICAL

Figure 28.17 lists the most frequently used *JSlider* methods. The first two methods, **setMinorTickSpacing()** and **setMajorTickSpacing()**, determine the spacing used for the tick marks. The ticks marks are not displayed unless we invoke the **setPaintTicks()** method with the value *true* as the parameter. Invoking the **setPaintLabels()** method with the value *true* adds numbers to the slider. Invoking the **setInverted()** method with the value *true* reverses the placement of

```
void setMinorTickSpacing(int spacing);
void setMajorTickSpacing(int spacing);
void setPaintTicks(true);
void setPaintLabels(true);
void setInverted(true);
int getValue();
void setValue(int value);
```

Figure 28.17 Frequently Used *JSlider* Methods

the minimum and maximum values. We use the **getValue()** method to obtain the slider's current value, and we use the **setValue()** method to change the slider's value.

Sliders use a *ChangeListener* that we implement as an inner class when we add a change listener to a slider. We use the **addChangeListener()** to add a change listener. The *ChangeListener* class contains a **stateChanged()** method that responds to slider events.

The *Temperature* Page

Figure 28.18 contains a *Temperature* page that uses sliders for the Fahrenheit and Celsius temperatures. Figure 28.18(a) shows the initial locations of the sliders. The minimum value on

(a) Initial Slider Locations   **(b) Sliders After User Moves Fahrenheit Slider**

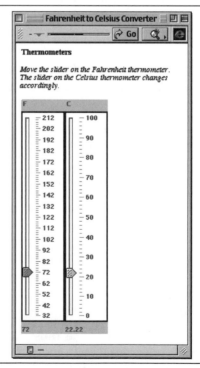

Figure 28.18 The *Temperature* Page

each slider represents the freezing point, while the maximum value represents the boiling point of water.

Only the Fahrenheit slider responds to events. When we move this slider, the page not only displays the Fahrenheit temperature and its Celsius equivalent: it moves the Celsius slider to the correct temperature. Figure 28.18(b) shows the page after the user has moved the Fahrenheit slider.

The *TemperatureSlider* Class Definition

The *TemperatureSlider* class definition uses arrays to store the *F* and *C* labels that appear above each slider. We also create arrays for the sliders, the temperature labels appearing at the bottom of the page, and the panels that hold the labels and sliders. Figure 28.19 contains the definition of the *TemperatureSlider* class.

```
import java.awt.*;
import java.awt.event.*;
import java.applet.*;
import javax.swing.event.*;
import javax.swing.border.*;
import javax.swing.*;
public class TemperatureSlider extends JApplet
{
    private Container contentPane = getContentPane();
    private static final String [] tempString = {" F ", " C "};
    private JSlider [] tempSlider = new JSlider [tempString.length];
    private JPanel[] tempPanel = new JPanel [tempString.length];
    private JLabel [] currentTemp = new JLabel[tempString.length];
    private JPanel screen - new JPanel();
    private int fahrenheit;
    double celsius;
    //put the init() Method Here
public double roundPlaces(double number, int places)
{ //round the number to the desired decimal places
        return Math.round(number *
        Math.pow(10, places))/Math.pow(10, places);
 }
}
```

Figure 28.19 The *TemperatureSlider* Class Definition

Because we construct the *ChangeListener* as an inner class, the *TemperatureSlider* class requires only an **init()** method and a **roundPlaces()** method. We use the latter method to round the Celsius temperature at two places to the right of the decimal point.

You might wonder why we're using arrays when we have only two sliders. Because the sliders use the same style, we reduce the code by half when we use arrays rather than individual sliders. This will become obvious when we examine the **init()** method.

The init() Method

We begin the **init()** method by creating a 2 × 1 grid layout for the *screen* panel. This panel holds the two slider panels. Next, we create the two sliders by using the following statements:

```
tempSlider[0] = new JSlider(JSlider.VERTICAL,32, 212,32);
tempSlider[1] = new JSlider(JSlider.VERTICAL, 0, 100,0);
```

The first statement creates the Fahrenheit slider. This slider has the minimum and maximum values 32 and 212, respectively. We set the initial slider position to 32. The second statement creates the Celsius slider. This slider has the minimum and maximum values 0 and 100, respectively. We set the initial slider position to 0.

We use a **for** statement to create the panels for the sliders and their labels. Each panel has a border layout. We place the *F* or *C* label in the north position, the slider in the center position, and the temperature in the south position of each panel. We also use the **for** statement to set the slider style. The style is a white background with a two-pixel black line border. The minor tick marks are two, the major tick marks are ten. Both the tick marks and labels are displayed.

After the **for** statement terminates, we add a change listener to the Fahrenheit thermometer. The method call is

```
tempSlider[0].addChangeListener(
    new ChangeListener(){
        public void stateChanged(ChangeEvent e)
        {
            fahrenheit = tempSlider[0].getValue();
            currentTemp[0].setText(Integer.toString(fahrenheit));
            celsius = 5.0/9.0*(fahrenheit - 32.0);
            tempSlider[1].setValue((int)Math.round(celsius));
            currentTemp[1].setText
                (Double.toString(roundPlaces(celsius, 2)));
        }
    }
); //End addChangeListener() Method
```

Notice the parameter passed in the **addChangeListener()** method. The parameter is a call to the *ChangeListener* class constructor. The *ChangeListener* object created by this constructor has only a single method, **stateChanged()**. This method is invoked when the user moves the Fahrenheit slider.

We use the **stateChanged()** method to obtain the current value in the Fahrenheit slider. We place this value in **currentTemp[0]**. We convert the Fahrenheit value to its Celsius equivalent. Sliders work with integers only, so we must round the *celsius* value to the nearest integer. The statement that does this is

```
tempSlider[1].setValue((int)Math.round(celsius));
```

Notice the type cast to **(int)** used to set the value for the Celsius slider.

To create the Celsius temperature label, we call **roundPlaces()** to round the temperature to two decimal places. We use the **setText()** method to place the value in the label. The statement is

```
currentTemp[1].setText(Double.toString(roundPlaces(celsius, 2)));
```

Figure 28.20 contains the definition of the **init()** method.

```
public void init()
{ //add the labels and scrollbars in layout
  int i;
  setBackground(Color.white);
  screen.setLayout(new GridLayout(1,2));
  tempSlider[0] = new JSlider(JSlider.VERTICAL,32, 212,32);
  tempSlider[1] = new JSlider(JSlider.VERTICAL, 0, 100,0);
  for (i=0; i< tempString.length; i++) {
      tempPanel[i] = new JPanel();
      //use border layout so that the scrollbars have more space
      tempPanel[i].setLayout(new BorderLayout(5,5));
      tempPanel[i].add(new JLabel(tempString[i]), BorderLayout.NORTH);
      tempSlider[i].setBackground(Color.white);
      tempSlider[i].setBorder(new LineBorder(Color.black,2));
      tempSlider[i].setMinorTickSpacing(2);
      tempSlider[i].setMajorTickSpacing(10);
      tempSlider[i].setPaintTicks(true);
      tempSlider[i].setPaintLabels(true);
      tempPanel[i].add(tempSlider[i], BorderLayout.CENTER);
      currentTemp[i] = new JLabel("     ");
      tempPanel[i].add(currentTemp[i], BorderLayout.SOUTH);
      screen.add(tempPanel[i]);
  }
  //Create a new ChangeListener
  tempSlider[0].addChangeListener(
      new ChangeListener(){
          public void stateChanged(ChangeEvent e) {
              fahrenheit = tempSlider[0].getValue();
              currentTemp[0].setText(Integer.toString(fahrenheit));
              celsius = 5.0/9.0*(fahrenheit - 32.0);
              tempSlider[1].setValue((int)Math.round(celsius));
              currentTemp[1].setText(Double.toString
                  (roundPlaces(celsius, 2)));
          }
      }
  ); //End addChangeListener() Method
  contentPane.add(screen, BorderLayout.CENTER);
}
```

Figure 28.20 The **init()** Method: *TemperatureSlider* Class

COMBO BOXES

We now turn our attention to Swing's *ComboBox* class. This class is equivalent to AWT's *Choice* class. Figure 28.21 contains a list of the *ComboBox* methods and their *Choice* equivalents. Identical methods are in clear; modified methods are shaded.

The *ComboBox* class replaces many of the *Choice* method names with names that convey more meaning. For example, the *ComboBox* class contains a **setSelectedIndex()** method that is equivalent to the *Choice* **select()** method. Both methods do exactly the same thing; however, the *ComboBox* name more clearly indicates the method's purpose.

ComboBox **Method**	*Choice* **Equivalent**
ComboxBox();	Choice();
void addItem(Object *obj*);	void add(String *s*);
int addItemListener(ItemListener IL);	int addItemListener(ItemListener IL);
int getItemCount();	int getItemCount();
int getSelectedIndex();	int getSelectedIndex();
Object getSelectedItem();	String getSelectedItem();
Object [] getSelectedObjects();	Object [] getSelectedObjects();
void insertItemAt(Object *obj*, int *index*);	void insert(String *s*, int *index*);
void removeItem(Object *obj*);	void remove(String *s*);
void removeItemAt(Object *obj*, int *index*);	void remove(int *index*);
void removeAllItems();	void removeAll();
void setSelectedIndex(int *index*);	void select(int *index*);
void setSelectedItem(Object *obj*);	void select(Object *obj*);

Figure 28.21 Frequently Used *ComboBox* Methods and Their *Choice* Equivalents

The *ComboBox* class is also more versatile than the *Choice* class, because we can construct combo boxes containing objects. For example, we can create combo boxes using strings only, icons only, or both strings and icons.

The *Telling Time* Page

Our illustration of combo boxes is a small English–Tibetan tutorial on telling time. The page contains an English panel and a Tibetan panel. The English panel contains the message *What time is it?* We display the phonetic Tibetan equivalent, *Chu tsö ka tsö ray?*, in the Tibetan panel. The English panel contains a second message, *It is ___ : ___ .* The two combo boxes form the time, as is illustrated in Figure 28.22. In this example, the user has selected 11:55.

We don't want to print the Tibetan time until the user has selected both the hour and minutes, so the page contains a *Done* button that the user presses after selecting the numeric time. We print the phonetic Tibetan equivalent of the user's time in the Tibetan panel. Thus, 11:55 in English is equivalent to *Chu tsö chu chik tang karma ngap chu nga nga ray.*

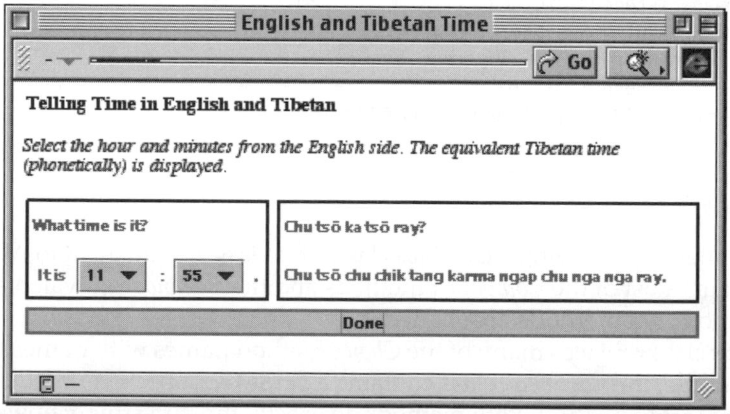

Figure 28.22 The *Telling Time* Page

The *TimeBox* Class Definition

The *TimeBox* class definition uses separate arrays to store the hours and minutes in English. We use a second set of arrays to store the Tibetan hours and minutes. We also use a string array to store the question *What time is it?* and its Tibetan equivalent, and we create a panel array to hold the English and Tibetan times. Figure 28.23 contains the definition of the *TimeBox* class.

```java
import java.awt.*;
import java.awt.event.*;
import java.applet.*;
import javax.swing.border.*;
import javax.swing.*;

public class TimeBox extends JApplet implements ActionListener
{
    private Container contentPane = getContentPane();
    private String [] englishHour = {"1", "2" , "3", "4", "5",
        "6", "7", "8", "9", "10", "11", "12"};
    private String [] tibetanHour = {"chik", "nyi", "sum",
     "shi", "nga", "trook", "d\u00FCn", "ge", "gu",
     "chu", "chu chik", "chu nyi"};
    private String [] englishMinute = {"00", "05", "10",
        "15", "20", "25", "30", "35",
        "40", "45", "50", "55"};
    private String [] tibetanMinute = {"null", "nga",
      "chu", "chu nga", "nyi shu ", "nyi shu tsa nga",
      "sum chu ","sum chu sho nga",
      "shi chu ", "shi chu sa nga",
      "ngap chu ", "ngap chu nga nga"];
    private static final String [] question =
       {" What time is it?",
       " Chu ts\u00F6 ka ts\u00F6 ray?"};
    private JLabel tibetanTime =
        new JLabel(" Chu ts\u00F6 _____ ray.");
    private JPanel [] timePanel = new JPanel[question.length];
    private JPanel answerPanel = new JPanel();
    private JComboBox hourBox = new JComboBox();
    private JComboBox minuteBox = new JComboBox();
    private JButton doneButton = new JButton("Done");
    private int hours, minutes;
    //Put the init() Method Here
    //Put the actionPerformed() Method Here
}
```

Figure 28.23 The *TimeBox* Class Definition

The *TimeBox* class definition contains two combo boxes, which we create by means of the following statements:

```java
private JComboBox hourBox = new JComboBox();
private JComboBox minuteBox = new JComboBox();
```

Each box has a corresponding integer that holds the index of the selected time: *hours* holds the index of the selected hour, *minutes* that of the selected minutes.

The init() Method

The **init()** method begins with a statement that creates a new border layout with a five-pixel horizontal and vertical gap for the content pane. Next, we place the times in the combo boxes, by means of the following statements:

```
for (i = 0; i < englishHour.length; i++)
  hourBox.addItem(englishHour[i]);
for (i = 0; i < englishMinute.length; i++)
  minuteBox.addItem(englishMinute[i]);
```

We use a separate panel, *answerPanel*, to hold the English time. As the *Telling Time* page illustrates, the English time combines string literals and combo boxes. We create the time by adding the literals and boxes to the *answerPanel* in the following order.

```
answerPanel.add(new JLabel("It is "));
answerPanel.add(hourBox);
answerPanel.add(new JLabel(" : "));
answerPanel.add(minuteBox);
answerPanel.add(new JLabel("."));
```

We use the *timePanel* array to store the English and Tibetan time questions and answers. Since these two panels have a similar style, we use a **for** statement to create the panels and add the information to them. The **for** statement is:

```
for (i = 0; i < question.length; i++)
{ //create the English and Tibetan Time Panels
    timePanel[i] = new JPanel(new GridLayout(2,1,2,2));
    timePanel[i].setBackground(Color.white);
    timePanel[i].setBorder(new LineBorder(Color.black, 2));
    timePanel[i].add(new JLabel(question[i]));
}
```

Within the **for** statement, we create a panel with a 2×1 grid with a two-pixel horizontal and vertical gap. Each panel has a white background and a two-pixel black line border. We place the time question in the first row of each panel.

After the **for** statement terminates, we add *answerPanel* to the English panel with the statement

```
timePanel[0].add(answerPanel);
```

We add the Tibetan time to the Tibetan panel with the statement

```
timePanel[1].add(tibetanTime);
```

We put the English panel in the west position of the content pane and the Tibetan panel in the center position. We add a border and an action listener to the *Done* button, and we place this button in the south position of the content pane.

Figure 28.24 contains the definition of the **init()** method.

The actionPerformed() Method

The action listener invokes the **actionPerformed()** method after the user presses the *Done* button. The first statements in this method use the **getSelectedIndex()** method to obtain the indices of the selected hour and minutes:

```
hours = hourBox.getSelectedIndex();
minutes = minuteBox.getSelectedIndex();
```

```
public void init()
{
  int i;
  contentPane.setLayout(new BorderLayout(5,5));
  contentPane.setBackground(Color.white);
  for (i = 0; i < englishHour.length; i++)
     hourBox.addItem(englishHour[i]);
  for (i = 0; i < englishMinute.length; i++)
     minuteBox.addItem(englishMinute[i]);

  answerPanel.setBackground(Color.white);
  answerPanel.add(new JLabel("It is "));
  answerPanel.add(hourBox);
  answerPanel.add(new JLabel(" : "));
  answerPanel.add(minuteBox);
  answerPanel.add(new JLabel("."));

  for (i = 0; i < question.length; i++)
  { //create the English and Tibetan Time Panels
     timePanel[i] = new JPanel(new GridLayout(2,1,2,2));
     timePanel[i].setBackground(Color.white);
     timePanel[i].setBorder(new LineBorder(Color.black, 2));
     timePanel[i].add(new JLabel(question[i]));
  }
  timePanel[0].add(answerPanel);
  timePanel[1].add(tibetanTime);

  contentPane.add(timePanel[0], BorderLayout.WEST);
  contentPane.add(timePanel[1], BorderLayout.CENTER);
  doneButton.addActionListener(this);
  doneButton.setBorder(new LineBorder(Color.red,2));
  contentPane.add(doneButton, BorderLayout.SOUTH);
}
```

Figure 28.24 The **init()** Method, *TimeBox* Class

All Tibetan times begins with *Chu tsö,* so we initialize a string with this text. The statement is

String time = " Chu ts\u00F6 ";

The remainder of the Tibetan time phrase depends on the user's selection for the minutes. If the user selected "00", which is in index position 0, we add the Tibetan hour followed by *ba ray* and a period to the *time* string. For example, if the user selects 1:00 as the English time, the Tibetan equivalent will be

Chu tsö **chik** <u>ba ray.</u>

If the user selected any other minutes, we add the Tibetan hour followed by *tang karma* followed by the Tibetan minutes followed by *ray.* For example, if the user selects 2:15 as the English time, the Tibetan equivalent will be

Chu tsö **nyi** <u>tang karma</u> **chu nga** <u>ray.</u>

Just in case you're curious, the literal English translation of the Tibetan time is

```
Chu tsö nyi tang karma  chu nga ray.
(Hour)   (2) (and)(minutes) (15)     (is).
```

Figure 28.25 contains the definition of the **actionPerformed()** method. Notice the **if...else** statement that forms the correct Tibetan time.

```
public void actionPerformed(ActionEvent e)
{//Get the Hours and Minutes and create the Tibetan time
   hours = hourBox.getSelectedIndex();
   minutes = minuteBox.getSelectedIndex();
   String time = " Chu ts\u00F6 ";
    if (minutes == 0)
      time = time + tibetanHour[hours] + " ba ray.";
    else
      time = time + tibetanHour[hours] + " tang karma "
          + tibetanMinute[minutes] + " ray.";
   tibetanTime.setText(time);
}
```

Figure 28.25 The **actionPerformed()** Method, *TimeBox* Class

LISTS

We discussed AWT's *List* class in Chapter 25. This class let us create single- or multiple-selection lists. Like many other Swing components, the *JList* class is more versatile than its AWT counterpart. The *JList* class constructor hints at the new features introduced in Swing. The syntax of the simplest constructor is

> **JList(Object [] ** *objectArray*);

As the syntax indicates, we create a new *JList* object by passing an array of constituent objects as the parameter. This means that we can create lists of icons or strings without using a **for** statement in the **init()** method.

The AWT *List* class provides two selection modes, single and multiple; the *JList* class provides three selection modes. We use the **setSelectionMode()** method to change the selection mode. Figure 28.26 contains the three selection-mode constants.

```
ListSelectionModel.SINGLE_SELECTION
ListSelectionModel.SINGLE_INTERVAL_SELECTION
ListSelectionModel.MULTIPLE_INTERVAL_SELECTION
```

Figure 28.26 The *JList* Constants

Notice that the *JList* class contains *two* multiple-selection modes. Setting the selection mode to **MULTIPLE_INTERVAL_SELECTION** indicates that the user may select several list items from anywhere in the list. Setting the selection mode to **SINGLE_INTERVAL_SELECTION** indicates that user may select several list items; however, the selected items must form one contiguous area.

The *JList* class provides all the methods of the *List* class; however, the *JList* method names have been modified to convey more meaning. Figure 28.27 contains the most frequently used *JList* methods and their *List* counterparts. The **getSelectedIndex()** method is the only identical method in these two classes.

As Figure 28.27 indicates, the *JList* **getSelectedValue()** and **getSelectedValues()** return an object or objects; the *List* counterparts return only strings. In addition, the **getSelectionMode()** method returns an integer representing the selection-mode constant, and the **setSelectionMode()**

JList **Method**	*List* **Equivalent**
int getVisibleRowCount()	int getRows();
int getSelectedIndex();	int getSelectedIndex();
int [] getSelectedIndices();	int [] getSelectedIndexes();
Object getSelectedValue();	String getSelectedItem();
Object [] getSelectedValues();	String [] getSelectedItems();
boolean isSelectedIndex();	boolean isIndexSelected();
int getSelectionMode();	boolean isMultipleMode();
void setSelectedIndex(int *index*);	void select(int *index*);
void setSelectionMode(int *MODE*);	void setMultipleMode(boolean *mode*);

Figure 28.27 Frequently Used *JList* Methods and Their *List* Counterparts

method requires a parameter that represents a selection-mode constant. The AWT equivalents use *boolean* values, because AWT provides only two list-selection alternatives.

The listeners for the *JList* and *List* classes also differ. The *List* class uses an item listener; the *JList* class uses *ListSelectionListener*. When the user selects a list item, this listener invokes the **valuedChanged()** method to handle the event.

We will create two pages that illustrate Swing's *JList* class.

The *Birder's Check List* Page

The first page contains a list of bird names. The user may select as many names as desired from anywhere in the list. As the user selects birds, we print the selected birds in a text area, along with the current count of birds observed by the user. Figure 28.28 contains a sample page.

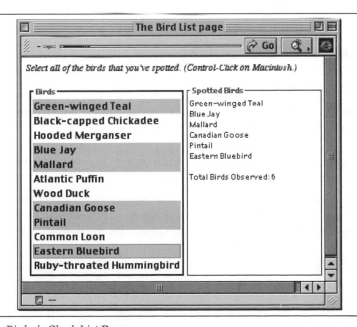

Figure 28.28 The *Birder's Check List* Page

The *BirdList* Class Definition

The *BirdList* class definition implements the *Birder's Check List* page. The definition contains an array of bird names and a list to hold the bird names. We declare this list with the statement

```
private JList birdersList;
```

The *BirdList* class definition also contains a text area, *outputArea,* that holds the list of selected birds and the bird count. Figure 28.29 contains the definition of the *BirdList* class.

```
import java.awt.*;
import java.awt.event.*;
import java.applet.*;
import javax.swing.*;
import javax.swing.event.*;
import javax.swing.border.*;

public class BirdList extends Japplet implements ListSelectionListener
{
    private Container contentPane = getContentPane();
    private static final String [] birdName = {"Green-winged Teal" ,
      "Black-capped Chickadee", "Hooded Merganser",
      "Blue Jay", "Mallard", "Atlantic Puffin",
      "Wood Duck", "Canadian Goose",
      "Pintail", "Common Loon", "Eastern Bluebird",
      "Ruby-throated Hummingbird"};
    private JList birdersList;
    private JTextArea outputArea = new JTextArea(30,10);
    //Put the init() Method Here
    //Put the valueChanged() Method Here
}
```

Figure 28.29 The *BirdList* Class Definition

The init() Method

The **init()** method contains several simple statements. We begin by constructing the list containing the bird names:

```
birdersList = new JList(birdName);
```

We set the selection mode to **MULTIPLE_INTERVAL_SELECTION,** and we add a list selection listener to *birdersList* by the means of the following statements:

```
birdersList.
    setSelectionMode(ListSelectionModel.MULTIPLE_INTERVAL_SELECTION);
birdersList.addListSelectionListener(this);
```

The remaining statements in the **init()** method create titled borders for the *birdersList* and the *outputArea* text area. We place the birder's list in the west position of the content pane and we place the text area in the center position. Figure 28.30 contains the definition of the **init()** method.

The valueChanged() Method

The list selection listener invokes the **valueChanged()** method each time the user selects or deselects a bird. We use a string variable, *output,* to construct a list of the selected birds. We initialize *output* to the empty string.

```
public void init()
{//initialize the bird list. Add the list and
 //text area to the content pane
   birdersList = new JList(birdName);
   birdersList.setSelectionMode(
       ListSelectionModel.MULTIPLE_INTERVAL_SELECTION);
   birdersList.addListSelectionListener(this);
   birdersList.setBorder(new TitledBorder
     (new LineBorder(Color.black,2),"Birds"));
   outputArea.setBorder(new TitledBorder (new
       LineBorder(Color.black, 1), "Spotted Birds"));
   contentPane.add(birdersList,BorderLayout.WEST);
   contentPane.add(outputArea, BorderLayout.CENTER);
}
```

Figure 28.30 The **init()** Method, *BirdList* Class

We use the **getSelectedIndices()** method to obtain an array with the indices of the selected birds. Once we have the array of indices, we can use a **for** statement to find the bird names. The **for** statement is

```
for (int i = 0; i < indices.length; i++)
    output = output + birdName[indices[i]] + "\n";
```

The body of the **for** statement adds the selected bird name to *output*. The current position in the *indices* array (**indices[i]**) provides the correct index to the bird name.

After the **for** statement terminates, we add the total number of observed birds to *output*, and we use the **setText()** method to place *output* into the *outputArea* text area. Figure 28.31 contains the definition of the **valueChanged()** method.

```
public void valueChanged(ListSelectionEvent e)
{//record information about the event
  String output = "";
  int [] indices  =  birdersList.getSelectedIndices();
  for (int i = 0; i < indices.length; i++)
      output = output + birdName[indices[i]] + "\n";
  output = output + "\nTotal Birds Observed: " + indices.length + "\n";
  outputArea.setText(output);
}
```

Figure 28.31 The **valueChanged()** Method, *BirdList* Class

Single-Select Lists and Icons

As our final example, we implement a *Bird Identification* page. The page contains a list of bird icons. When the user selects a bird, we print the bird's name in a text area to the right of the list. Figure 28.32 contains a sample page. Notice the scroll pane used with the bird list.

The *BirdIconList* Class Definition

The definition of the *BirdIconList* class parallels the definition of the *BirdList* class created in the previous section. The definition contains a *birdName* array, which holds the bird names. We use

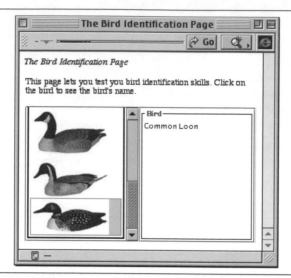

Figure 28.32 The *Bird Identification* Page

a shorter list than the one we created in the *BirdList* class. We add an array of file names that contains the *jpeg* files for the bird icons. We also add an array of image icons. The remainder of the *BirdIconList* class definition is identical to the corresponding part of the *BirdList* class definition. Figure 28.33 contains the class definition. The changes are highlighted.

```
import java.awt.*;
import java.awt.event.*;
import java.applet.*;
import javax.swing.*;
import javax.swing.event.*;
import javax.swing.border.*;
public class BirdIconList extends JApplet
      implements ListSelectionListener
{
    private Container contentPane = getContentPane();
    private static final String [] birdName =
       {"Green-winged Teal" , "Wood Duck",
        "Hooded Merganser", "Mallard",
        "Canadian Goose","Pintail", "Common Loon"};
    private static final String [] birdFile =
       {"greenTeal.jpeg", "woodDuck.jpeg",
        "merganser.jpeg", "mallard.jpeg",
        "goose.jpeg", "pinTail.jpeg", "loon.jpeg"};
    private ImageIcon [] birdIcon = new ImageIcon[birdName.length];
    private JList birdersList;
    private JTextArea outputArea = new JTextArea(10,15);
    //Put the init() Method Here
    //Put the valueChanged() Method Here
}
```

Figure 28.33 The *BirdIconList* Class

The init() Method

The **init()** method begins with a **for** statement that creates the bird icons. We've filled icon arrays several times in this chapter; the creating of the bird icons uses code similar to the code used in previous examples. The **for** statement that creates the bird icons is

```
for(int i=0; i < birdName.length; i++)
    birdIcon[i] = new ImageIcon(this.getImage
        (this.getDocumentBase(), birdFile[i]));
```

We use the *birdIcon* array to create the birder's list. The statement is

```
birdersList = new JList(birdIcon);
```

We set the selection mode to **SINGLE_SELECTION**, and we add a list selection listener to the birder's list:

```
birdersList.setSelectionMode(ListSelectionModel.SINGLE_SELECTION);
birdersList.addListSelectionListener(this);
```

We add borders to the birder's list and the text area. We place the birder's list in the west position of the content pane. The icons create a list longer than the applet's height, so we construct an anonymous *ScrollPane* object that contains the birder's list as its parameter. This lets us scroll vertically through the bird images:

```
contentPane.add(new JScrollPane(birdersList), BorderLayout.WEST);
```

We add the *outputArea* text area to the center position of the content pane.

Figure 28.34 contains the definition of the **init()** method.

```
public void init()
{//initialize the language list
   for(int i=0; i < birdName.length; i++)
      birdIcon[i] = new ImageIcon(this.getImage
         (this.getDocumentBase(), birdFile[i]));
   birdersList = new JList(birdIcon);
   birdersList.setSelectionMode
         (ListSelectionModel.SINGLE_SELECTION);
   birdersList.addListSelectionListener(this);
   birdersList.setBorder(new TitledBorder(
      new LineBorder(Color.black,2),"Birds"));
   outputArea.setBorder(new TitledBorder (new
      LineBorder(Color.black, 1), "Bird"));
   contentPane.add(new JScrollPane(birdersList), BorderLayout.WEST);
   contentPane.add(outputArea, BorderLayout.CENTER);
}
```

Figure 28.34 The **init()** Method, *BirdIconList* Class

The valueChanged() Method

The list selection listener invokes the **valueChanged()** method when the user presses a bird icon. We use the **getSelectedIndex()** method to obtain the index of the selected bird:

```
int  index  =  birdersList.getSelectedIndex();
```

The icon indices match the bird name indices, so we can change the text in *outputArea* with the statement

```
outputArea.setText(birdName[index]);
```

Figure 28.35 contains the definition of the **valueChanged()** method.

```
public void valueChanged(ListSelectionEvent e)
{//record information about the event
  int index = birdersList.getSelectedIndex();
  outputArea.setText(birdName[index]);
}
```

Figure 28.35 The **valueChanged()** Method, *BirdIconList* Class

➤ EXERCISES

1. **The *Favorite Seasons* Page.** Create a Swing version of the *Favorite Seasons* page appearing in Figure 25.1. Find icons that represent each of the seasons. Use the icons to create your lists.

2. **The *Favorite Food* Page.** Create a Swing version of the *Favorite Food* page appearing in Figure 25.8. Find icons for your favorite foods, and use these icons to create your list.

3. **The *German Phrases* Page.** Create a Swing version of the *German Phrases* page appearing in Figure 25.14.

4. **The *German List* Page.** Create a Swing version of the *German List* page appearing in Figure 25.19.

5. **The *Font Choice* Page.** Create a Swing version of the *Font Choice* page appearing in Figure 25.37.

6. **The *Ice-Cream Float* Page.** Create a Swing version of the *Ice-Cream Float* page appearing in Figure 14.19.

7. **The *Fonts* Page.** Create a Swing Version of the *Fonts* page appearing in Figure 25.38.

8. **The *Animals* Page.** Create a Swing Version of the *Animals* page appearing in Figure 25.39. Find pictures of the animals, and use icons.

9. **The *Inches to Centimeters* Page.** Create a page with sliders for inches and centimeters. When the user moves the *inches* slider, display the inches and centimeters, and move the centimeter slider to the correct position.

10. **The *Cups to Pints to Liters* Page.** Create a page of sliders for cups, pints, and liters. When the user moves the *cups* slider, display the cups and the pint and liter equivalents. Also, move the sliders for the pints and liters to their correct positions.

11. **The *Multilanguage Counting* Page.** Create a Swing version of the *Multilanguage Counting* page appearing in Figure 25.41.

12. **The *Multilanguage Weekdays* Page.** Create a Swing version of the *Multilanguage Weekdays* page appearing in Figure 25.43.

13. **The *Shakespearean Quiz* Page.** Create a Swing version of the *Shakespearean Quiz* page appearing in Figure 14.40.

14. **The *Multilanguage Greeting* Page.** Figure 17.41 contains English, Tibetan, and Spanish greetings. Add more *Hello* and *Good-bye* greetings in languages of your choice. Create a list of languages. Create radio buttons for the greetings. The user may select any number of languages. Print the English greeting, along with the corresponding greeting(s) in the selected language(s).

15. **The *Multilanguage Counting* Page, version 2.** Implement a *Multilanguage Counting* page by using sliders for the numbers.

16. **The *Survey* Page.** Create an opinion poll containing at least five questions. Give the user a 7-point scale, where 1 is strong agree, and 7 is strongly disagree. Use sliders. For example, the questions could deal with the user's evaluation of this book.

HTML Character and Numeric Entities

Figure A.1 contains the HTML character and numeric browser. The list contains only those characters that are recognized by Netscape and Internet Explorer.

Symbol	Character	Numeric	Meaning
&	&amp;	&#038;	Ampersand
<	&lt;	&#060;	Less than
>	&gt;	&#062;	Greater than
f		&#131;	Small *f* (florin)
"		&#132;	Dagger
†		&#134;	Ellipsis
‡		&#135;	Double Dagger
‰		&#137;	Per thousand
‹		&#139;	Single angle quotation
Œ		&#140;	*OE* Ligature
–		&#150;	En dash
—		&#151;	Em dash
			Non-breaking space
¡	&iexcl;	&#161;	Inverted Exclamation
¢	&cent;	&#162;	Cent symbol
£	&pound;	&#163;	Pound Sterling symbol
¥	&yen;	&#165;	Japanese Yen Symbol
§	&sect;	&#167;	Section Symbol
a	&ordf;	&#170;	Feminine Ordinal
¬	&not;	&#172;	Logical not
®	&reg;	&#174;	Registration mark
°	&deg;	&#176;	Degree
µ	&micro;	&#180;	Micron
¶	&para;	&#182;	Paragraph
•	&middot;	&#183;	Middle Dot
°	&ordm;	&#186;	Male Ordinal
1/4	&frac14;	&#188;	One-quarter
1/2	&frac12;	&#189;	One-half
3/4	&frac34;	&#190;	Three-quarters
¿	&iquest;	&#191;	Inverted Question
À	&Agrave;	&#192;	*A* grave
Á	&Aacute;	&#193;	*A* acute
Â	&Acirc;	&#194;	*A* circumflex
Ä	&Auml;	&#195;	*A* umlaut
Ã	&Atilde;	&#196;	*A* tilde
Å	&Aring;	&#197;	*A* ring
Æ	&AElig;	&#198;	*AE* ligature
Ç	&Ccedil;	&#199;	*C* cedilla
È	&Egrave;	&#200;	*E* grave

(continued)

Symbol	Character	Numeric	Meaning
É	É	É	*E* acute
Ê	Ê	Ê	*E* circumflex
Ë	Ë	Ë	*E* umlaut
Ì	Ì	Ì	*I* grave
Í	Í	Í	*I* acute
Î	Î	Î	*I* circumflex
Ï	Ï	Ï	*I* umlaut
Ñ	Ñ	Ñ	*N* tilde
Ò	Ò	Ò	*O* grave
Ó	Ó	Ó	*O* acute
Ô	Ô	Ô	*O* circumflex
Ö	Ö	Õ	*O* umlaut
Õ	Õ	Ö	O tilde
×	×	×	Multiplication
Ø	Ø	Ø	*O* slash
Ù	Ù	Ù	*U* grave
Ú	Ú	Ú	*U* acute
Û	Û	Û	*U* circumflex
Ü	Ü	Ü	*U* umlaut
ß	ß	ß	*SZ* Ligature
à	à	à	*a* grave
á	á	á	*a* acute
â	â	â	*a* circumflex
ä	ä	ã	*a* umlaut
ã	ã	ä	*a* tilde
å	å	å	*a* ring
æ	æ	æ	*ae* ligature
ç	ç	ç	*c* cedilla
è	è	è	*e* grave
é	é	é	*e* acute
ê	ê	ê	*e* circumflex
ë	ë	ë	*e* umlaut
ì	ì	ì	*i* grave
í	í	í	*i* acute
î	î	î	*i* circumflex
ï	ï	ï	*i* umlaut
ñ	ñ	ñ	*n* tilde
ò	ò	ò	*o* grave
ó	ó	ó	*o* acute
ô	ô	ô	*o* circumflex
ö	ö	õ	*o* umlaut
÷	÷	ö	Division
ø	ø	÷	*o* slash
ù	ù	ø	*u* grave
ú	ú	ù	*u* acute
û	û	ú	*u* circumflex
ü	ü	û	*u* umlaut
ÿ	ÿ	ÿ	*y* umlaut

Figure A.1 HTML Character and Numeric Entities

JavaScript Operators

Figure B.1 contains the JavaScript precedence hierarchy. The operators are arranged in order from the highest precedence to the lowest. Operators in the same row have the same precedence.

Operator	Description
. () []	Property, Function, Array
++ -- + - ! new void typeof	Increment, Decrement, Unary Plus or Minus Bitwise and Logical Not
* / %	Multiplication, Division, Modulus
+ -	Addition and Concatenation, Subtraction
<< >> >>>	Left Bit Shift, Right Bit Shift, Right Bit Shift: Zero Extension
< <= > >=	Less than, Less than equal, Greater than, Greater than equal
== !=	Equality, Inequality
&	Bitwise and
|	Bitwise or
^	Bitwise exclusive or
&&	Logical and
||	Logical or
? :	Conditional expression
= *= += -= /= %= <<= >>= >>= ^=	Assignment Operators
,	Comma operator (and)

Figure B.1 The JavaScript Precedence Hierarchy

The Perl Precedence Hierarchy

Figure C.1 contains the Perl precedence hierarchy. The operators are arranged in order from the highest precedence to the lowest. Operators in the same row have the same precedence.

Numeric Operator	String Operator	Other	Description
		()	Parenthesis, Function Parameter Lists
		[]	Array Subscripts
		{}	Associative Array Keys
		-	Dereference
++			Increment
	++		
--			Decrement
~ - +		! /	Bitwise Not, Unary Minus, Unary Plus Logical Not, Reference
**			Exponentiation
	= ~		Match
	! ~		Doesn't Match
* / %			Multiplication, Division, Modulus
	x		String repetition
+			Add
-			Subtract
	. (dot)		String Concatenation
<< >>			Left and Right Bit Shift
		-r -R	File is readable
		-w -W	File is writeable
		-o -O	File owned by
		-x -X	File is executable
			File exists
		-e	File has zero size
		-z	File has non-zero size
		-s	File handle is opened to a tty
		-t	
		exit eval	
		exp getpgrp	
		getprotobyname	
		gethostname	

Numeric Operator	String Operator	Other	Description
		getnetbyname	
		gmtime hex	
		int length	
		localtime	
		log ord	
		oct require	
		reset rand	
		rmdir readlink	
		sin sleep	
		sqrt srand	
		umask	
<<=	lt le		Less than, Less than equal
>>=	gt ge		Greater than, Greater than equal
== !=	eq ne		Equality, Inequality
<=>	cmp		Compare
&			Bitwise and
| ^			Bitwise or and Exclusive or
		&&	Logical and
		| |	Logical or
. .	. .		Range operator
		? :	Conditional expression
= += -= *=			
%= /= **= <<= = .= x=			Assignment operators
= &= |= ^=			
		'	Comma operator (and)
		( )	List operators
		not	Low precedence logical not
		and	Low precedence logical and
		or xor	Low precedence logical, Exclusive or

Figure C.1 Perl Precedence Hierarchy

The Java Precedence Hierarchy

Figure D.1 contains the Java precedence hierarchy. The operators are arranged in order from the highest precedence to the lowest. Operators in the same row have the same precedence.

Operator	Description
++ -- + -	Increment, Decrement, Unary Plus, Unary Minus
! (*Type*)	Logical Not ,Type Cast
* / %	Multiplication, Division, Modulus
+ -	Addition/String Concatenation, Subtraction
<< >> >>>	Left And RightBit Shift, Right Bit Shift: Zero Extension
< <= > >=	Less than, Less than equal, Greater than, Greater than equal
== != instanceof	Equality, Inequality, Object Type Comparison
&	Bitwise and, Boolean and
^	Bitwise Exclusive or (Xor), Boolean Xor
|	Bitwise or, Boolean or
&&	Conditional and (cand)
||	Conditional or (cor)
? :	Conditional expression
= += -= *= %=	
/= <<= >>= >>>=	Assignment operators
&= |= ^=	

Figure D.1 The Java Precedence Hierarchy

The Java *Character* and *String* Classes

INTRODUCTION

This appendix includes a brief description of the Java *Character* and *String* classes. The CD that accompanies this text contains demonstration programs for both classes.

THE *CHARACTER* CLASS

Figure E.1 contains a list of the most commonly used methods in the *Character* class. The class contains several *is* methods that check characters. For example, the **isDigit()** method determines whether the character passed as a parameter *is a digit*. The class also contains methods that convert a character to its upper- or lower-case equivalent and a method that identifies the type of character passed as a parameter. The type identification method, **getType()**, uses a twenty-nine point scale for the classification.

Method	Description
`boolean Character.isDigit(char ch);`	Return *true* if *ch* is a digit. Otherwise, return *false*.
`boolean Character.isLetter(char ch);`	Return *true* if *ch* is a letter. Otherwise, return *false*.
`boolean Character.isLetterOrDigit(char ch);`	Return *true* if *ch* is a letter or a digit. Otherwise, return *false*.
`boolean Character.isLowerCase(char ch);`	Return *true* if *ch* is a lower case letter. Otherwise, return *false*.
`boolean Character.isUpperCase(char ch);`	Return *true* if *ch* is an uppercase letter. Otherwise, return *false*.
`boolean Character.isWhiteSpace(char ch);`	Return *true* if *ch* is a white space (space, \n, \t, \r, \f). Otherwise, return *false*.
`char Character.toLowerCase(char ch);`	Return the lowercase equivalent of *ch*.
`char Character.toUpperCase(char ch);`	Return the uppercase equivalent of *ch*.
`int Character.getType(char ch);`	Return a constant representing the type of *ch*.
`boolean Name.equals(Character ch);`	Return *true* if the two *Character* objects are identical. Otherwise, return *false*.

Figure E.1 The Java *Character* Class

Two of the *Character* methods deserve special attention: **equals()** and **getType()**. The **equals()** method does not follow the syntax used by the other methods. All of the other methods pass a **char** literal, constant, or variable as a parameter. Each call uses the *Character* class as the object name. For example, a call to the **toUpperCase()** method might be

```
char ch = Character.toUpperCase('c');
```

This statement passes the literal *c* as a parameter. The uppercase equivalent is assigned to *ch*.

In contrast, the **equals()** method requires a *Character* object as a parameter. It returns a new *Character* object.

The **get_type()** method follows the standard *Character* method calls. What makes this method interesting is the constants it uses to identify a character's type. The **get_type()** method returns an **int** that represents the type of constant.

Figure E.2 lists the character constants returned by the **getType()** method.

Constant Value	Constant Name
0	UNASSIGNED
1	UPPER_CASE_LETTER
2	LOWER_CASE_LETTER
3	TITLE_CASE_LETTER
4	MODIFIER_LETTER
5	OTHER_LETTER
6	NON_SPACING_MARK
7	ENCLOSING_MARK
8	COMBINING_SPACE_MARK
9	DECIMAL_DIGIT_NUMBER
10	LETTER_NUMBER
11	OTHER_NUMBER;
12	SPACE_SEPARATOR
13	LINE_SEPARATOR
14	PARAGRAPH_SEPARATOR
15	CONTROL
18	FORMAT
19	SURROGATE
20	DASH_PUNCTUATION
21	START_PUNCTUATION
22	END_PUNCTUATION
23	CONNECTOR_PUNCTUATION
24	OTHER_PUNCTUATION
25	MATH_SYMBOL
26	CURRENCY_SYMBOL
27	MODIFER_SYMBOL
28	OTHER_SYMBOL

Figure E.2 The **getType()** Constants

THE JAVA *STRING* CLASS METHODS

Figure E.3 contains the most frequently used methods of the *String* class.

We can divide the methods appearing in Figure E.3 into three groups:

The Single-String Methods.   These methods include **toUpperCase()**, **toLowerCase()**, **charAt()**, **length()**, and **trim()**. The *String* and *Character* classes share the first two methods. The **length()**

Method	Description
char *str*.charAt(int *pos*);	Return the character at *pos*.
String *str*.concat(String *s*);	Return a string with *s* appended to the end of *str*.
int *str*.compareTo(String *s*);	Return negative number if *str* > *s*
	Return zero if *str* = *s*
	Return positive number if *str* > *s*
boolean *str*.equals(String *s*);	Return *true* if *str* = *s*. Return *false* otherwise.
boolean *str*.equalsIgnoreCase(String *s*);	Case insensitive version of **equals()**.
int *str*.indexOf(String *s*);	Return starting position of *s* in *str*. Return −1 if *str* does not contain *s*.
int *str*.lastIndexOf(String *s*);	Return starting position of last occurrence of *str* in *s*. Return −1 if *str* does not contain *s*.
String *str*.substring(int start, int end);	Return the substring from *start* to *end-1*.
int *str*.length();	Return the length of *str*.
boolean *str*.startsWith(String *s*);	Return *true* if *str* begins with *s*. Return *false* otherwise.
boolean *str*.endsWith(String *s*);	Return *true* if *str* ends with *s*. Return *false* otherwise.
String *str*.toLowerCase();	Return *str* in lower case letters.
String *str*.toUpperCase();	Return *str* in upper case letters.
char [] *str*.toCharArray();	Return a character array equivalent to *str*.
String *str*.trim();	Remove any leading or trailing spaces from *str*.

Figure E.3 The *String* Class Methods

method parallels the **length** field used for arrays. Strings use a method call to return the length of a string; arrays use a field name. Be careful—you're likely to confuse the two often. The **trim()** method removes any extra spaces appearing at the beginning or end of a string.

The String–String Methods. These methods require a string as a parameter. We can further subdivide the methods into three categories.

String Concatenation. The sole method in this group, **concat()**, creates a new string by appending the parameter to the string component used in the call. We can use the string addition operator, +, to achieve the same result.

String Comparison. Java provides three methods that compare the string used in the call with the string parameter. The **compareTo()** method returns a three-valued result; the **equals()** and **equalsIgnoreCase()** return a boolean.

String Search. The remaining methods determine whether the parameter is a substring of the string used in the call. The **indexOf()** method and the **lastIndexOf()** method return the index of the first or last occurrence of the parameter, respectively—these methods return a -1 if the string does not contains the substring. The **startWith()** and **endsWith()** methods determine whether the parameter is a prefix or suffix of the component, respectively—these methods return a boolean.

Other Methods. The two remaining methods create string slices (**substring()**) or convert a string to the equivalent character array (**toCharacterArray()**).

List of Figures

List of Programs

INDEX